The House

THE HOUSE
NEW ZEALAND'S HOUSE OF REPRESENTATIVES 1854–2004

JOHN E. MARTIN

Dunmore Press Ltd

©Crown Copyright 2004

First Published in 2004
by
Dunmore Press Ltd
P.O. Box 5115
Palmerston North
New Zealand
email: books@dunmore.co.nz
http://www.dunmore.co.nz

in association with

Parliamentary Service, Office of the Clerk and
The History Group,
Ministry for Culture and Heritage

Australian Supplier:
Federation Press
P.O. Box 45
Annandale 2038 NSW
Australia
email: info@federationpress.com.au
Ph: (02) 9552-2200
Fax: (02) 9552-1681

Text:	Garamond 10.5/12.5
Printer:	K & M Print Ltd
Cover design:	Anna Brown Design, Wellington
Layout design:	Tracey Stagg
page 1 photograph:	NZ *Observer and Free Lance*, 21 June 1890
page 2–3 photograph:	The buildings, c. 1928, ATL, F68827½

National Library of New Zealand Cataloguing-in-Publication Data

Martin, John E.
The House : New Zealand's House of Representatives, 1854-2004 / John E. Martin.
Includes bibliographical references and index.
ISBN 0-86469-463-6
1. New Zealand. Parliament—History. I. Title.
328.93—dc 22

Copyright. No part of this book may be reproduced without written permission except in the case of brief quotations embodied in critical articles and reviews.

Contents

Foreword		7
Chapter 1	Shaky beginnings, 1854–56	9
Chapter 2	Establishing the foundations, 1858–75	31
Chapter 3	Political realignment, retrenchment and depression, 1876–90	73
Chapter 4	From free-lance to disciplined private: the single party in the House, 1891–1912	107
Chapter 5	Escaping the 'trammels of the past': organised party government, 1913–35	147
Chapter 6	The consolidation of two-party government and Parliament, 1936–49	203
Chapter 7	Reform, efficiency and accountability, 1950–69	233
Chapter 8	Executive and Parliament: the balance at issue, 1970–84	271
Chapter 9	Redressing the balance: institutional reform and MMP, 1985–2003	303
Conclusion		337
Acknowledgements		339
Notes		341
Select Bibliography		369
Index		373

RT. HON JONATHAN HUNT MP

OFFICE OF THE SPEAKER
HOUSE OF REPRESENTATIVES
WELLINGTON, NEW ZEALAND

FOREWORD

This history was commissioned to mark the 150th anniversary of the first meeting of the House of Representatives in Auckland on 24 May 1854.

The project has been co-sponsored by the Office of the Clerk of the House of Representatives and the Parliamentary Service and managed by the History Group of the Ministry for Culture and Heritage (formerly the Historical Branch of the Department of Internal Affairs). Dr John E Martin was selected, in 2000, to research and write a history of the House of Representatives. It is my privilege and good fortune, as Speaker and Father of the House, to see this project come to fruition.

A parliamentary historian, Dr A H McLintock, was appointed in 1954 to undertake a history of Parliament project. Following publication of *Crown Colony Government in New Zealand*, Dr McLintock embarked on research on the Legislative Council but died before a history could be written. Drawing on Dr McLintock's researches, an extensively revised work was eventually completed by Professor G A Wood and published in 1983 as *The Upper House in Colonial New Zealand: A study of the Legislative Council in the period 1854-1887*.

In the meantime, Professor Keith Jackson had independently written *The New Zealand Legislative Council: A Study of the Establishment, Failure and Abolition of an Upper House*, published in 1972. The story of the House of Representatives has, however, not been told to any significant extent until now, despite its being one of the oldest continuously functioning legislative chambers in the world.

As a member of Parliament since 1966, I have witnessed and participated in political and parliamentary events over four decades. Dr Martin gives a comprehensive and often quite lively account of the House from its earliest days to the present – its life and culture, its proceedings against the backdrop of the times, its personalities, the accommodation and support services for the House and its members and staff.

He is to be congratulated on achieving a work of such quality and scope in a comparatively short time. Thanks are due, too, to those who have supported this project and helped it to be realised.

This book will be of interest not only to those who are or have been parliamentarians but to all who are interested in the place of representative institutions in our society. It will do much to fill a gap that has long been evident in New Zealand's written political history.

Rt Hon Jonathan Hunt
Speaker of the House of Representatives

Newly elected Speaker Jonathan Hunt addresses the House, 1999 (picture opposite).

Paul Fisher, Parliamentary Service collection

GRAND REFORM BANQUET.

Demonstration in favour of the immediate establishment of Representative Institutions in this Colony,

TO BE HELD AT THE

BRITANNIA Saloon,

ON THURSDAY, THE 1st MARCH, 1849,

CHAIRMAN:—

JOHN DORSET, ESQ.,

VICE CHAIRMEN:—

Major Baker, J. P.	James Kelham, Esq., J. P.
Kenneth Bethune, Esq.	William Lyon, Esq.
J. Boddington, Esq.	A. M'Donald, Esq., J. P.
Captain E. Daniell, J. P.	Samuel Revans, Esq.
J. Johnston, Esq.	W. B. Rhodes, Esq.

STEWARDS:

MESSRS.

A. de B. Brandon,	George Rhodes,
F. Bradey,	Joseph Rhodes,
Richard Barton,	David Scott,
William Dorset,	George Scott,
J. E. Featherston, M.D.	James Smith,
William Fox, J.P.	J. Varnham,
Major Hornbrook,	W. E. Vincent,
W. S. Loxley,	R. Waitt,
D. M. Laurie,	John Wallace,
J. Marriott,	J. H. Wallace,
John M'Beth,	George Waters,
Thomas M'Kenzie,	Thomas Waters,
Robert Park,	John Wade,
E. Roe,	F. A. Weld.

Dinner on the Table at six o'clock, precisely.

TICKETS 5s. EACH, INCLUDING WINES.

W. E. VINCENT, Secretary.

Wellington, February 23, 1849.

Chapter 1

Shaky Beginnings, 1854–56

Auckland was not particularly welcoming when the members of the new General Assembly gathered in May 1854 – the weather that winter was extremely wet and the townsfolk affected disinterest.[1] Moreover, the town was threatened by a move of the capital away from Auckland; the opening of Parliament highlighted this possibility. Aucklanders seemed to inhabit a commercial world, with the military and Governor's establishments providing some formality, different from the pastoral, rural world of the southern organised settlements. Government House behind the new Parliament Buildings and the large military barracks further back on the brow of the hill symbolised this contrast. The new Parliament Buildings, hastily thrown up just before the members arrived, was on the rise ('Constitution Hill') between Official Bay and Mechanics Bay on an extension of Eden Crescent. It lay on the fringes of the town, in a semi-rural setting surrounded by paddocks, not far from scenes of commercial interchange between Pakeha and Maori. The bustling centre of Auckland was thronged with Maori plying their trade in fruit and vegetables, pigs and poultry, wheat and flour, with thousands of produce-laden canoes and 150 coastal vessels arriving in the town each year.

The General Assembly first met on Wednesday 24 May 1854, at noon, for both Houses to take their oaths of allegiance to the Crown. The day, appropriately, celebrated Queen Victoria's birthday, but was very wet. Despite the rain, there was a spirit of celebration: 'the ships in harbour, as usual, were "dressed" in their gayest bunting – the Government Brig, "Victoria" … being magnificently decorated, fore and aft, from her trucks to her water line', and a 21-gun salute was fired from Fort Britomart at noon, followed by a salute given by the 58th Regiment in the Albert Barracks square.[2] After the swearing-in, the Acting Governor, Lieutenant-Colonel R.H. Wynyard, held a formal reception in the House that afternoon. Those attending were received by a guard of honour complete with a band and the Queen's Colour. The reception was followed by a grand ball that evening at the barracks.

With the opening of Parliament, New Zealand embarked on the road to fully representative democracy, which many settlers had assumed was an integral part of the colonising enterprise. Hopes were high and ambitions, previously fettered, were set free. The early proceedings of the House of Representatives were fraught with these expectations, making the first years notable for their drama but also vital in setting the pattern which subsequent decades followed. Members themselves were conscious of the importance of the occasion and the historical role that they were called upon to play as the new institution began to form about them.

Expectations of self-government

Migrants from the British Isles had come to New Zealand with firm views on the kind of government that should be instituted in their new country, even if the British government had initially shown little enthusiasm for taking New Zealand under its wing. Once this had been accomplished with the signing of the Treaty of Waitangi, the British Parliament showed little interest in the fledgling

Left: The Constitutional Association's 'Grand Reform Banquet', 1849. ATL, Eph-D-Politics-1849-01

colony. Others such as Edward Gibbon Wakefield had an eye to the opportunities provided by a new form of colonisation. Democratic self-government was part of his colonial vision. 'The colonists, being an instructed and civilized people would be as well qualified to govern themselves as the people of Britain … they might frame their own laws, in a Colonial Assembly … At all events, they must be governed, by whatever machinery, with a view to their good and contentment, which is the greatest good, instead of to the satisfaction of their governors only.'[3] He and others associated with the New Zealand Company had played a role in the first experiment in colonial self-government in Canada.

After the assumption of sovereignty the new colony was ruled by a Governor appointed from Britain. He was supported by an Executive Council of appointed, salaried officials to administer the country, and a Legislative Council, these same officials sitting with several senior Justices of the Peace, to pass measures into the statute book. The Governor and his officials really ran the colony, with the Legislative Council meeting only sporadically and briefly.

Immigrants came to New Zealand, tempered in the fire of British philosophical radicalism and Chartism, and pressed for self-government and for more democratic forms of suffrage. It was not long before the autocratic powers of the Governor came under attack. As A.H. McLintock described it: 'It is little wonder, therefore, that successive bands of the Company's emigrants, imbued with this doctrine, set sail with the determination as free-born Englishmen to transplant their rights and liberties and, incidentally, their glorious constitution, from the old to the new world and to assume as by natural right the full responsibility for the management of their own affairs – in essence, to enjoy the privileges of representative government with control of the executive and the colonial revenue.'[4] These young, politically animated colonists drew themselves up under the impressive-sounding banner of 'Constitutionalism' to take charge of the country's affairs themselves under an advanced liberal franchise. Their model was deeply influenced by what they had left behind them – the Westminster parliamentary system – although they sought to go beyond Westminster in the extent of representation demanded.

By the mid nineteenth century the British Parliament had evolved over many turbulent centuries from its distant origins in the thirteenth-century 'parlement', through the civil war and revolutionary fervour of the mid seventeenth century (which elevated the institution to a central position in the political firmament), to the constitutional settlement of 1689 which consolidated parliamentary sovereignty. From the eighteenth century into the nineteenth the institution matured into a form not too distant from today's, with elections, members representing constituencies, nascent 'parties' contesting for power, elected Speakers independent of both the Crown and party, rules of procedure governing debate and the passage of legislation, and 'Prime Ministers' wielding power through 'cabinets'.

The scene was set for New Zealand's representative institutions by the political reforms and agitation of the 1830s in Britain. The Reform Act of 1832 extended the franchise, while the Durham Report published in 1839 recommended responsible self-government for Canada. Chartist commitments to further reforms such as a universal male franchise, the secret ballot, equal electoral districts, annual parliaments, and the payment of members were brought to New Zealand by the early immigrants.

The British 'Westminster system' was a centralised form of legislature based on a small number of cohesive political parties (usually two) competing for power. A simple majority in the debating chamber determined who held power. New Zealand followed this model, with factional politics dominating in the nineteenth century and organised political parties developing from the 1890s. Like Australia, New Zealand took this model even further with a pronounced development of party caucuses. But first, following the assertion of sovereignty in 1840, the British government, together with the Governor, had to settle on a suitable means of representation – one that would satisfy colonists' aspirations but also ensure that the interests of Maori were not ignored. Self-government in principle was conceded from the outset, but the form that it might take was less obvious.

Shaky Beginnings, 1854–56

The Constitution Act

The New Zealand Constitution Act was passed by the British Parliament on 30 June 1852, following a decade or more of constitutional agitation in New Zealand's more southern settlements to move New Zealand beyond Crown Colony status. The Act created a central colonial legislature, the General Assembly, together with six subordinate provincial legislatures. The General Assembly comprised the Governor, the Legislative Council (whose members were nominated by the Governor for life) and the House of Representatives (whose 37 members were elected for terms not exceeding five years). The House of Representatives had extensive powers to make laws for the 'peace, order, and good government of New Zealand', as long as those laws were not 'repugnant' to the laws of England. The only matters reserved for the Governor were defence and 'native affairs'. The Governor remained Commander-in-Chief of the colony's military forces.

The franchise for electing members of the House of Representatives, restricted to males aged 21 and over, was based on property. Electors could vote in any district in which they held property. This allowed plural voting. In practice the property qualification proved little obstacle to the registration of adult males of all social groups.[5] Wage levels were sufficiently high and property ownership sufficiently widespread for the franchise to give almost universal adult male suffrage for Pakeha.

Maori political representation was not taken into account. Few Maori possessed property to qualify them for the vote because of the communal tenure of land. Governor George Grey treated the matter of Maori representation as one of personal patronage and paternalistic cultivation of particular chiefs, believing that his policy of amalgamation of the races might better prepare Maori for the introduction of representative government.[6] He then failed to act on the provision in the Constitution Act allowing the Governor to establish Native Districts 'for the Government of themselves'.

The Act also prescribed how Parliament was to function. The Governor was empowered to summon Parliament, to proclaim its time and place of meeting, and to prorogue or dissolve it. He also had the power to assent or refuse assent to bills, to amend and return them to the Assembly, or to reserve bills for consideration by the British government. Members of the General Assembly were required to swear an oath of allegiance or make an equivalent affirmation or declaration. The House of Representatives was to appoint a Speaker on its first meeting. The Legislative Council and the House of Representatives were to adopt 'standing rules and orders' for the orderly conduct of the two Houses, to regulate the relationship and forms of communication between them concerning votes and bills, and to set down the procedures for passing bills.

The most crucial aspect of the Act for subsequent political developments was the division between the powers of the General Assembly and those of the provincial governments. The General Assembly had paramount powers to control, supersede and render null and void any provincial laws that were repugnant to or inconsistent with any of its own legislation, and had control over Crown and Maori land, customs duties, coinage and currency, weights and measures, post offices, and much of the justice system and civil and criminal law.

The subordinate role of the provinces was underlined by their lack of financial powers. The General Assembly was to control all revenues from general taxation, duties and other sources, and the disposal of land. The surplus revenue, after general (central) government appropriations was to be divided among the provinces according to their contributions to the revenue. The place of the General Assembly was further reinforced by its powers to amend provincial boundaries and the number of provinces.

The relationship between the General Assembly and the Governor and the nature of executive government in the new order had been left vague in the Act. In the first two fraught years of parliamentary government the struggle between the Governor and the House over attaining full responsible government was paramount. New Zealand had gained representative government, but proper self-government would not be yielded until ministries fully responsible to Parliament, that is the elected House of Representatives, were formed. The continued existence of the Crown Colony government officials combined with the inability of the House to form a stable majority were major stumbling blocks. Although New Zealand gained responsible government in 1856, the powers given to the Governor, in particular his jurisdiction over 'native' or Maori affairs, were critical constraints to the future of the General Assembly in the next decade.

The Constitution Act was received officially in New Zealand at the end of 1852. Following Governor Grey's proclamation bringing the Act into operation on 17 January 1853, expectations were aroused that the country was about to attain both representative and responsible government, for which the constitutional associations had agitated strongly. Key members of such associations – in Wellington, Charles Clifford, Frederick Weld, Dr Isaac Featherston, William Fox and William Fitzherbert; in Nelson, Alfred Domett and Edward Stafford; and in Canterbury, James FitzGerald – were soon to become central protagonists in the fledgling Parliament.

The Constitution Act stipulated that the Governor should proclaim electoral districts, provide for the registration of voters and issue the writs for elections within six months. This was done by July 1853. Grey divided the country into 24 electorates, of which 11 were multi-member electorates, giving a total of 37 members for the House of Representatives. There were 12 members from the most populous province, Auckland; 8 from Wellington; 6 from Nelson; 5 from Canterbury; and 3 each from Otago and Taranaki. The numbers of people in the electorates varied greatly; there was torrid debate in the chamber down the years on this matter. In practice rural areas (and what amounted to the same thing, the minor provinces, until 1876) were over-represented on a population basis for many decades, both when electorate boundaries were determined by the parliamentarians themselves and following the introduction of the 'country quota' in 1881.

All elections were held by October 1853. Compared to the provincial elections conducted at the same time, those for the General Assembly aroused markedly less interest.[7] In a number of cases there was great difficulty obtaining candidates at all. In 13 of the 24 electorates, involving 20 of the total of 37 members of the House, candidates were elected without opposition.[8] Members were strikingly young. Most were in their 30s and 40s, and the average age was 39. Virtually all had been born in the British Isles, three-quarters in England. The Provincial Councils were strongly represented in the General Assembly, with 2 Provincial Superintendents and 11 other members of Provincial Councils sitting in the Assembly. There was a diverse mix of occupations. From the rural sector came 7 runholders and 4 smaller farmers; there were 9 from commerce, trade and manufacturing; men drawn from professional groups included 2 doctors, 2 army officers, 6 lawyers and 3 journalists. It was by no means a squatters' Parliament, although many had connections with the land, as might have been expected in a young colonial society. The House was highly educated, with nearly half of all members having a university education or equivalent.

With the elections completed, Wellington, as the centre of the constitutional agitation movement, celebrated with an 'election ball' held in the 'Ball Room' of Barrett's Hotel.[9] Decorated for the assembled throng of nearly 300, its two chandeliers were 'wreathed with evergreens and artificial flowers. The walls were hung with flags of various descriptions, interspersed with floral and other very appropriate decorations', while over the mantelpiece was a device 'emblematic of the Free Constitution' of 1852 with the names of Provincial Council members emblazoned in the centre. Five from the Council would also go to Auckland as members of the House of Representatives. There was dancing from 9 p.m. until nearly daylight. Wellington awaited with considerable anticipation the summoning of the General Assembly.

Calling the Assembly

But Grey failed to bring the General Assembly together.[10] This step in the process had been left vague in the Act – a meeting was to be held 'as soon as conveniently may be' after the return of the writs – and Grey temporised for as long as he could. This allowed the provinces to consolidate their position and severely handicapped the general government.

Suspicion of Grey's motives hardened as he failed to act, but initially only E. G. Wakefield, who had arrived in the country early in 1853, had the temerity to confront him publicly on the issue. He considered that 'government in New Zealand is in a great mess of illegality and disorder' because of Grey's 'unconstitutional actions'.[11] By late that year agitation mounted. Claims were made that Grey had 'substituted his own arbitrary will in place of the legitimate and legal acts of the New Zealand Parliament'.[12] Grey packed his bags and departed from New Zealand in December 1853 with the Assembly still not summoned. It was left to his inexperienced and hesitant deputy, Lieutenant-Colonel Wynyard, who was now also Auckland's Superintendent, to deal with the situation.

It was by no means certain where the first gathering of Parliament would take place. Auckland, the official capital since 1840, had a strong case.[13] Wellington felt that it had a strong claim too, particularly after the partitioning of New Zealand into New Ulster and New Munster, with separate capitals, under previous constitutional arrangements for New Zealand which were only partially brought into effect. However, the petition of the Auckland Provincial Council to the British government (backed by an apparent promise from Grey that Auckland should have the first sitting of the new general legislature) clinched the matter for now.[14]

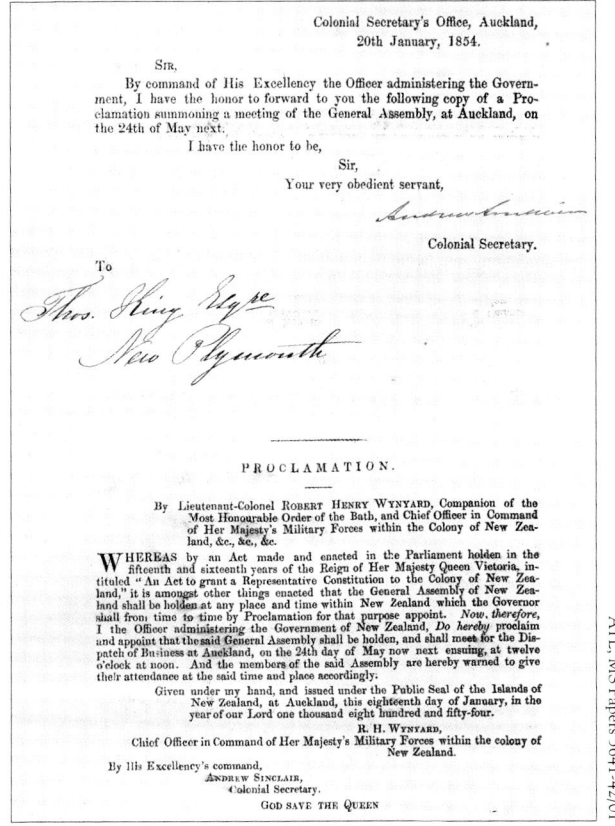

The members of the new General Assembly were given ample notice that it would meet for the first time on 24 May 1854.

On 18 January 1854 Wynyard issued a proclamation summoning the General Assembly to meet in Auckland on 24 May 1854.[15] The next task – much more difficult than it would seem today – was to assemble the members of both Houses in Auckland. For those who had the honour of representing New Zealand's far-flung electorates, attending the first session of Parliament was an onerous undertaking. They had to leave their farms, runs and businesses unattended for months. Sessions of Parliament had to be held outside the peak summer months of the colonial economy, when shearing, haymaking and harvesting took place and trade and commerce were most active.[16] The pattern settled into an opening of Parliament in June or July, with the session running for two or three months. By and large this mid-year opening was kept to for the next hundred years, although from the 1890s the sessions stretched into October or November.

It was no simple matter getting to Auckland, given the lack of regular shipping and the length of time it took to travel up the coastline. The government had to contract ships to pick up members.[17] A choice had to be made between the new steamer *Nelson* and the government brig, which had been commandeered by the Auditor-General to go around the various settlements in a desperate attempt to pull together the colony's financial accounts for the forthcoming General Assembly. The Otago members arrived in Lyttelton on the government brig on 2 April. On 7 April the *Nelson* also arrived in Lyttelton, to great excitement, as a speedy alternative for the trip to Auckland. Many, including Henry Sewell, James FitzGerald, David Monro, Frederick Weld and Francis Dillon Bell, abandoned the brig and opted for the next run of the steamer north on 11 May.[18]

Sewell's diary chronicles the steamer's progress to Wellington, then to Nelson (where the vessel

The House

Otago members found the trip to Auckland daunting. This was the suggested method of transport for William Cargill, the member for Dunedin Country from 1855 to 1859.

Cartoon by James Brown, Hocken Library

was stranded on the Boulder Bank) and New Plymouth, before negotiating the treacherous Manukau bar after waiting out the night and for morning fog to clear. The parliamentarians finally landed at Onehunga on 23 May, 12 days after leaving Canterbury and the day before Parliament was to open. The tide was falling, so the steamer had to anchor a mile offshore. The passengers came ashore in the ship's boats.[19] Sailors carried the women and children ashore, but the men were forced to take off their shoes and stockings and wade through mud and stones. The passengers had to carry their own baggage along the shore for half a mile before meeting the carriages sent to pick them up. The women and children were taken to a public house in Onehunga while the men continued in carriages along the rough track towards Auckland, six miles away, to arrange accommodation.

The bedraggled members reached Auckland at dusk and were put up with difficulty at hotels and lodging houses.[20] The FitzGeralds and other southern members rented 'St Kevins' on Karangahape Road, Grey's former house, with FitzGerald's wife Fanny keeping house for 20 people including her own children.[21] Soon the town took on a lively appearance as its social scene flourished with the influx. Newly arrived members joined the rounds of dinners and formal visits of Auckland's élite, the Governor's establishment, military officers and local dignitaries.

Meanwhile the government brig (with Wakefield, newly elected for Hutt, and the Otago members aboard) had taken two months to sail from Otago, and had arrived only the day before the steamer. It had been forced by head winds back through Cook Strait from the west coast and, much delayed, had sailed to Auckland up the east coast.

Opening the Assembly

The members assembled in the new Parliament Buildings. The building had still to be lined and was largely a bare shell.[22] The House of Representatives met in the upper floor chamber and the Legislative Council on the ground floor, 'a strange inversion of order', said Sewell. The chambers were simply halls with seating, with the public areas separated by a rail. The very plain, gabled, two-storey structure, too small from the start, was disparagingly nicknamed the 'Shedifice'. It was described variously as 'a great wooden barnshaped affair, which might serve for a Hospital, a Jail, or a Barrack – or if gutted be turned into a Methodist Meeting house' (Sewell), or a 'sort of cross between a barn, a bastille, and a union work house' (Fox).[23]

Fox also described the interior: you 'enter a long narrow room some five and forty feet by 20, with a great staring window at one end, a row of other staring windows facing the sun, opposite to you, a bar across one end making an apology for a gallery, and an erection at the other end which is the speaker's chair, but so exactly like a French bedstead and canopy, that you expect to see the honorable

Shaky Beginnings, 1854–56

The General Assembly buildings, to the right in this view, were above Mechanics Bay in a semi-rural setting. The more lavish Government House is behind to the left and the military barracks above on the skyline.

members head in a nightcap peeping over the tester.'[24] In front of the Speaker the Table stretched one-third of the length of the cramped chamber.

Hugh Carleton initially took the chair in the House of Representatives. He was described as the 'Father of the House', being the first member elected in the staggered elections the previous year. He was knowledgable if pedantic about parliamentary matters. Few others had much knowledge of parliamentary government and virtually none had direct experience of it. Wakefield, older and better versed in British politics, had briefed the Otago members on the long journey north.

Chief Justice William Martin wanted to administer the oath to members of the House of Representatives in the Legislative Council chamber below, but the House refused on principle. By insisting on having the oaths taken in its own chamber, the House indicated that it should not be toyed with. The Legislative Council quickly appointed a Speaker, but the House delayed its official opening for further discussions on the election of its own Speaker. After much politicking and some uncertainty about his religious persuasion and the fact that he was not from Auckland, the members settled on the Roman Catholic Charles Clifford, the Speaker of Wellington's Provincial Council.[25] Clifford had aspired to the position and had gained Wakefield's support. He was tactfully proposed by the most senior and respected Auckland member of the House, T.H. Bartley. With a southerner as Speaker, the House chose F.W. Merriman from Auckland as Chairman of Committees.[26]

Clifford would be at the centre of the parliamentary turmoil of the next two years, and had to make some invidious decisions. He was concerned to elevate the standing of Parliament and urged the adoption of regalia. He later presented the House with a mace. On his retirement Premier Stafford noted his 'natural urbanity', his dignity and his combination of 'justness with judgement, and firmness

Evans album, 1861, Auckland City Libraries, A11714

The General Assembly buildings from what was then an extension to Eden Crescent, now the site of the Supreme Court. The Bellamy's extension can be seen on the right at the rear.

of decision with the most conciliatory of manners' at a time when Parliament was dealing with 'great national questions'.[27] The experienced politician William Gisborne regarded him as a good choice. 'He combined ability, firmness, and impartiality with dignity and good temper.'[28]

The state opening of the General Assembly on 27 May proceeded with all the pomp and ceremony that could be mustered. The central symbolic trappings of mace, Black Rod and state robes were absent from this Parliament. Shortly after 2 p.m., Acting Governor Wynyard arrived and was received by a guard of honour of the 58th Regiment and a band playing the national anthem. In an embarrassing departure from British tradition, members of the House of Representatives were not formally summoned to the Legislative Council.[29] Wynyard proceeded into the Legislative Council chamber, where members of both Houses had gathered 'higgledy piggledy' in crowded conditions, and took the Speaker's chair. The strangers' (public) gallery was packed and people spilled over into entrances and passages.

In the Speech from the Throne, Wynyard described the establishment of a General Assembly as an 'experiment in constitutional government'. This was an accurate description, since New Zealand's parliamentary democracy was one of the earliest colonial examples. The Speech also laid down a challenge: 'it will rest with the General Assembly of these Islands whether New Zealand shall become one great nation, exercising a commanding influence in the Southern Seas, or a collection of insignificant, divided, and powerless petty States. To mould its various provinces into one united people, to create amongst them a feeling of common sympathy, and to inspire them with the pride of a common nationality, may well be the leading object of the Assembly'.[30] This would become the over-riding issue of Parliament as it navigated between the omnipresent and compelling concerns of provincialism and the need to rise above localism and take account of wider national interests.

These stirring sentiments were well received, but Wynyard's careful reference to *representative* self-government avoided the most central and immediate issue of all. The House was stunned that there was no mention of *responsible* government, for which all members and constitutional associations had been clamouring.[31] Immediately after the opening of Parliament, members began to discuss how to force the issue. Wakefield rapidly emerged as the leader in this matter, having experience of the issue in Canada and Australia, and having spent much energy agitating amongst southern members. He now worked on the northerners, who were not particularly enthusiastic about responsible government because of fears that Auckland would lose the power of the existing 'Officials' and possibly also the seat of government.[32]

Wakefield was a polarising magnet in the House. As Sewell said, 'nobody guides any body or follows any body, except that Wakefield's powerful mind goes about like a Stockman driving in wild cattle and reducing them into something like order. He is the informing principle and mainspring of the whole, but then there are all kinds of jealousies and alarms about him.'[33] Sewell's concerns were soon to be realised as the struggle for responsible government developed.

Charles Clifford, born in Liverpool on 1 January 1813, arrived in Wellington in 1842. After being in the forefront of Wellington's Constitutional Association in the late 1840s, he was elected to represent Wellington in the General Assembly. Clifford was elected as the first Speaker of the House on 26 May 1854. He was awarded a knighthood in 1858. Clifford remained Speaker until 1860, when he retired from Parliament and returned to live in England, where he died on 27 February 1893.

Practical matters

The House had a range of housekeeping matters to attend to immediately, some of considerable symbolic importance and others humdrum but vital to the functioning of the House. Select committees were set up and began work. The Speaker was authorised to regulate proceedings.

The matter of adopting a prayer to open proceedings was contentious. James Macandrew, a devoted member of the Free Church of Scotland, insisted on 'acknowledgement of dependence on the Divine Being'.[34] Walter Lee, a Catholic, moved that the House 'be not converted into a conventicle and that prayers be not offered up'. Others felt that the House should not commit itself to any particular religious persuasion and that a choice of prayers had connotations of a state-endorsed religion.[35] The Constitution in this view implied religious equality, as Weld, a Catholic, argued in his first speech.

Weld confided to his diary feelings that many others must have experienced on giving their first speech. The New Zealand General Assembly had adopted the British House of Commons' rule that members had to deliver their speeches bona fide in their own words 'in the form of an unwritten composition' in order to contribute truly to debate. Reading from detailed notes was forbidden. Weld confessed to being in 'a funk' and was relieved to have his first speech over with.[36]

In the end the majority accepted Wakefield's assurance that a prayer was a common practice in other legislatures and did not imply any endorsement of a state religion. The Catholic Speaker, Clifford, cleverly anticipated the situation and lined up a Church of England clergyman and good friend, the Rev. F.J. Lloyd from St. Paul's just down the road, disingenuously asking the Sergeant-at-Arms to go out and find the first clergyman he could, of whatever denomination. Lloyd was ushered in and conducted prayers. There was relief at getting over this first hurdle. Later a committee that included Clifford and Weld drew up a suitable form of prayer which was adopted by the House.[37] It was also agreed that the Speaker should conduct prayers. It eventually became a standing joke in Parliament that 'the Speaker entered the House, looked to the right, then to the left, and prayed for the country'.[38]

The next matter was standing orders.[39] The Standing Orders Committee reported back with the first set of standing orders, which was adopted on 9 June. The 123 orders dealt with the procedure of the House and its relationship with the Legislative Council. They established the general principle of following the 'rules, forms, and usages of the House of Commons', provided for the appointment of select committees and the receiving of petitions and private bills, asserted the authority of the Speaker, and regulated procedure and members' behaviour in the House. The House was to sit from Tuesday through to Friday, beginning at noon (except for Wednesday, the day allocated for private members' business, when the House sat from 5 p.m.) and continuing until 4.30 p.m. before adjourning until 6 p.m. and then working into the evening.[40] Government business was accorded priority on Tuesdays and Fridays – although it remained to be seen whether a ministry could actually be formed.

The procedure for passing bills was similar to that of the House of Commons. A bill would be introduced into the House without debate for a first reading. During the second reading, the member promoting the bill would give a substantial argument in its favour and outline its major provisions. This would be followed by debate, after which the House would consider it in the Committee of the Whole House ('in Committee') clause by clause, perhaps referring the bill to a select committee first. Following amendments, if any, the bill would move to its third reading and final passage through the House, before being referred to the Legislative Council for consideration and thence to the Governor for his assent.

In 1856 the House agreed to more substantial standing orders.[41] The most important addition was provision for changing the standing orders themselves: two-thirds of the House had to be present and notice of four sitting days given. This stipulation became a serious constraint on the development of the standing orders, particularly in dealing with obstruction, until it was changed in 1894.[42] It was a tall order to assemble two-thirds of the House, and any initiative to change the standing orders could easily be thwarted by members simply absenting themselves from the chamber.

Members soon raised the question of expenses for attending Parliament. The select committee considering the issue believed that Legislative Councillors should not be paid, not being elected representatives and thus requiring a double independence from the executive and the people. On the other hand it declared that elected members of the House should be provided for 'on a liberal rather than on a parsimonious scale'.[43]

At that time, private means were important for men with political ambitions. Those with some wealth could afford to indulge in politics as a gentlemanly and leisured pursuit. The cost of candidacy, the disruption to business of being away from home for several months a year and the cost of accommodation in Auckland were real deterrents to those of lesser means and made membership of the House much less attractive than membership of a Provincial Council, especially for residents of distant Canterbury and Otago.[44] When the time came to attend a session, a number of those elected resigned their seats rather than travel to Auckland. For the settler and trader Thomas King, travelling away from home and staying in Auckland was a considerable burden. He was very keen on compensation for expenses – otherwise he would be 'an absolute loser'.[45]

Wakefield argued that an allowance would enable representatives of a wider range of social groups to enter Parliament and that most legislatures, apart from the House of Commons itself, paid their members. FitzGerald, who was less keen on generous payment, said 'he did not mean to say one could drink champagne, ride a horse, or dine every day at Bellamy's upon it. But 15s. [shillings] a day to a working-man for legislating would be ample'. The House, led by Wakefield, voted itself an allowance of £1 a day (known as the 'honorarium') for out-of-town members for the length of time that Parliament was in session.[46] Those closer to Auckland who were obliged to leave their homes to attend were given ten shillings a day. In 1856 a flat rate of £1 was paid to members irrespective of where they lived – with members of the Legislative Council now included.

Parliament's accommodation needed substantial improvement. The House Improvement Committee's report said that the building required 'better means of seeing, hearing, and ventilating – reasonable accommodation for the members, the public, and the press … the structure is little better than an elevated barn, through which "The winds whistle cold and the sun glimmers red"'.[47] The House, incredibly, had no suitable clock or even a division bell, and a strongroom was required to guard against fire. There were also no toilets – the committee recommended that at least three water closets be provided close by.[48] Most importantly of all, there was no 'refreshment' room.

Providing 'for the comfort of members' was the phrase used to describe a New Zealand 'Bellamy's' in the tradition of the British Parliament. The House of Commons' Bellamy's was founded by John Bellamy in 1773 as a private arrangement with members, providing food and liquor. From 1848 more formal arrangements were adopted in the new Houses of Parliament, with a House Committee supervising and subsidising Bellamy's. In New Zealand's case, the proposed Bellamy's was a modest lean-to at the back of the building with entry from the lower lobby of the staircase.[49] A housekeeper (who lived in a cottage at the rear and rented out rooms to members) was employed.[50] The fare provided was very limited. 'There was a board supported by two trestles, on the board there was a clean table-cloth, and on the table-cloth were cups and saucers and a few plates of bread-and-butter.'[51]

Furnishing liquor was just as important for the comfort of members. In order to legalise this, the House passed the Licensing Amendment Act, suspending standing orders to do so. This, the first Act under representative government, has a certain delicious irony about it given the singular lack of progress on other legislation in the first sessions. Known as the 'Bellamy's bill', the Act permitted the sale of alcohol within the premises and indemnified those who had previously contravened the existing ordinance.[52] When the House attempted to defend its record in the first session, the action was mocked by newspapers and by Frederick Whitaker of the Legislative Council as 'setting up a grog-shop for members'.[53]

By the early 1860s a proper Bellamy's caterer, Mr James, had been appointed. The House Committee in 1863 agreed to meet at his store in Fort Street: 'to consider the scale of charges and to taste the wines'.[54] The tariff was agreed to and posted up. Admission was restricted to members, the Governor's secretary and Aide-de-Camp, key parliamentary staff and civil servants. Reporters could be admitted to the smoking room, where they might be served refreshments. Thus was the long-standing system of privilege holders and restricted entrée established.

The layout of the chamber did not work, so the position of the Speaker was soon swapped with the public gallery. He now had direct access to the Speaker's room and a committee room behind him. This required the addition of a second staircase outside the House for public access to the gallery. The members' entrance was on the downhill side of the building 'round a corner down a slippery bank, and then up a step ladder in an angle of the building'. Members had to ascend 'a corkscrew stair as nearly perpendicular as it is possible to be. Arrived at the top you stand on a platform just a yard square, with your nose against the narrow mean door of the House of Representatives; that is you stand there unless knocked backwards by some honorable member rushing out to escape a division'.[55] The two newspaper reporters, who at first had to make do on the floor of the chamber to the right of the Speaker, were crammed into a small hole cut in the wall of the chamber.[56] By 1864 the press gallery had been shifted to above the Speaker's chair, allowing ladies, previously quartered in the Speaker's room behind the chair, to have a tiny gallery of their own.[57]

Key officers of the House had to be appointed. This immediately became a constitutional issue, with Carleton arguing that appointments should be the Governor's prerogative, as it was the monarch's for the British Parliament. Eventually the matter was resolved in the Governor's favour and James Coates, previously employed on a temporary basis, was retained.[58] As described by Fox, the Clerk wore 'a suit of solemn black and scarlet stockings' and was seated just below the Speaker's chair at the

The House

Francis Eastwood Campbell, born in 1823, emigrated to Canterbury in 1851. He became Clerk of the House of Representatives on 21 July 1854 and was appointed as Clerk of the General Assembly in 1858, also acting as the General Assembly's librarian for some years. In 1868 Campbell became Clerk of Parliaments. He retired in 1889 and died on 27 September 1911.

head of the Table. 'Charged with the whole of the documentary business of the house, he revels in red tape and pigeon holes'.[59] Who was to appoint parliamentary officials subsequently became a matter of weighty constitutional significance. It caused a rift between the Speaker and the executive in the 1860s and 1870s. On the sudden death of Coates shortly after his permanent appointment, Captain Francis E. Campbell was appointed to the position on 21 July 1854.[60] Campbell was employed as Clerk of the House of Representatives for the next 35 years and became the mainstay of Parliament through its formative period.[61]

The House also needed a Sergeant-at-Arms for reasons of ceremony, to take care of routine administration and to enforce its proceedings if the need arose. Captain Philip Deck, previously master of the *Victoria*, was appointed on 7 August. He carried a white wand as a symbol of office and wore a white waistcoat, white gloves and black clothes.[62] His role in opening the proceedings of the day reflected Commons tradition. Fox described him as 'a sort of Legislative Policeman – armed with a white staff he begins his duties for the day by ushering the Speaker from his room to the Chair, announcing Mistar Speakar in a loud and triumphant voice which we presume is intended to strike terror into the groups of members who are irreverently chatting about the floor. He then seats himself in a special chair just inside the door'.[63]

The House employed a few messengers and temporary clerks during sessions, and by the early 1860s had established the formal positions of Clerk-Assistant and Second Clerk-Assistant.[64] Parliament, however, still lacked the ceremonial Gentleman Usher of the Black Rod of the Parliament. The appointment was a Legislative Council matter, and the House of Representatives jealously guarded its own position by obstructing any appointment. In the meantime the Governor's Private Secretary or Aide-de-Camp fulfilled the role.

Towards responsible government

The central and incapacitating issue through the first sessions of the House of Representatives was responsible government. It was difficult to consider anything else, since Wynyard had not prepared any business for the Assembly to deal with and the matter of who now had charge of government remained opaque. In resolving this issue the Legislative Council played little role beyond supplying additional members for the Executive Councils formed in these two years.

FitzGerald, in the Address-in-Reply to Wynyard's unrevealing Speech from the Throne, emphasised that the House saw no obstacle to ministers being responsible solely to the House and that legislation was not required to bring ministerial responsibility into effect.[65] Wakefield's motion for ministerial responsibility passed with one member dissenting. Wakefield then, however, entered into secret negotiations with Speaker Clifford over forming a ministry.[66] Wynyard offered the compromise of a

Shaky Beginnings, 1854–56

James Edward FitzGerald entered the House in 1854 representing Lyttelton Town and resigned in 1857. In spite of his central role in bringing about responsible government he was not suited to the rigours of politics. Returning to the House in 1862, FitzGerald was instrumental in introducing Maori representation and the Hansard system of reporting. He made a successful career as Comptroller-General after resigning again in 1867.

'mixed ministry', in which the Executive Council would be enlarged by a few members drawn from the Assembly. FitzGerald formed such a ministry, including Sewell and Weld together with Dillon Bell from the Legislative Council in addition to the Governor's officials.

FitzGerald's 'ministry' felt that full responsible government would come once the officials had been pensioned off, and celebrated its 'revolution'.[67] The combination of officials and elected representatives proved unworkable. The officials were in an ambiguous position. Wakefield (who had been left out of the ministry and took enormous affront at his omission) intrigued against the ministry. The 'flightiness' and headstrong nature of FitzGerald and indecisiveness of Sewell added to the difficulties of making the ministry work.[68] In the end FitzGerald resigned when it became apparent that the situation could not be resolved. Then Wakefield, in a badly misjudged bid for power, acted as unofficial adviser to Wynyard. On 5 August Wynyard presented his celebrated message no. 25 to the House, which argued that legislation and the royal assent were necessary to implement responsible government. This message stated his position forcefully. It was generally agreed that Wakefield had written it. Before an astonished House, Wakefield took part of the message out of the hands of the Speaker while it was being read, in order to alter what Wakefield claimed was a 'clerical error'.[69]

The majority in the House, now referred to as the 'Constitutional Party', saw this as part of Wakefield's diabolical plan to force a dissolution of Parliament and go to the country on a popular platform. It was reiterated that there was nothing to prevent the General Assembly providing retiring allowances for the officials, thereby inaugurating responsible government. The stalemate continued until 17 August, when Wynyard dramatically prorogued Parliament.[70] This produced a famous stormy scene in the House. Wynyard sent a message warning the House of his intention. As Sewell rose to respond, Wynyard's private secretary, who had been waiting behind the door to the chamber for this message to be read, re-entered with a new message proroguing Parliament for two weeks. As Governors' messages suspended all other business then before the House, in theory the House was now prorogued and could do nothing about it.

FitzGerald moved, amid cheers and cries of 'divide, divide', that standing orders be suspended so that debate could take place before the new message was opened. A fiery debate ensued. The Speaker attempted to disallow the suspension of standing orders, but the House insisted on taking a division on the question. Clifford said that he was 'in the hands of the House'. On the call for a division, Wakefield's opposition members attempted to flee the chamber and ensure that there was no longer a quorum, which would have meant that the suspension of standing orders could not be agreed to. Amid cries of 'Lock the doors!', the Sergeant-at-Arms (who thought that the Speaker had given him an order) locked the members' door. Some fleeing members clambered over the bar and into the public gallery, chased by Sewell, who locked the gallery door. When those in the gallery attempted to shout that there was no quorum and that the bell had not been rung, the Sergeant-at-Arms threatened to take them into custody. Meanwhile, the public in the gallery stood on the benches expressing a mixture of astonishment and derision, according to E.J. (Jerningham) Wakefield.

The Speaker conceded that the division bell had not been rung before the doors were closed, and ordered that they be opened. Wakefield's opposition group departed. Those remaining in the chamber played for time while a supporter rounded up absentees so that a vote could be taken. When two

21

additional members were found, to the cheers of those remaining, standing orders were suspended and a debate on the first message ensued.

Sewell's resolutions condemning both the prorogation and Wakefield's role as adviser to Wynyard were subsequently adopted. While they were being discussed in Committee some of Wakefield's supporters entered the House intent on breaking up the proceedings. James Mackay, the member for Nelson, 'marched in with his hat on, defied the chairman, flung a *Gazette* on the table and declared that the session was over,' shouting 'You are no House, you are prorogued. I have as much right here as you'.[71] (Members had to have their hats off when entering the chamber.) He marched about the chamber flourishing his umbrella and daring anyone to evict him. In the uproar which followed, Sewell and another member tried to manhandle him out but found the door closed. Mackay escaped, having lost his hat, and then 'met the charge of the committee, and beat an honourable retreat over the rail into the stranger's gallery waving defiance to his assailants with his trusty umbrella.'[72]

Mackay was in the end judged guilty of a 'gross and premeditated contempt of the House'. His umbrella became a treasured family heirloom, according to Alfred Saunders, later a member himself.[73] This disorderly incident was to some reminiscent of the seventeenth-century struggles of Parliament against Charles I. For others, such as Australian newspapers, the situation had descended into a disgraceful and appalling farce.[74] The first session of Parliament came to an end there and then.

During the two-week prorogation, Wynyard attempted to form a new mixed ministry from Wakefield's opposition group. This was Thomas Forsaith's 'clean-shirt' ministry, so called because he went back to his draper's shop and changed his shirt on being summoned. But it immediately lost a vote of confidence, 22 to 10, and resigned.[75]

There were to be no further ministries until the matter of responsible government was properly settled in 1856. Sewell assumed the role of de facto leader of the House. The majority of the House worked co-operatively with Sewell in voting supply and passing legislation while waiting for Britain's response to the request for responsible government. FitzGerald had become incapacitated by a descent into wild rage at Wakefield. In a fury at the politicking and obstruction of Wakefield and the Auckland members, he attempted to have the next session of Parliament shifted to 'a more central position', but failed because he had not consulted his supporters. Wakefield and his southerners walked out of the House rather than be seen to support Auckland on this issue. Nonetheless the vote was close.[76]

Compared with the first, prorogued, session a substantial body of legislation was passed in the second session and supply was granted, although in a rather unorthodox fashion, given the lack of a responsible ministry. The House worked late into the night pushing through bills and dealing with the estimates, half asleep and at risk of being 'counted out' through the lack of a quorum, but the business was done. The session culminated in a dinner on the floor of the House, with the Legislative Council chamber used as a 'drawing room'.[77]

This first tempestuous and unstable year of Parliament came to an end on Saturday 16 September 1854, brought to a close because the steamer *Nelson* was waiting to take members south.[78] At 3 p.m. Wynyard sent a message to the Speaker of the House. The Speaker and other members, led by the Sergeant-at-Arms, proceeded downstairs to the Council chamber where Wynyard, a guard of honour and a band awaited.[79] Wynyard prorogued Parliament until 5 July 1855, when additional supply would be required and by which time Britain's response to the request for responsible government should have been received.

Members dispersed to their homes, many with unbounded relief at finally getting away. The lovelorn Thomas King was 'tired of political life with its

Henry Sewell entered the House for Christchurch Town in 1854 and was appointed to the Legislative Council in 1861. A leading early member, he took part in a number of ministries. His journals are an indispensable source for the formative years of the House.

anxieties, cares and responsibilities – with my severance from my home and family'.[80] Members walked to Onehunga, while the ladies travelled in 'sundry vehicles' with the luggage in carts, only to find the tide out and no steamer. It began to rain. When the tide rose in the late afternoon, the ship's boat got close to the shore and painfully ferried the passengers the mile and a half out to the *Nelson*. Sewell, for one, swore that he would never again come to Auckland 'except under compulsion'.[81] Members' messages to their constituents were mixed. The beginnings of parliamentary government had been turbulent, and the shaky start meant that the attention of many turned instead towards provincial politics.

The British government had not been concerned about the constitutional situation in New Zealand until it heard about the impasse that had developed. It made its views on the matter crystal clear – ministers should be drawn from the majority party in Parliament and should be responsible to that institution immediately.[82] This determination became known in New Zealand at the beginning of June 1855, at the same time as the General Assembly was called for its third session. The issue at once died. In 1854 Wynyard's lack of confidence and indecisiveness, Wakefield's unfortunate role, the continued existence of an appointed Executive Council, and the cumbersome method of communication between the Governor and the House had resulted in unnecessary confrontation and blockage.

Parliament was called for a third short session of routine business beginning on 8 August 1855, with most feeling that fresh elections were necessary so that the country could place its full confidence in those elected to form a responsible ministry. A small rump of 19 members plus the Speaker attended. Many southern members boycotted the session in protest against its being held once again in Auckland.[83] Some members had failed to receive the official circulars summoning them in time, and arrangements for the new steamer *Zingari* to pick up members had been made belatedly.

Sewell resumed his de facto leadership and a Pensions Bill for the retiring officials was passed and supply voted for a further year, with the House trenchantly criticising the parlous state of the public finances.[84] Towards the end of the session the new Governor, Sir Thomas Gore Browne, arrived in New Zealand. He decisively prorogued Parliament, confirmed Britain's commitment to responsible government, assented to the bills passed by Parliament, and announced that the next session, too, would be held in Auckland.[85] It appeared that the troubles which had beset the first two years of Parliament were at an end.

The factional system

Elections were held late in 1855. Many sitting members had found the long trip to Auckland and the first sessions discouraging and did not stand again. Only a dozen of those previously in the House were returned. The House was virtually starting afresh. This was to be a recurring problem in the early years of the New Zealand Parliament. The dynamics of each session were shaped by the need to persuade members first to attend and then to stay for the entire session. Regularly, large numbers failed to arrive on time or resigned as the session loomed. Many left before the session had finished. Sewell expostulated: 'it is almost impossible to get fit men in the South to stand for the General Assembly … The great misery of our progress to the place of Assembly lies in the repeated stoppages, with the consequent renewal, at each remove, of the horrors of a sea-voyage.'[86] The travails endured by members travelling to Auckland were not ameliorated until the establishment of a regular, faster steamship service in the 1860s. Even then, disembarking at Onehunga without a jetty and getting into Auckland remained an ordeal, especially when the tide was out and the roads were wet and muddy. Accommodation was hard to find and expensive.

The government used the *Zingari*, another underpowered steamer similar to the *Nelson*, which had little accommodation, to bring members north.[87] There was an undignified scramble for berths. Some had to sleep on the floor and seasickness was prevalent. Otago members chartered their own vessel to ensure more rapid travel than in the brig in 1854, and opted again to return to Dunedin via Sydney!

Auckland was more welcoming than it had been in 1854. Most members found suitable accommodation, although Nelson members 'had a sleeping den opposite the Masonic Hotel' where they had to sleep three in a bed.[88] The town put on three public balls to entertain its visitors.

Unlike the rump of 1855, this session was attended by almost all members, including all six Provincial Superintendents and a large number of provincial councillors. Provincial and general government politics were closely intertwined. Thirty-two of the 44 Provincial Superintendents through the entire provincial period, and no fewer than 230 provincial councillors, were also members of the General Assembly.[89] Fewer than one quarter of members did not also serve on a Provincial Council at some point; about 60 per cent had served on a Provincial Council prior to entering the General Assembly. Another fifth entered provincial and national politics at the same time.[90] A.S. Thomson, an historian of the time, noted that 17 members of the new Assembly already held lucrative government appointments and another four had substantial private means.[91] There were, according to his count, 14 runholders and other farmers, 7 lawyers, 5 merchants and traders, 2 newspaper owners and 2 resident magistrates.

Better provincial representation brought members of considerable talent into the House alongside FitzGerald and Sewell. Stafford, Fox and Domett all became Premier at various times. Other new members such as Featherston, Bell, C.W. Richmond and William Fitzherbert also made their mark. Prior to Parliament's opening, the southern members gathered to decide on policy and a leader, but the process was cut short by the Governor's request to Sewell to form a ministry. Sewell subjected the House to a three-hour speech on his policies that did little for his cause.[92] With the difficult issue of pensions for the 'old' officials out of the way, Sewell became Colonial Secretary, Bell Colonial Treasurer and Frederick Whitaker Attorney-General.[93] In this manner responsible government became something of a reality, although a stable ministry still had to be achieved. The crucial difficulty was one of combining the provincial factions into a durable majority. Members would divide into 'centralist' and 'provincialist' camps over the way in which provincial interests might be reconciled in the General Assembly. While not signifying separate stable political parties, this distinction represented real differences along a continuum concerning the balance between provincial and general government powers.[94]

The warring provincial factions were evenly balanced, easily paralysing the House. The chamber was graced by some members merely making up the numbers, in Fox's acerbic estimation. There were the three 'comic performers' – 'Greenwood does the genteel comedy – Brodie the farce – and East the clown'. Fox continued unkindly: 'unfortunately none of the three had the taste to perceive that their performances were neither creditable to the house, nor appreciated in the dress circle.'[95] There were also the '"dumb dogs who couldn't bark" – "the chips in the porridge" – the empty vessels who would if they could, but didn't because they couldn't.'

Sewell's ministry was thought too 'centralist' and collapsed when Logan Campbell moved an amendment to the Address-in-Reply.[96] Sewell fell, 17 to 15, with one supporter apparently locked out for the division and unable to vote. Fox then attempted to form a ministry, but this was defeated two weeks later for adopting too 'provincialist' a stance. The arrival of the two Nelson members on the *Zingari* had changed the balance in the House. Ample leverage was available through a debate on the location of the next Parliament and Fox was brought down by a majority of one.[97] On 2 June 1856 Edward Stafford, Nelson's Superintendent, who was waiting in the wings, formed a ministry that lasted. Responsible government (with a 'centralist' cast) was at last securely in place.

Stafford and Fox were to become long-term protagonists in the House, with Stafford proving by far the more effective leader in government because of his pragmatic ability to form ministries out of the factional melée. Fox was far better in opposition, brilliant on attack and loyal to his supporters, but unable to administer a government. 'His brilliant wit, his telling attitudes, his great power of satire, and

… boiling-over indignation' suited the opposition benches, but when he headed a ministry, 'one of his ablest colleagues [would take] the bit and run away with him'.[98]

As Stafford had perceptively analysed, there were three factions or 'parties' in the House. None held a majority, but the largest was well represented in the centralist Sewell ministry and included Stafford.[99] The other two 'parties' were the separate provincialist groups based on Wellington and Auckland that had combined to defeat Sewell but could not otherwise agree, especially when it came to the seat of government. Stafford formed a coalition with the Auckland group, thereby securing a healthy majority in the House. In the process a system of factions, based largely on provincial interests, was established.

In this and following chapters, the term 'faction' describes a form of political organisation in Parliament.[100] Factions enabled relative stability and continuity to be achieved, but should not be confused with modern political parties. The term 'party', as used by contemporaries, referred to a faction and its supporters. Factions were persistent core groupings around which larger groups of parliamentary supporters clustered to build a majority. While these majorities were often fragile and impermanent, the factional nuclei were cohesive and long-lasting. Stafford's ministries of the 1850s and 1860s (in combination with colleagues such as Whitaker, Sewell and John Hall) and the so-called 'continuous' ministry of the 1870s and 1880s (involving a small, revolving core group which included Major Harry Atkinson, Whitaker, Hall and Donald McLean) exemplify the factional system. These entities were not distinguished by clear ideologies, but formed around dominant personalities who had the ability and will to pursue and assume power, and possessed political and administrative abilities.

Factionalism established the principle of majority rule and a cabinet system of government independent of the Governor and the Executive Council long before parties emerged. With the cabinet form of executive government came the concept of collective responsibility. Cabinet ministers voted consistently with the Premier on matters of importance to the government.

The formation of ministries under the factional system took place when members gathered for a new session. It involved a confusing welter of manoeuvering and forging of alliances.[101] As late as 1928 members came to Parliament and defeated an incumbent government after an election. The close confinement of members of the House as they made their way to Auckland allowed friendships and alliances to form and policies to be discussed. Once in Auckland, leaders would hold meetings, increasingly referred to as caucuses, to establish support.[102] Such meetings would be called after the start of a session only at times of need or crisis. These early caucus meetings were not the routine means of communication and policy formation that they became with the development of party politics.

Leaders of factions had to court the provincial blocs and independent members in turn – hoping to include those with administrative skills in cabinet – to assemble a workable majority. Personal friendships and family ties, patronage and ambition for political office and power, the promise of public works or other advantage for members' electorates, religious affinities and common business interests – all helped determine how members would coalesce into government or opposition factions. Leaders had to find a combination that gelled, while also satisfying the wider needs and expectations of the House, bearing always in mind that a balance of provincial representation had to be achieved. Members would divide in different ways on the balance between provincial and central affairs, the prosecution of the war against Maori, the way that revenue was distributed, and the location of the seat of government. Out of this confused environment emerged, nonetheless, ministries stable in their personnel and underpinned by a small core group of able, enduring and experienced politicians.

Leaders had their own personal followings or 'tails' of committed supporters. Members were expected to support rather than elect or otherwise choose their leaders. Internal loyalty rather than democracy was pre-eminent. It was expected that a member who pledged himself to a faction would continue to vote for that faction's leader or 'chief' throughout the session on ministerial or 'party' matters, unless he had explicitly declared his 'independence'.[103] If he was no longer prepared to give the ministry his vote, a member was expected to become independent rather than move into the opposite camp. To do otherwise and unexpectedly desert the ranks was considered dishonourable 'ratting'. Such commitments tended to terminate with the session and had to be negotiated anew for following sessions. These arrangements resulted in considerable stability in voting during sessions.

The essence of faction-building was the need to seek support beyond the factional core, which could not alone provide a majority in the House. As Premier, Stafford proved the expert in pragmatically mustering support in his quest for efficient government. It was necessary to draw in loosely attached individuals and even so-called independents. Those claiming to be independent of 'party' were said to favour 'measures, not men' and purported to act in combination with others only in pursuit of principle or the public interest. With more than two factions in the House, coalition became the necessary means of securing a workable majority. Failing this, the leaders of factions had to attempt to detach disaffected or otherwise loosely affiliated members of other factions or entice self-avowed independents into the fold. Coalition and other means of creating a majority inevitably pushed ministries into bipartisan policies. Members were distinguished more by being 'in' or 'out' of power than by distinct policies. The formation of a ministerial faction or 'party' would be accompanied by the coalescing of an opposition 'party' dedicated to defeating the ministry.

The Speech from the Throne and Address-in-Reply played a key role in the formation of ministries and oppositions. At first the Speech from the Throne represented the Governor's independent contribution, reflecting his position of power, but it quickly became a statement of the intent of a prospective ministry, 'an opportunity afforded Ministers to state to the House a programme of the proceedings which they intend to ask members' consent to – in fact, a statement of the ministerial creed by which the Government is to stand or fall.'[104] The Speech from the Throne was particularly important when parties did not come to the House with already agreed and well-formulated programmes. It followed the initial lobbying and coalescing of members into viable factions.

The Address-in-Reply constituted the response of the House to the Speech from the Throne. The House soon adopted the custom of the House of Commons of giving the most recently elected supporters of the ministry the opportunity to propose and second the Address-in-Reply and thereby make their maiden speeches. Correspondingly, the opposition began to use the Address-in-Reply as a vehicle for launching an attack; 'it is generally in the debate on the address in reply that parties begin to shape themselves'.[105] It became a tradition for the leader of the opposition to follow the seconder of the Address-in-Reply, thereby opening the attack on the ministry.

The issues that an opposition faction chose to make matters of confidence most clearly delineated the groups. A ministry's key policies and its financial proposals relied upon the confidence of the House. This history will adopt the convenient shorthand expression of 'no-confidence' to register the various ways in which oppositions sought to test the confidence of the House.

Aside from explicit motions of no-confidence in a ministry, motions regarded as 'ministerial' or 'party' questions that tested its continued existence concerned the Address-in-Reply, motions expressing broad censure of the ministry, the second readings of important bills, and supply. Often such challenges came by way of amending motions. When the election of a Speaker or Chairman of Committees was made a 'party' matter, this, too, could become a matter of confidence. At times opposition procedural divisions or other tactical motions were treated as challenges since they were an accepted means of testing the ministry's majority support, which could never be taken for granted. The continued confidence of the House in the ministry was at the heart of responsible government, and maintaining confidence was a feature of proceedings under the factional system.

A ministry would advance a legislative programme without seeking ratification from its supporters outside the cabinet. These members, for their part, were not bound to vote for the ministry outside of ministerial questions. A ministry's policies were scrutinised in the House on an ad hoc basis, and voting depended upon the intensive lobbying and temporary alliances that arose in the day-to-day flux of the House, shaped by pledges given at election time, by local and provincial allegiances, and by individual preferences and philosophies.

The factional system required the 'whipping' of members. Charles Elliott, the member for Waimea, was described in 1856 as Stafford's hidden hand in forming the first durable ministry in New Zealand's history. 'Even Stafford himself dances to his piping, heading the troupe of obedient performers who exhibit on their hind legs when he shakes his little whip.'[106] The whips also began to monitor the order paper, organise speakers for debates and generally make sure that a ministry's majority and a quorum would be maintained in the House; 'keeping a House' as it was called.[107] They sat close to the front bench, adjacent to the gangway to ease their access to both government and backbench members.

'Pairing' – agreement between members on different sides when one was absent that the other would refrain from voting – was part of the factional system and existed from the early days.[108] Pairs were increasingly arranged by the whips, although the practice was long considered a private matter and not officially recognised in the standing orders until 1951.[109] As Speaker Maurice O'Rorke stated in 1887: 'The House has never recognised pairing … [it] always religiously excludes the consideration of pairs – it is something outside the House, and a mere private arrangement between honourable members'.[110] Breaking a pair was a serious offence; it not only wrecked the arrangement of business in the House but besmirched the honour of the offending member.

Stafford remained Premier for the next five years, a remarkable feat in the circumstances. Cabinet positions and areas of responsibility remained relatively flexible. Stafford stated that he would lead the House during the session, but he did not take up a portfolio. Sewell, the Colonial Treasurer, had a 'sort of understood leadership', retaining his role of communicating with the Governor.[111] The absence of a strong Premier, a vague definition of 'cabinet', an unclear relationship between the cabinet and the Executive Council, and frequent ministerial absences from the seat of government meant that procedures remained loose. There was no formally prescribed process for government measures to be approved by cabinet, submitted to the Executive Council and introduced into Parliament.[112]

The Compact of 1856

With the Stafford ministry in place, the House could now proceed. Sewell presented a financial statement that became known as the 'Compact of 1856'. The question of how to allocate different powers and revenues between the provincial and general governments had plagued government up to this point. The agreement apportioned these controversial powers and revenues in a way that was acceptable to all the provinces except Wellington. The provinces were to administer their own land regulations and obtain the revenue from land sales to assist immigration and public works. The general government would obtain its revenue from customs duties, but not less than three-eighths of these duties were to be handed over to the provinces. The South Island provinces would repay the New Zealand Company debt, while those of the North Island would repay the loan for purchasing land from Maori. This agreement favoured the provinces, especially the wealthier southern ones, which had plenty of open land available for settlement. But it also endowed the general government with a legitimacy and powers it had not previously enjoyed.

The Constitution Act had to be altered. The New Zealand Parliament asked the British government for 'the largest possible measure of constituent powers' so that it could change the entire Act apart from 22 entrenched sections.[113] Britain amended the Constitution Act in 1857. The entrenched sections involved the Governor's powers to veto and reserve legislation, Britain's powers to direct the Governor in the exercise of these powers and to disallow Acts, and the political and financial relationships between the general and provincial governments.

View of Auckland from Britomart Barrack, 1852. Auckland became the seat of government in September 1840 when the British flag was raised there. In January 1841 Lieutenant-Governor William Hobson transferred his headquarters to Auckland and in 1842 the first immigrant ships began to arrive. In the next decade the settlement became the fledgling colony's bustling administrative, military and commercial centre. In the petition sent to Governor George Grey in 1853, arguing that Parliament should sit in Auckland, it was suggested that more than one-third of the country's European population lived within a radius of ten miles of the centre, and that the town's agriculture, commerce, shipping and exports far exceeded those of other provinces. Auckland's wish was granted, at least for the time being, and Acting Governor Wynyard called the first Parliament to Auckland for 24 May 1854.

With this vital work accomplished, a number of members left Auckland, reducing the House to a bare minimum of 25.[114] There was concern that the House would not be able to complete its business, and it was agreed that members absent without leave should have their names taken down and displayed in a prominent place.[115] Frequently the House was counted out for lack of a quorum. The situation became ridiculous. On one occasion, Wellington members, by leaving en masse, blocked the reporting of a motion to prevent the voting of money to facilitate the movement of Parliament to Wellington. 'The door was then opened [following the division, in which only 15 members voted] when in rushed, or tried to rush, the pro-Wellington absentees, but the Auckland members managed to get outside the door too soon for the Chairman to be able to count the quorum; and so, in this abrupt manner, the House was declared to be adjourned.'[116] Stafford was forced to issue a 'Call of the House', as specified in the standing orders, to assemble the two-thirds of members required to suspend the standing

Patrick Hogan, ATL, A-109-044

orders and get business through. This meant that those members still absent without leave were to be brought to the House in the custody of the Sergeant-at-Arms.

The other major issue of the session was responsibility for native affairs. Governor Gore Browne said that he would receive the ministry's advice and, if this differed from his own view, submit the matter to Britain. Sewell pointedly said that the reservation of native affairs meant that Britain had responsibility for 'peace and war', including paying for military defence, a matter that would soon assume great importance as Pakeha and Maori became embroiled in violent conflict over land.[117]

The General Assembly was now functioning in a permanent and efficient manner. A ministry had been formed, parliamentary officers had been employed and the buildings had been made usable, though they remained cramped, hot and architecturally undistinguished. The session of 1856, which had been both long and momentous in confirming responsible government and setting out the relationship between general and provincial governments, was prorogued with little fuss or ceremony. The members were pleased to be leaving, 'and there was an instantaneous scattering amongst the members of both Chambers, who were speedily en route to Onehunga to embark on their homeward way per *Zingari*'.[118]

CHAPTER TWO

ESTABLISHING THE FOUNDATIONS, 1858–75

In their first 20 years, New Zealand's representative institutions were sorely tested. A range of difficult, interwoven issues dominated Parliament. The tensions between provincial and general government remained. No sooner had Parliament begun to tackle improving the electoral legislation and creating a body of statutes required for the new order than the country was drawn into a bitter conflict over the alienation of Maori land and the exercise of sovereignty. The eruption of war dictated Parliament's proceedings through the first half of the 1860s. At the same time relations with the Governor were extremely difficult because of the divided responsibility for native affairs and war. The wars exacerbated divisions between North and South Island provinces, while strengthening the general government administratively.

As peace returned, Parliament faced the intractable issue of where the country's permanent seat of government should be. Parliament moved to Wellington in 1865. The institution then began to consolidate itself, extend the buildings it occupied, and develop methods of working that would serve it into the future. In the mid 1860s the suppressed provincial question reappeared in the form of a separation movement. The general government began to squeeze the provinces financially, and their predicament worsened towards the end of the decade, giving Julius Vogel the opportunity to increase markedly the powers of the general government. In the end the provinces were abolished.

By the mid 1870s the House of Representatives was ready to assume comprehensive powers of government. It inhabited substantial 'Houses of Parliament', and had developed well-established procedures after confronting such tricky issues as the relationships between the Speaker and the executive government and between the House of Representatives and the Legislative Council.

Despite the hopes of the early 1850s that the Legislative Council would become a colonial 'House of Lords', playing an independent and influential role, it became subordinated to successive ministries and the House of Representatives.[1] It initiated little legislation and while it was at times obstructive, its potential role as a check on rash government was not developed. Its major function, and a useful one on many occasions, was to amend legislation sent up from the lower House. In the period 1854 to 1875, just over half of all legislation originating in the House of Representatives was amended in the Legislative Council.[2] The contribution of the Council lay in co-operation rather than independence, and the two Houses developed methods of dealing with one another to smooth the passage of legislation. Joint conferences were convened, important addresses and resolutions moved jointly in both Houses, joint select committees established, and arrangements made for sharing papers, tabling bills and dealing with difficult private bills.[3]

Many viewed the Legislative Council with scorn, derision or indifference, as a feeble shadow of the House of Representatives, because its members were appointed rather than elected, in the first instance by the Governor and from 1856 by ministries. It was characterised as a runholding oligarchy

Left: Medallion shield, 1861 J.N. Crombie, *Auckland Star* collection, ATL, G3162

and was a useful scapegoat for governments that sought to portray themselves as expressing the popular will. In fact, the Legislative Council did not differ greatly from the lower House. The most that could be said was that it was an older and usually more conservative version of the House itself. It did not develop the exclusive or élite character envisaged for it in the Constitution Act. This is hardly surprising since the colony lacked a social stratum with aristocratic qualifications, even if some had aristocratic aspirations.

The Legislative Council's incapacity was compounded by its small size and the rapid turnover in its membership.[4] Its debates were desultory, its hours short, and its absenteeism rates high in comparison to the House of Representatives. The House tended to dump its legislation on the Council for approval late in each session.

The high turnover of members of the Legislative Council played into the hands of ministries. Successive ministries were able to appoint members sympathetic to their wishes. Stafford's appointments from 1857 detached the Council from provincial interests. It became more 'centralist' and conservative in character. In 1862 limits on its size were removed and the way was opened for wholesale ministerial patronage. The power to nominate members to the Council meant that ministries could 'swamp' or 'stack' the Council to suit their purposes. For some time the practice of ministries having one or two members of cabinet drawn from the Legislative Council gave the Council some status, and it retained its powers of obstruction. But the long-term trend was for it to become marginal.

Getting down to business – the 1858 session

Parliament did not meet in 1857, and was opened on 12 April 1858, again in Auckland.[5] The Wellington members and others were absent. Fifteen members chose to resign their seats, largely to avoid having to come up north.[6] Even the Speaker threatened to resign because of the expense of attending. Throughout the session it remained difficult to achieve a quorum or to call a division.

The session opened in refurbished General Assembly buildings.[7] Mrs Gore Browne and other ladies were seated in a special gallery to the right of the Speaker's chair. The public gallery had been enlarged, the chamber improved and a larger Bellamy's constructed. The area behind the Speaker's chair was reserved for members of the Legislative Council, but at times of popular interest was also used for members of the public, over protests from the Council.[8] Before long the House adopted the twin seats that are still used. These were described by Anthony Trollope: 'the members sit, like Siamese twins, in great armchairs, which are joined together, two-and-two, like some semi-detached villas.'[9] Problems remained with ventilation. The chamber was stiflingly hot when packed, even in midwinter; but draughts from open windows gave members rheumatism.[10] The General Assembly would not improve the buildings since they had been handed over to the Provincial Council in a complicated deal involving the new and expensive Government House up the road.[11]

Stafford's ministry dominated legislative business through a lengthy session.[12] Electoral legislation improved registration and voting procedures but the major impact of the session was to shift the balance between general and provincial governments in favour of the former. The financial arrangements of 1856 were sanctioned with modifications that shifted the pendulum back towards the centre.[13]

Edward Stafford, who entered the House for Nelson Town in 1855, was the pre-eminent parliamentarian and Premier of the period, the man best able to forge the perennial factions into durable ministries. When he resigned from Parliament in 1878, he had led three ministries spanning nine years.

The General Assembly gained a veto over provincial land legislation with the passage of the Waste Lands Bill while the New Provinces Bill, passed against the strong dissent of Speaker Clifford when the powerful Wellington 'ultra-provincial' contingent was absent, facilitated the creation of additional provinces.[14] In the long term, the effect of this legislation was to increase dissatisfaction with the provincial system and weaken the provinces. Southland separated from Otago, then went broke. Other provinces also experienced severe financial difficulties.

The question of who should control native affairs plagued government for a decade. In spite of apparently accepting the Governor's responsibility for native affairs, the House considered control went hand in hand with responsible government and prepared a resolution to this effect at the end of the 1856 session. In a compromise, administration was placed under the 'general oversight' of a minister, with final decisions still reserved for the Governor.[15] But the Assembly was able to, and did, legislate, and controlled the money devoted to native affairs, subject to 'the advice and consent of the Executive Council'. Britain approved Gore Browne's stand against further erosion of the Governor's powers, regarding the retention of control over native affairs by the Governor as a necessary if temporary state of affairs caused by the need to maintain British forces in the colony and the General Assembly's lack of effective authority in the matter.[16] In 1858 Parliament, taking encouragement from the compromise, announced a native policy and pushed through a number of native affairs bills that limited the Governor's role.[17]

Ultimately this struggle would result in the 'self-reliant' policy of 1865, under which New Zealand undertook to pay for 'self-defence' and the Governor's reserved powers over native affairs were removed. But in the meantime the issue paralysed policy. The Assembly voted money grudgingly and responsibility was divided. Native affairs became increasingly entangled with how much the colony would pay towards maintaining the military forces.

The ministry was under considerable pressure to get business through during the session of 1858.[18] The House agreed to sit for extended hours and limit the time spent on notices of motion in order to get all the measures through and allow members to catch the *White Swan* steamer home.[19] This productive session was prorogued in late August, with the relationship between the general government and the provinces settled, responsibility for land legislation determined, state revenue from customs duties assured, native policy and legislation formulated, and the electoral laws revised. A rudimentary legal structure had been created for the central state, and legislation passed on a range of basic functions of state from justice to marriage.[20] The government had at long last sorted out its accounts, which had been in chaos since the time of Grey. It was deemed not necessary to summon Parliament for a session in 1859.

The Governor and war in the early 1860s

As a result of population growth, the House of Representatives gained four seats for the 1860 session, taking the total to 41. From this time, the numbers in the House would grow rapidly as migrants flooded in. The principle for making such adjustments was set down in the Representation Act 1860, which increased the total number of members to 53, distributed evenly amongst the provinces. At the same time a special franchise was extended to miners, who would become a substantial political force in the 1860s.

The 1860 session was dominated by war. The late 1850s had seen increased Maori resistance to the sale of their land, and the rise of the King Movement in the Waikato. When some land at Waitara in Taranaki was offered for sale the government decided to accept it, against the wishes of the chief Wiremu Kingi, in order to break the deadlock over the purchase of Maori land. Surveying of the block of land at Waitara was obstructed, martial law declared and troops called in. The conflict escalated into war early in 1860. The Governor and the ministry were criticised trenchantly for refusing to call

The House

David Monro, born in Edinburgh in 1813, emigrated to Nelson in 1842 after graduating as a doctor from the University of Edinburgh. He was elected to the House for Waimea West in 1853, and became Speaker in 1861. Monro made strenuous efforts to strengthen the Speaker's role, but became involved in a political feud with William Fox. He was knighted in 1866 for his services, and retired from the Speakership in 1870. He sought re-election in 1871 but was unseated after an electoral petition. Monro regained a seat in the House in 1872 but resigned in 1873. He died on 15 February 1877.

Parliament, and for taking action and incurring expenditure without Parliament's authority.[21] But an increasingly confident executive felt that governing the country took priority over summoning the General Assembly. In prosecuting the war, Stafford's ministry and Governor Gore Browne drew closer together.

The 1860 session, originally scheduled for Wellington, was held in Auckland because of the war. It opened late – at the end of July – because the Speaker and the Wellington members had not arrived in time.[22] The balance of power shifted back towards provincial interests as Stafford's hold on power slipped. A full Wellington contingent, led by Featherston, made its presence felt. The opposition failed by a single vote to suspend the New Provinces Act after a member crossed the floor, but it did manage to pass legislation securing surplus revenue from land sales for the provinces, even though the measure was twice rejected by the more centralist Legislative Council.[23]

Many North Island members, led by Fox and Featherston, condemned the Waitara purchase, while the southern members – less well-informed, or less threatened – supported it. Drama occurred over an enquiry into the events that had led to the Taranaki war. Fox launched a direct assault on the Governor which, according to Saunders, departed from recognised practice in the House.[24] In the first such case, Archdeacon Octavius Hadfield (who knew Wiremu Kingi) and Donald McLean were called to the bar of the House to give evidence. They were escorted in by the Sergeant-at-Arms, 'a creditable looking elderly personage, with a white wand, white waistcoat, white gloves and black inexpressibles', according to Sewell.[25] Calling witnesses to the bar of the House was to be a rare occurrence.[26]

The Native Offenders Bill, which controversially sought to ban trade with 'rebellious' Maori, became a matter of confidence that Stafford only narrowly survived. On the night of its introduction the public gallery was overcrowded, as was the space behind the Speaker's chair and the adjoining antechambers.[27] With the House 'anxiously whipped', the bill passed its second reading by a small margin, and there was a tied vote on whether it should go into Committee.[28] Only the Speaker's casting vote allowed it to be continued with (although Clifford personally opposed the bill). Stafford, recognising the inevitable, had the bill

Hugh Carleton was the first member of the House to be elected, for the Bay of Islands, in the staggered elections of 1853. Until his defeat in 1870 he was known as the 'Father of the House'. He had a strong interest in parliamentary procedure and ambitions for office in the House, and was Chairman of Committees from 1856 to 1870. His scholarly background and interest in debate made him a force in the chamber, but he was also pedantic and bored those not impressed by his cultivated mannerisms.

discharged. But the opposition did not want the ministry to resign; as Fox said, 'As they had sown so let them reap'. He did not, in any case, have an alternative policy.[29]

In 1861 the opening of Parliament was again delayed on account of the Wellington members.[30] The elections had resulted in 26 new members (including Harry Atkinson and Maurice O'Rorke) entering the House, nearly half from Auckland.[31] The House remained evenly split over the war. David Monro was elected Speaker in place of Clifford. He was proposed by Dillon Bell who, according to Sewell, had aspirations to the position himself, as did Monro's seconder, Carleton, the 'Father of the House' and Chairman of Committees since 1856.[32] Bell, who had known Monro for 18 years, suggested optimistically that he was 'not distinguished for holding any extreme views' and would 'fill the chair with grace and dignity'.

Monro in fact was clearly identified as a supporter of Stafford and would run into serious conflict with Fox.[33] At times Monro's support for Stafford was openly expressed, even though he proclaimed the power of the Speaker and the independence of the legislature from the executive. He rapidly swotted up on parliamentary proceedings and the rules of the House and played an important role in rationalising its procedures, as would be evident in the new standing orders of 1865, and in asserting the administrative independence of the House from the executive.[34]

Stafford's ministry – termed the 'war ministry' in contrast to Fox's 'peace' or 'peace-at-any-price' party (as Stafford's supporters described it) – was poised on a knife-edge. Weld's resolutions attacking the Maori King Movement's assertion of a separate sovereignty were a feature of this session. The Governor said that he was not prepared to authorise the further involvement of British forces unless he had the full co-operation of the colony. This brutal message, sent independently of the ministry, was intended to strengthen Stafford's hand, but it embarrassed him, shocked the House and brought matters to a head.[35] Fox brought an explicit no-confidence motion into the House, with the issue turning on whether the war was an imperial or colonial responsibility. When Fox realised that he was one member short, people were sent 'all over town' to find the missing member, who was eventually discovered in the smoking-room. Meanwhile members such as C.R. Carter desperately 'spoke against time' to get to 5.30 p.m. Then it was the government's turn to play for time as it awaited the arrival of a newly-elected supporter, J.C. Richmond of Taranaki. With the ship bearing Richmond at the Manukau Heads, Fox finally called for a division. Stafford was defeated by one vote.[36] A five-year ministry that had given New Zealand politics stability came to an end. Fox immediately set about forming a ministry bringing together the interests of Wellington and Auckland.

The next four years were unstable, confused and conflict-wracked.[37] At each of the five short sessions between 1861 and 1865 a ministry was defeated or resigned. In 1862 the Speaker controversially broke a tie to throw the Fox ministry out. The Domett ministry resigned the following year before the confidence of the House was tested, and a coalition formed by Whitaker and Fox out of the war and peace parties lasted little more than a year before resigning late in 1864. The Weld ministry that followed resigned in 1865. It was only with the formation of another centralist Stafford ministry that stability returned.

The underlying problem was the tendency of any provincialist-based ministry to fragment and disintegrate once in power. This was compounded by the distorting effect of war on political patterns – it destroyed the provincialist/centralist dividing line and replaced this with a cleavage between a warlike south and a more moderate north. This was expressed in a movement to separate south from north, to spare the wealthier south the burdens of war. The war also diminished the role of Parliament

William Fox, Stafford's durable opponent, proved much more effective in opposition than in government. Having entered the House representing Wanganui in 1855, he left it for the last time after being defeated in the 1881 election. Fox led ministries briefly in 1856, for a year in both 1861–2 and (with Frederick Whitaker) 1863–4, and again from 1869 to 1872. His feud with Speaker Monro was a feature of the 1860s.

A medallion shield of the 1861 House. This was one of the first occasions that such a photographic record was made. The building at the top is Government House. Speaker Monro is in the centre, Sergeant-at-Arms Mayne with white wand is at the lower left and Clerk Francis Campbell is on the lower right.

and enhanced that of the executive, while discrediting governments grappling with its consequences. As the cost of war spiralled upwards the country got into financial trouble, with governments failing to restrain expenditure and seeking loans to make up the difference. The provinces got into chronic debt as a result of over-ambitious public works schemes.

After Grey had replaced Gore Browne as Governor, the Fox ministry, with an uncertain majority, saw its task as preventing Stafford from returning to power.[38] Fox avoided divisions, and although the government was defeated by four votes on one division this was not considered a matter of confidence and reason to resign. The opposition backed off, Stafford falling silent to allow the new ministry to do its work. A valedictory address to Gore Browne, introduced notably by the opposition, was undermined when the government majority in the House insisted on an amendment. Even then the address was supported only by the opposition half of the House. Others walked out in a calculated slight to the recalled Governor. In the end the ministry called it a day and advised Gore Browne not to keep the 'ghost of the Assembly in existence to meet Sir George Grey'.[39]

On his arrival in September 1861 Grey immediately assumed control of native affairs and the war while transferring financial responsibility for them to the colony.[40] With the abatement of hostilities in the north, the session of 1862 was held for the first time in Wellington. The refusal of the southern members to continue to travel to Auckland was a major factor. The omens were not propitious when the session opened a week late in mid July. The Governor and many members had failed to arrive. The *Harrier* (with Grey aboard) had been blown almost to the Chatham Islands by a storm, and the *White Swan* – conveying Premier Fox, many of his cabinet, other members, wives, officials and boxes of papers – had been wrecked near Uruti Point south of Riversdale in the Wairarapa.[41] The passengers survived but the boxes of government records disappeared out to sea. Replacements were sent down from Auckland on a following ship, and Fox completed his journey by the *Stormbird* in time for the delayed opening. In future years when a document was asked for in the House 'which it is thought inexpedient to produce, an excuse is given that it was lost in the *White Swan*.'[42]

The opening lacked the flourish that Auckland's military could provide. Two ranks of soldiers lined the road leading to the Provincial Chambers, 'but the band was contemptible, the only distinguishable instrument being the flagelet [flageolet – a recorder type of wind instrument] playing a Contre danse', according to Sewell.[43] In opening Parliament, Grey outlined his plans to undermine the King Movement through measures for self-government for Maori while at the same time preparing for a possible invasion of the Waikato should the need arise. Sewell saw clearly that responsible

Establishing the Foundations, 1858–75

Alfred Domett became a member of the House in 1855, for Nelson Town, and left it in 1866 for the Legislative Council, where he remained until 1871. Domett was Premier in 1862–3 during the wars. His long-standing literary interests led him to take a leading role in the establishment and development of the General Assembly Library.

government in the matter of native affairs was in 'abeyance'.[44] Stafford hammered away at the unclear responsibility for native policy as the ministry foundered, with South Island members being swept up in the separation movement that had spread from Otago.

The inevitable confidence motion eventuated through a member moving 'the previous question' in the debate on Fox's native affairs policy, so that the question under consideration was not put – a device to kill a measure. Fox's resolution stated that the ministry should be responsible for administering native affairs but not in effect bear the cost of such government or the wars. The vote on whether Fox's resolution should be put was a tie, broken by the Speaker's casting vote against Fox.[45] In House of Commons tradition, Monro's vote technically allowed further consideration of the issue, but this was unconvincing given the 'previous question' motion and the fact that two days' debate had already been allowed. In reality he was voting as a supporter of Stafford.

Fox resigned after some deliberation and was replaced eventually by Alfred Domett, who cobbled together a stop-gap ministry of moderates from Fox's and Stafford's factions which gave the south greater representation. The ministry was not too different in outlook from that of Fox. Grey retained his pre-eminence.[46]

FitzGerald and 18 others who had been in the House for the tumultuous first session of 1854 held a 'ten-year' reunion dinner in Bellamy's.[47] Among the singing, the champagne and the numerous toasts, there was a toast to that fearsome parliamentary weapon, 'Mackay's umbrella'. A song was even composed for the occasion. But in spite of the good-natured reminiscing, the session was characterised by ill tempered outbursts and votes that defied understanding as there was no clear majority. The various factions became increasingly frustrated.

The trivial 'clock' episode in particular created a rift between Speaker Monro and Fox. The Native Lands Bill (which established the means of future alienation of Maori land) gave rise to the longest debate in the history of the House up to that time, stretching through three very late evenings at the end of the session. Fox persistently obstructed progress; in the end the ministry had to send the bill to the Legislative Council the same evening to be passed.[48] While standing orders dictated that the House was to rise at 5.30 p.m., Monro instructed a messenger to stop the clock and put it back (it was by then showing after 5.30) so that the last stage of reporting the final division on the title of the bill after its third reading could proceed.[49] This unorthodox step became notorious. Monro, confronted by Fox, had to admit that his action had been irregular.

Further conflict broke out in Taranaki in May 1863. With Grey determined to invade the Waikato to bring the King Movement to heel, the Governor and Domett's ministry agreed to a campaign against Maori without summoning the General Assembly. The Waikato campaign began in July, as Domett completed plans to settle the Waikato following the confiscation of land. Grey pressed Domett to call Parliament to vote money for the war, but he refused.[50] In August Sewell protested to Domett, saying that Parliament had been 'practically suppressed' at a time when 'the most extreme and dangerous measures [were] being taken by Sir George Grey of his own authority, without and against law.'[51] Domett knew that his ministry was likely to lose office when Parliament met, and called it together only when the government had run out of money.

The General Assembly finally met in Auckland in October 1863, with four Otago members added to the House as a result of gold-rush immigration. The opening was thinly attended, however, with little more than half the members present. One reason for the low turnout was the lateness of the steamer *Wonga Wonga*, but resignations and a lack of enthusiasm for attending so late in the year also contributed.[52] Grey justified his actions and outlined the plan for military operations and settlement, but the ministry was in serious disarray. Domett was unable to find anyone in the Legislative Council willing to represent the ministry and decided to resign, fed up with both the autocratic Grey and the personal differences within the government, including Bell's 'overbearing' conduct.[53] He made no recommendation for a successor.

To the surprise of all, Grey asked Fox, who had arrived that day, to form a government. Whitaker (in the Legislative Council) consented to join Fox if he could be Premier, and on this basis a ministry was formed.[54] Fox became Colonial Secretary, Minister for Native Affairs and Leader of the House. Auckland dominated the new ministry, whose policies, largely continuing those of Domett, included a new loan to pay for the war and further settlement, and the active prosecution of the war by the executive government. This led to confrontation with Grey because Fox was much more determined than Domett to have his way. Fox was roundly criticised for reversing his position in now adopting a warlike stance. The disgruntled Domett was reported to have described the House as 'one vast urinary – every fellow piddling down another fellow's back!', even as it was enveloped by an atmosphere of self-congratulation.[55]

The new Fox–Whitaker ministry explicitly accepted responsibility for native affairs, the British government having emphatically relinquished it.[56] The ministry passed the Suppression of Rebellion Act, the New Zealand Settlements Act and the New Zealand Loan and Loan Appropriation Acts, laws that made the session notorious.[57] Sewell fulminated against them and the haste with which they were put through, feeling that the ministry was treating the House with derision.[58]

More organised obstruction followed. The House began to sit 'by relays', with the ministry bullied by one half of the House until they retired from the chamber and the other half came in.[59] The government then made Saturday a sitting day.[60] Because of continuing obstruction the House, remarkably, did not rise until 3 a.m. on Sunday – 'the minority kept the House sitting till midnight, when a number of members left; the sitting then continued till three or four on the Sunday morning; and the minority, by talking against time, absolutely ruled the majority.'[61]

As a result of the concerted stonewalling, the House agreed that there should be no further sittings on Saturdays. This was observed until the mid 1870s, when occasional Saturday sittings were again accepted with the proviso that they should terminate by 11 p.m. Stonewalling was still relatively unusual. It was adopted in response to a more organised and determined executive rather than as a standard tactic. The term 'stonewalling' itself was considered offensive under the standing orders.[62] The 1863 session ended meekly enough, with some members 'hastening to get on board the steamboat' to get home before Christmas while others battled on in a thin House.

After a session plagued by resignations and absences, Fox, not keen to hold another in 1864, argued that there was no constitutional reason to hold Parliaments annually.[63] Others such as FitzGerald pointed to the irregularity of continued government expenditure in the absence of authorised appropriations – which were usually granted for one year only. In the end it was agreed that Parliament should meet by March 1865. If arrangements for the shift to Wellington had not been completed, Christchurch would host the session.[64]

The seat of government

Settling on the location of the seat of government had plagued Parliament since the beginning. While many members from outside Auckland agreed that it should be shifted, it was another matter deciding where it should go. No ministry dared take a stand on the question. Voting was left to individual members. The obvious alternative of Wellington in the centre of the country had drawbacks. The

Establishing the Foundations, 1858–75

earthquakes of 1848 and 1855 were still fresh in members' thinking and Wellington's ruling triumvirate, 'the 3 Fs' – Fox, Featherston and Fitzherbert – was widely mistrusted as 'ultra'-provincialist.

In 1856 the question erupted in earnest.[65] Proposals for Auckland, Nelson and Wellington were lost in turn (as neither Wellington nor Nelson members would support the other), and in the end the House could only accept that the next session be held in some more central place that the Governor considered appropriate. But the Governor stalled, preferring to stay in Auckland, and Stafford's ministry declined to take any position on the matter, being deeply divided on the question. Stafford himself was a strong advocate of staying put. Following a select committee report which emphasised the cost of moving the seat of government, money was not voted for a move. A compromise was proposed by the Governor: Auckland should have the next session, with sessions then alternating between Wellington and Auckland.

Featherston had meanwhile cleverly invested in substantial Provincial Council buildings in Wellington. Completed in 1858, they were specifically designed to house the General Assembly and compared favourably with Auckland's. The chamber of the House of Representatives was much more spacious and had both a lower and upper public gallery and a proper press gallery. There was a substantial block of offices as well.

But the Taranaki war and the need for the Governor to remain in Auckland meant that the session of 1860 was again held there, on Stafford's advice and under threat of resignation by Auckland members, despite the understanding that Wellington would have it.[66] The war kept Parliament in Auckland in

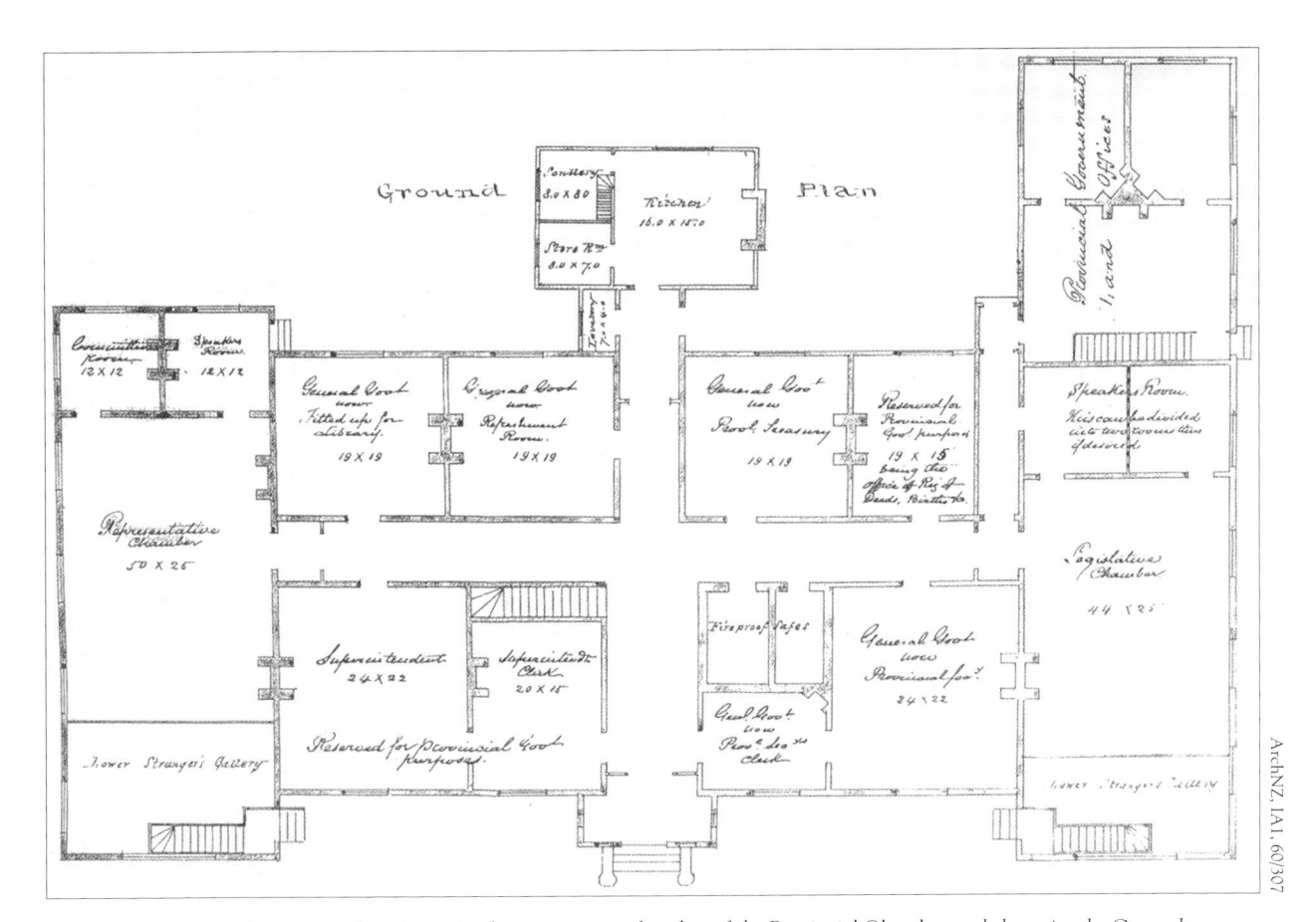

Wellington's Provincial Superintendent Isaac Featherston sent up this plan of the Provincial Chambers to help entice the General Assembly to Wellington. The building was on the site of the present Parliamentary Library.

1861.[67] Wellington's turn came in 1862, when peace returned. A motion to keep the Assembly in Wellington was defeated by only a single vote, with Fox and Weld voting for it, the south generally strongly in support, and Stafford leading the opposition.[68] It was agreed that the matter should be put into the hands of the Governor after a range of alternatives – Dunedin, Christchurch, Picton and Nelson – had been tossed into the pot.

The issue of the location of the seat of government was coming to a head. The substantial growth of population in Otago and the prosperity of Canterbury were shifting the demographic centre of gravity of the country southwards. The case for Auckland, based on the conduct of native affairs and the war, was now turned on its head. Sewell considered having the government in Auckland was pernicious – people were 'living upon the War and like greedy beasts of prey they are looking out for the fat morsels of Native Land, and Commissariat pickings'.[69]

In 1863, with Parliament having gained four more Otago members, the question was confronted. A group of Wellington and Nelson members agreed to put before the House resolutions that set aside local Cook Strait rivalries.[70] Domett's motion that the seat of government be moved permanently to the Cook Strait area was embodied in a formal resolution moved by FitzGerald that the Australian Governors should select commissioners to decide exactly where the seat of government should be.[71]

Stafford, knowing that some supporters of a shift were soon to sail south, attempted with Auckland support to adjourn the debate, but this was ruled out by the House. The question was put without further discussion on the motion of Fitzherbert. Stafford, apparently white with rage, shouted, 'I declare this proceeding to be most unfair – most unfair, Sir; and I shall leave the House', and he did, accompanied by Auckland members.[72] Stafford's words were ordered taken down for censure. When Stafford recovered his wits, he realised that FitzGerald's motion was about to be agreed to. When he attempted to re-enter the House, he and the others who had left with him found themselves locked out as the division was taken. The resolution was adopted unanimously in their absence. Initially there was no-one left to go into the Noes lobby (which meant the division could not be recorded), so FitzGerald and another supporter of the resolution, W.B. Rhodes, volunteered to vote 'no', making the official result 24 to 2.

Stafford's anger resulted from the standing order which allowed members to move for a division at any time without further discussion. This was very rarely used – ministries generally lacked both sufficient control over the House and the will to impose 'closure' by such means.[73] There was an understanding that speeches should take their course. Members could and did speak for many hours, and this is what Stafford had expected.[74]

Stafford's final attempt to block the move of the seat of government in a fuller House failed by 24 to 17, and the address conveying the resolutions to the Governor was adopted. The House agreed also to fund the necessary buildings associated with the shift to the tune of £50,000 – not only to house the General Assembly but also for government offices and a Government House.

The rift between Grey and the Whitaker–Fox ministry in 1863 was reflected in protracted manoeuvering over the location of the next session and developed into a constitutional crisis.[75] Whitaker, keen to leave office, suggested Wellington as a more convenient location than Auckland for the government. Grey objected strongly, dug his heels in and refused to attend a Parliament held anywhere but Auckland. Following a flood of memoranda (dubbed 'the Memorandummiad' by FitzGerald)[76] the ministry capitulated and agreed that members should be summoned to Auckland once again. In the end the Whitaker–Fox ministry resigned in September 1864 as a result of the deadlock with Grey, who was able to paralyse government in spite of ministerial responsibility for native affairs.

During 1864 the government had got into fiscal difficulties. Southern provinces such as Otago, led by Julius Vogel, urged separation of the south from the north, while Weld, speaking in Christchurch in the interests of the south, advanced the notion of colonial 'self-reliance' in providing both the finance and military resources to settle the conflict. As a result of the ministry's resignation, Grey was forced to call a very short session at the end of 1864. Southern members were particularly unhappy at being dragged back to Auckland.

At Grey's invitation, Weld managed to gather together a strong, predominantly southern, ministry on the basis of the withdrawal of British troops and their replacement by a small defence force, and a shift of the seat of government to Wellington.[77] The self-reliance resolutions asked Britain to withdraw its forces and institute full ministerial responsibility, because the prevailing system of 'double government' resulted in a vacillating policy and unnecessary expenditure. The resolutions were presented to the House but were watered down before going to Grey and being accepted.[78]

The Australian Commissioners deciding upon the seat of government visited Wanganui, Wellington, Picton, Port Underwood, Havelock, and Nelson before coming to the unanimous and obvious conclusion that Wellington was the best place, for which difficult task they were paid £4,085![79] With the fight to move to Wellington won, the people of Auckland rose up 'in rebellion'. A large meeting called for Auckland's separation from the other provinces.[80] Grey, who had reluctantly consented to the move in November 1864, and other Aucklanders, were glad to see the back of a House that had voted to take itself south. The 1864 session came to a hurried end in mid December, allowing members to get home for Christmas.

Frederick Weld was amongst the first members of the House, representing Wairau. He retired in 1866 after being instrumental in shifting the seat of government to Wellington, and serving as Premier in 1864–5.

The move to Wellington took place in early 1865. It was a substantial logistical exercise involving the Governor and his establishment, officials of the various government departments, the staff of Parliament and the Government Printer.[81] Public records and about 80 cases of library books were sent south by the ss *Queen* in late March 1865. The total cost of the move was £54,665, the bulk of which was spent on the purchase or building of offices, the General Assembly buildings, a ministerial residence, Government House, and compensation to officials. In an unseemly parting shot, the Auckland provincial government locked the General Assembly buildings and seized the furniture for dispersal around its own offices.[82]

The opening of the General Assembly was held over until late July 1865 as a result of alterations to the Wellington Provincial Chambers (themselves delayed by shortages of carpenters due to the disappearance of labour to the goldfields).[83] A library and more committee rooms were added to buildings that had already acquired a Bellamy's kitchen and other outhouses at the rear of the original premises.

On the whole, members found Wellington more congenial if rather cold in winter. J.C. Richmond wrote that 'the House of Assembly here is a much better building than at Auckland. It contains two halls with a sort of degraded Gothic window in the gables, standing some distance apart and connected by a range of offices. The refreshment rooms are clean reputable places. It stands on a terrace some distance back from the water and has a good view over the town and harbour.'[84] But Monro found the Speaker's rooms 'very unfurnished' and described being 'half poisoned with foul air' after the lengthy Address-in-Reply debate.[85]

Weld's ministry soon found Grey impossible to work with. It warned that it would resign if disagreements continued. Grey and the British military commander General Duncan Cameron were at loggerheads over the Taranaki–Wanganui campaign. The government was rendered even more helpless as expenses mounted. As the time for another session of Parliament approached, Weld decided to resign because of Cameron's inaction in prosecuting the war and the now-evident manipulation of affairs by Grey. The government had also exhausted its credit with the Bank of New Zealand and public debt had risen alarmingly. In Weld's mind the dual system of power over native affairs was constitutionally intolerable, especially as it looked increasingly likely that the colony

The Wellington Provincial Council chambers not long after their construction, c. 1859.

would have to pay for both the administration of native affairs and defence without gaining control over them.

Weld's intended resignation was pre-empted just prior to the opening of Parliament by a despatch from Britain accepting self-reliance. This coincided with General Cameron's resignation.[86] Stafford, supported by the Auckland and Otago members, was likely to head a formidable opposition. During the Address-in-Reply debate, Stafford launched into a personal attack on the ministry and headed a walkout of Auckland members. A division was not held because there was no teller for the 'Noes'. The government was nonetheless defeated emphatically soon afterwards, over a bill to make it more difficult to create new provinces.[87]

Matters came to a head with the financial statement, which brought home the reality of self-reliance and underlined the government's precarious fiscal state. The arrangements of the Compact of 1856 were no longer adequate because the wars and payments to service loans had inflated the expenditure of the general government.[88] Vogel mounted a sustained attack on the government, establishing his leading position in the opposition. He would prove a major force in government. The motion to end the financial debate became an issue of confidence and was won by the government by only two votes. Vogel's alternative financial resolutions resulted in an unseemly scene as the opposition, not wanting to seize that particular moment, tried to rush out of the chamber wholesale before the division was taken.[89]

Auckland convincingly lost its move to separate the two islands (precipitated by the move to Wellington) 31 to 17.[90] Vogel was one of several who missed the final and crucial division at 1 a.m.

through being 'drunk & asleep & did not hear the bell'.[91] After many close divisions, the ministry secured approval in principle for its financial policies but still teetered on the precipice. Censure of the ministry over an amnesty for Maori 'rebels' was carried on voices, but a division on the matter was prevented when opposition members fled the chamber.[92] Weld demanded that the motion be rescinded as a matter of confidence. The House did not want to take things so far and agreed to do so, with the opposition again absent. Thereafter business broke down. The Speaker had to cast a vote to save the ministry over its financial policy. Vogel complained bitterly of pairing mistakes that might have defeated the government. Stafford's Disqualification Bill (subsequently dropped), which would have removed two ministers from office, passed its second reading without a division.[93]

Weld's ministry resigned in any case. Stafford appeared to be the only alternative to avoid the looming threat to provincial revenues.[94] After a caucus meeting of the largely provincialist opposition, Governor Grey and Stafford came to an understanding. Grey would dissolve Parliament if Stafford was unable to secure supply and Stafford agreed not to interfere with Grey's authority over British troops.[95] With Weld and his supporters having left, the House was unable to resist this usurpation of power. Parliament was rendered powerless and the House was soon prorogued.

Settling in

Wellington welcomed Parliament for the status it brought, the additional business it generated and the injection of gaiety into the city's social scene. In the days prior to the session, members would arrive by steamer, arrange local accommodation and gather around the Parliament Buildings. Almost all would lodge within walking distance of the House in boarding houses or cheap hotels where they would be in constant daily informal contact with each other.

Sessions of Parliament, with their attendant social gatherings, gossip, political intrigue and scandal, provided a focal point for Wellington's winter social season.[96] The Governor was in residence, and the influx of parliamentarians and their wives and families stirred Wellington out of its torpor with a gay whirl of 'balls, opera, concerts, theatre, "at Homes" and dining'. Social life became even more exciting when Vogel became Premier (and Sir James Fergusson, Governor). The number of 'balls, receptions, drawing-rooms, and banquets as well as the less formal at-homes' increased.[97] Parliament organised its own balls and Speakers invited members to dinners that were often held in the chamber itself.

The space in the Provincial Council buildings was soon taken up. These had also to house government departments and the chamber had been designed for the smaller Provincial Council, which had many fewer than the 76 members that had to be crammed into it from 1868. The condition of the building caused alarm.[98] It lacked strength in its roof structure and had been attacked by dry rot.[99]

In 1866 a grand new 'House of Representatives' complete with a tower in wood was planned behind the existing building to free up space and allow for renovations. This did not go ahead because of Stafford's retrenchment. Instead makeshift alterations and renovations took place at the end of the 1860s.[100] The roof was strengthened, supporting buttresses added down the sides of the two chambers, leaks dealt with, attempts to improve ventilation made and the chamber refurbished. A new and more substantial kitchen and additional committee rooms were built at the rear of the buildings. Following an investigation of gas lighting, a large number of gaslights were installed in the roof lanterns of the chamber.[101]

After William Clayton, the new Colonial Architect, criticised the structure's lack of strength in 1870 there was progressive reconstruction of the buildings and substantial extensions along the southern Sydney Street frontage.[102] Clayton's report alarmed the Legislative Council sufficiently that a member produced some rotten and honeycombed wood in the chamber.[103] The Speaker referred to the buildings as being on their last legs, but ambitious plans for a completely new building were firmly quashed,

The first library building (at left) and committee rooms (middle) at the rear of Parliament Buildings in Wellington, c. 1870. With the move to Wellington, the library enjoyed more spacious quarters. In the first years in Auckland the parliamentary library was housed in a tiny room and shared with the Auckland Provincial Council. In 1860 the 750-volume parliamentary collection was moved to a larger room. Files of newspapers were transferred to the library so that 'an authentic record of the early political history of the colony' could be created. The newspapers were essential: they contained the only detailed record of parliamentary debates. It was agreed that a complete collection of New Zealand books be made, presaging the later legal deposit system. The library's first catalogue was printed in London in 1862. In 1863 the library shifted into a new single-room cottage behind the main building that could house 4,000 volumes. The author Alfred Domett, a member of the House of Representatives (1855–66) and then of the Legislative Council (1866–74), was described by Gisborne as the 'father' of the library, building up its classical collection in particular. W.T.L. Travers, Hugh Carleton and William Fitzherbert were other mainstays in the early decades.

partly because proposing new buildings might re-open the question of where the seat of government should be located.[104]

This matter had not been finally settled. Members persisted in agitating for another move.[105] It was alleged (shortly after a member had died in 1868) that there was 'malaria along the beach and even about the House', and a 'miasmatic influence' that might 'with epidemic fury, sweep off the people in hundreds. In short Wellington was the dirtiest town in the Colony.'[106] There was some truth in this. Wellington did not get a proper sewerage system until the 1890s. A more concerted effort was made in 1871 to shift Parliament to Dunedin for the next session in the hope that eventually it might return to

Establishing the Foundations, 1858–75

Auckland.[107] The House seemed agreeable, but Fox pointedly noted that his government strongly resisted the idea, and that it was the Governor acting on the advice of the ministry of the day who summoned Parliament. The ministry failed to act once the full cost of sitting in Dunedin became apparent.

In 1871 further work on the buildings began with additional strengthening of the roofs. Substantial extensions to provide a new library and offices for government departments were then constructed behind the existing buildings, causing considerable inconvenience to parliamentarians who were engaged in an exhausting session.[108] In 1873 the House's chamber was enlarged to accommodate the additional members and a new Council chamber was built at the rear of the newest extensions. The rotten white pine was removed from the old structure and a three-storey addition was built abutting the House at the front to provide new offices and committee rooms.

The overall result was a transformed set of buildings in a more elaborate Gothic style than the original, on the axis of Sydney Street.[109] Both chambers featured central 'lantern' glass sections for lighting and ventilation, decorated with Gothic iron railings. The remodelled and enlarged House of Representatives chamber had a moulded plaster ceiling, Gothic pillars, ornamental cantilevers and

This view from Sydney Street, c. 1880, gives a good impression of the westward extensions of the 1870s. From left to right: the Legislative Council block, library, Bellamy's, House of Representatives chamber, and a three-storey office block at front.

Photograph by R.H. Taylor, ATL, 18472

The Governor arrives at the Legislative Council chamber to open Parliament.

hammer beams. The previously featureless south wall was opened up with windows and given turrets containing winding staircases to the galleries. The new Legislative Council chamber was located to the west at the rear of the buildings. Its north elevation facing Hill Street looked out onto a carriageway running down the side of the buildings. The carriageway was used by the Governor when he opened Parliament. The state openings were held in front of the main entrance of the chamber.[110]

The buildings were fitted with gas lighting and underfloor water heating. A substantial smoking room was available and additional 'water closets' were provided, including some for ladies. A welcome innovation, following the Commons, was the installation of battery-powered electric division bells.[111] The Clerk had a switch at his table to activate them. Previously, divisions were sounded by a messenger running through the buildings clanging a large bell. The new chambers were ready for the opening of the 1873 session. They were marred only by the retention of the old shabby fittings, seats and desks, which were not replaced until the following year.[112] The new seating of 1874 was stepped, with the front two rows of desks on a low raised platform and a third row at a slightly higher level behind.[113] The Speaker sat at the east end of the chamber, with the government benches to his right and opposition to his left on the colder and draughty southern flank of the building.[114] The members sat on double padded leather couches in a horseshoe formation. The press gallery was above the Speaker, separated by a partition from the Hansard reporters. Opposite this was the ladies' gallery, and on either side of the chamber were the Speaker's gallery and the general public gallery.

New Speaker's chairs were fashioned for both chambers. The House's was described as 'a wooden structure like the head of a bed without the foot, with a cumbrous ornament like a table turned, carved legs upwards, upon the top.'[115] Beyond it lay the 'long table', much as it does today, 'with stationery cases, imposing tomes, and a supply of water, the only refreshment, except the flow of the soul, that members partake of in the Chamber'. Outside the chamber, the corridors forming the 'Ayes'

The interior of the chamber of the House, c. 1897, showing the moulded plaster ceiling, Gothic pillars, ornamental cantilevers, hammer beams and chandeliers. The reporters' gallery is above the Speaker's dais, with a large 'strangers' (public) gallery on one side and the other side reserved for Legislative Council members and those invited by the Speaker. The ladies' gallery faced the Speaker. Downstairs, twin-couch seats are arranged in a horseshoe formation similar to today's. As in the House of Commons, the government benches are to the right of the Speaker, facing the opposition across the Table of the House. On either side of the Speaker sat ministers' private secretaries, heads of department and honoured guests.

and 'Noes' lobbies were lined with racks containing *Hansard*, the *Journals* of the House, *Statutes*, and other publications for members' reference.[116]

The extensions of the early 1870s included an improved Bellamy's and an enlarged library. From the early days, Bellamy's had been the centre of parliamentary conviviality. C.W. Richmond described in 1862 how members got together nearly every night in Bellamy's 'for singing and joking and drinking whisky toddy'.[117] The new Bellamy's comprised a larger kitchen and scullery and a capacious dining room and tea room between the library and the chamber of the House.[118] Substantial sums were spent on a range of silver plate and cutlery, crockery and table linen ordered from Britain. Entrée to Bellamy's was a privilege which gave access to one of New Zealand's foremost restaurants and bars. Each year the list of the favoured few was published.

THE LADIES' GALLERY, PARLIAMENT HOUSE, WELLINGTON, NEW ZEALAND

The Graphic (London), 13 November 1880, ATL, C16700

In Auckland men and women initially sat together in the part of the hall that was designated the public gallery. In 1864 a separate area defined as the 'ladies' gallery' was created. The separation of females lasted until 1945. The provision of an open gallery for women distinguished the New Zealand Parliament from the House of Commons, where women sat behind grilles so that members would not be distracted by the sight of the opposite sex.

The ladies' gallery was integral to Wellington's social scene and had its own pecking order. According to Alfred Cox, the political 'ladies' seemed to have a preternatural ability to anticipate a sensation, and many members relied on this. The right of members' spouses to knit, sew, embroider and the like while watching the melée below has been preserved to the present day.

The 'widespread suspicion that much of the legislation of this period was being considered and carried in a miasma of whisky fumes' had some truth to it.[119] Bellamy's featured as a weapon in the political struggles and in the stories of the time. As member William Swanson described it, 'No doubt very free use is made of Bellamy's: there is no mistake at all about that. I have seen such results from the existence of Bellamy's in this House as I am sure have never been seen in any [Provincial] Council. I have seen the Native members … offer in this House to carry a member home and promise to put him to bed and not to hurt him, so that the proceedings might be carried on … I have seen this House cleared on a subsequent day so that no one should hear what took place – so that the dirty linen might not be washed in public, while the offending member was being reprimanded … I will tell you what I hear in the lobby from a distinguished leader of a party. I heard him say to a "whip" on the other side – "If you make any of my men drunk I will keep the talk up for a fortnight".'[120] A Bills Office clerk of the time had his office at the end of a passage from the chamber, separated only by a 'swinging green-baize door'.[121] He wondered at his popularity

The well-known 'dandy' Jackson Palmer, member for Waitemata, plays to the ladies' gallery. When Wellington's 'political ladies' were present, the evening session became more of a public meeting in which members addressed the women above. It was said that the ladies' gallery had been situated facing the Speaker to remove the distraction, but members soon got around this – some even spoke with their backs to the Speaker. When the ladies departed, the excitement subsided and routine business was resumed.

until he discovered that there was 'a trapdoor in the window at the side of my office, where liquor can be got from "Bellamy's".'

The most notorious incident involved Jerningham Wakefield, whose fondness for alcohol was well known.[122] In 1872, Fox's government whip attempted to secure Wakefield's vote by locking him in a committee room. Stafford's whip, hearing of this, 'got up on the roof, and lowered a bottle of whisky with a loosened cork down the chimney. When the division bell rang, the … Whip rushed up to the committee room to get his sure vote, but, alas it was "paralytic" under the table.' The government whip continued to ply Wakefield with alcohol, but he nonetheless voted with Stafford to throw out the ministry.

In 1875, as his alcoholism took its toll, Wakefield was removed from the House by the Sergeant-at-Arms 'disgustingly drunk'. He only just escaped being banned from Bellamy's and the library because of 'habits of drunkenness and uncleanliness' which rendered him a 'nuisance'.[123] He was soon rejected by the Christchurch electors after appearing at a rival's election meeting partially drunk, and died in ignominy in an Ashburton old men's home in 1879.

Although it was well patronised, Bellamy's was not approved of by all members. Those wedded to the temperance cause particularly disliked its provision of alcohol. In 1869 Carleton attempted to have the institution abolished in order to 'raise the character of the House … to preserve its influence in the country … [and to] dispel the general impression … that members were more solicitous about their own comforts than about the public welfare'.[124] To some members Carleton's challenge was a red rag to a bull, but one or two rallied to his cause. Hall charged that 'a pothouse bar could not have its array of drinks displayed more disgustingly' than Bellamy's. Nonetheless the exemption from the liquor laws that Bellamy's had enjoyed from the first days of Parliament continued, and was written into the consolidated Licensing Act 1881.

With the completion by the end of 1876 of the new Government Buildings on reclaimed land, government departments moved out of the complex.[125] The final renovations were made around this time. The old central section of the original Provincial Council building was substantially rebuilt, with the old Legislative Council chamber converted into offices and accommodation for the housekeeper. The General Assembly could at last enjoy fully its own commodious premises, which were now called rather grandly 'the Houses of Parliament'.

JACKSON PALMER playing to the (Ladies) Gallery.

Edward Jerningham Wakefield, the son of Edward Gibbon, was elected as member for Christchurch Country for the first Parliament of 1854–5, and returned from 1871 to 1875. His second term was clouded by his descent into alcoholism.

Conduct in the House

The Speaker's authority over members was backed up by both standing orders and the Privileges Act 1856, which gave him the ability to levy fines of £20 or imprison offenders for up to one month. The amount was raised to £50 in the 1865 standing orders. Members guilty of contempt could be fined, but this rarely happened. In 1877 H.H. Lusk, the member for Franklin, was found to have received payment from the Auckland City Council for assisting in drafting a government bill that gave advantage to the Council. He was fined £50.[126] In 1881, William Gisborne's disorderly challenge to the House during a notable stonewall resulted in a £20 fine (see chapter 3).

Other resources were available to discipline members. The Speaker could 'name' offenders and ask the House to pass judgement on the member's conduct. This would usually result in a motion that the member be 'suspended from the service of the House'. If carried, the member could not vote or enter the lobbies for the period specified. As a matter of honour members did not directly refer to each other by name in the chamber, but referred to the electorate which they represented. 'Naming' was thus a form of punishment by dishonour. In the nineteenth century the only example of this was over Vogel's actions in 1887 (see chapter 3).

The Speaker could also order an offending member to leave the chamber and, by resolution of the House, a motion condemning a member's actions could be passed. While such motions were rare and considered serious, being ordered to leave the chamber became common and was taken more lightly. As a newspaper correspondent noted, one might imagine that the offending member 'with a shadow of censure over his head would be cast into some dungeon, with an orderly on the mat outside the door', but when an offender was asked how he had spent his time 'he laughed and said he was in a very comfortable committee room, writing his Home letters, and he was very glad of the chance to do so!'[127]

The New Zealand House of Representatives carried over a number of traditions from the House of Commons, some arcane and some practical. In Parliament's early years, the standing orders required members to rise and take their hats off whenever messages from the Governor were read. They bobbed up and down like jack-in-the-boxes. Another rule from the beginning was the prohibition on reading speeches. This terrified new members and those not adept at speaking off the cuff. This prohibition remained in place until 1996. Much of the time members did not prepare speeches, a fact reflected in the quality of debate.[128] Vincent Pyke at one time said there were three kinds of members – 'there were the speechless members, who were never heard of except by their votes. Then there were the silly members, who talked nonsense by the yard. And, thirdly, there were the sensible members, who said very little, and said that little to the purpose.'[129] William Pember Reeves observed that 'Bores are never shouted or coughed down', since 'the House is too small, and nearly all the members are on friendly terms with each other.' The usual sign of disapproval was simply evacuation of the chamber. Some were noted for producing this effect. F.J. Moss cleared the House 'when he rises, more quickly than even Seddon himself, and has more often had the bell rung to get a House for him than any other member.'[130]

This sketch of a member delivering a speech from his desk in the 1870s is accompanied by a curious inscription at the bottom. Was the cartoonist casting aspersions on the veracity of the member? 'T. Ruth – pinx' – literally 'T. Ruth painted it'. It is possible that the sketch is of William Swanson, one of the Auckland 'rats' of 1879.

Parliamentary Library, untitled cartoon collection, 1870s

Some members' proclivities during debate were well known. Everyone tries to escape as Robert Stout pontificates.

A few members were genuine orators. Scobie Mackenzie adopted the method of Disraeli; he would write out speeches in full, prune them, commit the central points to memory, then throw the written speech away. This gave his speeches a natural spontaneity that disguised their careful preparation. He was able to best most in verbal duels: 'the words "Scobie's up" were as potent as any party whip to clear the lobbies ... Members discussing the situation over a bottle of wine at Bellamy's hurriedly emptied their glasses and returned to a fast filling House. Animation returned to the Strangers' Gallery and a look of expectancy was on every face.'[131]

The use of hats has already been mentioned. Members were not allowed to wear hats when entering or leaving the chamber or addressing the House, although they were generally worn in the chamber at other times. In 1863 Speaker Monro was exasperated at the Jewish new member Vogel's insistence on taking the oath on the Old Testament while wearing his hat. He explicitly included in his new standing orders of 1865 the provision that members' heads must be 'uncovered' when they were entering or leaving the House, or moving a motion during a debate. Members had also to take their hats off when a message from the Governor was read. But if a member wanted to raise a point of order when the doors were locked and a division taken, he had to do so from a seated position with his hat on. The reasoning behind this was the same as used in the Commons – to avoid giving the appearance of creating a debate. While this did not happen too often, when it did it produced hilarious scenes as members desperately scrambled for a hat – anyone's hat, whether it fitted or not – as they attempted to speak. This arcane requirement was abandoned in the 1929 standing orders.

It was generally understood that reading newspapers, books or letters, and smoking, were not allowed in the chamber, although snuff was provided, again following the tradition of the House of Commons. The Sergeant-at-Arms kept the House's snuff box filled. Sewell 'snuffs like a Scotchman, and not unfrequently he will break off in the middle of a speech, and on finding the three boxes before him all empty will cross the House to where sits Dr. Lee, to borrow his box for the rest of the day.'[132] Featherston once played a trick on Sewell. 'Bowing and advancing towards him with box in hand he attracted Sewell's attention, who was gently drawn to the opposite side of the House. He took a pinch of snuff, and in a fit of absence of mind sat down by the side of his opponent. And not only sat down, but rose up to speak before making the discovery that he had joined the Opposition.'[133]

The system for taking a division was the same as in the Commons. It persisted until 1996 and is still used for personal votes today. Members went into the 'Ayes' and the 'Noes' lobbies (corridors to the right and left respectively of the Speaker outside the chamber) where the appointed tellers would stand at the doors ticking off names from the division lists. There was plenty of scope for the manipulation of numbers when party organisation did not exist and voting lines were indistinct. The generally poor organisation of debates meant that they could suddenly collapse if members were out of the House or not expecting to speak.

The early years of Parliament were plagued by low and erratic attendance, but members were not prepared to lay down hard and fast rules on absences.[134] It was agreed only that when there was no quorum was shaming appropriate: a list of absentees was pinned up in a conspicuous place until the end of the session. A practice developed of members not turning up for the first weeks, believing that little was done at the start of a session. Desertions late in the session were also common. Facing an impending exodus of southern members, Stafford in 1866 threatened 'a call of the whole House'. Under standing orders this would have required names to be taken and absences dealt with by the House. It was agreed that, as in the House of Commons, a roll should be taken.[135] This also allowed a system of forfeiting the daily allowance for lengthy absences to be introduced.

In the early years 'counting out' the House – a mass exodus before the doors were locked – was an easy way of avoiding a division.[136] In 1860, after concern over this practice, the Speaker ruled that the procedure for establishing a quorum should follow that of the House of Commons. The division bell would be sounded and the sand-glass turned, giving members two minutes to return to the House before a count was taken.[137] The system did not work perfectly, and on occasion members were stranded outside the chamber.

The parliamentary record

Parliament took time to develop appropriate forms of recording its proceedings. For the first 12 years there was no official record of debates, only a rudimentary journal of the day's sittings. At first, the House published *Votes and Proceedings*, which provided a good daily chronicle of proceedings but was less successful in dealing with other material. In 1858 the *Journal* of the House was separated from the reports and papers tabled in the House, which were published as an *Appendix to the Journals of the House of Representatives*. This system, which used subject groupings of 'shoulder numbers' in the *Appendix*, was an improvement on the previous approach and has been maintained ever since. The Clerk of the House compiled the daily journal from his notes. Until 1868 this was printed each day as the 'votes and proceedings', then compiled weekly into the *Journals*.[138] In the early years printing was contracted out, but in 1864 the government established its own printing office to deal with the *Journals*, *Appendix to the Journals*, bills, the order paper, and a host of papers tabled and otherwise required to be printed, along with *Hansard* from 1867.[139]

Unlike in Britain, the press had unfettered access to the New Zealand Parliament from its first days. Indeed, the Assembly needed the reporters desperately in order to have a daily verbatim record of its debates. Other newspapers relied on the Auckland papers for rather belated reports; they could not afford to maintain their own reporters in the House. But the nature of the colonial newspapers led to considerable difficulties in maintaining an accurate, measured and reliable record.

Many prominent politicians owned or were involved in newspapers, which were with few exceptions highly politicised and polemical.[140] Edward Gibbon and Jerningham Wakefield, together with others, 'formed a sort of reporting society or club' in the first sessions of 1854 to take notes of speeches and supply them to the newspapers.[141] Sewell accused the Wakefields of inaccurate reporting and tampering with their own speeches to place them in the best light with copy 'embellished throughout with cheers'. A committee appointed to look at the issue made little progress.

Newspaper reports had other limitations. Errors inevitably crept in and reporting was uneven. At times speeches were reported virtually verbatim, but at others there was simply a note that certain members spoke on an issue without any information about what they had said. Moreover, as one observer commented, the:

> reports give you little notion of the reality. Some members, (such as poor old Domett for instance) whose speeches are dreary beyond belief and almost unintelligible as delivered in the House, contrive to figure well with rounded periods and flowing oratory in the columns of the newspaper – while others such as Fitzherbert, whose power of illustration and sarcasm you well know, Sewell who speaks much and often, or Fox who speaks at Railway pace, are shorn of their fair proportions, and their speeches reduced to mere notes … [it] makes some members, who usually talk to empty benches, apparently as prominent as those who electrify the gallery or are the life of the House.[142]

The desirable system of reporters working short shifts – necessary for full and accurate reports – could not be implemented without devoting more resources to the task, something the newspapers could never contemplate. Parliamentarians hankered after the example of Britain and various Australian colonies, where debates were reported either by newspapers which were subsidised or by a parliamentary reporting staff. The problem here was one of divided responsibility between the General Assembly and the executive; neither was keen to pay.

In 1856 Fitzherbert pleaded for 'accurate and authentic reports' on constitutional grounds. 'Without such public opinion, Responsible Government would virtually cease to exist, that chamber might as well have no reporters' or strangers' gallery, they might close their doors and transact their business in a small comfortable parlour.'[143] Fox, who had witnessed debates in the Commons, gave a brilliant speech on the importance of reporting that reflected the approach subsequently adopted in the New Zealand Parliament: 'they were bound, in all honesty and fairness, to give a plain unvarnished statement of what actually passed – as much condensed as they might think proper, but leaving no argument out, and putting none in, and giving to the speakers on both sides an equal share of space proportioned to their speeches.'[144] Nothing eventuated, but the practice was adopted of sending copies of all bills to the Auckland papers.[145]

So, the problems with newspaper reporting remained. An enquiry in 1861 highlighted factual errors, misreporting of speeches and inaccurate recording of divisions. Complaints mounted and in 1864 William Gisborne, Under-Secretary to the Colonial Secretary, suggested that the Assembly itself arrange for reporting. The *Journals* and the *Appendix* were clearly inadequate. 'That skeleton should be clothed with the flesh and blood, and be inspired with the vitality, of discussion.'[146] What was required was that everyone on a daily basis should have 'as regularly as his breakfast a flowing, accurate report interspersed with all dramatic incidents of debate'.

A select committee negotiated with newspapers to contract to provide the service – first the *Southern Cross* in Auckland and then, with the shift to Wellington, the *Wellington Independent* and the *New Zealand Advertiser*. But the contracts were not attractive. Reporting was tricky to arrange and there was no real guarantee of accuracy.[147] Meanwhile, the Wellington papers refused to report the debates in depth, as a rift developed with the government. This passive form of censorship added to Parliament's resolve.[148]

The Government Printer put forward an estimate for printing the full debates. This was considerably lower than the newspapers' offers and would allow easier control of revisions and earlier publication. A newspaper editor, C.C.N. Barron, offered to manage a parliamentary staff of reporters and a Hansard service was organised in haste just before the 1867 session started.[149] Stafford announced the trial and emphasised that a Reporting and Printing Debates Committee rather than the government would have complete control over the new *Hansard*.[150] The gallery over the Speaker's chair was set aside for the reporters and a transcription room was established adjacent to the printing office. Reporters would engage in a 'take' of a quarter to half an hour of shorthand in the chamber and then retire for the laborious process of transcribing their notes. A Hansard 'reader' was engaged in the Printing Office. Members could revise their speeches 'on the strict understanding that the alterations are to be confined to making the reports more in accordance with the remarks actually uttered in the House'.[151] Alteration was a constant source of temptation for members who were sceptical that *Hansard* had really recorded what they had said (or intended to say), or sought to make improvements for posterity. Members freely changed their proofs, delaying the printing of *Hansard* and incurring high costs. 'Thus a "bull" may be dehorned and a "bloomer" may quickly fade and pass away from the *Hansard* garden.'[152] This gave rise, paradoxically, to members flourishing their uncorrected proofs as the ultimate demonstration of what they had really said!

Barron's trial proved successful.[153] He continued as Chief Hansard Reporter for the next 29 years. New Zealand had established one of the first official and independent records of parliamentary debates, well ahead of Westminster which did not establish an official *Hansard* until 1909. The reporting provided substantial and consistent coverage in the so-called 'substantially verbatim' approach. *Hansard* was not completely comprehensive, however, since speeches relating to the first readings of bills other than the formal introduction were not reported, and from 1871 only amendments and divisions were recorded when the House was in Committee.[154] It was, nonetheless, the prime record for the House. The old partisanship of newspaper reporting was disposed of once and for all.

By the 1870s the reporters were employed on a permanent basis and returned for each session.[155] Hansard reporters were a special breed. They had to be able to write accurate shorthand at speeds of 180 words per minute or more, and do so with intelligence.[156] It was not a matter of mechanical verbatim reporting. Many fast reporters found that they were unable to cope with the reality of speeches in the House. The speeches were at one extreme roughly fashioned, poorly expressed, ungrammatical and repetitive, and at the other erudite and full of classical allusions, quotations and abstruse phrases. They were punctuated with interjections and procedural matters. Reporters had to exercise discrimination and editorial discretion simultaneously as they penned their shorthand. They had to be knowledgeable about political affairs, the procedures of Parliament, and the diverse allusions sprinkled through speeches.

Hansard staff, 1873–6: C.C.N. Barron (chief reporter) centre, and from upper left, clockwise, W. Drake, William Mitchell, Charles M. Crombie, Edward Downie and George Fisher. There was a serious gap in the official record of Parliament, the period 1854–66. In 1884, after urging by James Macandrew (who had been in the House since 1854) and James FitzGerald (who had been instrumental in getting Hansard off the ground in the first place), Premier Stout agreed that the early debates should be published. Maurice FitzGerald (James' son), who was suffering from incurable tuberculosis, performed this most meticulous of tasks without pay, devoting the rest of his short life to reconstructing the debates in a form akin to Hansard. *He consulted the principal newspapers, sought memoirs and notes of speeches from all the living members of both Houses, and compared the newspaper reports and other material he gathered with the* Votes and Proceedings *and* Journals of the Houses. *The 1854–66 debates were published in the latter half of the 1880s.*

Parliamentary Service collection

As soon as the House was being officially reported, the issue of the retrospective revision of *Hansard* was raised. This was seen as a threat to the integrity of the record.[157] Politicians also began to use their recorded utterances in the House for political purposes. Members were supplied with copies of the weekly *Hansard* pamphlets to distribute, and obtained special prints of notable speeches for circulation.

Standing orders and procedure

The standing orders of the 1850s soon proved inadequate. A select committee in 1863 concluded that comprehensive revision was required and that the revised orders should be based explicitly on those of the House of Commons.[158] Speaker Monro drafted new ones, using the 1854 version of Sir Thomas Erskine May's guide to parliamentary procedure issued by the Commons' Speaker, Lefevre. These were adopted in 1865.[159] Members' powers to terminate debates were expunged on Stafford's urging after a close vote of the House. (Fitzherbert had used them to terminate the debate on moving the seat of government in 1863.)

This action confirmed the House's tolerance of lengthy debates and opened up the possibility of concerted stonewalls. This issue proved a major preoccupation for the House whenever it considered the standing orders over the next 70 years. Meanwhile the only resource of governments facing a stonewall was to insist that the House continue sitting until the debate was concluded. Trollope observed that there was an excessive 'reference to papers [in speeches] … It seemed as though barrows full of papers must have been brought in for the use of gentlemen on one side and on the other. From this arises the great evil of slowness.'[160] Trollope also believed that members took delight in delay and revelled in the tyranny of their position while holding the floor. The practice of allowing unrestricted debate, as in the Commons, was carried to absurd lengths here. 'A Speaker … can hardly call the offender to order, – but he might have the power of putting out the gas', but only when midnight Saturday was reached.

The new standing orders were based on the principle that the full range of procedural matters should be spelt out. There were now sections dealing with a new Parliament and the opening and prorogation of Parliament, and much more detailed specification of procedure during sittings. They shifted the time that the House met to 2 p.m. as a result of the increased demands of executive government and select committees extending beyond the mornings. In 1868 the time of meeting was delayed further to 3 p.m.[161] It became common for governments later in the session to move that their business take precedence in order to hurry things along. The evenings would often continue until 3 a.m., with members drifting away after midnight and business continuing through the suspension of standing orders.[162] In 1870 the time was moved back to 2.30 p.m. This established the pattern followed thereafter. Attempts were made to shift the time back to noon, or even the morning, but, as their business increased, governments would not allow this encroachment on their time.[163]

In a departure from previous practice, Monro adopted the Commons' procedure of electing a Speaker prior to the swearing in of members. House of Commons precedent was followed also in the prescribed role for the three committees involving the entire House – the Committee of Supply (the appropriation of revenue), the Committee of Ways and Means (the raising of the money) and the Committee of the Whole House (to consider bills in detail).[164]

Private bills were difficult to deal with. They involved legislation of restricted application for the benefit of a limited number of people, and were sponsored by individual members and promoted by 'parliamentary agents'.[165] A Private Bills Office and an Examiner of such bills were created to deal with them. Railway bills were a common and important example, as were those concerning local authority public works. In 1865 Monro attempted to apply House of Commons practices to private bills, but it proved difficult to differentiate them from public bills.[166] Under Fox in 1870 a special select committee reviewed how private bills were dealt with. As a result, new slimmed-down standing orders for private bills which departed from British practice were adopted in 1871. These were vigorously disputed by Monro.[167]

From the beginning the House appointed a range of select committees each session.[168] They met in the mornings and on Wednesdays, when the House did not sit until 5 p.m. A number concerned with the administration of Parliament were routinely established at the opening of sessions – Standing Orders, Printing, Library, House (chaired by the Speaker and concerned with the running of the Assembly buildings) and Private Bills, for example.

Other committees were created for particular purposes. Privileges Committees dealt with matters of privilege arising between members of the House or between the House and outsiders. An Audit Committee was established in 1861 after the Audit Act 1858 created the position of an independent Auditor responsible to Parliament rather than the executive. The first Goldfields Committee was created in 1862; from 1865 it was appointed annually. In the 1860s many committees were created to deal with land issues, including the important Waste Lands Committee in 1864. The standing orders of 1865 created a regular Public Petitions Committee. It was large and particularly hardworking, as the number of petitions escalated into the hundreds each year in the 1870s, and many more later.[169] A Reporting Debates (and Printing) Committee was formed annually from 1867 after the establishment of *Hansard*. In 1870 a Public Accounts Committee was first appointed, in association with Vogel's ambitious development plans. This had been preceded from 1854 by other committees of a similar nature which had gone under various names.

In 1871 the first regular Native Affairs Committee (with the four Maori members on it) was appointed. Petitions from Maori were increasing in number, and this committee helped deal with what became a flood. Most concerned land, many relating to specific transactions. Some concerned the operation of the land laws and asked for the setting up of commissions of investigation or for the return of confiscated land. Some sought better Maori representation in Parliament. This committee played an important role in communicating Maori concerns, registering protest and making parliamentary representation effective.

The complexity of the process of passing laws also gave rise to committees. The Joint Committee (with the Legislative Council) on Standing Orders on Private Bills and the Committee of Selection (of Private Bills) were established in the early 1860s to deal with procedural matters. In 1877 a Joint Committee on Bills of the two Houses was formed. This decided whether a bill was public, private or local, and co-ordinated the two Houses' legislative programmes. In 1880 a Statutes Revision Committee was appointed to consider bills of a legal nature that might, for example, consolidate legislation. It became permanent from 1893. A Local Bills Committee met from 1888 as the number of local bills mounted; all local bills were referred to it.

The privileges of the House

The House was also concerned to clarify the extent of its authority and privileges. By the nineteenth century the House of Commons had successfully claimed privileges against the prerogatives of the Crown, against the authority of courts of law, and in relation to the House of Lords.[170] Here it was not a simple matter of asserting similar privileges. The precise relationship between the House and the Governor was negotiable; it was legally tricky to claim judicial privileges; and the role of the Legislative Council was uncertain.

A committee in 1854 found that the House did not have the 'inherent rights or privileges' of the House of Commons based on 'prescriptive and immemorial usage' and the judicial role of the Commons.[171] The only basis for privilege was that by common law the House was invested with powers necessary to its existence and to the proper exercise of its functions. It had a right to protect itself against all impediments to its proceedings. The committee suggested passing legislation to embody the powers of the House. This was done in 1856 through the Privileges Act, which asserted that witnesses could be compelled to attend the House and produce documents, and protected members, civil servants and witnesses against actions for libel for words spoken in the House. Reports and papers published by the House were also protected, and members were exempt from attending courts of law as witnesses or jurors.

From 1861, the more assertive Monro, as Speaker, adopted the symbolic form of assertion of parliamentary privilege that was used by the Commons on the opening of Parliament.[172] In this the House laid claim formally to privileges from the Crown. Monro later argued that the new standing orders of 1865 should be complemented by a new Privileges Act to consolidate Parliament's powers. The New Zealand Parliament did not have the power to punish those in contempt of its privileges; it had to rely on the courts. Monro also argued that members should have freedom from arrest and protection against personal violence, libel and slander.

The Parliamentary Privileges Act 1865 repealed the Act of 1856 and based New Zealand's parliamentary privileges wholesale on those of the Commons. The Act established the basic principles of statutory privilege in New Zealand, but in practice the House proved lacking in confidence when specific issues arose, and additional legislation was passed in 1866 and 1875.[173]

The most common problem – attacks on members in newspapers that Monro felt went well beyond what was tolerated in Britain – could not be addressed under existing legislation.[174] The press gallery emerged in the mid 1860s, and became a well-established, independent entity in the 1870s.[175] This highlighted the increasingly problematic relationship between the press and the executive government and Parliament. The connection of Parliament to the telegraph in the late 1860s and the formation in 1870 of the forerunners of the United Press Association greatly facilitated the reporting of Parliament and assisted in the displacement of local politics by national politics.[176] With the formation of press associations, the press adopted an independent and distinct identity that set it apart from politics and gave it organisation and a sense of cohesion. In the so-called 'Telegraph libel case' in 1870, the *Otago Daily Times* accused the government of holding up news to favour papers that supported the government. The resulting prosecution of the editor was eventually dropped. This was regarded as a victory for the press.

Edward Thomas Gillon was at the centre of developments in reporting Parliament. He had been one of the first Hansard reporters appointed in 1867.[177] After that session he worked as Clerk of Private Bills and of the Waste Lands Committee for two sessions. He was allowed for a time to act also as a political correspondent for newspapers, but in 1869 the propriety of this was questioned and he had to quit his parliamentary posts. He then worked for the *Evening Post* and eventually became its editor. He was also manager of the Press Association, which provided the bulk of the material for parliamentary reporting. Gillon virtually lived in the reporters' gallery, and was its chairman in the early days.[178]

By the 1870s more reporters inhabited the gallery. One of the earliest was George R. Hart, who represented the Christchurch *Press* and the *Wellington Independent* from 1871.[179] He was renowned for writing longhand at 'lightning speed', eliminating the need for shorthand and subsequent transcription. Wellington newspapers sent their own reporters along, and there were also parliamentary 'correspondents' – the 'special reporters' – whose more analytical and partisan reports appeared in newspapers that could afford to pay for them. Reporters were also beginning to write general columns on politics, parliamentary life, gossip and scuttlebutt, with a distinction between 'reporter' and 'correspondent' emerging.

In 1873 a dispute arose over press access to committee proceedings and changes made to the record of *Hansard*.[180] Gillon's *Evening Post* had published an inaccurate report of a speech. Speaker Bell sternly rebuked the reporter, refused to allow a defiant letter from Gillon to be printed in *Hansard*, and asserted his authority concerning the record. Bell became embarrassingly isolated when the House decided not to back him. After being lambasted by the colony's press, the usually imperturbable Bell refused to have anything more to do with the reporters' gallery, cancelled all reporters' permits, and washed his hands of issuing permits for the reporters' gallery. Responsibility for these matters was transferred to the Reporting Debates Committee. The *Post* continued its war against the Speaker by cheekily truncating a speech by Bell and by publishing other material on him that he regarded as malicious and untrue. The paper also obtained internal information about the Reporting Debates Committee from one of its members. Bell accused this member of bringing him into public contempt.[181]

One of the most celebrated incidents involving the press concerned the Oamaru *Evening Mail*'s accusation that Whitaker was a member 'of the Auckland land-speculating "ring"'. The newspaper's proprietor, George Jones, was called to the bar of the House as a result.[182] Vague rumours swept Parliament that a coal-hole was being readied as a temporary prison. In fact Jones was well looked after in a form of 'House arrest' by the Sergeant-at-Arms. He sat in a room during a debate that went on for seven hours, liberally supplied with refreshments and cheroots, and playing a violin while he waited. Jones remained defiant, the matter was made a ministerial one, and the House eventually agreed to endorse Whitaker's determination to take it as a libel case to the Supreme Court with full government backing, after rejecting a proposed select committee enquiry. Whitaker's case failed, however, and the Crown had to pay huge court costs. Jones received hundreds of congratulatory telegrams for his stand and was subsequently elected to Parliament.

One element of the privileges of Parliament was its power to determine the qualification of members for the House. The Constitution Act had not dealt with this and from time to time difficulties had arisen.[183] The issue was finally confronted in the late 1860s. Stafford in opposition attempted in 1865 to pass a Disqualification Bill that would have excluded current ministers on the grounds of their other employment.[184] Then as Premier he introduced in 1868 a bill that would have excluded provincial politicians apart from Superintendents from sitting in the General Assembly. This was shelved after strong provincialist resistance.[185]

In 1869 Premier Fox insisted that one member, Major Charles Brown (following Brown's vote against him on internal defence), choose between being commander of the forces in Taranaki and a member of the House.[186] This caused a row and the government won a narrow victory in the division. Brown was forced to resign. Fox pledged that he would come up with a better definition of who should be disqualified from Parliament. It was argued that Vogel's public works policies were increasing the risk of influence and corruption.[187] A Disqualification Bill was finally passed in 1870 – after much squabbling in the House – on the grounds that politicians should be free to vote without corruption or the fear of losing office.[188] The Act excluded from either House holders of paid public office and contractors for government work, bringing New Zealand into line with Britain and Australia.[189]

Stafford and Fox, 1866–9

Stafford took charge of a weak ministry after Weld's resignation in 1865. He had scant policy direction apart from a desire to reduce expenditure. Following fresh elections in early 1866, Stafford set about assembling a stronger ministry. The House was increased to 70 by 13 additional southern members, as a result of population growth in Canterbury and Otago. Twenty-seven members were new.[190] Domett and Walter Mantell had moved into the Legislative Council, Weld had resigned, and Sewell had been defeated. They 'felt that their world had changed and there was no longer a place for them in it' as a new breed of career-minded politicians made their presence felt.[191] Monro was re-elected Speaker, and the House adopted a mace into its proceedings.

The issue of provincial separation was the focus of the 1866 session as Auckland and Otago fought increased centralisation. The wars in Taranaki and the Waikato had finished, British troops were departing, and the convoluted machinations between ministry, Governor and General Cameron

Establishing the Foundations, 1858–75

Major T.V. Shepherd with the original mace, c. 1900s. For more than a decade the House had no mace – its ultimate symbol of authority. The mace originated in the weapons carried by the Sergeants-at-Arms, bodyguards to the King, who had powers of arrest without warrant. As power shifted to Parliament, the Sergeant-at-Arms and the mace came to symbolise the authority and privileges of the House of Commons. In 1866 – with the government not prepared to pay for it – retired Speaker Clifford gave the New Zealand Parliament its first mace, a smaller version of the silver gilt mace used in the Commons, incorporating New Zealand motifs.

Speaker Monro, who had prescribed the use of a mace in the standing orders of 1865, was also keen to adopt ceremonial robes for the Speaker and officials. The Speaker and Clerks should wear gowns and wigs for proper dignity. But such garb was not adopted until Speakers and Clerks had legal qualifications. Speaker Guinness was the first to adopt the wig, in 1903, and Clerk Hall did so in 1930.

This mace was destroyed in the fire of 1907. As in the Commons, it was brought in each sitting day on the shoulder of the Sergeant-at-Arms, who preceded the Speaker into the chamber. When the House was in Committee (with the Chairman of Committees replacing the Speaker and sitting at the head of the Table), the mace was stored under the Table.

Parliamentary Service collection

were no more. When Whitaker's Auckland separation resolution came before the House, Stafford demolished it. The separation movement soon became a lost cause as the provinces became more dependent financially on the general government and perpetually divided.[192]

Stafford soon reduced the share of general government customs revenue given to the provinces. This caused an uproar in the House and a 'sensation' in the country.[193] FitzGerald moved no-confidence without success. William Moorhouse then proposed a carefully worded amendment expressing a lack of confidence in the specific composition of Stafford's ministry rather than in Stafford himself. This resolution, carried 47 to 14, defused the situation. The result was a reconstruction of the Stafford ministry. This stronger, more capable ministry endured until 1869. Stafford had to carry on when many southern members had left, at which time the salaries of the Speaker and officers of the House were cut back by an ill-tempered House.[194] A.S. Atkinson sighed with relief at getting the formalities over with: '& so the play ended & the spectators & actors dispersed'.[195]

In 1867 Parliament opened with few members present. Stafford was angry at the low attendance. 'A miserably cold wet day & the band of the volunteers as discordant as the weather', said Monro.[196] Vogel was spoiling for a fight with Stafford but was easily defeated. The rivalry degenerated into personal conflict that boiled over into a dispute about whether the proposed Hansard service should be paid for by the government or left to the newspapers.

Vogel, who was easily able to goad Stafford, became the effective leader of the opposition – such as it was, with Auckland and Otago provincialism fragmenting and many provinces in financial difficulty. There were 'frequent and really childishly violent altercations' between Carleton as Chairman of Committees and Vogel during the session.[197] Vogel attempted to replace Carleton with O'Rorke, alleging partisanship. He engaged in behaviour that Stafford described as 'not only unusual, but improper and undignified'. The House agreed. When Stafford trumped Vogel's attempt to overturn the government's financial policy, Vogel refused to co-operate and in humiliating fashion had to attach a dissenting minority view to the select committee's report. Speaker Monro said that such an action was 'unheard of' and 'no precedent could be found' for it, and Carleton waded in with an admonition that Vogel 'had gone beyond his power'.[198]

But while its days were numbered, provincialism remained a powerful disruptive force. The debate on financial policy lasted six sitting days, the longest on record. The government proposed a new arrangement for dividing general and provincial revenues, and dealt with outstanding loans. This resulted in the temporary breakup of the provincialist bloc of Auckland, Wellington and Otago members, when Auckland members deserted to the ministry.[199] The revised financial arrangements improved the colony's finances and brought the provinces under greater control.

Stafford accelerated business by suspending standing orders and worked the House hard as the long session came to a close.[200] O'Rorke, who was missing his wife greatly, confided to her that 'your prediction of the session being as long as usual is likely to come true so I think you had better make up your mind to pay me a visit'.[201] The town was 'not so gay' as during the previous session and he had not yet been invited to any official dinners. Members complained at sitting until 2 or 2.30 a.m. 'night after night'.

In early 1868 Grey was ignominiously recalled and replaced as Governor by Sir George Bowen. Bowen was quite happy to follow the ministry's advice on all colonial matters. He was more interested in the trappings of office and personal comfort. From this time on, Governors by and large became nominal figureheads.

In the same year, Fox returned to a House which had grown by 6 to a total of 76, with 2 new West Coast representatives (as a result of the gold rushes) and 4 Maori members. Stafford easily won the vote on the policy of the government initiated by Fox, 34 to 25, with the support of two of the new Maori members.[202] For the first time a Maori member spoke in the House, through a hurriedly arranged interpreter. Tareha Te Moananui urged that the House enact wise laws to promote good, and that Maori and Pakeha work together. He was critical of the Native Land Court and asked Parliament to reconsider its role. A second Maori member, Mete Kingi Paetahi, followed. He urged respect for the authority of the law and the sovereign, and detailed how his peaceable Wanganui people had become entangled in the Taranaki confiscation process. The House then blithely continued to debate Fox's motion.

Both before and after the wars Maori had pressed for political representation. For some time it was argued that indigenous institutions such as Native Councils and runanga might meet the need.[203] The wars highlighted the lack of involvement of Maori in the political system. In the early 1860s Maori representation became an issue in Parliament. Some, such as FitzGerald in 1862, argued passionately for a 'full and equal enjoyment of civil and political privileges' by Maori.[204] Mainstream opinion in the House did not accept FitzGerald's grand vision, but was prepared to accept limited separate representation of Maori by European members.

In a context of maintaining the balance of seats between the North and South Islands, Stafford supported separate Maori representation. He encouraged Donald McLean to bring in a bill to that end in 1867. The alternative of a common franchise aroused fears that Pakeha voters could be swamped by Maori in some electorates. McLean was assisted in drafting his bill by FitzGerald. It proposed four representatives, three in the North Island and one in the South, to be elected by Maori on the basis of full manhood suffrage. Because of fears of manipulation by Pakeha and potential disturbance to the North–South balance, the bill was amended so that only Maori could be elected to the seats. It was agreed to by the House as an experimental measure for five years, until the individualisation of Maori land tenure led to substantial numbers of Maori voting on the general roll.

Elections were held for the new Maori members early in 1868.[205] Frederick Nene Russell, nephew of the renowned Waka Nene, was elected unopposed for Northern Maori. Major Mete Kingi Paetahi, a Wanganui chief, was similarly unopposed in Western Maori. Tareha Te Moananui was elected for Eastern Maori in a small but closely contested poll, and John Patterson from Kaiapoi for Southern

Maori, also in a low poll. In 1876 the four seats were made permanent and became a distinctive feature of New Zealand's political system, even though there was strong opposition to enhancing the ability of Maori to influence the shaping of ministries at a time when factional instability was increasing. What began as an experiment became entrenched as fears of swamping of the general roll by Maori and manipulation of their votes persisted.

It was difficult for the Maori members to participate in parliamentary debates and follow the intricacies of parliamentary procedure because of the language barrier. It is hard to identify any significant impact by Maori members on land legislation or the role of the Land Court, in spite of their strenuous criticism of the Land Court within the House.[206] Individuals' votes were important during close struggles for power, but did not translate into continuing influence once a ministry had been formed. Manipulation of Maori members' votes was not unusual. But their presence reminded the House and the government of Maori interests, and at times stimulated action on behalf of Maori that might otherwise not have occurred.[207]

Meanwhile, Stafford's feud with Fox, Bell and Vogel worsened. The ministry had to work hard to maintain its support as a more organised opposition emerged.[208] A protracted debate on Fox's motion of no-confidence came to a sudden and extraordinary close when Stafford and Fox were absent from the chamber when the debate petered out. Neither was expecting the crucial division at that moment.[209]

Early Maori members, Wi Parata, left (1871–5) and Mete Kingi Paetahi, right (1868–70). After Maori members entered the House Stafford and Fox, perceiving the usefulness of the Maori vote, suggested that Maori might also be appointed to the Executive and Legislative Councils. However, nothing was done. Four new and more active Maori members were elected in 1871 – Wiremu Parata, Wiremu Katene, Karaitiana Takamoana and H.K. Taiaroa. In 1872, Vogel appointed Parata and Katene to the Executive Council as ministers without portfolio, and two Maori were appointed to the Legislative Council. Parata and Katene retained their positions until 1876, establishing a tradition of Maori ministers without portfolio. But this was largely symbolic. They were there to convey Maori opinion, and attended the Executive Council only when issues affecting Maori were discussed.

The government co-operated with the opposition in the pandemonium that broke out so that a proper division could be taken. The government won comfortably.

On another test of confidence at the same time, moved by McLean over defence and native affairs, Maori member John Patterson had to be unearthed by the opposition from a 'safe place' where the ministerial whips had put him.[210] He complained of being pulled this way and that 'like a bullock or a pig'. Charles Heaphy reportedly beguiled him in the House 'by drawing pictures to amuse him' lest he escape. Only the casting vote of Monro saved the government on a tied vote. The convention that the Speaker support the government on matters of confidence and supply, on the grounds that he should always vote for further discussion and to maintain the status quo, was emerging.[211] The ministry fought on. Stafford outfaced the opposition, which now wanted to force a dissolution by disrupting business. He argued that having won the battle he should be allowed to proceed. A stonewall when the opposition 'set on half a dozen hardly sober nincompoops to insult the House' backfired, and Stafford gained the sympathy of the House.[212] But the government's proposals to marginalise the provinces further had to be ditched.

In June 1869, Parliament was assembled because of the renewed conflict involving Te Kooti in Poverty Bay and Titokowaru in Taranaki. The country, in the doldrums for some years, entered a depression. The wars had been a serious drain on the economy and had unsettled commerce. Agricultural prices were low, gold production had begun to fall, and the flow of immigrants had slackened. The colony's credit was in bad shape and public borrowing had declined.

Governor Bowen being absent, Parliament was opened by Commissioners who, along with the Speaker, 'managed to jam themselves into the upright canoe, & looked very much like 3 in a gig'.[213] As members assembled, expectations were high that Stafford would be challenged. There had been a loss of confidence in him as another war developed. Fox introduced a motion of no-confidence in the government's defence policy. As the debate came to a close, the *Nelson Examiner* exceeded itself with its description:

> From all quarters of the building – from Bellamy's, from the smoking room, from the library, from the terrace outside where legs are stretched and lungs cooled – members came hurrying into the House … The space devoted to the public, in a very few minutes were in a state of bumper; and even the ladies – Heaven save their sweet faces! – with heightened colour, and breathless excitement, rushed into their own little political paradise, and in an inconceivably short period their gallery was rustling with silks, and glowing with bright colours, and still brighter eyes sparkling with the expectation of a row.[214]

Fox was handed a note indicating that he had the numbers in the middle of his speech, and he abruptly ended the debate. He won 40 to 29, to sustained loud cheering.

Fox's new ministry included Vogel and McLean.[215] Stafford did not accept his defeat with good grace. The session was characterised by bickering, with Stafford using his procedural knowledge to obstruct. Fox also came into conflict with the Speaker over 'unparliamentary' forms of expression, among other things.[216] Monro's response was that the proper Speaker's role was not one of 'constant interference', which would lead to his being regarded as obstructive and 'only render himself powerless for good'; 'the real source of proper tone … lies … in the tone of feeling of the members themselves'.[217] This was a perceptive admonition that many following Speakers had to heed.

Given the parlous economic situation, grandiose plans for renewed immigration were afoot and constitutional reform was in the air. Vogel indicated that he would introduce an ambitious plan for development through immigration and public works in the next session, while E.C.J. Stevens stunned the House by introducing resolutions abolishing the provinces. Although these were put aside for the next Parliament to consider, the issue was unlikely to go away.[218] Fox's ministry fell into disarray as he proved weary of office. He attempted to persuade Bowen to dissolve Parliament, without success. After temporising, Fox rushed through bills towards the end of the session when members had begun to leave. The House had to sit on Mondays and commence at 2 p.m.[219] He retained a slim majority, but some bills had to be dropped. As the session drew to a close, Monro noted that 'the speech put into the Govrs mouth was so absurd that he cd hardly read it; and the whole audience was on the broad grin.'[220] Monro farewelled the southern members and they sailed that afternoon, sent off with three cheers.

Power plays

The late 1860s saw a complex struggle between the House, as represented by its Speaker, and the executive government and the Legislative Council. Aside from the abstract constitutional principles involved, the resolution of these issues had serious consequences for the manner in which Parliament was administered and legislation enacted.

In the early decades, Speakers were more political than they would become from the time of Speaker O'Rorke in the 1880s. An apolitical Speakership was difficult to achieve in a small and intimate House. Even in Britain the concept of a neutral, non-partisan Speaker was only just emerging in the mid nineteenth century.[221] Clifford introduced his own political views in two respects – his commitment to responsible government, which was understandable in the circumstances of the early sessions, and his provincialist, specifically pro-Wellington, leanings. Monro, a centralist, supported Stafford. He was active in debates and divisions while the House was in Committee, and was taken to task for his role as local member when he promoted a private member's Picton Railway Bill which Fox demolished by ensuring that royal assent would be withheld.[222] Because Speakers faced re-election, there was a strong incentive for them to participate in debates while the House was in Committee and to take part in public works estimates debates, particularly on matters affecting their own electorates. Monro's feud with Fox made it difficult at times for him to stand aside from the political fray, and his vote in 1862 defeated the Fox ministry. Dillon Bell's election as Speaker in 1871 restored a more tranquil relationship between Speaker and ministry.

Speakers, and in particular Monro, asserted their role as the defender of the House in reaction to the increased powers of the executive. Monro launched a concerted campaign in the latter 1860s to assert the power of Parliament. He was concerned to keep administration of the institution separate from the government of the day, a concern that still persists.

In 1867 Monro approached Stafford on the matter of his salary, which was voted on annually in the estimates. He argued that 'the Speaker was immediately placed in a false position and became the subject of a party discussion … it was most desirable that the Speaker should be in a position of the most perfect independence and impartiality.'[223] He also wanted to take charge of appointments of officers for the House and the buildings. Stafford drew up a bill that fixed officers' salaries but also specified that the Clerk of the House would be appointed directly by the government, with other clerks appointed by the government after consultation with the Speaker. Monro protested indignantly that he had been ignored and could not agree. The House passed the Legislative Officers Salaries Act 1867 to fix his and clerical salaries, but the issue of powers of appointment remained.

Another contested point was the issuing of writs for vacancies in the House. In 1858 Clifford had had the Election Writs Bill amended so that resignations during the parliamentary recess were forwarded to the Speaker first rather than to the Governor, a departure from British tradition.[224] In 1868 Monro, on a literal reading of the Act, broke with tradition and communicated directly with the Governor to have a writ issued for a vacant seat.[225] In the end Stafford conceded and Monro agreed that the law should be changed to bring the practice into line with that of Britain. The constitutional anomaly was

Julius Vogel entered the House in 1863 for Dunedin and Suburbs North, and retired in 1889. He is best known for his policy of economic development through borrowing in the 1870s. He led the House in the Waterhouse ministry of 1872–3, and was Premier 1873–5 and again in 1876. With Stout as Premier (1884–7) Vogel again took a central part in government.

removed in 1870 when the Regulation of Elections Act created the position of the Clerk of the Writs and a committee of the House to deal with writs.

Following the establishment of the Government Printing Office, friction developed over the lack of priority given to parliamentary printing compared to executive government business.[226] In 1868 the Printing Committee, endorsed by the Speaker, moved that the Government Printing Office be at the disposal of the House (rather than the government) when it was in session, but Stafford's government defeated the motion. The same year Monro refused to table a letter from the military which protested against the way the forces had been described by members of the House. Stafford wanted to table the letter 'by command' of the Governor. Monro and Dillon Bell argued that this would be an interference with the 'freedom and privilege of Parliament'; no-one, not even the Governor, could insist on the letter being tabled.[227]

The battle continued. With a grand new 'House of Representatives' in the offing in the late 1860s, Monro moved to take charge of Parliament Buildings and Bellamy's.[228] Stafford resisted and Monro backed off. The House Committee then asked Stafford to yield catering arrangements to the Speaker and itself.[229] Monro suggested that it was the Speaker's duty to deal with Bellamy's, as with other aspects of members' 'convenience' such as seating and the lighting and heating of the House. The government disagreed, but in the end conceded that the original legislation of 1854 allowing the sale of liquor in Parliament actually stipulated that this take place under the authority of the Speaker. Monro gained greater control over Bellamy's and administration of the buildings in association with a more effective permanent House Committee that would meet over the recess as well as during the session.[230] The House Committee subsequently formalised the operation of Bellamy's.[231]

The issue of responsibility for appointing officers of the General Assembly had not been properly determined in the early days. In 1857 Clifford tartly reminded Stafford that officers of the House 'should be solely responsible to the Speaker, & I believe this to be the opinion of the House, several times expressed'.[232] As the institution of Parliament grew, so did the need for staff. Monro urged the House to make 'some legislative provision for the appointment and control of the clerks and other officers of the House … He thought the attention of the House might be profitably occupied by considering its own organization, as the most important department of the constitution.'[233]

In 1862, when Monro recommended George Friend as Clerk-Assistant, Fox objected on constitutional grounds, arguing that all appointments, apart from the Speaker and possibly the Chairman of Committees, were to be made by the government, citing British and Australian precedents.[234] Monro disagreed – 'I consider it my duty, as [the House's] Chief Officer, to assert its independence of the Executive, and in doing this I am only carrying out a view of the matter which was strongly insisted on by my predecessor.' In Australia the general position was that officers were appointed by the government on the recommendation of the Speaker. The House agreed to follow this approach here.[235] This gave practical power to the Speaker and established a precedent.

Monro then raised the broader question of control of the legislative estimates (the money provided for running the General Assembly). Hitherto this had been the responsibility of the executive government, but there was good precedent from Britain for the Speaker to have charge.[236] Bell picked up the issue in 1872.[237] Stafford and Fox disingenuously disclaimed any practical responsibility for the executive while still asserting a responsibility in principle. The matter remained unresolved, with the executive government retaining ultimate control. But from this time on the Speaker drew up and submitted the legislative estimates.

The debate over the legislative estimates became the means for members to criticise government expenditure. To the irritation of governments, the House picked away at them every time they came up.[238] This was unfortunate for parliamentary staff anticipating salary increases beyond those fixed by statute in 1867. Members with axes to grind could exact retribution by reducing allowances for the Speaker and the salaries of officers of Parliament. Because of the continued conflict between the two Houses it was usually the unfortunate employees of the Legislative Council who suffered, but the problem was a general one.

In the late 1860s, a struggle between the two Houses tested the limits of their relationship and established the role of the Council for the future. The issue was whether the House had the same privileged position over money bills as the House of Commons. The ability of the Commons to grant taxation to the Crown was the source of its power historically, and it jealously guarded this privilege. In New Zealand the Constitution Act was silent on the matter.[239]

The weak ministries of the first half of the 1860s, beset by war, allowed the Council to adopt a more aggressive stance. In 1861 Fox was unable to prevent land revenue legislation being killed by it. There was some question whether the legislation constituted a 'money' bill. The following year, the Council amended the Native Lands Bill. The ministry was forced to accept the change, under protest that its privileges had been infringed upon. When both Houses sent to Britain for opinions, opposed views were received from British Crown Law Officers and Erskine May.[240] May stated that the amendment infringed on the privileges of the House and would not have been accepted in Britain. His opinion was written into the *Journals* of the House, but the matter remained unresolved.

The Parliamentary Privileges Act 1865 stored up further trouble, because it gave both Houses in principle the same privileges as those of the House of Commons. Some argued that this implicitly gave the Council the power to amend money bills. The matter was tested over amendment of the Public Debts and Loan Consolidation Bills in 1867.[241] Following a deadlocked conference, Stafford stage-managed a second conference, and got the original bill through. A protest to Britain by disgruntled Councillors who had been outmanoeuvred was – notably – not forwarded by the government.

Conflict between the two Houses was heightened by a stand-off over the appointment of a Clerk of Parliaments.[242] By British tradition and in the Australian colonies, the Clerk of the upper house held this position. In 1868 the Council refused to recognise the post, which Stafford had given the House's Clerk, Campbell, in 1865. The matter was not resolved until 1871, when the House of Representatives conceded that it belonged to the Council.[243] Campbell, however, retained the role until he retired. The Clerk of Parliaments Act 1872 confirmed this situation, but even then Fox hoped that 'none of them would live to see the day, when the other House would be in a position to exercise its privilege'.[244] His comments showed foresight, for Campbell continued in service for another 17 years.

The Council was less enamoured of Vogel's expansive policies than the House and the country, and attempted to assert its powers by opposing the Payments to Provinces Bill in 1871.[245] When the Council deleted a clause, the House responded that it had no power to amend a money bill. The dispute was again referred to Britain. The response was unequivocal – the Council could not amend such a bill.[246]

The Council was not deterred from challenging Vogel, who gave as good as he got, trying to limit the term of members' appointments to five years. In 1873, the Council seemed to take over the role of opposition by refusing to pass the Provincial Loans Empowering Bill, a popular measure in the House. Vogel contemplated swamping the Council with new members who would support his policies, but decided to reform it instead. Many agreed that it needed 'radical reform'. The Council continued to play opposition in 1874 by rejecting a Railways Bill and the Constitution Bill (Vogel's attempt to reform the Council). The conflict was increasingly overshadowed by the matter of the abolition of the provinces, however, and the strained relationship over money bills had largely been settled by the British opinion of 1872. Nonetheless, the House of Representatives had to remain on guard against Council attempts to enlarge its role.[247]

Leaving behind 'old landmarks'

The early 1870s were a watershed for Parliament as Vogel implemented his immigration and public works programme. The political correlate was the abolition of the provinces. Vogel's definitive financial statement was – unusually – delivered shortly after Parliament opened in 1870, to an expectant House and galleries. He would galvanise the country and stimulate prosperity by a massive development programme that would revitalise settlement through large-scale assisted immigration and public works.

Centralist Speaker Monro thought that Vogel's statement 'took everyone by surprise. One thing pleased me about it. I think they have given up the Provinces. It is worth 6 millions to accomplish that.'[248] Some could hardly believe what they were hearing and wondered whether the ministry had committed political suicide; ironic laughter and cheers broke out frequently.[249] The announcement set the tone for the session, particularly as it was known that the ministry would seek a dissolution if necessary.[250]

Most of the House went along with the proposals. Vogel's readiness to drop a proposed increase in custom duties kept his large majority. The Immigration and Public Works and Loan Bills passed with little opposition, and the policy received general acclamation throughout the country. The *Otago Daily Times* termed the plan a 'social revolution' and observed that 'the session ... will be remembered for many years to come as the most remarkable in our history'.[251] It considered that 'the old political questions which had previously absorbed the attention of the public were suddenly shelved ... No one henceforth will undertake to argue over the old controversy between Centralism and Provincialism ... The whole system of Provincialism is virtually abolished.' Vogel acknowledged that his policy had 'destroyed the old landmarks of party'.[252]

Monro decided to retire as Speaker. His health was no longer good, his wife was ill, and Fox was again Premier. Stafford, taken by surprise, broke down – 'the honourable gentleman, overcome by his feelings, was unable to proceed', noted *Hansard*.[253] McLean and Vogel responded in generous fashion for the government, but Fox was less well-disposed. As Leader of the House he refused to propose a vote of thanks, and thus no formal acknowledgement of Monro's contribution as Speaker was made.

The elections of early 1871, the first conducted by secret ballot and generally agreed to have been successful, endorsed Vogel's scheme in resounding fashion but also saw great changes in the membership of the House.[254] There were 33 new members out of a total of 78. Fox had obtained a theoretical majority – the question was whether it could be maintained as issues came before the House. He delayed the opening as long as possible in the hope that Vogel would return from London, where he had gone to raise loans, in time to strengthen his forces.[255]

When Parliament eventually opened in mid August 1871, Bell decided to stand for Speaker.[256] Monro proposed Bell, Fox acceded, and Maurice O'Rorke became Chairman of Committees in place of Carleton.[257] Bell was to be a different kind of Speaker from Clifford or Monro. He had always been seen as clever but lacking strong views, indecisive and easily led, with an ability to see unnecessary complexities in issues. He demonstrated these traits in a positive way as Speaker, showing imperturbability, independence and competence in

Francis Dillon Bell, said to have been born in France on 8 October 1822, arrived in New Zealand in 1843. In 1854 he was appointed to the Legislative Council. He was elected as the member for Hutt in 1855 but resigned in 1856. In the late 1850s he joined Edward Stafford and J.C. Richmond to buy a sheep station that was known as the 'Ministerial run'. Elected for Wallace in 1860, Bell was appointed Speaker in 1871 and knighted in 1873. After retiring from the House in 1875, Bell was reappointed to the Legislative Council from 1877 to 1882. From 1880 to 1891 he was Agent-General in London. Bell was made KCMG in 1881 and CB in 1886. He returned to New Zealand in 1896 and died on 15 July 1898.

administration.[258] In particular he made an active and independent contribution while the House was in Committee.

However, Bell had to be persuaded to recognise a fundamental equality of members before the Chair. On one occasion he allowed Fitzherbert to adjourn the House not long before the dinner break. A few days later J.C. Brown, when he found that his benchmates had, as a trick, shuffled his speaking notes out of order, attempted to follow Fitzherbert's example.[259] Bell pronounced that 'it can't be done for every member, and the honourable member must know that in this House there are members and members'. A fellow new member, William Swanson, came to Brown's rescue. He challenged Bell for being partial, and argued that all members had to be treated alike.

Monro, who had sought re-election as an ordinary representative, became embroiled in the first electoral petition heard under the legislation of 1858.[260] He had held Motueka by a single vote, the returning officer's. Fox stacked the committee hearing the matter, which found against Monro. The House agreed that the Governor should be asked to appoint Monro to the Legislative Council, an appointment equivalent to the customary peerage given to retiring House of Commons' Speakers, but Fox delayed announcing a decision until Monro, in a fit of pique, turned down the offer.[261]

Although he got rid of Monro, Fox failed to lead the ministry. He took a back seat to his ministers, and was incapable of controlling Vogel when the latter returned from London. Galvanised by the ministry's incompetence, Stafford finally agreed to lead the opposition.[262] The opposition's concern for financial responsibility was reflected in strong support for FitzGerald, who, as Comptroller, constantly struggled with Vogel over the accounts.[263]

The government's majority proved shaky. The session was noted for its long sittings, and members and parliamentary staff became 'thoroughly knocked up'. Neither Bellamy's nor the smoking room were available because of construction work.[264] Vogel's domineering approach and the ministry's failure to manage the House effectively by making concessions meant that the political and constitutional implications of Vogel's policies remained unrealised. Stafford observed: 'a Government may treat its supporters until, like overflogged coach-horses, they at last cease to care either for the sound or the lash of the whip.'[265] But Vogel warned he would shortly introduce what was in effect 'a new Constitution Act'.[266]

During the session of 1872, the parties were finely balanced and little of substance was achieved. Vogel decided 'to leave well alone' – 'the less we do this session, the better. We can plead heavy work as a good excuse for not producing the new Constitution Bill'.[267] Vogel was often not in the House, and Fox showed little leadership. The parties jockeyed for supporters and the ministry lost divisions. Stafford's no-confidence motion attacked the administration of the public works and immigration policy, the frequent absences of ministers from Wellington, and Vogel for ignoring the House and even cabinet. After an extraordinarily long debate, the ministry was voted out, after Jerningham Wakefield's celebrated vote for Stafford.[268]

Asked – for the last time – to form a new ministry, Stafford proposed little beyond a more careful approach.[269] Less than a month later, to his surprise, he lost office after complicated political jockeying. Vogel, who had taken over as opposition leader from Fox, moved a no-confidence motion amid accusations of undue influence from the railway contractor Brogden on the government.[270] Stafford attempted to call the division early by refusing to enter into a debate on the motion, knowing that some of Vogel's supporters were out of the House. He still lost by two votes, 37 to 35. There was some last-minute drama. Stafford changed his mind about the state of the House and attempted to speak again when the Speaker had taken the motion on voices. With Vogel shouting 'Too late, too late!', the Speaker allowed Stafford to speak. At the same moment government whip H.A. Ingles assured Stafford – 'It is all right' – that he had sufficient votes to win. Stafford declined to commence the debate, but unfortunately the whip had miscounted.[271]

Stafford refused to resign immediately, and asked the Governor for a dissolution on the basis that neither party had a clear majority. Bowen declined on a number of grounds, including fears that supply would not be granted.[272] Stafford's recent refusal to consider Bowen's lavish private expenditure claims probably did not help his chances. Bowen was also ill-disposed towards Vogel, whom he disliked as a Jew and an upstart, so he approached Fox instead. The former Premier refused and suggested G.M. Waterhouse of the Legislative Council. Fox was by now keen to leave politics and wanted 'new blood' introduced: 'there has been in this Assembly too much of interchange of office between certain old members of the political world.'[273] Having Waterhouse head a ministry proved a temporary expedient. Vogel, as leader in the House, was Premier in all but name. (Waterhouse resigned five months later – to the fury of Bowen – and Vogel became Premier on his return from overseas after Fox had played a caretaker role in the interim.) Vogel did not attempt to prolong the session, which subsided uneventfully.

Vogel dominated the House during the session of 1873 to the extent that the focus of conflict was between the House and the Council. He displayed a remarkably pragmatic capacity to keep going even when many of his initiatives had to be abandoned. Once again the session was characterised by large numbers of lapsed or rejected bills, but it was like water off a duck's back to Vogel.

During the 1874 session, the abolition of the provinces suddenly became a distinct possibility. When a bill was obstructed, Vogel, prodded by Stafford, angrily brought in resolutions to abolish the North Island provinces and confirm Wellington as the permanent seat of government.[274] The House was shaken out of its lethargy and the diehard provincialists made a final stand, led by a dissident cabinet minister, O'Rorke. After delivering an impassioned speech, O'Rorke took up his hat and papers and walked over to the opposition benches, before stalking out of the House to hand his resignation to the Governor.[275] The abolition resolution passed overwhelmingly, as Stafford and his supporters joined Vogel. The smaller provinces voted wholesale for the measure, while the larger ones were divided over it. The session closed with little else accomplished, but the stage had been set for one of the most fundamental changes in New Zealand's political history.

The 1875 session was a peculiar one. Daniel Pollen became Premier in a reconstructed ministry once it was apparent that Vogel would not return from Britain. Stafford and his supporters remained influential, although sitting on the opposition side of the House. Further moves to abolish the provinces provoked ex-Governor Grey to enter politics on a provincialist platform, threatening to sweep away 'the General Assembly in its present form'. He entered the House to rousing cheers and took his place on the opposition benches.[276] Grey warned that his supporters would take extraordinary measures in order 'to meet a revolution' and succeeded in having the Address-in-Reply debate adjourned.[277]

The ministry, meanwhile, had decided to abolish the entire provincial system during the current session. The opposition obstructed the Abolition of Provinces Bill for as long as possible. When the bill went into Committee there was a marathon debate which the House decided Hansard should report in full. Both parties divided their supporters into 'watches' with eight hours on duty and 16 off. As one reporter described the scene: 'An old party was on his legs muttering away to no one in particular, and certainly no one was listening. There were about twenty members in the House, generally stretched in all sorts of lazy but very undignified postures, some of them asleep', while Hansard reporters strove to catch some of the words concerning athletic exercises.[278] The press were quietly playing euchre. As the night wore on, 'possum rugs, spare coats, travelling caps of sleepy looking form and material, slippers of every possible device within the Standing Orders for getting through the night either asleep or awake gradually accumulated … the ringing of the bells invariably brought in enough workers in the Ministers' room, and of loungers in the library, Bellamy's, or the lobby to make up the necessary numbers.' The debate continued until an adjournment at 6.15 a.m., 'enough for a wash, breakfast, and a walk' before the House reconvened at 10 a.m.

In the end the ministry lost its resolve, adjourned the House and negotiated to amend the bill in return for lifting the stonewall. Abolition was postponed until after elections and the end of the session of 1876.[279] The opposition, virtually moribund since 1869, had been rejuvenated by Grey. The Abolition of Provinces Bill was read a third time and passed through the Legislative Council with ease.

The formative years

By the 1870s the General Assembly had unmistakably established its presence. The abolition of the provinces sealed the pre-eminence of central government. New Zealand now had a substantial if rather higgledy-piggledy Houses of Parliament. Parliament had a reliable system for recording its debates, and its procedures had been refined and formally prescribed over time. By the mid 1870s the relationship between the House and the Council had been sharpened by differences over Vogel's bold moves. Although the Council had adopted an aggressive stance, it was unlikely to triumph. The Council's willingness to reform itself offered one opening for it to remain a force, but that was a course fraught with danger.

Reforms in political representation – the miners' franchise, the four Maori seats, and the secret ballot – had not greatly disturbed the political order established in the 1850s, although changes to electorates had enlarged the House, which swelled from 37 to 78 by the early 1870s. Politics remained the domain of élite and propertied social groups, although colonial society was more open than Britain.[280] The House was filled with those who had built up a substantial stake in the country. Landowners, businessmen, merchants and lawyers predominated, supplemented by journalists, newspaper editors, retired officers and officials. By the 1870s the social composition of the House was shifting away from landowning towards professions such as the law. Members were generally well educated. Thirty per cent had a university education and a large number belonged to learned societies.

This political élite had almost without exception been born outside New Zealand, well over three-quarters in the British Isles. Those from England alone were more than half of the total.[281] Few early members had previously participated in politics, either in Britain or in New Zealand. By British standards, the colonial Parliament was middle-class in nature and radical in tone. In the absence of a weighty conservative establishment of church and land, it was made up of those from the middling ranks who had bettered themselves by migrating.

They were not by and large recent arrivals. More than half had emigrated before the first session of Parliament in 1854, usually in young adulthood. Consistent with the characteristics of an immigrant population, they were still relatively young when they entered the House. The average age of members during the first sessions of Parliament was less than 40. During the next 20 years, it rose to the mid-40s.

This cadre of politicians had some familiarity with the social and political issues besetting Britain, but had also gained experience in the colony before entering politics. This interesting combination of ideals and practicality was allowed full rein in the chamber of the House. But while the colonial offspring was different from the 'Mother' of parliaments back 'Home', there was an ardent wish that New Zealand should construct political institutions worthy of the comparison. In the debating chamber, settler pragmatism and middle-class self-improvement coexisted with Etonian erudition and eloquence. Members sought to recreate a familiar world in a rude and makeshift colony.

In these early decades the turnover of members was extraordinarily high, reflecting the difficulty of attracting representatives at a time of primitive transport and when politics was perceived as a part-time pursuit.[282] Resignation was a far more common way of leaving the House than defeat at the polls.[283] On average half of the chamber was fresh after each election, and there was a turnover of one third or more of the membership during each five-year term.

But it should not be thought that this made effective government impossible. A strong and durable thread was provided by a small core of 20 or so politicians who were in politics for the long haul. They were well-educated professional men who were keenly aware of current affairs and assumed key positions in successive governments. This gave continuity despite the frequent changes of executive. Ministries were led by Stafford, Fox and Vogel, and key cabinet ministers included Sewell, Whitaker, Reader Wood, Major Atkinson, McLean, Fitzherbert and C.W. Richmond.

From the mid 1860s, after the fall of Weld, the kind of person entering the House changed.[284] Men such as Vogel were more determined to make their own way and use politics as a means of

THE RETURN OF THE OTAGO PARLIAMENTARY THEATRICAL TROUPE.

"Slap bang, here we are again ;
Jolly dogs are we !"

Dunedin Punch, 4 November 1865

Vogel, Macandrew and others return to Dunedin in triumph after promoting the separatist cause and helping to bring down the Weld ministry. In the early 1860s southern provinces, and in particular Otago, felt that central government was not sufficiently responsive to their interests while the country was preoccupied with the wars in the north. The continued convening of Parliament in Auckland compounded the grievance. The separation movement had its beginnings in Otago in 1862, and caused the fall of the Fox ministry that year over the issue of responsibility for native affairs. In 1865 the collapse of the Weld ministry led some in Otago to advocate the merging of provinces, enhanced provincial powers, and the confining of the General Assembly to strictly federal concerns. With Parliament having been removed to Wellington, Aucklanders harboured similar thoughts, but the two provinces were unable to agree and their resolutions were defeated in 1866. Separation was now a lost cause.

advancement, and less interested in the constitutional debates which preoccupied the House in its early years. Vogel was brash and volatile, did not own land, and had a rough and tumble style shaped by his Australian goldfields experience. He did not brook authority easily. Vogel introduced into the House the more abrasive and domineering style that he had used in provincial politics against Otago's 'Old Identities'.[285] This new breed saw development of the economy and growth of the state going hand in hand, not only as a political philosophy but also as a personal crusade. Their arrival on the political scene reflected the gradual supplanting of the pastoral élite, the members of which were happy to debate matters of great moment from a largely disinterested position as long as the tenure of their runs remained undisturbed.

By the 1870s political representation too began to change. The elections of 1871 and 1875 saw governments going to the country on their policies for the first time. This advanced the concept of 'party' beyond the loose, ad hoc groupings that were factions in the House. It also extended the concept of representation beyond the vague notion of election in a general, usually propertied, interest. Popular participation in politics broadened. Greater numbers registered to vote, most seats were contested, and the numbers voting swelled.[286] Parliament became the centre of attention for an increasingly politicised population as the provinces faded.

The centralist/provincialist division had gone; the old generation of statesmanlike politicians who sought to speak for and interpret the 'general will' over and above the clamour of competing groups lost its influence. The new, more assertive politics was more directly linked to the interests of particular groups in society, both propertied and waged. This provided fertile ground for the eventual emergence of the Liberals and fully-fledged parties. But meanwhile the strength of the well-established factional system would be tested.

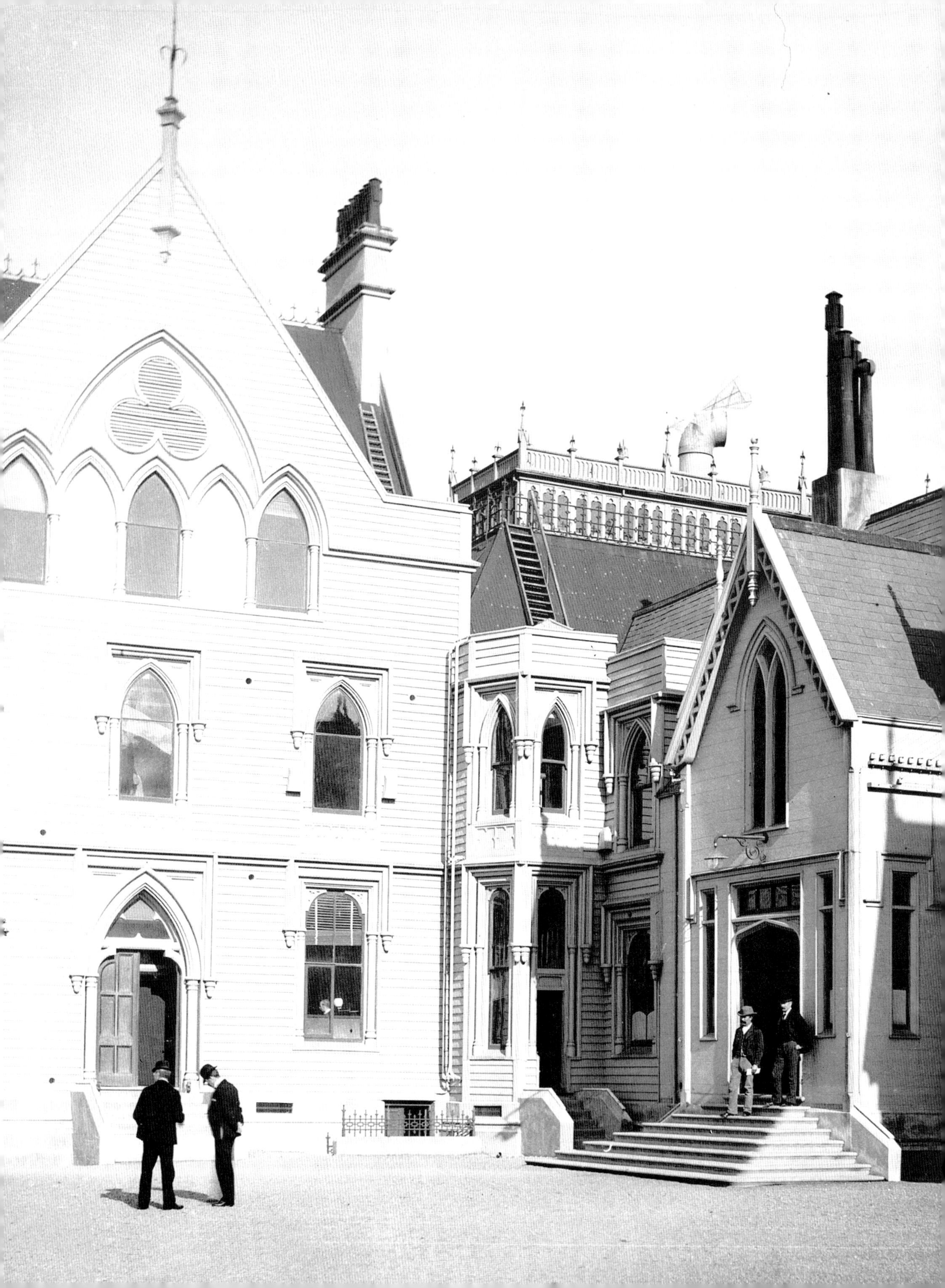

CHAPTER 3

POLITICAL REALIGNMENT, RETRENCHMENT AND DEPRESSION, 1876–90

With the abolition of the provinces, many political issues which had been ventilated in the provincial council chambers were thrown into sharper relief at the national level. Provincial responsibilities that had given rise to liberal and radical politics were, in particular, control over land, immigration and public works. The fiscal, native affairs and military responsibilities of the general government had given it a more conservative cast. The centralisation of politics displaced the pivot point of liberal and radical politics into Parliament, and George Grey became their vehicle. The fundamental issue was land, but to this were added over time taxation and tariffs, the administration of the state, and as depression took hold, retrenchment and the protection of industry.

In the late 1870s and 1880s, a clearer distinction began to emerge between 'conservative' and 'liberal' politics. But these terms are not to be regarded as party labels. There had always been a distinction between centralist, relatively warlike governments and more provincialist and peaceable oppositions. Now the battle lines in national politics were drawn more clearly as Grey entered the lists. The 'conservative' ministries were portrayed by their 'liberal' antagonists as holding on to power illegitimately and corruptly, and as using the state to foster their own interests and those of their business associates. The 'liberals' in Parliament attacked landed oligarchy and business 'rings', and pursued democratic reforms. These 'liberal' politicians were portrayed by the 'conservatives' as inciting the 'mob', and as an extreme, irresponsible and radical alternative to their cautious, steady, responsible, progressive and truly 'liberal' policies. The 'conservatives' for their part boasted of electoral reforms, and of progressive land settlement policies and social and labour legislation. Historians have tended to regard Grey's ministry of 1877–9 and (in a qualified sense) the Stout–Vogel ministry of 1884–7 as 'liberal' administrations which punctuated the domination of the 1870s and 1880s by a so-called 'continuous' conservative ministry which maintained its power through shifting combinations of the same politicians, particularly Atkinson, McLean, Whitaker and Hall.[1]

This divide between 'liberal' and 'conservative' ministries was not, however, clear cut. Factional government continued to exist, based on provincial and public works politics and the tension between the economic imperatives of development and retrenchment. The cement for factions was the dispensation of public works, now funded by the general government as part of Vogel's development scheme, and described as 'log-rolling' or 'pork-barrel' politics.[2] The potential for corruption in relation to land dealings, finance and railways lurked in the background, particularly as depression began to cripple the country. To the traditional image of an evil squattocracy of pastoralists was added those of land speculators and money-grubbing financiers. Opposed to them were politicians claiming to be

Left: Front courtyard of Parliament Buildings, 1890s Tyree collection, ATL, G11627½

working to ensure fully democratic representation and to help small settlers and wage-earning immigrants realise their aspirations. But one man's corruption was another's honoured promise in the never-ending scramble for public works. And the very fact that supporters of a faction would continue to vote for a government through thick and thin was regarded as evidence that they had been bought rather than of loyalty.[3] Acceptance of party loyalty had some way to go.

The factional system came under increasing pressure with the collapse of the old centralist/provincialist divide. When the largesse of public works dried up, factionalism lost its source of cohesion. Enlarged electoral participation, together with the novel methods that politicians began to employ in communicating with electors, pointed the way to the future. Meanwhile, old patterns persisted in the House as members grappled with the changes.

Old alignments break up

The elections in late 1875 revealed widespread support for the abolition of the provinces.[4] Grey's party had formed a concerted platform. He was bent on demolishing the power of the self-appointed 'governing class', breaking up the large estates, reducing borrowing and furthering democracy. Vogel advocated abolishing the provinces, borrowing and development.

Vogel resumed the premiership after the election, but his popularity had declined and the House received him coldly.[5] In the new House of 88 members, only half had sat in the previous Parliament; nearly 40 per cent were complete newcomers.[6] This made for an unpredictable session. Vogel reconstructed the ministry and sought to buy off key opposition members. Fitzherbert jumped at the opportunity to become Speaker, Vogel disingenuously saying that it was not desirable to make such an appointment a party matter.[7] Grey, as leader of the opposition, seconded the nomination, expressing sorrow that one of the strongest debaters had been removed from the fray.[8]

Fitzherbert's performance as Speaker was less assured. His lack of presence or decisive opinions became failings. One political observer said he allowed 'the ill-breeding of certain of the members to be freely imparted to the debate, and the whole tone of the House [was] lowered by the license allowed to the speakers. With eyes closed, and without motion, he would sit, apparently heedless of the course of events, like a figure freshly transplanted from Madame Tussaud's Exhibition'.[9]

Grey went onto the attack, determined to throw out the ministry by whatever means possible. The government, to its horror, lost the first division of the session, one requiring two-thirds endorsement, when Grey moved the suspension of standing orders. He then moved that the

William Fitzherbert, who was born in England on 15 August 1810, graduated from Cambridge in Classics and qualified as a doctor. After arriving in Wellington in 1841 he became an important figure in the local Constitutional Association. Elected for City of Wellington in 1855, Fitzherbert became a renowned debater who could speak for lengthy periods without notes thanks to his prodigious memory. He was a forceful, eloquent and sarcastic speaker noted for memorable phrases. Fitzherbert was Colonial Treasurer under Weld and Stafford from 1864 to 1869. Elected Speaker of the House in 1876, he was made KCMG in 1877. His lack of a forceful presence or clear opinions left him vulnerable to manipulation by those clever in parliamentary procedure. In 1879 Fitzherbert resigned from the House to become Speaker of the Legislative Council, a position he retained until shortly before his death on 6 February 1891.

secret sale of the Piako swamp to banker and land speculator Thomas Russell be halted. This motion was defeated, but only on the Speaker's casting vote.[10] Vogel rallied his supporters and adjourned the House. Many began to feel uncomfortable that the relationship between land speculation and political influence had been exposed, and the sale cast a long shadow over the session.

Grey swayed the House and galleries like no other with his passion and talk of the need to provide for the 'unborn millions' of the future. But he proved no strategist or organiser. Over time, he grew increasingly wild and irrational and obsessed about conspiracies.[11] He tried desperately to halt the abolition of the provinces by proposing separation of the two islands and attacked the Governor as being in the government's pocket. When Vogel responded he was admonished but not suspended for using unparliamentary language.[12] The Speaker's intervention came too late, after the matter had got out of hand.

The unrelenting personal attacks and the length of debates took their toll. Vogel was ill and exhausted and, when Featherston, New Zealand's Agent-General in London, died, Vogel secured the position for himself. The politically clumsy Atkinson formed a ministry. His debut did not go well when he messed up his cabinet appointments.[13] He sought to suspend standing orders to pass a corrective bill but was blocked. His ministry had to resign and was reconstructed.

It was in these circumstances that one of the most notorious stonewalls in the history of the New Zealand Parliament took place. W.L. Rees (an ardent Grey supporter) spoke for more than 24 hours on whether Atkinson's ministers should be disqualified from the House.[14] By now the art of the stonewall had become well-developed. The government controlled the business of the House, but the opposition decided how long it would take to get the business through.

Stonewalls often focused on the Committee stage of bills, when each clause was debated. Discussion of the short title of a bill was a favourite opportunity for stonewalling because free-ranging debate was allowed. Tactics for clauses of bills included moving amendments to delete individual words and substitute others, and moving that the Chairman report progress or that he leave the Chair. Either of the last two moves, if successful, would effectively kill the bill. They were used less to achieve this goal than as a means of obstruction. Another tactic was for members to rise together and then stage-manage a lengthy dispute over who should speak first. Debaters would resort to dictionaries, lists or their favourite hobbies in desperate attempts to keep their speeches going for as long as possible, sometimes with amusing consequences as the House sought any opportunity to relieve the dreariness of endless debates. In later years, stonewallers had to be careful to avoid the 'tedious repetition' that could foreclose the debate.

To mount a successful stonewall, the group had to plan its forces carefully and marshal its troops in shifts or relays to maintain the flow of speeches. The government, while not bound to put up speakers, had to maintain a quorum. Government members brought in rugs and pillows instead of dictionaries and lists. At times the galleries were cleared to minimise publicity for the stonewall.

Rees' day-long speech was a record. He took up the challenge shortly after 3 a.m on 15 September. After several hours speaking:

> a member of his party handed him a slip of paper on which was inscribed an inquiry whether a brandy and soda would be acceptable. Upon the inquirer receiving an affirmative nod, he bowed to the Speaker and went into Bellamy's. He presently returned with a carafe containing the desired beverage, which he handed to a messenger with instructions to take it to Mr R—. But one of Mr R—'s opponents either smelt a rat or the liquor, for he immediately rose to a point of order. Of course Mr R— sat down while the Speaker investigated the disputed point – which was 'that one of the messengers had brought some dirty water into the House.' The Speaker examined the carafe and had to admit that the contents were anything but *aqua pura*. So Mr R— had to proceed with his oration, fortified only with the genuine Adam's ale.[15]

During the stonewall, two members on opposing sides argued fiercely over the use of a couch in the lobby. One wielded a chair, whereupon the other hurriedly left the couch and complained to the Speaker that his life had been threatened. This allowed Rees temporary respite from his marathon as the Speaker extracted an apology from the offending member.

The Hansard reporters were eventually forced to give up reporting Rees' speech. The Speaker also wilted and retired, and was replaced by O'Rorke. With others taking over from Rees in the early hours of the following day, the Speaker announced that at midnight Saturday he would vacate the Chair until Monday morning. This did not deter the opposition, which continued until just before midnight on Monday evening. *Hansard* (which had resumed) recorded the date as 14 September whereas in fact it was now 18 September, as the House had sat continuously. This monumental exercise in futility caused a fracture within the opposition, with supporters deserting Grey towards the end of the session as his obstructiveness continued.[16]

Next session a member sought to have speeches restricted to 20 minutes.[17] He did not want the Commons' practice of putting down long speeches 'by clamour' and making 'unearthly noises' introduced here, but argued that something had to be done. Some thought the motion a joke; closure was anathema. It would allow 'a tyrannical majority to coerce the minority'.

The opposition's attack in 1876 included tightened-up provisions for disqualifying members.[18] Hunting out perceived corruption became an obsession. William Montgomery introduced a private member's Disqualification Bill, alleging the government was both rewarding its supporters and buying out opposition members. This measure was pre-empted by the government's short bill, which repealed all previous legislation and stated that those employed by the government were not eligible to be elected to the House, and that former members of the House were not to take up offices until a year after leaving it. Grey introduced significant electoral reform bills implementing full manhood suffrage and triennial Parliaments. These bills were defeated narrowly after barely being debated as virtually all in the House sought to bring the session to an end. Members deserted the House even though Atkinson delayed the steamers.[19] The remaining members made their way north on the *Stella* and south on the *Hinemoa* after a session that William Rolleston regarded as 'one of the weariest ever'.[20] Almost everyone agreed.

Grey's interlude, 1877–9

'What was to be the new "cry" that was to divide members?', asked Robert Stout.[21] His answer was liberal reform, but others thought the key distinction was between fiscal prudence and irresponsibility. The 'long depression' had the last say. The break-up of long-term political alignments followed as familiar provincial rivalries disappeared. The session of 1877, running from 19 July to 10 December, was the longest held up to that time. Grey had come with a comprehensive alternative platform, but the opposition was disunited.[22] Atkinson's ministry was little better. Atkinson asked for a 'political rest' from headlong borrowing and development, for completion of what had been begun, and for time to deal with the social implications of previous economic policies.[23] He showed

George Grey was the most influential political figure in nineteenth-century New Zealand. Under his first governorship (1845–53) much Maori land was purchased and the colony prepared itself for representative government, while his second term (1861–8) saw the protracted conflict of the land wars. Following his retirement from colonial administration Grey entered the House in 1875 as the member for Auckland City and immediately transformed politics, becoming Premier in 1877. After the dramatic defeat of his ministry in 1879, he remained an impassioned (if now embittered and increasingly isolated) orator in the House until his resignation in 1895, aged 83.

Political realignment, retrenchment and depression, 1876–90

little skill or interest in organising his supporters or selling his policies, which had little appeal to members whose electoral survival depended on continued public works. The government lost the initiative.[24]

Into September the government finally began to make some progress with the business of the session. The balance of power suddenly shifted when John Ballance, the future leader of the Liberal Party, deserted the ministry, taking his friend Stout and John Bryce with him.[25] Ballance proclaimed that two definite parties had 'formed, not upon temporary or fleeting questions or principles, but upon principles that will endure – namely, the principles of conservatism and liberalism'.[26] Grey began to talk in similar terms, but Atkinson and others rejected the distinction. Atkinson was beaten in the motion of no-confidence that followed, 42 to 38.[27] The majority included John Joyce, who had been rescued by the opposition from a room in which he had been locked by the government whip and made drunk. Celebrations ensued – J.W. Thomson produced his fiddle and played 'See the conquering hero comes', and 'high jinks were kept up all night'.[28] After Grey was elected leader of the opposition, the Governor, lacking any alternative, reluctantly sent for him.[29]

The sequel to the vote of Joyce was a court case taken against the respectable James Mackay, JP, for assaulting a member of the House, T.W. Hislop, with a horsewhip.[30] Mackay blamed Hislop for spreading a rumour that he had been implicated in getting Joyce drunk. Wellingtonians were appalled when Mackay was convicted, and at his proposed imprisonment. It was widely felt that a gentleman's honour had to be satisfied, even if it meant breaking the law. Following a petition signed by thousands and a deputation to the new Minister of Justice, John Sheehan, Mackay was released on the Governor's assent.

Grey formed a ministry with great difficulty, and Atkinson immediately challenged him by moving a no-confidence motion. The public was fascinated by the struggle, with the galleries 'crowded to suffocation'. But the government whips called a division, which caught Atkinson off-guard. Three opposition members were unable to reach the House in time.[31] Atkinson rose eight times to foil the snap division, 'until his face was livid with rage' as he was cried down by shouts of 'Adjourn!' and 'Sit down!' Grey 'cheered, clapped his hands, and laughed with the pleasure of a child'. The ministry squeaked home on the Speaker's casting vote.

For the remainder of the session the government desperately used 'talking against time', the order paper and standing orders to avoid another test of confidence.[32] Grey sought a dissolution to strengthen his precarious hold on power. To his fury, Governor Normanby delayed until after the end of the session and then declined – the last time a Governor refused a dissolution in New Zealand. This was part of an acrimonious standoff between Grey and Normanby. When the House refused to take out some controversial clauses in a bill, Grey made an extraordinary attempt to sabotage this decision. After advising Normanby to veto the bill, he left it out of the bills requiring the Governor's assent.[33] Asserting his constitutional role, Normanby withheld further supply from Grey's government by refusing to sign the Appropriation Bill until the offending bill was presented for his assent. Grey was unrepentant in spite of his unconstitutional actions, and the extraordinary session was closed by Commission. The belief was that Normanby had refused to read the ministry's speech.[34]

Grey managed to entice Ballance and Stout into his government, and undertook a triumphant national 'stump' tour of a kind not seen before.[35] More conservative politicians viewed this populist initiative with horror, but it worked and was the forerunner of a political style of leadership that others such as Seddon would adopt.

Grey and Macandrew dispense public works to Auckland and Otago in the late 1870s. Other provinces could go to the devil.

Parliamentary Library, untitled cartoon collection, 1870s

The Governor's speech at the opening of the 1878 session suggested that Grey would carry out his manifesto energetically.[36] Early in the session, Parliament took a novel break. Both Houses, with the Governor, sailed to Christchurch and then travelled by the first special train to Dunedin to celebrate the opening of the Christchurch–Dunedin line. However, 'most of the ministry, including Grey, stopped behind, either as not quite sympathising in what might be deemed a Vogelite triumph, or in order to profit by the opportunity of working up arrears'.[37]

When Parliament got back to Wellington, the government's Electoral Bill proposing complex arrangements to extend the franchise was headed off by Whitaker's simpler Parliamentary Representation Bill, which provided for full manhood suffrage.[38] There were serious differences in cabinet over the issue. The amendment of the Electoral Bill to introduce women's suffrage and abolish plural voting was greeted by opposition laughter and scorn at the shambles. The Council's abolition of the Maori ratepayer voting qualification caused Grey to explode and peremptorily withdraw all his electoral legislation.[39]

Sheehan, who was also Native Minister and Postmaster-General, became a key target for the opposition, which used all means to destroy him personally and discredit his policies. Grey proved incapable of acting as Premier, leader of his party or Leader of the House.[40] His autocratic nature, touchiness, insulting behaviour and general lack of control and respect for the rules of debate made for a chaotic session.

John Sheehan, the Minister of Justice in Grey's ministry, had a meteoric rise in Parliament after being elected to Rodney in 1872. He was the first New Zealand-born Pakeha to become a member of the House of Representatives and a cabinet minister. His fall was to be equally rapid. A fluent Maori speaker, he was also a brilliant tactician, acting as Grey's organiser and whip. His notable maiden speech emphasised the need for New Zealand-born politicans to take charge. 'I now stand alone. I shall not be long so. Others, like myself, will seek admittance. When they come in turn to the doors of this House – when they come rushing in … we shall have a better state of things than now exists'.* But he proved recklessly irresponsible with expenditure as a minister, and a poor role model in other respects. His brashness annoyed the older, more restrained members, while his well-known fondness for liquor and Maori women caused his downfall. His political career effectively ended with the defeat of the Grey ministry in 1879. Because of his controversial involvement in the purchase of land from Maori, he was soon deserted by Grey and scapegoated by others, and became an embittered pariah. He controversially married a 15-year-old girl in 1882, and died from pneumonia and cirrhosis of the liver in 1885, aged 40.

* *NZPD*, vol 12, 1876, p.16

Schmidt collection, ATL, F4198½

The colony now entered the 'long depression'. Gold exports fell dramatically, wool prices dropped, the land boom deflated and credit contracted. The opposition's search for an effective leader turned to the old stalwart Fox, in spite of his 'unfortunate craze on the liquor question'.[41] Fox's transformation into an ardent and leading temperance campaigner had largely overtaken his political

Political realignment, retrenchment and depression, 1876–90

inclinations. Meanwhile the ministry was starting to break up; cabinet no longer met and Grey dealt with ministers individually.[42] Grey forced Ballance and Stout to resign over a land speculation scheme. Renewed conflict with Maori surfaced in the form of confrontations with Te Whiti at Parihaka in Taranaki.

A new Speaker had to be found when the session of 1879 opened.[43] Fitzherbert wanted to resign in favour of securing the sinecure of Speaker to the more congenial Legislative Council. There was much negotiation and rumours flew about.[44] O'Rorke, the member for Onehunga, was put forward by Grey with the endorsement of Atkinson. Whitaker extolled his impartiality as Chairman of Committees, and his long experience was acknowledged. O'Rorke would prove an impartial, strong and long-lasting Speaker. He endured long enough to take the House into the twentieth century, he gained a reputation as the best Speaker in the Australasian colonies, and his abilities were remarked upon by overseas visitors.[45] As Speaker he continued to be active in Committee, and when 'trying to get some Onehunga grant passed, he ... will take advantage of any accident or of any negligence'.[46] He also had a reputation for going on drinking binges.[47]

George Maurice O'Rorke, the son of an Anglican clergyman and large landowner, was born on 2 May 1830 in County Galway, Ireland. After obtaining a BA with honours in Classics, he emigrated to Australia in 1852 and arrived in Auckland in 1854. He was elected to the House of Representatives in 1861 for Onehunga. In 1871 O'Rorke was appointed Chairman of Committees in the House, and he was a cabinet minister (1873–4) before resigning over the proposal to abolish the provinces. In 1879 he was appointed Speaker, and the following year he was knighted. O'Rorke, who became the longest-serving Speaker in the House, set the standard for impartiality. Some of his rulings were reportedly adopted in Australia and the House of Commons. He is famous for stating that he had never subscribed 'to the doctrine that the Standing Orders are the masters of the House; for I hold that the House is the master of the Standing Orders'. While renowned for firmness, O'Rorke allowed members some latitude, especially in relation to financial matters and no-confidence motions. He lost his seat in 1890, but was re-elected in 1893 and was again Speaker from 1894 until 1902. In 1904 he was appointed to the Legislative Council, where he remained until his death on 25 August 1916.

Parliamentary Service collection

'Verax', a seasoned observer in the House, had seen 'the business-like Clifford, the dignified Monro, the undecided Bell, the loquacious Fitzherbert, and the firm and impartial O'Rorke.'[48] The Speaker, in William Gisborne's words, had to combine a range of qualities rarely found in one individual. 'He must have a thorough knowledge of his duties, and fulfill them with firmness and discretion. He must be a man of the world, with the instincts of a gentleman and a high sense of the honour of the House. He must be able to control himself as well as others. He must be respected and popular; rule with dignity, conciliation, and with invariable firmness, be just in all his rulings, and without showing political or personal bias.'[49] Arthur Seymour, who had filled the position in 1873–4, became Chairman of Committees again.[50]

The 1879 session got off to an unusual start, with Grey attempting to suspend standing orders to approve a loan bill. The House rejected this move.[51] Fox's opposition wanted to confront the ministry immediately, and he moved no-confidence as an amendment to the Address-in-Reply, launching into a devastating series of criticisms of the ministry, attacking its profligacy and both Sheehan's expenditure and his moral character.[52] Grey's ineffectual defence of his ministry resulted in desertion from the ranks. When the division came, the government was handily defeated, 47 to 33. Rees immediately referred to those who had crossed the floor as 'the noble army of rats'.[53] A list of 11 'rats' was pinned on the door of the chamber. The hard core of Grey's supporters felt that the traditional pattern of shifting alliances needed to be replaced by pledges of permanent support for a party.

Both sides were disconcerted when the new Governor, Sir Hercules Robinson, acceded to Grey's request for a dissolution while insisting that no important or contested measures be introduced meanwhile and that the new Parliament convene as soon as possible. Robinson felt that Grey 'had been hoist with his own petard', but Grey had the gall to attempt to introduce his entire programme of electoral reform nonetheless, only to be sternly rebuffed by the House.[54]

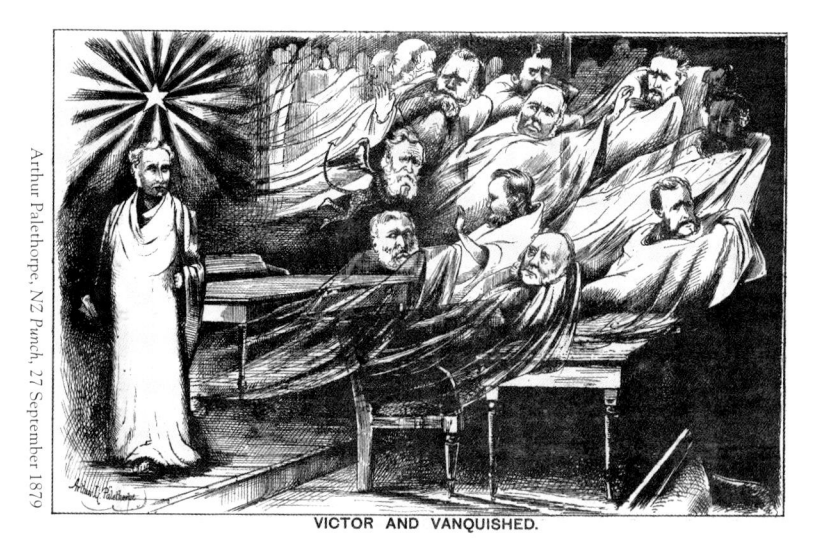

A number of members gained notoriety in 1879 for deserting Grey, who is shown here with a star above his head. They became known as the 'rats'.

There was not even a proper financial statement for this inconsequential session – Grey merely read out a brief statement with appended tables. No proper record of the financial statement passed into *Hansard* because the reporters did not have to take notes and – contrary to tradition – no printed copy was supplied.[55] Members wondered whether they were justified in accepting a full honorarium for sitting for little more than four weeks before Parliament was dissolved for the elections.

Grey's 1879 electoral campaign was unlike anything seen before, with a wide-ranging manifesto on 'Liberalism' and the organisation of Liberal Associations in the major centres and smaller towns.[56] The hard-fought election mobilised working people in a way not previously experienced but failed to produce a clear-cut result, even if the proposed electoral reforms were endorsed.

Hall and electoral reform

The House reassembled in late September with the whips working hard – key independent members and the Maori members were besieged. The opposition was strengthened by Hall's return from the

Council. With Fox having lost his seat, Hall became leader of the opposition.[57] Those with land, property or in business were keen to get rid of Grey and his land tax and James Macandrew and his expansive public works spending. With depression clouds gathering, retrenchment was in the air.

Grey refused to resign and adjourned the House in a futile attempt to consolidate support. Hall and Saunders slated the ministry for its administrative incompetence. The no-confidence motion came as an amendment to the Address-in-Reply, with Hall cleverly committing himself to liberal reforms. Pyke, Wiremu Te Wheoro, Ebenezer Hamlin and Whitaker remained in the chamber when the division was called.[58] The Speaker jolted Te Wheoro awake with the instruction that he had to vote. Hamlin and Whitaker descended on him for the opposition, but he turned and voted for the government, to loud cheers. Pyke stood in the gangway for a time, apparently uncertain, before going into the opposition lobby. The galleries in suspense awaited the result, and then an opposition member held up two fingers. Grey had been defeated, 43 to 41.

Grey still would not go – his ministry sat on the government benches for some days, until Hall announced that he would form a ministry, with Whitaker in the Legislative Council. The Governor accepted Grey's resignation but declined to ask his advice. Whitaker took charge of the Council for the next four years. He was described as a 'Triton among minnows' and 'our old wizard of the north' by Hall.[59] Hall was a hard-working member and a well-organised, earnest speaker who always marshalled his facts well.[60]

Hall required considerable skill in the fluid situation in the House, where Macandrew replaced Grey as leader of the opposition. Henare Tomoana thought he had extracted a promise of the appointment of a Maori as Native Affairs Minister with full salary and powers.[61] Disappointed, he deserted the ministry. Hall decided to battle on by continuing with the proposed electoral reform legislation, even as Macandrew brought in an explicit no-confidence motion.[62] The government used all the procedural resources it could to delay the division. The opposition for its part constantly obstructed Hall's introduction of electoral reform by repeated adjournments and 'previous question' motions, and began to assemble a majority.

The struggle was resolved by a spectacular crossing of the floor in the other direction – into the government's ranks – by four Auckland members, headed by Reader Wood and orchestrated by Whitaker.[63] They switched parties in return for 'written' promises, the most notorious of which was a 'fair' proportion of public works expenditure for Auckland. They also secured a commitment to electoral reform. The previous 'army of rats' was immediately replaced by the Auckland breed. Hall, now confident of a majority, outfaced Macandrew, who had to withdraw his motion. All hell broke loose as the opposition realised what had happened. The House was described as a 'bear garden'. New member for Hokitika, Richard John Seddon, put it bluntly: 'these four honourable gentlemen … broke their pledges to their party and betrayed them'.[64]

John Hall was first elected for Christchurch Country in 1855, and was a member of the House for 20 of the next 38 years. An excellent administrator, he served in several ministries, including as Premier from 1879 to 1882.

In the long run the episode contributed to breaking down the old personal and honour-based foundations of faction-building, and helped usher in parties bound by more formal and organised commitments. The interlude of the Grey government had given hints of the future of party politics – more clearly distinguished programmes, more inclusive appeals to the electorate, the extension of political organisation outside the House, and a greater role for electoral politics.[65] The widening of the franchise and burgeoning numbers of voters reshaped the political process. Interest groups began to seek a voice and express their points of view as they organised and became more articulate. Political philosophies and social reform became more attractive to the electorate than efficient administration and good government in the interests of colonial development, particularly as the depression took hold. But the House did not approve of the way in which the Auckland members had switched sides, and attempted to have relevant correspondence tabled.[66] When it became obvious that the new opposition would win, some government supporters rushed into the opposition lobby. This was a common if rather absurd tactic to avoid such issues becoming matters of confidence.[67] But in truth the opposition had splintered. The humiliated Grey became an increasingly solitary, disruptive and maverick force on the opposition benches.

Hall now guided the electoral reform legislation through the House. The Triennial Parliaments Act brought in three-yearly Parliaments and the Qualifications of Electors Act ushered in manhood suffrage, though plural voting was retained. When the year's work came to an end on 19 December, many members had already departed.[68]

With the installation of the Hall ministry, the country entered a decade of greater stability in politics. Elections were now held every three years, introducing a familiar electoral cycle. As William Massey pithily put it in 1920: 'during the first session we break in the colts; during the second session we do the country's work; and during the third session we prepare for the coming elections'.[69]

The actions of all governments in the 1880s were shaped by the problems of debt servicing, falling revenues and financing government expenditure without incurring deficits at a time when continued borrowing became more difficult as the country's credit rating fell.[70] Governments lost office as they grappled with these intractable issues by renewing or halting borrowing, by more or less severe retrenchment, or by increasing or introducing new forms of taxation. They were increasingly unable to retain power in a system based on factions through the traditional means of spreading around public works.

The system of factional politics based on personal leadership broke down under the weight of the depression and the increased size of the House. In a larger House, personal contact became less effective as a way of maintaining cohesive groups.[71] The House seemed more disorganised. Ministries were assembled out of uneasy coalitions as leaders failed to forge unity within their own ranks. The phrase that the House 'kept the ministers in and their measures out' was bandied around, reflecting the paralysis in government that developed during the 1880s.[72] The committed 'tails' of leading members such as Atkinson, Grey, Montgomery, Vogel and Stout shrank as independent members – 'rail-sitters', they were derisively called by the more loyal supporters of factions – rose to prominence.[73]

Paradoxically, the proportion of ministries surviving for a full parliamentary term increased – although the term was now only three years. The role of elections in changing governments became more important during this period. The lack of effective factional organisation disadvantaged oppositions more than it did governments and gave an impression of stability. Certainly there was a remarkably consistent pattern of voting for governments when it came to tests of confidence.[74]

Depression, retrenchment and stonewalling in the early 1880s

The session of 1880 was called early, for the end of May, because of the depression. The public works statement reinforced the gloomy mood and antagonised many members. Grey, Macandrew and Montgomery each led opposition factions, but a resounding defeat to a weak challenge made the opposition give up.

As the session developed, Parihaka dominated proceedings.[75] The government had to decide what to do with the prisoners taken in Taranaki. It introduced legislation so that it could continue to hold the prisoners without trial. The bill prompted three Maori members to approach the Governor, bypassing the House. This brought constitutional issues into the debate and caused serious divisions within cabinet.[76] Its Taranaki settler members, Bryce and Atkinson, threatened to resign if the bill did not pass and the prisoners were freed. The bill was passed convincingly enough, though some members had qualms about suspending habeas corpus.

Demands for substantial retrenchment mounted and civil service salaries were cut by 10 per cent. Staffs were reduced and departments amalgamated.[77] The organisation of the railways was centralised, with services cut and fares increased. Members, including Pyke, attempted to cut the vote for the

Political realignment, retrenchment and depression, 1876–90

controversial proposed Nelson railway by more than half, producing a confrontation between Seddon and Pyke.[78] Seddon had been caught asleep for the vote and on being woken shouted, 'I vote against Mr. Pyke'. Pyke jibbed at the ruling that Seddon's vote could be recorded and refused to sit down. He was ordered from the chamber but reappeared above in the reporters' gallery; the Sergeant-at-Arms had to remove him. Speaker O'Rorke suggested fining him, but the House recoiled from the prospect.

> *Vincent Pyke, a notable Otago local member and character, was always caricatured with a swollen red nose and an umbrella. He expostulated on the problems of servicing his Dunstan electorate, with its varied pastoral, agricultural and mining interests. It encompassed 'great mountains, aye, even unto the glaciers', and included valleys with no access to the rest of the electorate.* Dunstan had 14 polling places, and he spent at least a month each year travelling around the electorate, 'sleeping in uncomfortable beds, and eating ill-cooked food; I have to drink very dangerous liquors; and I am severed from the wife of my bosom during the whole time'. A city seat where the member could 'go a few doors down his street, deliver his speech and then retire to the bosom of his family, take his glass of grog, and go to bed' bore no comparison.*
>
> * NZPD, vol 57, 1887, pp. 383–4
>
> *'Hear, hear!' 'Yes!' 'No!'*
> *'Is that disorderly Mishter Speaker?'*
>
> NZ Observer and Free Lance, 12 July 1890

Pyke and Seddon often sparred in the House and were soon at it again. In 1881 after being needled on his humble origins, Seddon responded, using 'two adjectives and a noun which are never heard in any decent society'.[79] When Pyke threatened him with his walking stick he hit another member by mistake. The pair were separated, with Pyke hauled off into the lobbies still shouting.

By the end of the 1880 session the House had run out of steam and Hall had to drop various bills. Macandrew said that this would teach the government not to push measures through recklessly.[80] With the resignation of Native Affairs minister Bryce, Hall had to remodel his cabinet. But the opposition was in worse straits when the session of 1881 opened in June.[81] The Address-in-Reply died an early death, and it took the government to engineer a defeat of itself in one division. Richmond Hursthouse, a government whip, tried to push through railway legislation contrary to the government's wishes.[82] A member moved 'the previous question', whereupon Hursthouse admitted that he did not know what that meant and confessed that he and others usually headed into the wrong lobby on such occasions. When the vote came, O'Rorke, who apparently liked practical jokes, made Hursthouse a teller for the opposition, which won the division to abandon Hursthouse's own proposal!

J.D. Ormond, disaffected by Atkinson's property tax, deserted the government and eventually challenged it as a private member acting in association with the opposition. The House was stirred up – there were rumours of using ships to obtain absent members, people wandering around with division cards, and refusals to give pairs.[83] The challenge was not viewed entirely seriously, however, as the government reportedly converted the main lobby into a Tattersall's and offered odds of five to one that it would win. A reporter described the scene: 'Mercurial spirits flit about the House, and frequently are found at Bellamy's bar; while the inquisitive will haunt the reporters' room for news. Some men only speak when the ladies' gallery is full, others only when they have been mellowed by the cup that inebriates.'[84] Although defeated, the motion tapped a significant vein of discontent among government supporters, particularly over the paucity of new public works. Atkinson's cautious optimism was sufficient excuse for many to have inflated expectations of renewed prosperity.

The centrepiece of the 1881 session, the Representation Bill, shifted the basis for defining electorates from numbers of electors and communities of interest to population, modified by a 'country quota' of 25 per cent.[85] The latter had previously existed informally through the way that electorate boundaries were drawn up. The bill also increased general seats to 91. These were significant changes. In 1870 the number of European members had been increased to 74, and in 1875 to 84. In the 1880s the legislation altering representation would provide a focal point for dissatisfaction and a way of reducing the size of the House. In 1881 Sheehan viewed the changed electoral maps. 'I ... found four or five members of this House outside the door waiting for their turn, and looking exceedingly dejected and cast-down. I christened that place by the very appropriate name, as I think, of "The Place of Wailing".'[86] The changes reduced the representation of Auckland, Nelson and the West Coast, and increased that of Canterbury and Otago. This fractured the precarious party lines established in 1879, and gave rise to a stonewall of record length – nearly two weeks.

The members affected by the electoral changes, who included Grey and Seddon, got together to plan tactics. The Representation Bill passed its second reading unscathed, but then a monumental stonewall took place in Committee. This demonstrated how a minority in the House, even with the opposition completely fragmented, could obstruct proceedings.[87] The bill's opponents moved alternately and repeatedly that the Chairman report progress and that he leave the Chair, provoking division after division. The House sat from the afternoon of Tuesday 23 August until 2.30 a.m. on the following Thursday. More was to follow. Reporting was abandoned for a time, and the despairing government sought to modify the standing orders to give the Speaker the power of closure, a measure recently adopted in the Commons as a result of similar problems.[88] Then the stonewallers' tactics shifted to adjourning the House. Hall protested to no avail that this was an entirely new and illegitimate form of obstruction, and warned that he would not buckle under.

As the stonewall continued in the early hours, a sharp earthquake shook the chamber, making the House 'creak and tremble in a very alarming fashion', jolting the majority awake and causing everyone to rush frantically for the doors.[89] Dick Reeves (the 'Buller lion', described as a 'tall, dark, coarse-looking man ... [who] mistakes coarseness for power, and vulgarity for wit')[90] was reciting long quotations 'before two sympathisers and the skeleton of a Government quorum. Dick stood his ground till all but he had fled. Observing the Speaker tucking up his gown and making for a side entrance, he pointed to the walls of the trembling structure and shouted – not for the first time that day – "Sir, I beg to call your attention to the state of the House!"'[91]

ATL, F5255½

Richard Seddon, Premier 1893–1906, made a considerable impact on his entry into the House as member for Hokitika in 1879. His maiden speech went down in history for lasting two and a quarter hours. His energy and enthusiasm were renowned. On first acting as teller, 'in place of quietly standing by and counting heads, he was cavorting about the House and lugging less muscular members into what he considered the proper lobby. I have seen the gentleman similarly employed on the West Coast, but it was not legislators that he was rounding up.'* Seddon was soon acknowledged as one of the House's most incorrigible time-wasters – 'the arch obstructor of business, sometimes by order and at other times by choice'. His misplaced aspirate H's and Lancashire brogue were also often remarked upon. As his experience grew he became a skilled tactician notable for his grasp of standing orders.

* *LT*, 7 Nov 1879

Members delivered speeches on flora and fauna, on bees, and on various hobbies. Seddon discussed the effect of the property qualification on individual electors in his electorate, naming them in alphabetical order. At one point he announced in a stentorian voice: 'having finished K we'll now go to H__L', rousing government members from their slumbers as the stonewallers roared with laughter. (This became a standing joke in the House.) Seddon sat down after more than three hours. Tomoana offered to sing a waiata but was not allowed to do so. Those opposed to the measure spoke in relays, taking advantage of the rule allowing more than one speech per member while a bill was in Committee. Acting Chairmen had to take the Chair in relays.

Many resorted to sleeping on the benches; the elderly Grey was 'wrapped solicitously in scarves and overcoat and daily ushered to and from his lodgings'.[92] A Speaker's gallery ticket detailed government supporters' attendance. For light relief the card also suggested that Bellamy's would be providing free refreshments – 'See what we can do. We have got a majority; we can keep them here; and we are determined the party springs shall not run dry.'[93]

After 48 hours of no progress in Committee, Chairman Seymour refused to allow further motions to report progress or to make him leave the Chair.[94] Immediately William Gisborne (representing an electorate that was to be abolished) moved in disorderly fashion that progress be reported so that the ruling could be discussed. When Gisborne was reported to the Speaker, he called the Chairman 'a tyrant and a dupe of the Government', to applause from the gallery.[95] The Speaker was adamant that Gisborne be fined for the transgression. Hall regretfully moved that Gisborne be held in contempt and fined £20. The House voted for the fine, but then enthusiastic members raised more than £100 to cover it. O'Rorke held that the stonewall, far from being an exhibition on behalf of personal liberty, as argued by some, was a shameful exercise that abused the forms of the House 'to paralyse its powers, demoralize its members, and bring it into contempt.'[96]

One might have thought the stonewall would have ended there and then but this was not the case. Tactics shifted to moving new clauses, but when it became clear that the spectacle was over the galleries erupted in 'savage howls and hootings' and the Speaker had to threaten to clear them. Amid frequent calls for a quorum, the stonewall continued until 4.55 p.m. on Saturday 3 September, when the debate was adjourned for a final relatively short epilogue on the Monday. This finished at 4.15 a.m. with the bill being read for a third time.

Hall subsequently got the Standing Orders Committee to look at the issue of obstruction. The fundamental impediment to reform was the standing order stipulating that two-thirds of the House had to be present to alter the standing orders.[97] This was simply impossible to achieve, because the chamber emptied quickly when any move to make a change was threatened.

The government could now concentrate on the election, which it won without difficulty.[98] The battle lines of 1879 disappeared, replaced by renewed concern for local advantage. It was now generally agreed that parties had to organise on the hustings as well as in the House. This was particularly evident in Auckland and Otago, where party slates were organised.[99] For the first time, distinct worker organisations were identifiable in an election.

Hall resigned because of ill health and his difficulties in cabinet. Governor Sir Arthur Gordon precipitately and contrary to custom, summoned Grey against Hall's advice.[100] Hall was outraged by an 'attempt to transfer political power from one party to the other without the expressed will of Parliament'.[101] Grey tried to assemble support from a deeply divided opposition, while Gordon conceded that Whitaker would have to be asked to form a government. Whitaker of the Legislative Council became Premier, with Atkinson Leader in the House. The joint ministry was formed on the understanding that Whitaker's position was temporary.

The House met early again, in May 1882. The election of a Chairman of Committees provoked what amounted to a vote of confidence which the government won only narrowly after Atkinson unwisely proposed an Auckland 'rat', W.J. Hurst, for the position. When Atkinson backtracked and proposed Hamlin instead, the division was won.[102]

The government had a small majority. Atkinson lacked skills in organisation, but the opposition was as divided as before, with Grey refusing to accept Montgomery's leadership. As a result there was general disorganisation.[103] Rolleston's radical Land Bill – introduced against the wishes of some in cabinet but with the general support of the opposition – threw the House into more confusion.

The government was defeated on the second reading of a private member's bill, Tomoana's Maori Committee Bill.[104] Following a tied vote on the bill in Committee, the Speaker cast his vote against the government to keep the bill alive for the next session. One government supporter who thought that a member was going to vote for the bill, ran to the door and told a messenger to get the government whip. 'Don't you move, or I will brain you', was the reported response of an opposition member to 'the bewildered man in livery'.[105]

The opposition finally mounted a concerted attack, which the government easily beat off. Atkinson rammed through a great deal of business at the end of the session. His approach was to keep bills, and particularly the estimates, back as long as possible and then rush them through, believing that political machinations and endless debate were futile and best ignored or steamrolled over.[106] Hall was happy to get away. 'Gas & late hours are too much for me', he said, referring to the vitiated atmosphere in the chamber when the gaslights burned into the early hours.[107]

The parliamentary establishment in the 1880s

As the economy deteriorated, the institutional fabric of Parliament came under attack. Legislative expenditure suffered as retrenchment bit.[108] These reductions raised again the issue of the powers of the House and Speaker relative to the executive government and the Legislative Council.

Friction between the two Houses continued, especially over parliamentary salaries and appointments, since the House held the purse-strings. In the latter half of the 1870s, the Council had wanted its officers put on an equal footing with those of the House, with salaries set by statute. In an attempt to elevate its status in 1877, the Council attempted to appoint a Black Rod.[109] The House refused to allow this and struck out the vote. In 1880, miffed at the reductions imposed on it, the Council refused to reduce the number of its sessional clerks.[110] Retrenchment through the mid 1880s fomented continuing hostility.[111] When the Clerk of the Council refused to give evidence to the enquiry of 1886 concerning the retrenchment of legislative expenditure, this became a matter of privilege for the House.

In 1877 the authority of the Speaker over the buildings housing Parliament was questioned. Expenditure on maintenance had grown like topsy.[112] The arrangements were confirmed, but only on the casting vote of the Chairman of Committees. Speaker O'Rorke accepted that it was his role to provide the estimates to the House, and he had increasingly to defend legislative expenditure when it came up for debate each year. In the latter half of the 1870s hostility to the level of parliamentary officers' salaries erupted.[113] In 1878 attempts were made to cut the Speaker's salary and abolish other positions. When O'Rorke attempted to justify some minor increases in 1880, the battle began in earnest.[114] Hall desperately tried to beat off the attacks of ill-informed members who did not appreciate the work of the officers of Parliament and who were baying for blood. Council salaries were cut across the board and the Speaker of the House had £200 cut from his salary of £800.

The House came next. By now the establishment was considerable. In addition to the Clerk, the permanent employees included the Clerk-Assistant, Second Clerk-Assistant, Chief Messenger and Sergeant-at-Arms, a librarian, interpreters for the Maori members, a Reader who checked over all bills passed, an Examiner of Standing Orders on Private Bills (who also acted as clerk to the Local Bills Committee), a record clerk, and a clerk of works for the buildings.[115] Alongside the 6 Hansard reporters, 11 clerks, 13 messengers, 2 library assistants, 6 policemen and 12 charwomen were employed during the session. The constabulary provided a military atmosphere that was fitting for the many members who had fought in the New Zealand Wars and others who had served in India.[116] They wore blue uniforms with red and yellow piping, white belts, and white helmets topped with brass spikes and brass chinstraps.

The senior officers of Parliament had by now been employed for a long time.[117] Campbell had been joined by George Friend as Clerk-Assistant in 1862. Henry Otterson, the Second Clerk-Assistant, had started in 1875. The Chief Messenger, Michael Cosgrave, had joined the staff of Parliament in 1862 and was appointed to that position in the late 1860s. He held it for more than 30 years.[118] The nightwatchman, John Keefe, had been employed since 1869, and W. Letham, the custodian of Parliament Buildings and steward to Bellamy's, from 1873. Letham lived in a cottage by the gate at the corner of Molesworth and Hill Streets that had formerly been occupied by Cosgrave.[119] The tradition of long service that had become firmly established was endorsed by Speaker O'Rorke who said that the need was for 'officers specially trained for parliamentary work and having a special taste for the kind of work that has to be done here'. This would be ensured by promotion through the ranks rather than by 'importing strangers'.[120] Hall, O'Rorke and Gisborne stoutly defended the long and excellent record of Campbell as Clerk of the House, and after three divisions his salary was retained. The long-serving Friend also escaped the axe, but the Sergeant-at-Arms had his salary reduced by £100, prompting his resignation.[121]

The Hansard office also came under scrutiny as economies were imposed, but the retrenching members found it impossible to cut it back, even though they tried session after session. In 1879 the condensation of *Hansard* was looked at; next year attempts were made to abolish the reporters' salaries when other means of cutting Hansard had failed.[122] Cost-cutting attempts continued through the 1880s, but foundered on the hard fact that if Parliament wanted accurate and comprehensive reporting, it would have to pay for it.[123] The service had been set up on a shoestring compared with other countries, and the salaries were miserly.

George Friend, the son of an official in the East India Company, was born in London in 1838. After gaining honours at King's College, London and studying at Trinity College, Cambridge, he left for New Zealand in 1853. He was employed as a clerk in the Audit Department from 1854 and the Native Land Purchase Department from 1858 before being appointed as Clerk-Assistant to the House of Representatives in 1862. Friend occupied this position until 1889, when he replaced Major Campbell as Clerk, a post he retained until his death on 19 July 1898.

The wish of politicians to publicise their own cause also overrode the need for economies. There were strong demands for Parliament to be made more accessible and to advance 'the political education of the colony', as Hall put it, by increasing the circulation of *Hansard*.[124] While Sheehan claimed that *Hansard* 'was to be found in almost every hotel, club, or library – in fact, in all the public institutions', Fox facetiously said that 'it had never been his good fortune to see the farmers in his district with the plough-handle in one hand and *Hansard* in the other'.[125]

The House supplied members with more copies to distribute, reduced the annual subscription, and provided copies free to all local authorities and public libraries.[126] In the 1890s there were renewed efforts to increase circulation. The number of copies for members was increased substantially, and *Hansard* was advertised in post offices and other public buildings throughout the colony.

The office began to consider ways to increase the efficiency of transcription. An early form of typewriter – the 'Caligraph' – was tested and introduced in 1884.[127] These machines were not an instant panacea, but improved typewriters soon revolutionised *Hansard*. They avoided the large expense of sending proofs of typeset speeches to members, and speeded up the process considerably. Members' revisions no longer incurred large typesetting costs, and the final printed version could be available in days rather than weeks or even months.

The Houses of Parliament

Parliament Buildings housed a number of government departments until the construction of the Government Buildings on reclaimed land on Lambton Quay. When the departments left Parliament in 1876 their ministers went with them, and this eased the pressure on accommodation. Still, the state of the buildings left much to be desired as the number of members grew. The compromise of 1877 about responsibility for the buildings had resulted in divided authority and confusion, particularly when Fitzherbert was replaced by O'Rorke as Speaker, because O'Rorke did not live in Wellington during the recess. The Speakers and the government argued over the cost and extent of alterations and improvements. Money was spent without government approval.

Many members complained about the unhealthy condition of the precincts of Parliament, in particular the poor ventilation and the drains. In 1876 it was alleged that half of the House had fallen ill during the session and that the ventilation was disgraceful.[128] Despite opinions that the chamber should hold no more than 100, attendance was often nearer 300, and continued expenditure on fixing the ventilation problem had little effect.[129] In 1878 Speaker Fitzherbert referred to the drains under the floor of the chamber as 'a nursery and hotbed of zymotic diseases'. They were removed. Another member stated that 'they had lost member after member, who had gone from Wellington to die simply in consequence of the miserable and unhealthy state of the House'.[130] Draughts, too, were complained about. Members had to sit 'muffled up in great coats and their necks protected by comforters'.[131] Others declared the committee rooms 'not fit to be occupied by paupers', while the whips' rooms and Bellamy's were wretched.[132] Fresh air and space to take a little exercise in comfort were required. The water supply to the buildings and the toilets were also inadequate.

Atkinson got the House to agree in 1882 that the government would control the buildings during the recess (when most alterations and improvements would take place) and the Speakers would have control while Parliament was in session.[133] Now the vote of £10,000 previously designated for the library could be used to make the necessary changes to Bellamy's and offices.[134]

A range of improvements were made.[135] The furniture and interiors of both chambers were refurbished. The interiors of the buildings were whitewashed and repainted, the gas service supplying more than a thousand lights renewed, and fencing around the grounds replaced. The Council block was given an extension at the back, including a carriage porch where the Governor could arrive in style.

The substantial extensions at the rear of the original Provincial Council chambers, to provide a new Bellamy's and associated facilities for the comfort of members, were designed by Thomas Turnbull as a plain but spacious Gothic structure in brick.[136] Construction began at the end of 1882 and was finished in July 1883 shortly after the next session opened. New-fangled electricity was introduced into Parliament in what was the most substantial installation in the country at that time.[137] The chamber was first lit by electricity on 3 July 1883, appropriately for the reading of the public works statement. Gas was still used out of session and for heating and lighting corridors, committee rooms and the library until the 1890s.[138]

Bellamy's gained a new ground floor dining room accommodating 100, a servery, tea room and bar, and government and opposition whips' rooms, along with new lavatories.[139] Under the dining room was the wine cellar and bond store. On the upper floor there was a new kitchen, serving room, pantry and scullery, bathrooms, three committee rooms and the leader of the opposition's room.

Parliament Buildings c. 1885, seen from the rear near the tennis court, showing the Turnbull masonry extension of the early 1880s at left.

With the country tightening its belt, however, Bellamy's came under scrutiny. Some members wanted the subsidy on its costs eliminated entirely, others a reduction. William Swanson said that there was a 'division of the House into "nobs" and "snobs" … He objected to [Bellamy's] teetotally. If people chose to use very fine and expensive wines and food, and required the attendance of many servants, let them pay for them'.[140] In 1880 the subsidy was removed, the well-paid cook was fired, and prices increased.[141] A perennial problem was members who did not pay their bills, exacerbated by the system of credit or 'tick'.[142] In 1882 the House Committee threatened habitual offender Dick Reeves with legal proceedings if he did not pay up. Threats of legal proceedings against members continued, and in 1885 it was decided that defaulters would not be admitted to Bellamy's or the lobbies. But the institution continued to provide sumptuous dinners, engaging a professional French cook, reputedly the best in the country, in 1885. For the farewell given to William Larnach in 1887, 'roast turkey, braised duck and olives, saddles of mutton, fillets of beef with Madeira sauce, [and] quail on toast' were followed by 'nougat a la creme, Rhine wine jelly and diplomatique pudding'.[143] The bar reputedly supplied the finest liquor to be found in the 'Empire City'.

The 1883 extensions also featured a large 'promenade' lobby between the chambers with ornate rafters and a high ceiling. This great hall, known as the 'Lobby', was furnished with easy chairs and sofas and had double doors leading into the two chambers and other doors to Bellamy's, the library and committee rooms. Adjacent to it was 'Monte Carlo', the 'card-room of the House, where members whiled away a quiet hour in the mysteries of bridge, poker, and other tests of skill'.[144]

Part of the old library, c. 1890s, perhaps a writing room, lit by electric light and warmed by open fires. This photograph may have been taken as the books were being moved to the new library building. With the shift to Wellington, Ewen McColl was appointed 'assistant librarian'. The first separate catalogue of New Zealand books was printed by the Government Printing Office in 1866. A comprehensive classified catalogue published in 1872 listed more than 8,000 volumes. By the mid 1870s the library occupied six substantial rooms on the ground and first floors between Bellamy's and the Legislative Council chamber. Ambitious plans for a new (and fireproof) building came to naught in spite of the need for more space.

Following the extensions of the early 1880s, the library expanded into the section of the older wooden building vacated by Bellamy's. Plans to build a fireproof, two-storey neo-classical library adjacent to the tennis court behind the Legislative Council chamber failed to materialise. In 1887 attention moved to the site of the original Council chamber at the north-east corner of the complex. Retrenchment, the struggle for control over legislative expenditure, and the resignation of the librarian, James Collier, meant that the project was not taken further.

The Lobby immediately became the social hub of the buildings and a portrait gallery of some note.[145] It was a space where all sorts of extra-parliamentary activities took place, along with formal social gatherings and the daily stirring of the political pot – wagers such as Dick Reeves' bizarre exercise involving betting on the cuts to the honorarium, japes or tricks played on members, and the odd physical confrontation.[146] It also made a useful 'dormitory' during stonewalls. Members at a loose end would pull the leather-covered bench-like sofas out from the walls and arrange hurdle races, or engage in wrestling matches or other sporting activities.

Some members were better known for frequenting the Lobby and Bellamy's than for anything else. Henry Bunny, according to 'Verax', spent 'most of his time in the smoking-room or in Bellamy's, where he is quite a leader and law-giver, and may be truly said to "shine" in more senses than one.'[147] Others such as Rolleston found solace in the good company that could transcend political divisions. He remembered the 'friendly association of the dining-table' among members such as Grey, Bryce, Colonel Robert Trimble, and the brilliant, versatile conversationalist Scobie Mackenzie.[148] Mackenzie's generous personality and good humour around the House was legendary; on one occasion he was able to defuse a confrontation between 'two unnamed well-known and highly respected members, both of them elderly and sleekly rotund of person', who had come to blows in the Lobby.[149] They then repaired amicably to Bellamy's, where they shared a bottle of champagne.

Providing for Maori members

With the introduction of Maori members, Parliament had to employ interpreters. Notable later interpreters included Gilbert Mair and James Carroll.[150] The interpreter 'had to sit with two members on each side of him, and while he was whispering to them, in order to make them understand what had just been said, he must also listen to catch what members were saying on, and weave their words up in his brain, and then communicate them in another language.'[151]

By the 1880s there were three interpreters in Parliament.[152] They also informed the Maori members on a daily basis about what was happening, translated hundreds of petitions from Maori into English and all bills and parliamentary papers into Maori, attended the Native Affairs and other committees, and acted as interpreters when Pakeha members dealt with Maori. By the late 1880s the Maori members were more adept in English, but they still insisted on delivering their speeches in Maori. The practice of regularly having an interpreter in the chamber ceased in the first years of the new century as the four Maori members then spoke good English, although an interpreter was retained for the House for some time after that.[153]

Maori members naturally wanted to be able to communicate with their people. This required the translation of parliamentary matters into Maori, a principle that was only partly and intermittently accepted.[154] The revised standing orders of 1865 stipulated that Maori petitions be translated prior to being presented, and that the Governor's speeches to the House and bills 'specially affecting' Maori be translated and printed in Maori, but little was done.[155] In 1868, with Maori entering the House, it was resolved that a 'simple text-book' of parliamentary practice be published in Maori and that tabled papers be translated and relevant sessional papers translated and printed.[156] (Eventually the standing orders were printed in Maori.) In the Legislative Council,

Ewen McColl became assistant librarian in 1865 and librarian in 1878. After preparing a new, larger catalogue in 1880 he died the following year, perhaps in part from overwork. McColl was succeeded by Angus MacGregor, and in 1885 by yet another Scot, James Collier. Collier urged the establishment of copyright deposit, saw that the General Assembly's library might form the basis for a national library, prepared a national bibliography, and opened the library to students during the parliamentary recess. Following his departure in 1890 due to a breakdown in health, the library struggled along with unqualified and underpaid staff. For the next decade, second assistant, H.L. James, appointed only in 1889, was left to run the library as best he could.

Members assembled in the central meeting place, the Lobby, with its distinctive exposed rafters, c. 1900.

Walter Mantell called attention to the failure to translate documents and print them in Maori.[157] The revised standing orders of 1871 reiterated the requirement for translation and printing in Maori, but only a few translated bills appeared. Maori continued to ask for translations, but this occurred only on a limited, ad hoc basis through the 1870s.

In 1879 the Legislative Council, on H.K. Taiaroa's initiative, ordered that all bills translated into Maori be bound into volumes and put in the library. From this time on, more bills were translated and volumes deposited.[158] From 1889 to 1910, an annual series of relevant Acts were printed in Maori. However, bills and other papers were still not regularly translated, in spite of ministers' promises.[159] The requirement to translate bills and papers was then left to the discretion of the Speaker in the standing orders of 1929.

The issue of translating parts of *Hansard* into Maori was raised in the Legislative Council in the mid 1870s.[160] In 1875 W.T. Ngatata asked that Maori members' speeches be printed in the government's Maori newspaper, *Te Waka Maori*, and this was done to some extent. In 1877 the House agreed that the debate on the Native Land Court Bill should be translated and circulated. The material was printed, but not circulated by the government for 'political' reasons.[161] *Te Waka Maori* and the organ opposed to the government, *Te Wananga*, printed material selectively in the latter half of the 1870s, but both

Members gathered around the fireplace in the Lobby.

folded late in the decade.[162] Pressure to produce a Maori *Hansard* was maintained, even when the office was threatened with cuts.[163]

From 1881 a 'Maori' *Hansard* or *Nga Korero Paremete* containing the speeches of the four Maori members and other members' speeches on native affairs appeared. This filled the gap created by the disappearance of the newspapers.[164] The later volumes were larger, perhaps indicating that Maori members were speaking more often and at greater length than before. The reasons for the termination of *Nga Korero Paremete* in 1906 are obscure, but by this time most Maori, including the four Maori members, were conversant with English.[165]

Factional disintegration

In the latter half of the 1880s, as the factional system of politics disintegrated, governments looked beyond the House to the country for an alternative source of power and endorsement. Grey had already pioneered this approach. Leaders appealed over the heads of members to the electorate, and the threat of dissolution was used as a weapon to bring members into line (even if elections did not yet directly determine the shape of the House). In this manner New Zealand followed the example of the British and Australian Parliaments, in which party organisation was taking hold. Ministers who 'had been servants of Parliament' were now 'developing into servants of the people'.[166] But linkages between government and people remained undeveloped since there were not yet party organisations to bridge the gap. New Zealand politics entered a limbo of confused political alignments.

By the mid 1880s the press gallery had become part of the institution of Parliament. The 1885 press gallery included Tom Morrison (a long-standing member who was chairman), Edward Gillon, William Berry (who became a Hansard reporter the next year), and Albert Cohen, later fined £15 for publishing leaked select committee proceedings.

Delays in the extensions to the Houses of Parliament postponed the 1883 session until mid June.[167] Less than a third of members were present and the House was again disorganised. The ministry failed to hold any caucus meetings and conflict among opposition factions intensified.[168] Grey pushed for the reinstitution of a land tax and broke with tradition by proposing this directly after Atkinson's speech on finances. Atkinson's habit of rushing through the estimates gave rise to a petty stonewall, led by Seddon and Henry Fish and fuelled, according to one report, by whisky.[169]

Political realignment, retrenchment and depression, 1876–90

OVER THE SPEAKER'S CHAIR.
BY ELECTRIC TELEGRAPH.
(FROM OUR OWN CORRESPONDENT.)
WELLINGTON, Thursday.

The role of the telegraph in giving immediacy to reporting, and the fact that newspapers now included gossipy items, are suggested by this masthead.

NZ Observer, 9 July 1881

Grey's proposed land tax was moved by W.C. Smith as an amendment to the motion going into supply, but comfortably defeated, 42 to 28.[170] By promising to continue existing public works, Atkinson was able to hold on to his supporters. Grey was increasingly abusive, and at the end of the session members walked out of the House when he perversely attempted to introduce a notice of motion as Parliament was about to be prorogued.[171] He and a few others were left to make a futile protest in a pathetic close to the session as the quorum disappeared.

Whitaker soon resigned as Premier in favour of Atkinson and returned to his business interests. Atkinson was absent for the opening of the 1884 session on 6 June because of ill health. The political factions remained disorganised in spite of a number of caucuses.[172] Matters seemed topsy-turvy when two new members, A.K. Newman and M.W. Green, both ardent reformers, broke with precedent and lambasted the Speech from the Throne and the government in their maiden Address-in-Reply speeches.[173]

W.J. (Major) Steward, Montgomery's party whip, stepped into the breach and led the attack on the government, catching the Speaker's eye before Grey, who was seated in his usual place at the 'extreme end of the chamber', and directly proposing no-confidence in the government. The opposition won the motion easily, after a flaccid debate.[174] The following motion for a dissolution emphatically failed, however, because the opposition wanted the chance to form a government. But Atkinson agreed to dissolve Parliament as soon as temporary supply was granted, and the Governor agreed. Many members were sufficiently unconcerned about this foregone conclusion to take a pleasure excursion on the government steamer *Hinemoa* to Picton and Nelson over a long weekend.[175] The session came to an end when a motion attacking the Governor was lost only on the casting vote of the Speaker.

The election promised renewed hope. Vogel had been encouraged to return to politics, and promised to restore confidence in the economy, provide public works

Harry Atkinson, elected as member for Grey and Bell (Taranaki) in 1861, was one of the most prominent politicians in the House for the next 30 years, representing the 'country settler'. After entering cabinet in 1874–5 during the Vogel ministry, he was Premier three times (1876–7, 1883–4, and 1887–91) before leaving the House for the Legislative Council. A dogged and pugnacious pragmatic politician, Atkinson led the country through difficult times as Premier and Colonial Treasurer.

ATL, F23108½

The House

and promote settlement. Many thought that he could work his old magic and bring prosperity back to the country. For the first time during an election campaign, political leadership – Atkinson's caution versus Vogel's optimism – was a definite issue. Organised labour again made its presence felt.[176]

Wellington was a hive of activity when members reconvened for the post-election session, opened by Commission on 7 August 1884. The matter of a ministry and the situation of the various leaders was uncertain, with the previous government whip, George Beetham, pointedly placing his card on a seat to the left of the Speaker to show his allegiances had changed.[177] O'Rorke was re-elected Speaker for the fourth time by acclamation, but there were definite signs that government was poised on a knife-edge.[178] To avoid creating any opening for a challenge, Atkinson had left it to a private member to propose O'Rorke. Hoping to entice uncommitted members to support him, Atkinson played for time by resigning. The House was adjourned for more than a week while a ministry was found.[179] The Governor attended a delayed state opening on 19 August, with Vogel and Stout being asked to form a government that would be based on the numerically strong Canterbury and Otago contingents. Vogel immediately failed to sustain a majority.

Attempts to form other ministries followed. The *Evening Post* observed: 'there seems to be a complete deadlock. Each individual, or knot of little individuals, is determined to have his or their own way, and no terms of self-sacrifice or compromise will be listened to on any side.'[180] In early September, Stout and Vogel finally put together a workable ministry that promised public works and drew in Auckland support. Stout would be Premier and Vogel Treasurer, with the latter in reality at the helm. With the change of government, Hamlin's re-election as Chairman of Committees was strongly contested by Steward. Atkinson indicated that he would not attempt to defeat the ministry unless its policies were completely objectionable; he was content for it to undo itself.[181]

Robert Stout was elected to the House of Representatives as member for Caversham in 1875 and appointed as Attorney-General in Grey's ministry in 1878. He resigned in 1879 over his business dealings and returned to the law before re-entering the House in 1884. He soon became Premier, with Vogel as Colonial Treasurer (1884–7). Stout lost his seat in 1887 but was re-elected in 1893 after the death of Ballance, whose mantle he expected to assume. Outmanoeuvred by Seddon and unhappy at the development of organised parties in the House, he promoted the prohibition cause until his retirement in 1898. He then became Chief Justice of the Supreme Court until 1926.

Stout and Vogel, 1884–7

In this unpromising manner a government that was to prove remarkably stable over the next three years was formed. The new cabinet was a motley bunch of liberals and conservatives, but Vogel insisted that 'all fads and nonsense would be dropped'.[182] Vogel's sanguine financial statement would come back to haunt him.[183] He halved the property tax and proposed borrowing for railway lines and roading.

The government put up bills providing for both the private construction of railways and the government purchase of privately constructed railways. Cleverly designated as ministerial measures, cabinet held up the allocation of loans and other public works measures so that many members felt they could not oppose them.[184] But Vogel, Stout and Ballance, on the ruling of the Speaker, had to abstain from voting on the third reading of one such bill because of their 'pecuniary interest' in the Waimea Plains railway. The Legislative Council rejected this bill, to Vogel's dismay. He did not extricate himself from the Waimea Plains railway until 1886, at the cost of his political reputation and to his financial loss.[185]

During the 1885 session, with the depression worsening, Vogel had to abandon his optimistic financial policies. Grey's motion of no-confidence in the ministry amending the motion to go into supply was defeated on voices. He had lost all credibility.[186] The government also easily defeated Atkinson's no-confidence motion, which advocated retrenchment, 51 to 39. Further efforts to test confidence in the ministry were aided by the Speaker's casting vote in favour of continued debate but eventually defeated in a closer vote, 43 to 39. Vogel tried desperately to keep his supporters on side, but the proposal for a private Canterbury–West Coast railway was rejected. In revenge, affected local members supported a motion by Captain William Russell reducing the public works vote by £500,000. This passed, 44 to 29, despite the government's threat to resign.

During the lengthy debate, which finished at 4.40 on a Saturday morning, Hansard reporting stopped because the staff were 'overdone'. By the end of the session there was chaos and the government had become a laughing stock in both the House and the country at large. But the House could not settle on a viable alternative leader and continued to live with a government that lacked all credibility.

The government remained in power through 1886. The session began in early May. Atkinson undertook to accept the Address-in-Reply and get down to business.[187] A chastened Vogel produced a more realistic financial statement. The test of confidence came in the form of a motion by Montgomery that retrenchment should be made, and was won by the ministry comfortably, 44 to 28, as the House went into supply.[188] The threat of an early election kept its supporters loyal. But the ministry was defeated, 39 to 36, over legislation changing the representation of electorates which had been postponed to the very end. Even the cabinet was divided, with Stout voting for and Vogel against the bill.

The demands for retrenchment became stronger. In 1886 the House set up a special Legislative Expenditure Committee, headed by a member who had been crusading to force Parliament to make savings.[189] O'Rorke refused to serve on the committee, claiming it had been set up to pass judgement on him. He was infuriated when the committee failed to call either him or Fitzherbert, the Speaker of the Legislative Council, to give evidence.

The committee recommended reducing the number of European members to 71, abolishing payment for chairing committees, a substantial reduction in the honorarium, the employment of officers and Hansard reporters for the full year, and a reduction in the cost of *Hansard*. It argued that the government should be solely responsible for all expenditure on Parliament, but the House would not agree. The matter was overtaken by the defeat of the Vogel government in 1887.[190]

In 1887 Parliament was called even earlier, in late April, as the three-year parliamentary term would expire in August. To avoid consolidating support for the government, the opposition refused to debate the Address-in-Reply at all.[191] Vogel, a strong supporter of women's suffrage, had brought in a bill giving women the vote on the same basis as men and making them eligible to stand for Parliament. As the suffrage campaign gathered momentum, women petitioned Parliament and lobbied powerful supporters such as Ballance, Stout and Vogel. The bill received considerable apparent support on its second reading, although one member noted later that this was a 'fictitious majority'.[192] It became evident that the measure was not being taken altogether seriously. In Committee the bill was stonewalled and then narrowly defeated 21 to 19 in a 'snatch' vote by a thin House at 1 a.m., when some of its supporters had left. Women's struggle for the vote would continue for some time.

The government got its Representation Bill through, but while it was in Committee, Scobie Mackenzie (supported by two ministers) moved the so-called 'Mackenzie amendment', which slashed the number of European members to 71.[193] The bill was reintroduced after cross-party meetings, but again the two ministers voted for a reduction in the size of the House. The division was tied, amid allegations of members going into the wrong lobbies and being locked out. The casting vote of the Chairman of Committees kept the House at 91 members. The government was then defeated over its Customs Duties Bill, 42 to 38, after an opposition caucus decided to make it an issue of confidence. Stout advised the Governor to dissolve Parliament, and an election was held.[194]

Atkinson keeps it together, 1887–90

The Stout–Vogel government was roundly defeated in the 1887 election, which was notable for the prominence of economic issues – retrenchment, borrowing and taxation. Vogelite development was finished, and the protection of local industry came onto the agenda. Electoral organisations emerged for the first time, in regions such as Canterbury and Otago.[195] With the fruits of public works politics exhausted, new divisions emerged at the national level.[196] Propertied groups rallied to defend their interests against the threat of increased taxation and demanded swingeing retrenchment and free trade. On the other side, groups began to organise under radical banners urging settlement on the land, industrial development and tariff protection. In Sinclair's words, the move was 'towards the politics of class philosophy instead of the politics of public works'.[197]

Vogel resigned as the second session of 1887 opened in October, and Governor Sir William Jervois sent for Atkinson, knowing that the largest faction was the retrenching free-traders, who became known as the 'skinflints'. As Atkinson unhappily admitted, 'I undertook the duty of forming a Government … they were not a party in any true sense of the term, because they did not give in any allegiance personally to their chief.'[198] This was his predicament over the next three years. His cabinet became known as the 'Scarecrow Ministry' because of its threadbare existence.[199] The state of the House was summarised well by the *Otago Daily Times*. 'What with the Freetrade section, the "Skinflint" section, the Canterbury section, and the "Sitting on a Rail" section, our popular chamber exhibits a conglomeration of discordant and irreconcilable atoms … The Ministry are in a minority, and yet they can command a majority of votes. The Protectionists are in a majority, and yet they are split up into several sections … The Premier knows all this, and manages to pull the strings in order to prevent the discordant elements from being united.'[200]

As promised during the election, retrenchment was the order of the day. Ministers' and civil servants' salaries, and those of officers of Parliament, were to be cut and the number of representatives in the House reduced.[201] Also as promised, the honorarium paid to members of the House was reduced to £150. This gained overwhelming support. Atkinson reopened the vexed issue of responsibility for legislative expenditure. The number of European seats was reduced to 71 (later amended to 70). This gave members an incentive to keep Atkinson in power for as long as possible, even if the House was hopelessly disorganised, to avoid a dissolution.[202] The opposition veered from 'masterly inactivity' to a walkout and then to futile stonewalling.[203] The *New Zealand Herald* facetiously sketched what the walkout might look like. 'So soon as Sir J. Vogel finishes speaking the Protectionists will form in military order in the body of the House, and carrying their leader shoulder high, will march three times round the table to the music of the policemen's chorus from the "Pirates of Penzance" at the same time chanting "We go, we go; ta ran ta ra, ta ran ta ra, ta ran ta ra"'.[204]

Atkinson managed to hold the government together, usually with the aid of one or more of the factions of a hopelessly divided opposition. Having been goaded, the ailing Vogel accused one member of a lack of manners and alleged that messengers frequently had to assist members who were drunk.[205] He then suggested that 'one of the high officers of this House' had only been elected on pledging not to drink. This was a reference to O'Rorke himself, who was known to be partial to a drop and had on occasion been absent from the House as a result of drinking bouts.[206]

O'Rorke stated that he would 'name' Vogel. For the first time, one of the ultimate sanctions of the House had been invoked. O'Rorke ordered Vogel in his wheelchair to withdraw, cleared the public gallery, and had the Hansard reporters leave. For longer than an entire sitting the House debated the incident. It finally endorsed O'Rorke's action, but expressed regret that Vogel had been named. A defiant Vogel refused to accept the ruling and sought to have it taken out of the record.

As a result of an opposition walkout Atkinson managed to get through his resolution implementing retrenchment and postponing changes to the tariffs by 44 to 4.[207] However, the Representation Bill proved a stumbling block. A stonewall was mounted. With the government whips caught off guard, the opposition won a division delaying the implementation of the reduction in members until late 1889. The bill had to be recommitted, and Atkinson threatened to resign. He won the vote on the recommitted bill 29 to 16, with some government members walking out. They had previously voted for the amendment and did not want to be seen as 'stultifying themselves'.[208]

When Vogel was 'named' in 1887, this was the first time this ultimate sanction was invoked.

Towards the end of the session members were talking about the need to impose closure and everyone was getting fraught, but moves to restrict the reporting of long speeches failed.[209] The session continued to the bitter end as Atkinson tried desperately to get through business before Christmas, abandoning less important bills.[210] The session was finally prorogued at 4.50 a.m. on 23 December. Members from more distant electorates were unable to get home by Christmas.

Pressure to regulate working hours mounted as stonewalls slowed business and sessions stretched out. Since the mid 1870s, the House had attempted to reduce the hours of sitting, usually by blocking new business after 12.30 a.m.[211] Changes were made to the standing orders to this end in 1878, 1882 and 1887, but to little effect. Each time, ways around the restrictions were found. Another tactic to accelerate the work of the House was, after the initial weeks of the session, to give priority to government business on another sitting day in addition to the traditional Tuesdays and Fridays (which were formally prescribed in the 1871 standing orders). This practice was increasingly popular from the early 1870s, and was to be formalised for Thursdays in the 1894 standing orders.

When the next session was called in May 1888, the opposition was leaderless. Ballance, Seddon and Grey each had a small tail. This situation persisted through to August. No-one could be found to replace Vogel, who had left the country. With the opposition paralysed, Atkinson was spared any serious motions testing confidence.[212] He produced radical proposals of his own, independently of the Standing Orders Committee, to introduce closure to deal with stonewalls and other obstructive tactics.[213] He was determined not to make it a party matter, but was thwarted by opposition walkouts.

Atkinson came under sustained pressure from the 'skinflints', and finally had to deal with the issue of who held responsibility for the legislative estimates.[214] O'Rorke, who regarded the government's intervention as 'unwarranted, unconstitutional, and lawless', appealed to the House to preserve its independence, and accused the government of driving out Clerks Campbell and Friend.[215] In 1889 Major Campbell retired after 45 years. He had been Clerk of the House since 1854 and Clerk of Parliaments since 1865. He was getting elderly, and his enthusiasm had probably been diminished by the reduction of his salary.[216] With his retirement, the position of Clerk of Parliaments shifted to the Clerk of the Legislative Council. Friend now became Clerk of the House and Otterson his Clerk-Assistant.

The House put the matter of legislative expenditure to the vote, asserted its right to have charge of such expenditure, and then imposed cuts. The increases made since the senior officers' salaries had been set by statute in 1867 were systematically stripped away, and other salaries were reduced. The position of Examiner of Standing Orders on Private Bills, under attack for a decade, was finally abolished. Atkinson, piqued at this, absolved the government from any further responsibility for legislative expenditure, including on the buildings. This sounded the death knell for a proposed new library.

THE BREAK-UP FOR THE HOLIDAYS of the GOV.T SCHOOL

"Now my boys having finished your sum I will dismiss you, and those of you whom I do see again I hope will behave better next term"

Sum: If a little boy comes to Wellington to play for a month at £210 how much is that a day?

Answer £7 a day!

Observer and Free Lance, 25 June 1887

The honorarium paid to members always attracted much interest. During the prosperous 1870s, the allowance was steadily increased. In 1876, the House, against the ministry's wishes and in the face of public criticism, raised the honorarium to 200 guineas because the session was unusually long. Members increasingly sought greater financial security, especially as the 'long depression' began. Fixing the honorarium was always a vexed issue. Some wanted more generous payment to recognise public service and improve representation by attracting a wider range of people, and felt that this should be fixed by statute. Others tried to reduce the honorarium or even abolish it altogether, citing the example of the House of Commons, which did not pay its members. These differences reflected the divide between two views of politics: a part-time leisure pursuit of gentlemen, and a career for full-time professional politicians.

In 1880, in a climate of retrenchment, the honorarium was reduced by 10 per cent. In 1883 a bill to fix the honorarium was passed in the House but rejected by the Council, and instead the payment was again cut by 10 per cent. In 1884 the absurdity of the system was thrown into sharp relief when members received full payment for the first very short session, followed by another payment for the second session. This resulted in moves to cut the honorarium further, but instead the House at last passed the Parliamentary Honorarium and Privileges Bill, which fixed the payment per session at 200 guineas for those from outside Wellington, and £140 for local residents. In 1892 the Payment of Members Act replaced the honorarium with an annual salary. This recognised that politicians worked year-round, and at £240 was sufficient to enable working men to enter the House.

Atkinson's protective tariff blurred political divisions further because most of the opposition were protectionists while the government backbench was dominated by free-traders. The retrenchment/free trade faction, led by Ormond and Captain Russell and known as the 'Middle' or 'Country' party, finally severed its links with Atkinson over the issue, but the tariff measure went through comfortably with opposition support.[217] The opposition became even more disorganised, as was reflected in a disastrous test of confidence over the operation of the Representation Act as the House entered supply. The opposition whip failed to discuss the move with supporters, and the division was called in the end by the government whip, who sought to underline the chaos in the opposition's ranks.[218] The government won the motion 41 to 20, with some members, retrieved at the last minute from a ball, sitting glumly in their best 'bib and tucker'.

When the 1889 session opened in June, an opposition caucus unanimously elected Ballance as leader.[219] Finally they had someone around whom they could begin to organise. Atkinson and Ballance agreed to work together to despatch government business promptly to facilitate an early close to the session. They also agreed that the Representation Bill should take priority.[220] A ferocious stonewall was, however, mounted against the bill by members who feared for their seats. Ballance and a cross-party committee balloted members of the House on the issue of reducing the number of members, and attempted unsuccessfully to have the reduction rescinded.[221] Setting the country quota became a means of self-preservation for members and resulted in further confusion among parties. The fight opened a split between urban and rural and small-town members. Urban members stonewalled while the government provided nightcaps, mattresses and pillows for its supporters.[222]

The stonewall stretched from 24 July to 5 August, and saw the longest single sitting on record, at 124 hours 45 minutes, stretching from the evening of Wednesday 24 July to that of Friday 2 August.[223] Eventually a compromise emerged with a country quota of 28 per cent. The quota remained until 1945, giving rural areas relatively greater representation than others. Along the way the House abolished plural voting, introducing 'one man, one vote' on an amendment moved by Grey. Atkinson's government struggled on, devoting Thursday evenings, too, to government business, but being obliged nonetheless to drop a number of its bills.[224] Though both government and opposition were demoralised and apathetic, neither side was willing to face an election.[225]

By 1890 the government was in an even more parlous state than the opposition and Atkinson's cabinet disintegrated. The Premier was so enfeebled by a heart condition that he could hardly attend the House.[226] He was implored to continue for the meantime. The opposition began to talk about resurrecting the 'Liberal' banner, with candidates endorsed by party leaders standing on a common platform.[227] A motion testing confidence in the government's financial policies was moved by Ballance as the House went into supply. It was defeated 38 to 32, with some caught out of the chamber, after the debate collapsed when the government failed to put up speakers.[228] The supply debate continued in desultory fashion for nearly another two weeks.

The ministry's labour legislation, a response to the inquiries concerning 'sweating' in factories and other workplaces, fell foul of the combined efforts of the opposition and the 'skinflints', who stonewalled the estimates to impose further retrenchment upon the government.[229] After exhausting debate, the government conceded a dissolution if it could get the estimates through.[230] Further retrenchment was achieved, but there was little enthusiasm for persisting with the session. In its last weeks the maritime strike dominated proceedings. The session ended with 'a jumble of parties all

John Ballance was elected to the House of Representatives for Rangitikei in 1875, and became Colonial Treasurer in Grey's ministry in 1878. After being an important cabinet minister in the Stout–Vogel ministry of 1884–7, he assumed the leadership of the opposition in the House in 1889. Ballance became Premier when the Liberals came to power in 1891, but died of cancer in 1893.

THE POLITICAL TRUCE.—GOVERNMENT AND OPPOSITION ARMIES FRATERNISE.

The warring parties declare a truce to get parliamentary business through before the 1890 election. Vincent Pyke's mug is refilled (left), O'Rorke's braying is signified by the donkey's ears pinned to his hat (behind Pyke), Atkinson and Ballance shake hands (centre), and Hutchison and Whitaker (of the Legislative Council) exchange Bank of New Zealand notes (right).

trying to work out the problem of Party government, and getting themselves mixed up into inextricable confusion', according to the *Lyttelton Times*.[231]

By now many were reflecting on the political system.[232] The pathetic situation of the 'Scarecrow Ministry', the continued abuse of procedure exemplified in stonewalls, and the apparent inability of members to move beyond factions and log-rolling – all seemed symptoms of a system in paralysis.

Steward and a number of supporters advanced the concept of an executive elected from the House. This would, according to its advocates, reflect the general will of the House rather than that of a small majority, eliminate the antagonistic and gladiatorial aspects of debate, emphasise the merits of particular measures, and allow members to vote as individuals. As modern-style parties began to develop in the 1890s, an 'elective' (elected) executive became the rallying cry of those who deprecated such developments.

The vastly experienced Hall felt that time-wasting had reached ridiculous proportions and believed that 'parties' were once again divided by personal combinations rather than principles. Factions were no longer anchored in differences between centralists and provincialists, or distinguished by positions taken on native affairs or war policy. Saunders decried the 'public works system' as the demoralising cause of the decline of principle. A.K. Newman supported Hall in suggesting a system of closure such as had been introduced in the House of Commons. He also argued that a loss of confidence in a ministry should lead automatically to a dissolution of Parliament. Change was in the wind.

Political realignment, retrenchment and depression, 1876–90

Towards a new politics of party

Through the 1880s, depression had threatened the core values of New Zealand as an expanding colonial society based on continuing immigration and settlement and widening opportunities. Meanwhile the institution of Parliament had consolidated its position in national life. Despite the difficult times, there were no external threats to the legitimacy of an elected representative government, and the institutional weight of the House of Representatives grew. Indeed, political mobilisation strengthened and extended the democratic basis for the franchise. The limited protest that did occur sought redress from the legitimate authorities. As Rolleston observed, 'it is infinitely better to have Parliamentary pressure and agitation than growing discontent between class and class and that social feeling of unrest that will pervade the community, where wealth and poverty stand in great contrast, and where there are the jealousy and hatred that cover class animosity.'[233]

Central government had expanded considerably since the 1870s. It took over land legislation from the provinces, increased its powers of taxation, and established the Railways, Post Office and other new government departments. Both Atkinson and Pember Reeves described the system as 'state socialism'. The General Assembly dealt with more legislation following the abolition of the provinces, while still sitting on average for only 55 to 60 days a year. Keeping the House past midnight was now commonplace and a much higher proportion of sitting time was spent in the early hours of the morning, reflecting the concerted adoption of stonewalling and other obstructive tactics at a time when governments had increased business to get through. But with the decay of the factional system and the disabling of executive government during the 1880s, only about half of the bills introduced were enacted.[234] A third or more of bills came from private members, and substantial numbers of such bills found their way into the statute book. The Legislative Council, however, remained much as it had always been, a constitutional restraint on headlong change while the accountability of the elected representatives of the people was still being consolidated.[235]

Governments recognised that social and ameliorative policies were required in addition to policies promoting economic development, and began to question the efficacy of loan-based development. The demand for retrenchment did not fundamentally challenge the need for state intervention and a closer relationship between people and government to protect and develop further the kind of society that was desired.

In the 1880s the membership of the House of Representatives stabilised considerably in comparison with earlier decades. Its turnover declined to an average of around 30 per cent at each election.[236] Politics became more of a long-term commitment and a serious career. By the late 1880s almost all sitting members sought re-election. The 1887–90 Parliament showed just how much matters had changed. There were few newcomers; almost all members had previous experience in the House. The average age of members rose to close to 50 years. Two-thirds had been in the House for more than six sessions, a quarter for more than 12. The old-timers of exceptional durability were Atkinson with 29 sessions, Ormond with 30 and O'Rorke with 33.[237]

The proportion of locally born (European) members was starting to rise, although they were still only a small minority. Most of the 19 New Zealand-born members who sat between 1876 and 1890 entered the House in the latter half of the 1880s.[238] The educational level of politicians began to fall as the early cadre of well-educated British gentleman politicians was replaced. In the period 1876–90, one-third of all representatives had been educated only to the primary level; only one-fifth had a university education.[239]

Politicians were drawn from increasingly diverse backgrounds. Significant minorities now came from manual working backgrounds or had been employed in journalism, to supplement the continued major occupations of the law, farming, commerce and the professions. In the 1880s, journalism in particular became a common route into the House. Notably, the patrician runholder bloc had disappeared. John Studholme, who retired in 1881, was regarded by many as the last of the old breed.[240] Extensive pastoralism remained represented in the House, but only as one among other farming interests.[241]

A parliamentary tour party on a Cobb and Co. coach halts for a mid-day rest in the Pelorus Valley, Marlborough. Arduous journeys on horseback or by coach were the only way to service many electorates in the early days. Members usually travelled to and from Wellington by steamers, which the government would hold in port until the session ended. In spite of the spread of railways, members continued to use the government steamers in the 1880s. The North Island main trunk was making slow progress, and South Island members had to get across Cook Strait in any case. Some upper South Island representatives took advantage of special trains between Picton to Blenheim that were laid on by the government, while others travelled by train to and from provincial ports as the rail network expanded.

The ground was being prepared for a different kind of politician – hard-working, less educated and self-made, with a common touch. Seddon exemplified this new breed. These members viewed election to Parliament as the culmination of what they had worked for, rather than as an additional leisured pastime in which refined debating sharpened the intellect and allowed the exposition of philosophical and constitutional positions. In other words, for Seddon and his kind politics was a career. Parliamentary debating societies in many centres prepared ambitious budding politicians by providing a parallel to the real institution.[242] They appointed 'governments', 'Premiers' and other ministers, staged parliamentary debates on issues of the day, used parliamentary procedure, and even 'passed' legislation. A number of politicians, including William Pember Reeves, John Joyce and Thomas Mackenzie, gained their initial experience in such societies.

The broadening of the franchise and the greater involvement of working men in elections, the emergence of popular figures who stumped the country and engaged with the public directly, the increased recognition of the need to organise election campaigns – all these developments transformed the relationship between representatives and the people and led to the emergence of true parties.

With retrenchment the honorarium had been cut, but an emerging body of opinion wanted to put the payment of members on a footing which properly recognised the expense and commitment needed to be a member of the House. Proper payment of members would also, it was hoped, encourage broader representation, in particular of working men. The chamber was no longer a self-enclosed, rather cosy factional world in which members jostled for position and power without reference to those who had elected them. It was becoming more a microcosm of society and its concerns and interests. The assembled representatives began to feel increasingly accountable to their electorates.

What was missing thus far was the organisational cement for durable links between the chamber and the people. Grey's demagogic and populist approach had been too reliant on vague promises and charismatic appeal, had provided little or no sustained organisation, and had proved hopelessly inadequate to get business through Parliament. Atkinson's pragmatic and responsible alternative had taken little account of organising a party in the House and was discredited for its inability to gain support in the country.

Under these political pressures and the economic pressures of the depression, the previously successful factional system had broken down. Representative institutions appeared to be going backwards rather than forwards, resulting in a paralysis of government. But this was an illusion. The breakdown of the factional system in Parliament anticipated a new form of political organisation, one that would take the democratising processes better into account – the modern political party.

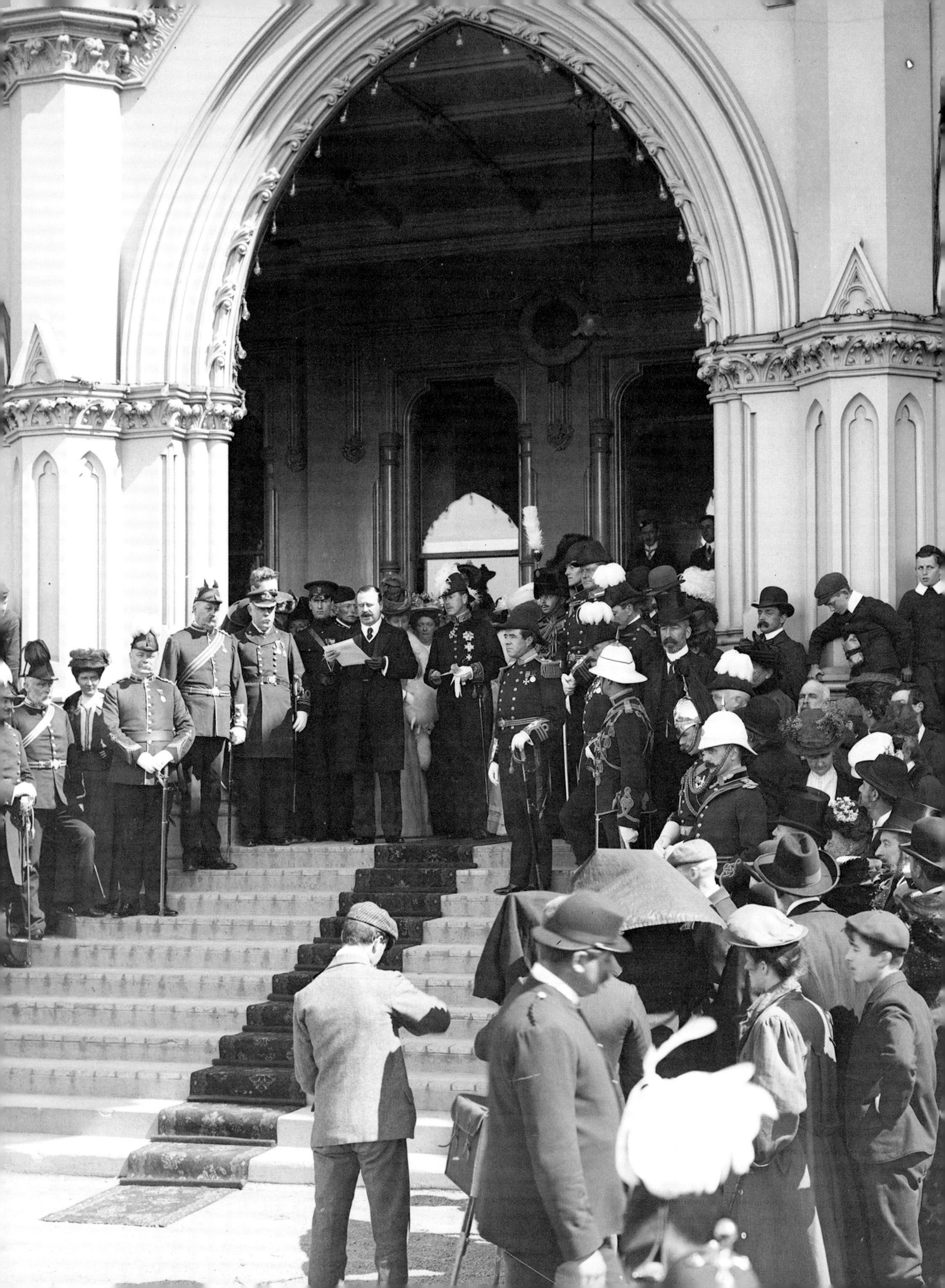

CHAPTER 4

FROM FREE-LANCE TO DISCIPLINED PRIVATE: THE SINGLE PARTY IN THE HOUSE, 1891–1912

There did not seem anything particularly remarkable about the 1890 election at the time, yet it has gone down as one of the most important turning points in New Zealand's history. The depression still had some years to run; retrenchment remained the priority in government; and the competing parties did not have greatly more concerted policy platforms for the election than before. But the sustained depression conditions, which had severely shaken the confidence of the country and led for the first time to net emigration from New Zealand, required a new mode of attack. The 'continuous ministry' had had its day. There was an increased willingness to look for more comprehensive solutions – by means of land legislation, financial assistance to settlers, village settlement, control over immigration, public works employment, recognition of trade unions, and protection of wages, working conditions and living standards.

Instead of reforming private members advocating 'faddish' measures, the state itself took a leading role. The centralisation and expansion of government after the abolition of the provinces encouraged this. Once a government was sufficiently cohesive and organised and enjoyed a popular mandate to take advantage of the central state, the political map would be transformed fundamentally. The Liberal government from the 1890s would raise state intervention to new heights, along the way setting in motion a process of party domination over Parliament. The Liberals also moved New Zealand politics along the road to modern parties. Participation in politics had expanded to the extent that working men not only had the vote and were using it to further their own interests, but were beginning to be elected to Parliament with the support of a burgeoning and organised labour movement.

Encouraged by full manhood suffrage, popular participation in elections had gradually risen by the mid 1880s. More comprehensive registration and higher proportions of votes cast were indications of this. The proportions voting increased markedly in the elections of 1887 and 1890.[1] A rising level of participation offered potential for a party that could mobilise the electorate more effectively. The Liberals seized this opportunity.

The election of 1890 is often seen as having turned on the conflict between capital and labour, with the new Liberal Party using state power to establish a sense of equality between capital and labour.[2] But at the time the distinctions between the contending groups were not so clear-cut. The major differentiating issue was the property tax rather than labour policy. It was land policy that was paramount, together with the need to reinstate strong and effective government. The Liberals did not go into the election with an obvious manifesto or a high degree of organisation, and the extent to which labour was united behind them varied. Many of the urban members from Atkinson's side also supported reformist labour measures.

Left: Prime Minister Ward declares New Zealand's Dominion status on the steps of the General Assembly Library, 26 September 1907 ATL, G8648

There was, however, greater agreement than before among the Liberals on the general principle of reform by means of the state. Trade union involvement in the election was unprecedented, and a substantial contribution was made by the radical Knights of Labour.[3] But for the most part, the labour movement remained external to Parliament, its voice being heard through a few members such as William Pember Reeves. The number of 'labour' members was never more than a handful, and some of them were soon estranged and became Liberal independents.

The beginnings of party government

After the election, Atkinson followed the traditional factional approach of waiting to see how the groups coalesced once Parliament had been summoned.[4] He was unsure just how the numbers might fall, so he called Parliament extremely early, in late January 1891. At a caucus, he resigned as leader and accepted the position of Speaker of the Legislative Council, having stacked the Council with his supporters.

With O'Rorke having lost his seat, the appointment of a Speaker for the House was bitterly contested as a test for formation of a new ministry.[5] The old order put Rolleston forward, while the Liberals proposed Major Steward. A full party contest took place for the first time; the Liberals won the vote, 36 to 29. The Liberal Party then assumed power and Ballance who became Premier, prorogued the House until June so that the new government could gather its thoughts and tour the country to assess its support. Ballance's cabinet followed the usual geographical balance but was notable for its youth and inexperience, for the different range of occupations represented, and for the number who had risen through the ranks.[6]

A party of a new kind was born – one that would not be assembled from the members present on the floor but was actively created outside the chamber.[7] In forming his ministry, Ballance, in contrast to previous practice, drew entirely from previous Opposition (from now on, reference is to the 'Opposition' as a cohesive body, rather than the 'opposition') members. He did not attempt to negotiate with the remnants of Atkinson's ministry. However, Ballance, like those before him, had spurned interference by the leader in the selection of parliamentary candidates.

When the more authoritarian Seddon came to power in 1893 after the death of Ballance, party considerations intruded much more noticeably into politics and the business of Parliament. Seddon saw himself as the leader of the Liberal Party at large rather than just the

William Jukes Steward was born on 20 January 1841 in Reading, England. He emigrated to Canterbury in 1862 and worked as a journalist before entering Parliament in 1871 as the member for Waitaki. Defeated in 1875, he was re-elected (for Waimate) in 1879. Steward was noted for his gentle manner and courtesy, and for his persistence – if not stubbornness – in promoting private members' bills over many years. From the late 1880s he was the leading advocate in the House of an elected executive, an innovation which would have prevented party government from emerging. Personally, however, he took enormous pride in being a stalwart Liberal Party man. In his later years as the 'Father of the House' he appeared rather eccentric, being tall and thin with a long beard, wearing a small skull cap, and adopting a rather wild appearance. Also noted for indecisiveness, leniency and very lengthy rulings, he was replaced by O'Rorke in 1894. Steward was knighted in 1902 and retired from the House in 1911. He died on 30 October 1912.

From free-lance to disciplined private: the single party in the House, 1891–1912

parliamentary party. He manipulated candidate selection, endorsed 'government' candidates, and stumped electorates in their favour. He obtained written undertakings from candidates to support the party on no-confidence motions and on its general policy. Later, official lists were issued that gave candidates a 'hallmark' or stamp of approval. He rewarded loyalty in preference to skill or intellectual prowess, and made greater demands on the allegiance of members in the House.

Seddon used caucus meetings more extensively than before, to establish and impose policies on the party and to hold it together in times of need.[8] This could only work when the leader's persuasive powers were effective. As one dissident Liberal, G.W. Russell, said, 'The Government rules, and when they get into trouble they ask their followers to meet in caucuses … this House is through Whips and caucuses reduced to a machine for registering Ministers' behests.'[9] At times Seddon would threaten dissidents.

Change was slower to come in the electorates than in Parliament. Ballance promoted a national Liberal Association to bolster popular support for the party, but this did not really flourish and failed to provide a basis for an extra-parliamentary party.[10] In 1899 Seddon formed a compliant Liberal and Labour Federation to support the parliamentary party and co-operate with it in drawing up election platforms. This also proved ineffective. It was left to the populist appeal of Seddon to provide the necessary link between the party in Parliament and the people.

For a long time the Opposition – and a number of more independent-minded Liberal members – refused to accept the implications of the changed political environment. Lipson suggests that backbench members of the House were converted from 'free-lance warriors' into 'disciplined privates' as political parties demanded greater allegiance.[11] This perhaps assumes that private members all along possessed more power than they actually had, but discipline did tighten and expectations of conformity were raised. Only a few could now be called genuine independents. There was a shift from ad hoc expressions of support at the beginning of sessions to ongoing support for the party, which now required a commitment to vote with the party on all matters before the House unless a free vote was explicitly allowed.

The agitation of the time for an elective executive was intended both to embarrass the domineering Seddon and to register a protest against party government. Bills proposing an elected executive were regularly introduced until 1912 by Major Steward, a leading independent Liberal. But while he foresaw the burial of party government 'unwept, unhonoured, and unsung', the truth was that what he heard 'were not the wheels of the undertaker, but the chariot-wheels of the Reform party' as it finally accepted the inevitable and forged its own modern party from 1909.[12] The ground had shifted for good, but meanwhile it was the independents, together with a regalvanised Legislative Council, that provided most of the opposition to the Liberals.

The Speech from the Throne opening the session in June 1891, together with the financial statement, signalled a vigorous programme of reform. The Opposition expected the inexperienced government to buckle under the onslaught, but it gave as good as it got. Ballance and Jock McKenzie pushed through a land tax, purchased large estates for subdivision and promoted closer land settlement, while Reeves devoted himself to labour legislation to protect workers. The new House was substantially smaller at 74 members. The seating had to be rearranged, closer to the Chair.[13]

The new Opposition leader, the impetuous and hot-headed Bryce, got embroiled in an argument with the Speaker over saying that Ballance 'ought to be ashamed of himself'.[14] Steward should have brought the House to order far earlier for much worse instances of unparliamentary language. Ballance then usurped the power of the Chair by asking Bryce to withdraw the remark. Bryce refused. The Speaker cleared the galleries and Bryce was censured, with the House voting along strict party lines. Steward, who lacked authority, made a late, ineffectual, appeal for restraint. As Reeves perceptively observed, 'the House supports a strong Speaker, but is disposed to bully weakness in the chair.'[15] Rolleston took over as Opposition leader when Bryce stalked out of the House, mortally offended. He resigned his seat after the government rejected his petition for the censure to be withdrawn. In another incident, Steward's lack of knowledge of parliamentary practice and vulnerability to manipulation by the government was exposed when he bowed to Seddon's demand that a member cease talking. This prompted accusations that Seddon was intimidating the Speaker.[16]

In the circumstances of Liberal ascendancy endorsed by the electorate, the Opposition faced a hopeless task. Neither the distant and rather haughty Rolleston nor his successor, the gentlemanly Captain Russell, were able to respond to the changed circumstances. Russell acknowledged that 'we may as well try and stay the waves of the ocean as the waves of democracy'.[17]

Speaker Steward had trouble controlling the House. Here, with his neck tied in a knot (to prevent garrulousness), he ineffectually tries to maintain order as Premier Ballance tweaks the nose of Opposition leader Rolleston. A reporter gleefully notes the disorder from the gallery.

Legislative Council obstruction to Liberal reforms made Ballance threaten an election. By the end of the decade, such confrontations had resulted in the Council becoming a moribund and discredited body.[18] Reform of the Council – including the introduction of seven-year terms for members – was generally supported, and legislation providing for this was passed in 1891. It was not so easy a task to stack the Council in favour of the Liberals. The obdurate Governor, Onslow, and then the incoming Governor, the Earl of Glasgow, both refused to make the new appointments to the Council which Ballance proposed. A constitutional crisis ensued. Britain's ruling that Ballance's appointments should be made was a huge victory for the Liberals and spelled doom for the Council. Ballance allotted four seats in the Council to labour representatives and appointed another eight party supporters. When the 1893 election endorsed the Liberal government, much of the force of Council resistance was negated. Seddon shifted the Council the Liberals' way by the late 1890s. Many of his appointees were of a low calibre, discrediting the Council. By the turn of the century it had become relatively powerless and was 'publicly reviled as an anachronistic and troublesome institution with little real value'.[19]

Atkinson died suddenly in the Legislative Council Speaker's room in June 1892.[20] His demise deeply shocked the House. When the Speaker announced his death, Ballance stopped in the middle of a speech and the House was immediately adjourned. 'Mr Speaker's voice suddenly breaks hoarsely across the proceedings, and his face is ashen and awe stricken as he rises … a deadly hush falls upon the listening House … A groan bursts from the House and the galleries'.[21]

The centrepiece of the 1892 session was the Land Bill. Jock McKenzie introduced the famed lease-in-perpetuity tenure that steered a middle course between the leasehold and freehold factions.[22] This took the wind out of the Opposition's sails and Rolleston waved the flag of surrender for the session, suggesting that the House settle down to practical work. The Opposition's only contribution was Buckland's facetious Washers and Manglers Bill, designed to highlight the Liberal government's propensity to control and regulate.[23] The fake bill was sufficiently convincing in its drafting that it passed its first reading, to the delight of the Opposition. In the latter part of the session, Ballance's cancer made it difficult for him to continue. The cabinet appointed Seddon acting Premier and he began to flex his political muscles. When he attempted to manipulate the House, a number of Liberals left the chamber and it had to be counted out.[24]

Ballance died on 27 April 1893. He was given a public funeral but erecting a memorial to him proved a protracted business.[25] Seddon finally unveiled a statue in 1897. It stood in the centre of the lawn in front of Parliament Buildings. When the grounds were relandscaped after the First World War, Ballance's statue was moved to stand more squarely in front of the General Assembly Library, while that of Seddon was placed in front of the new main buildings.

Ballance's death brought dissension within the Liberal cabinet to a head.[26] Seddon cleverly outmanoeuvred Ballance's anointed successor Stout, who had been out of the House since 1887. The caucus had little choice but to accept a fait accompli. Stout's planned glorious re-entry into politics became a damp squib, and a precedent was set for the election of a Premier by caucus. Seddon announced the new ministry and his premiership at the opening of the 1893 session, flourishing a *Gazette* notice before the House to underline who was in charge. He retained a number of portfolios, and appointed Joseph Ward to the key post of Colonial Treasurer.

The new politics and politicians

Seddon's confirmation as Premier put the seal on a new breed of New Zealand politician.[27] It also ushered in a gathering of power into the hands of the Premier. Seddon not only became virtually a one-man ministry, but also dominated Parliament by strengthening executive power and wresting control of its administration from the Speaker.

Men in the Seddonian mould who entered politics in the late nineteenth century were largely self-made. They had got where they had by virtue of hard work and the ability to take advantage of opportunities. They had little respect for authority or status, regarded self-reliance and self-help as crucial principles, and saw themselves as democratic in the sense of being at one with the people through a sharing of experiences rather than because of adherence to abstract principles. The state was there to be used for democratic purposes, and the Liberal Party was there to express the will of the people.

They were naturally ambitious – a seat in the House was the climax of their work. They were rough and rude in manner and dress, and survived through hard graft, belligerence and their wits rather than eloquent debating skills, being described by one conservative member as 'a horde of illiterate braggarts'.[28] Retaining their seats mattered above all else, and being granted a portfolio was their greatest blessing. Among such men, internecine rivalry could be more bitter than cross-bench warfare.

Masterton's Alexander Hogg, who had a background in radical journalism, was one such member. He was garrulous, unrestrained and lacked polish and tact, being 'squat and drab, habitually clad in a rumpled black frock-coat'.[29] Hogg became known as the 'Roads and Bridges Minister' for his determined advocacy of the interests of the backblocks North Island settler.

Some poked fun at the changing nature of the House. O.T.J. Alpers recounted misunderstandings over literary references and allusions, badly rendered French and the like.[30] Members who were seen as putting on airs and graces got short shrift. The uncouth Jock McKenzie attacked the young, educated and polished lawyer F.H.D. Bell (known as 'Baby Bell'): 'his very tone, his speech [is] typical of the high English Tory … by the time he has been three years in this House, he will change a good deal of that high-toned falutin' way'.[31] Bell evidently got the message – he resigned after a single Parliament and later, in 1912, he joined the more gentlemanly, cultured and restrained environment of the Upper House.

In the House, the differences between the Liberals and the Opposition were highlighted over the liquor issue. The Liberals had agonised discussions on the subject while the Opposition, less enamoured of the party approach, calmly accepted the matter as one on which they might cast a free vote. Stout led the prohibition charge and sought to undermine Seddon, but his approach to mustering support was the traditional one of faction-building. Seddon's tactical skills were manifest.[32] Following a stonewall and an incident in which Fish pulled off his coat and challenged another member to 'have it out' in the Lobby, Seddon introduced a more moderate bill that went through comparatively easily with some Opposition support. This most difficult issue was shifted out of the parliamentary arena and into local polls. Stout had lost his main chance to undermine Seddon.

Seddon declined to move into Premier House on Tinakori Road. Instead his large house at 47 Molesworth Street became the focal point of Wellington's political life. But the time when members of both Houses were invited en masse to receptions and entertainments had passed.[33] An invitation to a ministerial residence on Molesworth Street was not coveted. The Liberal government had no 'social position' and was composed of men of 'lower rank'.

The outstanding feature of the 1893 session was the enactment of female suffrage, long-discussed but always stymied. With stronger, more effective government restored to the country, there was a chance that previous votes in 1887 and 1890 in support of the principle might at last carry the day.[34] But the government was deeply ambivalent about whether women's votes would be to its or the Opposition's advantage. Key cabinet members including Seddon were set against the measure. Hall in Opposition made matters tricky by introducing his own female suffrage bills.

NZ Observer and Free Lance, 4 August 1894

PARLIAMENTARY CHARACTER SKETCHES.
No. 3.—MR HEE MET-CALF SMITH.

The New Plymouth and then Taranaki member dubbed 'Ironsand' or 'Heehem', E.M. Smith (1890–6, 1899–1907) created a role in the House for himself by mocking his own characteristics. The newspapers poked fun at him endlessly. He recited his own verse and accentuated his lack of grammatical polish and misplaced aspirate 'Hs'. He also dressed eccentrically.

In 1891 the government obstructed the measure persistently but eventually allowed a full debate. The House was packed and many women crowded the gallery. The unrolling of all 70 feet of the suffrage petition in the House caused much amusement.[35] The bill easily passed its second reading in a thin House, but was then wrecked by a new clause allowing women to become members of the House. This was too much. The bill fell in a close vote in the Council.

In 1892 female suffrage was more firmly on the agenda, making it difficult for the government to oppose overtly. A new petition had been organised, 180 yards-long. The bill passed in the House without much trouble but was amended in the Council in such a way that the government rejected it, whipping the party strongly to achieve the bill's demise. In 1893 Hall slowly unrolled an even larger petition of 26,000 women asking for the franchise. The petition came close to 300 yards. '"I shall require a little assistance here", he said presently, as the unrolled loops of paper began to embarrass him. A messenger stepped forward and soon the solid roll was bowling along the floor to the other end of the chamber, which it reached without being apparently at all diminished in size'.[36] By now few members wanted to be identified publicly as against women's suffrage. The government's bill passed through the House without incident, once Stout and Saunders had prevented Seddon from manipulating the order paper to delay its proceeding.

Sir John Hall, promoter of female suffrage, unrolls the massive 1893 petition in the House.

The bill had a tougher time in the Council. Both sides lobbied hard. While the bill was in Committee, a number of destructive amendments were narrowly defeated. The country watched with fascination. When Seddon attempted to manipulate the vote of a paired Liberal councillor two angry councillors precipitately switched their votes and the bill passed its third reading, 20 to 18.[37] Seddon grudgingly conceded, to applause in the House, that the bill would have to go through.

A very high percentage of eligible women enrolled and voted, but female suffrage did not greatly change voting patterns. The massive increase in the Liberal majority in the election of 1893 was more the result of the party's popular land and labour policies. Seddon consolidated his position, appealing to the people rather than the party.[38] The Opposition was decimated – only about 16 members remained. This small group was soon joined by a youngish farmer from Mangere, William Massey, who was elected at a by-election in 1894.[39] Before the end of the session he would be appointed whip and would assist in gradually organising a more effective Opposition.

When Parliament reconvened in 1894 there were many new members. O'Rorke had been returned again. As *Fair Play* noted wryly, the new House included a large number of prohibitionists, amongst whom were six preachers who would 'never, never patronise Bellamy's – except for lemonade', together with ten members of the radical Knights of Labour.[40] But many from the old order including Scobie Mackenzie, Rolleston, Dick Reeves, Fish and Fisher had now gone.

By the 1890s Bellamy's finances had reached crisis point. Discontinuing the service was seriously mooted.[41] The self-funding regime of the 1880s had not worked and the reduction in the number of members and influx of new members of a temperance persuasion spelled problems. In the early 1890s it came under concerted attack from the temperance lobby and in 1893, in response to new controls on drinking hours throughout the country, the bar was closed at 11 p.m. Matters

The House

John McLachlan, elected to Ashburton in 1893, was a Scots raconteur with a fondness for Burns and whisky. He would speak in the House while intoxicated, often using bad language. His début was inauspicious to say the least. Shortly the opening of the 1894 session, he fell into the harbour while wandering home to his lodgings, after mistaking wharf lights for those in a nearby chemist's shop. He was fished out after clinging to a piece of timber for a long time.

became serious at the opening of the 1894 session. The situation was not helped when a new member, John McLachlan, took a drunken plunge into the harbour while trying to find his way home late at night.[42] As the *Otago Daily Times* commented, New Zealand would acquire 'the reputation of a community which returns a Parliament which cannot be trusted in the presence of strong drink'.[43] Amid backroom politicking and talk of special legislation to allow the supply of liquor to continue, it was agreed that the supply would be maintained for that session since the liquor had already been ordered from Britain.

Seddon then cleverly orchestrated maintenance of the status quo.[44] He amended the existing legislation so that a poll of members would be held at the beginning of each Parliament to see whether liquor should be provided, requiring only a bare majority for prohibition. As a Legislative Councillor perceptively pointed out, this would result in no change, for the lower House would be split half and half and the upper House would remain firmly committed to such comforts. This is how it worked out in the first poll in 1897.[45] Polls were taken at the commencement of subsequent Parliaments, when it was remembered to do so. Support for abolition was always a minority and later declined to small numbers.

Both Houses agreed publicly that liquor should not be served on Sundays, to bring Parliament into line with the rest of the country. But Bellamy's remained open seven days a week nonetheless. Amended licensing legislation in 1904 apparently prevented the sale of alcohol in Bellamy's on Sundays and after 10 p.m. on other days, but Seddon would not have a bar of this in practice. In his view, the unrepealed 1881 provision excluding Parliament from licensing controls remained pre-eminent. Most members were only too willing to go along with this. With the consolidation of legislation in 1908 the restricted hours were incorporated into the Legislature Act, but at the same time Parliament continued with the provision in the Licensing Act that exempted it from the controls, thereby surreptitiously escaping the restrictions.

The temperance movement had some effect. The tradition of serving liquor in the Lobby and to members of the public in the strangers' waiting rooms ended.[46] Orders for liquor were no longer placed with British merchants and quality declined, to the chagrin of Councillors. Bellamy's reputation for the best liquor in Wellington disappeared – now the Scotch whisky 'was fiery enough to burn a hole in a blanket'.[47] As patronage declined and debts mounted, Bellamy's full restaurant service was abandoned and more economical meals were provided until Parliament provided renewed subsidies.

Despite the influence of the prohibitionists, Bellamy's remained a social centre and parliamentary life retained its lighter side. There was still plenty of conviviality, music and singing. A.L.D. Fraser was remembered for his genial nature, as a raconteur, and for playing the piano in Bellamy's.[48] Concerts were held in the Lobby on Saturday nights, drawing in members from all sides. Ward possessed a fine tenor voice and the Maori members James Carroll, Hone Heke and Apirana Ngata were impressive singers.[49]

A number of larger than life characters and inveterate drinkers still featured in the life of the House. George Fisher, also Mayor of Wellington and known as 'the people's George', was one.[50] He had observed Parliament since the early 1860s and spent a number of years as a Hansard reporter

From free-lance to disciplined private: the single party in the House, 1891–1912

from the early 1870s. He developed considerable powers of debate and oratory after he entered the House in 1884, but he was also alcoholic, argumentative and eccentric. When he died in 1905 he was replaced by his son F.M.B. Fisher, known as 'Rainbow Don', who was a similarly maverick and charismatic member and a powerful platform speaker. Roderick ('Roddy') McKenzie was described as a 'ranting, raving, roaring, rough diamond of a West Coaster, with "hair on his teeth" as the saying goes, and a voice which drives the Hansard men temporarily deaf'.[51] He, George Fisher and McLachlan were notorious for their large debts at the bar. O'Rorke, as Speaker, did not set a good example. Sidney Webb recorded in his diary: 'It is rare to meet in the streets a man who is in liquor, whereas the Speaker of the House [O'Rorke] is constantly absent incapacitated from his duties by drink.'[52]

Other characters populated the House. R.M. Taylor, an ardent anti-prohibitionist, was known as 'Rum' Taylor.[53] Complete with white bell-topper and long black frock coat, he was the funny man of the House and the universal butt of humour – but in a friendly manner, for he had no enemies. When he wanted to attract another member's attention in the House he would take a white handkerchief out of the pocket of his long black coat and wave it. He was soon replaced as member for the City of Christchurch by the young, charismatic T.E. ('Tea') Taylor, an independent, prohibitionist Liberal whose dramatic presence and entertaining oratory filled the House easily.[54] The contrast between 'Rum' and 'Tea' was

(OUR LEGISLATORS). "Wot! Put down Bellamy's? Great Scott! They'll be a wanting to put HUS down next!!!"

NZ Graphic, 16 September 1893

Members enjoying Bellamy's hospitality are shocked at the notion of banning liquor.

General Assembly Library collection, ATL, F91-35mm-E

T.E. ('Tea') Taylor, member for City of Christchurch, 1896–9 and 1902–5, and Christchurch North, 1908–11.

Back from Sydenham

NZ Observer and Free Lance, 1 July 1893

R.M. ('Rum') Taylor, member for Sydenham and City of Christchurch, 1886–93.

115

too good to pass up. 'Tea' Taylor gained a reputation as the 'stormy petrel' of the House, remaining a maverick independent who saw conspiracy and corruption everywhere.

The Liberals faced some difficulty over the Speaker when Parliament reconvened in 1894. Steward could not be prevailed upon to retire, but O'Rorke could hardly be overlooked. Seddon proposed O'Rorke, and he and Steward, as was the gentlemanly custom, went into the opposite lobbies to vote against themselves. O'Rorke won easily. All those who voted against him were 'temperance men' put off by his reputation for heavy drinking.[55] O'Rorke, although Liberal, was not a party man, and the notes for his acceptance speech (the speech was not reported in *Hansard*) stated that the Speakership should not be a party matter but a matter of confidence of the entire House. 'Your Speaker is clothed with power but what avails that power without your co-operation? … The only symbol of his power is the mace which a mocking age and mocking men delight to term a "bauble"'.[56] O'Rorke tried to reassert the privileges of the House in the face of Seddon's taking of power, but he was unable to resist the government taking control over expenditure on and the staffing of Parliament.[57] Within a few years O'Rorke became Father of the House and the only member left from the Parliament of 1861 (when a great many new members had been elected). In his latter years, O'Rorke's sense of judgement deserted him at times and he proved less effective at controlling the House.[58]

Seddon's assertion of executive power

Government business and the whips dominated sessions in a manner not previously experienced.[59] The Liberals had triumphed over the Legislative Council and resistance to their legislation diminished, but the middle years of the decade saw a backbench revolt against Seddon by left-wing independents and prohibitionists. The Opposition, in comparison with the Parliament of 1891–3, was more active and forced more divisions. Things could easily go wrong between government and Opposition whips. Towards the end of the financial debate in 1893, the understanding over speakers broke down and Seddon was forced to adjourn the House to save an embarrassing collapse of the debate.[60] Whip Mills reflected on the work: 'it's not such an easy job to "roll up the party" this session as last. The new members have got a nasty way of asking questions. Confound them, the beggars actually want to know what they are voting for now, whereas in the good old days the Whip had only to be liberal with his "shouts" at Bellamy's, and the votes were there up to time, just as they were wanted.'[61] Whips required definite and distinct characteristics that were not possessed by all and sundry – 'suavity, readiness, sound judgement, self restraint, wide information, insight into character, power of intrigue, a tough cuticle, and a case hardened unscrupulousness'.[62]

In 1894 McKenzie's Land for Settlements Bill was the focus of the session. McKenzie was akin to Seddon in character and as a populist, full-time, career politician.[63] He was dogged, extremely loyal to Seddon, and aggressive and rude in the House, seeing little use in observing gentlemanly procedures that might get in the way of his ramming through legislation. The bill's second reading was shepherded along. McKenzie was used to driving and rounding up sheep. 'The members are now his flock and if they stray they must be rounded up by the Whips.'[64] When McKenzie sought to adjourn the House to cut short debate in the early hours, virtually the entire

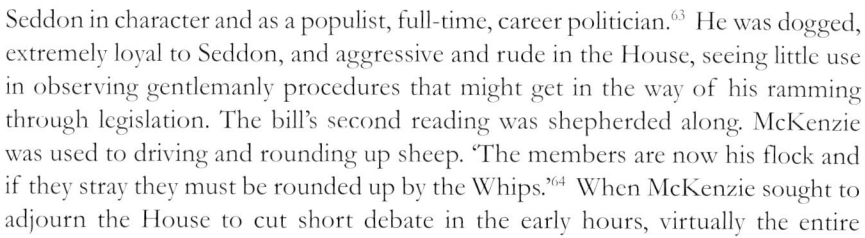

Jock McKenzie was elected for Moeraki in 1881 as one of a new, less-educated breed of politicians who became associated with the Liberals. As Minister of Lands in the Liberal government he introduced a range of legislation to dismantle large landholdings. A key member of the government, McKenzie was Acting Premier when Seddon was absent.

From free-lance to disciplined private: the single party in the House, 1891–1912

Opposition and a number of Liberals vacated the chamber in protest. McKenzie pointedly turned his back on the Speaker and addressed the nearly empty Liberal back benches.

The debonair Ward was the 'darling' of the press – not 'coarse like Seddon, decrepit like Buckley, boorish like McKenzie, waspish like Reeves, lugubrious like Cadman, nor languid like Carroll'.[65] He had a facility with figures and a tremendous speed of delivery which often bamboozled the Opposition and defeated Hansard. When Ward returned from Britain shortly after the 1895 session opened, having helped float a loan, he was received with rapture. The House adjourned in his honour and the ministry flanked his triumphal procession to Parliament.[66] Trees were planted in Parliament grounds to mark his achievement and 'Ward was piped into the House to the tune "Hard times come again no more".'

During the 1895 session Captain Russell brought the first outright motion testing confidence in the government into the House for a long time. The Opposition was defeated by 43 votes to 20, denting Russell's assurance.[67] A more successful attack on Ward over the tariff issue came from radicals in his own party, who joined with the free-traders. Government discipline collapsed and Ward's credibility fell as he was forced to revise his plans. Dissident Liberals continued to defy the party line and Captain Russell poked fun at Seddon's expectation that when he 'holds up his little finger' his party 'will dance accordingly'.[68] But in future Russell's policy would be to join with the government against the left wing of the Liberal Party. Seddon, fearing for the unity of the party, threatened to dissolve Parliament and to abandon planned legislation to bring it to heel.

The end of the session was dominated by Ward's entanglement in the affairs of the Colonial Bank of New Zealand, recently purchased by the Bank of New Zealand. The Opposition wanted to debate the merger of the banks and the government barely deflected a motion by F.H.D. Bell asking for legislation. The government's supporters felt increasingly disgruntled and punished the ministry by rejecting other less important legislation.[69]

By June 1896, sensationally, Ward's affairs were out in the open and he had to admit his insolvency in court. It was the only topic of discussion among parliamentarians. When the judge described Ward's business practices as illegitimate and dishonest, he resigned from cabinet in an attempt to salvage his political career. Seddon, seeking to shift the onus onto Atkinson's government of the late 1880s, agreed that a select committee would enquire into the banking legislation. This gave rise to the most notable instance of contempt of Parliament in New Zealand's history when William Watson, the president of the directors of the Bank of New Zealand, refused to divulge information relating to individual accounts even when summoned to the bar.[70] He was fined £500, which the Bank paid. Honour was maintained on both sides. The House had demonstrated that its authority could not be defied.

The Opposition, together with independent Liberals, almost defeated the government on Stout's motion to report progress as Seddon continued to force business through.[71] Towards the end of the long session, the patience of some Liberals had been stretched to breaking point by Seddon's demands, and only the Speaker's vote saved the day. Members had already rounded on Seddon for driving rather than leading the House when he attempted to overturn the order paper to go into supply unexpectedly late one night.[72] Seddon had to back off for once. Captain Russell railed at Seddon's control, suggesting that there was 'no limit to the autocratic power of the Premier … There is no longer a true Parliament in New Zealand, but merely a body of men collected together to record the views of the Premier'.[73] Seddon nevertheless continued to change the order paper at the last minute.

At the same time a broader revolt took place as the House refused to allow several bills to go into Committee.[74] Seddon had to adjourn the House immediately and whip members back into line. After threatening that the government would resign he agreed to drop some bills – the usual 'slaughter of the innocents' – and bring the session to a close. Seddon was not sad to see the back of members and was in no hurry to call them back to Wellington. 'The formal business was disposed of, and shortly after 3 o'clock the curtain was rung down, and a procession of cabs, and legislators carrying carpet bags, weighted with the golden honorariums, passed down the wharf to the steamers.'[75]

Seddon had amassed considerable power. With depression still affecting the country, his cuts in departments gained him the sobriquet, 'The Chief Executioner'.[76] In 1891, determined to take advantage of the weak Steward occupying the Chair, he had reopened the issue of legislative expenditure. Steward conceded that he did not want to present the legislative estimates in the House. In a close vote, the House made a symbolic reduction of £1 in the estimates to signal its wish that the government take charge. This gave Seddon his chance. As Minister of Public Works and then as Premier, he held the administrative reins. He dismissed any constitutional niceties airily. 'I have taken the commonsense view of it, and I care very little for these old traditions or musty precedents which are raked up occasionally, and as it were rammed down our throats'.[77]

Seddon argued that executive control over the estimates for legislative expenditure also meant control over the appointment of staff. Steward protested that Seddon's appointment of a shorthand writer was 'not in accordance with the intentions of the House' and tried in vain to resist. Seddon next fired various sessional officers after insisting that they work throughout the recess, contrary to tradition, the Speaker's view and a Crown Law Office opinion.[78] He then prevented committee clerks taking up Hansard appointments – their usual route of preferment – so that he could exercise his own patronage over the wider civil service and require new reporters to work during the recess.

Steward in desperation sought support from Australian practice, which confirmed that, constitutionally, the Speakers controlled appointments and legislative expenditure. But this made no difference. When Hall raised the question of the Hansard reporters as a matter of privilege, Seddon deflected it towards a committee with a majority of goverment members and enthusiasts for retrenchment. This committee backed him on the basis of the 1891 decision, thereby reversing the resolution of 1862 that appointments would be made by the government on the recommendation of the Speaker.[79] The authority of the Speaker over officers was to be limited to the session itself, but Seddon's insistence that the new reporters work for the government during the recess was never pursued. Speakers O'Rorke and Guinness both said they would refuse to insist upon it.

When the Speaker's opinion on control was reported back to the House, McKenzie said that Erskine May (the essential reference work on parliamentary procedure) should be burnt on a bonfire on the tennis court. The committee's report was finally agreed to along party lines in a thin House. Amendments ensured that the positions of Second Clerk-Assistant and above were protected, as were Hansard reporters engaged prior to 1893, and the interpreters. The Opposition kept gnawing away at the issue. It was reopened in 1898, when Seddon conceded that the Speaker would have control over parliamentary officers even though the government still controlled expenditure and made the appointments. A motion to this effect was agreed to in the House. It is likely that the constant criticism had worn Seddon down, and that in any case he could see no advantage in having day-to-day control.[80]

Rolleston, an acute observer of constitutional matters, believed it to be an abuse of constitutional powers and bitterly called Seddon's moves to assert executive control over legislative expenditure and appointments 'an absolute carelessness of the privileges and position of Parliament' as recognised in other British colonies.[81] The Legislative Council, fully aware of the implications of Seddon's demands, refused to be a party to the changed practice, and its Speaker continued to be responsible for the employment of the Council's officers and other staff.

As speeches swelled to fill the time available and speakers crammed more into their allotted time, extra demands were made on the Hansard staff. The enlargement of the Council further increased these demands. Seddon wanted *Hansard* to be more efficient and up-to-date, but publication was now much delayed and inaccuracies had crept in. Seddon publicly withdrew support for the now elderly Barron and criticised him in the House. A split developed among the reporters over loyalty to Barron, who was eventually forced to retire, accused of neglecting his duties and lacking an interest in *Hansard*. New appointment procedures were instituted, and the position of Hansard Supervisor was established to take over much of Barron's work.[82] Seddon also appointed new reporters who were in principle required to work through the recess. The extra reporters and the adoption of more efficient typewriters

From free-lance to disciplined private: the single party in the House, 1891–1912

for transcription made a big difference, and *Hansard* appeared more quickly.[83] *Hansard* now explicitly adopted 'substantially verbatim' reporting. The new Chief Hansard Reporter, J. Grattan Grey, soon ran into trouble with Seddon and the government as a result of articles critical of the Liberal government which he had rashly written in his other capacity as a journalist. He was sacked in 1900.[84]

Political patronage by means of distributing 'government billets' amongst party faithful and other supplicants reached new heights under Seddon. The end of the depression, the expansion of government and the new government's distrust of the old bureaucracy offered fertile ground. Positions as parliamentary messengers and charwomen became available.[85] The many parliamentary appointments made in the late 1890s as the establishment expanded drew further accusations of patronage. Seddon's practice of giving an annual gratuity to sessional staff did nothing to calm matters.

Hansard reporters, 1896.

T.E. Taylor created a scene in the House in 1898, when he accused Seddon and the Liberals of corruption in appointments.[86] The commotion began when Taylor said to Ward, 'Oh, you miserable coward'. His words were taken down, as the inexperienced Chairman Guinness wrestled with the House in the absence of O'Rorke, before Taylor was given the opportunity to withdraw and apologise. Meanwhile Ward had threatened Taylor with worse if the words were repeated outside the chamber – Seddon feared that physical violence might erupt. Fisher launched into a virulent attack on Taylor, suggesting that his accusations were the most 'degrading and disgraceful' example he had witnessed since the days of Domett in the early 1860s. Taylor was 'a man with a muck-rake'. This caused renewed uproar and Fisher had to back down.

The most notorious example of patronage, long remembered in Parliament, was the appointment of a previous member of the House and stalwart Liberal supporter, Colonel Fraser, as the new Sergeant-at-Arms.[87] Seddon had bought him off while manipulating candidates to stand in the 1893 election. In appointing Fraser, Seddon had contravened the established process that was dependent upon the recommendation of the Speaker. The issue became a matter of confidence in the government, but Seddon managed to salvage his appointment eventually, though with some delay because it had infringed the Disqualification Act. Some argued that Seddon's wresting of control away from the Speaker had led to demoralisation and a deterioration in the management of Parliament. The 'Speaker had become disgusted and had let everything go by the run'.[88]

The emergence of party patterns in the House was reflected in greater organisation of government business and more concerted exploitation by the Opposition of opportunities to challenge the government. The private member was squeezed between the two. Stout railed at the situation in which party ruled, and Captain Russell formally protested against the House 'degenerating into a body which had merely to ratify the will of the Premier'.[89]

Around this time, the custom was for private members to be allocated Wednesday sittings and for the first six weeks of the session, Thursdays, subject to the Address-in-Reply and financial statement taking priority. Speaker Steward had ruled in 1891 that private members' business could be superseded by government business without suspending the standing orders because the traditional practice of reserving days for private members was merely customary.[90] Seddon increasingly demanded priority for his heavy legislative programme. When he needed to, he took over Wednesdays, extended sittings into Mondays, began sittings in the morning, or suspended standing orders to accelerate progress in the final weeks of the session.

Seddon also took greater control over the appointment of select committees.[91] His changes to the standing orders in 1894 (see below) gave the chairmen of select committees a vote beyond the casting vote. He also edged awkward independent Liberal members out of committees. The selection of members had always been an informal process between the parties and factions, negotiated by the whips and formalised by the tendering of lists of members of different committees by the Leader of the House (that is, the Premier). While the composition of the committees reflected the balance of power within the House, it was not intended to have a 'party' cast. With a single party and a dominant Premier, the numerically small Opposition found itself incapable of maintaining an effective presence in the House when Seddon inflated the numbers on committees.

The business of Parliament

Seddon also exploited the facility adopted in the 1880s of allowing bills to pass all the post-Committee stages after midnight in the dying weeks of the session. This was confirmed in the new standing orders of 1894.[92] By the turn of the century a tradition had been established that the government, in the last two weeks of a session, could have bills read a second time, committed, and passed on the same day. This was the precursor to moving urgency in the House, and it led to numerous late-night sittings towards the end of sessions. In 1903 the revised standing orders explicitly allowed the government to move urgency 'in the public interest' without notice or debate.[93] As business increased, the session lengthened from three to four or even five months. Seddon often did not open Parliament until after mid-year, which meant proceedings frequently threatened to extend into December.

The mid-year opening was consolidated by the timing of the financial procedures. The need to pass Imprest Supply Bills – the means by which government spending was kept going until the Appropriation Bill was passed at the end of the session – dictated the timing of the convening of Parliament. The previous year's Appropriation Act authorised expenditure only until the end of the financial year, 31 March, but by convention a further quarter of the previous year's expenditure could be spent without additional approval. This allowed governments to continue until June without Parliament coming together. It became the practice to introduce an Imprest Supply Bill every fourth Friday to keep the money flowing.

Members wanted to get home well before Christmas. The New Zealand Cup in Christchurch in early November was also an attraction. This, the most prestigious horse race in the country and a highlight of the social calendar, had become something of a target date for the close of the session. Racing was close to the hearts of many parliamentarians.[94]

Asking for returns was the traditional means of attacking a government, and the number of returns proliferated in the 1890s as the Opposition adopted more aggressive tactics. They also questioned ministers more systematically. Members had been able to question cabinet ministers from the early days, but this had not been a co-ordinated strategy.[95] A ruling in 1892 recognised the practice more formally. Time for the increasing numbers of questions prior to public business was first designated in the standing orders of 1894. Seddon responded by refusing to answer questions in the House, by allowing them to accumulate, and by opposing requests for returns. In 1903 the revised standing orders required written replies on a supplementary order paper. By 1904 provision had been made for the adjournment of business so ministers could address questions more fully. Seddon began to withhold the supplementary order paper containing replies.[96]

By the turn of the century substantial and wide-ranging debate took place when the estimates first came into the House, headed by the vote for the House of Representatives which opened the estimates debate (with the rather redundant Legislative Council vote now completely submerged in the process). The discussion would open with a general debate, to which a sitting would be allocated. Then the estimates would be worked through in detail on Fridays when, with members keen to finish for the week, there was little incentive to debate the matter of going into Committee.[97] A general debate to open the estimates was formally endorsed in 1895 by the Chairman of Committees. It became a time when the House had a 'night out'. 'Any disorder is then order; the irregular is regular … The Government has to stand against the wall and beat off, as best it can, all the political cabbages, onions, jam-tins, fish-heads, and other things that may be thrown. Anybody can say anything about anything or nothing'.[98]

The strengthening of government control in the House came up against the practice of obstruction by stonewalling. When the Opposition obstructed the second reading of the Land Bill in 1891, Ballance indicated that his government would not tolerate the delay.[99] At 2.35 a.m. the galleries were ordered cleared and reporting stopped. Reporting began again at 5.25 a.m. after a motion for adjournment had been defeated and the bill was read. The two sides then argued over the place of obstructive tactics, before the Liberals walked out en masse and the House was counted out.

The government was increasingly prepared to use what was termed the 'iron-hand', acting peremptorily the moment it felt a stonewall was emerging. Two old stonewallers, Seddon and Fish, stymied such initiatives by the Opposition. Ballance considered legislation on the matter inappropriate and a closure rule too extreme, but conceded the difficulty of changing the standing orders under the requirement that two-thirds of the House be present. One member described the rule as a 'sentinel … guarding all the Mumbo-Jumbo … before it'.[100] Agitation for reform continued. To bring matters to a head, Seddon moved that the standing orders expire next session, while the Reporting Debates and Printing Committee – the so-called 'early closing committee' – recommended a truncation of *Hansard* to limit the length of speeches.[101]

Facing a new and inexperienced House in 1894, Seddon grasped the nettle. The Governor's speech starkly stated that revision of the standing orders would take precedence over everything else – 'under the honoured name of "parliamentary privilege" has been masked in practice the discomfort, if not slavery, of a majority of your members.' The 'license of prolix speech indulged in by a few' had prevented proper debate.[102] Seddon took few chances. He tabled a comprehensively revised set of standing orders complete with running commentary for the select committee to consider.[103] Unlike Atkinson in 1888, Seddon managed to get the new standing orders through, but only by persistence and compromise and

Henry Otterson was born in Nelson in 1846 and educated at Nelson College. Appointed as a committee clerk in 1870, he became Reader in 1872, Second Clerk-Assistant in 1875 and Clerk-Assistant in 1889. When Friend died in 1898 he became Clerk of the House. He compiled the much-used Notes on Procedure in Committee of the Whole *in 1897 and updated the* Rulings of the Speakers of the House of Representatives *that had been produced by Chief Hansard Reporter Barron in 1889. Otterson was made CMG in 1913, retired in 1915, and died in 1929.*

with a supine Opposition. O'Rorke and Steward worked in tandem to forge an acceptable consensus, and the House went through the proposed standing orders with a fine toothcomb, making many revisions.

The new standing orders regulated members' speaking time for the first time. Proposals for closure (in the form of members being able to move for a vote closing debate) were in the end defeated, and a rule limiting speeches to half an hour was substituted. An hour's speech was allowed for the Address-in-Reply and financial debates and for the Appropriation Bill, and also for moving the second reading of a bill or a motion of no-confidence. The right to adjourn the House was more closely defined, and only two hours could be spent on such motions. If there were not five members supporting the motion, a division could not be taken.

Restrictions were also placed on debate on bills and supply to hasten business. Ministers could insist that the House go into Supply without debate. When in Committee, members were allowed ten minutes on each point and could speak no more than four times on each question (each clause of a bill). The Speaker or Chairman of Committees could stop members speaking for 'continued irrelevance or tedious repetition'.

The standing orders could now be suspended or changed more readily. Their suspension without notice was allowed if 40 members were present, and they could be amended with four sitting days' notice and by an absolute majority of the House. Governments could and did move the suspension of the standing order requiring an absolute majority so that amendments to the standing orders could be made conveniently. The House's power to suspend members was spelled out in detail. 'Naming' resulted in a motion for suspension without further debate, for a period of up to a week in the first instance and for longer on subsequent occasions.

Some of the old stonewalling tricks had been stymied and the ultimate weapon against a stonewall – changing the standing orders to introduce closure outright – was now easier to obtain. But opportunities for stonewalling remained, particularly with the House in Committee.[104] And, as opponents of time limits had always pointed out, setting a limit had the unfortunate effect of encouraging people to speak up to that limit, and to speak faster. One result was that the size of *Hansard* continued to grow, even though there were substantially fewer members than in the past. But Seddon had achieved his broader goal of improving the efficiency with which government business went through the House. He continued to tighten his control and extend the dominance of government business. In this quest he was supported by one 'Twelve-o'clock Brown', an anonymous but notorious Liberal member who consistently supported Seddon's desire to keep the House sitting into the small hours.[105]

The passage of legislation providing old-age pensions was instructive.[106] Spotting electoral advantage, Seddon suddenly announced plans for an old-age pension in 1896. The Opposition, aided by radical

From free-lance to disciplined private: the single party in the House, 1891–1912

Liberals, managed to cut out means testing while the bill was in Committee. A furious Seddon stormed out of the chamber, whereupon the irrepressibly cheeky Liberal member for Riccarton, G.W. 'Ricketty' Russell, occupied his seat to continue with the bill. Seddon soon returned, 'fairly foamed', and turned the interloper out, before telling an amazed House that he would withdraw the bill. In 1897 he introduced a modified bill that passed its second reading easily. But in Committee the Opposition mounted a stonewall from 19 November to 3 December by moving endless amendments.[107] In a sitting lasting 28 hours, the stonewall was broken down after a monumental 89 amendments and 945 speeches, 147 by Seddon alone. But then the bill was rejected in the Legislative Council.

Seddon, undaunted, introduced the bill once more in 1898. In Committee it was debated continuously for 90 hours, beginning on Wednesday 21 September. More than 1,400 speeches were delivered. Seddon 'slumbered peacefully with his head on a crimson cushion and his ample body covered by a large opossum-skin rug'.[108] By Saturday morning, 'The floors were dusty and strewn with torn papers, looking as though a paper chase had pursued its devious way round all the desks and ended at the Premier's chair, where a veritable snowdrift lay about his feet. The Chamber bore unmistakable signs of having been used as a dormitory during the night. Almost every bench had a Ministerial grey blanket or an Opposition or Independent rug huddled into one corner, and stray cushions had the crushed and dejected look that pillows always wear in the morning. Here and there members were still endeavouring to snatch an hour's rest … Occasional remarks [came] from the recumbent figures'.[109] When the Chairman said that members should not speak while lying down, John Hutcheson asked whether it was possible 'for a member standing to be lying'. Such a double play on 'standing' and 'lying', relying upon the traditional unimpeachable honour of members, would be used again in the future during other stonewalls.

The interminable proceedings carried on until midnight on Saturday. After a Liberal caucus meeting on Monday morning, the government rallied for another gruelling week.[110] The bill was forced through clause by clause, and by Friday the stonewall was crumbling. The following Monday night the House was counted out before the bill was even reached. The final clauses then went through more rapidly, and the bill finally passed its Committee stage on the night of Thursday 6 October. This time it passed through a Legislative Council more effectively stacked by Seddon.

The exhausting process took its toll. Roddy McKenzie snapped when another member said in jest that McKenzie was not responsible for his actions (implying that drink had got the better of him). McKenzie refused to obey Chairman of Committees Guinness, and persisted in trying to get the words taken down.[111] He refused to give way even when Speaker O'Rorke was summoned and thundered 'Sit down, sir'. When he would not apologise immediately, McKenzie was 'named' and suspended for a week under the new standing orders. Still wrathful, he handed in his resignation (which was refused by the Speaker) and began to pack his bags while his wife and others sought a compromise. As tempers subsided, Seddon agreed to rescind the suspension if McKenzie apologised.

In the early 1900s Seddon again tried to introduce closure. The House refused, and he had to back off in 1903 when it perversely reversed his efforts by attempting to remove all time restrictions instead.[112] Those with the will to do so could still mount massive obstruction because the House would not countenance the equivalent of the Commons 'guillotine', in which definite time limits were specified for the various stages of bills and other business, or the closure of debate.

The 1896–9 Parliament was the most difficult of all for Seddon and his government. The Opposition gained vitality after the election, the left-wing Liberals

The suicide of longstanding member and previous cabinet minister William Larnach on 12 October 1898 shocked parliamentarians. He obtained a revolver and shot himself in J-committee room above the Lobby after locking himself in. After some hours a search was made, the door was broken down and his body was discovered. Seddon was called from the chamber and returned in a state of shock to announce Larnach's death. The House was immediately adjourned. His biographer speculates that he had received news of an affair between his third, much younger, wife and his favourite son that had been gossipped about for years.

became a highly vocal nuisance, and there were many new members in the House.[113] A brief session in April 1897 farewelled Seddon, who was off to Britain to attend Queen Victoria's Jubilee. The main 1897 session awaited his return in late September. His colleagues went out to the Wellington Heads on the government steamer *Tutanekai* to greet him, and a huge procession marched from the wharf to the main entrance of Parliament Buildings, where the bands 'struck a concord of sweet sound, [and] the melody of "Home Sweet Home" floated through the air and all the people sang'.[114]

In spite of this gratifying welcome home, Seddon had to fight a determined rearguard action to reinstate Ward in the House. The upshot was the expulsion of the left wing from the Liberal caucus, creating a loose independent party prepared to vote against the government on motions of no-confidence.[115] The Opposition stonewalled bills in Committee trenchantly. Sittings lengthened while the number of bills passed diminished. Only Seddon and McKenzie remained effective debaters for the ministry, although both were drained by ill-health and the long hours. The session was eventually prorogued at 4.15 a.m. on 22 December with large numbers of bills dropped.

Seddon began to hold more regular caucus meetings and appeared more conciliatory during the 1898 session as his grip weakened.[116] As party discipline tightened, alienated members such as 'Tea' Taylor and George Hutchison made increasingly outrageous allegations of corruption.[117] The Opposition mounted a stonewall to force Seddon to present the Public Works statement. Seddon's

James Carroll was an important Maori politician at the turn of the century. He had gained valuable experience of parliamentary life by working as interpreter in the House from 1879 to 1883. He defeated Wi Pere for Eastern Maori in 1887. Carroll attempted to draw Maori into mainstream politics and social and economic life. True to his beliefs, he shifted to the general seat of Waiapu in 1893. Carroll became an integral part of the Liberal government, knowledgeable about procedures and a much-admired speaker. In 1892 he was appointed as a member of the Executive Council representing Maori – a position not filled since Tomoana's brief tenure in 1879 – and from 1899 to 1912 he was Minister of Native Affairs.

In the 1890s, with many Maori having given up on the Pakeha Parliament, the Kotahitanga movement held a number of Maori Parliaments (Paremata Maori) that sought to provide an alternative forum. These won support from a number of earlier members of the Pakeha Parliament, and from serving Maori members. Prominent politicians, including Carroll, visited the Maori Parliament, but Seddon remarked that it was really only a runanga. The Maori Parliament urged a boycott of the Land Court but the move failed and the Kotahitanga movement faded away. The initiative passed to Kingitanga and the Kauhanganui (the Maori King's Parliament), which was established in the early 1890s at Maungakawa, near Cambridge.

Developing a relationship between two constitutional bodies – Maori and Pakeha – became less salient for Maori members by the turn of the century. Carroll provided an alternative approach. He was the key mediator for compromise measures that Parliament was prepared to enact, although he was unable to hold the demand for land at bay. District Maori Councils were established in 1900 under Carroll's direction. Seddon successfully confronted the Maori King Mahuta over his opposition to the Councils and the Kingitanga's self-imposed isolation. Mahuta was co-opted and became a member of the Legislative Council. Carroll's place in the Liberal cabinet was recognised when he became acting Prime Minister in 1909 and 1911, and his general contribution when he was made KCMG in 1911.

grey-bearded messenger brought in a 'possum rug and a crimson pillow' for him, and blue blankets for other government members were requisitioned from government stores. Soon Opposition speeches were interspersed with the 'snores of their recumbent audience', ranging from 'a gurgle and a gasp' to one that was 'musical and melancholy' and another 'wild, weird squeal' which proved to be coming from the chamber's ventilators. The government side of the House was a 'curious spectacle' of mummy-like figures topped by hats, handkerchieves and even sheets of blotting paper.[118] At daybreak the last speaker for the Opposition, the noted orator Monk, was able to run over time as the Chairman of Committees had fallen asleep and no-one had come to relieve him. Monk warbled on about 'the sunlight outside and the birds singing and the shameful waste of good daylight'. The stonewall ended with a rare victory for the Opposition next evening when Seddon agreed to bring the statement forward.

The 1898 session was also noted for an unnecessary altercation over including a map in *Hansard*. Jock McKenzie brandished in the House a map of Hall's Hororata estate that allegedly showed gross 'gridironing', a land-purchasing practice intended to exclude other purchasers and protect the estate.[119] Other members facetiously waved their own contributions to *Hansard* or displayed them hung over desks – maps, cartoons, and even a document supposedly written in Chinese characters. When the newly appointed Hansard Supervisor declined to comply with McKenzie's demand and the Speaker said the map could go in only by order of the House, the decision to publish it in *Hansard* was rammed through after a bitter struggle and only when McKenzie threatened to resign as a minister.

Jock McKenzie, armed with pickle jars, repels assailants during the controversy over the publication of the map of Sir John Hall's estate in Hansard. *McKenzie consumed pickles for his bad breath and was know to throw the jars when angry.*

Parliament and the press

The swelling powers of the executive under Seddon were met with a growing assertiveness by the press. Journalists wanted to be able to act as independent critics of the government and use any information that came their way, without disclosing their sources.

There had always been a close association between the press and politics.[120] In the early years, politicians frequently owned newspapers and used them as political platforms. The rise of a more commercially oriented journalism from the 1860s made newspapers more independent, but they usually remained aggressive advocates for factions and policies. A more independent press took time to establish. The *Evening Post*, under Edward Gillon, represented this new style, declaring that 'it neither truckles to Labour, nor panders to Capital, and it is always ready to support right against might'.[121] This more assertive approach by journalists was accompanied by the rise of popular 'sketches' that gave shorter, entertaining and 'picturesque' descriptions of political life and politicians. Cartoons and caricatures abounded and successful satirical journals were launched.

By the mid 1880s journalists were being drawn to the press gallery, which was becoming an identifiable entity with its own officials.[122] There was a tension and symbiosis in the relationship with Parliament. The politicians needed the reporters to get their views across to the electorate, while the reporters needed the co-operation of the politicians to create the 'news'. Both sides might distrust the other, but they lived and worked alongside one another, shared their time and drank together.

Reporters had been allowed to mingle freely with parliamentarians in the buildings, but were excluded from the inner precincts such as the Lobby in the mid 1880s after an editor foolishly divulged sources.[123] Relations became strained in the 1890s. The *Evening Post* criticised Seddon's patronage in parliamentary appointments as improper, and in 1894 Gillon declined to divulge the source of a leak.[124] Instead of the Speaker, Seddon took the initiative and banned the offending reporter from Parliament. The paper sought a legal opinion from Stout, who stated that the public could not be excluded from Parliament, and the ban was lifted.

The parliamentary press gallery and reporters, 1906. The gallery included some notable figures. From left: second, Charles (C.E.) Wheeler, Auckland Star, *who worked in the gallery until 1950; seventh, Malcolm Ross,* Christchurch Press, *an eminent mountaineer, photographer and war correspondent; tenth, G.H. Scholefield,* New Zealand Times, *historian and later General Assembly Librarian; and far right, M.C. Keane,* New Zealand Times, *later editor of the* Press.

The fact that a number of members of the House were also working journalists complicated the relationship between Parliament and the press gallery.[125] Incidents began to occur in which members passed on information or gave privileged access to journalists. This was particularly the case with

From free-lance to disciplined private: the single party in the House, 1891–1912

proceedings of select committees, which since 1856 under the standing orders could not be reported until tabled in the House. In 1881 the *New Zealand Times* had obtained access to proceedings of the Native Affairs Committee before they had been tabled.[126] There was a similar incident involving a select committee in 1883, while in 1890 the Speaker specifically considered an instance to be a breach of privilege.

In the 1890s such incidents became common.[127] It was just too tempting for many members – conscious of the need to foster their electorates – to co-operate with the press. A stand was taken in 1901 when it was established that the House would act on a breach of privilege after the Dunedin *Evening Star* published evidence prematurely.[128] Albert Cohen, a 17-year veteran who was chairman of the press gallery, refused to disclose the source of his information and argued that committee proceedings should be open to the public. While the House – with journalists amongst its ranks – was ambivalent, a majority decided Cohen should be fined £15. The *Star* and other newspapers ridiculed the decision and exhorted Parliament to follow Britain's example by opening up its committee proceedings. Instead the House became more determined, and when the *New Zealand Times* transgressed in 1903, Seddon thundered that 'the people were the masters of Parliament, not the Press'.[129] Emil Schwabe, the likely culprit (and a later chairman of the press gallery), was fined £15 and the newspaper £25. The Privileges Committee recommended that future offenders lose their access to the press gallery and be fined £100.

Ward took a softer line on becoming Prime Minister after Seddon's death in 1906.[130] The standing orders were revised so that committees could open proceedings to accredited reporters, while retaining the right to keep them confidential. The new standing order also clarified that the Speaker could exclude reporters from the gallery. Occasional breaches still occurred, but the House refrained from draconian action. Such trangressions were formally made breaches of privilege under standing orders in 1929.

Some members of the House, dissatisfied that diligent but perhaps boring members were seldom reported, while the utterances of the 'big men' and sensational or trivial episodes were covered, complained that 'Year after year the members of the Press of this colony have thought fit … to lampoon and deride members of this House. If you want to be magnified in the esteem of a member of the Press in this colony you must get drunk, and you must take off your boots in Parliament and put them on your desk.'[131] At this affront to their dignity the reporters in the gallery walked out, but this was not the last time they would hear this refrain.

The press gallery became a training ground for a cohesive cadre of top journalists.[132] The gallery was the country's prime reporting institution, and its occupants were the cream of political journalists, many of whom went on to edit major newspapers or otherwise distinguish themselves in journalism or politics.

Women began reporting Parliament from the ladies' gallery in the 1880s. In 1884 Laura Suisted, who was probably the first, wrote a column for the *Otago Witness* – 'Jottings from the seat of government' – under the pseudonym 'Scribbler'.[133] The 1890s saw the entry of a number of vigorous female journalists who wrote irreverent sketches of parliamentary life as the suffrage movement blossomed. Forrest Ross at that time went under the pen-name of 'Pamela'. Her columns in the *Press* were called 'Peeps at Parliament'. There was also 'Birds'-Eye' of the *New Zealand Graphic*. These women injected an amusingly wry, fresh, human dimension into their descriptions of life in the House. Their reports were written from the point of view of the cultured, politically aware woman of the 1890s.

The masthead for 'Birds'-Eye', a female parliamentary reporter.

NZ Graphic, 26 August 1893

'Birds'-Eye' asked whether it was 'the charming variety of the specimens sprawling over the cushioned benches below us which constitutes the attraction?' She continued: 'here we have them, old and young, bald and hairy, married and single, tall and short, long and broad, big and little, great and small, plain and cultured, loud men and gentlemen', and concluded that 'in short, there are seventy four varieties, and I'm tired of enumerating.'[134]

In 1898, some women attempted to gain entry to the press gallery itself.[135] One of them, Stella Henderson, was a brilliant law graduate, suffragist and founding member of the National Council of Women. The editor of the *Lyttelton Times* asked the Chairman of the press gallery to arrange for her to take the newspaper's seat, but the gallery voted against this.

The Houses of Parliament

Seddon interfered in the routine administration of Parliament Buildings and made improvements to the buildings and grounds to provide a more impressive backdrop to the triumphs of the Liberal government.[136] In 1893 there was substantial relandscaping of the grounds and the general appearance of the Houses of Parliament was tidied up. A new main entrance with double wrought-iron gates and stone pillars was placed on the corner of Molesworth and Sydney Streets. A carriage drive swept up the slope to the front of the buildings. During the recess of 1893–4, the remaining gas lighting was replaced by electric lights. The power came initially from generating equipment installed in a cellar, then from Wellington's general supply.[137] The grounds were lit by a powerful electric arc light on a pole in the middle of the lawn. One young lady was heard to remark on the changes: 'You know, dear, it is more up-to-date, now; of course, one misses the old trees, but the place did have an early settlement look about it with that narrow path, and the little pokey gates'.[138] From this time on the grounds were used for public events, such as the commemoration of the death of Queen Victoria, farewelling the troops for the South African War, and the declaration of New Zealand as a Dominion in 1907. In 1901, two guns captured in the South African war were placed on either side of Parliament's main steps.[139]

Seddon's upgrading of the buildings continued with substantial renovation of the interior, which had been neglected during the depression years.[140] In the early 1890s he plunged heroically – but unsuccessfully – into the seemingly intractable ventilation problem. Large electric fans, a huge cavity underneath the chamber to introduce fresh air, bunsen burners in the ceiling ventilators to create a more effective draught through large exhaust tubes in the roof – nothing seemed to work. In 1900 both chambers and the old section of the buildings were renovated, and the old library section was altered to form committee rooms.[141] From 1902, an 'officer in charge' supervised a team of custodians, a gardener, two nightwatchmen, Bellamy's staff and the charwomen.

Stella Henderson was employed by the Lyttelton Times *in the 1890s to report on Parliament, but was excluded from the press gallery. After protests from newspapers and a petition to Parliament, she was given a cubicle in the ladies' gallery. Henderson wrote her articles in the ladies' tearoom. Robin Hyde, a parliamentary reporter in the 1920s, described this cubicle as an uncomfortable and narrow bench.*

Canterbury Museum, 12945

Tyree collection, ATL, G11625½

The Houses of Parliament from Molesworth Street after the re-landscaping of the grounds, mid 1890s. The newly installed electric arc light takes pride of place on the lawn.

Parliament's efforts to build a new library, which had dragged on for many years, continued. Fire remained a serious threat.[142] By the 1890s, the library was overflowing, even though two further rooms in the decaying old northern wing had been commandeered – one a 'miserable den' and the other 'old worm-eaten rain-stained'.[143] Books had to be stored in two ministers' rooms, the ladies' tearoom and two committee rooms, and the shelf classification could no longer be kept up. The librarian, James, at last completed his magnum opus, a new general catalogue, in 1897.

In the same year Seddon suddenly announced that a new library would be constructed. A noted Wellington architect, Thomas Turnbull, was commissioned to produce designs.[144] His initial Gothic Revival design, including a tower and an ornate frontage, was considered too expensive, and a second, simpler design was accepted. This was for an iron-framed, three-storey structure with a brick exterior, tessellated terracotta-block floors and moulded plaster detailing that sought to evoke the Westminster Houses of Parliament. The design included a vastly improved library section, with special rooms for storing valuable items, a stackroom, newspaper and periodical room, writing room and separate reference library. The other half of the building would accommodate the Premier, cabinet ministers and select committees.

Seddon saw political advantage in building the new library, and moved fast during the recess.[145] Workmen pulled down sections of the old buildings and excavated the new foundations, and tenders were called. But then the building became embroiled in political controversy during a Wellington by-election. Allegations of extravagance and patronage were made. Seddon had to admit to acting precipitately, but because part of the existing buildings had already been pulled down, the government was committed to the new building even though the tenders were embarrassingly high. Members arrived back in Wellington for the next session to discover that the old structure had been pulled down and a new one was going up.

The new General Assembly Library provides a much more impressive main entrance to the Parliament Buildings, 1901. Ballance's statue (left) has been placed in a prominent position.

Under pressure, the government conceded that the design would have to be severely truncated. The third storey, the new section of offices, and the embellishment and ornamental work were removed. Only the library and the portico entrance section (housing the Premier's office, cabinet room and some committee rooms) would remain. John Campbell of the Public Works Department redesigned the building as two storeys that blended well with Turnbull's 1880s masonry extension behind it, if less well with the wooden structure alongside.

Parliament's joint Library Committee and Turnbull, protested vehemently at the changes, but to no avail.[146] The building went up rapidly and was finished just as the 1899 session began. The library section had fire walls separating it from the main entrance section, and an iron fire door closed off the main library entrance from the vestibule. Turnbull asked for his name to be removed from the commemorative tablet. The Wellington member Duthie said it would be a 'great libel' if Turnbull was considered responsible for the 'deformity about to be erected'.[147]

The new library, if somewhat less magnificent than originally conceived, still capped off the more impressive Houses of Parliament that reflected the enlarged role that Seddon had created for the Liberal government. For the first time the library's 40,000 volumes were comprehensively classified (according to the Dewey system).[148] A proper librarian befitting the new quarters had now to be appointed.

From free-lance to disciplined private: the single party in the House, 1891–1912

THE GENERAL ASSEMBLY LIBRARY

Jeremy Garvitch collection, ATL, F89362½

The Reading Room of the General Assembly Library. At front is a pedestal displaying the pen used by Prime Minister Massey to sign the Peace Treaty at Versailles in 1919. After the war, captured enemy flags were hung in the library.

Parliamentary Service collection

The fiction section of the General Assembly Library, with tables for members to attend to correspondence. A copy of the New Zealand Times lies on the back of chair, and on the table there are nib and quill pens in a rack, inkwells, a weighing machine for items to be posted, and stationery. Members made good use of these facilities. As the demands of constituents increased, they began to agitate for clerical assistance. While a few wealthier members were able to employ shorthand typists, most had to club together to employ clerical assistance at their own cost, or continued to hand-write their letters.

Seddonian patronage prevailed over the Legislative Council and the joint Library Committee, which wanted the appointment to be made from Britain.[149] Charles Wilson, a just-retired Liberal member and familiar figure around Parliament, was appointed.[150] He had been a journalist and newspaper editor, and had a substantial private library and a strong interest in literature. James remained as assistant librarian until 1923.

The library was beginning to provide a research facility, having built up an extensive historical collection of bound newspapers and periodicals. Parliament agreed to establish a manuscript and printed collection concerning 'the early history of the colony' that would include paintings and photographs as well as documents. It began to collate and index members' speeches – an activity facetiously termed the 'Paste-master-General's Department'.[151] In 1888 librarian Collier had suggested that copyright legislation be enacted, requiring deposit of all publications in the General Assembly Library.[152] The General Assembly Library Bill was passed in 1903. The Act required that two copies of all publications be deposited in the library, to constitute it as a 'national library'. As a result, Wilson was able to expand the New Zealand holdings tremendously and create a protected New Zealand collection. The library's collections and its use continued to grow as it attempted to cater to the growing interest of members in fiction. The range of outside people using the library was wide, which was understandable given its reputation and the lack of other good collections in Wellington.

Party developments

The Opposition appeared to have gained new strength in 1899, when the Liberals' ranks were divided and cabinet was weak. On two no-confidence motions, a number of left-wing Liberals voted with the Opposition. By the end of the session the government's effective majority had been whittled down to no more than a few. Still, the Opposition found it difficult to organise itself as a party. Charles Lewis, the Opposition whip, spoke of the need to marshal the troops to be constantly in the chamber. He found it hard to mount stonewalls with fewer than 20 members available. 'Night after night I had seen men going down. Every afternoon revealed an empty seat, and finally I had to lie up myself under an attack of influenza.'[153] Then as now, 'most of the real work is done in the Lobby, and the Whip's Rooms.' The Opposition succeeded in defeating the Workers' Compensation for Accidents Bill in Committee when Seddon's arm-twisting failed.[154] Seddon, searching for support among the Maori members, introduced a Maori Lands Administration Bill, but this, too, was defeated.

However, New Zealand's involvement in the South African War made it difficult to attack the government. When Seddon moved in the House on 28 September 1899 that a contingent of mounted rifles be offered to Britain, Captain Russell seconded the motion and it was passed overwhelmingly. 'A stirring scene followed. Led by Mr. Seddon, the members almost spontaneously rose and sang the National Anthem with great enthusiasm. The onlookers in the galleries rose at the same time, and joined in the hymn. Hardly had the last notes died away when Mr. Seddon raised his hand and asked for a true British cheer, which was given with the utmost heartiness.'[155]

Seddon worked to rid himself of meddlesome independents at the 1899 election, with some success, obtaining a substantially increased majority and a general endorsement of his policies. The Opposition, reduced again to a rump of less than 20, lapsed into impotent passivity.[156] Seddon readmitted Ward to cabinet. Ward returned to Wellington in triumph and promptly moved into the vacant Premier House, which once again became the centre of Wellington's social scene, as it had been in the time of Vogel, rivalling Seddon's residence on Molesworth Street.[157]

With the Opposition bereft and the left wing vanquished, conflict was largely found within the mainstream of the Liberal Party itself. Discontent over cabinet positions erupted into serious confrontation during the session of 1900 when, following the retirement of McKenzie, Seddon replaced him as Minister of Lands with a nonentity, T.Y. Duncan.[158] There was mayhem over a bill increasing

Public ceremonies increasingly took place at Parliament as the Liberals capitalised on their popular support. For this memorial service for Queen Victoria on 2 February 1901, the buildings were draped in black crepe.

ministers' salaries. After a sizeable dissident Liberal faction defied Seddon and the caucus, the Premier had to produce a modified version of the bill.[159] The same faction sought to alter the government's tariff proposals. Speaker O'Rorke began to exert pressure on Seddon to increase the number of permanent officers of the House and to improve the salaries that had been cut in the late 1880s. The confrontation between the two led to a division, narrowly lost, which sought to force Seddon to implement the Speaker's recommendations. The session was marked by the 'naming' and suspension of dissident left-wing Liberal, Fred Pirani, when he refused to withdraw an allegation that Roddy McKenzie had repeated a 'slander' circulated by Seddon.

A similarly fluid situation pertained during the session of 1901. A return to factionalism threatened, and Seddon came under great pressure to reform his cabinet. Organising a consensus through caucus no longer seemed to work; Seddon had to resort to more traditional techniques of personal negotiation. The year was notable for the death of Queen Victoria in January, and the visit to New Zealand of the Duke and Duchess of Cornwall and York. This included a reception at Parliament on 19 June, not long before the session opened.

The Opposition reached its nadir when it failed to muster any speakers for the Address-in-Reply at the opening of the 1902 session, then allowed the financial statement through with minimal resistance. It offered little opposition to bills and went into the election of 1902 without a leader.[160] Throughout

1902 Seddon still refused to consider reconstruction of his ministry. Matters drifted and the lines of difference between political groupings became increasingly blurred. With O'Rorke absent due to ill health for most of the session, Guinness took his place as Speaker.[161]

The election of 1902 (for which the number of general electorates was increased from 70 to 76, the number at which the House remained until 1969) was notable only for O'Rorke losing his seat. The longest serving and most acclaimed Speaker finally departed from the House. Surprisingly, the inert Opposition made moderate gains, leading Seddon to consider introducing a two-ballot system.

By now the Opposition, so long focused on criticising Seddonian 'autocracy' and corruption, was beginning to develop an alternative platform based on freehold tenure, an independent civil service and an elected Legislative Council (to prevent it continuing as Seddon's tame pet).[162] Adoption of the freehold would prove crucial in splitting the Liberals and cementing an alliance between the Opposition and the Farmers' Union.

With a reconstruction of cabinet in the wind, R. McNab refused an offer of the Speakership, and J.A. Millar refused the position of Chairman of Committees.[163] Cabinet remained unchanged, however, and Guinness was elected Speaker unopposed (even though Major Steward remained in the House). Guinness would follow in O'Rorke's footsteps, vigorously defending the privileges of the House and maintaining a scrupulous impartiality.[164] The ambitious Millar reluctantly accepted the position of Chairman of Committees.

Massey emerged as the Opposition's leader by taking the leading role in the Address-in-Reply debate in 1903.[165] He had proved a hard worker and effective organiser, though still a poor debater. Massey was aided by James Allen on financial questions, W.H. Herries on stonewalling and standing orders, and the hard-working but 'silent member' C.A.C. Hardy as chief whip. Hardy was assisted by another 'silent member', the gentlemanly, well-dressed Canterbury landowner Heaton Rhodes.[166]

Massey was determined to introduce a disciplined approach to the Opposition. He refused, for example, to commit the party to an irresponsible no-confidence motion over supply moved by a dissident Opposition backbencher. Duthie observed that a 'vote of want of confidence is no light matter, and it is ... beyond what is prudent ... without consultation with others'.[167] Massey attacked the Liberals on their inability to sort out the land question, and with the aid of disaffected left-wing Liberals began to win divisions. Massey's Opposition had begun to steal the Liberals' clothes, 'not only the coat, vest, trousers, and shirt ... but they have also appropriated the studs and buttons', grumbled Carroll.[168] Massey's strategy was to learn from the Liberal enemy.

Seddon continued to dangle cabinet positions in front of potential contenders, but stuck with ministers who posed little threat to him. In 1905 several discontented factions emerged for a time. The session was dominated by the so-

Arthur Robert Guinness was born in Calcutta on 11 January 1846, arrived in New Zealand in 1852 and worked as a lawyer in Greymouth. Elected for Grey in 1884, he was a strong Liberal supporter. Guinness became Chairman of Committees in 1893 and was Speaker from 1903 until his death on 10 June 1913. Knighted in 1911, he was the second-longest-serving Speaker (after O'Rorke). Active in advancing the interests of his constituents when the House was in Committee, he was nevertheless an impartial Speaker. He was noted for his dignity, courtesy and attention to detail. He also introduced the full-bottomed wig to the Speakership. His funeral was one of the largest ever on the West Coast.

called 'voucher' incident, in which F.M.B. Fisher accused the Premier of corruption, believing that Seddon's eldest son, Captain Richard Seddon, had received an unauthorised payment.[169] The House was transfixed and the galleries were packed. Seddon reportedly got out his handkerchief to dry his eyes before sending for his son. The pair consulted in whispers as everyone looked on with bated breath. The charges proved a political blunder, as the person in question proved to be one 'Richard Sneddon'. Amendments had to be systematically inserted in the existing *Hansard* record at each instance of Fisher's allegations.

From Seddon to Ward

The 1905 election was a triumph for Seddon in spite of the rejuvenated Opposition. He wrote that he was 'firmer in the saddle now than ever … with only a few new members (or in other words "young colts") to break in, the duties of the whips and the driving of the coachman will not entail much anxiety.'[170] But his triumph was shortlived. While returning exhausted from a visit to Australia, he died of heart failure. His death resulted in an outpouring of public grief never witnessed before in New Zealand politics. Parliament became a scene of mourning. It was hastily called on 27 June 1906 for a brief session, to lament the loss of Seddon and to vote supply before going into recess to await Ward's return from Europe.

Ward became Prime Minister on his arrival.[171] With the larger majority inherited from the 1905 election, the problem of discipline in the party had worsened. Ward's efforts to include the left wing in his cabinet only compounded the problem. The vacant post of Chairman of Committees went to Roderick McKenzie after he failed to make cabinet. The long-serving Major Steward was embarrassingly rejected in a vote. T.E.Y. (Tom) Seddon, who had been elected in place of his father, made his maiden address in moving the Address-in-Reply. Clad in the traditional evening dress with white tie and tails, he was extremely nervous at stepping into his father's shoes.[172]

Ward's professed consensual style of government meant in reality immobility. Disputes over land policy were to disrupt Parliament as Ward failed to deal effectively with the leasehold/freehold divide. The session of 1907, from 27 June to 25 November, was the longest since 1903 as the institution began to settle into a pattern of full half-year sittings. Confused voting patterns on Ward's tariff proposals suggested there was not much distinction between the Liberal and Reform parties, and vague notions of coalition or realignment floated about.[173] Ward threatened to dissolve Parliament and managed to keep the government together. To general surprise the noted independent and government critic, Thomas Mackenzie, declared his support for Ward.

Ward did not drive the House in the fashion that Seddon had done.[174] The government stuck closely to the order paper, did not sit late into the night, and introduced Monday evening sittings earlier in the session to get through business. Ward's less demanding approach had the unfortunate effect of lengthening sessions unduly, without getting through the amount of legislation passed in earlier years.

New Zealand's new status was celebrated on Dominion Day, 26 September 1907, with proclamations read on the front steps of Parliament and a vice-regal

Joseph Ward, elected for Awarua in 1887, made an immediate impact with his engaging manner, dress sense, and rapid speech. He became a Liberal cabinet minister, but had to resign from cabinet and then the House as his businesses collapsed and he became bankrupt in 1897. He soon returned to the House and became Prime Minister on Seddon's death in 1906. After resigning in 1912 he joined a coalition with Reform during the First World War. Ward lost his seat in 1919 but returned to the House in 1925 and miraculously became Prime Minister leading the United government in 1928. In failing health, he resigned in 1930 shortly before his death.

The Governor arrives for the last opening of Parliament before the buildings were consumed by fire, 1907.

Ward takes his place on the government benches as Prime Minister of the reconstituted Liberal ministry, 1906–7. The mace donated by Clifford in 1866 lies on the Table.

luncheon for members. Little did they know that this would be the last time that the Gothic buildings were the backdrop for a public occasion. Fire was an omnipresent fear for those working in the increasingly tinder-dry wooden Houses of Parliament. This fear had motivated the construction of the new library and prompted the planning of other new structures in masonry. Down the years a number of fires in the old buildings had exposed Wellington's limited capacity to deal with a serious outbreak.

The devastating fire that began early on 11 December 1907 was believed to have been caused by a short in the electric wiring in the ceiling of the interpreters' room.[175] The nightwatchman had checked the buildings at 2 a.m. before returning to his office to make a cup of cocoa. He heard what sounded like rain on the roof but proved to be an already substantial blaze. He sounded the alarm, opened the gates for the fire brigade and returned to attack the fire with a hose. The fire spread quickly through the old wooden parts of the buildings, including the two chambers, moving through the ceilings and roofs. By 3 a.m. it had broken through the south face but had not yet consumed the Legislative Council chambers nor crossed the Lobby to the rest of the 1883 masonry additions. As people salvaged whatever they could, the lawn began to look like a fairground, with crowds of spectators and 'chairs, fenders, papers, bureaux, and thousands of books'. Crowds also gathered on Sydney and Hill Streets. By 4 a.m. it was clear that the old wooden structure was doomed. It had been assumed that the new library and the masonry additions were safe, but fire now threatened Bellamy's and the main entrance portico section of the library building. By 5 a.m. Bellamy's had gone and firemen were battling desperately to save the portico section.

In daylight the full scale of the devastation was apparent. The library had been saved by its fire walls and fire door, but the rest of the buildings had been destroyed. Of the wooden sections only 'a couple of gaunt chimneys pointed their ugliness against an ashen sky, and thin wisps of the pungent blue smoke of smouldering wood smarted the eyes of people who stood to gaze at the remnant of the Parliamentary Buildings'.[176] The 1880s extensions had been gutted internally, the roof had collapsed, and the mortar in the walls had been weakened by the heat. There was also substantial damage to the main entrance portico section. Fortunately, the session was over and many papers had been shifted out, but the mace, lying forgotten in a cupboard, had been consumed.[177]

Parliamentarians were stunned and the country felt the loss keenly.[178] The buildings, prominently placed on the hill, were a familiar sight and had been home to a vast number of politicians, officials and journalists. Many of the country's treasured historical possessions had been displayed within it.

Crowds watch from Sydney Street (East) as Parliament Buildings are destroyed by fire on the morning of 11 December 1907.

The 1908 session opened in Government House across Sydney Street, hurriedly commandeered from a disgruntled Governor who hoped that the inconvenience would be temporary.[179] The House met in the ballroom, which was extended into one of the drawing rooms, while the Council occupied the conservatory that had been used as a billiard room. A covered elevated footbridge – christened acerbically by Massey 'The Twopenny tube' – was rapidly thrown up over the Sydney Street gully to provide a link to the surviving library building.

Conditions in the temporary chamber were cramped and uncomfortable. The members sat on chairs arranged in rows, and it was extremely difficult to find room for Hansard, the press or the public. Many had to be put on the floor of the House. Members of the public were to be found in the lobbies, and on one occasion several got locked in when a division was taken. Members' wives were arrayed along the windowed wall of the verandah, sufficiently close to their husbands to 'tap [them] on the shoulder and tell [them] to come straight home and not dally in Bellamy's'.[180] Members were tempted to wander and sit next to women 'for a little chat as a diversion from political labours'.

The House

Following the session, the 'ballroom' chamber was extended further by taking in the verandah, and proper seats and miniature desks were hurriedly installed, with the seating rearranged in a horseshoe. Parliament remained in these motley premises for the next ten years as the rebuilding was debated and then the new buildings slowly went up.

The 1908 session opened without the usual ceremony because of the lack of room outside the porch of Government House.[181] The major initiative was amended arbitration legislation strengthening the provisions against strikes. This was passed against a background of industrial strife that highlighted the growing gulf between the Liberals and sections of the labour movement. The government also passed the Second Ballot Act, designed to solve problems caused by split Liberal voting.

Ward now declared that there should be a 'legislative holiday'; in his view, most necessary reforms had been achieved. The election at the end of 1908 strengthened Massey's Opposition. The second ballot seemed to encourage the very disunity among Liberals that it was designed to minimise. In the cities, labour unrest was reflected in the appearance for the first time of a number of 'Labour' candidates. David McLaren became the first Labour member in the House. Belonging to the Political Labour League, which wanted an independent 'Labour Party', he occupied a lonely, awkward position in the House, oppressed by a sense of responsibility and preferring 'the battering ram to the rapier'.[182]

A ladies' gallery ticket for the 1915 session. Such tickets were highly prized, particularly in the years the House sat in the cramped temporary chamber in Government House.

A lonely Ward faces the Table of the House in the ballroom of Government House at the beginning of the session in the temporary premises.

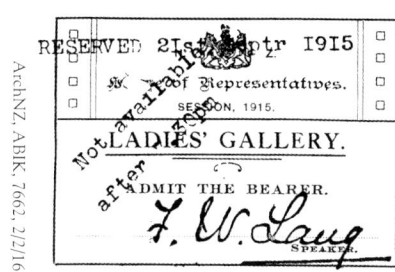

Ward reshuffled his cabinet. Thomas Mackenzie's astonishing elevation to cabinet so soon after deserting the Opposition, and Ngata's rapid promotion, fuelled disatisfaction.[183] Prior to the session, Speaker Guinness, by now one of the longest-serving members, made an extraordinary speech condemning Ward and warning that he was looking forward to a 'jolly good row' in Parliament.[184] He had to apologise, as for a time his re-election as Speaker 'hung in the balance'.

Ward attempted to galvanise public opinion by offering out of the blue to pay for Britain to build a 'Dreadnought' battleship. He made plans to visit Britain again, for an Imperial Conference. Intending

From free-lance to disciplined private: the single party in the House, 1891–1912

David McLaren, elected for Wellington East in 1908, was the first labour representative in the House outside the Liberal Party. Having organised the waterside workers, he was elected to the Wellington City Council in 1901 and was Mayor of Wellington in 1912–13. He lost his seat in the House in 1911, but other members representing labour – A.H. Hindmarsh, W.A. Veitch, J. Robertson and John Payne – were elected that year.

to call Parliament early for a brief session, he encountered a technical hitch because it was prorogued until 10 June 1909.[185] Ward had to gather members informally a few days earlier to approve the Dreadnought offer and his trip to Britain.

Parliament met formally on the due date for a session of only a week so that Ward could slip off to Britain. With Roderick McKenzie entering cabinet, the position of Chairman of Committees was again vacant.[186] Ward knew that the permanent fixture Major Steward was waiting in the wings and pleaded for unanimous support for his candidate, T.M. Wilford. However, he undermined his case by asserting that 'the majority must rule', and Wilford had unwisely canvassed actively for the job. Massey insisted on a division. Wilford was confirmed on condition that he refused payment for the position until the next session.

Ward was forced to sack the exuberant and loose-tongued Hogg from cabinet after he unwisely demanded radical land reforms.[187] At first his speech had sent the House into fits of laughter over his mispronounciation of French from a hotel menu, but when it turned serious one minister after another left the chamber until only an angry Ward was left on the front benches. There were wild scenes in the lobby afterwards as Hogg was roundly denounced. The rejuvenated Opposition under Massey, recognising the need to become a formal party, now adopted the title 'Reform Party'. It argued that it could administer the state better and more efficiently – without corruption, patronage or faddish radical left-wing elements – and began to campaign for the reform of the civil service. The House divided on stronger 'party' lines than it had done for a long time as a renewed spirit of bitterness entered politics.

While in Britain in 1909, Ward arranged for the purchase of a new gilt mace, more elaborate than the original and modelled on that of the House of Commons.[188] On his return, Parliament was convened in early October for a session that unexpectedly ran through until after Christmas. Everything was rushed. The House had to await the government's programme until well into the session.[189] Major Steward, as the oldest member and a past Speaker, was given the honour of formally moving acceptance of the new mace, which is still in use today.

Disintegration of the Liberals

Ward began to lose control over his party in a House which now had a majority of freehold supporters. The leasehold minority provided organised opposition both inside and outside Parliament to Ward's proposals for land tenure.[190] A concerted stonewall led by T.E. Taylor in early December obstructed other government business. Ward threatened to resign after this co-ordinated disruption. Party lines were reasserted after he announced the postponement of the Land Bill.

Members became disgruntled at spending long hours in the cramped, hot ballroom, with the blinds down and large numbers asleep on the benches.[191] The farming members were seriously inconvenienced as the session stretched into summer because of Ward's overseas jaunt. Half of the House had gone home for

Sergeant-at-Arms Major T.V. Shepherd with the new mace, c. 1909. Sergeants-at-Arms were often retired military officers. They wore a black evening suit, white shirt, white bow tie, medals and a black top hat on ceremonial occasions.

Christmas, but Ward still had the budget to deal with and the House sat until 11.55 p.m. on Christmas Eve. Massey skilfully kept a stonewall going – it was described as 'obstruction run mad' – for more than a week. He threatened division after division on a pound-by-pound reduction of £400 on the supplementary estimates that was estimated to require 15 miles of traipsing backwards and forward to the lobbies. Herries warned 'that if they did not [report progress] the turkey, roast beef, and champagne would have to be laid on the tables of the House – and ordered to be printed.'[192] The House had to be recalled for a 'one-day' sitting on 28 December. The sitting in fact lasted several days. Massey finally relented when Ward capitulated and said that the estimates would be reviewed next session. Members were able to go home when Parliament was prorogued close to midnight just before the New Year.

Ward proposed a compromise Land Bill in the session of 1910, but this only compounded the conflict between leaseholders and freeholders and had to be dropped ignominiously. When Wilford resigned as Chairman of Committees, Ward put forward James Colvin over protest from Major

THE 'PARLIAMENT SPECIAL'

Premier Ward's wife is presented with a posy as she and parliamentarians arrive at Taumarunui on the 'Parliament Special'. The government offered F.W. Furkert, the engineer in charge of the North Island main trunk railway, £1,000 to complete the link in time for the parliamentary party to travel to Auckland by rail in August 1908 to greet the American 'Great White Fleet', which was on a world tour. The Public Works Department laboured desperately, taking many shortcuts. The lines from north and south were joined just in time to allow the train to travel north.

Parliamentarians assembled in front of the 'Parliament Special'. Travel around the country had improved markedly since the early days of sittings in Auckland. From the mid 1890s a scheduled inter-island ferry service connected with rail services in both islands. The Union Steam Ship Company was prepared to delay vessels to suit governments, and even at times to waive fares. North Island members had used rail for some time to get to Wellington, but this could be complicated before the completion of the main trunk. Frederic Lang caught the train from Wellington to New Plymouth, travelled by coastal steamer to Onehunga, then another train into the Waikato on Saturday mornings.

From free-lance to disciplined private: the single party in the House, 1891–1912

Steward.[193] The issue was made a party matter, and Steward was forced to step aside. He died late in 1912, shortly after being appointed to the Legislative Council. As Bell said, this left a 'real void' in 'parliamentary association'. Since first entering the House in 1871, Steward had become an institution in his own right, even though constantly passed over for higher office.[194] The eulogies were many and heartfelt. The House adjourned until the evening as a mark of respect, and both Houses adjourned at the opening of the 1913 session to acknowledge his passing.

Ward tended to become the captive of pressure groups.[195] In response to an anti-gambling delegation, he allowed the issue to be discussed on the basis of a conscience vote, and bookmaking was made illegal. In response to prohibitionists, he suggested relaxing the criteria for referenda, causing much conflict within the Liberal Party and ferment in the lobbies. The measure was thrown out, but not before barmaids were effectively banned from bars and the local licensing option was introduced. The session, at close to 100 sitting days, proved the longest on record, and there was much fractiousness, with interjections becoming a problem.[196] Ward, exasperated by the Opposition's effective obstructive tactics, introduced Monday sittings and talked about introducing closure.

Members on board ship wearing lava-lavas during a visit to the Cook and other Pacific Islands in 1903. One of Seddon's ambitions was to extend New Zealand's influence in the Pacific, and in 1901 the Cook Islands and Niue were annexed. New Zealand's Parliament decided to survey its new possessions, and an extended visit on the steamer Mapourika *was made in April and May 1903. Thirty-three parliamentarians, plus senior officials and photographers went on the trip. They also visited Fiji, Tonga, Samoa and Tahiti.*

Substantial new political developments were taking place outside the House.[197] Labour asserted its independent and increasingly radical presence through the 'Red' Federation of Labour, while farmers pushed strongly for the freehold and were increasingly disconcerted by the government's inability to control industrial relations. Ward left for a six-month trip to Britain, including an Imperial Conference and the launching of the Dreadnought, leaving Carroll as Acting Prime Minister.

The 1911 session – intended to be a short one following the previous year's record-breaker – began late, towards the end of July, but under Carroll's benign eye little was achieved in the following month. The House came alive when Ward returned and presented a generous pre-election budget, and by the end of the session it was proceeding under 'urgency' in order to complete business by the end of October, in readiness for the election.

The election of 1911 resulted in a deadlock between the two major parties. There were four new Labour members and a similar number of professed independents whose allegiances were uncertain, although the independents had reportedly pledged support to Ward. Parliament had not seen the like since the 1880s. Frantic behind-the-scenes negotiations began. Ward tried to delay the session until June 1912, but the Governor, Lord Islington, protested and he had to call Parliament for mid February.[198] Islington pointed out that such delay was unconstitutional when the parties were so finely balanced; he warned that he might be forced to take action, since the government did not appear to 'possess the confidence of the country'.

Parliamentarians admire a motor car, c. 1905. Members witnessed the arrival of the first cars in New Zealand in 1898. William McLean promoted a private member's bill that year after he was prevented from driving his vehicles on Wellington's roads. He demonstrated the car to members in Parliament grounds, providing light relief towards the end of an arduous session.

Reform prepared for office.[199] As the House debated the no-confidence motion – for the first time in many years proposed as an amendment to the Address-in-Reply – Ward attempted to head off defeat by announcing that if the government won, he would no longer head it. He had also concocted several bizarre enticements to Labour. The Speaker had great difficulty maintaining order during a week of bitter debate and desperate manoeuvering. Three of the four Labour members finally declared their support for the government, and the votes of independents Harry Atmore and J.G. (Gordon) Coates now held the balance.[200]

From free-lance to disciplined private: the single party in the House, 1891–1912

The long-awaited confrontation finally arrived. As the Liberal Tom Seddon remembered: 'The galleries were packed. Members' wives, sitting near the seats of members, brushed aside messengers or even members who obstructed their view. All eyes were on Mr. Atmore and Mr. Coates. The Division Bells stopped ringing. Slowly members entered the "Ayes" and "Noes" lobbies and still Mr. Atmore and Mr. Coates had not stirred. At last they rose, stretched themselves as if they were rousing themselves from a slight slumber and then, to our relief and to the Opposition's chagrin, they entered with us into the "noes" lobby.'[201] The government survived on the casting vote of Speaker Guinness, who broke a tie by declaring for the traditional principle of voting for the status quo. This precedent became the anchor point for affirming the Speaker's casting vote from then on.

The shocked Massey could not believe that some chicanery had not taken place, while the excitement of the government knew no bounds. 'The Government Whip's room saw over-joyous Liberal members abandoning themselves to a celebration. Exulting members mounted chairs and delivered themselves of their feelings in speeches. Emotion overwhelmed the Liberal members like that which seized loyal citizens when Mafeking was relieved.'[202] The government gained some breathing space by adjourning the short session. In March Thomas Mackenzie was surprisingly elected as the new leader, with the front-runner Millar having been rejected by Labour as a turncoat. The aggrieved Millar and Roderick McKenzie walked out of the caucus meeting.[203]

When Parliament reassembled on 27 June, it became apparent that Massey was simply waiting for the inevitable. Mackenzie did not dare summon his caucus for fear of instant disintegration. He ignored the new manifesto trumpeted in the Speech from the Throne – as well as the new radical members of his cabinet – by urging a 'political rest'. After moving the inevitable motion of no-confidence during the Address-in-Reply debate, Massey refused to put up any speakers. His well-drilled party 'faithfully played the Sphinx' and the government desperately adjourned early as no speakers could be found. Finally, Massey called for a division over an adjournment. The government frantically tried to prolong debate while its forces were mustered.

When the no-confidence vote finally came in the early hours of Saturday 6 July, Reform won by 41 to 33.[204] All four Labour members voted for the government, but a number of independents including Coates and five disaffected Liberals crossed the floor. The most dramatic switch was that of Millar, who had lain in bed in the buildings for three days waiting for the moment. He now made a dramatic entrance in a dressing gown and pyjamas, a bent figure with the side of his face twisted by partial paralysis. As he made his way, a minister shouted 'Traitor' at him. 'Mr Millar on Mr Massey's benches – the old warrior of the maritime strike of 1890 with the Tories! Yet there he was. He slowly followed the leader of the Opposition into the lobby. Then he came over and conversed with some Liberal members. There were one or two pleasant sotto voce remarks. "The tumult and the shouting dies, The captains and the kings depart". It was daylight.'[205]

The Opposition burst into shouts of triumph at their victory but were silenced by an imperious Massey. He made a straightforward, polite speech acknowledging the victory before leading his supporters in a victorious 'crocodile' into Bellamy's where the party, aided by champagne and chicken, continued into the new morning with some performing a haka.[206] Parliament was adjourned for a few weeks. On its return, it was apparent that Reform would be able to maintain its majority. The era of single-party government and Liberal dominance had come to an end.

After the Battle.
There was rejoicing in the Massey Camp and a sound of hilarity floated out from Bellamy's —Daily

Spectator, 13 July 1912

Reform leaders Massey and Allen head for Bellamy's to celebrate their victory over the Liberals and assumption of government.

MR. HARKNESS as the Political Buffalo Bill, whipping up the votes.

J.G. Harkness, the Opposition whip, rounds up votes.

NZ Graphic, 26 August 1893

Party system in the House

The rapid consolidation of the Liberals in the early 1890s had given them an enormous advantage over the Opposition, which for more than a decade refused to countenance organising along similar lines. As a result it was disorganised and leaderless for substantial periods, and neither an effective critic of the government nor a viable alternative. Only with the emergence of Massey as leader and the establishment of the Reform Party towards the end of the first decade of the new century did the situation change.

The period was one of transition towards a modern party system. The inability of the Liberal Party to maintain its cohesion meant that true party government had not yet arrived.[207] Most notably in Committee, and particularly in the latter 1890s, the Liberal Party split on divisions. Its large majority made for an ill-disciplined rank and file. On the whole, the more compact Opposition displayed greater discipline in voting, but it was unable to become an alternative party of government. Liberal indiscipline remained marked into the new century, reaching a peak shortly after Ward became leader. The Liberal Party was no voting machine in the House, in spite of its dominance. Although renowned for some landmark legislation, the Liberal government experienced limited overall success with its legislation.[208] While nearly 200 bills were introduced under Seddon per session fewer than half were passed. Ward's success rate was higher, at around 60 per cent, but this was still nothing like the blanket adoption of government measures associated with a fully-fledged party system. Private members' bills also retained a significant place in Parliament's business. With an increased number of bills, the pressure of business in the House was substantial. The number of sitting days rose to about 70–5 under Seddon, but the proportion of time spent after midnight remained high. There was some decline in the length of sessions under Ward, apart from the exceptionally long sessions of 1903 and 1910, and the House sat less frequently after midnight.

The old anchorage of the General Assembly in provincial politics weakened and then disappeared.[209] In the 1887–90 Parliament more than one-third of the members still had provincial political experience. By 1912 virtually none had. This did much to sever Parliament's links with the nineteenth century. Local interests still played a vital role in Parliament, but these were now mediated by 'party'. Many Liberal members came into the House from local body politics – one-third had been mayors, half members of borough or county councils, and two-thirds had served on education boards or school committees.

There were larger numbers of New Zealand-born members in the House – over the entire period nearly one-third of the total – with the locally born found more commonly in the ranks of the Opposition, particularly after the turn of the century.[210] The Liberals remained predominantly British immigrants, and largely middle-aged. They were an upwardly mobile group, drawn largely from lower-middle-class backgrounds. Almost half had been small businessmen, with few farmers or manual workers. Their outlook was shaped by the personal insecurity many experienced during the depression of the late nineteenth century.

During the period of Liberal dominance, the general pattern of occupational representation did not change markedly, but there were some increases in the proportion of lawyers and journalists and decreases in the trade and commercial groups. Farming representation in the House declined slightly to just over a quarter of the membership, but this masked a considerable change. The old generation of 'squatter' politicians disappeared, replaced by the rising generation of small farmers.[211] From the election of 1911, farmer representation rose markedly and moved to the conservative end of the spectrum as the freehold was confirmed. More members came from manual working backgrounds, reflecting not only the drawing into the Liberal fold of some working men and trade unionists, but also the increased representation of men who had risen through the ranks. The educational level of members continued to fall. Nearly half had only a primary education.

The stability in membership that had emerged in the 1880s remained and was in some ways strengthened. The turnover rate by Parliament declined from the late 1880s until 1905, when a low point of 20 per cent was reached. Turnover then rose again as the Liberals went into decline, but a sizeable cadre of experienced politicians remained. By the end of the period nearly two-thirds of the House had served for more than six sessions, one-third for more than 12. Speaker Guinness had the longest service of all, at 35 sessions, followed by Walter Buchanan, Ward, Carroll and Allen (all 32), and Thomas Mackenzie (27). Consistent with the increased stability of the House, the average age of members increased somewhat from the 1880s to just over 50 years. There were now many members in their fifties, for the first time the largest single age group.

As election succeeded election, the governing Liberal Party held on to a greater proportion of its members in the House than the Opposition. The average age of Liberal members increased later in the period as the party went into decline and fewer new Liberal representatives were elected. Reform's ranks included newer and younger representatives. The disintegration of the Liberal Party resulted in a confused period of alignments – characterised as three-party politics – during which the concept of a political party developed considerably. The Liberal period was a transitional one, in which 'party' was only just taking shape. The new Reform and Labour parties would have much closer relationships with organisations representing sectional interests. These links would infuse the parties with new, energetic and New Zealand-born blood.

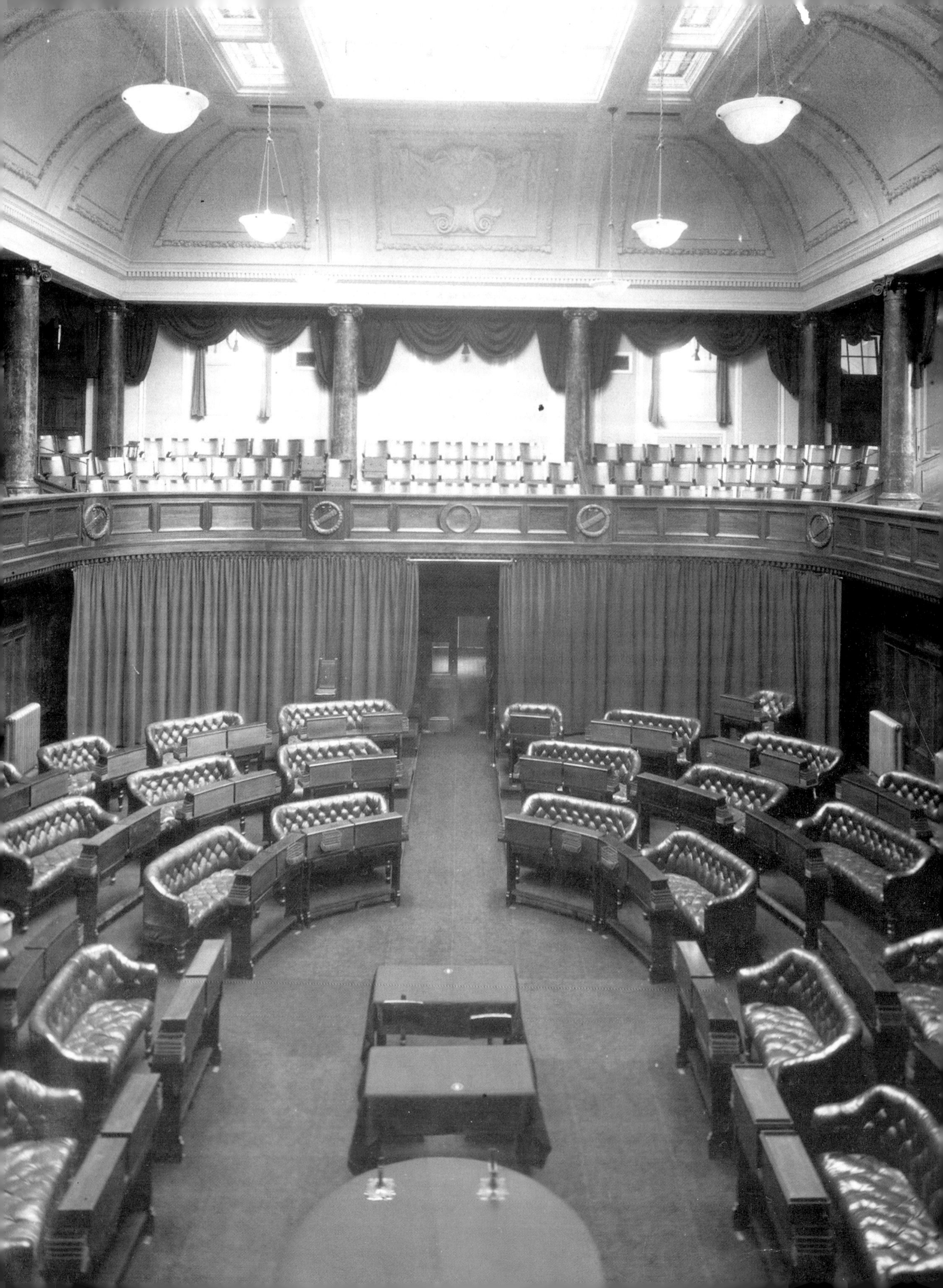

CHAPTER 5

Escaping the 'Trammels of the Past': Organised Party Government, 1913–35

At the end of the no-confidence debate that ushered in the Reform government, the leading Liberal Thomas Wilford reflected on the changes that were taking place in New Zealand politics. He exhorted the new Reform Prime Minister, William Massey, to continue with the progressive Liberal mission and 'shake himself free from the trammels of the past' – of old-style conservatism – by bringing together a variety of supporters in a broad party transcending old factional divisions.[1]

The rise of Massey represented the consolidation of party government and an abandoning of the old ways of conservative politicians, but it also introduced a time of confused alignments until the two-party system became established.[2] Massey had entered politics when a single party was first making its presence felt. By the time he died in office, he had helped establish an organised and disciplined party within a complex three-party system which arose with the rise of Labour.

This period saw dramatic changes in the way that the House conducted its business. But Reform, unlike the Liberals, would not be able to claim an easy pre-eminence in the House. Nonetheless, the developments set in train by Seddon were capitalised on. Executive dominance over Parliament was reinforced as party government was consolidated. By the 1930s this would include the curtailment of debate by time limits and the outright closure of debate.

William Massey was elected for Waitemata in 1894 and soon became a central figure in the Opposition to the Liberal government that became the Reform Party in the early years of the twentieth century. He led the Opposition from 1903 and helped introduce the modern, disciplined party to New Zealand politics. Becoming Prime Minister in 1912, he managed to retain power through the war and the confusion of three-party politics until his death on 10 May 1925.

Reform in power

Massey 'became something new in New Zealand politics: a "full-time" conservative politician, meeting the Liberals in continuous party warfare.'[3] He was an implacable party man, representing the interests of smaller farmers and settlers and heading a rural–urban alliance. In Wilford's words: '"My party, right or wrong", was, to my mind, his invariable practice. His devotion to his party bred quite naturally loyalty by his … party.'[4]

Massey's unrelenting character, organisational experience and abilities had given him the capacity to take on Seddon and then to exploit Ward's organisational and tactical weaknesses. He grew to be an agile debater with a great sense of anticipation, developed an excellent knowledge of parliamentary procedure, and would 'take up a

Left: House of Representatives chamber, c. 1920s E.T. Robson collection, ATL, F60073½

few sheets of paper covered with notes in large characters, and proceed to extemporise straight hits at critics all round the House, usually introducing a touch of ridicule, not unduly subtle but never in bad taste. He was at his best in attack.'[5] Like Seddon, Massey was able to read the mood of the House. As he put it, 'The House is a strange animal. You must learn to know that sometimes when it appears most dangerous it is really only mischievous, and will give way if you stand firm. At other times a slight squall may be the forerunner of a raging storm, and in that case you must be ready to compromise.'[6]

Massey believed that having 'sturdy freeholders, farming their own lands, and sending representatives of their own class to the Parliament of the Country' was part of the natural order of things.[7] His sternly Presbyterian beliefs were strongly anchored in religious texts, and he quoted readily from the Bible during parliamentary debates. He was a fervent British imperialist. His bucolic and bulky appearance – while easily lampooned – reinforced his claim to be a farmer politician.

Massey forged a cohesive Reform Party with a nucleus of trusted and able men – James Allen, William Herries, William Fraser, Heaton Rhodes and Alexander Herdman. Like Seddon, Massey ruled largely through personal authority and political acumen. His response to a deputation that he did not want any more ministers – 'give me six secretaries and I can run the whole country' – was taken as proof of his despotism, but it also reflected his political skills.[8] This is not to say that Massey ruled his cabinet or caucus with an iron hand. He regularly called caucus meetings – but to maintain support for himself and the government's policies rather than to make decisions. The primacy of cabinet was maintained and caucus was an instrument of executive power. Ward, meanwhile, continued the pattern of infrequent caucuses of an increasingly disorganised and diminished parliamentary Liberal Party.

Reform set about creating the first proper political party organisation in New Zealand's history. This was based on the Political Reform League formed in 1908, with Massey as its president.[9] Massey's relationship to the party outside Parliament was similar to Seddon's. Both dominated their organisations and used them as a link between Parliament and wider support in the country.

Massey relaxes on the government benches in the new chamber with Speaker Lang (wigless) in the Chair, c. 1919. In front of the Speaker is a bell and probably the Speaker's clock, and in front of the Clerk is the sand-glass used to time the calling of divisions.

Escaping the 'trammels of the past': organised party government, 1913–35

After a short adjournment following Mackenzie's defeat in July 1912, Massey's government took over.[10] The Liberals were banished from their quarters in Government House and found themselves occupying inferior accommodation in the library building. F.W. Lang, who had been in the House since 1894, was appointed unopposed as the new Chairman of Committees, filling the vacancy left earlier by James Colvin's appointment to the Mackenzie ministry.

Massey appointed his old allies to cabinet, forming a durable team that Gardner considered one of the strongest in New Zealand's history. In contrast to Liberal cabinets, Massey's was well-educated (including Cambridge and Oxford graduates). It was also more urban than rural, even if farming was the single most important occupational background. A majority were New Zealand-born.[11] F.H.D. Bell was appointed to lead the Legislative Council and to strengthen it as a revising chamber, rescuing it from the parlous position it had been reduced to under the Liberals. Bell formed a long-term partnership with Massey, acting as his cool, calculating partner behind the scenes. James Allen was Massey's loyal and able lieutenant in the House. Maui Pomare, who had voted for Reform in the final dénouement, was rewarded with a position without portfolio. Massey, who insisted on ministers being in their place in the House, had some trouble keeping Pomare in the chamber at times, because of his fondness for billiards.

Outside cabinet, a large contingent of much younger, inexperienced and less well-educated but ambitious men, became a long-term problem for Massey in maintaining party unity. These men were more representative of the small farmers – 'the Back Blocks cowspankers whom Mr. Massey has drawn into his net by promising them the new Jerusalem'.[12] Massey's problem was that, although he had won the vote of no-confidence, those pledged to support him comprised less than half of the House.[13] When the perennial Elective Executive Bill came up yet again, condemned by those in favour of party government as the vehicle of opportunists, rail-sitters and 'wobblers', it was defeated by only a single vote. Massey moved to strengthen his position. Thomas Mackenzie was appointed High Commissioner to London, and Reform won the subsequent by-election.

Following a conciliatory gesture over private members' business, the House was plunged into financial complexities, with Massey and Allen at loggerheads with Ward. The budget included a number of popular Liberal elements, and the government's strong-arm tactics over the intractable Waihi strike gained it additional popular support. Massey was able to maintain his majority, the only defeat coming when Tame Parata of the Council had his son Taare in the House slip a clause protecting Maori customary fishing rights into the Taieri Land Drainage Bill.[14] The Liberals, meanwhile, fell apart. Ward held back from reassuming the leadership, even while resuming hostilities with Massey. When the usual valedictories closed the session, Massey and Ward appeared genuinely in agreement that it had run smoothly and in good spirit.[15] Massey's promise of less taxing sessions seemed fulfilled, but could this be maintained?

The difficulties of government

Chairman of Committees Lang soon had more onerous duties thrust on him when Speaker Guinness died. Lang, who had been senior Reform whip for some years, was elected unopposed as Speaker at the beginning of the 1913 session.[16] A.S. Malcolm became the new Chairman of Committees.

The 1913 session proved easily the longest on record as Massey got to grips with the difficulties of government. Many bills were passed and long hours spent beyond midnight. But the session proceeded without any great acrimony, apart from the abolition of the second ballot. In September Ward was re-elected Leader of the Opposition and given a free hand in framing policy for a deeply divided and disorganised party. He continued to work well with Massey in the House.

A majority of the Liberal Party had favoured doing away with the second ballot, and the Mackenzie government had drawn up a bill to abolish it.[17] Reform, committed to its repeal, seemed to favour

Frederic William Lang was born in 1852 in London and came to New Zealand at the age of 19. After farming in the Waipa area he was elected for Waipa in 1893, Waikato in 1896, and Manukau from 1906. Lang was senior Reform whip for some years and was elected Chairman of Committees in 1912. He was Speaker from 1913 until he lost his seat in 1922. Keen to relax the formality of Parliament, he did not wear the full-bottomed wig as Speaker. He was knighted in 1916. Lang served in the Legislative Council from 1924 until his death in 1937.

preferential voting, but when the obstreperous orator P.C. (Paddy) Webb won Guinness's Grey seat for Labour on the second ballot, Reform was deterred from adopting a system that might advantage the Liberal and Labour parties in combination. When Massey declared his intention to simply abolish the second ballot, the Liberals sought to obstruct this.

A Second Ballot Repeal Bill was introduced but disappeared after being blocked in the House. When the measure appeared in a new guise as the third clause in an otherwise innocuous Legislature Amendment Bill, one of the longest stonewalls on record began. The battle commenced in earnest on Thursday 20 November. As described by Tom Seddon: 'The younger members called themselves "The Dog Watch". The debate in the daytime was conducted by the elders. The Dog Watch took over after the older members' day's work was done. The Dog Watch team had a natural leader, a regular Napoleon in tactics – Apirana Ngata.'[18]

In a previously untried manoeuvre, the Opposition began moving amendments and reading out alternative bills in full. The new Speaker called attention to the disruptive nature of the tactics and sought to appeal to 'the taste' of members as to whether they should continue. In an unprecedented move, Ward tried to move adjournment of the House to prevent discussion of the bill. Such a motion by a private member was eventually ruled out by the Speaker.[19] Meanwhile, Massey issued a veiled threat that he might introduce a standing order enabling closure, or even dissolve Parliament. The stonewall continued, largely by way of amendments to the title of the bill and motions to report progress. Members left the House at midnight on Saturday, to rejoin the battle at 2.30 p.m. on Monday.

On Sunday the Speaker and Chairman of Committees considered what to do. Malcolm resolved to adopt the strategy of 1881.[20] He threatened to suspend the standing orders and warned the House that he would do his utmost to bring the stonewall to an end. He had also drawn up a list of topics and expressions that members had used in order to make his rulings on repetition. (This innovation was to be a serious constraint to future stonewallers, as other Chairmen followed his example.)

In the end, Malcolm took the initiative on Monday evening and proposed the clause's second reading himself. Amid strenuous protest, he ruled numerous members out of order for irrelevance and ordered them to sit down – sometimes before they had started to speak. The motion was carried. A similar farce took place over adding the third clause to the bill. The Opposition then attempted to move futile and obstructive new clauses, but these were rejected and member after member was ruled out of order. The bill was finally reported at 3 a.m. The commonsense approach and persistence of the Chairman had won out. He had both avoided suspending the standing orders and provided an instructive lesson for the future.

The waterfront strike, which began in October 1913, made for a tense atmosphere. The government came into collision with Labour Party members John Payne and Webb as feeling mounted. Massey refused to give the House a chance to debate the issue. Ward and other members attempted to mediate a settlement, but to no avail. Members ventured onto the wharves during the strike to see what was going on for themselves, and a few got tangled up in the riots on the streets of Wellington.[21] Parliament and Massey's residence became the objects of strikers' attention, the temporary premises of Parliament being particularly vulnerable. On one occasion strikers appeared at the windows of the temporary debating chamber.[22] Massey received death threats and took to carrying a revolver in a 'conspicuously bulging hip-pocket'. The short but effective Labour Disputes Investigation Bill was rushed through at the end of the session. This placed restrictions on strikes by unions not registered under the arbitration system. Massey and Reform had proved themselves in battle. As the *Round Table* commented: 'The Government held its own throughout. It was never defeated in a division. It withstood some severe attacks on its administration, and went into recess stronger than before.'[23]

In 1914 Payne and Webb continued to make a nuisance of themselves, frequently giving vent to 'unparliamentary' language and challenging the proprieties of the House systematically. Webb pointedly said: 'Let members realize that this is not a gentleman's club, but a place of legislature'.[24] Payne tried to insist on having his accusation that Massey was susceptible to 'bribery and corruption' taken down.[25] Massey urged the House to name and suspend him, but he was given another chance to withdraw the words. As the Sergeant-at-Arms could not find him – to the mirth of some – the matter had to be postponed. When Payne again refused to withdraw the words, he was suspended. Near the end of the session he yet again refused to withdraw a statement and was suspended for a second time. Webb engaged in the same tactics and was likewise suspended. Labour members would continue to challenge conventions and the Speaker throughout the First World War. Lang's successor as Speaker, Charles Statham, was to ruminate that the standard of debate declined as those educated in English public schools gave way to the colonial born and bred, and in particular with the advent of Labour members.[26] He even undertook to compile a 'compendium' of unparliamentary words after there was a rash of such language at the end of a session and Labour's Charles Chapman attempted to recite a litany of them.

As the House engaged in this bickering, war clouds were gathering. Following the Canadian offer to Britain of an expeditionary force, Massey intimated that New Zealand might respond likewise. When someone attempted the opening bars of 'God Save the King', the entire House and galleries rose to sing.[27] Matters moved fast. On 4 August Massey outlined the preparations being made for war in a ministerial statement. He hoped that political differences would be put aside, and Ward committed the Opposition to co-operation with the government in principle.[28] At 1 p.m. the next day the Governor, standing on the steps of the library building, formally announced New Zealand's involvement in the war to a large crowd.[29] Political differences immediately arose as Ward wanted the financial statement to be postponed. When Massey said that it would go ahead as usual Ward had to keep to his commitment not to oppose it, but the Labour members and several Liberals filed out of the chamber when Allen rose to deliver the statement.

Members soberly got on with business and passed emergency legislation rapidly. Massey continued to win all the important divisions, but the election at the end of 1914 failed to give Reform a workable majority.[30] Reform won only 40 seats, while the Liberals won 32 and Labour, supporting Ward, 8. Six months of recounts, challenges and by-elections did not greatly change the result. Only when the new member for Northern Maori, Tau Henare, attended a Reform caucus after Parliament opened in late June 1915 did Massey gain a majority of 41 to 39.

By now the pressures to form a coalition government were irresistible.[31] William Downie Stewart, who persistently advocated the 'fusion' of the Reform and Liberal parties in the 1920s, urged them to merge: 'we shall then get for the first time for some years a proper alignment of parties in this House … there is no doubt that the Labour party will then emerge as a distinct and more substantial factor in the House than it is at present.'[32] Following arduous negotiations and the intervention of the Governor, during which Parliament conducted very little business, Massey and Ward agreed on a National cabinet of six members each, with Ward becoming Minister of Finance and de facto joint head of government. Cabinet found it tremendously difficult to reach unanimous decisions. It was agreed that the next election would not be held until six months after the end of war, despite Reform's promise during the 1914 campaign that the life of Parliament would not be extended unless the enemy was 'at our gates'.[33] The result was the disappearance of an independent Liberal Party and fragmentation in the House. Wilford became the spokesman for the Liberals.

The war took precedence over the usual parliamentary business, with shorter sessions fitted around the frequent visits to Britain by Massey and Ward. They became travelling 'political Siamese twins … held together by the ties of mutual suspicion'.[34] The tenacious and hardworking Allen, the Minister of Defence, capably ran the country in their absence, being Acting Prime Minister for a total of almost two years. The war also tended to exclude private members' bills and made the small number of Labour members the real Opposition. The rising cost of living, the introduction of conscription, and the imprisonment for sedition of leading labour agitators (including Webb) gave Labour plenty of ammunition.

Massey moved the adjournment of the House late in August 1915, noting the number of members' sons and brothers who had fallen as the Gallipoli campaign reached its peak.[35] The House congratulated New Zealand's forces on their conduct and bravery, and rose to sing 'God Save the King'. Parliament later farewelled Seddon and Downie Stewart for military service; they were to be joined by Gordon Coates and J.B. Hine. Under urgency, Ward passed a rapidly drafted but massive Finance Bill (which provided comprehensively for the financing of the war) in one night, with the House rising at 4.55 a.m. The National Registration Bill providing for the military registration of manpower was passed without a division, although Labour attempted to introduce a 'census of wealth' as well as of men.

In 1916 the session began and finished early. It was intended to be a 'war session', with the House passing important legislation introducing compulsory military service and funding the growing demands of the war.[36] Opposition to conscription became a major point of contention. William Veitch resigned from the Labour caucus because of his support for conscription. The Military Service Bill was passed with general support, but the small contingent of Labour members battled on to the bitter end, forcing division after division. On its passage, the National Anthem was again sung. Following the example of Britain and Canada, the life of Parliament was extended for a year by legislation. On finishing, the members rose and sang the Anthem again, establishing the tradition of singing the National Anthem at the end of sessions.[37]

The 1917 session commenced as soon as Massey and Ward arrived back in the country in late June. Parliament considered legislation to control less desirable aspects of social behaviour such as drinking, horse racing and gambling in the interests of 'economy and efficiency'. Amid agitation for the closing of public bars at 6 p.m., Massey declared that the matter would be a conscience vote – and that Bellamy's must conform to any such restrictions.[38] The vote over the Sale of Liquor Restriction Bill was close. While the government favoured 8 p.m., Massey had to accept an amendment for 6 p.m. closing. Intended to last only for the duration of the war, early closing remained in force for half a century. In 1918 a special session of a week in April allowed Ward and Massey to travel overseas once again. To the fury of Labour members, the life of Parliament was extended to December 1919.

The new Houses of Parliament

It took time to decide what to do about new Parliament Buildings. Government Architect John Campbell prepared sketch plans for rebuilding around the remnants of the existing structure.[39] The entire 1880s extension was soon rebuilt, with new internal walls strengthening the weakened structure.

Escaping the 'trammels of the past': organised party government, 1913–35

THE 'WINTERLESS NORTH TOUR'

The cavalcade of motor cars carrying parliamentarians on the 'Winterless north tour' halts at a small Northland settlement. As dairying became important in the early twentieth century, Northland members became what Taranaki members had been in the nineteenth – quintessential 'roads and bridges' politicians whose survival depended on securing public works funding to improve communications, especially roads. The route of the North Auckland main trunk railway line was obviously significant to local communities, and it was strongly contested. In January 1917 a delegation of 40 parliamentarians, together with farmers, businessmen, journalists and motoring buffs, left Auckland in 33 cars on a two-week tour organised by the North Auckland Development Board after agitation by Colonel Allen Bell, a later Reform member for the Bay of Islands who was a tireless propagandist for the development of Northland. Huge crowds gathered to see the convoy pass, and it was very successful in increasing awareness of Northland's problems.

Northwood collection, ATL, G4899

The convoy created clouds of dust while the roads remained dry, but then rain began to fall and the clay hills of the far north turned to mud and slush. There were days of fording rivers, bogged vehicles, and many punctures.

ATL, C20907½

When there was an unscheduled stop at Herekino because of the mud, the tiny settlement was unable to accommodate the hundred or more travellers. Some had to sleep in barns, and more in their cars. When a 13-mile stretch of mud that took four hours to navigate followed this experience, some abandoned the journey at Kohukohu. On the rear canopy of one car was written 'Gloria est pro patria mori' ('It is a glorious thing to die for one's country'), followed by 'Honour the brave with kicks'. A sign attached to the vital coil of rope read, 'The line that landed us political pulls once more!!', referring to the many times the parliamentarians had to pull cars out of the mud.

ATL, C2052½

View of the grounds of Parliament, Government House and the General Assembly Library, c. 1912. Quinton's Corner (later taken for the Cenotaph) is at far left. At centre the 'Twopenny Tube' links Government House and the library as site preparations for the new building commence.

Campbell also sketched roomy new, fire-proof Houses of Parliament on the Government House site in an Edwardian form of the Classical Revival style, with an elevated central dome. A new library would be housed in the new building, with a large, circular reading room as in the British Museum. Ward liked this plan, but Massey labelled it the 'maddest, wildest, and most extravagant scheme'.[40]

In 1910 the government reached agreement with the Wellington City Council for a comprehensive replanning of the site to give Parliament a consolidated block running from Hill Street to Bowen Street.[41] Sydney Street (West) was closed off and Museum Street shifted to line up with The Terrace. Bowen, Charlotte and Molesworth Streets were widened. This allowed building closer to the existing General Assembly Library and more generous parliamentary grounds.

In February 1911 Ward announced a competition for designs among New Zealand architects.[42] Detailed specifications were drawn up for a building on the present-day site between the library and Government House. Ward, under pressure from Wellington and Opposition members, conceded that the immediate building plans should be more modest. The first stage, including both chambers, would be constructed without interfering with Government House. The second stage – to comprise Bellamy's and a huge new library – would extend the building to the south and replace Government House.[43]

Thirty-three entries were received and judged by the former Government Architect for New South Wales, Colonel Vernon.[44] Campbell's two designs won first and fourth prizes, and were blended for the final design. The first prize-winning design provided the central dome and eastern elevation, the fourth prize-winning design the general plan and corner cupolas. The buildings were to be constructed of brick with stone facing and reinforced concrete roof and floors, with three floors and a basement. The Edwardian Baroque style was widely used for grand public buildings.

In Opposition Massey had criticised Ward's vision of magnificent new Parliament Buildings. On coming into power he ordered a moratorium, but foundations had already been prepared, a foundation stone laid (in March 1912) and extensive site preparation carried out.[45] Massey eventually and

Watercolour by Harold Matthewman, S.C. Smith collection, ATL, G19600

Government Architect John Campbell's final design for the new Parliament Buildings. The cupolas and dome were removed from the design approved by Massey's government, and the second half (left) was never built.

reluctantly approved the planned first stage, apart from the domes and ornamentation of the roof. Tenders for the first stage were submitted in October 1913, and that of £152,000 from Hansford, Mills and Hardie, a Christchurch firm, for a marble-clad building with granite for the ground floor, was accepted.[46]

Construction began early in 1914 with the removal of the 'Twopenny tube' and work on the eastern facade. At first good progress was made, and by later in the year the basement and ground storey were almost completed. But the target of two years proved hopelessly optimistic. There were difficulties in locating suitable marble – this was quarried near Motueka and shipped on scows to Wellington – and another quarry had to be opened up. The war restricted the supply of materials and created shortages of labour. It was announced that the building would not be finished until June 1917. By late 1915 the main floors of reinforced concrete had been laid and the walls of the imposing lounge lobby and the House of Representatives chamber had reached roof level. Construction of the northern and western sections was painfully slow. With members desperate to get out of the ballroom 'hothouse', Parliament moved hurriedly into the incomplete buildings for the second session of 1918. The buildings were dedicated as a memorial to those who had fallen in the war. Carved wreaths commemorating engagements and fields of battle adorned the faces of the galleries in the chamber.[47]

Parliament and the government were finally in their spacious new premises.[48] The Prime Minister had a suite of offices on the principal floor, which also housed the cabinet room, the Speakers' rooms, and rooms for orderlies and messengers. The Speakers had suites of offices, including reception rooms, dining rooms, bedrooms and bathrooms, so that they and their wives could live there during the session. Below, on the ground floor, were ministers' suites. Also on this floor were the Native Affairs Committee room, waiting rooms, messengers' and charwomen's rooms, the members' smoking

The top floor has been added to the new buildings and the levelling of grounds in front has been completed, c. 1917.

room, a supper room and rooms for the Hansard reporters. The restored section of the library building housed most of the select committee rooms.

The building was never officially opened. Construction dragged on into the 1920s, with the marble cladding going up at a snail's pace. In 1921 the contractor was told to finish the building before that year's session started in September. Work on the southern wall petered out in 1922, and this wall remained incomplete until the late 1960s because of uncertainty over the second stage.[49]

Inside the chamber, the traditional double padded seating (with flat-topped desks in front) in a horseshoe formation was retained. Hansard moved to the floor of the House. The reporters took five-minute turns, increased to ten minutes while the House was in Committee of Supply (when debates could be condensed by more than half), and 30 minutes while it was in Committee.[50] Turns were timed by a clock in the Hansard room, from which communication was made to the chamber by a bell-push. Later on, the reporters timed themselves in the chamber with a handsome large silver clock, with the ten-minute intervals indicated by a tap on the table as reporters silently left and came in.

Indigenous New Zealand materials were favoured for the new building. Besides the granite and marble of the exterior, rimu and other New Zealand woods were used for much of the interior joinery. The walls of the cabinet room were lined with Canadian bird's eye maple and walnut, donated by the Canadian government to cement links between the two countries.[51]

A committee appointed to advise on furnishings, which included Pomare and Ngata, considered incorporating Maori designs into the interior and furniture, including new desks ornamented with

Marble from the Takaka quarry arrives by lorry at the rear of the new buildings as they near completion, c. 1920. Note the unfinished nature of the southern face.

Maori motifs.[52] But the old plain heart kauri seats and desks remained in use despite their deteriorating condition, and Maori designs were confined to the new Native Affairs Committee room on the ground floor at the back of the buildings.[53]

The House made do with much of the old furniture until after the war, and the floors were not carpeted until 1923.[54] The acoustics in the new chamber were terrible at first, particularly in the galleries and at the back of the chamber. Large amounts of green felt, chair-coverings in the galleries and carpets on the floor of the House made an improvement. The ventilation and heating were not all that had been promised either. Dr Thacker, a member who made free use of the English language, claimed one evening that 'one could almost carry armfuls of human breath and excreta'.[55] Massey too complained of the stuffiness. The Minister of Public Works said that he would do what he could, but conditions were not improved even after Public Health Department experts commented adversely on them. As the House laboured well into the summer during the 1921–2 session, the problem became acute.[56] The sun beating down on the glass roof of the chamber virtually turned it into a conservatory.

The new galleries were more spacious, but the public was still made to feel it was there on sufferance. People had to enter from the rear of the building through what the *Dominion* described as a 'coal cellar', then 'creep in through a rat-hole up a blind alley' and an 80-step 'corkscrew' to the gallery.[57] The traditional rule that members of the public (including the press) had to remove their hats when entering the buildings (while parliamentarians' heads could remain covered) was not enforced under the less formal Speaker Lang. But in the early 1920s, Statham, a more traditionally minded Speaker, reimposed the rule. Labour members protested that what was good for parliamentarians should be good enough for others.[58]

The House

MAORI IN THE HOUSE

Apirana Ngata was elected for Eastern Maori in 1905. Soon after the turn of the century the role of Maori members changed substantially under the influence of the 'Young Maori Party', a loose association of like-minded individuals including Ngata, Peter Buck and Maui Pomare who were committed to working within the existing framework to improve Maori health, develop Maori land with state assistance, and foster Maori arts and crafts. Ngata was promoted to cabinet in 1909 as Minister for the Public Trust Office, and supported Carroll in the Native Affairs portfolio. Ngata was a loyal Liberal Party supporter, taking a wide view of issues and fraternising with Pakeha members in Bellamy's and the lobbies.

Ngata remained influential in Maori matters in Opposition, particularly through his relationship with Coates. Maori members seemed to be above party politics in this period. Coates made him Chairman of the Native Affairs Committee when he became Prime Minister in 1925. Ngata continued to promote Maori land development, and on becoming Native Minister in 1928 he initiated many land schemes. He was knighted in 1927, but had to resign from the government in 1934 because of irregularities in the administration of the schemes. He retained his seat until 1943, and died in 1950.

The Maori Affairs Committee Room, c. 1940s. This room was opened in 1922 when the new main buildings were completed. Massey, his ministers and many members attended the ceremony, which was followed by a banquet in the old Government House. Carvings denoting the entrance to a whare runanga were fixed to a wall and on the architraves of the doors. Making the room a whare runanga was an appropriate recognition of the committee's place in Parliament. It was here that Maori sought redress for their grievances, and here that the minister and the Maori members came together in non-partisan fashion. When Duncan MacIntyre became Minister of Maori Affairs in 1975, he declared that the room should be treated as a marae.

The Maori Affairs Committee Room was substantially renovated in 1955 under the supervision of John Grace, the private secretary to the Minister of Maori Affairs and a Tuwharetoa chief. Minister Corbett wanted it to be a 'show part of Parliament Buildings'. A large panel reproducing the Treaty of Waitangi was mounted on a wall, which also displayed coloured portraits of Carroll, Buck, Pomare and Ngata. Red and black kowhaiwhai decorated the ceiling and cornices, the replica whare runanga entrance was restored, and tukutuku was extended around the walls.

Peter Fraser, keen to challenge the more antiquated customs, instigated a futile crusade against the 'hats off' policy. He also agitated against excluding women from the public gallery. Britain had allowed them in when they gained the vote, yet here the restriction was maintained: 'It strikes a new member [that] there are notices up "No ladies must be admitted here", "Members only", and so on. We find in almost every portion of the House the sex line is drawn. Now, that line will have to go.'[59] But Fraser expected too much of the institution – women were refused admittance until 1945.

The new buildings served backbenchers badly. The failure to go ahead with the second half of the buildings left large numbers jammed into cramped quarters. Statham complained that members 'were compelled to stow themselves away in odd corners in the library, in the stack-room, in the attic, and even in the cellar with a chair and a table'.[60] Not being the official Opposition was a disadvantage for Labour, whose eight members were 'jammed into a small badly ventilated room' in which they almost suffocated if the door was closed.[61]

As the number of parliamentary staff grew, pressure on accommodation intensified and the Leader of the Opposition was banished to the dingy rear of the library building.[62] Eventually there was a 'spontaneous revolt' by members, who complained of instances of six to a room and an omnipresent 'constant clicking of typewriters'. One member was installed 'in a dark and dreary hovel', while Labour's Robert Semple inhabited a 'dug-out' that had previously been a lumber room.

Old Government House remained an essential part of the complex. The conservatory became variously a messengers' room, the post office and the tea room, while the ballroom became the Social Hall used for the frequent official functions. Before long, the pressure on space in the main buildings meant that some ministers and their assistants were located on the upper floor. Later, other members had to be housed there also.

Bellamy's, in the rear of the building, could expand. It retained its reputation for a fine table and liquor even if it was housed in premises of rather decayed grandeur.[63] But maintenance work on the buildings remained minimal, and when Labour came to power in 1935 an even more parsimonious approach was adopted. Women were not admitted to the dining room, but a special tea room was provided for members' wives and daughters, female friends and 'lady press reporters'. There was a separate Hansard and Press refreshment room, a private secretaries' and clerks' room, and a small visitors' bar known as the 'Dog Box', all clustered near the main members' bar.

The grounds were comprehensively relandscaped into the form that is broadly retained today.[64] In 1915, a statue of Seddon was erected squarely in front of the new buildings. Quinton's Corner, where Bowen Street met Lambton Quay, became a triangular island on which the war memorial was erected later. The main gates into the grounds were placed at that corner. A drive swept up the hill to a large forecourt in front of the buildings. The main entrance was reached up steps which gave access to the principal floor of the building. The grounds required a substantial contingent of gardeners. In the 1920s a nursery behind the buildings also served other public gardens and domains in Wellington.[65] The grounds once again became a venue for public occasions. From 1920 the Returned Soldiers' Association held its Anzac Day commemorations on the grass in front of the buildings, where a temporary cenotaph was erected before the permanent monument was built outside Parliament's main gates.

Providing for members' needs

As the buildings went up, parliamentary staff became more closely integrated into party government. When Massey came to power in 1912, the portfolio of the Legislative Department was created and the two parliamentary administrative arms associated with the Speakers were drawn together, formalising the de facto situation that had existed since 1891, when Seddon took control of legislative expenditure.

The completed new buildings, c. 1928.

    The Clerk of the House headed the Legislative Department and gained formal authority over all of Parliament, including the library, Bellamy's and Hansard, except the Legislative Council.[66] One of Reform's major planks was civil service reform. The Legislative Department soon felt the effect of this as the government attacked Liberal patronage in Parliament.[67] Many elderly sessional messengers, orderlies and clerks dating back to the days of Ballance and Seddon were precipitately retired (albeit with generous pensions) amid protest from various members.[68] In 1915 A.F. Lowe became Clerk of the House in place of Henry Otterson, who retired after 45 years' service. In 1920 Lowe moved to the better paid position of Clerk of the Legislative Council and Clerk of Parliaments after Leonard Stowe died. Stowe had been Clerk of the Council since 1865.[69]

    The institution of Parliament grew substantially, nonetheless, after Reform came to power. With Lowe moving, Clerk-Assistant E.W. Kane was promoted to Clerk of the House. He had strong ideas about reorganising the Legislative Department. During the retrenchment of the early 1920s, there was a thoroughgoing review of the department. Its budget had more than doubled since 1914 and now included funding for the Law Drafting Office.[70] To the well-established tradition of employing older, needy men in ancillary positions in Parliament was added the demand to find suitable positions for returned soldiers. The sessional establishment had expanded markedly since the war.

    New Clerk Kane considered that discipline was poor, that the Sergeant-at-Arms was not properly supervising staff, and that there were too many staff with overlapping duties.[71] He recommended cutting a number of positions and reducing salaries. Bellamy's in particular, was ripe for reform. Payment of the wages of Bellamy's staff by vote in the 1890s had become a comprehensive subsidy of the service. Bellamy's charges were increased, the number of sessional messengers and orderlies was cut by 20 per cent, and waiting staff and charwomen were cut back.

The popular Sergeant-at-Arms, Major Shepherd, had resigned in 1915 due to ill health. He was replaced by Commander Cecil Horne, who had held the position in the 1880s. Horne was also fondly regarded.[72] When he died in 1920, he was replaced by Major H. Browne. According to Kane, Browne barely turned up for the session. Most of his administrative functions were stripped from him, and the position became largely symbolic. The custodian took over general responsibility for sessional employees, in addition to having year-round charge of all the buildings.[73] From 1929, the standing orders specified that, subject to government control of Legislative Department expenditure, the control and administration of the grounds, buildings and staff was vested in the Speaker for the entire year.

Neither the library nor Hansard were much affected by retrenchment, and the library's collections grew steadily. When Charles Wilson retired in 1926, the appointment of a new Chief Librarian proved controversial.[74] Dr Guy Scholefield, a journalist and historian, was appointed. The Libraries Association protested vigorously, pointing to Scholefield's lack of library experience.

Preceded by the Sergeant-at-Arms, Major Sandle, Speaker Statham and Clerk Hall mount the steps of Parliament after presenting the Address-in-Reply to the Governor-General on 13 October 1935.

By this time, the library held more than 110,000 volumes and had expanded its fiction collection considerably.[75] Despite his alleged deficiencies, Scholefield brought the library into the modern era. He introduced a card system for issues to replace the cumbersome process of entering details in ledgers and day-books. The elderly male library assistants began to disappear; staff were now expected to have university degrees and library qualifications. Increasing numbers of women were employed.[76] Scholefield also began to provide a reference service, a response to the research needs not only of members but also of government departments and students.

Scholefield persuaded Prime Minister Coates to add archival functions to the Librarian's responsibilities.[77] As 'Dominion Archivist', he actively pursued the development of a national archives. He took in a range of provincial and general government and other papers, and built up the newspaper collection. He also began to compile a union list of newspapers in New Zealand. After he had travelled overseas in 1935, an official documents section was established. This had exchange arrangements with libraries in Britain and the United States.

Hansard had settled down since the tempestuous days of Seddon, but staff dissatisfaction with the poor career structure remained.[78] After the retirement of the Chief Reporter, Silas Spragg, in 1923, Hansard was reorganised. The traditional source of reporters dried up because high-speed shorthand became a dying skill among male newspaper reporters. Female typists had to be brought in to help. A new salary structure with more attractive promotion prospects was devised. The attrition of staff remained a problem, but female reporters would not be employed. In 1927, F. Manderson and A. Sutherland were appointed from the clerical ranks of the public service, breaking the tradition of hiring newspaper reporters.[79]

The House

Further retrenchment took place in the Legislative Department during the depression of the early 1930s. In 1931 parliamentary staff had their wages reduced by 10 per cent and lost previous bonuses.[80] The government-appointed National Expenditure Commission of 1932 initially recommended substantial cuts in the Legislative Department but, probably for political reasons, these were not included in its final report.[81] The number of staff was reduced by attrition and their work altered. On the retirement of the Second Clerk-Assistant, the position was amalgamated with that of Reader. When W.E. Dasent, the Clerk-Assistant, retired in 1933, G.F. Bothamley took up the position, and H.N. Dollimore, who was described as 'one who will later be capable of filling the highest office', became Second Clerk-Assistant.

Parliamentary life

The self-enclosed, intense and intimate male culture of the House faded as the traditional ferment of seven-days-a-week informal politicking in the precincts that had acted as a substitute for formal caucuses subsided. Many members returned home for the weekends. In the old buildings, members had lived and worked in the Lobby and eaten together in the adjacent Bellamy's. A strong tradition of socialising had accompanied the long hours. The new, more spacious accommodation dispersed members into twos and threes scattered about the various buildings.[82] To attend committee meetings they might

A.T. Bothamley, the Gentleman Usher of the Black Rod – the Legislative Council's equivalent of the Sergeant-at-Arms – in formal dress and with the official Black Rod, c. early 1930s. Full evening dress was worn on the state occasions upon which Black Rod played his ceremonial role. Bothamley had filled the position on an acting basis since 1892, following a dispute between the two Houses over the creation of the position which went back to the 1870s. At that time he used a longer plain black wooden staff akin to a billiard cue. Bothamley assumed the role formally when a Black Rod was appointed officially in 1914. The Black Rod shown here is still in use today. It was presented by Governor-General Bledisloe to the General Assembly in 1931. Fashioned in London, this was similar to the one used in the House of Lords.

The Bothamley family had an extraordinary connection with Parliament, where father and sons served for close to 80 years. Arthur Thomas Bothamley was first employed by the Legislative Council in 1871 and became Clerk-Assistant in 1878, a position he held until 1925. He was awarded an ISO in 1924, and retained the position of Black Rod until 1937, the year before his death. Bothamley's successors as Black Rod were retired military officers. His son Grafton Francis Bothamley worked in the House from 1906 as a sessional clerk and was permanently employed as a clerk from 1913. He was promoted to Clerk-Assistant in 1933 and held the Clerk's position briefly in 1945–6 before his retirement. Another son, Charles Mildmay Bothamley, joined Parliament as a committee clerk in 1917 and worked his way up to become the Clerk of Parliaments and of the Legislative Council from 1934 until the abolition of the Council in 1950.

Escaping the 'trammels of the past': organised party government, 1913–35

The Governor, Lord Liverpool, Lady Liverpool, Prime Minister Massey, Ward and others at a parliamentary cricket match, Basin Reserve, 1915. Cricket was a popular recreation for parliamentarians. Into the twentieth century, many also bred and trained horses and administered racing clubs.

have to go to the library building; for Bellamy's they would cross to old Government House. The old-time socials, dinners and musical evenings were no longer held.

In the early twentieth century, as members began to travel more frequently, demands for better travel concessions increased. South Island members wanted free rather than subsidised travel and concessions during the recess. Members also wanted recompense for their hire of cabs and motor cars.[83] Those from North Island areas not serviced regularly by trains or steamers, such as the East Coast, had to travel long distances by motor car, service car or mail car at their own cost. Travel was also difficult in the central North Island. W.T. Jennings, who held the Taumarunui seat, was known for his 'feats of great endurance in travelling to the recesses of his undeveloped district, and [making] himself equally at home in the navvy's camp and the kainga'.[84] He was followed in the electorate by C.K Wilson, who travelled on horseback. 'Except on paper there were no roads to these new farms … the tracks had turned into quagmires … We rode, I think, some seven miles until [Wilson] met us – a mud man riding a mud horse. The road was from one foot to three feet deep in slush. Sometimes the horse stepped into a hole and I wondered if it would really be able, this time, to pull itself out.'[85]

By the 1920s rail travel was effectively free for members, most of whom went home for the weekends and returned on Tuesdays.[86] Parliament now provided annual steamer passes for both the Wellington–Lyttelton and Wellington–Picton runs, as well as other steamers. These passes allowed free travel, and special accommodation if this was available.[87] From 1929, with sittings finishing at 5.30 p.m., members found it easier to get away on Fridays. Later the House shifted Friday's sitting forward an hour by sessional order each year, so that members could get away at 4.30 p.m. and catch the Limited north. By the end of the 1930s sitting days were rearranged to enable members to go home at weekends, and aircraft were even made available when the inter-island ferry timetable was inconvenient. Some members still stayed in Wellington over the weekend, enjoying 'something in the nature of a Savage Club organised by members'.[88] As John A. Lee remembered, members gathered together 'around the fires in the library or whips' rooms' and achieved 'a social intimacy as they yarned'. On fine Sundays they walked in the gardens and on the hills around the city.

Salaries had not been raised since 1901. In that time there had been substantial inflation. Members' pay was simply inadequate by the end of the war – less than what a tradesman could earn, and far below what parliamentarians were paid in other countries.

TRAVEL PASSES

Members' travel to and from Wellington for sessions was covered by parliamentary vote. They hung the railway passes granting them free travel from their watch chains or around their necks. These round medallions about the size of a shilling made of blue enamel and gold were regarded fondly as symbolic badges of office. Until the mid 1970s they were solid 9 carat gold; thereafter they were made in silver with a hard gold finish. The medallions remained in use until the mid 1980s, when they were replaced by mundane plastic credit cards.

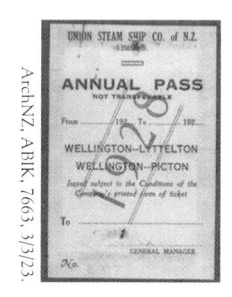

Private collection

A Union Steam Ship Company annual pass for inter-island ferries, 1928.

ArchNZ, ABIK, 7663, 3/3/23.

The member for Kaipara, Gordon Coates, was often the last to board the train. Here he chats to the engine-driver. Coates stayed at the Wellington Club during the week, and caught the Limited Express north on Friday evenings. Arriving in Auckland the following morning, he would pick up his garaged car and breakfast at the Northern Club, before driving to Matakohe in Northland in three hours, arriving early on Saturday afternoon. Leaving home on Monday afternoon, he would be back in the House the following afternoon.

NZ Free Lance collection, ATL, F92658½

A first-class rail pass for Mrs W.H. Field, the wife of the member for Otaki, 1927.

Phillip O'Shea, New Zealand Herald of Arms

Escaping the 'trammels of the past': organised party government, 1913–35

Messengers brought the Evening Post into the chamber at 4 p.m. each day. Some members found the practice of erecting a 'barrage' of newspapers against speakers offensive, and in 1929 the Standing Orders Committee tried to prevent the 'circulation' of newspapers in the House. It was pointed out that in the House of Commons only books and papers necessary for the debate could be read in the chamber. But others were just as keen to maintain the practice, and pointed out that members would simply step into the lobbies to pick up a copy and then return to the chamber. The proposed change was dropped.

In 1919, a deputation representing virtually the entire House urged Massey to improve matters so that members could 'live in reasonable comfort … commensurate with their legislative responsibilities'.[89] L.M. Isitt observed that the demands of the public on the time and money of parliamentarians were endless. 'We are supposed to give to everything that comes along. In connection with every bazaar, every football club, every public movement, the member of Parliament is supposed to head the list … day after day and week in and week out, two-thirds of my time is given up to meetings and interviewing all sorts of people … I practically do not do any business, as I leave that to my manager'.[90] The Labour members, lacking other sources of income, were the worst off. They could afford only cheap boarding houses, and some reportedly lived in 'garages' while in Wellington. M.J. Savage and W.E. Parry shared a room on Hill Street and ate at Bellamy's.[91]

The honorarium was increased substantially – from £300 to £500 – following the election of 1919. However, in 1922 it was reduced by 10 per cent to £450 in line with public service-wide cuts as New Zealand's economy entered uncertain times. Later in the decade, pressure to increase the payment mounted, and almost the entire House laid siege to Prime Minister Coates, led by T.K. Sidey and a committee.[92] The committee drafted a bill to provide for substantial increases and a contributory superannuation scheme.

Some looked askance at the £100 Christmas bonus awarded to members in 1929 in lieu of an increase in salary.

165

When the government was challenged to a vote, it put off any changes until after the election because of public sensitivity on the issue. It was left to Ward's new government to act. On the last day of the 1929 session, members voted themselves a £100 sessional allowance dubbed the 'Members' "Xmas Box"'.[93] As the depression deepened, the honorarium was cut by 10 per cent in line with the wage and salary cuts of 1931, and by a further 10 per cent the following year. It was gradually restored to £450 by 1936, but this was still meagre payment.

Three-party politics

The Labour Party formally declared its existence in 1916.[94] At its first annual conference in 1917, on the motion of H.E. (Harry) Holland it was agreed that the Labour Party would form a separate party in Parliament (led by A.H. Hindmarsh), with its own caucus to which members would be bound. Previous Labour members, while an identifiable group, had not acted in such a concerted fashion, being more akin to independents of a 'labour' persuasion. W.A. Veitch, Hindmarsh, and particularly the maverick John Payne were very much in this mould. The war had resulted in Labour member Webb losing his seat in controversial circumstances.[95] Harry Holland won it in 1918.

The creation of an organised Labour Party brought a new dimension to politics. Labour became a serious contender for power following the election of 1919. It made strong showings in by-elections and local body elections. Holland's win, together with Peter Fraser's and Bob Semple's overwhelming victories in Wellington electorates imbued the small party with radical energy.

Labour became a highly disciplined parliamentary party.[96] The old-style, amateur 'socialist' activists and craft unionists of the Liberal period were replaced by a cadre of professional politicians. Labour was committed to making decisions by majority vote, and there was extensive consultation among its members. The party was strongly influenced by its successful Australian counterpart, in which caucus had a central place. The caucus elected its leader, and also 'decided the order of speakers in parliamentary debates, allocated seats on the front bench, approved the introduction of private members' bills and decided the approach to government legislation'.[97]

Holland warned a startled House in his maiden speech that he came 'to effect a change of classes at the fountain of power … we shall often shock the unthinking members of this House, and … often infuriate the intolerant members. But one thing is certain: we shall in the end succeed in converting the intelligent section.'[98] That remained to be seen. Labour's path to power was to be tortuous, and for a long time its members were ostracised by others. There was a cultural and social abyss to be bridged. Clyde Carr remembered that they 'were not even welcomed to the billiard tables in the members' lobby'. On a lighter note, Carr described how the rough West Coast Labour member James O'Brien and a colleague engaged in lighthearted 'heated and acrimonious vilification of each other' to the extent that 'a dear old gentleman "from another place" [the Legislative Council] thought bloodshed would certainly follow, and summoned the Sergeant-at-Arms.'[99]

Allen, Parliamentary Portraits

Paddy Webb was elected for Grey for the Social Democratic Party in 1913, one of the first Labour members in the House. He resigned in 1917 to challenge the government in a by-election after being imprisoned for three months for making seditious statements. He won unopposed, but lost the seat in 1918 after being absent for the session as a result of his further imprisonment for two years for refusing to be conscripted. He was prevented from standing again by legislation which disqualified conscientious objectors for 12 years. Webb won Buller in 1933, and held it until his retirement in 1946. He became Postmaster-General, and Minister of Mines and Labour, in the first Labour government.

Escaping the 'trammels of the past': organised party government, 1913–35

The members' lounge in Parliament Buildings, with billiard tables.

Holland's stirring sentiments provoked laughter, but Labour soon proved a well-informed, aggressive, organised and determined critic of the government, dangling before voters the lure of an alternative social order. Labour began to develop a substantial external organisation, with a national executive, a large membership that included affiliated trade unions, and Representation Committees in all electorates.[100] During the 1920s, dominated by the parliamentary wing, the party consolidated and gradually moved from revolutionary socialism to working for social change by democratic and parliamentary means. Candidates were required to sign a pledge to support the party platform and to vote in the House in accordance with the majority in caucus.

The second session of 1918 was the first to be held in the new chamber. Labour tried to present itself as the real Opposition by amending the Address-in-Reply.[101] The House sat from late October through the height of the influenza epidemic. At least 18 members were laid low, with the Labour caucus particularly affected. The epidemic resulted in the death of Labour's leader Hindmarsh and Reform's David Buick. Holland became the new leader of the Labour Party. Massey briefly adjourned the House in mid November so that ill members could regain their health to deal with a concerted onslaught of business before he and Ward returned overseas to the Peace Conference. He was forced to adjourn the House again because of the severity of the epidemic, and then to close the galleries. The House farewelled Massey and Ward once again, and awaited the return of Captains Coates, Hine and Seddon. Downie Stewart had already returned to the House, and Massey had spoken of the contribution made by some 100,000 New Zealand men in the war.

As the Labour Party became a real force, support for the National government waned. Towards the end of the war Reform approached the Liberals about a possible 'fusion' of the two parties, but was spurned. Ward suddenly brought the coalition to an end in August 1919, just before the session was due to start. He immediately issued a radical manifesto designed to demarcate his Liberal party from Reform and provide the basis for a rapprochement with Labour. Massey was left high and dry and had to contend with serious rumblings within his own caucus concerning his leadership and the Reform cabinet.[102] He included the returned war hero Coates and two from the discontented 'Progressive Reform' group in a new cabinet.

Despite Ward's precipitate actions, Reform and the Liberals could always find common ground against their mutual foe, Labour. At the start of the 1919 session, Ward promised not to bring down the government straight away, and the House witnessed the strange spectacle of members from both major parties remaining silent during the Address-in-Reply. It was left to Labour to test confidence in the government. The motion was lost 28 to 5 after a mass exodus of Liberal members from the chamber.[103] The breach between the Liberals and Labour widened. Some Liberals considered throwing their hand in with Reform and voted consistently with the government. Massey was able to stagger through the session and into the election that had been twice held over because of the war, and was finally held at the end of 1919.

As the House polarised between Reform and Labour caucuses were held more frequently.[104] The Liberal Party frequently split on divisions and was described as a substantial body of 'critical freelances'. On a number of occasions, the Liberals fled the chamber rather than vote on Labour's no-confidence motions. On others, the Liberals moved motions against the government, then when Labour joined them, voted against their own motion rather than support Labour. The longstanding traditions of the House, based on a ritualistic opposition of two parties, were thrown into confusion. As Holland frequently and bitterly complained, much of the Liberal Party was keeping Reform in power.[105]

Labour strove to become the official Opposition and used private members' bills to forge an alternative programme. Savage advocated motherhood endowment, Howard workers' compensation, and Fraser unemployment insurance.[106] Labour struggled valiantly to offer day-to-day opposition to the government. 'All-night sitting … supper adjournment at 10 o'clock, Ministerial benches usually almost empty, Labour benches usually putting up at least a decent show. It's Labour members, of course, who talk at least nine-tenths of the session's shining hours away. The Government emulates Brer Rabbit – lies low and says nuffin' … Up in the room used by the Labour Whips and others, usually somebody would be studying something … that at the very least should be said for the Labour veterans'.[107]

Massey lacked a strong sense of direction after the war.[108] Handicapped by small or non-existent majorities, he steered the government in response to public opinion, listening carefully to the 'people's voice' and not venturing policies that might disturb the precarious balance. The Women's Parliamentary Rights Bill enabling women to be elected to Parliament was introduced with little fanfare. It had been lobbied for on and off since women gained the vote. The bill was passed in a single sitting without a division.[109] Three women stood in the 1919 election. None was successful, but Reform's Ellen Melville ran the winning candidate close in the Grey Lynn seat. She stood unsuccessfully on a number of subsequent occasions.

The 1919 election result reflected the newly polarised political forces. The licensing poll seemed about to usher in prohibition until the votes of soldiers from overseas narrowly reversed the result. Religious bigotry, not usually found in New Zealand politics, became evident as the Protestant Political Association made its presence felt. Massey, although encumbered by a number of 'Independent Reform' candidates pledged to support him only on votes of no-confidence, won a workable majority for the first time with 47 seats. Labour slightly increased its representation to eight, having provided a strong alternative policy platform and for the first time contesting a majority of the electorates. Micky Savage, D.G. Sullivan and Bill Parry entered the House. The Liberals, caught in the middle, fell to 19 seats. Their leading figures Ward, G.W. Russell and Carroll lost their seats. For a time the ailing W.D.S. Macdonald became leader. When he died suddenly in 1920 he was replaced by Wilford, who proved unable to keep the disintegrating party together.[110]

During the 1920 session confusion between the Opposition parties was cruelly exposed when the financial debate suddenly collapsed without warning.[111] Massey, to amusement, was able to thank the House for allowing the budget to go through without criticism. Statham, who was now an independent, denounced the influence of party in the House and introduced a motion for an elected executive. In his opinion, 'the difference between the Reform party and the Liberal party is the difference between Tweedledum and Tweedledee so far as policy is concerned'.[112]

Parliamentary collection

View of old Parliament Buildings and St Mary's from across Sydney Street, watercolour by Katherine Holmes, c.1898.

Parliament Buildings from Molesworth Street, oil painting by F.C.H., 1906.

ATL, G416

The parliamentary complex. From left to right, Bowen House, the Beehive, Parliament House and the Parliamentary Library.

Simon Woolf photograph

Paul McCredie photograph

Parliamentary Library after refurbishment.

Paul McCredie photograph, Parliamentary Service collection

Parliamentary Library foyer.

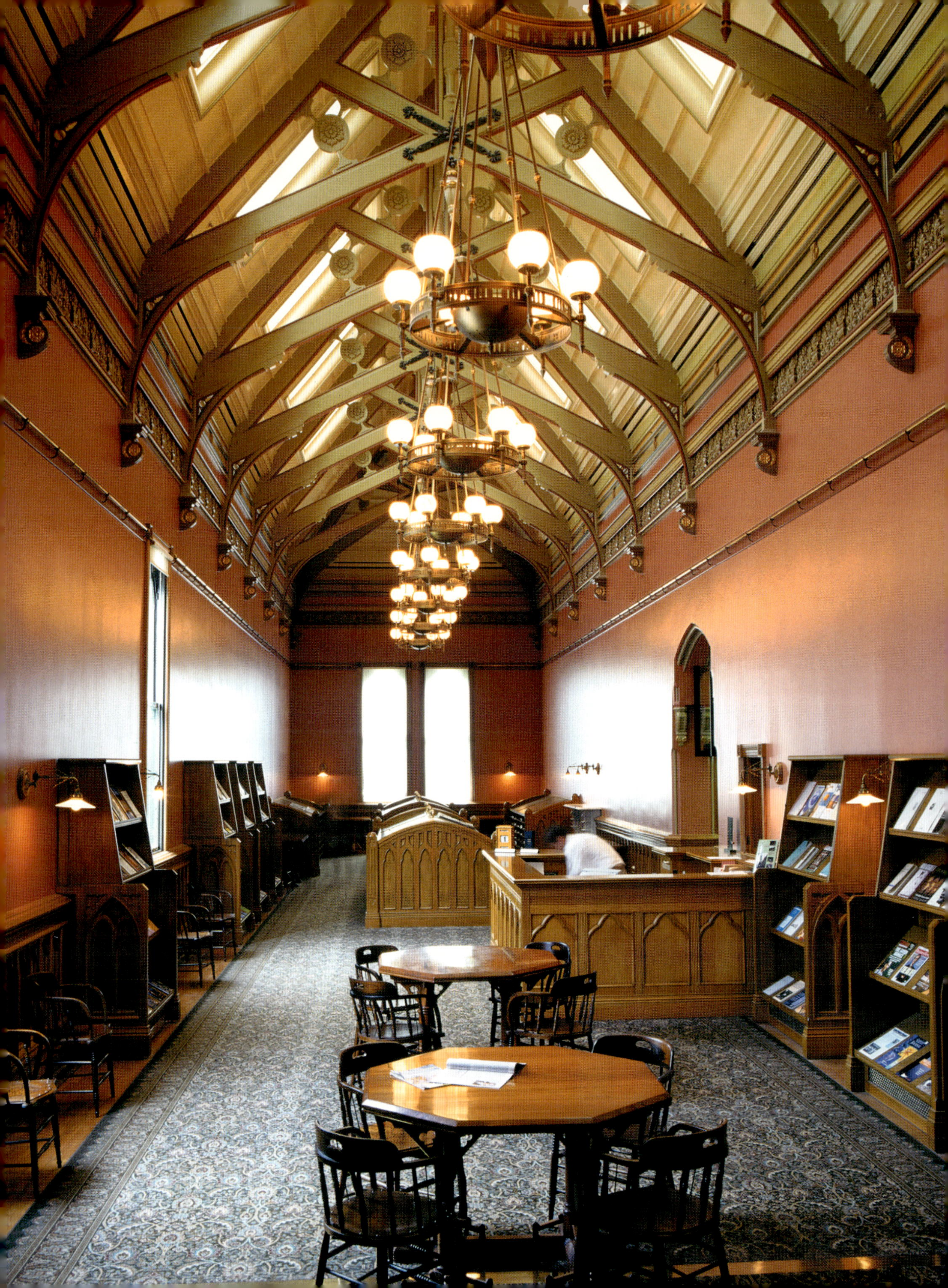

Parliament House and the Beehive by night.

Grant Sheehan photograph

Left: Parliamentary Library reading room.

Paul McCredie photograph, Parliamentary Service collection

Above and below: State opening of Parliament, December 1999, by Governor-General Sir Michael Hardie Boys.

Paul Fisher photographs, Parliamentary Service collection

Paul McCredie photograph, Parliamentary Service collection

Legislative Council chamber, Parliament House.

Governor-General Sir Michael Hardie Boys delivers the Speech from the Throne, December 1999, accompanied by his wife and flanked by the Prime Minister, Helen Clark (left), and Leader of the Opposition, Jenny Shipley (right).

Paul Fisher photograph, Parliamentary Service collection

Entrance lobbies for the first to the third floors, Parliament House.

Paul McCredie photograph, Parliamentary Service collection

The Grand Hall in Parliament House, previously the members' lounge.

Paul McCredie photograph, Parliamentary Service collection

Paul McCredie photograph, Parliamentary Service collection

View of the House of Representatives chamber from the chair of the Clerk of the House.

The original Maori Affairs Committee Room, Parliament House, opened in 1922.

Paul McCredie photograph, Parliamentary Service collection

The new Maori Affairs Committee Room, Maui Tikitiki a Taranga, Parliament House, with tukutuku – Nga toru kete (the three baskets of knowledge) – and carvings (left to right) of Maui, Taranga, Hinetitama and Tanenuarangi on the wall.

Paul McCredie photograph, Parliamentary Service collection

Opposite: Detail of carvings in Maori Affairs Committee Room, Maui Tikitiki a Taranga. Top, kowhaiwhai and carving above main doorway lintel inside the room. Bottom left, Maui, and right, Taranga, Maui's mother.

Norm Heke photographs, Parliamentary Service collection

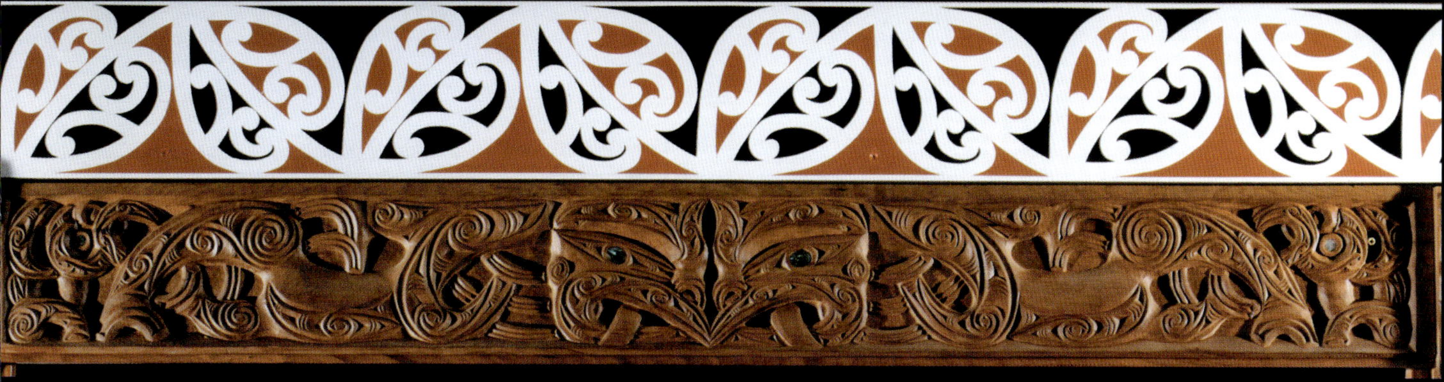

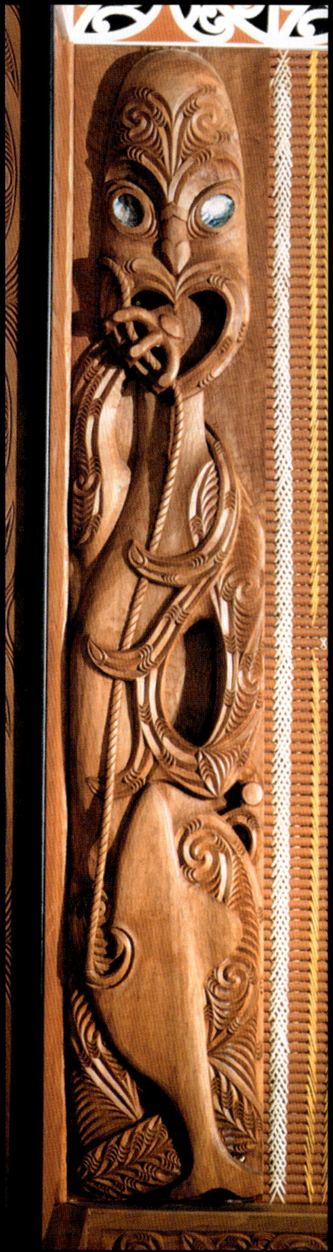

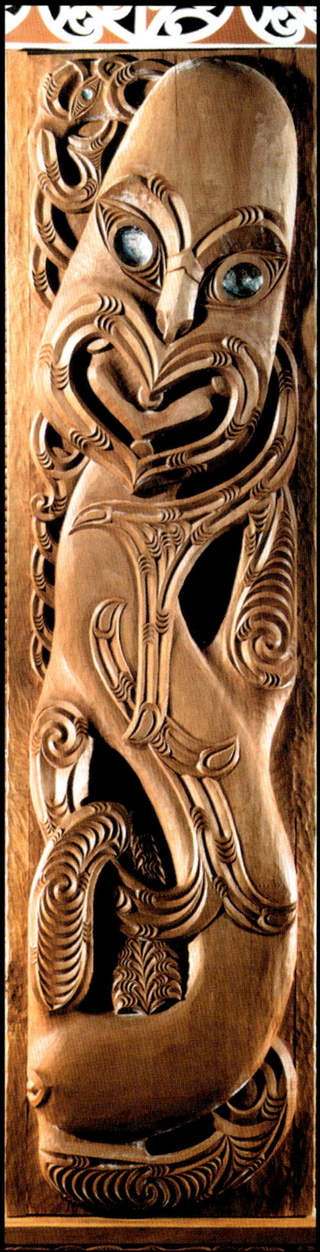

Paul McCredie photograph, Parliamentary Service collection

The Speaker's office, panelled in Canadian bird's eye maple and walnut, originally the cabinet room in Parliament House. The Speaker's desk is the table used by Seddon's cabinet and at right is the mace.

Doorways at Parliament House. Left – carved main entrance doorway to Maori Affairs Committee Room, Maui Tikitiki a Taranga. Centre – bronze gates at the entrance to Parliament House. Right – carved main entrance doorway to Pacific Room.

Parliamentary Service collection

Paul McCredie photograph, Parliamentary Service collection

Internal courtyard Galleria, Parliament House, with artwork, 'These are matters of pride', by Malcolm Harrison.

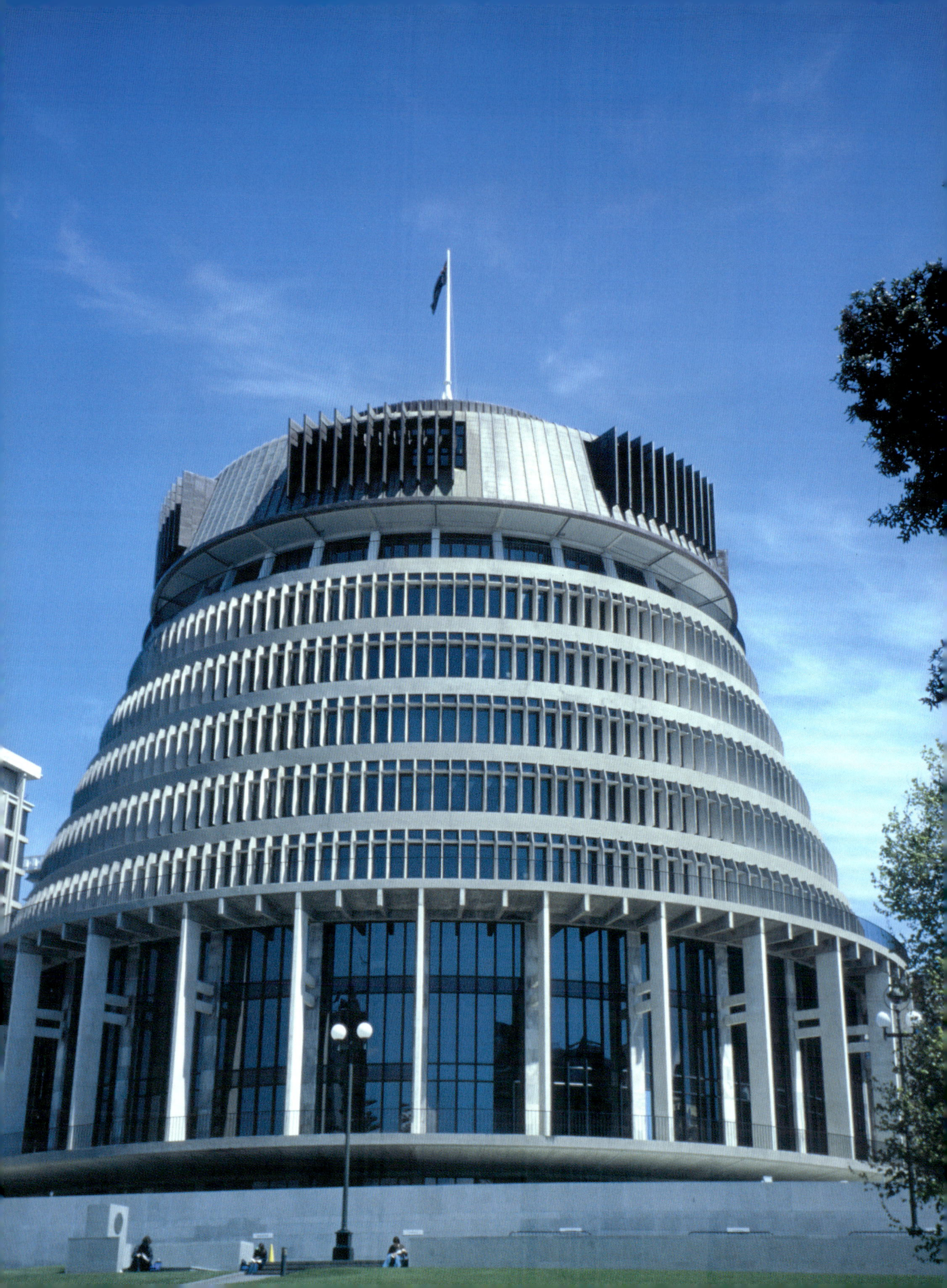

Escaping the 'trammels of the past': organised party government, 1913–35

The place of the independent was increasingly difficult. 'The party man says that the Independent's task is to square the circle – to run, more or less aimlessly, in a circle during session, and square it to his constituents.'[113] This put the dilemma rather nicely – in the House the independent had only his own principles and the need to account to his electorate as points of reference, but these could prove very difficult to put into practice when 'party' increasingly provided the steady guideline. Massey would not have a bar of prime ministerial power being so drastically usurped by his old friend Statham's highly unorthodox move.[114] Holland agreed with Massey – for him, party government was the *sine qua non* of politics since it was the extension of class interests. He preferred the Australian system of the caucus of the dominant party selecting cabinet members and the Prime Minister allocating portfolios – an arrangement that would be adopted by the future Labour government.

Massey's front bench, 1922 – from left: E.P. Lee, G.J. Anderson, W.H. Herries, Massey, D.H. Guthrie, W. Nosworthy. ArchNZ, ABGX, 7574, box 3, folder (a)

Parliament met for a week and a half in March 1921 before Massey attended an Imperial Conference in England. When his trip was treated as a matter of confidence, the government prevailed without difficulty.[115] The dour Bell became Acting Prime Minister and had to deal with a deteriorating economy as the short-lived postwar boom came to an end. Parliament reconvened in late September 1921. Members required considerable powers of endurance for a long session that lasted through a hot summer until mid February 1922. This was the first occasion on which Parliament had sat for a full session through a summer. Massey was keen to address the backlog of legislation that had built up since the war and because of his absences.[116] The Liberals fared no better than before with a motion of no-confidence during the Address-in-Reply, and when Labour proposed its own the Liberals walked out.

Left: The Beehive – the executive wing of the parliamentary complex – designed by Sir Basil Spence and the Ministry of Works. Gavin McLean photograph

Late in the session Massey introduced the Public Expenditure Adjustment Bill, which cut public service wages and salaries by 10 per cent. This met with stern resistance. McCombs, who was known as the 'Labour Party adding-machine', was in his element, revelling in cost of living statistics.[117] Holland complained about the half-hour limit to debate and, with the agreement of the House, was able to speak for longer. He promised a 'fight to the finish – the division bells must ring on every clause'.[118] Labour members mounted a stonewall, moving amendments and forcing divisions in Committee. Holland proclaimed that Labour had demonstrated that it was 'an effective opposition'. In a confirmation of this, when the Liberal George Witty moved a symbolic reduction in the estimates and was supported by Labour, the Liberals then chose to vote against their own motion. Within a few months, at the end of June 1922, members returned wearily to the chamber. The government hoped that the session would not be too long and this proved the case. Labour's Fraser expressed the hope that principles and measures would take precedence over men, in other words that organised parties would become pre-eminent.[119]

Such sentiments did not seem prophetic in the light of Massey's role in the election of 1922. Very much in the mould of Seddon, he took personal charge in the absence of a strong party organisation. He had to battle against the impact of the recession and government retrenchment. The advance of parties seemed stymied. Reform and the Liberals floundered around in search of some new organising principle. Labour made spectacular gains, nearly doubling its representation to 17, while Reform was reduced to 39, with Speaker Lang and Chairman of Committees Malcolm losing their seats. The Liberals remained stuck at 19 seats.[120]

With five professed independents, Reform seemingly could not muster a majority – but neither could anyone else. Massey's political skills and the deep rift between Liberal and Labour provided a resolution. Massey again suggested fusion, and called an early short session in February 1923 to determine who was the government. The 27 farmers in the House protested; they had work to do at home.[121] The Liberals rebuffed the fusion proposal, so Massey worked on the independents and secured the vote of Isitt, a dissident Liberal. Because other independents and some Liberals would not support Labour in a no-confidence motion, this was sufficient to keep Massey in power.

Massey also dealt with the problem of the vacant Speakership. Sir John Luke, who was also supported by the Liberals, would have been Massey's preference if Reform had obtained a viable majority. Lacking this, Massey looked to the Opposition and latched onto Statham, who was relatively youthful and had the added qualification of being a barrister. Massey put forward Statham; Holland responded with McCombs to test the Liberals' allegiances.[122] With Ward watching from the gallery, the Liberals voted as a bloc with Reform and Statham was installed as the first New Zealand-born Speaker.

It remained to be seen how the parties would line up over the separate no-confidence motions tendered by the Liberals and Labour. Holland's mastery of the standing orders was evident in his successful moving of an amendment to the Liberals' test of confidence during the Address-in-Reply. He secured the inexperienced Speaker's agreement, overriding Massey's challenge. Both Liberal and Reform maintained an eerie silence while Labour's new recruits 'expounded the Labour creed on strictly orthodox lines'.[123] When Labour's motion was put, the Liberals walked out, leaving Isitt, Harry Atmore, Allen Bell and Witty to vote with Reform. The government won 40 to 18. Labour was initially astonished, then responded with caustic 'Good-byes'. The Liberals then marched back in. Labour and Atmore supported the Liberal motion, but Reform won by 39 to 36. The House was then adjourned to June with Liberal support. When Labour tried to stonewall over the move, the Speaker struggled to impose his authority. South Island members seemed likely to miss their ferry, but they got away at 7.40 p.m. when Massey pre-empted the Speaker and correctly prevented notices of motion on a 'government day'. The House finally adjourned.

While Massey had retained power, the circumstances in which he had done so severely restricted his freedom of manoeuvre. Isitt's long-term position was unclear, and some Reform members persistently bucked party discipline in the following years. Massey threatened a dissolution more than

Charles Ernest Statham was born in Dunedin on 10 May 1875, educated at Otago Boys' High School and became a lawyer. Elected for Dunedin Central in 1911 as a Reform supporter, he became disillusioned with Massey's government. After attempting to form a Progressive Reform Party, he was an independent member by 1919. He increasingly became an advocate for the private member and an elected executive. In 1923, with Massey not wanting to lose his slim majority, Statham became the first New Zealand-born Speaker.

He proved a firmer and more traditional Speaker than Lang, and refused to take part in Committee proceedings. He favoured a greater measure of House of Commons' tradition and dignity, wore the full-bottomed wig, and had a special chair manufactured from which to preside. This high-backed 'Empire Chair' was made by a Dunedin period furniture specialist who was one of Statham's constituents. It had the New Zealand coat of arms above the head. Statham was made Knight Bachelor in 1926. His Speakership was made difficult by the complex three-party system, but he developed a thorough understanding of parliamentary procedure and standing orders and became an outstanding as well as longstanding Speaker, with some ranking him equal with or superior to O'Rorke. His argument that the Speaker's electorate should be uncontested – as in the House of Commons – was unavailing, and his majority dwindled steadily. He retired in 1935, but was appointed to the Legislative Council in 1936, and returned to Wellington to work as a lawyer. He died in 1946.

once. He and his whips had to be ever vigilant not only to 'keep a House' but also to guard against snap divisions. As Massey remarked to Downie Stewart: 'Never try to carry on a Government with a majority of only two or three; it is hell all the time'. He described the three-party system as 'wretched' and a 'curse', and was reported to have told a sick Reformer: 'I won't have members going to bed merely because they are ill. If they want to die, they must die in the House!'[124]

The session from mid-year 1923 was short and hurried, so that Massey could again get away to Britain. The House sat on Monday for most of the session, and worked late into the night. The Address-in-Reply test of confidence confirmed Reform's hold on power. To Massey's immense irritation, the Liberal and Labour parties delayed business so that Massey had to rush to board his ship a day before the session closed.[125]

Massey returned for the 1924 session, which opened at the end of June. His small majority was intact, but his health was poor. Over the years he had given many eulogies on the deaths of old and retired members (who were usually referred to as 'crossing the bar' of the House), but few can have affected him more than the death of his stalwart chief party financier and trusted ally of old, Walter Buchanan.[126] The session was very busy; nearly 100 bills were passed and long hours were worked.

An amendment to the Gaming Act to liberalise totalisator licences produced a stonewall which would have been pressed through into Saturday 'but for the fact that Reform members ... desire to attend a race meeting'.[127] Reform members came rugged up to the chamber and had the lights turned down to aid their slumber, while those speaking lowered their voices to the same end. One member moved that progress be reported because of the ranks of sleepers.

The stonewall placed the Chairman of Committees, J.A. Young, under severe strain. It ended abruptly when Young, failing to hear McCombs' call for a division because of the 'hum of conversation', put a clause of the bill.[128] The Opposition initially protested by using 'improvised head coverings' to raise points of order. Holland – wearing a hat many sizes too large for him – refused to provide tellers for the vote. Then Labour and some Liberals trooped out of the chamber in protest at the alleged refusal of the Chairman to accept the word of a member. Eventually, after Massey had been consulted, the House went into Committee again, rapidly divided on the same clause, and the stonewall ended. The boycotting members did not return to the chamber until the Speaker returned to the chair.

Coates takes the helm

By the end of the year Massey was unwell and had to relinquish much of his work. Early in 1925 his health collapsed entirely.[129] After his death on 10 May, his body lay in state in Parliament Buildings. With the old master gone, it was no easy task to find a successor. Most of his old benchmates had either predeceased him or retired. The much younger Gordon Coates was elected as the new Reform leader.

Coates seemed to bring a refreshingly different style to the government. He was known as a man of action, of bluff, straight responses and an informal 'breezy unconventional' approach. As Bassett describes him, he 'dressed immaculately, was urbane, smoked in public, liked dancing and was extremely physical. There was a hint of unorthodoxy that appealed after years of stuffiness in high places.'[130] Coates was open with the press, giving briefings to reporters in the toilet that were dubbed 'pisshouse politics'. As he washed his hands afterwards, he would on occasion sprinkle the journalists playfully and say, 'Receive the Prime Minister's blessing.'[131] He would also give tips for the races and shout reporters drinks in Bellamy's. Coates was at his best engaging in bonhomie in the House, dealing with deputations, and travelling around the country talking with the 'common man'.

But Coates proved hesitant as Prime Minister. He lacked the obsessive devotion to politics of his predecessors, did not appear to think strategically about preserving or enhancing his power, and manifested a 'take it or leave it' attitude when matters demanded concentrated and sustained attention. He retained Massey's cabinet virtually unchanged, and failed to tackle the issue of 'fusing' Reform and the Liberals.

Wilford had slowly moved the Liberal Party closer to Reform, but neither party was willing to surrender its identity.[132] When Coates pledged to complete Massey's programme, Wilford proclaimed that he had 'banged, bolted, and barred the door' to a new party. With Wilford's health breaking down, George Forbes became the new leader and the party became known as the National Party. With Forbes and Coates as the new leaders of their respective parties, and with the emergence of Labour as the real Opposition, the scene was set for the next decade.

Meanwhile the usual games were played during the 1925 session. In June, Labour challenged the government in one of the fastest no-confidence motions on record as the House went into Committee of Supply immediately. The debate took just 20 minutes. When the division came, Fraser suggested that 'All those in the middle walk out' – and the Liberals did so.[133] Labour's second no-confidence motion during the Address-in-Reply produced a similar result. The noted independent Harry Atmore

Gordon Coates was elected to Kaipara in 1911 and held the seat until his death. Initially an independent Liberal, he joined Reform to defeat the Liberals in the House in 1912. Coates served with distinction in the war, being awarded a Military Cross and bar. He was appointed to cabinet in 1919 and became Prime Minister in 1925 after the death of Massey. Defeated in 1928, his Reform Party joined with United in 1931 to form a coalition government. Coates took a wide range of portfolios, including Finance after the resignation of William Downie Stewart in 1933. Out of office again when Labour gained power, he became increasingly distant from the National Opposition and accepted Prime Minister Fraser's offer of a place in the war cabinet in 1940. Coates died in Parliament Buildings on 27 May 1943.

Escaping the 'trammels of the past': organised party government, 1913–35

exhorted Coates to form a 'National Government' and abandon the destructive impact of party politics.[134] This motion was amended by Labour to promote fusion between Reform and the Liberals and an end to the three-party system. The government took these as a matter of confidence. On Labour's amendment, the Liberals felt able to support Coates. Atmore's motion was lost 34 to 30, indicating that Reform had a stable majority against the joint forces of the Liberals and Labour. More tests of confidence followed, leading the government to protest that the situation was getting ridiculous. By the end of the session people were beginning to wonder whether Coates was such a breath of fresh air after all. The government's financial statement was tardy and uninspired, and little policy direction had emerged.

Having won the election in 1925 and become Prime Minister, Coates addresses the House.

The parliamentary fray was becoming more restrained, however.[135] Coates was popular in the House, and the absence of unpleasant 'scenes' was remarked upon. Holland and other Labour members had by now become part of the parliamentary establishment and well-integrated into the forms and courtesies of the House. Holland and Fraser in particular were very careful to observe parliamentary traditions, and Fraser showed considerable interest and expertise in standing orders and procedure.[136]

Statham's firm hand had undoubtedly helped. In the years since O'Rorke, a practice had grown up of members conversing and interrupting during speeches. 'There is a constant hum of conversation, a general air of inattention, and such a running fire of interruption, interjection, and retort, as would not be permitted elsewhere'.[137] Statham reapplied stricter rules about behaviour and insisted that members make their speeches without reading from detailed notes. He counselled members to consult with him in private or raise points of order before procedural matters got out of hand in the House, rather than subject him to the 'unparliamentary expressions' and 'black looks cast towards the Chair' that he was forced to endure.[138]

The election of 1925 was a triumph for Coates and his new kind of campaigning, which relied less on Reform Party policies than on a presidential-style populist tour. The slogans were: 'Coats off with Coates'; and 'More business in Government, less Government in business'.[139] Reform swept back into office with 55 seats. Labour was reduced to 12 and the National Party slumped to 11, with 2 'Liberal' independents.

The resignation of the cabinet minister C.J. Parr in 1926 made the Eden seat the scene for a clash between Labour and National over who would become the official Opposition. The ubiquitous Ellen Melville declared herself an independent Reform candidate, split the vote, and allowed Labour's H.G.R. (Rex) Mason to win. Labour was at last the official Opposition. In May, Holland claimed the Opposition benches, the whips' and other Opposition rooms, and the privileges of Leader of the Opposition.[140]

Coates kept on a number of old hands in cabinet. The Reform ranks were elderly, rural, conservative and conspicuously lacking in debating skills. Labour took delight in pointing out their lack of vitality. They were unkindly described by John A. Lee as 'Elderly men of Victorian sentiment … washed out of their armchairs into the House, where they had busied themselves in trying to turn the political clock back … It was yester-day trying to govern to-day, when the country was crying out for men with a vision of the future.'[141] Reform Party discipline slackened, and vote-splitting became a real problem with the enlarged majority.

Ward had re-entered politics as the member for Invercargill. When the 1926 session opened (it was shortened because of Coates' forthcoming attendance at the Imperial Conference), his arrival in the chamber to be sworn in 'caused a stir, as members rose to shake his hand'.[142] Insisting on calling himself a 'Liberal', he rose to second the re-election of Speaker Statham and made an extraordinary statement on his independence from party that was greeted by laughter. He thus pre-empted Holland, who had to swallow his pride and merely congratulate the Speaker on his election. But Ward's speech accurately reflected the parlous state of the National Party, which had fragmented.

Coates somehow overlooked the Governor-General's speech, which had to be thrown together at the last minute.[143] The speech divulged little that was new. He then omitted to speak to the government's policy during the Address-in-Reply debate. The session was notable for social legislation and other measures regulating services and controlling business that antagonised the Reform Party's right wing. Reform maintained its majority and got its measures through, but in the case of the Motor-omnibus Bill only with the aid of Labour as a substantial minority of Reform members voted against the government.

The 1927 session proved no better for Coates. Again the Speech from the Throne gave little away – Coates seemed unaware of the need to publicise his government's policies. The Reform caucus remained divided and several members left it. In the absence of clear government policy, private members' bills filled the void, creating more trouble for the government. Labour picked up another seat after R.F. Bollard, the Minister of Internal Affairs, died suddenly of pneumonia. Parliament ground to a halt as Reform tried to buttress its fortunes in the by-election.

When Labour members obstructed a bill to restrict the application of the Arbitration Act against which the labour movement was mobilising, most of it was dropped.[144] Coates was also embarrassed by the fate of the Licensing Amendment Bill, which he had naïvely introduced as a private member, allowing a free vote. Assuming his 'statesmanship' would carry it through, Coates found that he was able to please no-one. The bill was drastically rewritten in Committee by prohibitionists. Coates was forced to report progress, but he then refused to move its third reading and its passage was taken over by a Reform member, E.P. Lee. The much-altered bill passed the House with the support of many Reform members, including several ministers. Coates brought his influence to bear in the Legislative Council to have it restored to something like its original shape, but the House refused to countenance this and the bill was shelved. Coates was equally discredited in the eyes of the prohibitionists and the licensing trade. This session was the longest on record, at 105 sitting days.[145] Restricting the hours of sitting, or even the anathema of outright closure, was again mooted.

The 1928 session began with a concerted Labour onslaught over rising unemployment. Also facing criticism from business interests, the government was now paralysed. The new 'United' Party, formed by Veitch and including Forbes' National Party, organised for the election at the end of the year.[146] The new party sought to combine a resurrection of the old Liberal Party with an assertion of values of individual liberty.

Escaping the 'trammels of the past': organised party government, 1913–35

In September, out of the blue, the United Party elected the elderly and frail Ward as its leader.[147] Reform, which had been preparing to counter Labour, now found itself distracted by United. In an election meeting, Ward misread his notes and made a fateful promise to borrow the incredible sum of £70 million in a single year. Far from destroying United's chances, this error proved the secret to its success in the election. People were looking, as they had in 1925, for someone to wave a magic wand and return the country to prosperity. It was time to try the old financial wizard Ward. Reform suffered an unexpected and disastrous reverse, being reduced to 28 seats. United won 27 and Labour 19. Four independents supported Ward. Half of the old House and a great deal of experience had gone – an unprecedented degree of turnover – and United had many of the newcomers. Coates, who had come into the House as recently as 1912, was now one of the most senior parliamentarians.

Parliament was called for 4 December 1928, in deference to the old tradition that the confidence of the House should be tested, even though Coates knew that Labour would support United. Statham was re-elected Speaker unanimously.[148] Holland stated Labour's position. 'We hold the key … How we turn the key will depend upon the circumstances'. Coates began to present reports to the House, to the exasperation of Ward, who wanted to take power immediately. On 7 December Ward suddenly called for a division over one such report. 'There were hurried consultations on the benches of United and Labour, and "alarums and excursions" by the two Labour Whips.'[149] But everyone bar one from Labour voted with Coates, and the government won by 43 to 33. This gave Reform a very brief reprieve.

When the inevitable no-confidence motion eventually came, Coates displayed his best qualities in a lengthy valedictory speech. Following warm applause, only Reform voted against the motion, which passed by 50 to 28. More than 16 years of Reform government had come to an end. Coates rose from his seat and exchanged greetings with his opponents, who were 'spontaneously lining up to shake his hand'.

Ward was tempted to go to the ballot box again to obtain an outright majority, but the Governor-General counselled him strongly against this. Ward had to rest content with a caucus of untried members and an uneasy alliance with Labour. His cabinet was very inexperienced. Four ministers had not even been in the House before.

Political uncertainty, depression and parliamentary reform

The next three years saw a most peculiar arrangement. First Labour, then Reform propped up a weak and indecisive United government, which survived for a full term. No single party could gain a clear majority. Meanwhile, some formative developments in parliamentary procedure, more suited to strong party government, took place as depression engulfed the country and the need for strong measures became evident. The overriding issue was the control of debate in the chamber. During the 1920s, reform of the standing orders had been considered, but no progress was made.[150] In 1928, an arduous session, the question was discussed once more after Dan Sullivan boasted that Labour's 'capacity for self-expression is a well that never runs dry'.[151] Holland goaded Coates on the need for 'more business in government' in reforming parliamentary procedure, and Fraser thought that closure might have to be looked at.

Ward activated the Standing Orders Committee. He had long agitated for daytime sittings, and finally saw his chance.[152] The acknowledged experts in standing orders – Ngata, Fraser and McCombs – were made members of the committee, along with Ward, the Speaker, and the Reform and Labour leaders. The committee rejected closure (which was advocated by some Reform members, including Coates) but enthusiastically recommended wholesale revision of the standing orders.

The recommendations adopted by the House included reduced sitting hours and time limits on speeches. On Tuesdays to Thursdays the House would sit from 2.30 p.m. to 10.30 p.m., and on Friday

The new standing orders of 1929 limited the speaking times of members.

from 10.30 a.m. to 5.30 p.m. to allow members to get away for the weekend. A speaking limit of one hour was retained for the financial statement, but Address-in-Reply speeches were reduced to 30 minutes and those in Committee from 10 to 5 minutes. Significantly for the future, the standing orders themselves could be changed without the previous notice required simply by moving a motion.[153]

The flexibility of the new standing orders was immediately exploited to push government business through, particularly towards the end of sessions. Governments also took advantage of being able to extend the hours of sitting to midnight, use private members' time, take precedence for government business, and require Monday sittings. The hours members had to endure in the chamber were thus not reduced in spite of the changes.

The alliance between United and Labour was soon tested when Coates moved a surprise no-confidence motion as an amendment to the financial debate.[154] Reform's motion was rebuffed. Later in the session, Reform mounted a stonewall of some 50 hours over the most contentious measure of the session, an amendment to the Land and Income Tax Act. Reform had eight 'shift operators' to keep the debate going, while United and Labour combined to keep a quorum, with most sleeping in a brilliantly lit chamber that looked like 'a sanatorium verandah'. The 'tedious repetition' rule was applied by the Chairman of Committees after 24 hours' debate on a clause. When the division came at 5.40 a.m. members poured into the chamber, several without collars and some without shoes. One collarless minister 'had his hair combed by a friendly Reformer'.[155] The government conceded a minor change and the stonewall came to an end. But when Holland moved to censure the government for failing to restore public service salaries, alignments switched. Forbes got cautious support from Reform to win.[156] Ward was by now seriously ill, and was observed 'falling about the passages' in Parliament.[157] In May 1930 he was forced to resign as Prime Minister as his government had lost all momentum. Ward died on 8 July 1930. The House adjourned for a week and he was given a state funeral.

On Ward's death, 'Honest George' Forbes became Prime Minister after being narrowly elected as leader of the United Party. He was considered an uninspired leader thrust into unenviable responsibilities. Gardner describes him as being bizarrely 'transmuted from leader of a party in decline to head of a nation in crisis'.[158]

Forbes was stolid, taciturn and presented an unruffled and distant persona in the House. He was described as impervious to the many interjections that were

George Forbes was elected for Hurunui in 1908. He became Liberal whip in 1912 and was elected leader of the 'National' Party in 1925. When Ward resigned in 1930, Forbes became Prime Minister. He determinedly adopted measures he believed necessary to deal with the depression of the early 1930s. On the defeat of the coalition in 1935 he was Opposition leader for the 1936 session. He resigned his seat in 1943 and died in 1947.

Escaping the 'trammels of the past': organised party government, 1913–35

made during his speeches, and seemingly made no effort to produce an effect. Forbes did, however, have considerable debating skills, a good memory, and that most essential of skills in a party leader, an ability to assess the mood of the House. Like Massey, when he made decisions he stuck to them. His imperturbable manner, friendliness and courtesy were also useful attributes. During the depression, his decisiveness became intractability and stubbornness as he promulgated and defended unpopular measures.

The alliance between United and Labour was soon virtually at breaking point. Labour stayed with the government only to prevent Reform getting its hands on power. Urgency, available since 1903 but little used, now became a key tool for effecting government business. Forbes invoked urgency with gay abandon during the remainder of the 1929 session. It was also used liberally during the 1930 session for the vital Unemployment Bill and other measures.[159] The government argued that this was the only way in which 'the Government could have some control over the business of the House'. Labour began to protest at the practice, and some wondered whether the revised standing orders simply meant enhanced government power over the House.

The alliance reached breaking point when, late in the 1930 session, the government abandoned an amendment to the Industrial Conciliation and Arbitration Act, sponsored by the Alliance of Labour, that would have confirmed preference in employment for trade union members.[160] When Reform threatened a stonewall, the government caved in and called a division to adjourn the debate. Reform combined with United to win the vote by 35 to 16.

Labour split from United during the recess as it became clear that expenditure cuts and wage reductions would be imposed once Forbes returned from an Imperial Conference in London. Forbes talked of no 'dole' for the unemployed and promised severe retrenchment. Following a conference in January, the Reform Party began to support the government formally in early 1931.

The government convened an emergency session of Parliament in March 1931 because of the deteriorating economic situation. The depression was to prove disruptive to the traditional seasonal pattern of the sessions. Some took up most of the year. From the start of the session, Forbes took the entire week, including Mondays, up to midnight, and Saturday mornings, for government business.[161] Holland immediately moved no-confidence as an amendment to the Address-in-Reply debate. Reform sat silently while Labour put up one speaker after another. When the division came, the motion was defeated 50 to 20, with Reform and various independents supporting the government. When Labour tried again, Forbes moved urgency to cut debate short and this was passed 44 to 17. Further amendments followed amid a welter of withdrawals of words as Labour vented its spleen and the Speaker intervened.

Urgency would soon prove insufficient in the face of one of the most strenuous struggles ever mounted in the House.[162] It was taken for a Finance Bill which brought in 10 per cent cuts to public service salaries and allowed the Arbitration Court to amend awards. The struggle began when the bill went into Committee. Labour stonewalled all week until Forbes moved that progress be reported and the House rose at 2.45 p.m. on the Friday. Urgency was evidently insufficient. At 7.30 p.m., to Labour's astonishment, Forbes said that he would introduce closure. This standing order would allow members to move 'that the question be now put' without notice. Such a motion, to which 20 members must agree, would be decided without amendment or debate. If carried, the clause of the bill or other matter under consideration would itself be put forthwith, without further amendment or debate. The new standing order, based on a South African example, had been drafted within cabinet. With feelings running so high, neither the Speaker nor the Clerk had wanted to be involved.[163]

This move generated a ferocious debate which lasted from Saturday until the early hours of the following Tuesday. The debate followed familiar lines of argument: freedom of debate and the rights of the minority versus the need to be able to expedite business. The new standing order was eventually adopted, with some amendments, by 48 to 21.[164] Coates led a group of members in putting some constraints on its use. Closure could be ruled out by the Chair if it was 'an abuse of the rules of the House, or an infringement of the rights of the minority' (following the House of Commons), and it

Forbes and Coates bring into action the new standing order on closure adopted in 1931 to deal with Labour's stonewalling. Harry Holland suffers the consequences.

would lapse after the present Parliament. The latter provision caused Labour members to walk out en masse in protest against a measure they considered would apply only to the Labour Party in Opposition.

While Savage warned that the 'party machine is to be the judge as to when the closure is to be applied', hardheaded members such as C.H. Clinkard (who usually said little) complained that Parliament had degenerated into a 'talking shop'.[165] Forbes said bluntly that the changes of 1929 had been an experiment dependent upon the goodwill of members – and they had failed. The provision for closure that operated in the Parliaments of all other dominions was now required.

The House moved back to the Finance Bill. At 4.30 on Tuesday afternoon, Forbes moved the first closure motion, to prevent Labour continuing to move endless exemptions for those on lower wages. After Labour chorused 'Gag!', W.A. Bodkin, the Chairman of Committees, carefully explained his ruling that the motion for closure could be put while members listened intently. The motion passed 48 to 26, with some independents voting with Labour, and Parry shouting, 'Sandbaggers to the right!' The Chairman ruled out further amendments after consultation with the Speaker.[166] Late that night came the second motion for closure. The third came after midnight, and the fourth on Wednesday evening. The bill was reported shortly before midnight on Wednesday and received its third reading at 3 a.m. The relieved Forbes then adjourned the House until the following Wednesday.

The government had managed to push through the Finance Bill. There had been more than 70 divisions during nearly 100 hours' sitting over nine days. The closure mechanism proved sufficient to limit the impact of the stonewall and get the measure through. This fundamental shift in the practice of the House, which had taken 60 or more years to come to pass, was justified by the emergency nature of the session.

Speaker Statham soon consulted the Speaker of the South African House of Assembly over the closure rule.[167] While appreciating that he did not have to give reasons for accepting the motion, he wanted to give careful consideration to the nature and length of the debate, and the impact of closing debate on the legitimacy of Parliament. Subsequent Speakers' decisions ruled out early closure motions – plenty of opportunity for debate had to be given.

Reform continued to support the United government through the next session, from late June

1931, but Forbes suspended legislative initiatives to force the issue of a coalition between the two parties. Coates, who remained opposed to Reform fusing with the United government, moved only that an all-party expenditure committee be formed.[168] This committee met in late August, at which time sittings of the House were confined to the evenings. While Labour proposals stymied its work and United had no interest in making progress, the committee provided the catalyst for coalition.

Coalition and two-party alignment

Reform and United eventually agreed to form a coalition government on 17 September 1931. Forbes remained Prime Minister, but Reform took half the positions in the new cabinet of ten. Coates, now Leader of the House, held a range of portfolios, and Downie Stewart became Minister of Finance. Meanwhile the work of the House came to a virtual standstill as a result of the many adjournments. Later in the session Holland tested the new coalition with a motion of no-confidence but found it solid.[169] As the House thinned out near the end of the session, with members leaving to tend their electorates, uncertainty reigned. After much equivocating, Forbes finally divulged that the election would be held in three weeks' time.

The election proved a major difficulty and distraction. Both Reform and United had already chosen their candidates. The coalition merely asked the country to trust it to respond effectively to circumstances. With more than one 'anti-Labour' candidate in many electorates, vote-splitting was a major concern.[170] The Labour Party won 24 seats, the coalition 51. There was a small number of independents. In an ominous sign for the government, Labour won the most votes of any party, but for the moment the coalition had consolidated its hold on power. While continuing to test the confidence of the House during the Address-in-Reply debate, Labour focused its attacks on the measures introduced to cope with the depression.

The government's crucial initiatives were pushed through using urgency and closure during a special early session which lasted from late February to early May 1932. The galleries were packed, with the unemployed flocking to Parliament to witness the passage of the emergency measures. The House sat from Monday to Friday, 2.30 p.m. to midnight, exclusively for government business. One of the government's first actions was to reinstate the closure standing order, after it became clear that Labour would obstruct proceedings to its utmost.[171] The Industrial Conciliation and Arbitration Amendment Bill, which made awards voluntary, was passed by invoking closure 15 times against Labour's stonewall. Closure was also applied to the unemployment relief legislation.

According to Lee, Statham was forced to relax the strictures on unparliamentary language and turn a blind eye to deliberate provocation as Labour fulminated against the government. Even so, Fraser and Lee

J.C. Hill, Auckland Star, 23 April 1932

During the depression there was agitation to reduce the size and cost of the House. Here Forbes contemplates cutting expenditure with the 'Economy Commission' broom while the 80 members remain safe in their seats.

were suspended from the House when they refused to withdraw angry statements they had made – Lee had called the House 'a Parliament of curs'.[172] Ill-feeling mounted. Lee led Labour members in the lobby in singing 'We'll hang George Forbes on a sour apple tree', and Labour prophesied revolution and insurrection. Shortly afterwards violent disturbances broke out in the major centres. On 10 May 1932, 3,000 striking relief workers who had gathered at the Basin Reserve marched on Parliament. Coates received a deputation, but the crowd around the Cenotaph grew restless and a group broke away and began smashing windows along Lambton Quay.[173]

The Public Safety Conservation Bill, drawn up in the wake of these riots, was rushed through in a single sitting under urgency. Closure was applied six times while the National Expenditure Adjustment Bill, which imposed wage and salary cuts and retrenchment on the public service, was in Committee. Closure was also applied to the Finance Bill on several occasions while it was in Committee. This bill, among other things, extended the life of Parliament for a year. This was a bold move in peacetime. Labour claimed that its purpose was to prevent the decimation of the government at the polls.[174] On one occasion closure was even moved by a private member when, according to the Chairman of Committees, the extent of tedious repetition had reached unbearable levels. Most of the House was pleased to troop into the Ayes lobby.

During the lengthy second session of 1932, which began in late September, the House sat for more regular hours but urgency and closure were used frequently to push business along. This session lasted until March 1933, with a Christmas break. Pressure for a devaluation of the New Zealand currency

A demonstration on the steps of Parliament, c. 1932. The expansive new Parliament grounds soon became the rallying point for protest against governments. The 1920s, and in particular the depression years of the early 1930s, saw demonstrations as the unemployed gathered to vent their feelings.

Escaping the 'trammels of the past': organised party government, 1913–35

had been mounting.[175] This issue seriously divided the coalition. Farmers hoped that it would increase their earnings, but manufacturers, importers, the banks and Treasury were all opposed. Cabinet was gradually persuaded, but Downie Stewart felt he had to resign as Minister of Finance. Coates, who had masterminded the change of policy, became Minister of Finance in his stead and became in effect 'the government'. Forbes was happy to remain the titular head and leave the hard work to his deputy.

Coates capitalised on his position by pushing through a range of measures. With extraordinary energy, he launched into unorthodox policies that strengthened state intervention, gaining reluctant endorsement as he went along. Late in the session, the House was ordered to sit from Monday to Saturday until midnight to cope with the volume of legislation. Labour sternly resisted the Sales Tax Bill on the grounds that it severely affected wage earners.[176] Closure was applied, and Forbes even threatened to legislate by Order in Council. After 23 hours of debate on the bill, the Chairman indicated that he had had enough and in one instance accepted a closure motion after only four speakers. Closure had come to stay.

When Holland died in 1933, Savage became the new Leader of the Opposition and Webb returned to the House after a long absence. Believing that Holland's death was in part caused by excessive work, Labour campaigned for more substantial secretarial assistance.[177] Coates was amenable. The position of Leader of the Opposition received statutory recognition and Savage was given an allowance to employ a private secretary.

The House was becoming accustomed to changed patterns of work. Parliament took a breather after the whirlwind weeks of early 1933 and did not meet again until September. This session was more leisurely; the House reverted to the hours and days agreed to in 1929. But the use of urgency was now commonplace. The government came up against an unexpected hurdle when, at the behest of the horse-racing industry, it promoted the Gaming Amendment Bill for a private member.[178] Forbes was challenged for giving no reasons of public interest for moving urgency – a fair, if technical, point. The government was defeated on its motion and the bill was withdrawn. This proved too much for Roy Sellars of the New Zealand Racing Conference, who was in the public gallery. He confronted W.J. ('Big Bill') Polson as he came out of the chamber, accusing him of blocking the bill because he had voted against urgency. Fisticuffs ensued. The most notable measure was Coates's Reserve Bank Bill, vehemently opposed by the banks.[179] Labour, which wanted outright government control of banking, resisted the measure trenchantly but unsuccessfully. New Zealand gained a central state bank of issue.

With economic conditions improving, the session of 1934 was uneventful but exceptionally long. It opened at the end of June and meandered on until early April 1935. Urgency was again used frequently, but with Coates distracted by an investigation into an Auckland financier, the government did not push its business through and the Labour Party seized the opportunity to introduce a large number of private members' bills.

Coates continued on his interventionist way in 1935, creating the New Zealand Dairy Board, providing for a Mortgage Corporation and assisting those with rural mortgages. But the coalition was running out of both time and support. Coates' decisiveness had resulted in desertions from the coalition, and his measures now often went through only by narrow margins. The towns and cities came to see New Zealand as a 'country governed by the farmer for the farmer', in Burdon's words.[180]

A short session was held from the end of August to late October 1935 to present the budget after Forbes and Coates returned from London. There were few divisions as the parties prepared for the election. A substantial number of bills were passed rapidly, including a record number of 26 bills in one sitting.[181] Speaker Statham announced that he would retire at the end of the session.

A well-organised Labour Party was confident it would take power. Coates felt that he could no longer work with Forbes while Reform's and United's party organisation had withered away.[182] The newly-formed Democrat Party and the New Zealand Legion offered criticism from the right of Coates' 'socialistic' interventionist policies, and other independent and Country Party candidates did not support

THE PARLIAMENTARY PAPER CHASE (LAST LAP).

J.C. Hill, Auckland Star, 7 November 1934

Forbes and Coates pedal desperately towards the finishing line, pursued by Savage and other Labour Opposition members. The rush of bills towards the end of the session was traditional. The pressure told on members, and the House would engage in a 'mock Parliament' on the final day of the session while waiting for the Council to pass the Appropriation Bill. The ladies' gallery would be crowded to watch the practical jokes and tomfoolery, which would culminate with the motion to adjourn the House. In 1888 the practice of calling the House into the Council chamber to hear the proroguing of Parliament (until 1875 by the Governor, then by Commissioners) was abandoned. From then on, the Premier (as Leader of the House) moved the adjournment, and then the Governor proclaimed the prorogation in the Gazette. Often a division was called on this motion, more to record those remaining to the bitter end than as a real contest. By the 1920s the humorous custom of negativing the adjournment motion had developed, and the Speaker had to be inventive to bring proceedings to a close. The practice continued during the first Labour government, and by the 1940s this division was described facetiously as the only truly non-party vote left in the House. By now a one-vote majority was engineered, usually recorded by absurdly appointed tellers and with a distribution of votes that mocked the usual lines of difference in the House.

the government. The electorate faced a bewildering kaleidoscope of choices. Coates, although belatedly producing a manifesto, was unable to shake off his association with the depression, and his promises were qualified by economic practicalities.

Changes in the House

The period 1913–35 saw the consolidation of a modern pattern of business in the House.[183] Sessions grew longer and the traditional, compressed winter session became a rarity. Sessions were also disrupted by prime ministerial overseas travel, war and depression. Sprawling debates, stonewalls and extended sittings were controlled by the 1929 standing orders and by the introduction of closure in 1931.

Escaping the 'trammels of the past': organised party government, 1913–35

ELIZABETH McCOMBS: FIRST WOMAN IN THE HOUSE

Elizabeth McCombs followed her husband James McCombs into the House on his death, being elected to Lyttelton for Labour with a large majority in 1933. Following the 1919 election (the first for which women were eligible to stand), a number of women had tried to get into Parliament. Ellen Melville was the most persistent, but none had succeeded. McCombs had a substantial impact as the first woman in the House, making her mark as a fearless and fluent speaker who fitted into the parliamentary Labour Party well. She was deluged with correspondence from women, advocated women's issues, and made trenchant attacks on the government's depression policies. Her health was poor, however, and she died on 7 June 1935. Her son, Terence, was elected in her place for Lyttelton.

Advisory Committee on Women's Affairs collection, ATL, F150372½

Party leaders jostle on the steps of Parliament to welcome Elizabeth McCombs. The institution had to make some adjustments. The 'No Women Permitted' sign over Bellamy's dining room was taken down, the wording of the swearing-in ceremony was altered, and the Governor-General had to refer to 'members' rather than 'gentlemen' in the Speech from the Throne. McCombs was not allowed into the inner sanctum of the bar, not that she would have wished to do so, being a longstanding temperance advocate.

Minhinnick, NZH, 15 September 1933

A hatless Elizabeth McCombs, wearing a severe and simple dress, is escorted into the chamber by members and inspected by Coates and Forbes – all dressed as women. McCombs' first entrance into the House was the subject of speculation as to what she might wear. (Lady Astor had worn a hat when she entered the House of Commons, but McCombs refused to do so.) As she was escorted by the whips to her husband's former seat on the front benches, members on all sides applauded loudly and the crowded galleries cheered deafeningly. After she bowed and took her seat, Forbes, Coates and other members of the government crossed the floor to congratulate her. On her desk were two bouquets, one from the ladies' gallery and another from 'an admirer'.

J.C. Hill, Auckland Star, 23 September 1933

Unemployed gather at the main gates to Parliament grounds, 10 May 1932. Shortly afterwards a section of the crowd broke away and smashed shop windows along Lambton Quay.

Average daily sitting hours fell from about eight to six or seven. Governments with a concerted and compact programme of legislation began to dominate the House and get their measures through. The total number of bills introduced declined substantially, but many more ended up on the statute book. In the 1920s, three-quarters or more of bills were enacted, close to the rate that would characterise the fully fledged two-party system.

These fundamental changes were associated with three divergent trends: increased turnover of members, aging of the House, and a reassertion of farmer influence. Turnover by Parliament increased from 1905 onwards, and returned to close to one-third of members in the 1920s.[184] The number of experienced politicians in the House had declined by 1918, when Carroll, Ward and Allen had 36 sessions apiece, followed by Massey and William Fraser with 28. The decline in experience continued through the 1920s. Despite the turnover, Parliament aged markedly because the new entrants often came from older age groups. By the time of the 1931–5 Parliament, the House was looking elderly indeed. The average age of members was 56, with more than three-quarters in their fifties or sixties.

This aging was associated with a substantial increase in the proportion of farmers (to more than one-third) and in the number of New Zealand-born politicians in the House. Over the whole period, the proportion of locally born members virtually doubled to nearly 60 per cent. The number of members with backgrounds in law, journalism and manual work declined noticeably in these years, but the new category of trade union secretary comprised more than 10 per cent of the total membership as the Labour Party made its mark. There was a much clearer differentiation between the occupational groups aligned with the Reform and Labour Parties than there had been between previous rival groups in the House. The peak of farmer representation was reached in the 1920s but this pinnacle was to be short-lived. The agonised history of the United–Reform coalition brought the pre-eminence of the farmer politician into question, and Labour was poised to shift the composition of the House dramatically.

By 1935, political confusion had lasted more than a decade. Parliamentary and democratic processes had survived, but by New Zealand's standards, there had been disturbing disorder and violence against a background of unemployment and poverty. Quite where the country might head remained difficult to predict, though the well-established structure of Parliament gave grounds for confidence for the future. Meanwhile, parties had consolidated their presence and the skeleton of a two-party system had emerged. Parliamentary procedure had evolved considerably since the nineteenth century, with executive government enjoying greater powers. It remained to be seen how these enhanced powers would be used as party became pre-eminent.

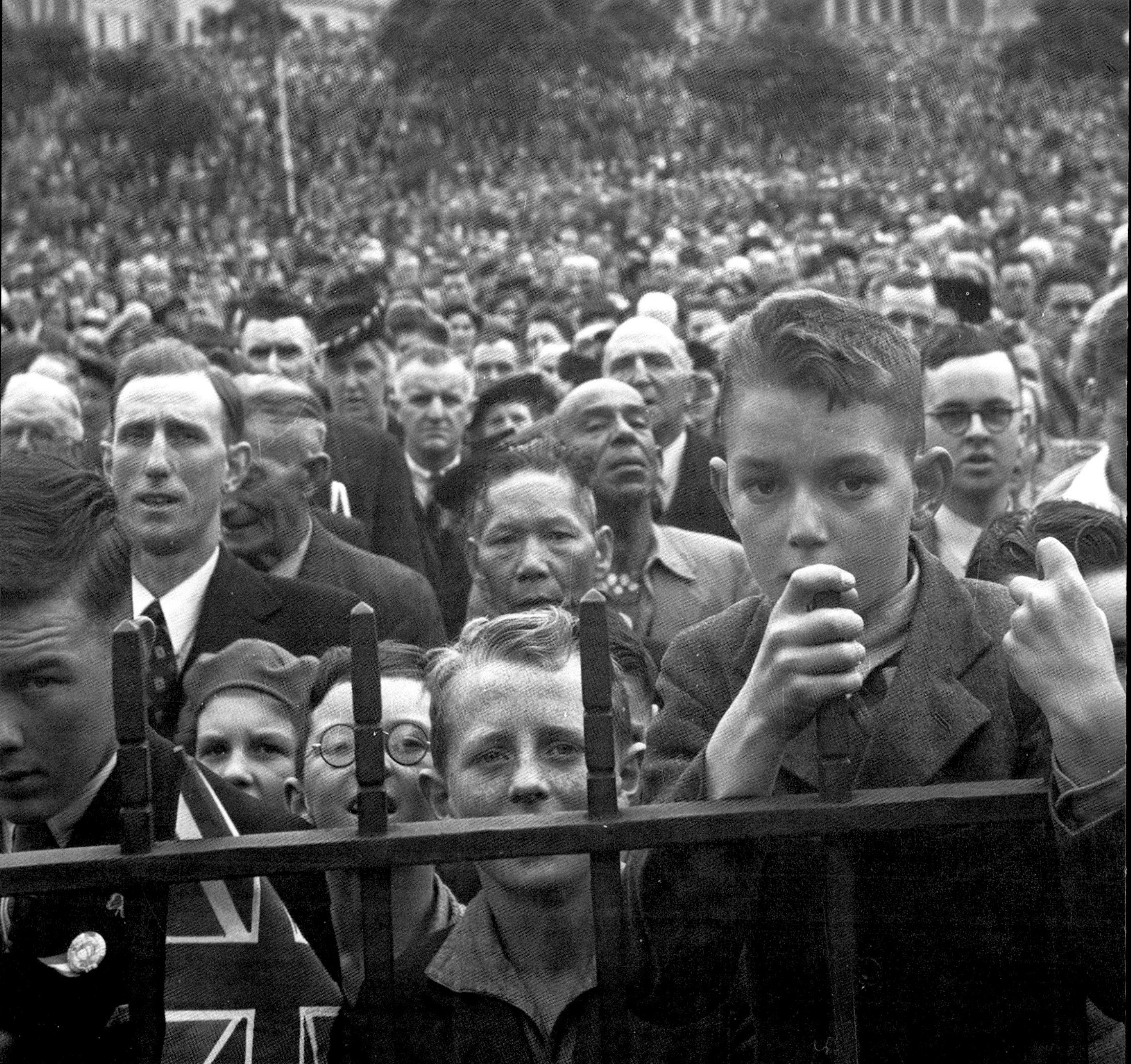

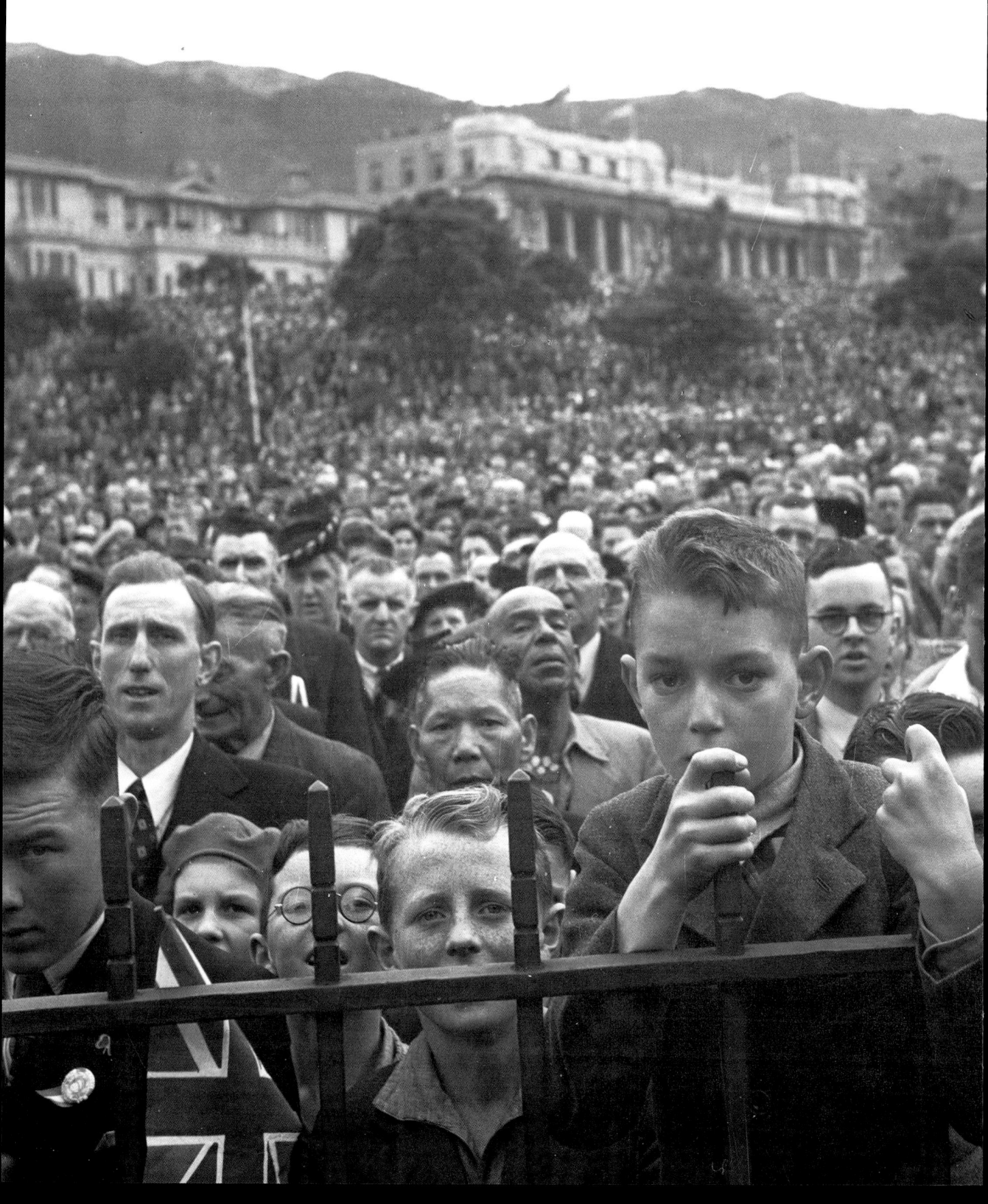

CHAPTER 6

THE CONSOLIDATION OF TWO-PARTY GOVERNMENT AND PARLIAMENT, 1936–49

Party and Parliament

The 1935 election was a landmark in New Zealand's history, ranking alongside that of 1890. It brought to power a new political party that established the welfare state. It also resolved the confused three-party political pattern since Liberal single-party rule. The development of the two-party system forged much closer links between election platforms, governments and legislative activity.[1]

In the nineteenth century, public opinion had been kept at a safe distance from the chamber. It was the opinions and affiliations of the assembled members that defined the public good and determined who would form governments and their policies. Parliament had considerable discretionary power. During the transitional period around the turn of the century, when Seddon was master, a greater role was conceded to public opinion. It became the role of the government to take a lead with its policies, but only after consulting and broadly reflecting the wishes of the electorate. As more organised parties put up detailed election platforms in consultation with their extra-parliamentary membership, legislative activity began to bear a closer relationship to election platforms. The function of elections shifted from deciding on the virtues of individual candidates to weighing up the merits of rival party manifestos and choosing governments. Administrations were no longer formed from within the flux of support in the House. They were chosen from the rival parties vying for the electors' approval in elections. This gave weight to the notion of an electoral mandate and to the platforms put up for voters to consider. It also emphasised the need for communication between parties and governments, and between parties and the population at large.

The Labour Party provided the model for the development of modern parties. The more conservative forces in New Zealand politics were again reluctant to follow suit, just as they had been in Seddon's day. Reform's party organisation fell away in the 1920s and the coalition muddled through the depression, refusing to contemplate a genuine 'fusion' of the anti Labour conservative groupings. The breathtaking accession of Labour to power and its demonstration of the advantages of an extra-parliamentary party organisation finally convinced the opposition forces that their only course was to unite and create new foundations for a political future. The parliamentary leader and party could no longer act unilaterally; the persistent nightmare of electoral vote-splitting had to be banished, and an intermittent and loose organisation which existed only during elections was no longer sufficient.

In 1936 a new National Party emerged from the remnants of the old coalition, led by Adam Hamilton.[2] National was founded on the principle that a decentralised and permanent mass organisation

Left: Crowd at VE celebrations, 8 May 1945 John Pascoe collection, ATL, F1527¼

would exist parallel to but outside the parliamentary party, with formal membership and a complex hierarchical structure of branches, electorate committees and divisions, all headed by a national council. The extra-parliamentary National Party controlled its members and organisational structure, managed its affairs independently, selected parliamentary candidates, organised education and propaganda campaigns, and consulted with the parliamentary party over policy through a joint policy committee. Local electorate committees selected parliamentary candidates, subject to the approval of the national council. The parliamentary wing of the party, however, was autonomous in the House. As the architect of the party's constitution, E.E. Hammond, expressed it: 'When the selected candidates win we say "Goodbye" to them at the gates of Parliament. The Organisation has done its work in giving the necessary assistance; it is then up to the Members to do their part as legislators'.[3]

Within two years a mass party of more than 100,000 had been built up and the parliamentary party had become a cohesive if still small unit in the House. During the 1938 election campaign, vote-splitting was almost completely eliminated and concerted efforts were made to persuade the electorate of the advantages of an alternative to the Labour government. The National Party's discipline in the House was evident in the complete lack of cross-voting on the floor of the House, even though in theory members remained free to vote according to conscience.[4] Sidney Holland, elected to the leadership in 1940, demanded that members support the party's election policy if National were elected.

The Labour Party in government also built up its mass membership, particularly by enacting compulsory unionism legislation that greatly increased the numbers in trade unions affiliated to the party.[5] Since the mid 1920s Labour candidates had been selected from a list approved by the party's national executive. The executive became increasingly powerful and closely integrated with the parliamentary wing, particularly after Labour became the government.

Within four decades from the 1890s, a loose factional form of politics had been replaced by a much more highly organised one. New Zealand's two-party system emerged rapidly and decisively and became more strongly entrenched than in other countries. Its unitary and centralised political system, its small size, and the small size of the House all encouraged this.[6] The powerful party organisations and discipline imposed through caucuses facilitated cabinet dominance of government. The electoral system, which gave governments power on the basis of a simple majority of single-member electorates, and the short parliamentary term of three years, gave rise to a political pattern in which two parties vied for office.

Reaching the people

Labour won the 1935 election in a landslide. It held 55 seats once the members for Southern and Western Maori declared their support for the government. The Reform–United coalition secured only 19 seats. There were four disaffected coalition members and two independents. Labour leader Savage selected the first cabinet, contrary to the expectations of some who thought that the caucus would do this.[7] Savage agonised over the list and in the end deleted a disappointed W.E. Barnard, making him Speaker instead.

Barnard became a proficient Speaker with a more relaxed style than Statham. From now on Speakers would be party appointees, expressed symbolically by their nomination by the party whips.[8] Barnard also occasionally participated in debates when government measures were in Committee, a practice not endorsed by Statham. Barnard was a leader of the credit reform faction in the Labour Party, an advocate of the power of caucus, and an associate of Lee. When Lee was expelled from the party in 1940, Barnard resigned from Labour but not from his seat.[9] He remained Speaker until defeated in 1943.

As the party system stabilised, a more strongly defined career path to the Speakership developed: from party whip to Chairman of Committees, to Acting or Deputy Speaker, and finally to Speaker.

The consolidation of two-party government and parliament, 1936–49

The position became, in the words of a later Speaker, Roy Jack, a 'spoil of office'.[10]

The Labour Speakers who followed Barnard took an active part when the House was in Committee.[11] For F.W. Schramm, Speaker 1944–6, this was to some extent understandable because he was also Chairman of the Statutes Revision Committee and it was useful for him to explain amendments to bills in Committee. However, he also voted with the government in divisions. R. McKeen, 1947–9, did not speak in Committee but always voted in divisions because of the government's small majority in the House. R.M. Macfarlane, Labour's Speaker 1957–60, also voted with the government in Committee to bolster its one-vote majority.

In the early 1930s the Labour Party advocated broadcasting parliamentary debates so that citizens could take an 'intelligent interest' in national affairs. The party knew that most major newspapers were conservative and biased against the labour movement. Labour saw broadcasting as providing an opportunity to bypass the conventional media and reach out directly to the people. The coalition government refused to consider broadcasting Parliament; Speaker Statham also opposed the idea.[12]

Before the 1935 election, Labour announced that it would broadcast Parliament in conjunction with a state-controlled national radio service, concentrating on 'important debates on matters considered to be of interest to the people – things that materially affected them'.[13] The new cabinet acted immediately and had the necessary equipment installed in the House before the session began. While some felt that this should have received the blessing of the House, many saw it as a significant and worthy move. As one political commentator observed, in 'the heroic

Michael Joseph ('Micky') Savage was elected for Auckland West in 1919. He succeeded Harry Holland as leader in 1933 and became Prime Minister when Labour won the 1935 election. The first Labour government ushered in the social security system, and Savage was remembered fondly for this notable contribution to the welfare state after he died in office in 1940.

The possibility of broadcasting debates in the House arose in 1934. The coalition government was not interested, but cartoonists speculated on the likely effects.

1930s … a national radio channel was a technological novelty and a large radio audience was deeply involved in the sharp ideological conflicts' of the day.[14]

When Parliament opened on 25 March 1936 the proceedings were relayed to the four national stations – the first regular broadcasting of a Parliament anywhere in the world had commenced.[15] The official commentator, press gallery reporter Charles Wheeler, sat behind the Opposition backbenches in the far corner of the chamber, assisted by a relay operator with headphones who monitored and mixed the sound. Next day, the formal opening of Parliament was also broadcast. Microphones were located on the steps of the main entrance, in the Legislative Council in front of the dais, and in the House. Wheeler provided continuity, 'speaking in subdued tones close to the microphone, so that the august silence might not be disturbed by this modern innovation', as all awaited the Governor-General in the Council chamber. He then sprinted to the House to resume his description as the Speaker announced that the members were returning to the chamber.

Labour's Micky Savage (as Micky Mouse), perched on Semple's head, battles with Forbes, standing on Coates' shoulders, as they go hammer and tongs at each other in the chamber.

When the House commenced business, the debates were broadcast. The intention was to reproduce the actual sense of the debates, including interjections. A number of sensitive, non-directional microphones hung from wires above the members, picking up every remark, whisper, cough or rustle of papers. When the division bells rang the technician switched off the microphones and played a record so that the 'light-hearted banter and conversation' of members going into the lobbies would not be broadcast. Red lights above the lobby doors indicated when the House was on air. The person providing continuity had to bridge the gaps, attempt to cut out any unwanted or embarrassing conversations and explain unforeseen events. Bursts of laughter over a member falling asleep in his seat had to be dealt with without giving the game away. The operators needed considerable skill to switch microphones on and off and regulate the volume. They had to master 'split second timing' and possess a 'strong knowledge of where MPs sit (and their wandering habits in the House)'. Technician

The consolidation of two-party government and parliament, 1936–49

Ken Collins 'got to know the peculiarities of any member's expression, tilt of head, or position of arm or hand if he suddenly got the urge to interject'.[16]

The government controlled the broadcasting of the House. Savage announced which debates would be transmitted and organised the lists of speakers privileged to go to air. Broadcasts usually took up the three hours after the supper adjournment, finishing at 10.30 p.m. The two parties put up their major speakers, who were sometimes joined by an independent. Backbenchers did not get a look in.[17] More traditional politicians – and many on the Opposition benches – blinked in the unaccustomed glare of publicity and felt that the new medium was being exploited for political purposes.[18]

The *Radio Record*'s columns showed that the broadcasts were well received, even if the characteristic commotion of the chamber was now revealed. The Speaker received numerous complaints about the din and the lack of order from a shocked public. Colin Scrimgeour, controller of the Commercial Broadcasting Service, described listening to debates as similar to following a wrestling match.[19] One member was astonished when he heard a broadcast: 'knowing something about the dignity of this House, I was astonished to realize the false impression I would have gained if I had not been a member … The broadcast gave the impression of a Donnybrook Fair, and brought back memories of forty years ago … an up-country race meeting and the gathering afterwards at the local "pub"'.[20] Other members suspected that their best efforts were not being transmitted faithfully.

Some thought that broadcasting revealed the poor quality of speeches in the House.

There were some hitches. Speeches did not always go to plan. When they finished early, the announcer had to fill the awkward interval. On one occasion, broadcasting was interrupted when the Speaker struck his bell so forcefully while his microphone was still on that the transmitter was overloaded and put out of action. In 1939 during the second reading of the Reserve Bank of New Zealand Amendment Bill, Labour members' speeches were broadcast but the transmission was terminated when the Opposition began to speak.[21] Fraser apologised for this incident, which had arisen because of a misunderstanding. On other occasions, transmission was interrupted by power failures or other technical difficulties.

Backbench agitation persuaded Savage in 1937 to broadcast all debates in the House from

2.30 p.m. to 10.30 p.m. on Tuesdays, Wednesdays and Thursdays, and 10.30 a.m. to 5.30 p.m. on Fridays. This did not end all complaints, as the government still controlled the time transmission ceased, and could leave its speaker with the final word. At first the government considered establishing a special parliamentary station for this service, but in the end 2YA, which had the most powerful transmitter in New Zealand and covered much of the country, was used. As time went on, further microphones were added to reduce the irritating background noise and focus better on the speakers.

When war broke out in 1939 broadcasting was circumscribed rather than stopped.[22] A censorship officer was stationed in the House, and the Speaker had a red light above his chair to indicate when speakers had been taken off air. He had little compunction in cutting transmission if a speech strayed too close to a matter of national security, but at times members failed to discipline themselves, forcing the Speaker to signal repeatedly. On one occasion Minister of Defence Fred Jones transgressed so frequently that the Speaker sent for him and admonished him sternly. Secret sessions got around some of the problem. *Hansard* was also carefully scrutinised, and members' questions which would go to air required prior approval from the Speaker. In 1941 New Zealand, like beleaguered Britain, adopted the BBC's practice of observing a minute's silence for prayer following the chimes of Big Ben. This required a brief interruption to parliamentary debates at 9 p.m., when the Speaker and members rose for the minute after the chimes were relayed from the chamber by radio.[23]

The debating chamber, 1947. Labour Speakers, preferring a more comfortable plain lounge chair, banished Statham's impressive chair to the basement. The supporting cables and suspended microphones needed for broadcasting are visible. Some felt that broadcasting encouraged the formal delivery of rehearsed speeches and took away the immediacy and 'cut and thrust' of spontaneous debate. But by the 1940s a more conversational style had developed and broadcasting revealed that parliamentarians were much like everyone else.

The broadcasting of Parliament soon became an accepted part of political life.²⁴ Members consciously tailored their remarks to the public, as they had played to the galleries in earlier days. Parties and members soon manipulated speaking slots to gain maximum advantage from the broadcasts – 7.30 p.m. to 9 p.m. was regarded as prime time. Ministers and the Leader of the Opposition sometimes delayed proceedings to speak at this time. Broadcasting reduced members' enthusiasm for afternoon debates to such an extent that debates sometimes collapsed. Whips had to keep this in mind when organising and supervising debates. One occasion which went awry was one of the first major speeches made by H. Johnstone, member for Raglan.²⁵ W.J. Broadfoot, the chief Opposition whip, tried to ensure that Johnstone made his speech in the evening. At 4.30 p.m., when the notably taciturn Tiaki Omana rose to speak, Broadfoot asked Johnstone: 'Are you ready to go? This joker might only last five minutes.' The prediction proved accurate and Johnstone had to follow, missing the opportunity to have his speech broadcast.

The broadcasting of parliamentary proceedings, together with Labour's Official News Service, which was personally administered by Savage, became part of the pervasive impact of radio on New Zealanders. By these means the government sold its policies to the public.²⁶ The news was put together in the Prime Minister's office (later through the Tourist and Publicity Department) to be read by the New Zealand Broadcasting Service. This tight control over news lasted until the 1960s. Savage's revered persona was largely forged by radio broadcasts as the government used the new medium effectively to put its message across. Budget night was listened to avidly: 'thousands of both country and city dwellers sit beside their radios in hopeful anticipation of tax reductions', it was said.²⁷ Members like Lee received 'fan mail' from listeners. At times the broadcasts attracted a lot of attention – both favourable and critical – and newspapers were filled with letters to the editor on the subject.

The Opposition was disconcerted by Labour's seizure of this effective means of propaganda. While the broadcasting of debates was relatively even-handed, the government had the whip hand in other kinds of access to radio. But by the mid 1940s, a stronger National Party saw advantage in using the airwaves. It gained in confidence and had more effective speakers. Holland, now convinced of the efficacy of broadcasting Parliament, said that radio had come to stay in the chamber – it 'was one of the things the present Government had done which had turned out to be right'.²⁸ On the other hand, after the death of Savage and his replacement by the dour Fraser, and with Labour losing its reforming drive and increasingly on the back foot, the government lost enthusiasm for the medium.

The election of National in 1949 saw an acceptance of government control over radio. The broadcasting of Parliament was substantially improved.²⁹ Additional

New Zealand Broadcasting Service announcer Mr Ensor in the control room at the back of the chamber, c. 1953–4. From the 1960s speaking in the House in the afternoon became more popular as members realised that the public would be watching TV in the evenings rather than listening to Parliament. According to Robert Muldoon, his old mate, Geoffrey Sim, the member for Waikato, 'rarely spoke in the House but most days in the late afternoon he would interject provocatively until called to order by Mr Speaker. As soon as Mr Speaker referred to the Member for Waikato, he would chuckle and leave the chamber knowing that, back home in the cowshed at milking time, his constituents had been told that their Member of Parliament was there in the chamber on the job. He could then amble down for a quiet pre-dinner drink ... in Bellamys.'*

* Muldoon, 'A politician's view of the press gallery', p. 78, in Comrie and McGregor (eds).

microphones were installed, and the operators shifted into a specially constructed soundproof control room with a large observation window. Parliamentary broadcasts remained popular – 2YA had the largest audience in the country when Parliament was on the air.

Labour gets to work

The first session under a Labour government lasted from late March to late October 1936. Momentous legislation was passed, most notably statutes governing industrial relations and working conditions and restoring wage and salary cuts made during the depression. Savage introduced a mid-winter adjournment to compensate for the length of the session. Labour learned quickly how to use the levers of power. The new Chairman of Committees, E.J. Howard, observed that he had a number of books thrust into his hands when he became Chairman, including several volumes of Erskine May and previous Speakers' decisions, but that the job really required common sense.[30]

Labour used urgency regularly, and closure became one of its key tools to push legislation through. The Opposition argued that closure should be used only as an emergency measure. Fraser later argued ironically: 'What is right for a Conservative Government … surely cannot be wrong to-day for a Labour Government; surely it cannot be wrong to follow such a splendid example.'[31] In fact the procedural innovations were vital for carrying through Labour's programme.

Closure was applied to two crucial measures early in the 1936 session – the Reserve Bank of New Zealand Bill, which established state control over the bank, and the Primary Products Marketing Bill, which provided guaranteed prices for dairy farmers. When the disgruntled Opposition challenged applying closure for the former, the Speaker pointed out that the second reading had taken five sitting days.[32] Closure was to be used extensively in the following sessions. What had been introduced as an emergency measure had become a routine part of parliamentary procedure. Eventually it did not have to be invoked so often; Savage observed acerbically that the government had made its intentions amply clear.[33] The Second World War largely ended concerted obstruction in the House.

Labour uses closure to rush through legislation in 1936.

Another Labour innovation was the Statutes Amendment Bill – an omnibus bill at the end of sessions in which non-controversial minor amendments to various Acts were cobbled together into a

The consolidation of two-party government and parliament, 1936–49

STATE OPENING OF PARLIAMENT

Railways collection, ATL. G23743½

The Governor-General, Lord Galway, reviews troops at the state opening of Parliament, mid to late 1930s. The formalities associated with the state opening looked even more dramatic against the backdrop of the new buildings. In the nineteenth century the local artillery battery had given the Royal Salute from the rear of the old Parliament Buildings. It was later fired from the terrace outside the General Assembly Library, but from 1925 the new Point Jerningham battery gave the Salute as the Governor-General left Government House in Newtown for Parliament.

As the Governor-General arrived, the guard of honour opposite the steps of Parliament gave a Royal Salute and the band played the National Anthem. His Excellency inspected the guard and entered the building, to be met by Black Rod. After the dignitaries and senior military officers moved into the Legislative Council chamber, removing their headgear, the Governor-General (who kept his on) passed through their ranks and took up his position on a dais in front of the Speaker's Chair.

The Governor-General then commanded Black Rod to summon the House of Representatives. Black Rod bowed three times as he left the Council chamber, moved to the House and knocked three times on the door (which had been locked). On the Speaker's command the door was opened and the bar of the House was removed. After Black Rod informed the House that the Governor-General desired their attendance, members processed into the Council chamber, led by Black Rod (who bowed and then backed out of the chamber), the Sergeant-at-Arms (carrying the mace), and the Speaker. When the Speaker entered the chamber he bowed three times along the way before being seated. The Leader of the Legislative Council handed His Excellency his speech to be read. When he had finished delivering the speech, the Governor-General left the chamber preceded by Black Rod, handing the Speaker of the House a copy of the speech as he passed. As the Governor-General left the grounds the guard gave another Royal Salute and the band played the National Anthem again.

single large piece of legislation.[34] Finance Bills had in the past incorporated miscellaneous minor amending legislation, and they had been used twice to extend the life of Parliament. Rex Mason, who introduced the first Statutes Amendment Bill in 1936, did not see anything particularly notable about the event – he merely wanted to hasten the end of the session.[35] The Act amended 51 Acts in 82 sections. Use of this instrument of convenience (with minor modification) became routine. From 1955 the bill was referred to the Statutes Revision Committee, and its passage agreed to on the understanding that its clauses would not be controversial and that each amending provision would be limited to two clauses (enacted as separate statutes).

The 1937 session opened late, in September. Savage had been in Britain for the coronation of King George VI and an Imperial Conference, and Nash overseas for trade negotiations. The session ran until March 1938 and was largely concerned with tidying up legislation, with the assistance of a co-operative Opposition. Nash, cabinet and special caucus committees spent much time wrestling with the scope and financing of an ambitious and comprehensive social security scheme.[36]

This session was closely followed by the pre-election session, which opened at the end of June 1938. Its centrepiece was the much-heralded Social Security Bill, which had originally been intended to go to the House towards the end of the previous session. It was now held out by Labour as an election lure, with the payment of benefits to commence after the election.[37] Nash outlined the bill in detail in the House, and concluded by stating that: 'If it brings the benefits I believe it will bring, then once more this country will be "God's Own Country".'[38] The Opposition found it difficult to oppose the bill trenchantly, saying only that Labour did not have a monopoly on enlightened social legislation and emphasising the cost. It put up only formal resistance while the bill was in Committee, apart from a procedural amendment modifying the financial arrangements that was ruled out of order. Hamilton preferred to 'leave it to the Government and also to the electors, who can make their choice … in the near future.'[39] That October the government won a massive endorsement. Labour's proportion of the vote soared to 56 per cent, a level never again attained by any party. Labour maintained its overwhelming majority with 53 seats, compared to National's 25. There were now only two independents.

Contingencies of war

The Speech from the Throne at the opening of the next session at the end of June 1939 focused on the growing threat to peace as well as the inauguration of the social security scheme. Following the declaration of war on 3 September, Fraser (the Acting Prime Minister, with Savage ill) declared his confidence that 'a united Dominion … will place itself at the disposal of the Government … to further the common cause.'[40] At the end of the session, Fraser adjourned the House rather than proroguing Parliament, to enable it to come together rapidly if necessary without the usual formalities.

By this time the revered Savage was seriously ill.[41] He returned to the House for the last time on 6 October, just before the session finished, to give what was effectively a valedictory speech. He soldiered on until early 1940, when a confrontation with John A. Lee ended in Lee's expulsion from the Labour Party. Savage died in March and was given a state funeral on a grand scale.[42] Fraser was elected the new leader and Prime Minister, with Nash as his deputy. In an apparent concession to the power of caucus, Fraser accepted that it should elect the cabinet. However, his leadership skills and the circumstances of war ensured that this did not seriously inhibit executive power.[43]

As the war went badly in early 1940, and with the example of the British 'National' government before them, Hamilton and Coates (who was by now estranged from the National Party) discussed a similar arrangement with Fraser. The Prime Minister called an urgent session of Parliament at the end of May to rush through emergency measures. He told the country that the government would take virtually unlimited powers to prosecute the war, and warned that it was impossible to tell when the

The consolidation of two-party government and parliament, 1936–49

session might finish.⁴⁴ It continued until early December. The traditional pattern of convening Parliament in the second half of the year was seriously disrupted during the war. Sessions often straggled on through much of the year, punctuated by long adjournments.

By regulation Parliament could now hold secret sessions, a step already adopted in Britain.⁴⁵ These were specific sitting days devoted to vital wartime business. All galleries (including the press gallery) were cleared, all doors locked, guards posted, and the roof regularly patrolled for eavesdroppers.⁴⁶ *Hansard* was not taken, and Fraser issued only brief, innocuous statements. There were five secret sessions during the 1940 session, and 18 in total during the war. Members were also reminded by the Director of Publicity, J.T. Paul, to be careful with their remarks during open debates – for example, they should not refer to the adequacy of the defence forces or the capacity or willingness of the community to meet the war effort. Throughout the war the Speaker had the onerous duty of acting as censor of the House, in close consultation with Paul. He checked all questions to ministers, revised the *Hansard* proofs and monitored members' speeches as they went to air.

Some Opposition members protested at the restrictions, but as the seriousness of the situation became apparent, Parliament subsided into quiescence.⁴⁷ The bumptious new National member F.W. Doidge, a former member of the press gallery, called Parliament a 'wax works' that hardly met and acted as a rubber stamp for the Labour Party and trade unions.⁴⁸ With the Opposition numerically small, the parties agreed that two government speakers would follow each Opposition one.⁴⁹ This gave an advantage to the independents, Lee and Atmore, which drew complaints from both parties as Lee gloried in his role.

Fraser persuaded Hamilton and Coates to join a war cabinet in July 1940. This precipitated a change of leadership in the National Party later that year, when the more dynamic and energetic Sidney Holland became leader.⁵⁰ Holland had experienced a meteoric rise since his election five years earlier. He was an ebullient fighter and a vigorous and aggressive debater, and possessed an exceptional memory. National argued that partisan politics should be put aside in the interests of the war effort, and that the party should form part of a National government. Holland, however, would accept nothing less than a fully 'National' government, which was anathema to Labour, although Fraser personally was more receptive to the idea. The difficulties involved in forging a wartime coalition were never resolved.

In 1941 Parliament sat from March to October. An election was due late that year, but as the war situation worsened enthusiasm for holding it waned. At the end of the session Fraser introduced a Prolongation of Parliament Bill that would postpone the election for a year.⁵¹ He described an election as 'unthinkable' in the circumstances, and not wanted by most people. The Opposition agreed grudgingly, on the understanding that there would be as little contentious party legislation as possible. Fraser congratulated the House for its co-operative spirit.

In December 1941 Japan entered the war and the threat to New Zealand became much more tangible. Before Christmas Fraser called Parliament together for an emergency session which continued from February to December 1942. Censorship over Parliament was tightened. Holland baulked at the secret sessions and at the extent to which information was withheld from the public, but Fraser was able to carry Parliament with him.⁵² He would brief the House on developments, and assured it that matters could be raised without being obstructed by the standing orders.

With a possible invasion looming, the Public Works Department hastily constructed a reinforced concrete war cabinet complex underneath the main vestibule of Parliament Buildings. This included a generating plant, cabinet room, telephone exchange, and typists' and cipher rooms.⁵³ It was to be the

Peter Fraser was elected for Wellington Central in 1918. He soon became a skilled parliamentarian and was an extremely hard worker. On the death of Savage in 1940 he assumed the Labour Party leadership and became Prime Minister, leading the country through the Second World War. Fraser died in 1950, having returned to the Opposition benches after the defeat of his government the previous year.

'nerve centre' of the country's defence. Emergency Precautions Scheme and Home Guard units were formed for Parliament. The buildings were blacked out at night and patrolled 24 hours a day. Access was strictly controlled. Covered trenches were dug in the grounds in front of the buildings for the public, and concrete shelters were erected at the rear for members and parliamentary staff.

In 1943 – when the Japanese threat had lessened – a substantial timber-framed, asbestos cement-clad penthouse was built on the roof of Parliament Buildings to house the Prime Minister's Department and his growing staff, many of whom worked on ciphers.[54] The new cabinet room, adjacent to the Prime Minister's suite of offices, was well-lit and spacious, with 'a plain maroon carpet on the floor, heavy brown curtains and venetian blinds. The furniture [was] austere and antiquated but not antique. It consist[ed] of three tables and a variety of straight-backed, leather-seated chairs'.[55] Maps of the world and the Pacific hung on the wall. The Opposition criticised the expenditure as being 'in the style of a Hollywood star'. The roof-top penthouse became known as 'Frasertown' and the floor below 'Nashville'.[56] The 'temporary' penthouse remained until destroyed by fire in the early 1990s.

By June 1942 Fraser had cleverly manoeuvred round the resistance of his colleagues and persuaded Holland to join a larger 'coalition' grouping – the 'War Administration' – comprising seven Labour and six National members. The smaller war cabinet (augmented by Holland) continued to meet, as did Labour's domestic cabinet. This created a complex decision-making structure. The parties agreed that the life of Parliament should be extended to up to 12 months after the end of the war. Parliament would approve yearly extensions on the motion of the Prime Minister.

The 'coalition' did not last. Government intervention in a coal strike and its take-over of the mines caused a rift, and National left the War Administration in September 1942. Coates and Hamilton rejoined the war cabinet and (with two supporters) voted with the government on a no-confidence motion over the government's handling of the strike, thereby severing their ties with the National Party. The government won the division easily, 47 to 17.[57]

In late May 1943 after much argument, a secret session of Parliament approved Churchill's proposal to keep New Zealand troops in Europe. Fraser displayed considerable mastery in convincing National and Labour alike to support this extremely difficult decision, which was contrary to Australia's action in pulling its troops out.[58] At this point Coates, who had worked hard for the war effort, collapsed and died in his office at Parliament. The government postponed the budget and the House was adjourned. Fraser and his colleagues felt the loss acutely. Coates was given a state funeral.

Coming out of war

With the collapse of the War Administration, the agreement to postpone the election also lapsed, and an election was held in September 1943. National marshalled its forces and Hamilton rejoined the party. The death of Coates had removed the last potential threat to the consolidation of the two-party system. Labour's majority was more than halved. But for the votes of soldiers overseas, its majority would have been small. With the defeat of Barnard, a new Speaker had to be found. After the Labour Party caucus agreed to put up the elderly and ineffective lawyer F.W. Schramm while Fraser was absent through ill-health, Fraser felt that he had to accept this choice.[59]

With National's benches swelled by new members, the party regained a sense of purpose.[60] Older members identified with the depression, such as Forbes and J.G. Cobbe, had gone. The parliamentary party was now organised into caucus committees in preparation for its anticipated assumption of power, and in 1944 a research department was established. The 1943 election manifesto, which was to be carried forward to 1946 and 1949, was consistent with this new-found vigour. It proposed National as an alternative government that would implement postwar reconstruction and bring in a 'new order' based on freedom from Labour's controls.

The consolidation of two-party government and parliament, 1936–49

The country quota weighting representation towards rural areas was abolished in 1945.[61] It had continued in spite of the shift of population towards towns and cities. The rural-based Reform Party had enjoyed considerable advantage from the quota. Labour, strongly dependent upon urban voters, had not, but in 1935, Labour won sufficient support from rural areas to lose some of its enthusiasm for abolishing the quota. With the loss of this support in the early 1940s, Labour's hostility towards the quota hardened again. The Electoral Amendment Bill – which also changed the population basis for calculating electorates in favour of Labour – was pushed through under urgency and using closure.[62] The bill was passed after a week of late nights, with Holland commenting that it was all about saving Labour's 'political skin'. On its passage, Labour members sang 'The Red Flag'. When National responded with 'God Save the King', Labour broke into 'God Defend New Zealand'. Party feeling had clearly revived during this session, which saw the country coming out of wartime stringencies. For the first time in many years a member – the chief Opposition whip, Broadfoot – defied the authority of the Chair and had to withdraw from the chamber.[63]

Labour's majority was cut to four by the 1946 election. Though Holland was bitterly disappointed at being again denied the Treasury benches, another new cadre of talented young National backbenchers entered the House. The electoral changes, combined with its now-established hold over the Maori seats (referred to as the 'Maori mandate' or 'brown mandate'), had kept Labour in power.[64] The defeat of Schramm saw Robert McKeen, the Chairman of Committees, elected Speaker.[65] His reputation for getting business through Committee rapidly had impressed the efficient – if not authoritarian – Fraser. Having weathered the war, Fraser adopted the practice of not convening Parliament until the last possible moment in order to retain control.

The four Maori members were now all Ratana supporters.[66] E. T. Tirikatene, the first Ratana member, entered the House in a by-election in 1932 as a Ratana Independent. He immediately presented a large petition which sought statutory recognition of the Treaty of Waitangi. Tirikatene was followed by H. T. Ratana in 1935. Both P.K. Paikea, elected in 1938, and Tiaki Omana (1943) stood under the banner of the Labour Party. Paikea was appointed to the Executive Council as a member representing Maori in 1941. After Paikea's death in 1943, Tirikatene took over this position. The alliance between Ratana and the Labour Party, which had been forged in 1936, did not translate into a great deal of influence in the House, even when the Maori members effectively held the balance of power in the late 1940s. The Minister of Maori Affairs wielded greater power. The Maori members were accommodated together in a single room under the steps to the main buildings. They worked closely together, guided by the pan-tribal Ratana philosophy and their primary goal of 'ratification' of the Treaty of Waitangi in legislation.

With Labour's small majority, the two parties were at loggerheads over pairing.[67] The government's chief whip, A.S. Richards, had been taken ill. With Holland unlikely to be co-operative, Labour threatened to revise the standing orders to introduce voting by proxy in case of sickness.[68] A conference between the parties was necessary to sort the matter out. After Speaker McKeen decided to vote in divisions in Committee, there were several incidents. Once Fraser was stranded in the Prime Minister's suite when the lift was intentionally run down to the basement and left with its doors jammed open with a chair. He made it to the chamber via the stairs in time for the vote. On another occasion Moohan, Langstone, Paikea and Semple were clustered around a radio listening to a popular wrestling match with the volume turned up so that the deaf Langstone could hear. They missed hearing the division bells and failed to vote.

The pairing issue was smoothed over for the following session. However, in 1949 a mix-up over pairs resulted in the defeat by one vote of a closure motion which Fraser moved in Committee during supply, in spite of Speaker McKeen's vote for the government.[69] Holland, in gentlemanly fashion, refused to take advantage of this moral victory and allowed the substantive vote to be put, while Labour's whips feverishly attempted to work out what had gone amiss.

This incident represented, at least technically, a defeat for the government. But serious motions of

> On the death of his father in 1943, 23 year old Tapihana Paraire ('Dobbie') Paikea followed him into the House as the representative for Northern Maori. Paikea was one of several Maori members (Eruera Tirikatene was another) who sought the right to speak in Maori, sometimes – often on Fridays – to much mirth from his fellows. The translation gave no indication why, but it later transpired that he was sending his wife messages about his impending return home.
>
> The provision for interpreters in the House had lapsed when the Liberal government was defeated, and in 1913 Speaker Lang ruled that Maori members should speak in English if they were able to do so. An interpreter could be arranged in advance if required. The use of Maori became more of an issue when Ratana members entered the House in the 1930s. After Labour's Speakers relaxed the ruling, at the Speaker's indulgence Maori members could speak briefly in Maori as long as they provided an immediate translation. In 1951 Speaker Oram reimposed Lang's ruling. Some time later, the practice that Maori members could make brief addresses in Maori if they translated them immediately re-emerged.
>
> Parliament eventually accepted the principle that Maori should be a second official language for New Zealand. Under the standing orders of 1985 members were explicitly able to speak in either English or Maori, a practice soon reflected in the Maori Language Act 1987, which made Maori an official language. Members began to use Maori in the House as the Speaker acknowledged that the old ruling no longer applied. In 1990 Koro Wetere caused an uproar by replying to questions in the House in Maori and refusing to supply an immediate translation. Peter Tapsell eventually offered a translation. In 1992 the Standing Orders Committee recognised that Parliament needed to develop an interpretation and translation service to ensure that its commitment to allowing Maori to be spoken was realised.
>
> On becoming Speaker in 1993, Tapsell set a precedent by singing a waiata. He suggested that the daily prayer might be rendered in Maori on occasion, and that other brief use of Maori for formal matters would be appropriate from time to time. This should, however, be translated immediately out of courtesy, and its extended use in debate when many others could not understand it would be unacceptable. Ceremonial prefaces to speeches and similar contributions from the gallery such as waiata on occasions of significance to Maori were increasingly common by the late 1990s, and the demand for translation both in the House and in select committees increased. Since 1997 an interpreter has been available.

no-confidence fell into disuse as the two-party system was consolidated and the focus shifted towards turning governments out in elections. Hamilton had introduced rather camouflaged no-confidence motions in 1938 and 1939 during the Address-in-Reply debates. Then the war intervened.[70] Following the 1946 election, National did not challenge the government in this way even though Labour's majority was small. Party discipline was sufficient to ensure that the numbers would be there – as long as pairing worked efficiently. No-confidence motions were advanced as a means of forcing debate on important topics that would otherwise not be debated. Holland confessed to using a no-confidence motion for this purpose in 1948, when severe electricity shortages were discussed.[71] Urgency was taken and the broadcasting time was extended.

With the disappearance of opportunities to throw governments out on a division, motions of no-confidence became ritualistic declarations and criticisms. The Leader of the Opposition's day-to-day role of managing the business of the House in concert with the Prime Minister (as Leader of the House), including opportunities for criticism and censure, took precedence.[72] In principle, the Prime Minister controlled the order paper within the constraints of the standing orders, but this was subject to consultation with the Opposition, and the smooth running of the House required co-operation.

The consolidation of two-party government and parliament, 1936–49

PRESS PHOTOGRAPHY

An enterprising member of National's front bench smuggled a camera onto the floor of the House in 1948 and caught Nash speaking. The bewigged Clerk sits at the Table in the foreground. In spite of the introduction of radio broadcasts, the House was very reluctant to accept the visual recording of events in the chamber. Shots of an empty chamber might be taken with permission, but photographs from the public gallery remained forbidden and the terms on which newspaper photographs could be taken continued to be strictly regulated.

Evening Post, 12 March 1954

Parliamentary Service collection

The first record of a state opening of Parliament by a news photographer inside the Legislative Council chamber. This was taken in 1957 by Morris Hill of the *Auckland Star*. Governor-General Lord Cobham is flanked by the Prime Minister Holyoake and Leader of the Opposition Nash.

On the adjournment of a day's sitting, the Leader of the Opposition could formally ask the Prime Minister to outline the order of business for the next sitting day, and during supply the Opposition chose which estimate items were to be discussed. The Prime Minister was obliged to allow time for Opposition motions of censure and to give the Leader of the Opposition the right of reply to a prime ministerial statement. By tradition, the Leader of the Opposition made the call for a division to be taken: following a nod to the Speaker or Chairman of Committees, 'Ring the bells!' rang out.

In 1949, with a beleaguered Labour government in serious decline, Fraser stalled before calling Parliament. National had been organising for the next election since 1946. Fraser chanced his arm over the contentious matter of introducing compulsory military training, which many in the Labour Party strongly opposed. He had to compromise on a referendum and seek the support of National. In moving a no-confidence motion, Holland criticised the government for being beholden to the labour movement.[73] Labour had an aging contingent and was burdened by the unpopular wartime controls which remained in force. National's younger and more vigorous group promised greater freedom and a change from the old order.

Providing for members' needs

From the mid 1930s the work of members was assisted by a reorganised Legislative Department. When Clerk Kane moved to the Legislative Council in 1930, Speaker Statham insisted that a legally qualified outsider from the Law Drafting Office, T.D.H. Hall, replace him.[74] Legal expertise subsequently became particularly important, as some of Labour's less experienced Speakers, such as McKeen and Macfarlane, did not have legal backgrounds. All the subsequent Clerks (with the exception of G.F. Bothamley) – H.N. Dollimore, E.A. Roussell, C.P. Littlejohn and D.G. McGee – have been barristers and solicitors. People with legal qualifications were increasingly recruited for the senior clerical ranks.

Hall was also employed to reorganise the Legislative Department. Appointments had been made haphazardly and many staff were elderly and had no specialised training. Hall found it difficult to reorganise the department in conditions of depression, expenditure cuts and low salaries. Nonetheless, by the mid 1930s the ranks of the 'Old Brigade' of officers who had been in their jobs since the nineteenth century were depleted. W.E. Dasent, who had risen from a position as sessional clerk in 1891, retired from the Clerk-Assistant's position in 1933. In senior positions only the Black Rod, A.T. Bothamley, and the Hansard Supervisor were left from the old days.

Labour had long made a fuss about the conditions of employment of ancillary parliamentary staff. Under the Labour government, the wages and conditions of

Thomas Donald Horn Hall (known as 'T.D.H.') was born in Wellington on 4 October 1885 and educated at Wanganui and Wellington Colleges. He entered the public service in 1901 as a cadet, briefly in the Railways Department and then in the Department of Agriculture. Hall rose to clerk in 1905, and to senior clerk in 1920 after serving in 1 NZEF during the First World War, obtained an LLB from Victoria University College and was appointed Assistant Law Draftsman in Parliament's Law Drafting Office in 1921. In 1930 Hall replaced E.W. Kane as Clerk of the House of Representatives, a position he retained until 1945 in spite of failing health. He edited the Index of Laws of New Zealand *in 1930 and was awarded a CMG in 1939. Fraser, an expert in parliamentary procedure, regarded Hall's stewardship of the House in combination with Speaker Statham as extremely effective. Hall died in 1970.*

messengers and others were improved. Messengers were no longer laid off at the end of sessions, but redeployed to government departments. Savage boasted that staff would be 'better provided for than they have ever been since there has been a Parliament'.[75] Attempts were made to apply the 40-hour, five-day week, with additional staff employed to compensate for the reduced working hours. But the government accepted that Bellamy's staff had to work longer during sessions, and the early-morning charwomen failed to obtain improved wages or hours. They were granted a sessional bonus instead. The charwomen eventually petitioned the Speaker and Prime Minister Savage, and secured some improvements.[76] Sylvia Jackson, who was employed as a charwoman in 1927 and stayed in the job for the next 30 years, remembered walking to Parliament Buildings from Kilbirnie at 3 a.m. through the tram tunnel. Later she bicycled; then a special early morning bus was provided.

Hansard, which had proved remarkably resistant to change, was reorganised under Hall.[77] By the mid 1930s it had become difficult to attract new recruits, as pay rates were not keeping up with general wage movements. The reporting profession lost its status as lower-paid female reporters replaced males. When elderly reporters retired, even though the 'feeling had been growing that shorthand-writing is a fit occupation only for young women, and that their work is good enough', the introduction of female reporters was still not to be contemplated.[78]

The Chief Reporter wanted more staff, but Hall wanted fewer reporters and female typists to transcribe their notes.[79] The Speaker concurred – but felt that young male typists would be better. Six were appointed in 1937, opening a new career path for Hansard reporting staff. They included J. McLean and A.B. Conway, both of whom would later head Hansard.[80] Transcriptions were made in a large room occupied by all the reporters and typists, dictating and typing alongside one another. While the typewriters did have 'silencing' cabinets, the noise can be imagined.

From the end of the war the reporting process changed. A second reporter now

A Hansard typist's unfortunate mistaken rendition of the 'right' honourable gentleman. Madeleine Hely began work as a Hansard typist in 1948. The typewriters were housed in boxes in an attempt to reduce the noise produced by three women typing to reporters' dictation. This part-time sessional work was intensive and involved late nights. The women took in the reporters' ten-minute 'turns' in succession, rapidly producing three accurate copies to be forwarded to the Editor for checking before going to the printer. The women lunched in Bellamy's in the 'typists room' established during the war, but at first they were not allowed to have their evening meals there. Eventually this right was conceded because of the lack of cafés open nearby. They had to sit well away from the men, at 'a small table in a dimly lit area'. After late sittings they were allowed to go home by shared taxi, but with all staff having the same privilege this often took some time. On one occasion Nash found the women still waiting late at night and stayed with them until their taxi arrived. Casual Hansard typists were poorly paid and most did not stay long. By the late 1950s a small core of permanent staff had been established.

undertook back-up 'check noting' alongside the reporter who was engaged in a ten-minute 'take'. The second reporter concentrated on interjections, unusual names, and other matters which the other reporter might miss or record incorrectly. After ten minutes, the second reporter would begin his own 'take', assisted by a new second reporter. At the end of each 'take', reporters left the chamber to dictate notes to the typists.[81] As the sitting proceeded, the shifts were shortened so that the reporters would finish their dictating at about the same time at the end of the day.

During the war female typists replaced the young male typists because of labour shortages. Before long, a permanent pool of female Hansard typists was established. Fred Manderson, known as 'Mandy', became Chief Reporter in 1944. He was the first Chief Reporter without a background in newspaper reporting. Manderson became Editor of Debates in 1953, when Hansard was reorganised, and retired in 1957.[82]

G.H. Scholefield's long-held ambitions for the library were realised as better times returned. Once again the library expanded its holdings, and increasing use was made of the reference section and its archival and historical collections.[83] Scholefield published resources to assist with research into New Zealand's history – the *Union Catalogue of New Zealand Newspapers* in 1937, and the *Dictionary of New Zealand Biography* and a revised version of the *Parliamentary Record* in 1940. By the late 1940s the library was bursting at the seams with close to 200,000 volumes. Scholefield retired in 1948. Sir Gilbert Campion, the retired Clerk of the House of Commons, considered that the library provided 'one of the best parliamentary services in the world'. This statement was proudly recorded in the library's annual report.[84]

Hall retired as Clerk of the House in 1945, having been prevailed upon to stay on during the war. Fraser wanted Hall and former Speaker Statham to write a manual on parliamentary procedure.[85] Hall agreed to work on this in his retirement, believing that New Zealand had lagged behind developing Westminster practice and that a comprehensive overhaul of the standing orders was required. He was particularly concerned about the rights of minorities and private members in the House – a losing battle as the two-party system became firmly established. But Fraser did not want to reopen the issue of standing orders, and the new National government was not interested in taking the matter further either. In the end Hall's work lapsed after he had completed a draft manuscript.

With Hall's retirement, G.F. Bothamley, the previous Clerk-Assistant back from the navy, was appointed Clerk temporarily, in recognition of his service, on the understanding that he would shortly retire.[86] In 1946 he was replaced by H.N. Dollimore, who was to serve as Clerk until 1971.

With the failure of successive governments to proceed with the second stage of the 'new' Parliament Buildings, the old wooden Government House continued in use. As

Henry Nelson (Neil) Dollimore was born in Gisborne in 1905. He attended Pleasant Point District High School before joining the public service in 1921. After working for the Stamp Duties Department and then the Railways Department, Dollimore joined the Legislative Department in 1929. He studied law part-time while working his way up to Record Clerk in 1932 and Second Clerk-Assistant in 1933, gaining an LLB at Victoria University College. He became Clerk-Assistant during the Second World War when G.F. Bothamley re-entered military service. He was appointed Clerk of the House of Representatives in 1946, after a short tenure by Bothamley (1945–6). Dollimore was awarded a CBE in 1968. He prepared the publication Parliament of New Zealand and Parliament House *in 1954 (issued as a revised edition in 1973) and retired in 1971. Dollimore died in 1991.*

Parliamentary Service collection

the building deteriorated, hygiene became an issue and staff left. Strategically placed flowerpots and rubbish bins dealt with the perennial leaks. Semple, Labour's Minister of Works, described Bellamy's as a 'rat-den' that was 'unfit for human habitation, for the serving of meals, or the dispensing of liquor', and was concerned that the entire structure might collapse in another earthquake like that of August 1942. Another member alluded to a 'stench' that made members go downtown for their meals, and to the deployment of many cats to deal with the rats. Rodents remained a problem in the building for many years. Once rats chewed through the plastic piping of the beer pump in Bellamy's, resulting in substantial losses.

Semple promised that the structure would be removed. In the meantime, the House Committee recommended substantial reconstruction work.[87] Extensive renovations and extensions in wood and fibrolite were undertaken during a lengthy adjournment of the House in 1944. This involved demolishing the ground floor and removing the distinctive tower at the south end, which was seen as an earthquake hazard. New dining rooms, a kitchen, pantry and bars were provided. The dining rooms were arranged around a central kitchen. Except during the rush hour before dinner, a single barman could run the whole show by moving between the bars' separate compartments and counters.[88]

The new Bellamy's was still makeshift and cramped. The kitchen was outfitted with surplus equipment from the departing American forces. There was standing room only in the cramped 'dog-box' bars, and almost no furniture. A report in *Truth* that women were to have their own bar caused alarm. Speaker Schramm telegrammed Acting Prime Minister Dan Sullivan 'to see that this ladies bar lounge forms no part of the new structure'.[89] He was assured that it would not.

New Zealand was the only Parliament to persist with 'Bellamy's' as the name for its catering establishment. A bureaucratic attempt to rename it the 'Catering Department' following the refurbishment failed dismally. The members did not like it, and everyone ignored the new signs, kept the old ones and kept using the traditional name.[90] By 1950 'Bellamy's' had been formally adopted again.

From the late 1930s, in recognition of the greater amount of work being done during the parliamentary recess, Bellamy's provided a meal service and opened a private bar for limited hours outside of the session. During the war years, the demands on its services escalated as sittings stretched further through the year, the number of functions increased, and ministerial staff grew. By the early 1940s losses mounted and the bar could no longer support the other services; meal prices had not changed since the early 1930s. The government – which by means of subsidy had continued to pay the salaries of Bellamy's staff – took control from the House Committee. It did not help that Fraser's internal audit found several thousand pounds to be missing from the bar takings over the years.[91] The manager and a senior barman were dismissed, the staff was reorganised, and the losses were stemmed. A new manager was brought in, and Bellamy's was subjected to a regular government audit – although it was made clear that the accounts would not be made public.

Executive and parliament

By the late 1940s, the two-party system was entrenched.[92] The party whips, working with their leaders, exerted a stranglehold over members by granting leave, arranging pairs and the speaking order in debates, and approving the introduction of bills, questions and notices of motion. Only two independents had been returned in 1938 – Atmore and C.A. Wilkinson. Both were long-serving and had strong local backing. In 1940 Lee became a third independent, after being expelled from the Labour Party. In 1943, Wilkinson retired and Lee was defeated. Atmore's death in 1946 made the genuinely independent member extinct.

There were still opportunities, however, for individual members acting within the party structures to have an influence.[93] The party caucuses met regularly on Thursday mornings when Parliament

Harry Atmore was elected for Nelson in 1911. The last in a tradition of independent local constituency members, he was renowned for his advocacy for his electorate. Generally a Liberal supporter, he helped keep the government in power in early 1912. He was particularly accessible to his constituents, preferring to ride a bicycle rather than use a car and answering all requests for assistance personally. As Minister of Education in the late 1920s he oversaw a progressive report incorporating ideas that were later taken up by Fraser and the Labour government. Atmore became an advocate of social credit and although usually supporting the Labour government he was critical of its monetary policy. Just two weeks after announcing that he would retire from politics, he died on 20 August 1946.

was in session.[94] Labour's meetings were more formal, with written rules of procedure and time limits on speeches. In the 1940s National adopted a system of caucus committees that paralleled the select committee structure. Labour followed suit in the 1950s. Caucus committees worked with relevant ministers or their shadow equivalents and the whips to provide a stance on proposed legislation and speakers for debates. The caucuses played a key role in cementing general loyalty into voting support on specific issues. While internal caucus mechanisms necessarily remained obscure to the public, they were clearly efficient in promoting party discipline. As Labour member Paddy Kearins said: 'All legislation is really passed before it ever comes into this Chamber. The caucus of the Government party decides – and rightly so, I think – what will pass and what will not pass in this Chamber. What happens in this Chamber are mere formalities … There is no other way we can work … There are many conflicts and many bitter struggles. They do not take place in this Chamber. It is only gallery play that we see here. They take place in the caucuses.'[95]

Private members' participation in debates in the House, while filling *Hansard*, was not especially incisive. There remained many opportunities for the average member to speak, unlike in the House of Commons. The inevitable tendency – abetted by the party whips – was to fill the time available. As Warren Freer ruefully remembered, on one occasion he was roundly abused by both sides because he refused to speak for an hour during the budget debate.[96] Such behaviour was not playing the game at all. Overseas commentators referred to a poor standard of debate.

The party system and the increasing emphasis on efficiency in the House combined to eliminate the old 'characters' from Parliament. While they were ill-disciplined and often took up undue time, such members had provided colour and entertainment. Without them, debates tended to be drab, set-piece stand-offs between the two parties. The Address-in-Reply debate, while free-ranging, was a disorganised and rambling exercise in which government members advanced the interests of their electorates and the Opposition levelled general criticisms against the government. The financial debate similarly lacked organisation and was often characterised by set speeches rather than genuine debate.

In 1953 the *Dominion* lamented that 'standardised' personalities had become dominant in an environment of 'ruthless, highly-developed party machines'.[97] Semple, soon to retire, was one of the last of the real characters. He would bash the top of his desk with great force, and was notable for his barrages of strongly phrased language and for his verbal duels with National's R.M. Algie, jousts which they – and the entire House – enjoyed. Semple also engaged in vitriolic exchanges with Stan Goosman over their favourite topic, public works. At the end of one altercation 'Semple strolled over to Goosman and said: "That wasn't bad, was it?" and they went off for a drink together.'[98]

The consolidation of two-party government and parliament, 1936–49

GIVING VENT

Cartoons frequently referred to hot air rising from Parliament. The session which began in June 1934 continued until April 1935 and included a warm February. The chamber had always been ill-equipped to cope with sittings during hot summers. Despite the introduction of closure, sessions lengthened and the public viewed Parliament as spending too long talking about too little. The New Zealand Parliament remained unusual in the amount of time it allowed members to contribute to debate – other Parliaments granted far less. During the war Fraser clamped down and gave extensions only to party leaders or other prominent speakers. In the more relaxed postwar environment extensions were seldom withheld, and once again members let their tongues get the better of them. Attempts in 1951 to restrict speaking times and the practice of granting extensions failed. A standing order was drafted but then dropped – members were just too fond of their 'freedom of speech'.

J.C. Hill, *Christchurch Times*, 21 February 1935

The Address-in-Reply was the traditional opportunity for members to 'blow off steam'. Here party leaders Forbes, Coates and Holland make their contributions.

NEW ZEALAND'S "HYDE PARK."

J.C. Hill, *Auckland Star*, 3 October 1933

Allen, *Parliamentary Portraits*

One of the most flamboyant members, Bob Semple, was elected for Wellington South in 1918 as one of the early Labour members, but soon defeated. He returned to the House in 1928 and remained until his retirement in 1954. He was known for the colour of his language and for his ripostes in the House. He was Minister of Public Works in the first Labour government.

223

T.K. Sidey was the assiduous local member for Caversham, 1901–8, and Dunedin South, 1908–28. The patron of countless societies, he seemed to attend virtually every possible public function. He replaced Steward as the most notable champion of private members' bills, crusading for daylight saving and promoting other bills. First introduced in 1909, his New Zealand Local Time Bill soon attained the status of a 'hardy annual'. It was to be a long fight. He finally got his due reward in 1927 when the Summer Time Act advanced the time by one hour during summer on a year's trial. After a rash of complaints from the country, the government reduced the change to half an hour, again just for one year. In 1929 Sidey, now in cabinet (having been appointed to the Legislative Council), was able to get the measure permanently onto the statute book.

Other departed personalities were A.E. Glover, Dr H.T.J. Thacker, W.D. Lynsar, Frank Langstone, John A. Lee, and David McDougall, 'who wore a gay tartan waistcoat and … refused consistently to allow extensions of speaking time to anyone but the party leaders and opening speakers'. Gwen Watts, the wife of National member Jack Watts, described 'Bill Bodkin – or "Billy the Bod", as we called him – with words tumbling out of his mouth in a never-ceasing cascade; W.J. Broadfoot, "Broady", hunched, suave and white-spatted … [and] Harry Morton, owner of a private plane and a wooden leg, the latter often removed and left lying disconcertingly on the floor of the House'.[99]

On the other hand, some members were renowned for their taciturn nature.[100] Peter McSkimming, who was completely out of place in the House, contributed only four one-minute speeches and one interjection in his three years. He refused to attend most of his last session of 1935. Warned that he would be penalised £2 a day for failing to attend, he saw this as 'the cheapest money he had spent for a long time'. The Labour members James Munro and Peter Neilson refused to participate in debates unless ordered to do so by the whips. When cajoled into contributing, Neilson strung together quotations ranging from the Bible to Stalin. No-one had the heart to pull him up for reading his speeches.

Private members' business was inevitably squeezed out.[101] Minimal time was allocated for private members' bills, which had declined in importance. In most cases they were ruled out because they involved appropriations (which could only be made by the government). The Address-in-Reply and financial debates cut substantially into the time reserved for private members. After the financial debate was concluded, the government would move precedence for its business. Of the time theoretically available to private members, more than half would be taken by the government.

Questions took up more than a third of the time available to private members, and this was where they made their major contribution. During question time there was usually a full attendance of the House, and an interested gallery. The Speaker called the parties alternately. Ministers were allowed five minutes for their answers before a bell went. Members then jumped up in an attempt to catch the Speaker's eye for the next question.[102] Members could not ask more than one question until all had had an opportunity. While question time almost invariably proceeded along party lines, it was not unknown for other, usually local, concerns to cut across these. Eric Halstead remembered one occasion on which a single question regarding Auckland public works occupied the entire afternoon, with both Labour and National members from Auckland combining against all other members. However, question time had its limits as a critical forum. There was no provision for supplementary questions, as in the House of Commons, and ministers were not required to reply and address the question.[103] The tendency was towards political rhetoric rather than penetrating inquiry.

The consolidation of two-party government and parliament, 1936–49

The scope for independent action by private members was potentially greater in select committees, but these played a relatively minor role, and little time was available for their deliberations. One commentator suggested that they were 'competent enough to be useful to the House, but not independent enough to be dangerous to the government'.[104] Over time, the mornings had been whittled away, leaving only Wednesdays for select committees to meet. Friday mornings had been taken for the House in 1929 to allow members to get away for the weekend. In the 1930s weekly caucus meetings came to be held regularly on Thursday mornings. Tuesday mornings had always been unpopular with members who wanted to spend long weekends in their electorates. With the advent of air travel, they were used to fly back to Wellington.[105]

Select committees were chaired by government members but were not particularly influential at this time.[106] There was no general requirement to refer bills to them, and they had no power to initiate independent enquiries. Nevertheless, they could, in a largely non-partisan manner, correct and recommend minor amendments to a reasonable proportion of the legislation that was passed on to

James McCombs (left), wearing borrowed flying gear, prepares to fly to Christchurch after missing the Friday night ferry to Lyttelton because of a division in the House, c. early 1930s. Air travel became increasingly popular after the Second World War. The Legislative Department arranged bulk travel arrangements with NAC. Members were notorious for holding planes up. Some of the older ones, not keen to take their chances in the air, continued to catch the train or ferry. Air travel changed the dynamic of sessions. Members could easily return home each week, and their presence in Wellington during the recess was no longer unusual. Bellamy's and the library closed down in the weekends.

them. The Statutes Revision Committee (largely populated by lawyers) played a particularly important role in scrutinising the technicalities of legal bills and Statutes Amendment Bills.

The Local Bills Committee enabled members to promote bills sought by local bodies and shape the resulting legislation in a relatively non-partisan way. The Public Accounts Committee considered the annual estimates of Parliament – but usually with the aim of uncovering embarrassing details rather than scrutinising financial management and accountability from a wider perspective. This committee provided a minor if haphazard check on ministers and government departments, limited by the speed at which it had to work. The role of the Public Petitions Committees was much reduced following the depression. There was a spectacular decline in the number of petitions presented annually to the House after the establishment of the welfare state. The number of petitions concerning Maori land also declined.[107] The work of the Public Petitions Committees remained considerable, but it was strictly advisory. The government made the final decisions on the merits of individual petitions.

Voting in the House represented the most obvious and complete subjugation of Parliament to the party system. Despite the claims of Labour and particularly National that members were still allowed a measure of freedom in exercising their vote, extremely strong party discipline was exerted in the House. There were very few examples of independent voting. The directive against crossing the floor was particularly strong in the Labour Party. National theoretically allowed members a free vote on matters they had not pledged themselves to during elections, but day-to-day voting patterns were highly predictable. The result was almost always known before members trooped into the lobbies.[108] This discipline was to be maintained in following decades.

The only remaining opportunity to vote independently was the infrequent free or 'conscience' vote on a contentious social or moral issue. Such votes usually polarised the House. Even on these issues, the extent to which voting was truly 'free' was debatable. For National in particular, even when free votes were explicitly granted, the tendency was for a party line to prevail.

But party discipline was not simply imposed externally upon individual members. Both parties insisted that members retained choice in their voting behaviour, even if all the indications and the day-to-day voting patterns suggested precisely the opposite. This can be explained in terms of the continued insistence by members that they could vote differently if they so chose. Rather than being dragooned into the lobbies, members entered them voluntarily. They chose to vote with their party because of the strong loyalty and collective cohesion that were integral to the powerful bonds of the mass party organisations. These bonds were enhanced in the House as members were inducted into its culture of party solidarity.

The party caucuses were crucial to maintaining this cohesion. Ambition, too, played its part, for the rewards of office were clearly given for loyalty and service as well as ability. In a small House of only 80 members, and with a substantial proportion of the majority party in cabinet, the prospects of promotion for the loyal and hard-working were good. Party solidarity was further strengthened by members' increasing workloads and specialisation, which encouraged co-operation to keep business going. The party structures allowed Parliament to function effectively. As select committees acquired an increased role, members specialised in particular areas and ensured contentious issues were aired and sometimes resolved before they were debated on the floor of the House.

With independents disappearing and the role of private members diminishing, the rise of 'delegated' legislation, usually by means of Orders in Council promulgating regulations, was viewed with concern. The government was able to frame regulations without scrutiny by Parliament. In theory, Parliament had some oversight over regulations because they were tabled in the House, but government control over the order paper meant that they were only rarely discussed. National deplored the increasing use of regulations while Labour was in power, but was not at heart opposed to the practice. The Clerk put the prevailing attitude clearly. 'We don't like the way you do this but we will take note of it for future reference when we take over the reins of Government.'[109]

The issue of delegated legislation had first arisen after the First World War. The war years had seen

The consolidation of two-party government and parliament, 1936–49

considerable growth in legislation which gave the Governor-General, ministers or departments powers to make regulations that were necessary to give effect to or for the purpose of the legislation. Concern about such legislation was expressed in the 1920s, and by the early 1930s some critics of it were becoming voluble. Professor R.M. Algie condemned the practice trenchantly. He became a National member in 1943, and Speaker in 1961.[110] He pointed out that at the turn of the century only one-fifth of legislation empowered the drawing up of regulations; by 1916 the proportion had increased to one-third, and by 1931 it was almost one-half. Moreover, there was no systematic method by which regulations could be monitored, since they were published in the *Gazette* (if at all) in an ad hoc fashion.

In 1936 Labour passed a Regulations Act which provided for publishing regulations in annual volumes. From this time, the extent to which regulations were being issued became clear. In the mid 1930s they numbered hundreds annually. A peak was reached in the early years of the war.[111] The Emergency Regulations Act 1939, in particular, augmented the government's powers of delegated legislation. The Act allowed for regulations to have the same force as an Act of Parliament, and to override legislation inconsistent or incompatible with them. Then the Economic Stabilisation Emergency Regulations of 1942 (followed by the later Economic Stabilisation Act 1948) provided effective tools for the control of the economy. Concern about the practice continued to be expressed and Algie pursued his quest to strengthen the authority of Parliament. He suggested, as did others, that a special select committee review all regulations as they were drafted. Labour was forced to an all-night debate and the application of closure in 1947 over legislation extending the life of wartime regulations. Holland described the measure as 'making New Zealand a completely communistic State' and 'the most far-reaching and important' bill in the government's history.[112] The subsequent Emergency Regulations Select Committee reviewed wartime powers, but its terms of reference were restricted and its life strictly limited.

The changing House

The Labour Party's elevation to government changed the composition of the House decisively.[113] After the 1935 election, two-fifths of members were entirely new to the House and their average age fell substantially, to just over 50. As the two-party system stabilised in the following years, turnover declined and the average age increased again. But by the end of the period, the parliamentary experience of members still remained somewhat less than it had been in the early 1930s, and a greater range of age groups was represented in the House. The 1946–9 cohort of members provided substantial continuity into the postwar period, however, with the average sojourn in the House rising to 20 years.

Some of the most experienced members had departed in 1943. Ngata, with 38 years of service, was defeated in the election. Coates, with 32 years, died earlier in the year, while Forbes decided to retire after 35 years. By 1949 Labour members were the longest-serving – Fraser had been in the House for 31 years, Parry for 30, and McKeen for 27. Apart from these stalwarts, the experience of the bulk of the House dated from the election of 1935 and after. The practices of the two-party system soon became second nature to most members, since they had known nothing else.

After the 1935 election the proportion of members of the House born overseas (slightly more than one-third) was higher than before, reflecting the substantial number of Labour members born outside New Zealand.[114] National was solidly New Zealand-born. The proportion born overseas declined in subsequent Parliaments.

Farmers remained the most important single group in the House after 1935. Although their representation diminished to some extent, the entry of farmers into Labour's ranks partly counterbalanced the collapse of the coalition.[115] Farmers comprised nearly one-third of all members, followed by manual workers and trade union officials at one-fifth, with business, law and professional groups each about one-tenth of the total. Much of the larger working-class group (which was –

unsurprisingly – confined to the Labour Party) now comprised manual workers in contrast to the previous period when organising trade unions had been a path into politics. The small shopkeeper and trade group made a notable contribution to Labour. The proportion of lawyers and journalists continued to decline, while that of other professional groups rose. Journalism, in particular, was no longer a common route into the House. The educational level of members rose again, in spite of the influx of less well-educated Labour members in 1935, as people with post-primary and university educations were elected for National.

Through its period in government, Labour lost many of the farmers and small businessmen that it had gained in 1935 as a result of the depression. It also began to lose its manual workers. National attracted more lawyers and company directors and a few accountants, making it more representative of urban interests. Mitchell summarised the differences by suggesting that Labour drew its members from the working and middle classes, while National relied more on the upper middle class.

The longstanding issue of members' pay became even more important after Labour's election, since there were fewer men of independent means in the House. But while governments were sympathetic to an increase, the times had not been opportune.[116] In the 1940s the salary was still lower than the level set in 1920, although the cuts of the early 1930s had been restored. The impact of inflation left members making invidious comparisons between their incomes and those of tradesmen or wharfies.

Labour was not keen to increase members' salaries. It put workers' wages first; then the war intervened.[117] Labour members were in fact not too badly off, since they had the benefit of a scheme whereby cabinet ministers pooled their salaries with those of ordinary members into a fund which was shared equally among all their comrades in the House. The Opposition and one or two Labour cabinet members were not happy about this. A National member, H.G. Dickie, who was about to retire with failing eyesight and poor prospects, deplored the paltry payment that he and fellow National members received in comparison. Labour's Attorney-General, Rex Mason, later described the pool as a 'mad scheme whereby Ministers had to relieve the poverty' of others and make themselves poor in the process.[118]

In 1944 a special select committee came to some hard-hitting conclusions.[119] Parliamentarians in other countries were paid much more. Despite the need for economic stabilisation during the war, it was 'essential' that action be taken to remedy this 'intolerable' situation. The work of members was now decidedly full-time and sessions had become protracted. Members should not be expected to supplement their income from other work or unearned income. Travelling expenses were considerable in spite of the concessions, and other expenses had escalated as a result of additional parliamentary and electorate work. On average, members' net incomes after expenses were substantially less than half the gross salaries of and considerably less than the current award rates for skilled manual workers.

Fraser accepted the committee's report and the salary was returned to the 1920 level of £500, supplemented by a tax-free allowance of £250. Labour's egalitarian but inequitable pooling scheme was ended. It was generally agreed that a demanding and responsible job should be remunerated appropriately, even if there would inevitably be public disquiet about pay increases. The *Dominion*, while conceding the case for an increase, suggested the move was ill-timed when there was unrest over pay concessions to various groups of workers as wartime stabilisation measures began to break down.[120]

The next step was to provide proper superannuation to replace the antiquated discretionary 'compassionate' allowance granted to impecunious retired members and their widows. Nothing had been done about superannuation for members during the depression, in spite of agitation. In 1945 a Members' Superannuation Committee was appointed to work in the recess.[121] The predicament was underlined by the case of G.M. Thomson, who had served six years in the House and 14 in the Legislative Council.[122] He had not been reappointed to the Council at the age of 83 when his term expired in 1932. Being eligible, he applied for the miserly state old age pension of 17s 6d a week. His friends put together a trust fund to provide him with a small annuity instead. When his circumstances became known, the government offered him a special pension of £100 a year, but he died shortly afterwards.

The consolidation of two-party government and parliament, 1936–49

THE WEIGHT IN THE BOAT.

Member of Parliament: And if anything untoward should happen, thank God that at least I will be provided for.

J.C. Hill, Auckland Star, 12 November 1932

It was reported that members had 'sunk party differences' to provide themselves with pensions. This move did not find favour with the cartoonist or the public during the depression.

The 1945 committee's recommendation for a proper superannuation scheme was accepted, and this was established by Part V of the Superannuation Act 1947. At the last minute, National was embarrassed by extra-parliamentary opposition to the scheme and had to vote against it.[123] Members were to contribute 10 per cent of their salaries and would qualify after nine years' service and at 50 years of age.

Following the entry of Elizabeth McCombs into the House in 1933 (she died in 1935), women made gains only slowly. Spokeswoman for the welfare of women and children became an accepted role for women members. In 1938 Catherine Stewart was elected for Labour. She had difficulty getting a room to work in, since members usually shared rooms. Janet Fraser arranged for her to occupy a large room vacated by the new Chairman of Committes, McKeen.[124] She was also allocated a single seat in the chamber, positioned so that the ladies' gallery had a good view of her. The colourful and energetic Mary Dreaver had, at an early age, decided that she would eventually stand for Parliament, and she had worked alongside Savage to that end. She entered the House through a by-election in 1941 after considerable experience in local body and Labour Party affairs. Dreaver urged that women should contribute to the making of 'domestic legislation' because of their experience in the home.[125] She and Grigg publicised the Women's Land Service by entering the chamber in its uniform. After losing her seat in 1943, Dreaver became the first woman appointed to the Legislative Council in 1946.

Mary Grigg, the first female National member, was elected unopposed in 1942 after her husband, the member for Mid-Canterbury, was killed on active service. Her prime concerns were children, the

The House

family and welfare. She married William Polson in 1943 and retired from Parliament at the election of that year, but remained active in the National Party. Her view was that 'unless it is brought to their notice, the men Members of the House seem to be completely unaware' of women's point of view. 'We need a great many more women in Parliament'.[126]

The entry into the House in a 1943 by-election of Mabel Howard, the daughter of the former stalwart Labour member Ted Howard, caused a great stir. She came from a background of socialist trade union organising, and was adept at public speaking and dealing with men in a rough and tumble environment. She was less tolerant than her female predecessors of some of the anachronistic customs of Parliament.[127] When she attempted to have a bath in the basement, she was stopped by a messenger who pointed to the 'Gentlemen' sign. She pointed to the 'Members Only' sign in return, and gained access after threatening to climb in through the window. She also protested against the rule that prevented women members inviting females onto the floor of the House, behind the Speaker. Alister McIntosh, the secretary of the war cabinet, observed that 'when roused, she can combine the qualities of a tiger and a Billingsgate fishwife'.[128]

Howard made a confident maiden speech and immediately wanted women appointed to the House Committee to provide better services to members. This provoked a comment from an unidentifed male member – 'And serve the drinks'. For her pains she was dispatched to the committee, a common destination from then on for women, who were presumed to have the requisite domestic acumen.[129] Howard entered cabinet in 1947 on the death of Dan Sullivan as Minister of Health and Minister of Mental Hospitals, with special responsibility for women and children. She was Minister of Social Security in the second Labour government. Hilda Ross won Hamilton for National in a by-election in 1945. Ross had a great deal of energy and was diligent in attending debates, 'hour after hour … upright in her place following every speaker'.[130] She was also appointed to the House Committee, and in the 1950s became its 'chairman'.

In its composition Parliament responded to the changing nature of New Zealand society. The broadening of representation reflected the emergence of a more complex society with larger secondary and service sectors and a place, albeit still minor, for women. The influence of farmers, while still remarkably strong by international standards, had diminished. Likewise, the role of the 'political' professional groups of lawyers and journalists that had been so marked in the nineteenth century was eroded. A wider range of professional and service occupations were becoming represented, including ministers of religion, doctors, teachers and accountants. The

ATL, F68071½

Mabel Howard represented Christchurch East and then Sydenham from 1943 until her retirement in 1969. As Minister of Health (1947–9) she was the first woman in cabinet. She was later Minister of Social Security (1957–60). The eccentric and at times naïve Howard could be relied upon to provide entertainment in the House. She is remembered for waving two large pairs of bloomers in the House in 1954 to emphasise the non-standard sizing of women's garments. No-one laughed, not wanting to feel her wrath. She had previously held up the dress she had bought for the opening of Parliament, which had shrunk severely after one wash. Howard seemed to be fascinated by the General Assembly Library's stock. In 1954 she suggested that the library held salacious literature that was issued on request. Some years later, when the reading habits of members were under scrutiny, she alleged that almost all the books in the parliamentary library (presumably the fiction collection!) were murder stories. Truth's resulting story led to the exclusion of the paper's reporters from the library for a year. In her last years in the House, suffering from ill health and a failing memory, Howard was looked after by the young newcomer J.L. Hunt. She was made to retire in 1969 under new Labour Party rules.

The consolidation of two-party government and parliament, 1936–49

Hilda Ross was elected for Hamilton in 1945 and held the seat until her death in 1959. She became a member of the Executive Council in 1949 (responsible for the welfare of women and children) and was appointed Minister of Social Security in 1957.

parliamentary cadre began to move up the social scale and become more highly educated as educational levels in the country improved.

By the end of the 1940s the House of Representatives had been transformed through the consolidation of the two political parties. The long transition of politics from a leisure pursuit of members of factional bands to a full-time vocation of party members had been accomplished. Fewer government bills were now introduced, but government legislation was virtually guaranteed success.[131] Under the tighter government control over parliamentary business, daily sitting hours declined to five or six and the practice of sitting until after midnight virtually disappeared. This pattern of the efficient dispatch of business and a very high success rate with legislation would characterise Parliament thenceforth as the executive maintained its authority.

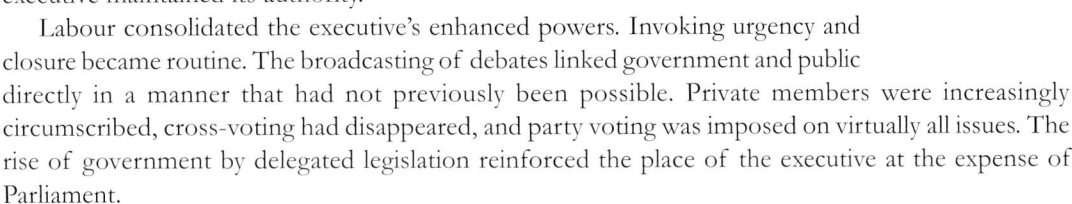

Labour consolidated the executive's enhanced powers. Invoking urgency and closure became routine. The broadcasting of debates linked government and public directly in a manner that had not previously been possible. Private members were increasingly circumscribed, cross-voting had disappeared, and party voting was imposed on virtually all issues. The rise of government by delegated legislation reinforced the place of the executive at the expense of Parliament.

The two-party system and the pre-eminence of the executive had become so entrenched that people began to question the future of Parliament. In Britain one commentator, Hollis, asked in his book, *Can Parliament Survive?*, whether driving a flock of tame sheep through the division lobbies would be better than what existed.[132] Was Parliament still an independent, sovereign source of power that expressed the will of the people? Or had it been reduced to the role of a critic on the sidelines? Parliament was clearly a very different place from the forum for complex factional struggles that it had been in the nineteenth century. But where did its future lie?

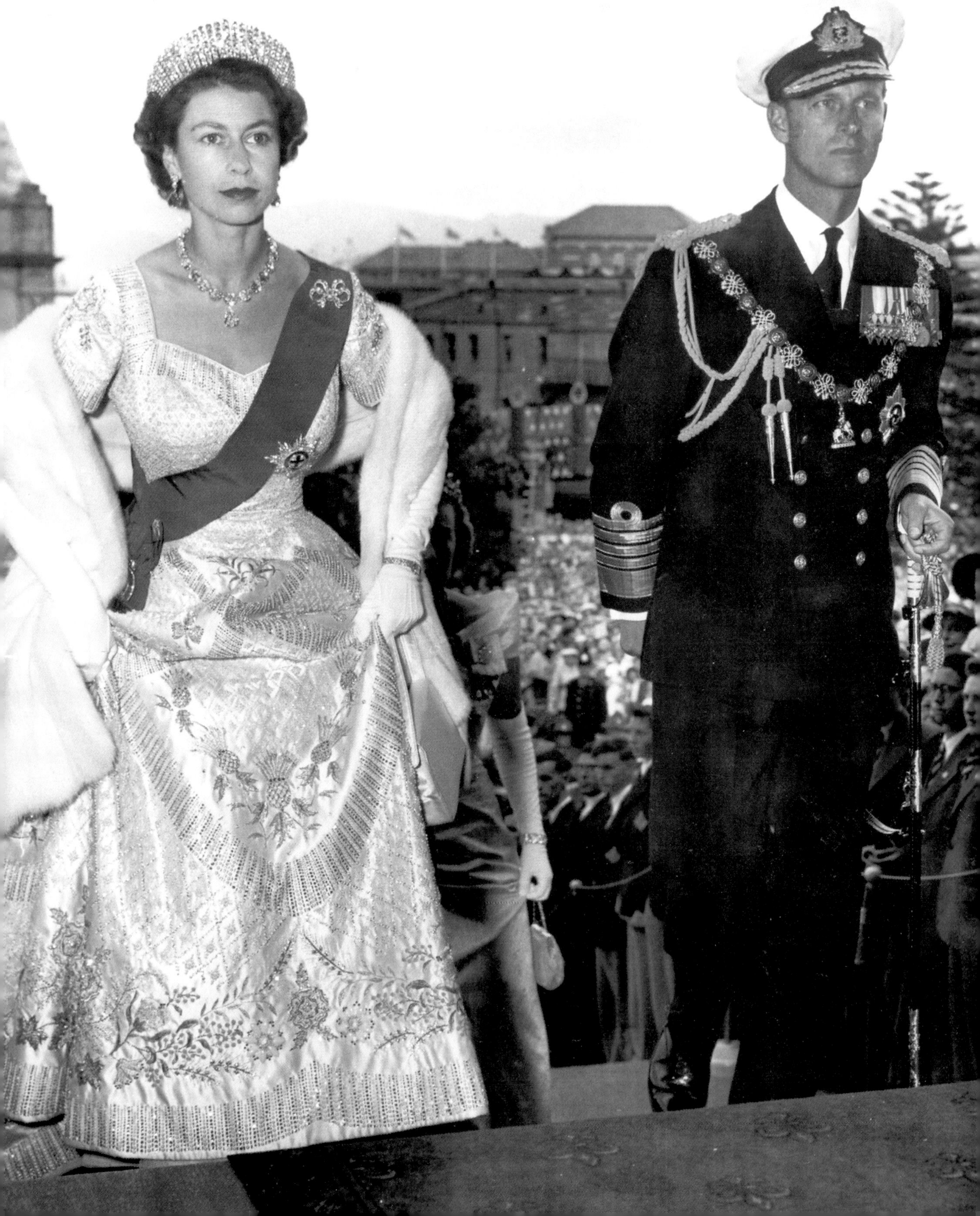

CHAPTER 7

REFORM, EFFICIENCY AND ACCOUNTABILITY, 1950–69

National easily defeated Labour, 46 to 34, in the election of 1949. The new government was determined to restore Parliament to the more prestigious place it had occupied in the past, in its ceremonial trappings if not in the standing of the private member. The dominance of parties was here to stay, but National believed that the iron grip of the executive consolidated by Labour and the war should be relaxed. Parliamentary procedure was to be reformed to improve the institution's public image and in the interests of greater efficiency. But on taking over National found that the huge expansion of government in the postwar decades centralised power in executive hands, a development aided by the abolition of the second chamber.

Sid Holland, the new Prime Minister, was energetic and genial, and seemed naïve, but was in fact shrewd. His down-to-earth bonhomie enabled him to relate well to his caucus members and to the public, in contrast to the ascetic Labour leaders Fraser, Nash and Nordmeyer, who did not fraternise much with other members.[1] Martin Nestor, Holland's longtime researcher and aide, found him generous, tolerant and approachable, but also impatient and impulsive. He saw Holland as neither a deep thinker nor widely read, but as well attuned to political developments and respected in the House. He created a highly disciplined caucus and was ruthless about attendance in the chamber. He proved able to manage a strong team and ran cabinet in a business-like fashion, while allowing initiative by delegating responsibility.

The core of Holland's cabinet included Keith Holyoake, Bill Sullivan and T.C. Webb, together with a number of older members. Holyoake, Holland's deputy since 1946, represented the rural section of the party. He became New Zealand's first official Deputy Prime Minister.

The previous Speaker, McKeen, was not put forward again. While his ill health may have been a factor, party appointment of Speakers was now well-established. Matthew Oram had been tipped for Minister of Education but his poor relationship with Holland saw him appointed Speaker instead. Oram was 'literally taken in hand by the two Whips and led, with some show of token physical resistance, to the Speaker's chair', continuing the tradition of symbolic reluctance to assume the mantle. He made his position apparent from the start by asserting that if he was anyone's man, 'he was the backbenchers". 'I shall do my best to ensure that the rights of private members, and of the minorities as well as those of the majority, are adequately protected.'[2]

Oram was a strong conservative, mindful of traditions and determined to restore a more dignified and neutral Speakership. He did not participate in Committee

Sid Holland, elected for Christchurch North in 1935, became National's leader in 1940 and Prime Minister in 1949. A shrewd and energetic leader with a common touch, he created a disciplined parliamentary team and cabinet. Holland retired shortly before the 1957 election because of failing health.

ATL, F3834½

Left: The Queen, wearing her coronation dress, and the Duke of Edinburgh enter Parliament Buildings for the royal opening of the special session of Parliament, 12 January 1954. Evening Post, Phillip O'Shea collection

Matthew Henry Oram was born in Christchurch on 2 June 1885 and attended Wellington College and Victoria University College, graduating with an MA and LlB in 1912. He became a lawyer in a Palmerston North partnership and developed a strong interest in educational matters. After being a Palmerston North Borough Councillor (1920–7) he stood for Parliament in 1935 for the Democrat Party. Having won Manawatu for National in 1943, he was appointed Speaker in 1950 after National came to power. Oram was keen to restore a greater sense of tradition to Parliament and was regarded as a fair and effective Speaker. He urged that the Speaker's position not be subject to the vagaries of elections and suggested that the Speaker be accorded higher status, as in other Parliaments, so that the executive did not outrank Parliament. He was knighted in 1952. On his resignation in 1957 he became President of the Constitutional Association that was campaigning for parliamentary reform. He died in Palmerston North on 22 January 1969.

proceedings. He strictly policed the rule proscribing the reading of speeches, challenging the speaker and then watching them closely, sometimes asking for the notes to be sent to the Table while the speech was still being delivered.

Confirming the centrality of the House and parties

When the new government opened the 1950 session in the traditional month of June, it heralded the abolition of the Legislative Council.[3] Through the early twentieth century, the Council had continued meekly to ratify government legislation, making a minor contribution through its revising role. Reform of the Council was closely intertwined with politics and had little to do with improving its position. The existing system of nominating Council members left the government of the day in control and also afforded an attractive means of patronage. There was little compelling reason to abolish the Council, although a substantial Liberal section in the House in the first decade or so of the century – led by prohibitionists and constitutional reformers such as Major Steward – wanted to reform it. Massey seized on this sentiment to drive a wedge into the Liberals by proposing that the Council be elected.

Once in power, Reform introduced legislation providing for an elected Council. After much manoeuvering this was passed in 1914, with heavy qualifications. Parliament would have the opportunity to reconsider the measure, it would not come into operation until after the election later that year, and nominations would continue meanwhile. Reform of the Council became stymied, however, after Massey obtained a majority on it through new appointments. Massey's failure to obtain a clear majority in the House was followed by an agreement with Ward that the matter would not proceed until at least a year after the wartime coalition had ended. After the war, implementation of the reforming legislation was postponed indefinitely.

After 1935 Labour stacked the Council with its supporters. During the 1940s, when National proposed outright abolition, Fraser found himself in a difficult situation. He wanted to retain a weak Council as a mechanism for dispensing patronage, but some Labour members were keen on abolition. Holland, on the other hand, had to steer around National's proclivity for two chambers. In 1947 Holland introduced a private member's bill to abolish the Council.[4] He later withdrew this on condition that the constitutional impediments to abolition be removed. Parliament then finally adopted the Statute of Westminster in full, a matter New Zealand had not moved on since Britain had enacted it in 1931. The New Zealand Parliament gained unconstrained legislative powers, including the ability to alter previously entrenched provisions of the Constitution Act. Parliament would now be able to ask Britain to amend the New Zealand Constitution Amendment Act 1857 in preparation for the abolition of the Council. Fraser then managed to fend off both a referendum and Holland's abolition bill in 1949.

With National in power, the brief Legislative Council Abolition Bill passed in the House without difficulty. Holland promised to explore the possibility of an alternative second chamber, but stated that in his opinion a revising chamber was unnecessary. He appointed 25 new members – the so-called 'suicide squad' – to make sure that the measure went through the Council. The bill passed, by 26 votes to 16, after the most protracted debate for years. W.J. Polson, the Leader of the Council, who had been appointed by National to bring about its demise, eventually imposed closure on the debate.[5] The recently appointed members maintained a stolid silence while longer-serving colleagues expressed their regrets. The Clerk of Parliaments, C.M. Bothamley, solemnly presented the bill at the bar of the House in person – a very unusual act. He rapped at the doors, advanced to the bar, bowed, and handed the bill to the Serjeant-at-Arms to give to the Clerk of the House and the Speaker. The Council sat for the last time on 1 December 1950.

The final gathering of the Legislative Council, 1 December 1950. Jack Marshall (a committed supporter of bicameralism) was one of the few watching from the gallery. The leader of the 'suicide squad', Bill Polson, expressed regret that he had been the instrument of abolition. Just before 6 p.m. the members linked arms in the centre of the chamber and sang 'Auld Lang Syne' and the national anthem before leaving.

Standing orders made redundant by the abolition of the Council were deleted, and others revised to suit a single-chamber Parliament.[6] The opening ceremony was modified slightly. To compensate for the loss of the Council's revising role, bills which had been substantially amended in Committee could be reprinted and recommitted to undergo further scrutiny prior to their third reading. Contrary to the Speaker's wishes, control of the Legislative Council chamber, the Executive Council room and ministerial offices passed to the government. Other minor changes were made to procedure. Question time moved closer to House of Commons' practice. Pairing was officially acknowledged in the standing orders for the first time.[7] The anachronistic 'moving the previous question' method of halting debate was finally removed.

The grip of the two parties over Parliament was tightening. In Crick's words, 'declining effectiveness of the House' was paralleled by 'rising efficiency of the Executive'.[8] Labour's practice of appointing cabinet committees to make delegated decisions was formalised and extended by National, which also introduced a cabinet secretariat. The power of cabinet over caucus became more pronounced as cabinet, organised more systematically, became a highly cohesive bloc of nearly half the caucus.

Caucus remained important. Politics had not become a matter of 'government by caucus', as the traditional opponents of the rise of party government would have it. But neither was the caucus merely a mechanism for expressing grievances. It was integrated into the political decision-making

POLITICAL MECHANICS

Using technology to record votes was considered during the revision of standing orders in 1951. The idea resurfaced from time to time until party voting was adopted under MMP in 1996. Interest in modernising voting methods went back a long way. In 1901 McNab, estimating that the 1,245 divisions between 1896 and 1900 had wasted 13 working days, proposed voting by electric buttons or switches linked to the Speaker. Ward made the same suggestion in 1907, and the matter came up again in 1917 after other Parliaments adopted the practice.

process as a necessary but subordinate element. Caucus provided essential lines of communication and could on occasion block or substantially revise specific measures. It was a vital link between the government and the outside world. By acting as sounding boards for their electorates, local members played an essential role in shaping policy and maintaining governments' hold on office. The system of caucus committees made a substantial contribution to policy formation.[9]

The whips became increasingly important as party discipline tightened. Their work included ensuring a majority in the House at all times; granting leave; providing personnel for select committees; co-ordinating committee work; allocating rooms and seating in the House; providing speakers for debates and deciding on their order; involvement in caucus and party meetings; assisting new members; relieving the Chairman of Committees and Speaker in the House; and consulting with the Prime Minister on parliamentary business and orders of the day.[10] Once the Labour whips went temporarily on strike over an argument with their leader, Walter Nash. On retiring to Bellamy's 'in disgust', they were delighted to find the chamber in pandemonium in their absence.

The whips had to be highly organised, determined and to some extent ruthless in imposing discipline and in dealing with members who might otherwise prove unreliable or absent themselves from the House without adequate reason. Trust between opposing whips was essential for the smooth running of the House, particularly over pairing for divisions. This custom was so strong that if members unintentionally broke their pairs by remaining in the chamber when the doors were locked they had to vote with the opposing party. On one famous occasion, Prime Minister Holyoake had to vote with Labour on a bill in 1971, producing a tied division.[11] After half an hour of discussion, the Speaker voted with the government to keep the bill in the House.

The so-called 'free vote' – available more readily within National than Labour, and granted on moral issues such as capital punishment, liquor licensing, indecent publications and gambling – allowed members to ignore party lines.[12] In 1953 the government allowed its members a free vote over a controversial measure involving liquor licensing in the King Country.[13] Labour moved an amendment to the bill that would allow Maori to vote in a separate poll. The amendment was defeated 38 to 33, but only after nine National members and one Labour member, Patrick Kearins (representing Waimarino – the King Country electorate), crossed the floor in opposite directions. Labour was not tolerant of such a departure from party discipline, and Kearins was forced to retire.

The well-known independently minded National member, Ralph Hanan, was one of those who crossed the floor. In 1954 he unavailingly urged more liberal use of the free vote.[14] In his view, Labour was 'rigidly tied to the party machine' in regarding even a minor defeat of the government as a major victory. Free votes remained few and far between, however. There were further instances in the 1960s, but these were exceptions proving the rule that party discipline was tight.

Private members' bills now got very little time in the House. A few were still considered seriously if the member could garner sufficient support. D.M. Rae's National Historic Places Trust Bill of 1952, which the government took up and passed in 1954, was a notable instance. Rex Mason's crusade for decimal currency in the form of Decimal Coinage Bills in the early 1950s was another. Eventually the government accepted his proposal and adopted decimal currency in 1967.[15]

Rex Mason was a very unusual Labour member. He lived in Wellington from 1935 and continued to do so while Labour was in Opposition, servicing his Auckland electorate through monthly constituency clinics. A lawyer, he was strongly intellectual and independent in his views, with a commitment to monetary reform and Theosophism. He was Attorney-General in the Labour governments of 1935–49 and 1957–60. By 1966, when he retired, he was the Father of the House with more than 40 years of service, having exceeded even Ngata's length of service.

ArchNZ, National Publicity Studios collection, ATL, C26208½

The band of the First Battalion, Wellington Regiment, leads the guard of honour from the grounds after the state opening of Parliament on 26 September 1951. For the revamped ceremony in the early 1950s, trumpeters on the balcony overlooking the main steps played a fanfare as the Governor-General arrived, and as he inspected the guard of honour, RNZAF Vampire jets flew overhead in formation. As the Governor-General processed to the Council chamber trumpeters sounded another fanfare from the gallery. After the abolition of the Legislative Council, members no longer had to stay behind the 'bar' in the Council chamber when they processed in.

The National government was determined to restore more ceremony and a greater sense of occasion to Parliament.[16] The old social whirl of the opening and the session had been lost in Labour's time and during the war. Openings had become relatively drab, and there were few official social gatherings. The first parliamentary ball since 1938 was held in the old wooden buildings in 1950. Speaker Oram also reinstituted the traditional Speaker's dinners to which a select group of members were invited. Together with Lady Oram, who became well-known for her hospitality, he provided nightly suppers in his apartment in the buildings, 'bringing together those who [had] done battle during the day'.[17]

Following the abolition of the Council, the opening ceremony was revamped to be made more impressive and colourful.[18] The social proceedings became more inclusive. Holland threw a huge afternoon tea reception for everybody that was attended by the Governor-General. The next day, Lady Oram held an 'At Home' for female members of the House, the wives of members and senior parliamentary officials, and 'lady editors' from newspapers. The upper social echelons of Wellington were once again able to enjoy themselves when Parliament opened for business. From this time on – including Labour's term in office in the late 1950s – the opening of Parliament provided a substantial

Reform, Efficiency and Accountability, 1950–69

> [Cartoon: Mr Speaker's new chair under an umbrella amid pots, pans, jugs and basins catching leaks. Sign on chair reads "NOT TO BE SAT ON TILL AFTER LUNCH ON TUESDAY". Header: "MR SPEAKER'S NEW CHAIR WILL BE PRESENTED TO THE HOUSE TOMORROW AFTERNOON. – NEWS –". Caption: "AH! NOW THAT WE'RE GETTING A NEW CHAIR, MAYBE WE'LL GET A NEW ROOF!" Credit: Choate, with permission from his son, Paul Choate, NZH, 19 November 1951]

While the Speaker had acquired an impressive new chair in 1951, Parliament Buildings still required much attention, having become dilapidated during Labour's time in power. Leaks were a perennial problem. Barnard and later Labour Speakers had preferred a less formal and more comfortable lounge chair. The impressive piece of furniture that Statham used had been relegated to the basement and then given to his widow. Oram wanted to reinstate the traditional dignity of the Speaker. Conveniently, a British parliamentary delegation presented a new chair to the House in 1951 in recognition of the centenary of 'full parliamentary government' in New Zealand (the Constitution Act 1852). The gift was also a response to New Zealand's own recent gift of despatch boxes made of puriri to the House of Commons on the occasion of the opening of its new chamber after the war. The new chair was made of English oak with a carved headboard, upholstered in green hide, and had New Zealand's coat of arms in gold at its head. The occasion was accorded full dignity. After a state luncheon, the Serjeant-at-Arms formally removed the bar of the House and the chair was ceremoniously carried into the centre of the chamber by orderlies followed by the Commons delegation who sat alongside it.

spectacle for Wellington, including parades, bands, aerial salutes, impressive processions of parliamentarians and distinguished guests, and receptions.[19]

Thoughts also turned to celebrating the centennial of Parliament in New Zealand in May 1954. Dr A.H. McLintock was appointed parliamentary historian in 1952. He produced *Crown Colony Government in New Zealand*, published in 1958, which dealt with the constitutional developments leading up to the establishment of representative government. The ceremonial opening of Parliament by the new Queen, Elizabeth II, on 12 January 1954 gave impetus to the centennial celebrations.[20] Parliament commemorated the centennial on the original site of Parliament in Auckland in late May 1954.

CENTENNIAL

Queen Elizabeth II inspects the guard of honour, 11 January 1954. National's efforts to celebrate the centennial of the New Zealand Parliament were enhanced when the new Queen opened Parliament next day. A royal tour had been eagerly anticipated for some time – this would be the first visit of a reigning monarch – but with the death of King George VI it had been delayed. The tour was wildly successful and long remembered. After the Queen delivered the Speech from the Throne, members returned to their own chamber to endorse an address to the Queen before Parliament was prorogued until June.

Prime Minister Holland and Labour leader Nash admire the 'Constitution' of New Zealand's Parliament. The centennial of Parliament in New Zealand in 1954 was commemorated by a memorial on the original site of Parliament in Auckland – a grassed area where two old pohutukawa trees stood behind the Supreme Court bounded by Anzac Avenue and Parliament Street. Parliament travelled to Auckland for a state luncheon in the Auckland Town Hall on 24 May 1954, followed by a Parliamentary Ball in the evening. Members travelled north again in 1956 for the formal unveiling of the memorial – a bronze plaque on a granite base set in a raised bay of garden walls, shrubs and plant troughs.

National asserts itself

When National came to power, trouble had been brewing on the waterfront for some time. In September 1950, with the waterfront idle, the government briefly proclaimed a state of emergency.[21] In February 1951 the government proclaimed a state of emergency and issued draconian regulations to deal with a dispute which had become the most serious in New Zealand's history. In some countries emergency powers could only be taken after the summoning of Parliament, but the Public Safety Conservation Act 1932 included no such requirement.[22] The government used servicemen to work the wharves and deregistered the union, but the watersiders remained defiant and the dispute dragged on into mid-year. When Nash asked for an early convening of Parliament, Holland delayed for as long as possible. He was secretly considering advising the Governor-General to dissolve Parliament and going to the country over the strike.[23]

Reform, Efficiency and Accountability, 1950–69

When Parliament was finally convened in late June, Holland obtained retrospective approval from the House for the emergency regulations. Labour attacked the government vigorously during the Imprest Supply debate, and on 4 July Nash moved no-confidence by amending the Address-in-Reply and challenged the government to call an election.[24] A week later, Holland dropped a bombshell during the debate on the government's actions. He announced the dissolution of Parliament and the calling of an election. For the first time since 1887, Parliament would not go its full term. On the same day, the watersiders conceded defeat.

The Labour Party was taken completely by surprise, although it put a brave face on events. 'Hard-boiled journalists … a phlegmatic tribe that is not easily roused, rushed the nearest telephones'.[25] National won four more seats in the election, an endorsement of both its tough stance during the waterfront dispute and its moves to tighten up industrial legislation. The confrontation and the election did much to consolidate National's hold on power. Labour, greatly weakened by the retirement of Parry and the defeat of Terry McCombs, Fred Jones and Reg Keeling, now lacked a core of skilled debaters in the House.

After the confrontation of 1951 the two parties were for a time more polarised in the House. One National member remembered that he had been a 'hatchet man whose job it was to break up the Opposition if they were doing well. If the minister's own men weren't good, one or two hatchet men would move in'.[26] He was followed by a 'tail twister after I'd stirred the pot'. In 1952 Labour confronted Speaker Oram with open and sustained defiance, referred to by the *Dominion* as an 'unedifying spectacle'. Fred Hackett was ordered out of the House after refusing to withdraw an unparliamentary remark. Then, in a most unusual event, A.G. Osborne was suspended and 'named', having been asked to withdraw and apologise over his protest regarding a 'barrage' of interjections.[27] The Speaker appealed to members to co-operate, especially over interjections. While suggesting that he was somewhat pedantic, the newspaper judged Oram to be fair to both parties. Eventually the House subsided.

The number of divisions, however, remained relatively low. They came largely on major policy issues associated with the Address-in-Reply, bills, and the estimates.[28] The House tended not to divide on procedural matters such as closure or urgency, which were now an accepted part of the way the government prosecuted its business.

A significant minority of the New Zealand electorate remained unhappy with the two-party system. In 1953 the Social Credit Political League emerged as a third party, resurrecting the ideas of Major Douglas that had attracted the left wing of the Labour Party in the 1930s. Its chances were quickly dismissed by the *Dominion*: 'New Zealand politics are strewn with the wreckage of third parties that have made a fleeting appearance'.[29] However, it made a good showing in the election of 1954 and became an irritant to National.

Following that election, in which National lost five seats (it now had 45 to Labour's 35), new members rejuvenated both major parties. Labour became more vigorous, helped by those such as Henry May. When Labour failed to muster speakers for the financial debate that year, Holland got the call and rose to close the debate peremptorily, but Speaker Oram denied Holland's right to reply and allowed May (who was ill) to endeavour to keep the debate going.[30] He did so impromptu for an hour with virtually no notes. May, Mick Moohan and Jim Kent made up for Labour's poor organisation. Before long, May was assuming the responsibility of whip. He had the valuable skill of being able to judge the mood of members and the direction debates were likely to take – to 'read a House'.

The government had to be much more careful in marshalling its forces for divisions. In late September Labour almost defeated the government over the closure of the Nelson–Glenhope railway.[31] Ministers had to be summoned from their beds in the early hours of the morning and the division was won only 34 to 33. Holland bluntly told his members that absenteeism must cease and that the whips must be informed of all absences.

Henry May was elected for Onslow, Wellington, for Labour in 1954. He soon became a key member of Labour's team, and was senior whip from 1958 to 1972. He lost his seat in 1975 after being Minister of Local Government and Internal Affairs in the third Labour government. May had the unenviable task of maintaining Labour's one-vote majority in the late 1950s. Agreements between the whips were serious undertakings. The rare instances when they broke down were usually inadvertent or the result of a misunderstanding or lack of communication, but they immediately placed in jeopardy the foundation of trust upon which the system relied. The necessity of co-operation between whips, and their ability to discipline their troops, is suggested by a story from the late 1960s. May and National whip A.E. Allen collaborated to catch out a National member who had been playing tricks. May sent out three Labour members so that the government could win the division by one. Later Allen returned the compliment with a vote similarly organised to catch out a Labour member. Allen confessed that he had himself as a whip conspired with Prime Minister Holyoake so that they could attend the night trots at the Hutt racecourse. In taking elaborate precautions to sneak away unnoticed, they failed to realise that the meeting had been cancelled because of bad weather. They had to return sheepishly to the chamber to the applause of members who knew what was going on.

In the mid 1950s Speaker Oram advocated changes to the standing orders.[32] He felt that the place of the private member was being unduly encroached upon and wanted six Wednesdays reserved for private members' business. Before the war there had been an interval of several weeks before private members' bills were squeezed off the order paper, and Prime Minister Fraser had allowed his backbenchers some latitude over second readings. By the mid 1950s the government was taking precedence for its own business as soon as the financial debate was over.

The second issue was the taking of urgency. Oram argued that this should be applicable only to a single bill or other matter, and should be explicitly justified in terms of the public interest. Urgency, he suggested, was being invoked too frequently by 'successive Leaders of the House as a convenient method of controlling the business of the House in the interests of the Government'.[33] He wanted the government to move for extended sittings rather than taking urgency. Holland and the government resisted Oram's proposals because they considered it would hinder government business. Previous Speakers had not insisted on reasons for urgency; the Prime Minister was presumed to be the best judge of the 'public interest'. Oram failed to have changes made.

The 1957 session became a bidding war for the impending election. Both parties dangled tax concessions before the voters as the new tax payment system (PAYE – 'pay as you earn') was to come into effect. Holland, in failing health, remained in the Prime Minister's seat while Holyoake unofficially led the House. Holland retired shortly before the election, leaving Holyoake with little opportunity to make his presence felt. National was saved from an embarrassing defeat in its first division under Holyoake only by the vote of the Chairman of Committees, after some members had gone home on the understanding that there would be no vote.[34]

Labour in power, 1957–60

Labour won the 1957 election narrowly, by 41 to 39. Its majority in the new House would be only one once a Speaker was chosen. The party was ecstatic, nevertheless, and its caucus meeting on 5 December was accompanied by music, cheers and a haka from Maori members.[35] Nash decided to put forward Robert Macfarlane (a member for 18 years, and party whip) as Speaker to avoid having him in cabinet. When Macfarlane rose to protest, Jock Mathison reportedly hissed at him, 'Shut up you fool, it's the only offer you're going to get!'

Macfarlane proved an ineffective Speaker. In the words of Norman Kirk (elected in 1957), he was 'perhaps the worst Speaker ever … [He] would dither this way and that, ruling one way and then changing his decision again. When [member] Algie, stood up to say, "Perhaps this would help the Speaker", poor Bob would cower.'[36] Macfarlane found it difficult to control the House. Hard of hearing with his wig on, he reacted slowly when dealing with disorder, and was uncertain about procedure. After belatedly shouting 'Order! Order!', perhaps following a failure to rule, he would threaten the next interjector with ejection. Clerk-Assistant Eric Roussell would desperately bring over the Speakers' Rulings with his thumb against the relevant item, and Chairman of Committees Keeling would cite the relevant ruling.

Labour's return to office did not get off to the best of starts. A brief session was called extremely early in January 1958 to put through the promised £100 tax rebate, but this stretched to eight sitting days amid conflict between the two parties. Labour's slim majority created great difficulties from the very start. This was the first time there had been such a narrow margin since the emergence of the two-party system.[37] On the return from the ceremony at Government House to present the Speaker-elect, Holyoake took charge of the liquor cabinet for the usual function in the Speaker's rooms and began pouring generous drinks. In the end a doctor had to be summoned to a Labour member who passed out in the Chairman of Committees' room. Some National members were likewise incapacitated, so Labour would have preserved its majority had a division been called.

Labour nearly lost the first division when it did come – on the tax legislation. Warren Freer, who was in the shower, failed to hear the bells.[38] Nash then got into difficulties over the Address-in-Reply, refusing to enter the debate, abruptly adjourning the House and proroguing Parliament. He accused the Opposition of reneging on debating arrangements. Holyoake was furious at losing his chance to wade into the government, and the bitterness persisted into the next session.

Nash now had to deal with a balance of payments crisis that threatened to undercut Labour's promises. For the full session, which commenced in June 1958, Holyoake threatened to withhold pairing on matters other than 'principle' – such as no-confidence or military training – as Holland had

Robert Mafeking Macfarlane was born in Christchurch on 17 May 1900. He joined the Labour Party in 1919 and became a trade union organiser. In 1938 he was elected Mayor of Christchurch, a position he held until entering military service in 1941. Elected to the House for Christchurch South at a by-election in 1939, he was Labour's senior whip (1947–51), and was re-elected as Mayor of Christchurch in 1950. Upon being made Speaker in 1958 he resigned the mayoralty. Following Labour's term in government (1957–60), he re-entered local politics while continuing to hold the seat of Christchurch Central until his retirement in 1969. During his Speakership Labour had a one-vote majority in the House, and he voted when the House was in Committee. He died on 2 December 1981.

done in 1947.[39] Labour won the no-confidence division 40 to 39. Many divisions were called during the session and pairing remained an issue throughout the Parliament. On one occasion Hugh Watt had to leave his sick bed in his dressing gown. On another a Labour member hobbled into the chamber on walking sticks to record his vote. 'Dobbie' Paikea, 'notoriously ill and absent' in previous sessions, experienced a miraculous 'recovery' which he attributed to all 40 Labour members praying for him. National worked hard to embarrass the government. Leading Opposition member Jack Watts, who practised law, was frequently called from work and would be seen 'streaking out of his office and running up Lambton Quay to vote'.[40]

Nash soon extended sittings to midnight to force business through so that he could take an overseas trip. This provoked an outburst from Tom Shand, who had already raised the ire of the Chairman of Committees by omitting to bow to the Chair. Amidst many interjections, Shand accused Nash of gagging the House.[41] Macfarlane took this as a reflection on the Chair and 'named' Shand, following which the House suspended him. National was outraged and Holyoake attempted unsuccessfully to have the House discuss the ruling. (This move was a direct challenge to the Speaker's authority. By tradition it would have languished at the bottom of the order paper and so not come before the House.)[42]

Labour's strong party discipline kept the struggling government together in what became a very bad-tempered session.[43] The government introduced a budget that went down in history as Nordmeyer's 'Black Budget'. Ministers glumly entered the House to deliver bad news that hit working people in the pocket and stunned Labour's backbenchers. Holyoake had Nash on about raising taxes. A trivial dispute developed over whether Nash had qualified his statement; there was an appeal to *Hansard* and the radio tape of proceedings in the House. Raymond Boord, the Minister of Broadcasting, delayed over Holyoake's demand for the tape, but Nash felt betrayed when he finally yielded.[44]

Some thought that the House would soon become unworkable, but party discipline held.[45] Labour's senior whip, May, played a key role in keeping the government's majority intact. The Speaker found it difficult to gain co-operation and the introduction of government business into the House was not well planned. Members were often kept up late, and irritability mounted. Macfarlane had to vote with the government while the House was in Committee (as previous Labour Speakers had done) to sustain its majority. National proved better organised than the government and won many tactical battles.

The House was much better behaved the following year, 1959.[46] Nash proceeded carefully, and too cautiously for some. He avoided long sittings and the use of closure, and did not take urgency towards the end of the session. The political games continued nonetheless. With Watt in hospital, the government secretly flew government whip Ritchie Macdonald (who had been in Christchurch awaiting a trip to Antarctica) back to Wellington to spring him on the Opposition during the Imprest Supply debate.[47] But Holyoake was wise to the situation and, after going on endlessly about pairs, never called a division. In 1959 Kirk suffered a mild heart attack in Bob Tizard's room.[48] Desperate to keep the news from National – and from Nash, who might fuss 'like an old chook' – May concocted a suitable story. After Nash had the House adjourned, Kirk was smuggled out to a doctor.

The government's loss of the initiative was reflected in the withdrawal of its most controversial measures – the Political Disabilities Removal Bill (easing the use of trade union funds for political purposes) and the Police Offences Amendment Bill (repealing legislation associated with the 1951 waterfront dispute). The latter bill had been subject to a no-confidence amending motion by National.[49] Holyoake defied the Speaker by refusing to withdraw a statement he had made rebutting an attack, and got away with it when Labour realised that if they pressed the matter pairs would be withdrawn and they could lose their majority. On one notable occasion three National members crossed the floor to vote.[50] Nash's attention was increasingly fixed on external affairs and his own travels around the world to meet leader after leader.

The session of 1960 had a more bitter tone as the next election loomed. The number of divisions far exceeded the 1958 figure and closure was invoked frequently.[51] When the Chairman of Committees, Keeling, allowed Nash grudgingly to withdraw a remark 'because I must', National protested vehemently and Hanan immediately 'apologised' in the same words.[52] Hanan was ordered to withdraw for defiance when he refused to apologise properly. The Police Offences Amendment and Political Disabilities Removal Bills were passed despite stern National resistance, but the Crimes Bill (also introduced in 1959) which would have abolished the death penalty and liberalised the law on homosexuality was again allowed to lapse.[53]

The experience of the late 1950s was not edifying for the future of the two-party system. The House lacked dignity and the debates were long and wearisome. The public was becoming increasingly critical of tedious displays by its parliamentarians, and pressure was building up for both a streamlining of procedure and a strengthening of the effectiveness of Parliament. Reforming the conduct of parliamentary business had long been talked about, especially by National, which now promised reform in its 1960 election manifesto.[54] But would Parliament's dignity be restored if members were paid adequately for their chosen vocation?

Solving the pay-fixing problem

The amount paid to members in 1920 had finally been restored in 1944, but inflation meant that they soon became discontented with their pay again. A compounding factor was that the abolition of the country quota in 1945 had enlarged rural electorates and increased travelling costs.[55] The Clerk of the House urged Holland to establish an independent body outside the political arena to fix parliamentary salaries and allowances. A select committee was not considered an appropriate way of dealing with the problem since full public endorsement was sought. In 1951 Holland appointed a Royal Commission (which included ex-Speaker Barnard) to do the job.[56]

Most members could not afford decent living quarters in the capital. At one end of the spectrum, National's Harry Lake stayed at a first-class hotel. Jack Watts was one of a number of other National members who could afford a better class of accommodation – the Hotel Waterloo.[57] Holland had been appalled, however, by the living conditions in Wellington of members without private means. Rental accommodation was in short supply and as prices increased few could afford to stay in hotels. Inferior, rented, shared rooms with meals at Bellamy's was the life of a typical member like National's

From left Rob Muldoon and fellow Opposition National members Talboys, Talbot, Gordon, Harrison and Venn Young in their flat in Hawkestone Street in the early 1970s.

Evening Post collection, ATL, F2272½

J.G. Barnes.[58] More than half a dozen Labour members bedded down at the People's Palace in Cuba Street, and a few even attempted to live in Parliament Buildings. Backbench members continued to live cheek by jowl in boarding houses, rented rooms or shared flats near Parliament into the 1970s.

Members pressed their case hard before the Royal Commission. The burdens on them were manifold.[59] They had to purchase their own typewriters, hire secretarial staff at their own cost, or handwrite letters. Those in rural areas covered large mileages in their own cars during the recess to service their electorates, often over rough, metalled roads. Some clocked up 10,000 or even 20,000 miles annually. The Buller electorate was particularly far-flung and difficult of access, running from the Marlborough Sounds to Farewell Spit and down the West Coast. The four Maori members, especially the Southern Maori representative, were particularly disadvantaged in this respect.

The time required to service electorates was widely acknowledged. Much electorate work was undertaken by members' wives, especially when their husbands were attending Parliament. No electorate assistance was provided but a minority, mostly National members, paid for their own.[60] Some made use of local community facilities such as council offices, Plunket or RSA rooms. When at home, members had to be on call to their constituents to take up cases with government departments, write copious correspondence in response to calls for assistance and advice, attend many functions and sporting events, open shows and bazaars, attend meetings and lunches, and return the hospitality they enjoyed.

The submissions said that parliamentarians were still grossly underpaid for an onerous and responsible job that involved long hours, much travel and many sacrifices, often to the detriment of family life, particularly for those who lived outside Wellington. Holland argued strongly, and from experience, for the Leader of the Opposition to be better paid and have more assistance.[61]

The Royal Commission enunciated guiding principles that would allow more generous provision for members. The Commission argued that 'the work is full-time professional work', that the level of payment should not deter those who would otherwise earn 'a reasonable reward in other occupations' and might 'lose too heavily' by entering Parliament, and that those without private means should not be discouraged from a career in politics.[62] It added that salaries should not be so high that they became the prime or only motive for becoming a member. Payment should 'maintain

Neville Colvin, EP, 29 September 1951

Members look forward to an increase in their salaries with the appointment of a Royal Commission by Prime Minister Holland in 1951. As usual, the public are less receptive.

the holder of any office comfortably and honourably, but not luxuriously', and be commensurate with the 'responsibility, authority, and dignity of each office', disregarding private means and based on the assumption that the member was a family man. The concept of not losing too heavily reflected the ethos that entry into Parliament was still seen to some extent as a sacrifice in the public good.

The Commission recommended substantial improvements that were promulgated by Order in Council after ratification by the House.[63] Members' salaries were raised substantially, and a new graduated allowance awarded according to the difficulties involved in servicing electorates, with categories ranging from inner-city to entirely rural.

With public reaction in mind, successive Commissions trod gingerly along the path of raising members' salaries. The increases attracted little adverse public comment, however, and salaries continued to be fixed this way until the early 1970s. The Commission of 1955 improved salaries and allowances, and gave special allowances to Maori members. Southern Maori by now encompassed not only the entire South Island but also the lower part of the North Island.[64] The Commission's recommendation that the government establish a typing pool for members was eventually implemented in the 1960s. The Civil List Act was amended in 1955 so that salaries were regularly reviewed by Royal Commission after each election.

Increases were received at times with embarrassment, particularly when the government urged wage restraint on others, as in the late 1950s and late 1960s. But parliamentary salaries eventually reached relative parity with comparable professional groups. By the late 1960s even the ratification by the House of the recommendations was proving politically embarrassing. The Commission of 1970 recommended that, in the prevailing conditions of inflation, salaries be looked at more frequently. This was done by an annual review of other wage movements and adjustment of salaries.

The last Royal Commission on members' remuneration convened in 1973.[65] This discarded the previous notion of self-sacrifice and suggested that economic considerations should not limit increases as they had in the 1960s. Fair remuneration became the watchword and, in the light of increasing select and caucus committee work, the salary was raised substantially and the allowance increased, upon which it was observed that 'parliamentarians joined doctors and lawyers as among the highest paid in the community'.[66] The following year, regulations gave the Higher Salaries Commission power to fix salaries, removing the issue entirely from the realm of Parliament itself – to the relief of members. Thereafter the issue became more one of maintaining relativity with the private sector. This was explicitly built into the instructions to the Higher Salaries Commission from 1977.[67]

Dogboxes and Beehives

A parsimonious Labour government and the war had left Parliament Buildings in poor condition. In 1936, with New Zealand's centennial celebrations being considered, their completion as part of a planned 'government centre' had been mooted, but this remained on the drawing board.[68] In 1949 Fraser again raised the issue of completing the buildings, suggesting that a modern, functional design be adopted.

By now the hotch-potch parliamentary complex was coming under fire.[69] Accommodation for backbenchers, particularly those in the Opposition, remained dingy and cramped. The Leader of the Opposition occupied three dimly lit rooms off the portico at the front of the library building. The remainder of the Opposition was jammed into rooms on the ground and first floors at the rear of the building that was nicknamed 'Siberia'. This section – the 'west wing' – was increasingly regarded as an earthquake hazard. Jack Marshall, when in Opposition, had to be content with sharing a small, narrow back room in the library building that contained a table, a chair, and a couch which they took turn about on during all-night sittings.[70] Government members were more fortunate, with most housed in the main buildings but others in the old wooden buildings. Members desperate for furnishings engaged in surreptitious raids. Freer remembered that 'when any member died or was defeated members immediately swooped on his room like a swarm of locusts. You would see his desk, his chairs, and his wardrobe if he was lucky enough to have one … being carted along the corridors at midnight'.[71] The main buildings were now considered dark, gloomy and inefficient. The offices of the Clerk and his staff were regarded as particularly impractical. The buildings were full of odd corners, being 'a queer kind of place, full of strange little cubbyholes containing old furniture, firewood, teapots, biscuit tins and crockery'.[72]

The National government was keen to upgrade the buildings, though some members wanted them knocked down. Holland suggested that £1 million might be required for new buildings.[73] The concept was floated of a 'Parliamentary Court' which would retain the main buildings and library, get rid of the old wooden buildings, and add further structures.

Meanwhile, the old wooden buildings received a new asbestos roof in 1952 and new foundations and a rebuilt dance floor in the rickety Social Hall in time for the royal opening of Parliament in early 1954. Substantial refurbishment of the parliamentary complex had been planned in anticipation of this royal visit, and some work was eventually accomplished on a much-reduced budget, but only after the new Queen had departed.[74] The buildings were repainted inside and out, apparently for the first time in more than 30 years. The roof of the library building was renewed and remodelled and the wing wall of the entrance to the building was strengthened because of the earthquake risk. It had been decided by now that the building was worth preserving for its historical merits.

In the mid 1950s the government further improved the premises. Backbench members had their rooms furnished with new standard items – an office desk and chair, an 'interviewing' chair, an armchair and a settee with 'plastic leather cover', a combined wardrobe and bookcase, a small table and a hard-wearing haircord carpet.[75] The cabinet room in the rooftop penthouse was refurbished. A special oval table and chairs made from selected indigenous woods provided by the Timber Merchants' Federation in 1957 was the centrepiece.[76] The room remained austere, however, into the 1970s, with only a large map and a few Tourist and Publicity photographs on the walls. In 1957 also, the old turn-of-the-century kauri seats and desks in the chamber were replaced with new ones of the same twin-couch design, and the fire protection systems of all buildings were upgraded.[77] The buildings were again spruced-up in the early 1960s. Most members still had to share rooms, although women such as Mabel Howard and Esmé Tombleson had their own.

Completion of the main buildings remained on the agenda as a 'hardy annual'.[78] In 1953 Holland conceded that Parliament was 'a collection of dogboxes' and that the buildings should be completed. In 1955 a group of ministers put proposals for a modern block to cabinet. The main buildings should be 'rounded off' at the main entrance steps, and a higher building of five to seven storeys constructed at an angle to the marble block on its southern side. No further progress was made, and when the Labour government was elected the matter fell into abeyance.

With the re-election of National in 1960, Minister of Works Stan Goosman released a drawing, based upon a tentative Ministry of Works plan, of a 12–14 storey block on the site of the old wooden buildings.[79] Reaction was mixed. Shortly afterwards the government formed a special ministerial committee (including both political parties) to consider a new building. Opinion was split on whether to retain the main buildings or replace them with a modern structure.

The Ministry of Works and Government Architect Fergus Sheppard were convinced of the need for a modern structure and thought that the main buildings should not remain for too long because of the earthquake risk.[80] For Sheppard, completion of the main buildings would be 'tantamount to turning the clock back'. Most members of the ministerial committee favoured completion in modified form, however, believing this would produce a unity of style and suggesting that it would probably be more enduring than building in a 'modern idiom'.

Reform, Efficiency and Accountability, 1950–69

Holland sings mournfully as Parliament Buildings fall around him. The new National government was keen to upgrade the existing buildings. Holland approved money for some necessary upgrading, including improving the Opposition quarters in the library building by installing proper lighting and laying carpets. But it proved politically impossible to find the sums required to rebuild Parliament.

The old wooden Government House leaked, its upper floors shook at every step, and filing cabinets had to be propped up because of sloping floors. The marked unevenness of the sprung dance floor in the Social Hall could not be rectified. There were regular infestations of mice and rats. Maintenance was skimped on, and the kauri timber and elegant carved woodwork was covered by yellowing Public Works paint and grime.

Minhinnick, NZH, 15 November 1951

It was decided that some amplification was required in the chamber. In 1954 microphones and small box speakers were installed on members' desks in the farthest regions of the cross benches, and for Hansard and the press gallery. But the overhead microphones still picked up excessive noise, to the extent that the Speaker clamped down on conversations on the floor of the House and had the microphones over the whips moved. By the mid 1960s there were amplifiers throughout the chamber but complaints were still made about the balance between the speakers. In 1975 the overhead microphones were removed and individual microphones were installed on all desks.

Neville Colvin, EP, 23 April 1953

In 1962 cabinet agreed in principle that an architect 'of recognised world-wide standing' be invited to report on the buildings, but that the ministry be responsible for design and supervision. Sheppard drew attention to the impending visit of Sir Basil Spence, who had an impressive reputation for his design for the postwar Coventry Cathedral, which combined modern and traditional elements.[81]

The ministerial committee engaged Spence in 1964 and, disturbed by the suggestion of considerable earthquake risk, commissioned an engineering survey. Spence was asked to consider whether the main buildings should be completed or knocked down, or a new building constructed adjacent to them. Spence urged retention of the main buildings alongside a startling new building conceived as symbolic of executive government power.[82] Before long this new building would be known as 'the Beehive'.

Spence argued that a modern circular tower would provide a focal point for the modern buildings of the Government Centre rising around Parliament. The new building carried through the basic 'propositions' of the main Parliament Buildings with its matching Takaka marble veneer, the height of the columns of the lower section, the size of its windows, and its balance of light and shade.

The first pencil impression of the 'Beehive' concept in Sir Basil Spence's notebook. Spence recommended retaining the existing main buildings, but argued that completing them would run against architectural thinking. He rapidly produced his startling 'Beehive' pencil sketch, apparently 'on the back of a napkin' during a dinner with Holyoake. While the ministerial committee tried to come up with suitably prosaic titles for the new building, the term 'Beehive' soon became entrenched. Holyoake revealed that it was coined when Spence asked him for boxes of matches to illustrate the concept. When he piled them up he saw the 'Beehive' brand name and the term was adopted thenceforth. Subsequently Bryant and May produced special 'Beehive' matchboxes for sale to members.

The concept impressed the committee; it pronounced that the building 'could become a source of national pride and international interest'.[83] The *Dominion* called it a bold concept, but some were less enamoured. Most architects supported a modern new building but wanted its design opened up to competition. One argued that completing the main buildings would 'impart the dignity and serenity which our unfinished Parliament deserves'. Others did not believe that such a radical scheme could be drawn up in a few weeks, and regarded the Beehive as a 'stunt' and 'a kind of shock tactic'. Spence denied that it had been dreamed up without thought. The Government Architect's position in the controversy was clear. 'To return to neo-classicism would relegate N.Z. to the position of a backward nation', while the Beehive demonstrated 'progressive determination'.[84]

Spence's detailed coloured sketch was unveiled in the House in August 1964 'to a chorus of mixed comments', Sir Basil Arthur saying it was 'a shocker and should be scrapped'.[85] But both political parties swung in behind the ministerial committee and the government decided to press ahead. The Government Architect was given the unenviable job of translating Spence's sketch into something workable. Not the least of the practical issues were the structural problems of the tapering cone from floor four upwards and the difficulties of the circular design with a central 'drum' core.

Spence was retained as a consultant for the sketch design stage and worked with Sheppard in developing the plans. In spite of the government's determination all along that the Government Architect would be responsible for the design, Spence seems to have remained hopeful that he might have a role in the detailed design.[86] But when sketch designs were completed and approved in mid 1965, Holyoake announced that Spence would not be retained.

Once the decision was made, the first phase of the work would be to complete and extend the south wall of the main buildings to provide additional accommodation. Then some of the old wooden buildings would be knocked down, the remainder shifted to the rear of the construction site, and construction of the Beehive could begin. Parliament was poised to make a radical statement of its new place in the world through a bold expression of the position of the executive arm of the state.

Services to members

Under Clerk Dollimore, the staffing of the Legislative Department was stable after the war, nearly 150 employed year-round and another 100 for the session.[87] When the Hansard Copy Supervisor retired in 1953, the Hansard office was reorganised to integrate the reporting and editing functions. Since their establishment under Seddon, the Hansard supervising staff had sat uneasily alongside the reporting staff.[88] Attempts at reorganisation in the early 1920s and 1930s largely failed, but the position of Hansard Supervisor was gradually downgraded and then renamed 'Hansard Copy Supervisor'. In 1953, an Editor of Hansard was appointed to take charge of the office as a whole, and the position of Senior Reporter was created.

Hansard reporters in the chamber furiously take down speeches in shorthand. In the 1960s speakers sped up noticeably, with the development of a more conversational style and as they were forced to say more in less time. Many now exceeded 200 words a minute – Norman Kirk and Martyn Finlay were especially fast talkers. Others, like Holyoake, Tirikatene and Jack Marshall, had a more leisurely style, while Nordmeyer was remembered for his impeccable delivery. Although tape-recording was adopted as a back-up from 1964, Hansard was convinced that shorthand reporting should continue, in order to take down speeches and interjections appropriately, something that well-trained Hansard reporters did as a matter of course. The discrepancy between what was actually said and what appeared in Hansard was considerable, as the reporters rendered often extremely disorganised and chaotic speech into organised prose.

Ron Burt sketch, 1960, Parliamentary Service collection

There was a growing shortage of top-flight male shorthand reporters from the early 1950s. But while the Public Service Commission, already using women for its own reporting service, pushed hard for their introduction, Hansard argued that they were 'physically and temperamentally unsuited to the long, late hours of concentrated work'.[89] Editor Sutherland, fearing 'wastage' through marriage, said that 'Only as a final resort would we consider the employment of women reporters'. Hansard wanted to reinstate the 1930s scheme through which young male shorthand writers had been recruited.

Change eventually came. In 1960 Manderson was brought out of retirement for two years, and Hansard conceded that women would have to be employed.[90] In May 1962 two reporting positions, for either men or women, were advertised at equal rates of pay. All ten applicants were female, and Mrs Rosalie Hall and J. Hunter were appointed. Hansard continued to make strenuous but almost always futile efforts to secure male reporters from overseas; meanwhile more women were appointed from the ranks of judge's associates, conference reporters and senior public service shorthand-typists to fill positions.

Bellamy's, housed in the old wooden buildings, remained a substantial operation. Since the time of Prime Minister Fraser the policy had been not to elevate the fare beyond what was acceptable to the public.[91] The facilities comprised the members' dining room, a tea room and dining room for members and their families, a senior staff dining room, and a typists' dining room (a wartime concession made to cater for the additional senior typists working for ministers and the Legislative Department).

Hansard's reporting staff in front of the dais for the chair in the Legislative Council chamber, 1962. At front: Mrs R.V.I. Hall, A.B. Conway (Chief Reporter and Assistant Editor), J. McLean (Editor), T.F. Reilly, Mrs J. Hunter. Behind: C.R. McColl, E.B. Cooper, M. Quirke, B.A. Snowdon, W. Wellbrock, A.A. Edwards. The first female Hansard reporters, Hall and Hunter, were appointed in 1962 to join the seven men, shortly after Jock McLean became Editor of Debates. Both had been in Hansard's typing team. Hall was certificated at 200 words a minute, had taught shorthand for 25 years, and was the principal of a business college. She had been a Hansard typist since 1956.

Parliamentary Service collection

In 1950, the National government decided to make Bellamy's more self-supporting as its balance sheet improved, and insisted that it assume responsibility for its assets. Bellamy's finally raised its heavily subsidised meal prices, which had changed little since the 1920s. Prices were increased from time to time thenceforth but remained reasonable. The government was forced to fund a new kitchen in 1955. From the latter half of the 1950s the loss made on food fell substantially, and sales of alcohol resulted in handsome overall profits.

The bar complex provided separate cubicles for members, their visitors, senior staff, Hansard and press staff, and messengers. During the session the bars remained open for extended hours and on Sundays, and over the recess limited private bar facilities were available. From 1957, when attention was drawn to the longstanding departure from the licensing laws, Bellamy's closed at 10 p.m. and did not open on Sundays.[92] Bellamy's maintained its own cellar, tested the proof of the imported spirits, and broke down and bottled spirits for sale over the bar and by the bottle or case to members. Bellamy's provided its own high quality branded liquor exclusively for members, alongside the usual range. Until 1967, with limited import licences, particularly for whisky, bottle store purchases were rationed. Whisky was sold by the bottle only to members and top privilege holders. A single bottle would be put up in the bar at a certain time, and whisky would be available only until it was finished. Prices remained just below wholesale rates, and three-quarters of overall sales were made through the bottle store.

Older National and Labour members still consorted regularly in Bellamy's, particularly on Friday lunchtimes and during the dinner break. The atmosphere encouraged a convivial intermingling, with political differences temporarily forgotten as exploits on the rugby field or the latest betting excitement were dissected. As Tizard remembered, 'There was Mick Moohan's corner at one end of the members' bar and the three "Ms" had left their mark at the other – Massey, Murdoch, and Maher.'[93]

The male culture of the institution was slow to accept the presence of women in the precincts of Parliament. In 1949 Iriaka Ratana was elected for Western Maori in place of her deceased husband. She did not participate greatly in debates but worked hard behind the scenes.[94] In the 1950s there was still only a handful of women members, and their contributions were not particularly notable, although

Reform, Efficiency and Accountability, 1950–69

Iriaka Ratana won Western Maori for Labour in 1949 despite considerable criticism of her candidacy. The first Maori woman member in the House, she had been involved in the pan-tribal Ratana movement since the 1920s and succeeded her late husband, Matiu Ratana, the leader of the Ratana church. She retired in 1969.

Hilda Ross was briefly Minister of Social Security in 1957 before Mabel Howard assumed the same portfolio in the Labour government. Howard was not a successful minister and had to be supervised closely. In 1960 Esmé Tombleson, a strong-willed farmer's wife and previously a senior public servant in Australia, won the marginal Gisborne seat for National. She held it for the next 12 years and at one time was tipped for cabinet, but Holyoake was not keen to appoint women as ministers.

Women had to steer a tricky course between the traditional expectation that they would concentrate on women's issues and aspiring to a broader perspective that might lead to promotion. As Tombleson put it. 'She [owes] it to the nation as a whole to delve into certain aspects of life to help womankind, but at the same time she must realise she must not go too far along these lines or no man will vote for her. But if she becomes too male in her outlook, too interested in industrial and scientific matters, she will find she has every woman complaining she is not looking after women's affairs.'[95]

Parliament remained in many respects a male preserve. Margaret Hayward remembered Clerk Dollimore remarking, 'Of course you know we don't like skirts around here'.[96] There was an unfortunate

The Parliamentary Press Gallery in front of Bellamy's, 1966. Speaker Algie is in the wig, centre front, with Mrs B.F. (Fran) Collett second on his right. Also included are the long-serving reporters (at front) Eric Benton, third from left, and Cedric Mentiplay, far right. Behind, Ian Templeton is third from left, and Neale McMillan fifth from left. Fran Collett was the first female reporter in the gallery, entering in 1965 for the Press Association. She had to agree not to take advantage of the gallery's bar privileges. The press gallery remained a bastion of male culture for some time, with poker schools and heavy drinking sessions. In the 1970s the number of female reporters increased rapidly and the nature of the gallery changed.

incident in 1965 when a drunk press gallery journalist commented on a gold bracelet worn by Mabel Howard, insinuating that she had slept around to obtain it. After the Speaker considered banishing him from the gallery, the newspaper removed him.

The separate public gallery for women was maintained until 1945 when a petition from J.P. McDavitt, Eastbourne's Town Clerk, asking that husbands and wives be allowed to sit together in the galleries propelled the House into the twentieth century.[97] In November 1945 men and women came together for the first time when an elderly Palmerston North couple sat together in what had been the ladies' gallery. A rule still prevented women other than members gaining access as of right onto the floor of the House to sit to the right of the Speaker's chair.[98] Howard and Ross unsuccessfully urged its abandonment. This matter was raised again by Rona Stevenson and others such as Whetu Tirikatene-Sullivan from the mid 1960s. Tirikatene-Sullivan would sit in the visitors' area to make the point. A.E. Allen, the Speaker for the 1972 session, was less ruled by precedent and allowed women onto the floor. He also opened the Speaker's ladies' gallery to both men and women.

Drinking in Bellamy's remained an entrenched male privilege, even though the rules were silent on the matter.[99] In the 1940s women members were excluded from the bars and women (other than female members) were excluded from the members' dining room. From 1953, with Ross chairing the House Committee, invited female guests could enter the members' dining room during the recess. Women members could now use the bar – though few did. Other women continued to be excluded from the bars on the excuse that additional facilities would need to be provided for them.[100] By the 1970s times were changing. Women now had equal access to the dining rooms, subject to the usual privilege restrictions. In 1971 women working in Parliament Buildings, such as ministerial private secretaries, press gallery and Hansard reporters, were allowed into the bar.

National's 'Young Turks' of the early 1960s, who were housed in adjoining rooms off the ground floor corridor, preferred to socialise in their rooms and bought bottles from the bar to enjoy a 'pre-prandial potion' while talking politics.[101] Prime Minister Holyoake is also said to have issued an instruction that members abstain from drinking in the members' bar after 5 p.m. They should either go into the guests' bar or buy bottles to take away to their rooms and drink with their colleagues. Apparently Leslie Munro, a heavy drinker, was believed to be 'leaking' information when in his cups. Such more exclusive drinking practices were subsequently adopted widely within the National caucus. The Young Turks also organised parties involving the press gallery and other parliamentary staff such as typists and librarians. Muldoon continued to socialise and drink with backbench members and the press gallery after becoming a minister in 1967. His (and Shand's) openness and accessibility to journalists and the public alike was remarked upon in the late 1960s.[102] In Opposition in the early 1970s, Muldoon led a group of National backbenchers who drank and socialised into the night, plotting a more aggressive approach against Labour than their leader Jack Marshall would contemplate.

From the time of Scholefield, the General Assembly Library consolidated its position as a major research and reference library as well as servicing parliamentarians. It strengthened its reference services to members with increased numbers of staff trained to respond to enquiries. From the 1930s newspapers were indexed to assist this process.

The concept of an integrated National Library lurked persistently in the background, calling the General Assembly Library's independent future into question. When new Parliament Buildings were considered at the end of the first decade of the twentieth century, it had been assumed that such a library would be centred on the General Assembly Library. Librarian Charles Wilson hoped for magnificent quarters akin to the British Museum Library in the planned second stage of the buildings.[103] These did not come to pass. When the issue resurfaced in the 1930s it was again thought that the General Assembly Library would take control of a national institution. At this time an ambitious 'Government Centre' was planned, involving the 'creation of a dignified and harmonious architectural composition with Parliament Buildings as a central and dominating feature'.[104]

BELLAMY'S

The members' bar, 1968. When women guests were allowed into Bellamy's in the early 1970s, Whetu Tirikatene-Sullivan immediately took one into the members and guests' bar for a celebratory lemonade. Although the bar's ambience did not live up to the hard-won 'privilege', its female patronage was soon substantial. As described by Hayward it was a small, shabby room with two chairs and a small table. From 1973 typists and secretaries were also allowed into the bar. Tom Scott remembered Bellamy's in the mid 1970s, just before its demise, as 'a ramshackle old wooden structure that leant against the south wall of the main building. It was always busy. You came down rickety stairs through an air-lock of cooking smells, tobacco smoke and hops. Early evening it had the casual gaiety of a benign riot. The bar was one of those continuous counter affairs you still find at the odd country racecourse. Thin partitions segregated the various castes. At the far end messengers got a bare wooden floor. Next door the press got stained lino. The Members and Guests and Members Only bars graduated to greasy carpet flecked with cigarette burns. People entered the cubicle befitting their status, hung up coats, tucked briefcases against the walls, and checked the stainless steel warming drawers to see what tasty morsels were left over from lunch. Sometimes there were crumbed oysters and sweetbreads but mostly it was fish in limp jackets of batter, but once fortified they were ready to battle through the crush to the bar.'*

* Scott, *Ten Years Inside*, p. 10.

The members' dining room, 1968. While Bellamy's continued to pride itself on its liquor, the food was plain and more akin to that served in a well-provided home than a top restaurant, though still cheap. However, menus show that the chef could still put on a sumptuous dinner for visiting dignitaries.

The run-down cubicle-like messengers' bar, 1968.

But the balance of competing library institutions shifted and instead of absorbing other libraries, the General Assembly Library was itself swallowed up. It had already lost its Dominion Archives function on the retirement of Scholefield in 1947, although the archives remained stored in the attic until 1954. The National Library Service, formed in 1945, had a huge collection in desperate need of decent permanent accommodation, and the specialist archival and rare book collections of the Alexander Turnbull Library were also poorly housed. Interdepartmental discussions concluded in 1956 that the three libraries should be grouped into a single National Library, controlled by the Department of Education and housed in a new building adjacent to Parliament. This should include only a small separate parliamentary section providing reference and research services as well as newspapers and recreational reading for members. In 1958 a National Library select committee adopted the thrust of this 1956 report.[105] The Friends of the Turnbull Library poured public vitriol on proposals that seemed to threaten their precious 'jewel', but the staff of the General Assembly Library could only express their qualms internally, although Chief Librarian J.O. Wilson did mount a rearguard action. Most members do not seem to have been much bothered.

After further reports urging the formation of a National Library, cabinet agreed to it in principle in 1963. The National Library Bill was introduced into the House and passed in 1965, after attempts were made to exclude the General Assembly Library from its coverage.[106] The Statutes Revision Committee strengthened safeguards for the General Assembly Library after representations from the Library Committee of the House. The Library Committee would be able to require the National Library to provide services to Parliament, and the Chief Librarian of the General Assembly Library would have delegated powers. Parliament was also granted three representatives on the Board of Trustees for the new library. The General Assembly Library became part of the National Library on 1 April 1966.[107]

By the late 1960s the library's collection had expanded to more than 300,000 volumes, and it provided privileged access to nearly a thousand outside readers annually, and many more research students. The library's reference section now had seven staff, mostly qualified librarians with a range of degree backgrounds and including a research officer with economics and statistics experience.[108] The library was used less by members than it had been in the past, when they had attended to correspondence or caught up on reading. The availability of members' rooms, party research units (from 1970), increased workloads, declining interest in using the library for literary stimulation, members' disappearance back to their electorates – all were factors in the declining usage.

Following the merger, the General Assembly Library remained in its historic premises and the National Library continued to be dispersed in 15 locations around the city. Whether the library's services had been improved by joining the National Library remained a moot point. Wilson was sceptical, given that staff numbers were still insufficient and a low priority was given to providing services to Parliament.

Reforming the House

New Zealand's economy improved greatly after 1958 and Labour was able to reduce taxes and improve social security benefits, but the 'Black Budget' still dominated the election of 1960.[109] The well-organised National Party won a majority of 12 seats and brought a number of notable backbenchers into the House. Labour's substantial losses included Philip Holloway (retired), Ray Boord, Reg Keeling, and Bob Tizard who lost the Tamaki seat to Rob Muldoon. The Labour Party was to experience considerable organisational difficulties in the House during the early 1960s, especially after Deputy Leader C.F. (Jerry) Skinner died in early 1962. There was a poor attendance by members, particularly on Friday afternoons, and a lack of discipline in the ranks.[110]

National had promised substantial reforms to Parliament in its election manifesto.[111] These included

Keith Holyoake represented Motueka (1932–8) and Pahiatua (1943–77), and became Holland's deputy in 1947. Briefly Prime Minister in 1957 after Holland retired, he was then Leader of the Opposition (1957–60). After National won the 1960 election he was Prime Minister until he relinquished the leadership in 1972. Holyoake was appointed Governor-General in 1977.

eliminating 'tedious repetition and long-drawn out debates', 'increasing the rights and responsibilities of private members', reducing the length of the Address-in-Reply and budget debates, greater provision for discussion on specific subjects and investigation by select committees, greater scrutiny of regulations, and the establishment of a 'Citizens Appeal Authority' (Ombudsman).

Holyoake was to be Prime Minister for four terms. He became the master of consensus politics by running cabinet as a team of strong characters who included 'Gentleman Jack' Marshall, 'Moses' Hanan, the 'Marlborough maverick' Tom Shand, and Muldoon.[112] Holyoake was also a master of parliamentary procedure and standing orders, and extremely effective both at forging relationships in the House and making himself available to the public. Holyoake became known as 'Kiwi Keith'. He was very encouraging of new backbenchers. Michael Bassett remembered his 'good natured wanders around the backbenches chatting to anyone whether in opposition or government'.[113] In contrast to Holland, he favoured a greater role for caucus, and introduced a much more democratic style into both caucus and cabinet. Teamwork was emphasised and extensive discussion was allowed in cabinet. Holyoake often waited to the end and weighed up the balance of opinion before announcing his own view.

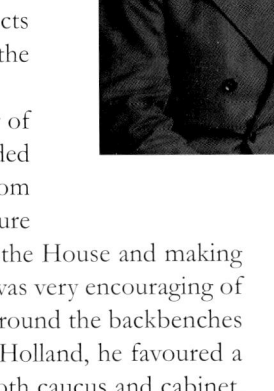

The new role for caucus was graphically illustrated by the debate over the proposal for a Nelson cotton mill that had been inherited from the previous Labour government's policy of industrialisation.[114] A group of new and assertive backbench National members, including Muldoon, criticised the proposal, questioned the Minister of Industries and Commerce, and in concert with pressure groups and the National Party at large reversed the decision to proceed. This was one instance in which differences between caucus and cabinet were resolved in favour of the former. It was indicative of a gradual shift of caucus from a sounding-board to a body more actively concerned with policy. But the episode also revealed how the House itself could be bypassed in decisions.

Ronald Algie was elected Speaker when the new Parliament opened in 1961. Algie was a somewhat reluctant Speaker – he had been hoping for a cabinet post – but he was a former Professor of Law and had both a good grounding in and a determination to reform parliamentary procedure. When the moment came to take the Chair, he refused to follow tradition and feign unwillingness by being dragged to it. 'Such playacting, he felt, was out of touch with modern conditions.'[115] Algie was a strong advocate of parliamentary and constitutional reform and a very effective debater. He oversaw a substantial strengthening of the role of the House. Hindered by poor eyesight, he learnt the standing orders by heart so he could respond immediately when a ruling was required. The Clerk had to prepare his papers with an especially large typeface.

The appointment of a new Chairman of Committees did not proceed so smoothly. Roy Jack had been at the forefront of the turmoil of the late 1950s, frequently challenging rulings of the Speaker and Chairman of Committees and gaining a reputation for partisan debating.[116] When National put him forward, Labour vigorously opposed his candidacy and it went to a division. Nonetheless, as Nash later conceded, Jack proved an excellent Chairman.

Amongst the new intake of National members were Muldoon, Peter Gordon and Duncan MacIntyre, who were christened the 'Young Turks'.[117] This group, and others in the substantial influx of 1960 such as Harry Lapwood, later the senior government whip, were part of a generation with Second World War service who were to be more assertive in caucus. Along with Brian Talboys, who had entered Parliament in 1957, and later David Thomson and (J.R.) Dick Harrison (1963), Rob Talbot (1966), and Frank Gill (1969), they formed a close cadre into the 1970s.

Ronald Macmillan Algie was born in Wyndham, Southland, on 22 October 1888. In 1915 he graduated with an LLM from Auckland University College, where he became the first Professor of Law in 1920. After retiring in 1937 to head a conservative publicity organisation for the National Party, he won the Remuera seat in 1943. An advocate of parliamentary and constitutional reform, Algie became one of the strongest debaters in the House. He became Minister of Education in 1949 and gathered other portfolios in 1951. In favour of bicameralism, he was the driving force behind the 1952 report of the Constitutional Committee to consider alternatives following the abolition of the Legislative Council. In his early seventies when National regained office in 1960, he took the Speakership and oversaw extensive changes to parliamentary procedure. He played a key role in revising the standing orders in 1962, the introduction of the Public Expenditure Committee, and the increased scrutiny of regulations by the Statutes Revision Committee. He retired in 1966, having been knighted in 1964. He was awarded an honorary LLD by the University of Auckland in 1967 and died on 23 July 1978.

Warrant of fitness.

Cabinet minister Algie observes that life in the House has its hazards. Algie was one of the most renowned debaters of the time.

With caucus discussions becoming more heated and Gordon's voice in particular carrying effectively, the chief whip stationed someone outside the caucus room door to ensure no-one else became acquainted with proceedings.[118] The enlarged role of caucus was not always appreciated by senior ministers – Shand was manhandled by two backbenchers during arguments over voluntary unionism in 1961.

Muldoon made his mark immediately. Given the honour of moving the Address-in-Reply in 1961, he carefully prepared a maiden speech that included the controversial topic of the International Monetary Fund.[119] Before Muldoon began, Speaker Algie reminded him that members should not read their speeches but that he would show indulgence as long as the speech was not controversial. This patronising comment was taken personally by Muldoon. Algie reciprocated, often cutting Muldoon off halfway through points of order throughout his Speakership.

National planned to introduce much legislation in 1961, including licensing law reform and the introduction of voluntary unionism. This resulted in the longest session in terms of sitting days since 1950. Abolition of the death penalty, considered under Labour, was now enacted. National gave its members a free vote, with most favouring retention.[120] Hanan, as Minister of Justice, introduced the Crimes Bill, which retained the death penalty for certain types of murder. He was in fact strongly opposed to capital punishment, and worked diligently for an amendment requiring full abolition. The 'atmosphere was electric' as members went into the lobbies. The result was 41 to 30 for the amendment, with Labour voting as a bloc along with ten National members (including Hanan).

The major focus of agitation for parliamentary reform was the possible reintroduction of a second chamber in association with the adoption of a written constitution.[121] While Holland had succeeded in abolishing the Legislative Council, the matter of a second chamber had been left unresolved. Throughout the 1950s and beyond, constitutional issues remained in the public consciousness. This was difficult territory for National, whereas Labour simply avoided it.

Concern had been raised by the draconian emergency powers taken by the government to deal with the 1951 waterfront dispute. The National Party also wanted to protect constitutional rights. Holland's promise to consider alternatives to the Legislative Council resulted in a Constitutional Reform Committee report of 1952. Its recommendation of an appointed Senate was not received enthusiastically.[122] Holland was not displeased at the indeterminate outcome.

Continued constitutional concerns led to the passage of the Electoral Act 1956. This entrenched provisions such as the definition of electorates, the franchise and the life of Parliament. Entrenched provisions could not be altered other than by referendum or by a majority of three-quarters of the House of Representatives. This protection was not sufficient for advocates of reform, and in 1957 the Constitutional Society was formed. Before long it was focusing its efforts on a second chamber. It launched major campaigns, including petitions to Parliament in the early 1960s, and made submissions to the Constitutional Reform Committee in 1964.[123] Its efforts were reflected in a deep split within the National Party on the issue, but the public showed little interest. In 1965 Deputy Prime Minister Marshall, a strong advocate of reform, conceded that public support was lacking and stated that the government had no plans for an upper House. The issue effectively died as concern shifted towards other means of enhancing Parliament's effectiveness, such as increasing the size of the House.

Procedural reforms, 1962

Members shared a desire to make Parliament more relevant and efficient. Under Holyoake the government introduced measures reducing the power of the executive, such as the creation of an Ombudsman and various 'quasi-autonomous' bodies ('quangos'), and relaxed control over censorship and broadcasting.[124] Holyoake wanted to raise the standard of debate in the House and generally streamline its business. He promised to appoint a select committee to revise the standing orders, and suggested introducing one-night debates on salient issues to generate public interest.[125] Speaker Algie was determined to improve the conduct of the House and make its proceedings more efficient and dignified.[126] Parliament's public image had deteriorated since the days of the first Labour government and the first broadcasts. Algie wanted to revise the prayer, restrict the extent of debates, give greater power and time to select committees, and replace the ineffective Public Accounts Committee.

The report of the Standing Orders Committee, chaired by Algie, recommended substantial revisions along the lines of the House of Commons. These were in large part accepted by the House.[127] While it did not go so far as to drastically shorten the Address-in-Reply and financial debates (as in the Commons), the length of speeches in the Address-in-Reply was reduced from 30 to 20 minutes, and in the financial debate from an hour to 30 minutes. (Further truncation of the Address-in-Reply would have been unwelcome to the government, which used this time to prepare its programme.) As a quid pro quo for the loss of debating time, private members were granted time on Wednesdays for notices of motion.

Other reductions, in aggregate, significantly reduced the time spent on dispatching business. Question time was made more topical and focused. It was altered from a weekly two hours on Wednesdays to a daily half hour of 'oral' questions which were answered immediately, with the right to ask supplementary questions at the discretion of the Speaker. A separate category of 'written' questions was created (previously all questions had been regarded as written). The House adjourned for half an hour at 10 p.m. on Tuesdays and Thursdays for members to have their say on a substantive motion concerning an issue of the day. Friday sitting hours were brought forward to allow members to get away earlier for the weekend – they were leaving early in dribs and drabs anyway.

Algie and the Standing Orders Committee wanted to strengthen select committees and hoped that each member would need to serve on only one. In the early twentieth century select committees had been an integral part of the business of Parliament, but their role had diminished as party government advanced.[128] Many of the more important bills had once been referred to select committees after their second reading, with relevant ministers attending to explain the provisions, members of the public giving evidence, and public servants being cross-examined. By the 1950s, however, select committee business was dominated by petitions. Only a small minority of bills were referred to them. (The mandatory consideration of local bills by the Local Bills Committee and scrutiny of more technical bills by the Statutes Revision Committee were exceptions.)

The role of select committees was now revived. More bills were referred to them, and a number of related committees were amalgamated. Select committees met more often during the 1960s, with two mornings a week during the session (Tuesday and Wednesday, especially the latter) devoted to their business.[129] As select committee work lasted for more of the year, members made more frequent trips by air to Wellington.

Another committee, known as the 'Algie' committee, reported on delegated legislation to safeguard against abuses of executive power, one of Algie's long-standing concerns.[130] It recommended that bills be drafted with precision, that emergency regulations and those altering taxation have a limited life, and that all regulations be laid before Parliament. It also recommended that the Statutes Revision Committee be established by standing order, sit during the recess, and consider all regulations.

The changes made in 1962 proved effective. Speaking time was reduced and the Address-in-Reply and financial debates occupied only about four and nine sitting days respectively.[131] Both sides were prepared to go along with the new procedures and there were fewer late nights. The government heeded the Standing Orders Committee's urging, in recognition of the fuller parliamentary year, that it adjourn the House periodically for a week during the session, as in Australia. This was to allow ministers to catch up with their work, select committees to handle business, and members to deal with their electorates. The more powerful Statutes Revision Committee suggested amendments to a majority of bills, but scrutinised few regulations.[132]

The establishment of the office of Parliamentary Commissioner for Investigations (or Ombudsman) was of more significance. This was set up in 1962 as a check on executive power and bureaucracy.[133] To ensure his independence, the Ombudsman was an 'officer of Parliament', appointed by the Governor-General on the recommendation of the House of Representatives. This proved a highly successful innovation. It satisfied a public demand for the consideration of grievances that had previously been ill-served by petitions to Parliament. The existence of the Ombudsman further diminished the already attenuated role of petitions to Parliament.

Question time was much improved. Ministers were able to answer on behalf of others, there was no backlog (as had previously plagued the system), and written answers provided a useful new way to obtain statistical and other information.[134] The number of questions increased markedly in the mid 1960s. The press gallery ran an annual 'King of Quiz' competition to find who had run up the most questions. Paddy Blanchfield was a frequent winner, while Ethel McMillan was dubbed 'Queen of Quiz'. The topical one-night debates – usually on international affairs – that National had introduced under Holland on an ad hoc basis proved successful in both arousing public interest and airing members' debating skills.

On one such occasion, the colourful Léon Götz – who had lost his right arm and an eye in an explosion, had a tattooed torso, wore an eyepatch, and was known as 'the pirate' – brought a nondescript box into the chamber. The Speaker assured members that this was appropriate – after all, 'boots, shoes, garments, bananas, and so forth' had previously been brandished, and this was not a bomb![135] The box proved to be a geiger counter, which Götz used to demonstrate a point about the lack of danger from atomic-bomb testing. Labour's Moohan shouted, 'Try it on your head' – to roars of laughter, as many believed that Götz had a steel plate in his skull.

On the other hand, the attempt to give private members more opportunities to contribute failed in the face of party pressures.[136] The 10 p.m. adjournment debate rapidly gained the cynical epithet 'Hancock's Half Hour' (a reference to the popular British comedy) because of the antics of members desperate to make a mark in their allotted five minutes. 'They go like trains and impose great strain on *Hansard*', said the Clerk, while the *Evening Post* commented that 'often they have generated more heat than light'.[137] Before long party politics intruded and the adjournment debate became a confrontation between leading National and Labour debaters. The time allotted for private members' notices of motion on Wednesdays was also taken over by the parties and became an occasion for futile posturing through endless motions.

The Speaker tried hard to improve members' conduct and a greater degree of order returned to the chamber in the early 1960s. National's use of closure declined noticeably after it was invoked extensively in 1961 for major legislation (and turned down on a number of occasions). Algie was at times sorely tested as Speaker. His tendency to revert to a schoolmasterish style when dealing with errant members was not always well received. His decision to break early for lunch one Friday because of disorder provoked a 'Heil Hitler' raised arm from one member and facile 'schoolboy' requests to go to lunch from others.[138] At one time he lost patience with the 'constant barrage of interjections' and threatened to 'name' offenders. During the 1964 session there was once again extensive use of closure motions, and Labour unrest over what they regarded as Algie's excessively rigid control and pedantic approach. This resulted in notices of motion regarding his rulings.

The most significant change in 1962 was the creation of a strong Public Expenditure Committee.[139] The previous Public Accounts Committee had been an inactive and powerless body, constrained in its work by the limited time available to scrutinise the estimates. Its primary use had been as a launching pad for Opposition attacks in the Committee of Supply. From 1932 it could only consider issues that were referred to it by the government or the House. This hardly ever happened, and reports back to the House were even rarer. Nor was the Committee of Supply an appropriate or effective forum for scrutiny of the annual estimates. After the war, delegation by cabinet of financial powers involving ever larger sums took place.[140] There had also been a tendency to make payments under permanent appropriations to avoid parliamentary scrutiny.[141] The power of the House to alter departmental votes directly during the estimates debate (the traditional means of protest) was no longer effective – the last occasion on which this happened was when £5 was symbolically lopped off the Department of Agriculture's vote in 1930.

The Public Expenditure Committee quickly made its mark once questions of membership and chairing had been resolved in favour of the government.[142] Its 12 members examined the estimates and reported on possible economies, scrutinised the public accounts and those of Crown corporations, and, in collaboration with the Controller and Auditor-General, inquired into matters referred to it by the House. It had the power to sit over the recess and to appoint its own subcommittees. It significantly augmented Parliament's ability to call the executive to account.

From its inception the Public Expenditure Committee took an independent and vigorous stance, led by its Chairmen, the independent-minded Bill Sheat and then the energetic Muldoon.[143] It became an important source of backbench power and a means of promoting parliamentary careers. Under Muldoon its role was broadened considerably to include discussion of policy matters. The Committee did not feel bound to agree with the Controller and Auditor-General, and undertook a number of independent investigations of public bodies beyond the bounds of parliamentary appropriation. It also followed up on its recommendations to check whether the government had taken account of them, made trenchant criticisms of government actions, and had its reports debated in the House.

These changes helped give Parliament a higher profile. Although members now had less time for speeches during set-piece debates, their opportunities to make an impact were increased by the greater role of select committees and the increased pertinence of question time. Private members' days were less squeezed because of the shorter Address-in-Reply and financial debates, and more Wednesday afternoons were available for their notices of motion, even if this time was largely taken over by the two parties.[144]

Further refinements

Pressure to increase the number of members in the House built up as the population grew and as members' workloads got heavier. The number of seats had remained fixed at 80, including the four Maori seats, since the turn of the century. For some time members such as Algie, and some academic political scientists, had advocated a substantial increase to redress the imbalance of power between the executive and Parliament.[145] Both Holyoake and the new Labour leader, Norman Kirk, supported this proposal. The reformers also suggested that the parliamentary term be extended to four or five years to enhance long-term planning, that Parliament be made more efficient, and that members be assisted by party research units.

The 1966 election barely changed the balance between the two major parties, with National now on 44 seats and Labour holding 35, but Social Credit's Vernon Cracknell won Hobson and the party gained 14.5 per cent of the overall vote. From this time, third parties became an important consideration in New Zealand politics.

With Algie having retired, Roy Jack (also a lawyer) was appointed Speaker when the new Parliament convened in 1967. Jack gained a reputation for impartiality. Like Oram before him, he was keen for the Speaker to adopt a more neutral stance, as in the House of Commons. He denounced attempts to persuade him to vote while the House was in Committee, seeing it as 'a clear affront to the Speaker and, through him, to the House, to have the Speaker traipse along to the Lobbies in his ceremonial attire and join a party voting line'.[146] Jack was also careful to distance himself from party politics in other ways. He noted ruefully that while Speaker he never frequented Bellamy's dining room or bars, or even the billiard room.

Speakers had to learn the art of letting go, ignoring or 'failing' to hear some of what was said in the House in the interests of long-term peace and the facilitation of business. On occasion this latitude could misfire. A Labour member called Sir Leslie Munro 'a senile old gentleman' while Speaker Jack was apparently dozing.[147] Munro ignored the interjection and attempted to carry on with his speech, but an enthusiastic and inexperienced National backbencher tried to insist that the Speaker rule the expression unparliamentary. Jack claimed that he had not heard the offending words, but to the delight

> *Roy Emile Jack was born in New Plymouth on 12 January 1914 and educated at Wanganui Collegiate and Victoria University College, graduating with an LLB. He served in the RNZAF during the war and then became a barrister and solicitor in Wanganui. He served on the Wanganui City Council from 1946 to 1955. Jack was elected for Patea in 1954, and was appointed Chairman of Committees (1961–7), and then Speaker from 1967 until early 1972, when in a cabinet reshuffle under new Prime Minister Jack Marshall he was made Minister of Justice and Attorney-General. Jack was knighted in 1970. Reappointed as Speaker in 1976 when National was re-elected, he soon fell ill. He announced his retirement but was determined to continue for as long as he could, and died in the Speaker's suite on 24 December 1977. A vigorous debater in the House, his nomination as Chairman of Committees in 1961 did not go unopposed, and his re-election as Speaker in 1976 was controversial in those highly partisan years. He was described by Muldoon as being in some ways unworldly but with a passion for Parliament and its rules of procedure. He brought a meticulous and rigorous approach to bear upon parliamentary procedure, had a strong sense of precedent, formality, and an insistence upon etiquette. He was an accomplished violinist whose playing could be heard from the Speaker's suite late in the evening.*

Parliamentary Service collection

of the Opposition the member persisted and the phrase was reiterated. Finally, after it had been repeated four times, Jack asked for a withdrawal and an apology. Meanwhile Munro was left 'looking at those windows up there and saying, "God protect me from my friends".' In another incident that led to a breach of privilege, Jack either did not or did not want to hear Harry Lapwood's interjection – 'Go back to your pipis' – during Maori member Matiu Rata's speech.[148] When the *New Zealand Statesman* newspaper called this lack of intervention racial prejudice, it was made to apologise for the accusation.

The standing orders were reviewed in 1967.[149] Kirk had toppled Nordmeyer (who had taken over from Nash in 1963) as leader of the Labour Party in 1965. Labour was unhappy at the restrictions on debate and regarded the 10 p.m. adjournment debates as 'no credit to Parliament'. Kirk had risen rapidly through the ranks to become a leading backbencher and debater with a good grounding in standing orders. He had set himself the goal of memorising these and the Speakers' Rulings one page at a time during the prayer each day.[150]

The 10 p.m. adjournment debate was abandoned. The number of Imprest Supply debates in a session, reduced to two in 1962, was increased to three again to give the Opposition greater opportunities. Although successful, question time had truncated debate too much, and an hour was now reserved on alternate Wednesdays for more extended debate on questions. Notices of motion had overloaded Wednesday's order paper. Now they were struck out after four weeks, and debate on each motion was restricted to an hour, with speeches reduced to ten minutes. Fridays were increasingly unsuited to debate on the estimates because of members' travel. The government could now choose any two days during the week for this debate.

The revised standing orders covered the process for considering breaches of privilege in some detail. Rather than ad hoc Privileges Committees being appointed when alleged breaches were raised on the floor, a standing Privileges Committee would be appointed every session. The Speaker would decide on the prima facie merits of each case before it went to the Privileges Committee.

The Standing Orders Committee concentrated on removing archaic 'flummery and rigmarole', as Holyoake put it, in the area of finance.[151] The major changes included simplifying the introduction of government bills; streamlined procedures for Imprest Supply Bills; abolishing the Committees of Supply and Ways and Means; delivering the budget in the House rather than in Committee, and having the financial debate during the second reading of the Appropriation Bill; using a second Appropriation Bill to deal with supplementary estimates; and making this second bill's third reading a wide-ranging debate on 'public affairs' at the end of the session.

Government bills previously introduced by a message from the Governor-General could now be introduced directly by ministers. (This old requirement technically pertained only to bills involving appropriations but had been extended, probably as a precaution, to all bills.)[152] This allowed all members access to copies of bills on their introduction, which had not previously been possible. It unfortunately also encouraged expanded debate on the introduction of bills – a matter that Speakers had to address.[153] Pro forma second readings of bills no longer required ministers to rise three times – bobbing up and down to amusement and amazement in the galleries. Local bills could now be referred directly to the Local Bills Committee during the recess (this committee was now convened for the entire Parliament) so it could cope with the heavy workload. The Standing Orders Committee rejected proposals for the mechanical recording of votes and the greater reporting of proceedings in Committee.

The House found it necessary to work for most of the year. The committee suggested that the government consider convening Parliament earlier. Nordmeyer had pressed for this in 1964.[154] With a session from March to November, punctuated by periodic adjournments, business would not be rushed through at the end, the House would be able to ratify government decisions, and there would be more time for committee work. Holyoake responded that National had already done a great deal to streamline business and opposed convening the House on a fixed date.

The revised standing orders and wider events were both influential in setting a new pattern for the House.[155] Muldoon, who became Minister of Finance on the death of Harry Lake, delivered the first 'mini-budget' in the House to deal with a rapidly emerging economic crisis. Holyoake took urgency for this in an all-night sitting, to the chagrin of the many Social Credit supporters who had travelled to Parliament to hear Cracknell's maiden speech. Parliament sat from late April until late November, with the most sitting days since 1936. The Labour Party, as it had done in the 1920s and early 1930s, put up a number of private members' bills in a concerted attempt to present an alternative to the government. Three adjournments assisted members and the government to conduct their other business, including select committee work. There were many divisions and the government had to make considerable use of closure as the turbulence in the economy and society was reflected in the House. Nonetheless, the session was not a 'stormy and fractious' one.

The changing context

During the relatively stable, two-party postwar decades, the turnover of members declined to between 15 to 25 per cent at each election. This was not accompanied, however, by an aging of the House.[156] There was a compression into the middle-aged groups (the forties and fifties), with fewer really young or old members. Parliament had become a second career for those already well established in an occupation. The average age of members declined gradually from a peak of 55 years in 1951 to 51 in the 1966–9 Parliament.

The 1960s saw the beginning of social changes that were to be reflected in the representatives elected to the House. It became less necessary for budding politicians to have lucrative careers before contesting a seat. Improved parliamentary salaries allowed younger aspirants to make a career out of politics. Most were full-time, not just in the sense of the hours they put in but in their commitment to the vocation.[157] Members were younger and often had no other income. Almost all were married, and many had young families to care for.

> Paddy Blanchfield, who represented Westland for Labour from 1960, was 'the bard of the West Coast, one of the real characters of Parliament who has provided many humorous interludes, and has always managed to capture something of the spirit of the people he represents.'* This is part of the poem with which he farewelled the House in 1978.
>
> > Now Time has rung the curtain, we six will leave the stage;
> > We'll bow to Mr Speaker and sadly turn the page;
> > I shan't forget these members, as south my footsteps roam,
> > For the pigeon's on the Miro and now I'm going home.
> >
> > I'll miss my old opponents on benches 'cross the floor,
> > I'll miss those members' luncheons at Bellamy's next door;
> > But when I leave the Chamber and walk away alone,
> > I'll leave no hate or rancour, when Westland calls me home.
> >
> > Farewell to all-night sessions and clang of division bell,
> > When nerves are frayed and tempers displayed,
> > Sure it's just like living in hell;
> > Yet I'll miss all my fiery colleagues who fight like gladiators of Rome;
> > 'Cos the tree ferns shade and the peaceful glade
> > Whisper, 'Paddy, it's time to come home'.
>
> * NZPD, vol 421, 1978, pp. 4290, 4295

Under Nordmeyer and then under Kirk, the Labour Party modernised itself and introduced new, younger blood. It grew increasingly distant from its trade union base.[158] Nash, Howard and Nordmeyer were relegated to the backbenches, while the Father of the House, Mason, had to retire after 40 years of service in 1966 under a new party policy that members must retire at 70. J.L. Hunt succeeded him in New Lynn, becoming the youngest member in the House at 27. National, too, reduced the age of its members over time.

The death of the 86-year-old Walter Nash in 1968 marked the disappearance of the old breed of Labour politician associated with the first Labour government – immigrant, self-educated and based in the labour movement.[159] Nash was given a state funeral with his casket placed in the vestibule of Parliament, draped in purple. He had attained the status of the grand old man of New Zealand politics, succeeding Mason as Father of the House and remaining on the backbenches until his death.

With the postwar dominance of the National Party, farmers remained by far the single most important occupational group in the House in the 1950s and 1960s, if now almost matched by lawyers and professionals taken together. Farmers continued to comprise about 30 per cent of all members. In the National caucus – but not cabinet – their proportion was nearly half. New Zealand remained internationally distinctive for the dominance of farmers in its legislature.

Farming was followed by the professional group – which had doubled its representation – and 'business', both with about 20 per cent. There was a decline in those with manual worker and trade union backgrounds. Few members were other than New Zealand born. By the 1960s, local body politics was less used as a platform for a national political career. Instead members went into national politics directly, earlier, and with higher professional and educational credentials.

The most significant change was the greater presence of professional groups and the weakening of the traditional Labour rank and file – an increased 'professionalisation' of members both in the sense of making politics a career and in the groups that were drawn upon. By the end of the 1960s, Labour was becoming dominated by professionals and others from service sector groups, most with tertiary qualifications. National members came from middle-class and more affluent backgrounds, and were often farmers or self-employed. The average level of education rose substantially in the period, with the previous gap between National and Labour narrowing by the end of the 1960s. By then few had only a primary education, more than half had a secondary education and two-fifths a tertiary education. Some social distinctions remained, however. About a quarter of National members had attended élite private secondary schools.

The parliamentary ranks comprised a diverse range of well-educated men – and a few women – in the prime of their lives. The characteristics of the two main political parties had converged. What did this promise for an institution that many saw as increasingly archaic?

Speaker Algie addresses the crowd while unveiling a plaque commemorating the centennial of Parliament in Wellington on 26 July 1965. The unveiling was followed by a special luncheon for more than 500 put on by Bellamy's, and an evening function in the Town Hall. A postage stamp depicting the original Wellington Provincial Council buildings was issued, television documentaries were made, and a school bulletin on the institution of Parliament was published.

What of the future?

The House was working harder and more efficiently with the same number of members.[160] The number of bills dealt with had gone up since the 1950s, when National began drafting separate bills for miscellaneous measures rather than incorporating them into an omnibus Finance Bill. From 1955, the Statutes Amendment Bill was also split into separate bills after its second reading.[161] More importantly, the legislation that went onto the statute book was longer and increasingly complex. The annual volumes were far thicker than before. In the 1950s the House had remained substantially a 'talking shop' for discussing government policy (more than 40 per cent of the total time) as well as a mechanism for transacting government bills (27 per cent).[162] The lengthy Address-in-Reply and financial debates contributed greatly to this, as did Holland's introduction of regular informal foreign affairs debates. The increasing importance of legislation was reflected in the allocation of time to bills in the 1960s (34 per cent), with considerably less given to general discussion of government policy (24 per cent). Sessions were becoming somewhat longer, but at the same time daily hours were reduced, and in particular the number of late-night sittings diminished markedly. The House was conducting its business in a much more civilised fashion, by this indicator at least.

The criticising and publicising function of Parliament that was reflected in question time experienced a resurgence. The number of questions asked in the House returned to the high levels of the turn of the century, in spite of a tightening up in the kinds of questions allowed by standing orders. The scrutinising role of select committees was enhanced with the establishment of the Public Expenditure Committee and the shifting of select committee work from petitions to bills. Select committees worked longer hours and their work became more important. By the mid 1960s they considered between one-third and two-fifths of all bills proposed, made more enquiries, and undertook more work in the recess.

While the Standing Orders Committee, the government and most members seemed satisfied with the internal reforms of the 1960s, perceptions were different outside Parliament.[163] Here the perception was that the reforms were too little and too slow, and that the power of the executive branch was gathering apace. The reputation of Parliament was declining. Its rituals seemed increasingly archaic and its debates irrelevant. Was the House simply to be the 'nation's political playhouse', as Mitchell put it?[164] Observers urged that the number of seats be substantially increased (perhaps to 100 or even 120) to give governments a greater reservoir of talent from which to draw for cabinets, to allow select committees to function still more effectively, and to redress the caucus balance between cabinet and backbench. The ambition of most members was to get into cabinet, the prospects for which were good if one stuck around in a safe seat.[165] This acted as an effective constraint on independent action.

Pressure mounted for sessions to start earlier and continue for longer through the year, with periodic adjournments for governmental and committee work. Parliament, it was argued, should be given more power through its select committees, the proceedings of which should be open to the public, allowing an exchange of information and views and improving the image of Parliament.

The public was not impressed by behaviour in the chamber. One embarrassed visitor saw members 'with mischievous-little-boy expressions, interjecting from behind their hands towards their own microphones' and 'bellowing abuse across the floor. A sort of animal feeding-time-at-the-zoo noise … accompanied the remarks of one speaker', while 'Shut up!' and 'Shut up yourself, you great ape!' seemed to summarise the debates.[166] Many people found the personal attacks and destructive criticism of the adversarial culture in the House distasteful, while accepting the need for an Opposition and retaining a strong element of trust in and goodwill towards the political system. While conflict on the floor of the chamber was nothing new, it raised issues concerning the pay and performance of members now that Parliament was regarded as a professional career. Was this the best advertisement the institution could offer, with the ideals of the first Labour government's broadcasting of Parliament in mind? Should the public be paying handsome salaries for this sort of behaviour?

Interest in the broadcasting of Parliament had faded. The availability at the turn of a knob of uninspired debates or petty back-biting fuelled criticisms of the institution. A survey in the late 1950s suggested that listeners had begun to switch off, but members refused to abandon what they saw as a key ingredient of democracy.[167] There was little support for anything except the transmission of debates in full. *Truth*'s view was that radio broadcasting had become a 'sacred cow' that could not be touched, even though Parliament no longer attracted a wide audience. The lack of reliable information on the number of listeners made the issue difficult to assess.

In 1962, the opening of Parliament was televised for the first time. This became a regular event.[168] Although two television journalists now joined the press gallery, the House would not entertain the possibility of filming proceedings in the chamber. When in the early 1960s the New Zealand Broadcasting Corporation asked for permission to film the Address-in-Reply debate and the closing of the session, the request was firmly rejected. Speaker Jack also opposed televising the House. He was well aware of the propensity of members to play to the gallery and spout propaganda while on radio. His view was that 'To televise the whole of our proceedings would be unthinkable but to televise edited excerpts would, I believe, result in a weeping sore of discontent from one, or other, or both, sides of the House. And human nature would make it certain that self-consciousness and playing to the gallery would be greatly increased. Television, like fire, is a good servant but a bad master.'[169] There was also concern that the chamber would be turned into a 'movie studio', with hot dazzling lights, cables and other equipment disrupting proceedings. Television remained restricted to ceremonial occasions.[170]

By the mid 1960s Parliament was attracting the attention of protesters. New Zealand's decision to become involved in the Vietnam War alongside the United States and Australia provoked considerable protest. In May 1965 there was a 'sit-in' in the corridor outside the Prime Minister's office as the House decided to send combat troops to Vietnam.[171] By the late 1960s, disruption had become more serious. The outdoor ceremony for the opening of Parliament in 1968 had to be cancelled, and the Governor-General entered Parliament Buildings by a side door. The guard of honour remained outside the grounds, because it was thought that marching solders with rifles and fixed bayonets would be provocative.

Parliament, like society at large, was entering a less stable time. New Zealand's place in the world was changing and being challenged.[172] The relatively tranquil and prosperous period that had begun after the Second World War and been buttressed by exports of primary produce to Britain was ending. Involvement in the Vietnam War and Britain's entry into the European Economic Community posed new questions. Social issues such as equal pay and others raised by the women's movement, the testing of nuclear weapons in the Pacific by the French, abortion, homosexual law reform, apartheid and sporting contacts with South Africa, and compulsory military training were all to change New Zealand's political landscape.

The established pattern of strong government through a two-party system was now challenged by pressure groups which sought a place in the political order at a time when traditional party identifications were weakening. Television was rapidly becoming the primary medium for political comment and criticism, and played an increasingly important role in election campaigns. Labour had modernised itself, improved its organisation, introduced a younger cadre of members, and chosen a strong, dynamic debater in Kirk as leader. Social Credit had hopes of becoming a major force by riding a wave of protest against two main parties whose differences were increasingly difficult to discern. The traditionally very high voting rate in general elections (90 per cent or more) had begun to decline. Ways had to be found to increase public participation and attract younger voters.

In 1965, with the demographic imbalance between the two islands widening as Auckland's population exploded, an amended Electoral Act provided for a fixed 25 seats in the South Island, with the number in the North Island rising in proportion to its population. In the electoral redistribution of 1967, four more North Island seats were created for the election of 1969, bringing the number of European seats to 80 and the total to 84. This did not greatly change matters, but it opened the way for a substantially larger House that was to have a greater impact.

In 1967 the issue of extending the parliamentary term to four years was put to the country in a referendum. Nearly 70 per cent voted against the proposal. A feeling that politicians should be regularly held to account outweighed any sense of the logic of longer-term planning. As Kirk put it, in a unicameral system in which Parliament was not highly regarded, 'the real protection for the citizen is the right to elect a government every three years … We are asking people to dilute their democratic rights to enable Governments to do things they would not dare to do in a shorter term.'[173]

Parliament had to attract members of higher calibre and become more responsive to the public or become increasingly irrelevant in the face of extra-parliamentary political action. As the executive had progressively asserted its power – first in the person of Seddon in the 1890s, then by the rise of parties, war and ambitious social programmes – the place of Parliament had become less apparent. While it was no longer the seat of decision-making power – if it ever had been – the challenge to Parliament, in the words of Bernard Crick, was to reconstruct its functions of influence, advice, criticism, scrutiny and publicity.[174] These elements of democracy should reinforce the most enduring characteristic of the modern Parliament – enabling a 'continuous election campaign' to be waged between the parties. These issues would have to be confronted, but meanwhile executive power was to be strengthened in response to new protest movements. In the short term, society was to become more alienated from those who sought to represent it.

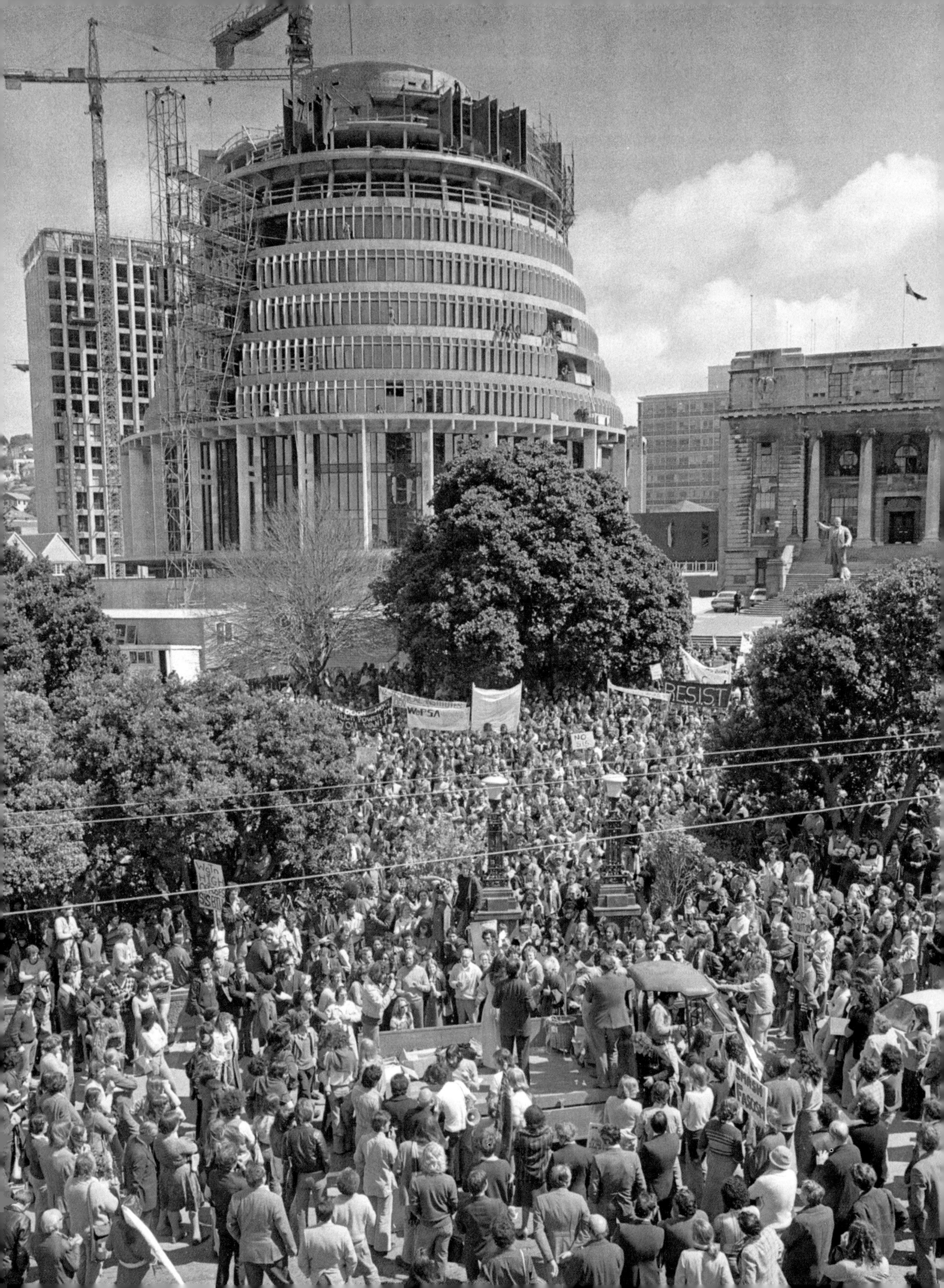
WePSA
RESIST

CHAPTER 8

EXECUTIVE AND PARLIAMENT: THE BALANCE AT ISSUE, 1970–84

In the late 1960s the bipartisan approach to foreign affairs established under Fraser broke down as New Zealand's involvement in the Vietnam conflict created powerful divisions.[1] Fraser had appointed a Foreign Affairs Committee following the war to educate and brief members on New Zealand's foreign policy. He also tabled treaties in the House, made confidential papers available to government and Opposition members, and had the Department of External Affairs' annual report tabled and printed. An intimate relationship developed between External Affairs (later Foreign Affairs), the Prime Minister's Department and the Cabinet Office, facilitated by their common location in Parliament's penthouse.

Over time, the House became less involved in foreign affairs. The Foreign Affairs Committee was not particularly active, and less access was granted to papers as the government became more conscious of security issues. Holland's practice, later confirmed by standing orders, of topical one-night debates encouraged some discussion of foreign affairs, but most members – their attention still firmly focused on local electorates – had little knowledge of or interest in the outside world.

In the mid 1960s the Vietnam War became a polarising issue. The major parties now strongly diverged on foreign policy, and from this time foreign affairs featured in the general debates and during question time. Vietnam, sporting contacts with South Africa, French nuclear testing in the Pacific, overseas trade and immigration policy, all received attention. At the same time, more members broadened their experience by travelling overseas. The days were passing when an old-timer such as Charlie Bowden could demonstrate naïvety on a parliamentary tour to Europe.[2] Stopping off in Paris for a few days, he got lost when he refused to take the Metro because he thought the signs were for a 'house of ill fame' rather than the underground railway.

Protest inside and outside Parliament

New Zealand now experienced organised protest demonstrations. These enlarged popular participation in politics, challenged government policies and often made Parliament grounds a battleground for a range of political and moral ideologies as people debated not only political matters, but also issues such as abortion, homosexual law reform and the place of religion in society.[3] The emergence of protest movements went hand in hand with the new role of the mass media, especially television. Government-scripted news was abandoned and reporting freed up from political control. Before long, current affairs programmes such as *Compass* and then *Gallery* were being screened on television.[4] Political reporting became increasingly assertive. Interviewers took a more independent line and questioned politicians closely as the conventions of giving them questions in advance and treating them with reverence were discarded. Newspaper reporting followed television's lead, casting off the 'journal of record' role in

Left: *Protest against the Security Intelligence Bill, 1977* Dominion Post collection, ATL, EP/1977/4060/20

Protesters against the Vietnam War at the opening of Parliament, 1969. Demonstrations at the opening of Parliament became common in the late 1960s. Parliament grounds became a more public place that was used not just for official occasions and political demonstrations but for all sorts of events. As demonstrations became more frequent and larger, Parliament took greater control of its grounds.

favour of political comment and analysis and more politicised and sensationalist fare. The press gallery became more aggressive and investigative.[5] Politicians had to adjust to having their personalities and images projected through the visual and immediate medium of television rather than by lengthy speeches reported in newspapers.

Although it lost the 1969 election by 39 to 45, Labour was invigorated first by its new intake, then by unexpectedly winning the Marlborough by-election that followed Shand's sudden death.[6] Along with the death of Ralph Hanan earlier that year, this weakened National, which fell into disarray. Labour dominated the House, with members clamouring to speak. Pressure mounted to replace Holyoake, cabinet members fell ill, and the government could not respond effectively to Labour's attacks.

Kirk was complemented by Arthur Faulkner and Jonathan Hunt, who could 'get to their feet, stall, hold off, while an expert goes to get his notes.'[7] Labour could also rely on the booming 'bellow' of Timaru's Sir Basil Arthur, described as 'Boom-Boom' and the party's 'tail-gunner', who liked to spar with Rob Talbot, the National member for Ashburton. Arthur sat behind Rowling and Tizard and on one occasion when he was in full cry, Rowling, feeling the brunt of the speech, jokingly 'turned around and said "Speak up, Bas", which he did. He went up about ten decibels. [Tizard] went down in the seat and Rowling withdrew a white handkerchief and held it up in terms of surrender.'[8]

When the Queen opened Parliament in 1970 some in the crowd booed and jeered as the royal party arrived. The session was prolonged and dramatic. For the first time since the late 1950s, the government on a number of occasions had to rely on the vote of the Speaker to stave off defeat. Towards the end of the session Labour began to refuse pairs. Once the government was defeated (36 to 35) on a clause of a minor bill when the sleeping Leslie Munro and David Seath failed to hear the division bells.[9] It then had to call on the Speaker to defeat Labour's successful amendment. From then on Munro was known as the patron of the 'sleepers' club', and Seath as its president. The introduction of a payroll tax precipitated one of the longest and most vitriolic debates for a long time. Holyoake in the end moved that the bill be considered part-by-part rather than clause-by-clause.[10] The imposition of a petrol tax resulted in the longest continuous sitting of close to 30 hours since the depression, with the government being saved by the casting vote of the Chairman of Committees, A.E. Allen.[11]

The session was also notable for Labour's antagonism towards the Speaker. Opposition notices of motion disputed Jack's rulings on closure and related matters. Kirk's valedictory speech created a precedent by avoiding the usual platitudes in favour of being overtly provocative and political. Another precedent was set by the length of the session, which lasted from March to December.

The session of 1971, from February to December, also demonstrated that there was another way to proceed with business. Parliament began early for a special session to pass legislation controlling wages. Dispensing with the usual outdoor ceremony, because of excavations for the underground carpark and Beehive, allowed Parliament to avoid any demonstrations. The government proved more effective this year.[12] In mid-year Holyoake interrupted the budget debate to announce the terms of New Zealand's arrangements for access to the EEC, after lengthy meetings of cabinet. Matters again became heated. In September, a tied division over closure of the estimates debate was broken by the casting vote of the acting Chairman of Committees.[13] In October Labour members walked out en masse over the Speaker's alleged bias. Kirk again left an unpleasant taste when the House was wound up by insisting on amending the traditional motion to adjourn to criticise the government. Other Labour members refused to follow his lead, and Holyoake made an effective rejoinder.[14]

Holyoake finally stepped down in early 1972. Marshall became Prime Minister and appointed a reshuffled cabinet. He criticised Kirk for suggesting that the government was ignoring Parliament – 'Parliament does not make the decisions. Parliament is there to consider, to criticise, and to comment',

Labour members Hunt, Gordon Christie and Bob Tizard (wearing a towelling hat) were leaders of the 'jackets off' campaign. In the 1960s Parliament's dress code remained formal despite changing standards in society at large. Younger Labour members grew their hair longer and wore coloured shirts. Tizard failed to introduce polo-neck sweaters without ties. Members had to wear a tie or a coat buttoned up to the neck. Tizard remembers a National member coming into the chamber in pyjamas covered by an overcoat. While this was buttoned, his ample stomach was spilling out and his navel was visible.

With women having been allowed for some time to have their hats off, Freer and Tizard launched a 'jackets off' campaign. Deputy Speaker Allen relented during an early special session in the warmth of the late summer of 1971, but still required a neat shirt and tie. As debates warmed up that November, Opposition members defied the Speaker by removing their jackets, and donned them again only under threats of suspension. Tizard insisted on wearing a garish orange towelling hat right under the Speaker's nose to underline the issue, since the traditional wearing of hats still applied. Neither Holyoake nor Kirk endorsed the campaign. A survey showed that most members favoured retaining jackets, and Speaker Jack would not countenance change. The more lenient Speaker Whitehead later abandoned the jacket rule.

Evening Post, 9 December 1971

he stated trenchantly, in case anyone had any misconceptions.[15] Some among Labour wanted the House to have more power – but how would they feel in government? Speaker Jack entered cabinet, so Chairman of Committees Allen – who lacked legal qualifications – became Speaker for the session, prior to his retirement.[16] Allen's tactful, firm control and earthy sense of humour made him a 'roaring success'. While his appointment was uncontroversial, that of Richard Harrison as the new Chairman of Committees was. The Opposition argued that it was unprecedented for a junior whip to be so elevated – and that Harrison had insufficient knowledge of standing orders and made arbitrary decisions. However, the session as a whole was less eventful. Marshall and Kirk worked well together.

The general trend, however, was towards a more combative House. With the number of divisions rising, the Parliament of 1969–72 saw the onset of a more 'divisive' House both in the literal sense and in the extent of disorder and conflict, often of a personal nature.[17] The intensifying conflict was reflected in a pronounced shift in the number and kind of alleged breaches of privilege. Outside the chamber the clamour also rose – for engagement with controversial issues of domestic and foreign affairs, and for the reform of Parliament itself. In mid-1972, not long before the election, a new party reflecting environmental concerns – the Values Party – emerged. While it made a modest electoral impact, it did raise public awareness of the possibility of an alternative to the mainstream parties and policies.

Further institutional reform

In 1970 publicly funded party research units were established in Parliament, following a recommendation by that year's Royal Commission on Parliamentary Salaries and Allowances.[18] It had been argued for some time that a parliamentary 'research secretariat' was needed, especially for backbenchers and the Opposition. From 1944 the National Party had a small research office headed by Martin Nestor, whose effectiveness was well-remembered by Labour members.[19] Labour lacked similar resources. Backbenchers were on their own even for typing correspondence. As Fraser Colman commented: 'It was often more speedy and sensible to write one's own correspondence in longhand, or, as I used to do … take it home – I had the good sense to marry a shorthand-typist.'[20] The lack of a centralised filing system or newspaper clipping service was a serious limitation. The library could not meet members' research needs because it was unable to provide politically focused ammunition. The limited amount of time the library's reference staff could spare was devoted to finding books, compiling bibliographies, making photocopies and summarising material for speeches.

The research units were expected to assist Parliament's scrutinising function, but not to the extent advocated by Crick and practised in the well-funded United States Congress. They comprised a director, two researchers, a clerk and a typist, working under the chief whips. From 1973 they were expanded to ten staff each. With the election of Social Credit's Bruce Beetham in 1978, a single researcher was allocated to this third party.[21] As the caucus committee system strengthened, the units turned towards a collective servicing function rather than assisting individual members. They built up files of newspaper clippings and other materials, prepared background papers and notes for speeches inside and outside the House, and helped with parliamentary questions.

Reforming parliamentary procedures remained on the agenda. In 1972 amid concern about its heavier workload, the House adopted the recommendations of the Standing Orders Committee.[22] The opening one-day debate on the Legislative Department estimates was abandoned, and discussion of the estimates was confined to 16 sitting days on the understanding that the Opposition could select the classes it wanted to debate. In a further concession to the Opposition, this debate now included matters of policy, which were removed from the ambit of the Public Expenditure Committee. The changes proved effective.[23]

Marshall agreed to an experimental joint whips' committee to settle on limits for debates. This was to work well for a time but fell into abeyance as conflict intensified after Muldoon became leader of the National Party.[24] The Standing Orders Committee also suggested that the House spend less time debating private members' bills, which often had two 'second readings', the first on their introduction. A second reading was usually allowed as a courtesy (but with no expectation of further consideration, as such bills generally involved appropriations).[25] These changes expedited business and little time was spent in the chamber beyond midnight.

Select committee work was made more efficient by reducing the number of members required (for most committees, from ten to seven) and by appointing committees for entire Parliaments so that they could work through the recess. Bills could now be referred directly to select committees after their first readings, and when reported back to the House without substantial amendment could be taken as a whole rather than clause by clause. However, it was felt impossible to alter sitting hours to free up more time for committee work during the session. Although the Standing Orders Committee recommended suspending sittings on Wednesday afternoons to facilitate committee work, this was not taken up. Instead the practice developed of short recesses of one or two weeks at about six-weekly intervals during sessions to allow committees to catch up with their work. This gave the work of select committees greater prominence.

Kirk and Hunt wanted to change the parliamentary timetable substantially. They urged that Parliament become a 'more continuous process', with the House adopting an explicit timetable, carrying over bills from one year to the next, and sitting for only three days a week, three weeks in four, for ten months a year.[26] This issue was addressed after Labour came to power in late 1972.

By the late 1960s the role of the Public Expenditure Committee had diminished.[27] Muldoon and other active committee members were now in cabinet, the government no longer heeded its recommendations, and the committee did not follow up on its work. Its reports were no longer debated in the House as they were now tabled very late in the session, and activity during the recesses diminished. From 1972 its discussions on the estimates could no longer include matters of policy.

When Labour won office, on Kirk's initiative Hunt took the chair of the committee to counter Muldoon.[28] Hunt stated that it would present a programme of reports to the House rather than relying on a single annual report, and more substantial investigations into expenditure were planned. These ambitions were not realised, although reports were again followed up more diligently. Most importantly, the estimates could not be considered in depth because of the lack of professional expertise. In 1973 an officer was appointed to the Legislative Department to provide independent, non-political advice. This was followed by the attachment of a liaison officer from the Audit Office, which strengthened the committee and improved the quality of its reports. The new party research units also helped to boost members' contributions to the committee.

The Public Expenditure Committee's profile and level of activity were raised significantly when the hardworking W.F. (Bill) Birch was appointed its chairman in 1976. His firm views on the role of the committee as a restraint on the executive and government departments were soon implemented through post-expenditure reviews of overspending departments and a revival of the work of subcommittees.[29] But the committee's reports were often not debated. In 1982 three permanent subcommittees were created to monitor areas of government activity, enhancing its scrutinising role. But it is a moot point whether such a powerful select committee boosted the control of the House over the executive or created an alternative power base for ambitious backbenchers.

Labour returns to office

There was euphoria when Labour won the 1972 election with a huge majority, 55 seats to 32. Mike Moore was elected at the startlingly young age of 23. Many older National members had either retired or been swept away. Labour left 'Siberia', accommodation for the Opposition that now showed signs of age as a result of Holyoake's parsimony.[30] Kirk had been the only one to have half-decent rooms at the front of the library, just off the portico, but even these were pretty dismal. 'The furniture was old,

Norman Kirk, elected for Lyttelton in 1957, became leader of the Labour Party in 1965. He led Labour to victory in 1972 and made an immediate impact as Prime Minister. After suffering from ill health for some time, he died in office on 31 August 1974.

Woolf, Parliamentary Service collection

the walls needed painting, the carpet square was ragged and the worn leather couches were unsightly.'[31] The stunned and much depleted National Opposition, which included new members Jim Bolger and Bill Birch, entered its new quarters without enthusiasm.

Labour refurbished members' offices, making more extensive use of carpets – Muldoon remarked on winning power in 1975: 'It's always good to have Labour in for a term. All the lino's gone.'[32] Historically he was not strictly correct, for National in the 1950s had dealt similarly with Labour's own years of neglect. Kirk's view was: 'Let's make [National] as comfortable as we can – then they will never want to get into Government'.[33]

From this time on, the expectation that the Speaker would have legal qualifications was abandoned. Stan Whitehead, a strong debater but with no legal background, was elected to the position. Like previous Labour Speakers, he attended caucus meetings and took part in debates, but the issue of his voting in Committee did not arise with such a large majority.[34] Whitehead had a good sense of humour and was tolerant, but proved insufficiently firm as the chamber became more turbulent, thanks to Muldoon and some Labour backbenchers.[35]

Kirk gave his ministers a complex, overlapping set of responsibilities to check their independence and enhance his own role. This sometimes caused confusion and conflict. Matiu Rata became the first Maori since Ngata to hold the Maori Affairs portfolio, while Whetu Tirikatene-Sullivan, the first woman in cabinet for 12 years, took tourism.[36] Rata and Tirikatene-Sullivan had entered Parliament in the 1960s aged 28 and 35 respectively, carrying the hopes of Maori for a younger generation of representatives.

S.P. Andrew collection, ATL, F20004¼

Whetu Tirikatene-Sullivan, of Ngai Tahu and Ngati Kahungunu descent, was elected for Southern Maori in 1967 in place of her father, Eruera Tirikatene, who had died. She had been a very fast verbatim court reporter and worked as a secretary for her father, often travelling around the vast Southern Maori electorate with him. Her selection to stand for the seat came after the belated discovery that the chosen male candidate could not speak Maori. She became Minister of Tourism, Minister for the Environment, and Associate Minister of Social Welfare in the third Labour government.

Tirikatene-Sullivan was keen to make Parliament more receptive to women and families. She was the first woman to give birth while a member. Determined that this would cause as little disruption as possible, she was back in the House less than two weeks after a caesarean birth in 1970. She looked after the baby in her room in Parliament, and took her round the electorate in a carry-cot in her car. She had two other babies. As her children grew up they would come to her room in the afternoons to do their homework before being picked up by their father. In the evening the family regularly dined together in Bellamy's. Tirikatene-Sullivan, like her father, would represent Southern Maori for about 30 years, being known as the 'Mother of the House' by the time she lost her seat in 1996.

Executive and Parliament: the balance at issue, 1970–84

Matiu Rata was elected for Northern Maori in 1963. He was Minister of Maori Affairs and of Lands in the period 1972–5. Under him the Treaty of Waitangi Act 1975 was passed, leading to the creation of the Waitangi Tribunal. In 1985 amended legislation extended the Tribunal's jurisdiction back to 1840, and the relationship between Maori and the Crown was placed on a new footing. Rata, however, had left Labour and resigned from Northern Maori in 1980 after a disagreement with Bill Rowling. He then formed the Mana Motuhake Party but was never re-elected. He died in 1997.

With the Labour victory, the pace of parliamentary reform appeared to quicken, but so, too, did conflict between the two parties. The reforms fell foul of the instability of politics. Labour had promised to summon Parliament in the second week of February and to divide sessions into two parts. It did establish a pattern of long sessions punctuated by recesses, heralding what would, a decade later under another Labour government, become a permanent feature of the parliamentary calendar.[37] But for now the strategy backfired because the government was not ready with its legislative programme when Parliament opened on 14 February 1973. There was a long recess (from March until June) while this was sorted out.

The Opposition, exhorted by Holyoake to get stuck in, gained the upper hand over Labour's inexperienced ministers, and the government at times failed to maintain a quorum.[38] Hugh Watt was the only minister with previous cabinet experience. Kirk gave as good as he got, but his ministers often remained buried in paperwork in the chamber, 'papers piled up about them, noses down, scribbling away, apparently oblivious of the debates'.[39] Kirk sometimes despaired of the quality of his front bench. The 'fearless and fearsome' Muldoon could reduce Labour to a 'leaderless rabble' when Kirk was out of the chamber, according to Templeton.[40]

On National's side, Marshall's gentlemanly approach was eclipsed by Muldoon's 'counterpunching' debating style.[41] Muldoon mobilised caucus support for an aggressive approach, had the senior and junior whips Lapwood and McLachlan as drinking mates, and socialised and kept in touch with backbench concerns and issues. Marshall, by comparison, was rather isolated from his colleagues, with whom he did not drink or socialise. His refined, finely honed speeches read well but did not carry the House. Muldoon, while not a dramatic orator, was extremely effective in delivering devastating, precise speeches that showed mastery of the material. He could think rapidly on his feet, had a quick wit, and responded to interjections ruthlessly. Hunt, who had the salutary experience early in his career of interjecting while Muldoon was speaking and being 'cut to pieces', strongly advised others not to do so.[42] Muldoon was prepared to push parliamentary procedure to the limits and sometimes beyond as he challenged Whitehead, whom he thought biased.

Progress on the government's legislative programme was slow, and there were notable incidents of disorderly behaviour and defiance of the Chair. Challenges to the Chairman of Committees, Ron Bailey, included an Opposition notice of motion criticising his performance.[43] At the end of July, Muldoon was ordered to withdraw from the chamber for defying Bailey

Robert Muldoon, the Minister of Finance, plays for the parliamentarians against the diplomats at Karori Park, 1971. When Parliament arranged annual cricket matches with the diplomatic corps, Mick Connelly took the captaincy. He and Bill Rowling were the leading batsmen.

and refusing to apologise in a proper manner. He had to be escorted out by the Serjeant-at-Arms. This followed a debate over members' wives that got out of control. Muldoon and Watt had sparred, with Watt bursting into tears and having to leave the House. Kirk, livid, was reported to have said to Marshall quietly but threateningly: 'Don't you ever let that creature [Muldoon] do that sort of thing again.'[44]

Having been unable to get a large number of bills through in 1973, Kirk (with the Opposition's endorsement) adopted the innovation of holding them over rather than letting them lapse. These bills included the controversial New Zealand Export-Import Corporation and New Zealand Superannuation Corporation Bills. Exhaustive consideration of the latter by a select committee included vitriolic attacks by Muldoon against the proposed scheme.[45] Hunt threatened to have him removed from the room.

Pressure to increase the number of representatives in the House had been maintained. The mounting work of select committees could not be done effectively as members engaged in 'musical chairs' in moving between them.[46] As one member described it in the mid 1960s: 'I had the misfortune to be on four select committees, and on one occasion all four were meeting. In helping to make quorums, I had to go from one committee to the other. I have known occasions in this Parliament when, to enable the Government to get a vote through in a committee … the Government majority turned up five minutes before we voted; they had not heard the discussion, but they were there for the vote and then went away.'[47]

The session of 1974, at 118 sitting days, was the longest ever, and one of the most contentious, opening on 4 February and closing on 8 November. From its early weeks it became bogged down, and Speaker Whitehead proved ineffective in dealing with points of order.[48] Muldoon was a persistently disruptive influence, and the government drifted as a result of Kirk's illness. Kirk decided to let Watt

Acting Prime Minister Hugh Watt delivers a speech in 1974, with Roussell in the Clerk's seat and female Hansard reporters taking notes.

lead the debate on the budget in early June, but could not resist summing up at the end of the debate. Increasingly distracted by interjections, he flagged and could not complete his speech before slumping exhausted in his seat.[49]

The legislative programme was swollen by the bills carried over and by many private members' bills. Muldoon – who had by now toppled Marshall as Leader of the Opposition – promised that Labour's superannuation scheme would be repealed as soon as National got into office. Acrimony intensified. On Muldoon's first day as leader in July, Labour made a determined effort to counter him. Points of order proliferated and interjections 'flew thick and fast'. According to Labour's Michael Bassett, National's chief whip, Harry Lapwood, threatened 'to push [his] teeth down [his] throat', while Rob Talbot offered to give him a black eye.[50] In concert with George Gair, Muldoon organised a systematic onslaught against weaker ministers. Muldoon continued to harrass the Speaker and criticised the new Chairman of Committees, Hunt, for taking part in debates. From this time onwards, the Speaker was to order members to withdraw from the chamber frequently. That such a sanction had become commonplace reflected declining standards of behaviour in the House.

The protracted struggle over superannuation dominated the session. Kirk decided that the bill should not be put through Committee part-by-part. Over 67 hours in Committee in early August, 589 speeches were made, 222 divisions taken and closure moved 104 times. The House sat through Saturday and until midnight, with Kirk now seriously ill.[51] Hunt recalled how Labour kept 40 members in the House at all times, rostered into teams, while on the other side Gair organised National teams to obstruct progress. During the session 355 divisions were taken.

Kirk died in the evening of 31 August from a heart attack. The House was shocked, for the gravity of his illness had been kept secret. Holyoake said in a generous tribute: 'It is almost impossible to believe that his big frame will not fill that empty seat … again.'[52] Parliament was adjourned for two weeks. Kirk was given a state funeral, which was particularly poignant – as Ballance's had been – because of the hopes and aspirations that he had come to symbolise for New Zealand as a nation, particularly for Maori and Pacific Islanders.[53] Labour elected Finance Minister Bill Rowling as the new leader and Prime Minister. Meanwhile New Zealand's economy began to experience difficulties as a balance of payments crisis followed the export boom.

Neither the conduct of the session nor its length was sufficient to shock members to make substantial changes to the standing orders.[54] Given the incessant use of closure to get business through, the Clerk of the House attempted – unavailingly – to get the Standing Orders Committee to adopt a 'guillotine' in preference to closure. Friday's sitting hours were changed to 9 a.m. to 1 p.m. to facilitate the return of members to their electorates.[55] Bills could be held over from one session to the next. The increased number of questions – more than double that of 1972 – saw the daily time allotted extended to 40 minutes.[56] A limit of two hours was imposed on bills' introductory debates. Outdated private bills' standing orders were revised and a new position of Deputy Chairman of Committees was created. The committee urged also that members refrain from vexatious notices of motion, and the Speaker was given authority to vet notices – but this made little difference.[57]

With Rowling less persuaded than Kirk of the advantages of an early start, Parliament opened in late March 1975.[58] This session featured notable free votes on private members' bills concerning homosexuality and abortion. The Electoral Act Committee, chaired by Hunt, produced a majority report on enlarging the House to 121 members to lighten workloads, increase the pool of talent and possibly increase the number of Maori seats.[59] National opposed the resulting Electoral Amendment Bill, and since the alteration of such entrenched measures required 75 per cent support, the bill failed after lengthy and bitter debate in Committee.[60]

Parliament's role in protecting its privileges changed considerably at this time. Since the nineteenth century hearings of alleged breaches of privilege had been rare, usually concerned with newspaper reporting, and relatively uncontroversial. The task of the Privileges Committee – comprising the Attorney-General (in the chair), the Prime Minister and his Deputy, and the Leader of the Opposition and his

Deputy – now became increasingly contentious. In a heated chamber, members themselves came under scrutiny. When in 1975 Muldoon published an article alleging a lack of impartiality on the part of the Speaker, he was brought before the Privileges Committee. After a stormy debate a majority found that a breach had been committed. This was only the fourth occasion, and the first since 1912, that a member had been found to have breached parliamentary privilege.[61] Muldoon insisted that a transvestite Wellington night-club performer, Carmen, be called before the committee for allegations made on television concerning the sexual activities of members. Carmen admitted there was no foundation to the claims and had to apologise. The committee described this as a 'tasteless and contrived affair'.[62]

As the political temperature rose and such incidents proliferated, the Privileges Committee became more politicised. Muldoon described it as a 'kangaroo court'.[63] Alleging breach of privilege became merely a form of retaliatory action, to the extent that from 1979 Parliament adopted the House of Commons' procedure in its standing orders. Members now had to raise the matter in writing privately with the Speaker first. Many vexatious complaints of breach were made; virtually no allegations were taken up.

With members also invoking privilege much more often to protect statements made in the House, the legal relationship between Parliament and the public became more contentious. Consideration of a charge of breach of privilege became more judicialised, involving the hearing of witnesses, written submissions and legal representation. In 1980, the Privileges Committee considered a complaint that senior minister Duncan MacIntyre had misled the House over his involvement with an application by his daughter for a marginal lands loan.[64] The committee decided that, to sustain the charge, there must be 'proof on the balance of probabilities' that a member had intended to mislead the House. The proof required was of a very high order, and by majority decision a breach of privilege was not found. From 1982 the Speaker, at the urging of the Privileges Committee, more actively weeded out trivial and technical charges of privilege that did not need to occupy the time of the committee.

As the 1975 election approached, debate became increasingly bitter and Rowling regularly imposed urgency to get business through. The demands of the long sittings, the conflict-riven House, and harassment of the Speaker took their toll on Whitehead, who suffered a heart attack in August and never really recovered. Hunt took over. Aided by a good understanding of standing orders and 'a schoolmasterly determination to brook no nonsense', he brought the House under firmer control.[65] Marshall, retiring after 29 years in the House, felt 1975 had been the most acrimonious session of his career – he wanted 'personal attacks and character assassination' taken out of Parliament.[66] In a controversial valedictory speech, Muldoon advised the Speaker and the Chairman of Committees to lean more towards the Opposition and to listen and pause before ruling.[67]

The election campaign, one of the most spectacular in New Zealand's history, was noted for Muldoon's barnstorming roadshow, which packed halls, and for the powerful influence of television. The 1970s saw the decline of a mass-based, two-party system, the rise of television, and the projection of the personalities of political leaders into the mass media to a much greater extent.[68] Muldoon appreciated the power of 'political television' and used the medium very effectively to speak directly to the voters. National's overwhelming victory completely reversed the 1972 result.

Outgoing members pack up after the defeat of the Labour government, December 1975. From left: Jack Ridley, Aubrey Begg, and Michael Bassett.

Executive and Parliament: the balance at issue, 1970–84

Executive power

As National was re-elected, the Beehive was rising into the sky. The symbolic association was apt, for Muldoon as Prime Minister was to orchestrate a strengthening of executive power that fundamentally altered the political landscape. It was as if all the postwar elements of increased executive power that had been associated with the two-party system, and which had functioned benignly in circumstances of relative prosperity and tranquillity, became concentrated and exaggerated in changed circumstances. New Zealand was now struggling with instability, inflation, recession and unemployment. The ultimate outcome was, paradoxically, a definite reversal of the balance between executive and Parliament rather than the further entrenchment of executive power.

Rob Muldoon delivers his last budget, July 1983. Elected to Tamaki for National in 1960, he retained the seat until his resignation in 1991. He became Minister of Finance, 1967–72, and Prime Minister, 1975–84.

Muldoon worked hard and had an excellent memory for detail. He was decisive, and could grasp key issues immediately and absorb a huge amount of information.[69] He also had an extremely good knowledge of standing orders, and was to be the last Prime Minister who viewed the House and its procedures and debates as central to the functioning of government. He respected the institution's rituals and rules while exploiting them to the hilt for political advantage.

Muldoon promised a more open style of government – both in relation to the general public and within cabinet and caucus.[70] However, his force of personality and his combined roles as Prime Minister and Minister of Finance led him to dominate cabinet and usually caucus, aided by whips such as Birch who gained a formidable reputation as a hard worker and as an operator who could get business through.[71]

Given the many new backbenchers, Muldoon had limited flexibility in choosing his cabinet. This situation reinforced longstanding concern over the limited pool of talent available for governments in such a small House, and would contribute to parliamentary reform.[72] Following Rowling's initiative, Muldoon established a separate Prime Minister's Department. The Press Office in the department was reorganised and a group of journalists appointed. The office became more overtly political and was closely integrated with the policy process, leading to a more general acceptance of the management of news.[73]

Muldoon's autocratic tendencies were accentuated and he became more isolated. As his socialising and drinking sessions in the precincts largely came to an end, he had little contact with backbenchers.[74] The loyal Colin McLachlan was one of his few remaining 'mates'. Muldoon's attitude to the media changed after he achieved power.[75] He had previously used it to attack Labour. Now the boot was on the other foot. The new style of investigative journalism was spearheaded by men such as Richard Long, Tom Scott and Colin James, who annoyed Muldoon, and before long a confrontational atmosphere developed.[76] He called the three leading press gallery journalists – Long, Richard Harman and Dick Griffin – 'the three dicks'.[77] Another press gallery irritant was Scott, who injected a novel, irreverent tone into his reporting, 'making Parliament a warmly human place in which fallible mortals grappled with their exalted tasks'.[78]

Muldoon refused to convene Parliament until mid 1976, a delay that some, particularly in Labour circles, saw as unconstitutional. To be fair, Muldoon had previously criticised Labour's approach to sessional timetables, arguing that the Public Expenditure and other select committees could not adequately function without a substantial recess, that members were unable to service their electorates, and that their health suffered from protracted sessions.[79] He believed in the traditional, compressed session, suggesting that a 'parliamentary Parkinson's Law' took over, with debate swelling to fill the time available, if the discipline imposed by shorter sessions was relaxed.

Immediately after the swearing in of his government, Muldoon effectively abolished Labour's superannuation scheme, as promised in National's election manifesto.[80] For this alleged constitutional impropriety he was taken to court. Chief Justice Wild found that Muldoon had suspended the law without the consent of Parliament, contrary to the Bill of Rights of 1688. This case (*Fitzgerald v. Muldoon*) was a landmark in reaffirming that the executive could not suspend the law.

National's huge majority and the entry of a younger generation of backbenchers made for a more lively relationship between a cabinet dominated by ex-servicemen and an energetic caucus. Two new backbench National members – Mike Minogue and Marilyn Waring – took a central role in the executive/Parliament debates that followed.[81] Waring – elected at the age of 23 – chose to sit in the front row of caucus directly in front of Muldoon, and rapidly made her views known. She was soon appointed to the powerful Public Expenditure Committee (subsequently chairing it). She remained on the committee until 1984. Minogue immediately criticised the growth of executive power and bureaucratic secrecy, and was soon at loggerheads with Muldoon. In contrast, Labour was greatly weakened. Many of those elected in 1972 had lost their seats, the party's debating strength was much diminished, and its organisation by the whips was deficient.[82]

Public protest became more visible again with Muldoon at the helm, and the bitterness of the election campaign spilled over into the House. The opening of Parliament, protected by heavy security, was disrupted by a demonstration of many thousands.[83] After Labour held a public rally on the steps of the General Assembly Library in April to protest against the government's tardy calling of Parliament, party-political rallies in the grounds were banned. Speaker Jack said that he did not want a 'Hyde Park Corner' atmosphere.[84]

Once Parliament was in session there was much turbulence. Urgency was taken often and many hours were spent in the chamber after midnight. This pattern, which was to characterise following sessions, was an eye-opener for new members.[85] Labour refused to endorse Jack's re-election to the Speakership, arguing that he had shown a lack of discipline in the previous Parliament, having had to withdraw from the chamber himself.[86] The Opposition fought the repeal of the superannuation legislation tooth and nail. Hunt introduced a bill requiring Parliament to be summoned within 90 days of an election and preventing an early dissolution of Parliament by the Governor-General without Parliament's consent, as had recently happened to the Whitlam government in Australia.[87] Hunt was later suspended for a day after being found – by majority report – to have committed a breach of privilege by saying in a radio interview that Jack was weak and should be replaced.[88]

Confrontation in the House reached a climax during a fierce exchange over the supplementary estimates in early November. Labour blocked the estimates, with finance spokesman Tizard breaking

The Maori 'tent embassy'. The land march arrived at Parliament in October 1975 after winding its way down from Northland. Initially it appeared that hundreds would remain on the main steps. When Acting Speaker Hunt asked Roussell what could be done, the Clerk suggested that he retire to the Speaker's flat and pray for a southerly and rain. This weather duly arrived and the numbers thinned out, apart from a few who slept in tents pitched on the lawn. Hunt gave approval for them to remain, but the incoming Prime Minister, Rob Muldoon, ordered police to remove them. Thirty-six arrests were made. The resulting court case confirmed that Hunt's authority had lapsed once Parliament had been dissolved. Muldoon's direction was therefore valid. The law was later changed to give the Speaker continued authority after the dissolution of Parliament.

tradition by speaking on the second reading. Muldoon was outraged and National countered with a barrage of points of order that prevented Tizard from speaking. The debate degenerated into personal abuse. Amidst a 'gaggle of interjections', Muldoon drew attention to Moyle's 'effeminate giggles'.[89] When Moyle riposted that Muldoon's accountancy firm engaged in dishonest practices, Muldoon accused Moyle of having been picked up by the police for homosexual activities. The Speaker ordered both men to withdraw and apologise and Labour walked out wholesale, whereupon the estimates went straight through.[90] The following day Labour walked out again as Muldoon rose to speak.

Controversy swirled around the House as Moyle denied that there was anything in what Muldoon had said and gave explanations for the incident. Muldoon then offered to table the relevant police file. In the end Moyle resigned during the recess, and an enquiry on which Rowling insisted found that Muldoon had not breached rules concerning access to police files.[91] Apparently the incident, which had occurred in June 1975, had been common knowledge around Parliament. Muldoon claimed that he had heard of it through a press gallery journalist. The 'Moyle affair' cast a pall over Parliament,

283

The Security Intelligence Bill provoked considerable protest in 1977. Here a large crowd gathers in the grounds on 14 October with the nearly complete Beehive looming in the background. Following another protest in the grounds on 18 October, demonstrators went into the chamber, singing 'God Defend New Zealand' and hissing, clapping and chanting from the gallery. A New Zealand flag draped over the balustrade fell onto the floor of the House. The galleries were cleared and four people who refused to leave were arrested.

Dominion Post collection, ATL, EP/1977/4060/20

creating an atmosphere of intimidation and fear of retaliation that particularly affected Labour members. Rowling, who had attempted to have the Standing Orders Committee reconvened to consider the standard of conduct in Parliament, said in the valedictory for the session that the public image of Parliament had never sunk so low and that the session had been disastrous.[92] David Lange was elected in Moyle's place in 1977, in a by-election for the safe seat of Mangere. His potential was recognised from the start. Amidst sustained applause at the end of Lange's notable maiden speech, Harry Lapwood shouted out, with some foresight, 'Watch it, Bill [Rowling], he's breathing down your neck.'[93]

The 1977 session was long, abrasive and characterised by divisive legislation. The relationship between Minogue and Muldoon deteriorated to breaking point after Minogue appeared on television to criticise the Security Intelligence Service Bill. Muldoon called him disloyal and, although the affair was patched up, the underlying division remained. The bill's passage was accompanied by huge demonstrations and disturbances in the public gallery that resulted in the arrest of some protesters.[94]

Considerable controversy surrounded cabinet minister David Thomson's restrictive private member's Contraception, Sterilisation and Abortion Bill for which there was a free vote. It inevitably caused serious rifts within National.[95] After exhausting debates and many amendments, the bill was passed at the end of the session. To formalise the Labour government's practice, the Legislature Act was amended to allow Parliament to carry out its business between sessions and between Parliaments. Bills could be held over, and members could engage in select committee work before being sworn in. On the night before the session closed, Labour walked out in the early hours after Muldoon failed to honour a promise that the session would be wrapped up.[96] The government's response was to put through more bills.

At 118 sitting days, the session equalled 1974 in length. From September, Dick Harrison had stood in as Speaker, as Jack was incapacitated following surgery. Jack died in the Speaker's suite on Christmas Eve. Another event marking the passage of time was the retirement of Holyoake, the Father of the House, after 40 years of service stretching back to 1932. Holyoake was controversially appointed Governor-General.

When Harrison was elected as the new Speaker at the beginning of the 1978 session, he made more than the traditional symbolic reluctance to assume the mantle as he was led to the chair.[97] He proved firm, handled the chamber fairly and managed to maintain his good humour. He had to deal with the entry of Social Credit into Parliament, which created procedural difficulties when speakers were called, and contend with increased disorder in the chamber. Harrison devised a useful new sanction, the 'sin bin', under which members left the chamber for a period to 'cool off'.[98] But the practice – giving them a 'yellow card', as later Speaker Hunt, termed it – meant that ejection became more commonplace, and for a time in the 1980s the number rose alarmingly.

To the shock of National, the leader of Social Credit, Bruce Beetham, won the 1978 by-election in the blue ribbon National seat of Rangitikei following Jack's death. Beetham joined two 'independents' – National's Gavin Downie, who had disagreed with candidate selection procedure, and Gerald O'Brien, who had failed to be reselected by Labour – on the cross benches. Meanwhile, in the first such instance for some time, two National members crossed the floor to vote against a clause of the government's Industrial Law Reform Bill. In a rather strange spectacle, Labour endorsed the clause.[99]

During this session Labour stonewalled the supplementary estimates. In late September, the House sat under urgency through a night and into the following day.[100] By morning the Hansard staff had collapsed from exhaustion and were sent home, leaving only a tape recorder to record proceedings. The House was thrown into consternation but the Clerk, alert to the situation, explained that this had happened before, during the notorious stonewall of 1876. Hansard returned that afternoon to loud applause. Further late nights followed the next week, notable only for Rata's singing of an old Maori lament in the early hours.[101] Prominent members retired at the end of the session in early October. Blanchfield delivered a parting poem of his own composition, Finlay reflected on political power with the aid of Thomas Gray's 'Elegy', and Gordon and Lapwood cracked jokes liberally.[102]

As the election approached, Rowling promised a '15 step' reform of Parliament that included Labour's proposal for a revised parliamentary timetable. National responded by promising a Standing Orders Committee. Muldoon was concerned about the 'childish farce' of notices of motion and how the estimates debate had developed, with matters of policy fair game in a contentious and partisan environment. In general, however, he favoured the status quo.[103]

National went into the 1978 election with some foreboding, because of the re-emergence of Social Credit and rising unemployment. National won the election but with a substantially reduced majority and slighter fewer votes in total than Labour. National's new cabinet was younger and less dominated by farmers. Muldoon had lost key supporters through retirement and the defeat of Bert Walker. Young, liberal, free-enterprise National backbenchers such as Ian McLean, Michael Cox and Doug Kidd now formed an assertive 'alternative caucus'.[104] Muldoon emphasised the need for discipline and team cohesion – crossing the floor was a serious matter, he warned.

There was a substantial delay before Parliament was called. The opening in mid May 1979 was disrupted by a large demonstration.[105] Muldoon intimated that he would reduce income tax while Parliament was in recess, but after Labour criticism, backbench concern and opposition from former

John Richard Harrison was born in Hastings on 23 May 1921. He was educated at Wanganui Collegiate School and graduated from Canterbury University College with a BA in 1941. During the latter years of the war, as Major, he commanded a company of the 23rd Battalion. Elected for Hawke's Bay in 1963, he was appointed junior government whip (1970–1), Chairman of Committees (1972), senior Opposition whip (1974–5), Chairman of Committees (1976–7), and acted as Speaker when Jack fell ill in 1977. He became Speaker in 1978 and held the office until 1984. Knighted in 1980, Harrison died in 2003.

leader Marshall, he agreed to bring Parliament together again earlier. Taxes could only be altered by Parliament, not by regulation.

The new National breed was to the fore in the Address-in-Reply debate, calling for a reduction in regulations and controls.[106] Muldoon was forced to abandon planned fiscal regulation in the face of vociferous opposition from his new backbenchers.[107] His inclinations were manifest nonetheless in a National Development Bill that was made necessary by the government's determination to build the Clyde dam despite likely delays in securing planning approval. This bill required many late nights for its passage.

This major energy project and others were later collectively known as 'Think Big'. The plan was orchestrated by Birch, Minister of Energy and National Development, in response to the impact of the two 'oil shocks' of the 1970s. While the House was in Committee Geoffrey Palmer attempted to include in the National Development Bill the requirement that Orders in Council be ratified by Parliament. Although Labour lost the division on the amendment, 46 to 41, three dissident National members – Minogue, Waring and Ian Shearer – crossed the floor. Speaker Harrison voted for the measure.[108] Waring later observed that she 'had crossed the floor and on a few occasions, with the knowledge only of the Whips and the Prime Minister, I had left the House because I did not wish to vote', without censure.[109] Labour protested against Harrison's vote with a notice of motion censuring the Speaker. The National Development Act was opposed by many, including the Coalition for Open Government, which was led by a former Ombudsman, Sir Guy Powles. The Act typified the excesses of executive power that were now seen as characteristic of the Muldoon government.[110]

The promised review of the standing orders resulted in minor changes made in the early hours of the morning at the fag end of this session.[111] Beetham, who had been excluded from the Standing Orders Committee, referred to it as a 'cosy two-party club'.[112] Further streamlining of procedure took place. Third readings were to be confined to the general principles of the bill, with speeches limited to ten minutes each. Imprest Supply debates were limited to four hours and the supplementary estimates to four and a half hours. Private members' bills – which had increased in number substantially from the late 1960s – would get less time. Any requiring appropriations were to go no further than an introductory debate unless they were referred to a select committee.[113]

Traditionally the Prime Minister had also been Leader of the House. This was now made a separate responsibility, and given to David Thomson, a senior cabinet minister, marking the beginning of a withdrawal of the Prime Minister from the day-to-day fray of the House. Muldoon was an acknowledged master of parliamentary procedure, but he had apparently conceded that his temperament and responsibilities created difficulties in organising the business of the House.[114] Later Prime Ministers were far less involved with parliamentary procedure or interested in taking a central role in debates. From this time the Leader of the House regularly announced the planned business for the week on the preceding Friday morning.[115]

Select committees were strengthened considerably, as all bills were now sent to them after their first reading.[116] They were becoming a much more integral part of Parliament, often meeting three mornings a week and opening their proceedings to the public. From 1967 committee chairs and ministers were able to make brief public statements while committees deliberated, and on occasion committees allowed the press access when considering controversial issues.[117]

After the election of Labour in 1972, select committees became more active and were opened up to the media. They met over the recess, following the example of the Public Expenditure Committee from 1962 and the Local Bills Committee from 1966. Some began to examine the estimates related to their terms of reference.[118] More ad hoc committees were also appointed. By the 1980s virtually all committees were open to the media. However, the traditional injunction against the publication of committee proceedings prior to their being tabled in the House remained. In 1976 television reporter Simon Walker was found guilty of a breach of privilege for divulging select committee proceedings, and in 1984 a reporter and the *New Zealand Times* were called before the Privileges Committee for a similar transgression.[119]

Advisory officers were employed to support the work of committees, following the experience of the special committee set up in 1970 to examine compensation for personal injury, for which counsel was provided.[120] Two permanent officers were appointed to service committees, and others were to be employed on an ad hoc basis when needed. As people became more aware of select committees, the number of submissions to them increased considerably.

In the 1970s nearly half of all bills introduced into the House were considered by select committees, largely after their first readings (including a substantial proportion of private members' bills).[121] The number of petitions rose again after the decline in the middle decades of the century. Hearing petitions became a substantial, if subsidiary, activity for committees.[122] The focus had shifted, however, from individual petitioners and personal grievances to petitions from organisations about public policy. National's back bench wanted committees to be able to consider amendments to bills that were broadly consistent with their policy direction, and pressure for committees to be able to initiate enquiries mounted.[123]

Labour wanted much more. Just before he retired, former Attorney-General Martyn Finlay described existing reforms as merely a 'popular parlour pursuit'.[124] Hunt – Labour's spokesman on such issues – called the changes 'timid, frightened, archaic, and conservative'. Geoffrey Palmer told the House that while the standing orders held 'the key to the reform of Parliament', at present they ensured that it remained a 'creature' of the executive.[125] Labour's amendments were defeated. Ralph Maxwell's Reform of Parliament Bill, intended as a check on the executive and embodying Labour's 1978 election manifesto proposals, including a revised parliamentary calendar, was also rejected.[126]

The entry of Palmer into the House through a by-election in 1979 was to have profound consequences.[127] Coming from a background of academic constitutional law, he was an energetic and enthusiastic crusader who would transform the perspective of the erstwhile cautious and conservative Labour Party on such matters. After a meteoric rise to power he would be extremely influential in reforming the electoral system and Parliament.

The Beehive

Following the decision to proceed with the Beehive, the south wall of the main buildings was completed by the end of 1968.[128] This slightly extended the side of the building and added 30 rooms, easing the accommodation problem and providing much-needed additional toilets, but it did not greatly improve the look of the south wall. Ministers, members and the Law Drafting Office then moved out of the old wooden buildings, the front section of which was quickly knocked down in late 1969.[129] The preserved rear was moved back towards Museum Street and extended as temporary accommodation for Bellamy's and the post office. New offices for many government members were built above the temporary Bellamy's, while 'Lockwood' buildings at the rear of the library were pressed into service.

Meanwhile, the Government Architect provided a disturbing report on the main buildings' lack of integrity in a severe earthquake. The risk to the chamber was particularly high.[130] The Commissioner of Works tried to smooth troubled waters by suggesting that the report was rather pessimistic; perhaps an independent engineer's report should be obtained? Holyoake thought that the 1964 report, which suggested that strengthening was feasible, offered sufficient reassurance, and the Ministry of Works was asked to investigate strengthening the chamber.[131] Unenthusiastically, the Ministry looked at fitting external columns. It emphasised that strengthening would have a limited effect at considerable cost – the buildings would still be unable to withstand a major earthquake. Why spend the money when the buildings would eventually have to be pulled down anyway?

National member W.L. Young in 1973 in the 'Lockwood' office he occupied at the rear of the buildings as the pressure on accommodation worsened. This part of the precincts was known as 'Siberia'.

Work on the Beehive began with the excavation of a deep basement and underground carpark.[132] The stage I contract for the podium, underground carpark and basement (including a national Civil Defence Centre), let to W.M. Angus, was completed in 1972. The parliamentary forecourt was then restored with patterned paving, raised flowerbeds and a frontage of native trees and shrubs. The facade of the main buildings was lit at night. Stage II was let that year to Gibson and O'Connor, with a projected completion date of December 1977. Construction was to be in two parts, so that the building up to floor three could be used before the entire structure was completed. This staged approach would allow Bellamy's to move in and the remaining portion of the old wooden buildings to be demolished, enabling in turn the completion of the Museum Street Annex of the Beehive, which was to house the Law Drafting Office, a carpark and a swimming pool.

The walls of the lower floors made extensive use of marble, and the exterior of the podium was clad in Coromandel granite to match the main buildings. All internal timber finishing was indigenous, with tawa and rimu used extensively.[133] New furniture, largely in tawa, was manufactured locally. The furnishings were designed by the Ministry of Works, predominantly in brown and russet tones. Bellamy's would use the same tableware in all dining rooms; the crockery was commissioned from Crown Lynn and incorporated a stylised Maori motif. 'Lounges' with comfortable low seating replaced the old-style 'bars' with high counters. Artworks were commissioned for the public areas.

As construction progressed the House Committee voiced qualms about the practicality for Bellamy's of the Beehive's circular multi-level design.[134] The heart of the problem lay in the many service outlets and the need to distribute food and liquor over three floors. The Tourist Hotel Corporation (THC), which had been approached to take over the ailing institution, wanted many changes to the layout. It also slated the catering and demanded full control of staff, salaries and expenditure.[135] Parliament agreed to the THC's terms, and the location of Bellamy's services was much revised. Parliament guaranteed that the THC would not have to bear any loss, and would be paid a management fee for operating the service. Any profits would go towards maintaining Bellamy's. The quality of the food was considerably improved.

Dominion Post collection, ATL, C5707½

The Beehive's foundations – a massive circular nine-foot-thick raft-like structure – were a 'hive of activity in concrete and steel'. Note the completed south wall of the main buildings, and in the foreground the remains of Bellamy's.

The increased number of members (from 84 to 92 by 1978) proved difficult to accommodate, especially when the temporary offices on the rear upper floor of the old wooden buildings were demolished for the construction of the Beehive.[136] Opposition members moved into the 'Lockwood' buildings at the rear of the library and further temporary accommodation was provided between the older rear portion of the General Assembly Library and the main buildings. These offices were then also known as 'Siberia'.

Bellamy's moved into the Beehive over the 1975–6 summer recess with new staff. The Queen duly unveiled a commemorative plaque in the reception hall in February 1977. The building was formally 'topped-off' by Muldoon in May 1977.[137] Progress on the upper floors was slow and the cost of stage II escalated significantly as a result of increased labour and material costs, the variations made necessary by the unusual design, and under-estimates of some expenditure, particularly on the swimming pool.[138]

In September 1979 the executive moved into the Beehive, which became a striking symbol of the

The Beehive nears completion, c. 1977. It had three 'social' floors on its lower levels: an impressive reception foyer on the ground floor with a grand staircase to the first floor, a first-floor reception room for state banquets, members' and other dining rooms, bars and lounges, as well as a television and radio interview room and a theatrette. Floors four to seven comprised 18 ministerial suites and meeting rooms. Floors eight and nine were allocated to the Prime Minister's Department and Prime Minister's suite respectively, while the tenth floor housed the cabinet room.

state, used in countless publications and associated with the executive powers exercised by the National government.[139] Muldoon brought with him his old furniture, including his chair passed down from Holyoake, and at his insistence the old oval cabinet table in indigenous woods was moved into the tenth-floor cabinet room.[140] Security was beefed up. Traditionally it had been minimal, with a lone police officer in the entrance lobby complementing the many elderly and sometimes rather frail messengers.[141] There was no check on visitors coming and going. For the first time official security guards were employed and identification cards were required for entry. The division bells were now to be rung for five minutes to allow ministers to get to the House for divisions. The time allowed was determined by having the oldest messenger available walk from the upper floors of the Beehive to the chamber. By early 1981 the two-storey Museum Street Annex behind the Beehive was also finished.

The completion of the Beehive meant much greater public access to Parliament Buildings and the grounds.[142] Regular guided tours of the main buildings had been instituted in the early 1970s, with the highly decorated Maori Affairs Committee room a feature. Now that the reception hall and Bellamy's were finished, groups could use the facilities if hosted or sponsored by a member – not only 'parties of constituents' but also 'book-launching ceremonies, school parties, farewells to bands, welcomes to visiting footballers, and State luncheons'.[143] From 1987 annual 'Parliament Weeks' and from 1994

290

From left: John Banks, Jonathan Elworthy, Warren Cooper, Marilyn Waring and Philip Burdon on a run around Wellington's waterfront. In the 1970s members participated in the emerging fitness boom. Clerk Roussell provided an example to emulate. He had represented New Zealand in both tennis and badminton, had a low golf handicap, and was an enthusiastic jogger. With Dr Gerard Wall in the House from 1970, members had expertise close at hand to minister to their needs, particularly back complaints. The 'Wall treatment' involving manipulation of the neck and spine was very popular. With Roussell's encouragement, Speaker Jack donned a tracksuit for discreet late-night jogs around Parliament grounds and Thorndon. Holyoake did not approve of such newfangled recreational pursuits. When a sweaty and panting new member, Warren Cooper, passed by his ministerial car on the forecourt and stopped to ask Holyoake how he kept fit, he retorted that he attended the funerals of 'young fellows' who had killed themselves jogging. By the 1980s squads of younger members setting off from Parliament on lunchtime runs were becoming a familiar sight.

NZH, 24 April 1982

biennial 'Youth Parliaments' were held to promote the institution to schoolchildren. The latter involved questions to 'ministers', debates, and 'select committee' work.

The press gallery had clamoured for improved accommodation for years. As the gallery expanded in the 1970s, its situation became dire, with nearly 40 journalists crammed into five rooms and other weekly newspaper reporters without any space at all.[144] The completion of the Beehive enabled the gallery to expand and a communal social room on the second floor of the main buildings was made available. A small television studio was developed adjacent to the chamber, and the Beehive had its own television studio.

By now the press gallery had lost its premier position in journalism, and political reporting was no longer a lifetime career. Reporters were much younger, many were female, and they left the gallery much earlier (often for more lucrative positions in public relations). Turnover was rapid and accumulated experience was at a premium. In the early 1980s reporters' lack of understanding of parliamentary privilege was commented upon pointedly by the House. Reporting was 'much less than adequate', with an undue focus on 'dramatic incidents', a lack of 'analysis or balance', and a failure to report select committees systematically, according to the Standing Orders Committee.[145] In 1984 there were 60 reporters housed in 15 rooms, and another 12 weekly journalists. At this time there were 12 women in the gallery; by 1991 there were 20. Into the 1990s women began to take a leading role in reporting Parliament as the old male culture disappeared. Journalists such as Jane Clifton, Jane Young and Linda Clark made their mark.[146]

The campaign to replace the main buildings with a modern earthquake-resistant structure continued, with the Labour government of the early 1970s seeming particularly keen.[147] Independent reports concluded that the buildings would be a hazard even in moderate earthquakes and that, while they could be strengthened to withstand a moderate to strong earthquake, it was not possible to guard against a severe one. Some limited strengthening could improve the buildings, but this should be regarded as temporary and not an alternative to eventual demolition.

The Ministry of Works again proposed demolition in 1973.[148] It also recommended that the General Assembly Library be demolished and the entire site apart from the Beehive be redeveloped in stages. The Minister of Works accepted this and in 1975 recommended demolishing the existing buildings, the temporary accommodation of Parliament in a planned conference centre complex, and an architectural competition for new buildings. Treasury questioned the move, saying that Works had prejudged the issue and not adequately investigated alternatives. The matter was delayed until after the election.

The rear of the library building (the west wing), the walls of which had been weakened in the 1907 fire, was an immediate and dangerous earthquake risk. A 1975 report concluded that this section must be demolished. A number of politicians still believed the entire library building should go – 'they're going to pull down this old dump once we're out of it'.[149] A further report in 1981 suggested that the main library building must be either strengthened or demolished. Demolition was ruled out by this time, however, because the building was now regarded as having architectural and historical significance and had received an Historic Places Trust classification.[150]

Unbridled power?

The House continued to be turbulent and difficult to control. Labour's Richard Prebble, who was adept in using the standing orders, gained a reputation as 'the scourge of the Government' and got into frequent confrontations with the Prime Minister. Muldoon accused him of 'a contempt for the Speaker and the Chairman of Committees that is unprecedented … the habit of interrupting Mr Speaker and the Chairman of Committees when they are on their feet, and the open public disagreement with their comments, does considerable damage'.[151] This may have been a case of the pot calling the kettle black, but the problem was real.

The 1980 session was long and fractious, and much occupied with the liberalisation of shop trading hours.[152] Muldoon's authoritarian tendencies were accentuated and his relationship with the news media went from bad to worse. He refused to be interviewed on television by Simon Walker or Ian Fraser, then banned journalist Tom Scott from his press conferences.[153] In 1983 Muldoon and his cabinet refused to co-operate with the *Dominion* after it published leaked information and in 1984, to outraged protest, he moved to charge rent for the press gallery's accommodation, banned tape recorders from his interviews and press conferences, and complained to the Speaker about the behaviour of one journalist.[154]

In the early 1980s the gallery was also having to confront other issues.[155] Accreditation was one – the gallery was now 50 to 60 strong, and demand for entry continued. Another was the introduction of new forms of newsgathering such as Newztel, operated by two former National press secretaries, which provided information in text on television screens. The Speaker insisted on Newztel being allowed into the gallery, in spite of resistance from journalists on the basis that it was politically orientated and not a genuine news organisation. In 1984 the gallery attempted to control its size by revising its rules to restrict access to those who covered political issues and reported Parliament.

Both major political parties were in strife during 1980. Muldoon highlighted the lack of discipline in Labour's ranks by organising concerted desertions of the chamber to show that the Opposition did not have the 20 members needed for a quorum in the House. Chief Opposition whip Hunt engaged in similar tactics.[156] Dissatisfaction with Muldoon's leadership culminated in the abortive 'colonels' coup'. A challenge was mounted while Muldoon was overseas, only to collapse when deputy leader Brian Talboys hesitated to take over.[157] Talboys resigned from the position and was replaced by MacIntyre. The loss of another safe seat to Social Credit in a by-election when Gary Knapp won East Coast Bays added fuel to the flames.

Rowling, for his part, narrowly survived a no-confidence motion in the Labour caucus. The split within the party between the Rowling and Lange factions was epitomised by the 'alternative budget' of Roger Douglas, published as Social Credit surprisingly scored higher than Labour in an opinion poll.[158] At the end of the session Muldoon had to be ordered back into the chamber to apologise to Lange for calling him a 'liar'.[159] The Prime Minister had stormed out, pursued by anxious National colleagues. He was eventually found and escorted back by the Serjeant-at-Arms. Speaker Harrison admitted that this was 'one of the most difficult and distasteful actions' he had had to deal with.

The 'fish and chip brigade'. Coup leaders Lange, Bassett, Douglas and Moore eat together immediately after the special caucus meeting that confirmed Rowling's leadership by one vote, 12 December 1980.

The 1981 session was overshadowed by the controversy over the tour to New Zealand by the Springbok rugby team. Muldoon saw electoral advantage in sitting on the fence. Parliament did not meet until well into the year, and the session was relatively short and notable for the complete lack of use of the closure motion. During the Address-in-Reply there was an extended debate on the tour. The House eventually passed a motion urging the New Zealand Rugby Football Union to reconsider its invitation to the Springboks to tour, but National would not countenance Labour's motion to refuse them visas. Waring was forced by National to vote against this motion. She was 'frogmarched' into the House by two colleagues, reportedly screaming and yelling.[160]

When the Rugby Union went ahead with the tour the House, like the country, was completely polarised over the issue. Hunt recalled that members usually sat together at breakfast in Bellamy's. During the tour the whips instructed Labour members not to raise the topic because of the risk of fights.[161] Talboys had to withdraw from the chamber for refusing to retract a comment made during a heated exchange over the tour, leaving to applause from the government and boos and cries of 'Shame!' from Labour.[162] He later redeemed himself by giving what was regarded as the best speech in years on issues associated with the tour, drawing applause from both sides of the House.

After the Springboks arrived security was tightened, plainclothes police swarmed over the buildings, and the public gallery was closed as protesters marched on Parliament. Serious disruption of its business was anticipated.[163] Members watched from balconies as the demonstration moved off into Molesworth Street, where it was was broken up with some violence by police using their new long batons. In early September protesters attempted an organised 'joint prayer' as Parliament reconvened for the evening and were found to be in contempt by the Privileges Committee. The participants were banned from Parliament for 12 months.[164] The sympathetic Labour Opposition argued that previously pamphlets, ping pong balls and even an overcoat had been dropped into the chamber without it being considered a matter of privilege. The government responded that the 'prayer' had been a political demonstration. A substantial number of long-serving members from both sides of the House retired at the end of the 1981 session, including the Father of the House, Warren Freer (after more than 34 years), and Talboys and Labour's Bill Fraser (24 years).

In the election late that year, the Springbok tour controversy won National some provincial seats but lost it support in the cities. It also starkly posed in the minds of a broad section of the community the issue of a repressive state, and again raised the issue of a political system that kept in power a government that garnered fewer votes overall than the Opposition.

Along with a number of energetic Labour members who would soon make their mark, including Helen Clark and Michael Cullen, the election brought into the House National members such as John Banks, Simon Upton (aged 23), and Ruth Richardson. Upton and Richardson became known as 'Hansel and Gretel', with Upton acting as National's philosophical conscience and Richardson confronting Muldoon with her own brand of economics. Upton remembered how, at their first caucus meeting, Richardson 'plonked herself in the front row of the caucus and calmly and crisply announced the terms of her engagement with the Prime Minister … She said that he was entitled to the undivided loyalty of members of the caucus, and, in return, she expected full and frank disclosure of all issues. There was a horrified silence, and then Sir Robert said: "We don't do things that way here."'[165] New National members less enamoured of Muldoon's policies, including Richardson and Banks, joined the 'alternative caucus' oriented around economic liberalisation.[166]

With Harrison as Speaker, National's effective majority in 1982 was only one if Labour and Social Credit voted together. Social Credit talk about holding the 'balance of responsibility' was not merely a flight of fancy, given some of Muldoon's obstreperous backbenchers. Beetham made a concerted if misguided attack on the practice of pairing.[167] John Luxton was appointed Chairman of Committees after Social Credit attempted to put up Jonathan Hunt against his will.[168] When the House was on air, Labour attempted to direct debate towards its numerous private members' bills and away from government business.[169]

Shortly after the session began in April, the Speaker was forced to use his casting vote to break a tie on the introduction of a bill when a minister, Warren Cooper, was away at Government House.[170] The government was vulnerable. In August another tied vote was avoided only when Muldoon slipped into the chamber seconds before the doors were locked. In November the Speaker broke a further tie after another minister, Birch, did not hear the division bells while being interviewed for radio.[171] Harrison felt that he should reconsider the convention regarding the casting vote, given the precarious state of the government. He restated the principles that had guided all Speakers since the 1870s, with the qualification that they could vote in accordance with their conscience on third readings of bills which were conscience issues.¹⁷²

National decided to go ahead with the Clyde dam, which required empowering legislation because a court decision over the lack of a water right had delayed the project.¹⁷³ In July, complicated negotiations began with Social Credit. Beetham and Knapp, who had voiced adamant opposition to the dam, were briefed and toured the area and, convinced that Muldoon would go ahead anyway by executive decision, decided to support the empowering legislation in return for concessions. The legislation went through, but the Social Credit members were discredited by their switch and they renounced any support for the government thenceforth.¹⁷⁴ Muldoon was once again vulnerable.

In 1982, other issues plagued the government. Richardson, with Waring's support, attempted to introduce a bill for a referendum on extending the term of Parliament, but was eventually dissuaded by Muldoon.¹⁷⁵ An Income Tax Amendment Bill (No. 2) that sought to prevent tax avoidance retrospectively was extremely unpopular amongst National voters. The energetic free-enterprise member Derek Quigley resigned from cabinet after criticising 'Think Big'. Meanwhile, unpopular executive power expanded with the introduction of a wage-price freeze. Muldoon was forced to amend the Economic Stabilisation Act to clarify its powers in the face of a legal challenge to the wage regulations made under it.

Chief whips Don McKinnon (National) and Jonathan Hunt (Labour) confer.

Further controversies befell the government in 1983 as its free-enterprise faction became increasingly vocal.¹⁷⁶ Parliament was called for an unusual one-day sitting at the end of May to deal with an increase in motor registration fees. When the government introduced the bulk of its legislative programme later in the year, it was saved from the threat of an early election by two dissident Labour members and Social Credit. John Kirk (Norman Kirk's son) and Brian MacDonell cut loose from the Labour Party towards the end of the session and formed an alliance with Social Credit that was known as the 'Gang of Four'.¹⁷⁷ Meanwhile, the two disaffected National members, Minogue and Waring, crossed the floor to vote against the Industrial Law Reform Bill which abolished compulsory trade union membership. The clause on youth rates was defeated in Committee when Waring, Minogue, Kirk and Social Credit voted against it.¹⁷⁸

A threat to National also arose to the right, outside the party, with the formation of the free-market New Zealand Party by the businessman Bob Jones, who was disgruntled at Muldoon's 'socialistic' economic interventionism, which now included the regulation of mortgage interest rates and an extension of the wage freeze. Key lobby groups such as Federated Farmers and the Employers' Federation edged away from the interventionist and protectionist environment that had been created by the government.

David Lange, who had succeded in replacing Rowling as leader of the Labour Party in February 1983, strenuously attacked Muldoon in the House, pointing out that Parliament had hardly met until the middle of August. For the first time since Kirk, Labour had a debater who could match, if not better, Muldoon, who was by now tired and isolated. Labour baited the Prime Minister and Lange showed scant respect for the Chair.[179] When Keith Allen, the Minister of Customs, became incoherent and had to leave the Table while the House was in Committee dealing with one of his bills, Labour accused him of being drunk and forced a division to get him back.[180]

Muldoon's increasingly battered mental state was evident when he broke down at the news of the death of Holyoake in December 1983.[181] In the House Muldoon said that Holyoake – who had supported him in preference to Marshall – was 'the greatest political figure of our time'.[182] Many long and heartfelt tributes were paid to a longstanding parliamentarian and Prime Minister, whose skills at creating consensus and managing business in the House were increasingly admired at a time when magnified and intractable conflict seemed the order of the day.

Muldoon had to plead with his caucus to support his Finance Bill as a serious rift developed. Quigley, Richardson and Dail Jones crossed the floor to vote against the interest rate controls in the bill, but the 'Gang of Four' voted for the measure.[183] Muldoon also transgressed the understanding of the 1970s that the Opposition could decide which classes of estimates to debate. His view that the agreement was not binding was supported by the Speaker, but this only worsened the animosity within the House.[184]

Muldoon extracted assurances from the dissident National members that they would not cross the floor during the election year of 1984. The touted freedom of National members to vote as they wished could not be sustained with such an insecure majority. The public watched the display with mounting unease. Journalist Tony Garnier observed ominously: 'Many people now believe Parliament is beyond reforming itself, so they are talking of the electorate applying its own sanctions.'[185]

By 1984 National's hold on power was precarious.[186] Parliament did not meet until June. On seven occasions in the two weeks after the opening the whips failed to assemble a majority, but Muldoon was always able to dragoon the dissident Labour members or Social Credit into voting for the government. Labour gathered its strength while National staggered on. Banks put it caustically: 'The Cabinet was tired. Many were fuelled by gin when they rolled into the House late at night only to be cleaned up and cleaned out.'[187] Muldoon rose to defend his ailing colleague, Allen, following reports of unusual behaviour caused by a combination of alcohol and diabetes.[188]

Legislation dealing with an industrial dispute at the Marsden Point oil refinery expansion project was rushed through, bypassing the select committee. Palmer called this a 'travesty of parliamentary proceedings' and an 'outrage'.[189] National members rushed into the chamber to make up the quorum of 40 needed to suspend the standing orders. A snap election loomed as Muldoon saw no way out of the dilemma. Waring, who had announced her retirement, decided to leave the National caucus when she was denied government speaking slots because of her support for a Nuclear Free New Zealand Bill sponsored by Labour in the hope of precipitating an early election.[190] Muldoon regarded the bill as a matter of confidence and National defeated its introduction by a single vote, with the support of the Labour dissidents. Minogue, Waring and Social Credit voted with Labour. MacDonell, according to Muldoon, voted with National only thanks to a 'casual encounter' that morning.

Matters came to a head on the evening of 14 June, while the Address-in-Reply was still being debated. Protracted meetings between Muldoon, Waring and National Party officials resulted in Muldoon emerging from a caucus meeting to announce a snap election to the assembled, incredulous, news media. National, led by an exhausted and struggling Muldoon, lost the election disastrously to a confident and well-prepared Labour Party which would usher in changes almost no-one would have dreamed of even a few years earlier.

A changing House

Parliament and those inhabiting its precincts had changed greatly in the preceding decade and a half. The 1970s represented the end of an era for the Legislative Department. With the opening of the

Beehive, the well-established mingling of staff, members and ministers in the main buildings was no more. Women were making their presence felt throughout Parliament, and a number of longstanding senior employees retired. There also loomed the first reorganisation of the department since the retrenchment under Clerk Hall in the early 1930s.

From the mid 1960s the parliamentary establishment grew as a result of the House's growing administrative needs. Dollimore retired as Clerk of the House in 1971, having suffered ill health in his last years.[191] He was replaced by Eric Roussell, who had worked under him as Clerk-Assistant since 1947. In 1976 Charles Littlejohn, the Clerk-Assistant, succeeded Roussell as Clerk on his retirement. Party research units were established in 1970, and from the mid 1970s all members had secretarial assistance. This, together with the employment of female Hansard reporters and the greater numbers of female press gallery reporters, began to transform the male-dominated atmosphere.[192] For the first time large numbers of women were visible in the halls of power.

Hansard expanded as the demand for its services grew.[193] Tape-recording of debates as a back-up had been introduced in 1964. The reporting of proceedings in Committee was considered then, but deemed too expensive. Instead, a master tape was used as a check when necessary. From 1973 as a back-up to their notes, reporters took their own portable tape recorders with stethoscope headphones into the chamber and plugged them into the amplification system. The introduction of word-processing from the late 1970s greatly quickened the production of *Hansard*.[194] The shortage of shorthand writers led to talk of taping debates and using teams of transcribers and subeditors.[195] In 1979 the sole remaining male Hansard reporter, Eddie Cooper, left. Bill Rowling observed that 'the men have lowered the flag on yet another area that was once a male bastion'.[196] When Eileen Edwards took up the position of Editor of Debates the following year, the organisation became comprehensively feminised.

Charles Philip Littlejohn was born in Paeroa on 11 January 1923. He worked for the Lands and Survey Department from 1940 as a cadet and clerk, and moved to head office in 1951. He served in the RNZAF during the Second World War. After joining the Legislative Department as Clerk of the Journals and Records in 1954, he was promoted to Second Clerk-Assistant and Reader in 1964 and to Clerk-Assistant in 1971. He completed an LLB in 1957, was admitted to the bar in 1965, and was awarded LLM in 1969 for a thesis on parliamentary privilege. Littlejohn was an acknowledged specialist in constitutional law. He became Clerk of the House of Representatives in 1976. He was awarded a CBE in 1985. He retired the same year, but continued to give advice on the reorganisation of the Legislative Department.

The character of the House changed rapidly during the 1970s. In the elections of 1972 and 1975, sharp reversals of party voting gave rise to high levels of turnover in the House – about one quarter and nearly one third respectively.[197] There was now more independence in voting behaviour, with new members less socialised into the norms of fraying party discipline. But at the same time the dominance of government business in the postwar period was reinforced. Now 45 per cent of the time of the House was devoted to government legislation, about one-fifth to general government policy and another fifth to questions and answers.[198]

The average age of members declined significantly to just over 45 in the 1981–4 Parliament, thanks to a combination of the higher turnover of the 1970s and a declining age of entry. One quarter of members were now in their thirties, and the average age on entry into the House had dipped below 40 for the first time. The extent of parliamentary experience declined markedly as a result. With a greater number of younger members, changes of government, and higher expectations of promotion, the length of time served before elevation to cabinet began to lessen. It was no longer two or more Parliaments; some now came through after three years.[199]

Members worked harder, with select committees playing a much more active role and working longer hours, the House sitting for longer sessions averaging more than 100 sitting days, more bills being introduced and papers and notices of motion tabled, and many more questions asked in the House.[200] The National government caucus and its committees became particularly energetic and played an important role as a vehicle for the ambitions of new members. An increasing number of specialist caucus committees had bills referred to them.[201]

New Zealand's changing society and the increasing importance of white-collar, professional occupations was registered in Parliament. By the 1980s, farmer representation had halved to 15 per cent. Manufacturing lost all of its previous (albeit small) representation, and the traditionally significant categories of manual labour, trade union organiser and journalist also virtually disappeared. The diversity of occupations characteristic of the mid twentieth century diminished as professional groups swelled to well over half of the total, including law at 15 per cent. The other significant group was people engaged in commerce (17 per cent). Such occupations made marked gains in the 1975 election in particular, and by 1984 they dominated the House.

The professional group included teachers, lecturers, doctors and public servants. There was a moderate increase in the number of women and greather ethnic diversity. Winston Peters, Rex Austin and Ben Couch, of Maori descent, all held general seats for National, and the first member of Yugoslav origin, Labour's Fred Gerbic, entered the House. Gerbic spoke in Croatian in his maiden speech in 1980.[202]

Labour had substantially reorientated itself by 1984. Almost three-quarters of its ranks were in professional and other salaried white-collar groups; there were very few manual workers or trade union officials left.[203] Farming remained the single most important occupation among National members, but a 'generation gap' appeared between the farmers and a new, younger group of professionally qualified, well-educated members who lacked the previous reference points of depression and war. This separated backbenchers from Muldoon and his older cadre of supporters.[204]

By now virtually all members had at least a secondary education and two-thirds were educated to the tertiary level. There was little difference between the two main parties. Some 70 per cent of those with tertiary qualifications had gained them at university, with law by far the most common qualification. Lange described this new style of member, epitomised by National's Jim McLay, who entered the House in 1975, 'as one of the "new wave" members of Parliament. He is professional, articulate, and from an early age he had a clear idea about what he wanted to do within Parliament, carefully working towards that end at university, and thereafter.'[205] But older members such as Tizard felt that worldly wisdom was being lost. In times past, members 'were already formed and influenced by the life they had led up to that time. Now we have a much larger number of young men and women that this place influences. They come in here and it is Parliament that influences them.'[206] Moreover the old cross-party sociability, based on male camaraderie, had disappeared. Members no longer drank together in Bellamy's, played snooker together, or met each other on the golf course or sweating it out on the squash court up the road in Kelburn.

Following in the footsteps of Waring in 1975, a number of energetic and well-educated young women were elected to the House: Ann Hercus in 1978, and Helen Clark, Margaret Shields, Ruth Richardson and Fran Wilde in 1981. The number of female members had increased to eight by the 1980s, and their impact was greater. Dorothy Jelicich had become the first woman to move the Address-in-Reply in 1973; in 1984 Fran Wilde was the first woman appointed as a whip, and then (as Acting Speaker) the first woman to take the Chair in the House.[207]

Women parliamentarians were keen to challenge a culture that they saw as sexist, and to change the parliamentary timetable from the anachronistic latter half of the year, which they bluntly stated catered more for sheep than people, especially those with families.[208] Clark found it deeply frustrating that politicking was centred around 'being one of the boys', including late-night drinking. Progress was slow and had to take place on many fronts, symbolic and material, trivial and important. When some National members began to refer scathingly to 'lady members', Acting Speaker John Luxton corrected them and said that reference should be made only to members' electorates and not to their gender, marital status or other attributes.[209] Pressure began to mount for the provision of daycare for the children of members, but a childcare centre did not eventuate until the early 1990s.[210]

Although work in Wellington had grown substantially during the period, the electorate demands on representatives did not diminish.[211] A survey in the early 1980s indicated that members spent at least 30 per cent of their time on constituency work. They had to offer 'surgeries' or 'clinics' for their constituents. The pattern remained one of answering messages on Friday evenings, holding consultations on Saturday mornings, attending local functions on Saturday afternoons and evenings, and following up on cases on Mondays.

The billiard tables in the lounge provided the major form of recreation and were the centre of social activities for many parliamentarians. The game was taken very seriously, and championships were keenly contested. On the wall behind are the shields for the parliamentary snooker and billiards championships, which were contested from the time Parliament moved into the new buildings after the First World War. The first winner of the Hunter shield for billiards, presented by Sir George Hunter, the member for Waipawa (1896–9, 1911–30), was Maui Pomare in 1919. Pomare, the member for Western Maori (1911–30), presented the shield for snooker. E.H. Clark of the Legislative Council first won this in 1921, followed by Pomare himself in 1922. The billiard lounge was exclusively for members. Messengers and other staff were not even allowed to go through. National and Labour had their own tables, and there was one mixed table. The lounge fulfilled much the same function as had the large central Lobby in the nineteenth century.

Labour members Dorothy Jelicich (left) and Mary Batchelor play pool in the billiards lounge, 1975. The inner sanctum of the lounge was for members only and the few women were not particularly welcome, although Mary Dreaver was known to play the odd game. Even in the 1980s women members tended to feel excluded. Tirikatene-Sullivan had successfully pressed for an area in the lounge to be devoted to newspapers and magazines, but this was merely a tiny, screened-off corner.

Ruth Richardson with her nine-week-old daughter Lucy. Richardson had planned to give birth to her first child in 1983 during a recess. When the House was called back unexpectedly early, she had to attend the chamber because of National's tiny majority. Although Chief Labour Whip Hunt had offered her a pair to breastfeed the baby in Parliament Buildings, Labour in the end denied her this since its female caucus members felt that she had not supported them over getting a childcare centre in Parliament. Richardson wanted a room close to the chamber, and was eventually given one in 'Siberia'. She cared for the new-born baby with the aid of her husband and a nanny. When she first went into the division lobbies to vote, the infant in her arms was regarded as a 'stranger'.

Much of this heavy burden was undertaken by members' spouses, virtually without acknowledgement. Some members paid for other assistance out of their own salaries, or relied upon volunteers.[212] By now 40 per cent had electorate 'offices', roughly half at their homes. Those with local offices tended to be younger, urban Labour members who favoured the introduction of paid electorate secretaries. National and older members were less keen on this. They probably valued the close personal relationships that had traditionally been forged with constituents; those in wealthier electorates had less demand made on them by social welfare, housing or immigration cases.

The demands of parliamentary life were seen as a reason for marriage breakups among the many members with young families.[213] Divorced members, once a rarity, were becoming commonplace. Backbenchers, who could spend only Saturday to Monday in their home electorates and even then had little time for their spouses or children, were considered most at risk. Cabinet ministers were able to bring their families to Wellington.

By the late 1970s, the long-suffering wives of members were making their presence felt. They complained of the hours and the work that they had to put in as unpaid electorate secretaries.[214] A meeting of prominent wives led to the formation in 1978 of a Parliamentary Wives' Association chaired by Pat Talboys. Their concerns included replacing the wives' room lost when the old wooden buildings were demolished, security at Parliament, the need for paid electorate secretarial assistance, flats in Wellington where they could stay with their husbands, superannuation, and a recess in the August school holidays.[215]

More radical parliamentary reform, long in the wind, was now becoming a distinct possibility. The election of 1981 discredited the first-past-the-post (FPP) electoral system. National retained power, even though it again secured fewer votes in aggregate than Labour.[216] Social Credit gained about 20 per cent of the vote but ended up with only two seats in Parliament. Various commentators, along with Social Credit, suggested proportional representation as a means of reform.[217]

The strongly developed 'majoritarian' form of government that had prevailed since the first Labour government – a cohesive two-party system producing a single majority party executive, and a unitary and centralised government – functioned well in a homogeneous society.[218] But the system was less able to accommodate issues arising in the 1970s, a time of economic uncertainty, declining prosperity relative to the rest of the developed world, growing social diversity, and well-organised social movements, including Maori pressing for greater recognition of their status under the Treaty of Waitangi. People began to sheet problems home to an electoral and political system that allowed a strong executive to govern while neglecting or ignoring a range of demands. Had New Zealand's system become an 'elective dictatorship', in the words of Britain's Lord Hailsham?[219]

The Muldoon years, when traditional party identification weakened, saw both a strengthened executive and an increased estrangement of Parliament from sections of society involved in or sympathetic to social movements that wanted to broaden political participation beyond its traditional confines. New Zealand's historical consensus on the relationship of the state to the economy and the country's place in the world fragmented at the same time as its leader seemed to have adopted an antagonistic and arrogant political style. Muldoon increasingly fought a rearguard action on both the domestic and international fronts. He offered a traditional view of the role of the state in the economy (as opposed to free-market liberalism) and maintained a stance in foreign affairs that subordinated policy to trade, sought a strong relationship with Britain and the United States, and reacted against the anti-nuclear and anti-apartheid movements.

By contrast, the incoming Labour government of 1984 seemed to offer a break with the past and a new consultative style. It would combine (in a contradictory tension) radical economic reforms with a strong anti-nuclear stance and a 'liberal internationalist' orientation. This challenge to previous panaceas broke asunder New Zealand's historical insulation from the world, both politically and economically. But Labour too, in pursuing radical economic change, came to be seen as arrogant and breaking its promises. Under Labour, the demands for constitutional reform were to become increasingly compelling. Meanwhile, the forces for change had been unleashed.

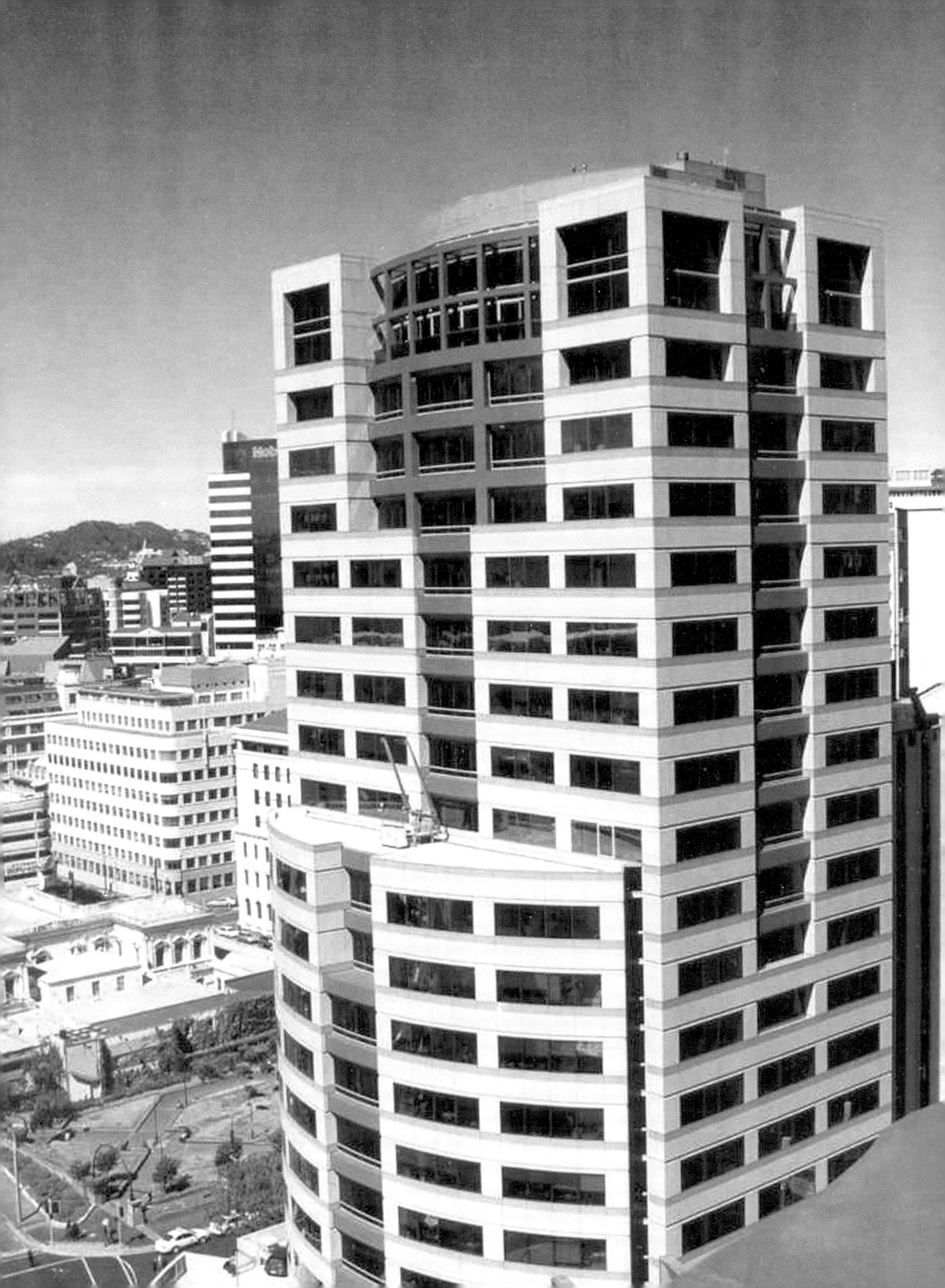

CHAPTER 9

REDRESSING THE BALANCE: INSTITUTIONAL REFORM AND MMP, 1985–2003

The Labour government launched with gusto into a far-reaching reshaping of the state. It immediately gained a reputation for radical reform, outrunning public opinion in an attempt to achieve as much as possible as fast as possible. Its anti-nuclear position fundamentally reoriented New Zealand's international stance. The currency was floated and government regulation of the economy reduced. The tax system was reorganised and a comprehensive sales tax (GST) introduced. The public sector was reformed and state trading enterprises opened up to market forces. The government also fundamentally recast the relationship between Maori and the Crown by declaring its commitment to adhere to the principles of the Treaty of Waitangi and allowing claims for breaches of the Treaty since 1840. Education, health and social policy were reformed. This reforming zeal provoked a deluge of legislation.

The new government also made unprecedented changes to Parliament. These changes reflected decades of concern about how the two-party system concentrated so much power in the executive, concern that had grown with Muldoon's further assertion of executive authority. Parliament would never be the same again.

The reforming onslaught commences

The 1984 mid-year snap election put parliamentary business out of kilter. The budget had to be presented in November and the House sat right through 1985 after a summer recess. This long session began a new pattern in which Parliament was not prorogued in traditional fashion at the end of the year, but simply adjourned. The adoption of three-year sessions from 1987, and the refurbishment of the buildings in the 1990s, meant that ceremonial state openings became relatively rare.

Geoffrey Palmer had crusaded to reform Parliament and protect it against excessive executive power since entering the House and publishing *Unbridled Power?* in 1979.[1] Palmer wrote the 'Open Government' sections of Labour's manifesto of the early 1980s. These proposed substantial reform of Parliament and sweeping constitutional and electoral changes. Lange saw this policy as heralding a 'new style' for government, which had 'operated bereft of principle, responsibility and accountability. Power has become seriously concentrated. The role of Parliament has been seriously undermined … The New Zealand Parliamentary system is out-of-date, inefficient and basically anti-democratic.'[2] This document set the agenda for the new government.

Left: View of Bowen House from top of Beehive Parliamentary Service collection

Maori women perform a karanga at the state opening of Parliament in August 1984. The new Labour government introduced a Maori dimension into the ceremonial opening. While the 21-gun salute, guard of honour and trumpet fanfare remained, there was a haka as the Governor-General arrived, and a powhiri provided by the tangata whenua, Te Ati Awa. Following the Speech from the Throne, the procession filed out of the chamber to the strains of the national anthem, sung by schoolchildren in both Maori and English. 'How Great Thou Art', also in both languages, was sung as they returned to the House. In 1993 Colonel W.C. Nathan, OBE, was appointed the first Maori Black Rod. In summoning the House he addressed the Speaker in both English and Maori. The following year Ihapera (Ipi) Cross became the first Maori Serjeant-at-Arms.

Dominion Post collection, ATL, EP/1984/3875/23A

Labour proposed a multitude of changes to Parliament: abolition of the Legislative Department and the establishment of a body to supervise parliamentary services; more power to the Speaker in running Parliament; revision of the Legislature Act 1908 to free the administration of Parliament from executive control; the reorganisation of select committees; a revised calendar; a mandatory delay of three months during the passage of legislation; and secretarial assistance for members in their electorates.[3] It also committed itself to a Royal Commission on electoral matters that would reopen such basic issues as the method of voting, the number of members, the use of referenda, and the length of the parliamentary term. Labour promised other broader changes, including a Bill of Rights, consideration of privacy issues and the repeal of legislation considered repressive of civil liberties, an assertion of the rule of law, restrictions on regulations and bureaucracy, and enhancement of freedom of information and the lawmaking process.

After National's defeat, Muldoon was unwilling to deal with a foreign exchange crisis that Labour said required a devaluation. A potential constitutional crisis centred on uncertainty over whether, and when, a defeated government had to act at the direction of its successor. It was resolved when National's Attorney-General, Jim McLay, conceded that an outgoing government should act on the advice of an incoming government, even if it disagreed with that advice, 'on any matter of such great constitutional, economic or other significance that [it] cannot be delayed until the new government formally takes office'.[4]

This and other uncertainties were cleared up in the Constitution Act 1986. This Act assumed a continuous Parliament, which meant that those elected but not yet sworn in could be appointed as ministers, and that ministers could remain temporarily in their positions after an election defeat. The House of Representatives (and by implication the government) was to be regarded as existing even if Parliament was dissolved or had expired. Parliament was to meet within six weeks of the last day for the writs for the election to be returned. In the same year the Electoral Act was amended to make it absolutely clear that members entered office the day after the return of the writs and left office on polling day at the next election. Thus the substantial gap between elections and the House meeting that had been traditional since the beginning of Parliament in New Zealand was done away with.

The Constitution Act also dealt with a number of other historical anomalies. Speakers were to remain in office even when Parliament was dissolved (or had expired); parliamentary business could be carried over to the following session or to another Parliament; the term 'General Assembly' was to be replaced by 'Parliament'; and the General Assembly Library – about to be reintegrated with Parliament – was to be called the Parliamentary Library. The Act also attempted to clarify that the Governor-General had to assent to bills passed by Parliament – the previous powers (which had long fallen into disuse) of reserving or amending bills were removed.[5]

Deputy Prime Minister Geoffrey Palmer was very influential in reshaping Parliament in the second half of the 1980s.

Changing the pattern of business

Labour soon moved to change the standing orders. The 1985 revisions, heralded by the Deputy Prime Minister and Leader of the House, Palmer, as 'the most dramatic and the most important set of changes made this century to the way the House works', were indeed significant.[6] Parliament returned to the longer sessions, punctuated by adjournments, first introduced by Labour in the early 1970s. Three weeks of sittings were to alternate with a fourth week of adjournment and the House was to meet for only three days a week. Mondays and Fridays, and where possible Tuesday mornings, were to be kept clear for electorate work. The daily sitting time was extended to compensate, making the hours 2 p.m. to 5.30 p.m. and 7.30 p.m. to 11 p.m. Urgency now extended sittings only to midnight; further extension meant invoking a new 'extraordinary urgency' provision that was to be used only twice in the next decade. Entire sittings were now broadcast.

Changes enhanced debate and smoothed the flow of business. The time limit for speeches was halved to ten minutes and the time spent on procedural matters was reduced. The estimates debate was reduced to 13 sitting days. Wednesday evening was made available for private members' bills. Oral notices of motion were abolished in favour of written notices, vetted by the Speaker, that would remain on the order paper for only one week. Such notices had long been a vexed issue. They consumed an inordinate amount of time, yet virtually none of the nearly one thousand raised annually by the early 1980s were actually debated. There was now provision for a two-hour general debate on Wednesday afternoons that might cover private members' written notices of motion, select committee reports or ministerial replies.

The quorum for the House was reduced from 20 to 15 to free up members for other business. The Speaker's powers were strengthened by formally incorporating Speaker Harrison's 'sin-bin' approach in the standing orders. The regular daily question time at the beginning of sittings was entrenched by restrictions on when government bills could be introduced. Question time was now 45 minutes. Up to six topical 'questions of the day' could be asked in place of oral notices of motion prior to the tabled questions.

Question time gets lively under the fourth Labour government.

The standing orders included a more flexible rule on reading speeches that recognised existing practice. Since Oram's hardline approach, the application of the rule had been relaxed by successive Speakers. It was increasingly difficult to enforce. If a member denied that a speech was being read, this had to be accepted – the routine response was, 'I am speaking from rather full notes'.[7] Members often challenged speakers to annoy or distract them. In 1969 Speaker Jack ruled that because of these vexatious challenges, only the Speaker could draw attention to the reading of a speech. By 1982 Speaker Harrison admitted that he would not intervene because of the difficulty of judging whether reading was taking place.[8] In the 1985 standing orders, reading a speech was forbidden only if it did not reflect the member's 'own views and interests'. Speeches could be read if 'factual information or technical detail or legal argument' needed to be presented accurately or if specialised knowledge was involved.[9] As reading became more frequent, the art of debating declined.

The existing structure of select committees was abandoned and the function of the committees was enlarged, greatly enhancing their potential place in Parliament and increasing the accountability of the executive.[10] Clerk of the House David McGee considered that select committee scrutiny was 'the most distinctive aspect of New Zealand's legislative process. Many overseas Parliaments do not use such a mechanism to anything like the same extent or directly involve such a large proportion of the public in the parliamentary process.'[11] This key plank in Labour's reforms built on the gradual changes since the 1960s. It was seen as both a response to and a substitute for the enlarged powers of the government caucus committees.[12]

Thirteen new 'subject' committees with fewer members (five) were formed, aligned to ministerial portfolios and with wide terms of reference. They were able to scrutinise the policies, administration and expenditure of government departments. Committees could initiate their own enquiries and, unless secrecy was specifically required, all were open to the public and the media during the hearing of evidence. In an effort to keep the executive and Parliament apart, ministers would no longer be members of the committees covering their portfolios. They and the Speaker were to serve only on the Standing Orders and Privileges Committees (and the later Officers of Parliament Committee).[13] The Electoral Law and Regulations Review Committees also continued in existence. As a result of the changes, additional select committee staff were required.[14] The select committee advisory service was expanded in 1987 from two to 13 full-time equivalent staff to cover all the committees.

The government offered the Opposition three chairs of committees.[15] National felt that its role as Opposition might be compromised, but did accept the chair of the Regulations Review Committee, to which Doug Kidd was appointed. From this time it became a convention to appoint the chair of this committee from the Opposition. The committee now played a more active role than before in controlling delegated legislation. In 1989, having identified some 400 obsolete or unnecessary sets of regulations, it drafted legislation that enshrined the power to disallow regulations.

The Public Expenditure Committee was abolished, with its work on the estimates shared out among the subject committees.[16] The new Finance and Expenditure Committee, which monitored financial management, had its scrutiny of the public accounts strengthened in 1986 and again in 1994. The Government Administration Committee dealt with public sector management issues. The Petitions, Private Bills and Local Bills Committees disappeared, with their work now shared around the subject committees. The Library and House Committees also went out of existence, as the Parliamentary Service Commission took over their functions.

Legislative Department to Parliamentary Service

Labour came into office intent on abolishing the Legislative Department. When Palmer was made its minister in order to achieve this, he stated that no-one knew how the department had come about. It had no legal definition of its functions, and had operated on the basis of custom and tradition.[17] Many members favoured abolishing it.[18] In addition to Palmer's constitutional arguments, it was felt that the government would always be parsimonious if it retained control over the resources of Parliament. The Prime Minister had held the purse-strings as minister in charge of the Legislative Department – and neither Holyoake nor Muldoon had been liberal.

The Legislative Department had grown in a patchwork manner, its components cobbled together as the need arose. Staff therefore identified more with their particular group than with the overall organisation. The Clerk had to administer an increasingly large and complex institution and its staff, yet was employed primarily on the strength of legal and procedural skills and experience. Previous reviews had suggested a need to modernise if not radically reorganise the department.[19]

The State Services Commission (SSC) favoured an all-embracing 'House of Representatives Commission' with a department employing public servants. The Clerk suggested an autonomous 'Parliamentary Service' with its own legislation and conditions of employment, headed by the Clerk outside SSC control.[20] Because of the particular working conditions within the Legislative Department, it was not subject to the State Services Act 1962 and had never strictly come under the control of the SSC. Nonetheless, the minister in charge had referred issues concerning salaries and conditions of employment to the SSC, and had always accepted the resulting recommendations.

The proposal to cabinet largely adopted the Clerk's position. Eventually it was decided that the constitutional and administrative functions should be separated into organisations headed by the Clerk and a new General Manager respectively. The Parliamentary Service Act 1985, which went through the House without controversy, preserved the special situation of those working in Parliament in the newly constituted Parliamentary Service and in the Office of the Clerk. The Speaker now became effectively the minister responsible for the vote of the Parliamentary Service and the Office of the Clerk, a role consolidated in the Public Finance Act 1989.[21] The Clerk's job returned to its core function of constitutional support for Parliament, advising on parliamentary law and procedure, helping the Speaker and members and keeping Parliament's records. David McGee, the Deputy Clerk, was appointed Clerk of the House in 1985 on Charles Littlejohn's retirement. In a first for a non-parliamentarian, Littlejohn was granted the honour of being permitted to address the House.[22]

David Graham McGee was born in Tynemouth, England, on 11 December 1947. He graduated with a BA (Hons) in 1970 and came to New Zealand in 1972 as a '10-pound' immigrant. McGee joined the Legislative Department in 1974 as an advisory officer to select committees. He completed the law professional examinations and became a barrister and solicitor in 1977. McGee became Clerk-Assistant in 1976 and Deputy Clerk in 1984. He was promoted to Clerk of the House of Representatives in 1985, the year he published Parliamentary Practice in New Zealand, *which immediately became the standard reference work. An extensively revised second edition was published in 1994. McGee was made a Queen's Counsel in 2000. In the early 1990s he was a member of the Electoral Referendum Panel which oversaw the public information campaigns related to the referenda on the electoral system. By 2002, when he was made a Companion of the New Zealand Order of Merit, he was regarded as a leading parliamentary Clerk in the Commonwealth.*

Parliamentary Service collection

In the mid 1980s the first women took up senior positions in the Office of the Clerk – Adrienne von Tunzelmann as Deputy Clerk and Carol Rankin as Serjeant-at-Arms. The reorganised office comprised two arms to service the House and select committees. The old system of sessional committee clerks supplemented by a couple of advisory officers was replaced by an expanded and unified select committee office whose permanent employees carried out both secretarial and advisory functions. The Clerk of the House of Representatives Act 1988 clarified the independent responsibility of the Clerk. The office now had its own vote and controlled its own staff.

From the early 1990s the Office of the Clerk checked the validity of signatures on the petitions for referenda that were provided for by the Citizens Initiated Referenda Act 1993. The introduction of MMP (Mixed Member Proportional representation) in 1996 created new demands, including a comprehensive revision of the standing orders. In an effort to ease the transition to the new environment, the Office of the Clerk initiated induction sessions for the many new members who were entering the House under MMP, published a guide on the work of select committees, and updated the Speakers' Rulings.[23] The burgeoning role of select committees placed additional demands on the office.

The Parliamentary Service was responsible for administering the buildings and grounds, Bellamy's, the library, Hansard and services to members. The Parliamentary Service Act also created a Parliamentary Service Commission (PSC) to oversee the Parliamentary Service. This was chaired by the Speaker and included the Leader of the House, the Leader of the Opposition, and four members appointed by the

House.²⁴ The commission worked much like select committees, in a bipartisan fashion and without the need for the Speaker to use his casting vote. The General Manager of the Parliamentary Service had delegated authority from the SSC to determine conditions of employment. While this was confirmed by the State Sector Act 1988, in practice there was increasingly close conformity with public service conditions.²⁵ Peter Brooks became the first General Manager in 1986. On his retirement in 1992 he was replaced by John O'Sullivan, who retired in 2003 and was succeeded by Joel George.

Providing for members

The PSC created five committees – House, Library, Staff, Ad Hoc (Whips) and Members Services – to oversee functions previously covered by select committees. It enhanced services and improved personnel administration and internal communication to integrate parliamentary staff better.²⁶ The most popular Labour reform was the provision of paid electorate secretaries for all members (initially half-time, then full-time from 1987).²⁷ Funding also covered rent, furniture and equipment for electorate offices. The paid secretarial support was taken up with alacrity.²⁸ The Parliamentary Service struggled to contain expenditure. The pressure of members' demands was difficult to deal with, and the boundary between legitimate parliamentary purposes and party political ones was hard to define or police.

The library was renamed the Parliamentary Library and separated from the National Library in 1985. The separation had been discussed since the late 1970s on the basis that materials not needed to support Parliament would go to the National Library.²⁹ Since these holdings had been a major reason for the original merger, there no longer seemed any compelling reason to keep the Parliamentary Library within the National Library. The transfer of archival materials, books and newspapers began in the early 1980s. Separation simplified administration, clarified the purpose of the library, ended the dual role of the Chief Librarian, and freed up the Parliamentary Library from servicing scholars and researchers. As it concentrated on its core services, the Parliamentary Library focused more on serving members. A computer service and a link to the Department of Statistics were established and an information service section commenced in 1980.

Bellamy's found it difficult to remain financially viable in the 1980s.³⁰ Meal prices were increased, but it still lost money. A review conceded that it was impossible to make ends meet, given the demands made of the service. It acknowledged that Bellamy's was run as efficiently as it could be. The PSC wanted to concentrate the facilities on the third floor to save money, but both major parties opposed this and the government stepped in to prevent it, installing a new ministerial suite on the third floor instead. Reorganisation of Bellamy's was limited to upgrading the cafeteria to provide fast food, and a

By the mid 1980s women were being appointed to senior positions in Parliament. Carol Rankin (depicted here) was Serjeant-at-Arms and Adrienne von Tunzelmann, Deputy Clerk of the House. There was also some relaxation of the decorum observed in the chamber and galleries. The Clerk and his assistants adopted less formal attire. With the extension of sessions into the summer the rule on the wearing of jackets was relaxed but ties remained a requirement. Speaker Burke and the Clerk reduced formality by wearing their wigs only for the formal part of the day's business and on state occasions.

Neale McMillan, Parliamentary Service collection

The first meeting of the Parliamentary Service Commission, 2 October 1985. Round the table from left: Michael Cullen, Don McKinnon, Jonathan Hunt, Speaker Wall, Jim Bolger, John Terris, and Rob Storey. On McKinnon's suggestion, members were deliberately mixed up around the table. Although party loyalty subsequently reasserted itself in the seating arrangements, the understanding that matters should not go to a vote and that decisions should be reached by consensus proved durable.

redesign of the third floor dining rooms and kitchens. The privatised THC was no longer interested in running the service. In 1991 Fishers Catering was contracted in its place. Staff numbers were cut, the privilege dining room and staff bar closed, and facilities relocated. Prices for food and liquor went up, but remained comparatively low.

The shift of Parliament during the refurbishment of the buildings in the early 1990s adversely affected patronage. The ministerial dining room was closed and the members' and guests' dining room was opened up to all parliamentary staff and guests. The return of Parliament to the refurbished buildings, the increased provision of fast food, and a substantial rise in the demand for catering for functions subsequently increased the use of Bellamy's. Over time, the menu was reoriented towards more healthy food such as salads after complaints about the previous 'fatty' and 'stodgy' fare.

With more resources needed to modernise support services, the Parliamentary Service budget rose considerably in the late 1980s, as did staff numbers. Parliamentary expenditure on travel, postage and printing soared.[31] The new National government elected in 1990 was determined to cut government expenditure through the Cabinet Expenditure Control Committee (the 'razor gang'), which was concerned about the substantial growth of the Parliamentary Service. After Hansard was reviewed, its staff numbers were reduced and it was moved to the Office of the Clerk, a location consistent with that office's responsibility for keeping the parliamentary record.[32] The messenger contingent was cut back when Parliament moved into Bowen House while the refurbishment was taking place. The traditional messengers, many of them former servicemen or retired public servants, were replaced by younger people, including women, for whom working in Parliament was just another job.[33]

In 1987 personal computers and printers were installed in all members' offices and a large number of mini-computers and terminals provided an 'office automation system'.[34] Division bells – so loud that they were sometimes sabotaged by stuffing them with paper or unscrewing or wrenching them from their fixtures – were replaced by an electronic version in 1987.[35] Some now complained that these were too quiet; others found them irritatingly loud, but sabotage was now virtually impossible. In 1988 a Parliamentary On-Line Information system (POLI) gave members and staff access to databases concerning bills, acts, *Hansard*, the newspaper index, and later, the Parliamentary Library catalogue. Terminals appeared in most members' rooms.

Hansard underwent great change at this time. When it was transferred to the Office of the Clerk, the old pattern of sessional work disappeared, but not before a difficult court case concerning changed working conditions and pay. Hansard staff now worked five days a week throughout the year. The recording and transcribing of debates changed dramatically. Text was transmitted electronically to the printer, and in the early 1990s high-speed shorthand was replaced by recording on digital audiotape.[36] Digital recording made *Hansard* immediately available on personal computers and eliminated the cumbersome handling and storage of tapes. Recordings were transcribed electronically and then integrated with interjections and procedural points, which were still better reported by shorthand 'monitors' on duty in the chamber. The traditional 'substantially verbatim' style shifted closer to a truly verbatim style, with less refining of the spoken word. The size of *Hansard* expanded greatly, as the estimates debate and proceedings in Committee were reported in full, as sessions grew longer and as written questions swelled to many tens of thousands.

The abolition of the Legislative Department increased the autonomy of parliamentary services, expanded services available to members, and strengthened the role of the Speaker. While some felt that the Parliamentary Service had become a new bureaucracy, most agreed that the change was for the better. Parliament had regained control over its own administration, resulting in some shift in the constitutional balance between Parliament and the executive.[37] But when large sums of money were involved – for major building works, the reorganisation of Bellamy's, the move to Bowen House, and greater resources for parties – the executive remained in charge. Its need to control expenditure made it difficult for the government to yield power to, consult effectively with, or even inform the PSC on such major issues.

Carrying on with business

Because of the snap election in 1984, the new Parliament opened in mid August. The new Labour government introduced a Maori dimension into the state opening. Sir Basil Arthur was elected Speaker, although not before Muldoon gave an edge to proceedings by pointing out that Arthur had recently been required to withdraw from the chamber. Muldoon's intervention infuriated the

Traditional elements associated with Parliament remained. The Serjeant-at-Arms, Wing Commander R.M. McKay, leads Speaker Wall down the steps to be presented to the Governor-General on 29 May 1985. They are followed by Clerk of the House, C.P. Littlejohn, and Deputy Clerk, D.G. McGee.

government and Arthur looked 'like he'd been hit with a plank'.[38] To National's surprise, Labour adjourned Parliament after only a week to hold its consultative 'economic summit' in the debating chamber. National members were annoyed that they were not invited to this event, and Norman Jones insisted on attending, sitting in his own seat. When Muldoon lost the National leadership to Jim McLay late that year, he refused to stay on the Opposition front bench.

Arthur soon fell ill, and relinquished his duties in late February 1985. John Terris, the Chairman of Committees, acted as Speaker. When Arthur died at the beginning of May during an adjournment, there were few obvious candidates for the post. When the House reconvened at the end of May, it elected Dr Gerard Wall Speaker. Michael Cullen warned members that Wall would bring a very different style to the Chair, including a commitment to the rights of backbenchers and a strong sense of rectitude. There was joking about a new 'sin bin' in the form of a playpen in the centre of the chamber, and about a Speaker's pistol to deal with unruly members.[39]

Wall rapidly asserted himself. He enjoyed robust debate but ruled 'with a rod of iron', according to Labour's senior whip, Austin. No-one was 'spared his cold, controlled wrath', as Tom Scott put it.[40] Wall's memory and detailed grasp of the standing orders were complemented by his decisiveness. He tolerated no nonsense, and was quick to block irrelevant questions, political jibes and endless points of order. Question time ceased to be raucous as stunned members wondered what had hit them.

But Wall's rigid approach antagonised the Opposition. He clashed repeatedly with members as the Opposition became increasingly exasperated at Labour's handling of business.[41] After Wall rebuked members for not bowing to him as they crossed the floor for divisions, many National members made exaggerated bows and salutes. When three were ordered out as Wall tried to assert his authority, another half dozen followed in protest, calling out 'Disgrace!' and 'Silly old man!' as they left. Merv Wellington frequently had to withdraw and was 'named' twice. When the House collectively drew breath for the valedictories in mid December 1985, not all agreed that the changes had been to the good. The long session had been extraordinary.[42]

The session of 1986–7 gave rise to a record number of withdrawals.[43] Wall had to order Prime Minister Lange and the new Leader of the Opposition, Jim Bolger, out of the chamber together twice. After losing the leadership, Muldoon had been ridiculed by Labour and largely ignored by National. He returned to the front bench under Bolger but remained truculent. National's senior whip, Robin Gray, was instructed to 'deal with Muldoon' when the former leader undermined one of Bolger's speeches, causing the House to burst into laughter.[44] Reporters overhead Gray try to admonish Muldoon, which drew the response: 'Don't come and whip me, young fella, I'll do as I want'.

Dr Gerard Aloysius Wall was born in Christchurch on 24 January 1920. He was educated at St Bede's College and studied law at the University of Canterbury before qualifying as a doctor from the University of Otago. He became an orthopaedic and plastic surgeon. Wall was elected for Porirua in 1969 for Labour. He became Speaker in 1985 after the death of Sir Basil Arthur. In 1987 he was forced to retire on grounds of age. Wall was particularly keen to improve the parliamentary precincts. He advocated a new Parliamentary Service building, argued for the preservation of the older Parliament Buildings, and advanced the cause of a parliamentary precinct. He was knighted in 1987 and died on 22 November 1992.

Parliamentary Service collection

Muldoon gave notice of a motion of no-confidence in Wall, alleging partiality towards the government.⁴⁵ Such motions had been notified on rare occasions since the 1960s when the chamber got particularly heated. They were a way of letting off steam and quietly disappeared off the bottom of the order paper. Now, for the first time, such a motion was debated. National members, however, were wary of supporting Muldoon. Palmer and Hunt stoutly defended the Speaker, pointing out that National's Tony Friedlander had been sent from the chamber seven times since 1985. When Muldoon issued a press statement on the matter, he was suspended for three days for breach of privilege.

Speaker Wall's draconian approach drew upon his rugby experience.

Things did not improve. Winston Peters was ordered out of the chamber amid turbulence during the financial debate in 1986.⁴⁶ When he refused to go there were calls for Serjeant-at-Arms Carol Rankin to 'hit him with your mace' or even 'hit him with your handbag'. Others followed, including Muldoon, and when they returned without the Speaker's permission they were ordered out again. Muldoon initially refused to go, creating further difficulty for Rankin. He finally left, but was 'named' and suspended for a day.

Another troublesome member was John Banks. After entering the House in 1982, he followed Holyoake's advice to 'breath through the nose' for only a short period. He was ejected from the chamber twice in 1983, and had a physical confrontation with Cullen in 1985.⁴⁷ Next year, after other National members had to withdraw while the Homosexual Law Reform Bill was in Committee, Banks suggested that Chairman of Committees John Terris was partial. He was 'named', suspended for a day and found in contempt by the Privileges Committee. Early in 1987 he was 'named' and suspended for an unprecedented seven days for questioning the Speaker's impartiality and making gestures at him, after three other members were ordered out.

Fran Wilde had introduced her private member's Homosexual Law Reform Bill in 1985. Parliament had found it awkward to deal with homosexuality. In 1960 Attorney-General Rex Mason had included a clause reducing the penalties for homosexual acts in the consolidated Crimes Bill, but this was withdrawn after strong opposition.⁴⁸ In 1968 a petition of the Homosexual Law Reform Society included statistics which led the *Evening Post* to suggest that at least four members were probably homosexual.⁴⁹ Parliament decided that a breach of privilege had been committed – the headline lessened 'the esteem of Parliament in the eyes of the public'. The *Post* was forced to publish an apology, albeit much qualified.

The society again sought reform after the 1972 Labour landslide brought younger, more liberal Labour members into the House. Mary Batchelor introduced a private member's bill which met concerted opposition from Kirk and in Labour's caucus, so the society persuaded National's Venn Young to introduce a Crimes Amendment Bill instead. The bill was referred to a special open select committee, but views diverged strongly and it was defeated on its second reading in 1975.

Wilde's bill split the parties. Debate focused on the age of consent. An 800,000-signature petition, sponsored by three members and opposing the legalisation of homosexual acts, did not sway the House. It voted 47 to 32 in favour on the bill's second reading.[50] The bill was considered in Committee in March 1986, and its first part went through, 41 to 36, but the anti-discrimination measures were lost. In early July a crucial division on not closing the third reading debate was won 43 to 42, with George Gair's vote tipping the balance. The first part of the bill was passed shortly thereafter, 49 to 44, amid loud cheers and celebrations from its supporters. This legalised homosexual acts by those aged 16 and over.

At the election of 1987 some notable older Labour members – Speaker Wall, Fraser Colman, Eddie Isbey and Frank O'Flynn – retired. Wall was not keen to retire but had to under Labour's rules. Lange described O'Flynn as one of a dying breed because of his love of the House. 'He was one of the members who would still be anxious to be on every speaking list, would still make notes, write his speeches by hand, [and] send the notes down to the House'.[51] Labour's reforms had not improved the efficiency with which Parliament conducted its business. The average number of hours per sitting rose markedly after the new standing orders came into operation.[52] The new Wednesday general debate was a success, but sitting to 11 p.m. was too taxing, and reserving Wednesdays for private members proved too generous. The House reverted to rising at 10.30 p.m., and to compensate the slot for private members' business was reduced to alternate Wednesdays. Private members' business had swelled substantially – particularly as National tried to resurrect bills drafted while it was in government – and interfered with the government's legislative programme. The government had to resort to urgency often, there was a last-minute rush of bills, and many had to be held over. By now half the time of the House was devoted to government bills.[53] The spectacle of a chamber in turmoil, together with Labour's breath-taking reforms, raised the issue of reforming Parliament from the outside in the minds of the public. Palmer's internal reworking of the institution did not seem to have produced the desired results.

Political crisis

Labour won the election of 1987 convincingly, buoyed by the stock market and property booms. The result seemed a reassertion of the two-party system, as Social Credit disappeared from the House.[54] National, still in disarray in the changed political landscape, now included in its ranks free market advocates such as Jenny Shipley, Murray McCully, John Luxton and Maurice Williamson.

Labour was still in a hurry. Only seven weeks separated the adjournment of the House prior to the election and the meeting of the new Parliament in September 1987. Kerry Burke replaced Wall as Speaker. He applied the standing orders more flexibly, proved much more lenient, and acrimony diminished. Internecine warfare within Labour contributed to a decline of antagonism between the parties. Withdrawals from the chamber ceased – Burke was determined that no such interventions would blot his reign.[55] The House remained combative, nonetheless, and the number of divisions was still higher than in the early 1980s.

Labour pressed on frantically, passing more statutes than ever, but it was now in turmoil over the party's underlying unresolved conflicts.[56] The boom collapsed shortly after the election. After the

Redressing the balance: institutional reform and MMP, 1985–2003

announcement of a new wave of economic reforms, including Douglas' flat-rate income tax, Lange dismissed him in December 1988. Early next year Lange called for a pause for 'a cup of tea'. Political paralysis ensued. Labour had experienced a few defections from its ranks since the late 1970s.[57] Now Jim Anderton left to form the NewLabour Party in 1989, taking a significant chunk of Labour's more left-wing supporters with him. (NewLabour later combined with other minor parties to form the Alliance Party.)

The first session of the new Parliament continued to the end of 1989. The government remained racked by conflict. In August 1989 Lange resigned after caucus voted to return Douglas to cabinet. Geoffrey Palmer became Prime Minister. The government, in spite of its large majority, was humiliated by a tied division on closure when some members failed to vote because the bells had been turned down for a fashion show in the Beehive. The Chairman of Committees voted against the government to continue the debate.[58] Just before the election in October 1990, Palmer was replaced by Mike Moore. With the writing on the wall, many senior Labour members announced their retirements.

Workloads had increased greatly because of the unremitting legislative programme.[59] The number of bills rose and they were considered more thoroughly, oral and written questions swelled, and papers laid on the Table multiplied. By 1990 the sitting day had lengthened to an average of more than ten hours as urgency was taken frequently. The amount of time under urgency rose to one-third of sitting hours. The previous lengthy adjournments disappeared. Burke, speaking for many in referring to a state of exhaustion in the House, advocated shifting the balance away from the chamber and towards committees to improve efficiency.

Select committee work remained dominated by legislation in spite of the intention to increase their powers of scrutiny. There was insufficient time to assess policy or expenditure and committee reports were hardly debated, even though from 1986 the government was required to respond to them. On occasion, insufficient time was allowed for committees to consider important measures.[60] Austin (the first female senior government whip) noted that her job was increasingly onerous because of the mounting committee workload. Most committees now sat for 11 months of the year and dealt with many public submissions.[61] The expansion of the executive and the exclusion of ministers from select committees meant there was a shortage of government backbenchers available to do the work. Substitutions were prevalent and absences frequent. Committees had to sit while the House was sitting, during the short adjournments and on Tuesday mornings – when members wanted to see their secretaries, finish electorate work, and get letters typed.[62] Isbey would reportedly 'explode' if asked to attend select committee meetings on Tuesday mornings.

Executive dominance over Parliament persisted despite Palmer's reforms. Urgency was taken frequently and legislation pushed through in unseemly fashion.[63] In 1988 the State Sector Bill was drafted hastily, and the many amendments made by the select committee were not available to the House during the second reading. The same situation arose for the second reading of the Public Finance Bill in 1989. On three occasions in the late 1980s urgency ran through the entire week. The Radiocommunications Bill of 1989 had its second reading and consideration in Committee under urgency immediately after being reported back from select committee with substantial amendments that were not available to the House.[64] In the final two weeks of the session ending in December 1989, sittings ran continuously through from Tuesday to Saturday evening, with the dates recorded in *Hansard* simply as 5 and 12 December.

Greater flexibility in the treatment of bills developed. On occasion, parts of

Jim Bolger won King Country for National in 1972. A cabinet minister in 1977–84, he made a notable contribution as Minister of Labour. Bolger replaced Jim McLay as Leader of the National Party in 1986, and became Prime Minister in 1990. He remained in the position until December 1997, when he was toppled by Jenny Shipley. Bolger oversaw the difficult transition to MMP, and was able to keep his government in office while parties fragmented. He also forged a coalition with New Zealand First in unlikely circumstances in 1996. He retired from the House in 1998 and became Ambassador to the United States.

bills would be taken out of legislation being considered by the House and hurriedly passed in advance. From the early 1980s the traditional single omnibus Statutes Amendment Bill was supplemented by others, such as the Law Reform (Miscellaneous Provisions) Bill in which numerous legal reforms were lumped together. Labour also introduced the practice of making substantial amendments by supplementary order paper while in Committee and frequently put bills through Committee part by part.[65] Governments found such devices too useful to ignore, even if the Opposition complained that its members had to help fix up badly drafted legislation in select committees.

On his retirement in 1990 Palmer reiterated his concern over executive domination and conceded that the new powers of Parliament and its select committees had not developed as he had hoped.[66] On the eve of the election, the *Evening Post* commented that: 'For all of Mr Palmer's early efforts to improve the process and potential of the Legislature, it concludes a second term of Labour domination as much in the shade of the Beehive as ever it has been.'[67]

The 1990 election gave National a huge majority of 39 seats, as the country recoiled from Labour's reforms, its perceived broken promises, and the hopeless disarray into which the government had fallen. National's leader, Bolger, promised honest and credible government.

Labour was decimated, losing cabinet ministers such as Phil Goff and Margaret Shields, Speaker Burke and his deputy John Terris, and both Labour whips. The large influx of 39 new members formed 40 per cent of the House. National's massive majority created a huge backbench that would prove unruly. Previous governments had been able to expand the number of executive positions to retain their dominance over caucus, but this now proved impossible.[68]

The new Parliament opened at the end of November 1990 inauspiciously. While Robin Gray was elected as Speaker without opposition, Labour opposed Jim Gerard as Deputy Speaker and Chairman of Committees. Moore proposed Murray McCully instead, because he wanted his 'small band' to feel what it was like 'to be in the line of fire'. But the tactic misfired. Some Labour members deserted the party for this first division. Others ran a gauntlet of sneers and jeers as they went into the lobby to vote.[69]

Gray remembered how he imposed his authority early in his tenure by outfacing a challenge made by Lange through points of order – even though he realised that he was wrong. He found the Speakership lonely because he had to isolate himself from a party with which he had been closely involved as a whip.[70] Conscious of the need to be fair-minded, Gray sat in the middle of Bellamy's and invited members from both parties to dine with him.

The House was soon adjourned. National had come to power to find that a large budget deficit loomed and that the Bank of New Zealand had to be rescued from bankruptcy. Its plans stymied, the government announced a Christmas 'economic package' of cuts to social welfare benefits, health and housing, and proposed radical reform of industrial relations. The country realised that another government was to take a different path to the one promised during the election campaign.

The House was recalled early in January 1991 for an emergency debate on the Gulf War, held in the new Bowen House chamber.[71] Some questioned the way in which the government announced its commitment to support the multinational force without a ministerial statement in the House, and Labour obtained an urgent debate on the matter. The Gulf War underlined the inadequacy of procedures to call the House quickly, it being necessary to prorogue Parliament and commence a new session. Changes were made to the standing orders in 1992 to allow more flexibility. The House was involved to a greater extent in later decisions to make military commitments – to Bosnia in 1994, East Timor in 1999 and Afghanistan in 2001.[72]

National pushed its legislative programme through under urgency. It had promised to rectify Labour's 'abuses of Parliament' in its 1990 election manifesto, to 'regain public respect for the institution'. Parliament's standing orders were to be examined, particularly the use of omnibus bills, the bypassing of the select committee process, and the use of urgency to force bills through rapidly.[73] But in government, National adopted the same practices as Labour to get its business through. At the end of

April 1991, the government pushed through the Employment Contracts Act (which revolutionised New Zealand's industrial relations) against stern Labour resistance. The bill required 22 applications of closure and 71 divisions while the House was in Committee.[74]

Finance Minister Ruth Richardson's subsequent 'mother of all budgets' was extraordinary in more ways than one.[75] It was the first budget to be telecast live; and it introduced sweeping, unpopular changes to social welfare benefits, accident compensation, housing and health, including charges for public health services. The government, however, failed to implement its campaign promise to remove the surtax on national superannuation that Labour had introduced in 1984.[76] The budget, along with a number of important associated bills and other measures, was taken under urgency over seven days, with one all-night sitting under 'extraordinary urgency', and hundreds of divisions. Hunt labelled the struggle the 'Battle of 91'. It gave rise to one of the longest sittings ever, from Tuesday 30 July to Saturday 3 August (67½ hours), followed by the first Monday sitting since 1958.

Muldoon disagreed with the direction National took with Richardson's 'redesign' of the welfare state. He resigned from Parliament at the end of 1991. His valedictory speech remarked on changes in the House, including the greater presence of women, which he admitted he had had difficulty dealing with.[77] He died not long afterwards, in August 1992. Bolger observed that for '31 years Sir Robert lived and breathed the atmosphere of Parliament'. Paul East remembered that with his 'deep love' for the institution, Muldoon had 'ensured that the debating chamber was the centre of political life'.[78]

The reshaping of the public sector and deregulating of the economy demonstrated the power of the executive, and its ability to act in ways not foreshadowed by election promises. The changes from Muldoon to Douglas and then to Richardson had not diminished the role of the executive. To the public and commentators, this suggested that more radical measures were needed to curb executive dominance. After all, this dominance was rooted within the ranks of the party in power – in strong party discipline and in the subservience of caucus to cabinet.

The transition to MMP

The pressure to reform Parliament mounted. Like Labour in the 1980s, the Bolger government was seen as betraying voters, in particular because of the welfare cuts and the failure to abolish the surtax on national superannuation.[79] Labour's 1984 election promise of a Royal Commission on electoral laws would have far-reaching consequences.

When the Royal Commission reported in favour of proportional representation at the end of 1986, neither major party was enthusiastic.[80] Proportional representation, it suggested, would be substantially fairer to minor parties, would yield greater representativeness, particularly for Maori, and would enhance the legitimacy of the political system. It would also result in a more effective Parliament, it was argued, by strengthening its role and providing a check on the executive. The commission recommended a 'mixed member proportional' (MMP) electoral system, in which members would be elected both from geographic electorates and from party lists. To make this system work, the number of members should be increased to 120 and and Maori seats abolished. A referendum should be held on whether to introduce it.

Although Palmer pressed Labour to act, the report remained buried until Lange mistakenly promised in the lead-up to the 1987 election that a binding referendum would be held. Following Labour's re-election, the report was considered by a select committee, which in late 1988 rejected MMP in favour of less sweeping change.[81] While attention was focused on Labour's internecine battle, defeated Social Credit member Gary Knapp and others barricaded themselves in a room in Parliament Buildings in support of a referendum on proportional representation.[82]

The electoral issue resurfaced at the 1990 election. The Electoral Reform Coalition pressed for MMP. During the campaign, National accused Labour of breaking its previous election promises and promised to hold a binding referendum. Labour agreed reluctantly to an indicative referendum.[83] Many believed that proportional representation would not be endorsed in a poll.

National honoured its commitment by organising a dual referendum. The first, in 1992, would ask whether change was sought, and if so which of four alternative electoral systems was preferred. The second referendum would be held in conjunction with the 1993 election if a majority had voted for change. This would pose a choice between FPP and the most popular of the 1992 options. Publicity was given to the views of new members such as Christine Fletcher, who was appalled at the 'gang warfarism' and the 'personal bullying, and the excesses produced under the confrontational politics' of FPP. Public confidence in Parliament remained very low.[84]

In the 1992 referendum 84.7 per cent of voters wanted change. MMP was the most popular option, supported by 70.5 per cent. Many members of the House were shocked by this result.[85] The Royal Commission's recommendation and strong lobbying by the Electoral Reform Coalition had been effective.

As the referendum result came in, an Electoral Reform Bill was drafted, in anticipation that change might be demanded. This set up the terms of the binding referendum of 1993, gave details of MMP, and made provision for a second chamber. The Electoral Law Committee made a number of important changes on such matters as establishing an Electoral Commission, the nature of Maori representation, raising the threshold for party representation to 5 per cent, and sidelining the idea of a second chamber. Maori resistance to the abolition of the special Maori seats resulted in this recommendation of the Royal Commission being dropped.

Murray McCully spoke for the Electoral Law Committee in saying that 'members of the committee decided that they had a duty to the House, and, indeed, to the country, to forge a consensus that would enable us to fashion a workable and consistent model of an MMP system, acceptable in all its key components to the majority.'[86] The entire House engaged with the Electoral Reform Bill to an unprecedented extent. All saw that their political futures were at stake. Party lines and caucus cohesion broke down as members grappled with the consequences of such momentous change. After many public submissions and extensive discussion, the bill was reported back to the House in July 1993, four months before the second referendum. Despite attempts to amend it (and the withdrawal of the whips for the Committee stage), the bill was passed unaltered in August.

In 1993 a narrow majority of 53.9 per cent favoured MMP in the second referendum. The die was cast. Factors such as the long-term fracturing of party alignments, greater social divisions, a broad desire for better representation, economic difficulties and broken election promises, all helped to precipitate this radical change. The reform was aided by some serendipitous events and it came about despite the strongly held view of some prominent politicians that the existing system was best and the fear of many that they might lose their positions. The support for FPP by members, the public's lack of esteem for Parliament and the executive, and the perceived betrayal of voters by successive governments, produced a strong demand for greater accountability and for politicians to be punished for their sins. Under MMP, the number of seats parties gained would be in proportion to their share of the total vote. Sixty enlarged general electorate seats remained, supplemented by 55 from party lists, which were allocated to top up the totals to the proportion of the national vote each party received. A further five electorate seats were reserved for Maori representatives.

Radical changes to the House were expected. Probably the most fundamental was increased representation of social groups other than 'Pakeha, male, middle-class professionals'.[87] It was also anticipated that the two-party system and strong majority government would break down, and that power would shift from the executive towards Parliament. With more parties represented, there would be minority or coalition governments. Minority governments would require a constant mustering of support within the House, with day-to-day inter-party bargaining to get legislation through. It was believed that this would give rise to a 'more conciliatory and consensual' approach to government.[88]

Within the House, a shift to a multi-party environment would require changes in procedure to give all parties and members fair debating time, altered seating arrangements in the chamber, and additional resources to enable the parties to contribute to debates and select committee work. The role of Leader of the Opposition might become tenuous as evenly balanced parties outside government competed. The Speaker – traditionally drawn from the ranks of the majority party and subject to re-election like other members – might need to become more independent. The most likely change, building on those of 1985, would be further strengthening of the roles of select committees and individual members. The larger House would allow greater specialisation and more time in committees, while the breakdown of the two-party system would encourage committees to shape legislation, form policy and scrutinise the government more actively.

As the introduction of MMP loomed, the disintegration of the two-party system accelerated. National experienced defections from the early 1990s. Winston Peters was forced to resign as Minister of Maori Affairs in 1991, but continued in the House as a destabilising backbencher until expelled from National in 1993.[89] The last straw had been Peters' sabotage of a triumphal moment in the House for the Minister in Charge of Treaty Negotiations, Doug Graham, following the settling of the Sealord deal with Maori over the allocation of fisheries.[90] Peters took National to court over his expulsion, resigned from Parliament, and won the consequent by-election in Tauranga as an independent before forming the New Zealand First Party.

Following Richardson's 1991 budget, National's legislative fervour dissipated as hostile public reaction to its social policies mounted and as its majority was eroded. The use of urgency declined and average sitting hours fell back to a more civilised seven or eight hours a day with a consequent improvement in behaviour in the chamber.[91] At the same time, the annual number of sitting days fell to 80 or 90, where they were to stabilise. The number of bills passed fell to about a hundred, a volume that was maintained into the MMP period.[92]

In 1992 Parliament revised its financial procedures.[93] Scrutiny of public expenditure had languished following the abolition of the Public Expenditure Committee in 1985. The sessional programme had become confused and difficult to follow, and the Public Finance Act 1989 had to be taken into account. Because of the failure to obtain bipartisan agreement within the Standing Orders Committee, a special debate was held in the House.[94] In the revised standing orders, approval of the estimates was separated from the review of departmental spending. Committees would now look at the newly created state-owned enterprises and from 1994 other governmental organisations. The time devoted to each item was specified, along with a new timetable for appropriation processes during the parliamentary year.

As the 1993 election approached party leaders conceded that the country had effectively left FPP behind, given the endorsement of change in the first referendum.[95] The election appeared to produce a 'hung' Parliament. Special votes eventually gave National a one-seat majority. Labour had 45 seats, and the Alliance and New Zealand First 2 each. The Alliance gained nearly 20 per cent of the votes. New Zealand First got nearly 10 per cent, with Tau Henare taking Northern Maori.

There was still the issue of the Speaker. Bolger, after quietly sounding out Lange, approached a disaffected Labour member, Peter Tapsell.[96] Labour, now led by Helen Clark, decided to allow Tapsell to become Speaker, believing it was unlikely to win if another election had to be held. Peters called Tapsell's appointment a 'charade' and mischievously proposed the previous Speaker, Gray.[97] Gray declined the nomination and Tapsell was elected. Bolger and Clark presented their agreement as 'MMP politics in action'. While following Burke and Gray in wearing a wig only for the formal part of proceedings, Tapsell insisted on members wearing jackets in the House, shaming some by glaring at them.[98] The requirement that men wear jackets and ties remains.

National appointed a large executive with 27 members. The most notable change was the replacement of Richardson as Minister of Finance by Birch. With MMP on the horizon, Richardson resigned her seat after seeing the Fiscal Responsibility Act 1994 onto the statute book. She regarded MMP as 'lowest-common-denominator politics – a recipe for political paralysis'.[99] As the economy improved, Birch oversaw budgets that were much more low-key than Richardson's.

The House

The 1993–6 Parliament was a transitional one. The pace of government activity slackened further and towards its end urgency was taken only with the support of both major parties.[100] In 1994 more private members' bills were introduced as the government found it difficult to block them. There were signs of a new consultative style, with wider discussion before some legislation was introduced. A bill removing the right of appeal to the Privy Council was withdrawn because the Labour Party opposed it, while the Food Amendment (No. 2) and Fisheries Amendment Bills went through after extensive consultation. The government was blocked 39 all (with the Chairman casting his vote in favour of the Noes) on a procedural division in June when Banks failed to respond to the bells.[101]

As members positioned themselves for the new world of MMP, arrangements in the House became more complex. In September 1994 Ross Meurant resigned from National and set up the Right of Centre Party, with which National was now in coalition. In November Peter Dunne left Labour and formed Future New Zealand. Graeme Lee left National and formed the Christian Democrats in May 1995. In June a centrist United Party comprising six members from Labour and National was formed, joined by Dunne. When Meurant lost his under-secretary posts following his refusal to resign from the directorship of a bank, the coalition broke up in August 1995, in effect creating a minority government.

At the end of the year the smaller parties were outraged when National and Labour agreed to alter an entrenched provision in the Electoral Act (which required 75 per cent support in the House). They believed that this change in the ballot paper would boost support for the two major parties by discouraging 'split' voting.[102] In March 1996 United agreed to a coalition with National, while Michael Laws left National for New Zealand First. This made National a minority government.[103] But it could still rely on other members in votes of confidence and for supply. In April there were two more desertions from National to New Zealand First, but Laws had to resign after admitting that he had misled Parliament over the authorisation of a poll in his electorate. When Bolger promised that a general election would be held within six months, the House decided that a by-election need not take place. The House was now evenly split. National, United and Graeme Lee comprised 49 of the 98 members (including the Speaker). The country awaited its first MMP election with a mixture of anticipation and bewilderment.

Peter Wilfred Tapsell was born in Rotorua on 21 January 1930. He was Ngati Whakaue on his mother's side. After distinguishing himself at Rotorua High School he went to Otago Medical School on the prestigious Ngarimu scholarship. He graduated in 1954 and became an orthopaedic surgeon. Tapsell won Eastern Maori for Labour in 1981, having been Deputy Mayor of Rotorua. He was a cabinet minister in the 1984–90 Labour government. In 1993 he became Speaker in unusual circumstances – National had a one-seat majority. He was the first Maori Speaker, and the first Speaker from the Opposition since the 1920s. He sought an improvement in parliamentary behaviour and standards, and was stricter about the use of language and formality of dress. A conservative and a traditionalist, Tapsell was noted for his own dress – he always had a flower in his lapel.

An 'Open House'?

Meanwhile, the public perception of Parliament sank to an all-time low. Opinion polls showed that trust in politicians slumped in the late 1980s and remained very low.[104] Parliament was increasingly concerned to revamp its public image. The changing role of the press gallery did not help. The relationship of journalists with politicians was just as symbiotic as in the past, but competition made the need to sensationalise and give a slant to a story stronger. The 'journal of record' approach fell out of fashion. Journalists discarded canons of objectivity they considered old-fashioned and unsustainable in favour of a cultivated scepticism.[105]

While politicians remained as unhappy as ever about how they were reported, parties saw the media as a resource to be exploited. The appointment of a press gallery member, Gerry Symmans, as Muldoon's ministerial press secretary in 1976 heralded this new approach. In the mid 1980s the Labour government began to hire journalists (including some from the gallery) as press secretaries. Communication became a key element of the government's strategy. In the years that followed, cadres of politically appointed press secretaries and public relations personnel became integral to politics.[106] This development did not result in increased public trust in politicians, especially as governments failed to honour election promises.

Labour's reforms of the 1980s included greater public access to Parliament. Citing the successful Canadian example, Palmer was keen to televise Parliament. Others were wary, believing that members would play to the camera and that filming might reveal an empty House or poor behaviour. TVNZ undertook a live trial of question time from 17 to 19 June 1986.[107] Producer Alistair Carthew was optimistic that the broadcasters would have control – 'so that if there's a disturbance in the chamber or a particularly interesting interjection, you can cut away and get a shot' – but there was little chance of that.[108] Panning across the chamber was banned, and the Canadian approach of providing a visual version of *Hansard* was adopted. There were simple shots of speakers' heads and shoulders, and a focus on members delivering their speeches.

The trial was relatively uneventful, aside from Winston Peters' accusation concerning the grounding of a Cook Strait ferry, and loud interjections from Muldoon (not caught on camera).[109] Journalist Tom Scott compared members with the soap opera *Coronation Street*. But the experiment proved costly and the presentation stilted, and the House was cautious about taking it further. Speaker Wall opposed televising the House. TVNZ estimated that few viewers would watch telecasts regularly.

Speaker Burke was more in favour of allowing television cameras in the House than his predecessor. A select committee decided that more regular televising should commence and that a Broadcasting of Parliament Committee should be established – but the filming should be at no cost to the government. The committee also conceded that a more flexible approach to filming than the one adopted in Canada would be appropriate. This began inauspiciously on 31 May 1990 when speeches were drowned out and there were taunts about members' appearance.[110] A code of practice was agreed to, but in 1992 members were filmed reading newspapers and talking on telephones in the chamber. The filming of National outcast Winston Peters walking from the Clerk's desk to his new seat at the back of the chamber specifically transgressed the agreement. TV3 reporter Bill Ralston told the Speaker that he 'was not his editor'. It was agreed to consider revising the rules so that 'film of general behaviour in the House', as well as speeches, might be screened.

In the event, lack of funding has limited the extent to which television cameras have appeared in the House. Television companies have been lukewarm about providing a free service.[111] The budget has been televised live since 1991 and question time has been filmed when controversial issues have arisen. The presence of cameras appears to have had little impact on members' behaviour or public perceptions of Parliament. In 2003 the Standing Orders Committee advised the government to fund the installation of permanent cameras and encourage filming of select committees to enhance the importance of their work.[112]

In 1994 following concern about the under-reporting of Parliament, daily and weekly round-up reports on National Radio (*The Day in Parliament* and *The Week in Parliament*) were commenced, with funding from the Office of the Clerk. These have been more informative than television in presenting Parliament's business to the public.

Parliament Buildings became more shabby and neglected in the 1980s. Demolition remained a possibility but the heritage value of the buildings was increasingly appreciated, and strengthening became more viable as new base isolation techniques could provide better protection against earthquakes.

The PSC planned a very substantial new 'Parliamentary Service' building (twice the floor area of the main buildings) behind Parliament as temporary accommodation while the old buildings were strengthened and refurbished.[113] Cabinet approved this in principle in 1986. Following the election in 1987, the government decided to enlarge the executive to 28 members, with ministers and associate ministers outside cabinet. The larger executive meant that accommodation in the Museum Street building (which was to have been demolished) was now needed. The proposal was scrapped.[114] Members of the PSC were furious at the lack of consultation and Chairman Wall, whose 'dream' it was to construct the building, protested strongly. Cabinet approved only temporary strengthening of the vulnerable west wing at the back of the library.

In the late 1980s the Historic Places Trust gave the main buildings an 'A' classification, considering them worthy of permanent preservation.[115] At the same time, engineering reports reiterated the seriousness of the earthquake risk. Politicians were concerned. Austin experienced a sharp earthquake while in the second-floor whips' office. As journalists rushed along the corridor and down the stairs, she saw the 'floor boards parting company with the wall'.[116] The PSC wanted to construct a smaller building behind Parliament, but the government wanted Parliament to move into the Bowen House tower block being developed by Government Property Services across Bowen Street and this went ahead.[117] Bowen House was to be linked to the Beehive by an underground passageway, and a temporary debating chamber was provided adjacent to the new block at 3 The Terrace.

In 1989 a public competition for strengthening and refurbishing the older buildings of Parliament was advertised – the country's largest conservation project. All additions since the early 1920s would be removed. The options ranged from the greatest possible retention of the original buildings to constructing new buildings within the facades of the old.[118] When he announced the winners, architects Warren and Mahoney and engineers Holmes Consulting Group, Speaker Burke declared that the buildings would be strengthened to 'national monument standard', with a 'very high value' put on conservation and enhanced public access. Parliament set its sights on making the buildings key heritage structures for the nation. Parliament Buildings would become an 'Open House' for the people of New Zealand.

As if to reinforce awareness of the hazard, an earthquake struck during question time on 21 February 1990. Prime Minister Palmer and other Labour members dived under the Table, Helen Clark was seen 'crouched cocoon-like on the floor', an unnamed member 'plonked a pillow on his head', and another 'hid under a sheepskin rug' (a comfort that was increasingly favoured by members for their benches at that time).[119] The sitting was suspended, and as the House was evacuated onto the lawn members reflected on what might have been. In January 1991 Parliament moved into Bowen House.

The estimated cost escalated, and the project was suspended for a time by the incoming National government. Acting Finance Minister Doug Kidd suggested it might be better to 'bulldoze' the buildings, retaining only the facades, or to leave them empty until money was available for the refurbishment. He earned the sobriquet 'bulldozer Kidd' from Bolger, who was more supportive.[120] In the end the government gave approval.

Mainzeal Group secured the construction contract and work began in 1992, but was interrupted by fires. A fire in the penthouse of the main buildings was not serious because the wooden structures were to be swept away, but in October 1992 a more significant fire took hold in the library foyer and badly damaged the staircase, plaster work, stained glass and roof.[121] A third fire destroyed some original urinals dating back to the early 1880s in basement toilets at the rear of the library.

Redressing the balance: institutional reform and MMP, 1985–2003

This fire destroyed the old penthouse roof additions to Parliament Buildings as the refurbishment began.

Dominion, 27 July 1992, Parliamentary Service collection

A fire in the library during the refurbishment provoked this thought on the place of politicians and press gallery journalists in the scheme of things.

IT'S FAR WORSE THAN WE THOUGHT. —THERE ARE NO JOURNALISTS OR POLITICIANS TRAPPED INSIDE…

Tom Scott, Evening Post, 21 October 1992

323

The first stage of the work was to cut the buildings free from their original foundations, excavate new basements and instal 417 base isolators to separate the buildings from the ground and protect them against earthquakes. The main buildings, previously separate structures, were rebuilt as a single unit. The walls were strengthened with reinforced concrete, and new wings were built on the second and third floors. A new 'Galleria', using Takaka marble and Coromandel granite, was created from an internal courtyard. A large hanging artwork was commissioned to enhance this striking space for exhibits. The new Maori Affairs Committee room (Maui Tikitiki A Taranga), in a prime location on the ground floor, was furnished with carvings and tukutuku work.

The ground floor of the main buildings was designated for select committee rooms, the first floor for the Speaker, the government whips and the Clerk of the House, the second for government members, and the third for the Leader of the Opposition, Opposition whips and members. A major consideration was to locate as many members as possible close to the chamber but, with the impending enlargement of the House under MMP, a number would have to be located in the Museum Street annex and Bowen House.[122] The creation of the 'Grand Hall' from the billiard lounge reflected the new resolve to open up the buildings to the public, but members were not too happy about sacrificing their inner sanctum. Locating select committee rooms rather than their offices on the ground floor of the main buildings was another bone of contention. The refurbishment also involved restoring the library building, whose west wing at the rear was replaced by a new block with vastly improved storage facilities. The work included recreating the nineteenth-century Lobby as the library's reception area and newspaper reading room. The redevelopment of Parliament grounds to reflect the original style of the 1920s was based around a number of large old pohutukawas and the cabbage trees along the frontage. Views of the buildings from Molesworth Street were opened up.[123] The opportunity to get rid of the many parking spaces on the forecourt was seized – this unattractive aspect of the precincts had been a matter of contention for decades.

Queen Elizabeth opened the refurbished buildings on 2 November 1995. Parliament began moving back in from January 1996, and the House first met in the restored chamber on 20 February. The refurbishment heightened public interest in Parliament and its heritage. Visitor numbers increased markedly. A shop and visitor centre were established and regular tours instituted. The Legislative Council chamber and the Grand Hall proved very popular for a range of functions.

With the increase in the number of members under MMP and the need to refurbish the interior of the Beehive, Broadcasting House behind Parliament was levelled, over considerable public protest. The new building on the site intended to house the executive temporarily did not go ahead, however. The select committee considering the issue tinkered briefly with moving the Beehive on rails onto this site to allow the main buildings to be completed to the original design.[124] After the matter became a political issue, the government renegotiated the lease on Bowen House instead. The Beehive was refurbished floor-by-floor from 2001. The site of Broadcasting House became a park.

MMP on trial

New Zealand's adoption of an MMP electoral system meant that the internal workings of Parliament had to change dramatically. The existing standing orders – structured around a two-party system with a simple government-opposition dichotomy – were inoperable in the new environment.[125] As electoral reform became likely and the two-party system progressively fragmented, Clerk of the House McGee made a case to the Speaker in 1992 for substantial reform of Parliament.[126] This intervention, which attracted much public attention, contrasted strongly with the traditional approach of informal, internal discussions, but reflected the changing environment. McGee suggested making procedure relaxed and more productive. The negative public perception of Parliament should be countered by 'moral leadership', in particular from a Speaker with enhanced status. The House should become more publicly acceptable, interesting and relevant. The Speaker should have greater discretion to manage the House, and should remain in office once elected regardless of changes of government. The annual programme of the session should be restored, the grip of party speaking discipline and whipping relaxed, and debate in the chamber made more meaningful, with its decorum and authority improved.

In 1996 the standing orders were changed substantially and procedure made more efficient. The Clerk's suggestions were adopted to some extent, and the standing orders were couched in more accessible language. They became operative on a trial basis later that year, prior to the first MMP Parliament.[127] An annual sitting programme based on the calendar year was adopted. The Address-in-Reply debate was confined to the triennial opening of Parliament. The Prime Minister was to provide a statement of the government's programme at the beginning of the second and third years of the parliamentary term, as an implicit test of confidence in the government. These statements were to be followed by a 15-hour debate. Sitting hours were changed and the weekly total hours were reduced. The House was to rise at 6 p.m.; there was to be only one evening sitting, on Wednesdays until 10 p.m., and a morning start on Thursdays at 10 a.m.

Debating time was cut back. The Address-in-Reply was reduced to 21 hours in total, and speaking time in general restricted to five to ten minutes. The weekly general debate was reduced to one hour. An overt 'guillotine' for the passage of legislation – trenchantly and persistently opposed throughout the history of Parliament – was finally adopted. The introductory first reading debate on bills was abandoned and replaced by the attachment of enlarged explanatory notes to bills. Second readings were now limited to two hours, with 12 ten-minute speeches. Debate on select committee reports on bills (now made after the second reading) and on the third reading were also confined to two hours. For the Committee stage, time limits applied only when agreed upon by the Business Committee.[128] Hansard now reported the estimates debate and debates in Committee in full. The obsolete rule prohibiting the reading of speeches was finally dropped. Question time was made more topical by doubling the number of questions for oral answer to 12.

During debates the Speaker's call was now to be based on voting strength, the opportunity for each party to speak, seniority, interest and expertise. The voting process was dramatically simplified.[129] There were now three types of vote – voice, party and personal. As before, the Speaker would ask for the 'Ayes' and the 'Noes'. If there was disagreement on the 'voices', a formal party vote would take place, with whips or others on duty announcing their party's votes.[130] Pairs – impractical in a multi-party Parliament – were done away with. The party vote included those outside the chamber and others who had authorised a 'proxy' vote. Personal votes were held on 'conscience' issues. In these cases, members would still go into the lobbies to be counted for a division. The Speaker's casting vote was abolished. In the event of a tie, the matter was lost. The Speaker's vote was now counted in the party vote.

The House no longer needed a quorum to sit, but 20 members had to be present for a vote to be taken.[131] The titles of Chairman and Deputy Chairman of Committees were replaced by Deputy Speaker and Assistant Speaker respectively. The formal position of Leader of the Opposition was retained, in spite of vocal opposition from smaller parties. It was to be held by the leader of the largest opposition party.

A Business Committee now planned the work of Parliament in the more complex environment.[132] This became a vital part of the House. Chaired by the Speaker and comprising one member from each party with six or more representatives in the House, together with one representative of lesser parties, it arranged the annual programme and weekly business of the House, specified the order of business and selection of speakers and times, and recommended the membership of select committees. It operated on a consensual basis and could over-ride the standing orders if necessary. This was a substantial shift of power away from the executive, in the form of the Prime Minister or Leader of the House, in determining business.

Select committees' powers to amend bills were increased substantially. Amendments agreed to unanimously were automatically incorporated into bills for their second reading. Amendments agreed to by a majority on the committee were to be considered by the House at the end of the second reading.

Select committee membership was expanded to a standard eight, and aggregate membership across all the committees was to be proportionate to a party's presence in the House. The attendance of ministers was now encouraged, but they could not vote. Select committees had to report on bills within six months, to prevent the use of delaying tactics to obstruct government measures. At the same time, following the Fiscal Responsibility Act 1994, more effective reporting to the House on the country's finances by the Finance and Expenditure Committee was introduced.[133] Much more information was given to the House in a planned manner, and the budget was presented and approved earlier in the year.

Parliament also grappled with the intractable issue of parliamentary privilege. Members more frequently made statements in the House that others thought defamatory.[134] The Standing Orders Committee had drafted a consolidating bill in 1989 to deal with the issue, but this had fallen by the wayside. David Caygill's private member's bill of 1994 (which sought sounder foundations for allegations of wrongdoing and better support for accused parties) suffered a similar fate.[135]

A long-running court case in the early 1990s highlighted the problem. Television New Zealand sought to use statements made in the House by the previous Minister of State-owned Enterprises, Richard Prebble, as evidence in a defamation action brought by Prebble against it. Unusually, the House, through Attorney-General Paul East, made submissions to the court on parliamentary privilege. Eventually, the Privy Council found in 1994 that privilege applied in this case – only the House could pronounce on words spoken in the chamber. Besides statements of members, those made by witnesses to select committees were also protected. The judgement was 'one of the most significant' on the matter of privilege, in the opinion of Clerk McGee.[136]

The 1996 standing orders gave greater protection to those giving evidence to Parliament. The New Zealand Bill of Rights Act 1990 required Parliament to observe natural justice in its inquiries while the controversy over alleged corporate tax fraud (the 'wine box' affair) in 1994 focused attention on

The symbolic end of an era on the main steps of Parliament, 6 September 1996. 'Applause peppered with a few bravos and boos marked the official dissolution of the final first-past-the-post Parliament yesterday', commented the Evening Post. *Hugo Judd, Official Secretary to the Governor-General (seated), signs the proclamation dissolving Parliament, witnessed by (from left) Milton Hollard (Clerk-Assistant) David McGee (Clerk), Angela Hauk-Willis (Department of Internal Affairs), and Ailsa Salt (Deputy Clerk).*

Redressing the balance: institutional reform and MMP, 1985–2003

Parliament's powers of inquiry, the place of tabled documents in the House, and the role of evidence to select committees.[137] Procedures were established to protect witnesses appearing before select committees, to allow responses to ad hominem allegations made in the House, and to disqualify members from select committees where there was potential for bias.

The country geared up for its first election under MMP. The Electoral Commission mounted a huge publicity campaign and voter registration was high. The election in October 1996 produced surprising results. National gained the most party votes and seats (33.8 per cent of the party vote and 44 seats). Labour slumped to 28.2 per cent of the party vote and 37 seats. New Zealand First took all five Maori seats – the so-called 'tight five' – and 17 seats in total. The Alliance won 13 seats, ACT 8 seats, and Dunne of the United Party won Ohariu-Belmont after National decided not to contest it.

A coalition was necessary but to the surprise of most commentators and the fury of Labour, National joined with New Zealand First.[138] The extremely detailed coalition agreement took what seemed an interminable time to conclude. It was not signed until the day before Parliament assembled on 12 December. Peters was appointed Deputy Prime Minister and to the newly created position of Treasurer, with Birch underneath him as Minister of Finance. The coalition parties maintained their own identities and appointed their own whips. An overall management committee and the Leader of the House were appointed jointly.

The House entered the enlarged and refurbished chamber 120 strong. The election of a Speaker and Deputy Speaker proceeded along traditional, two-party lines.[139] The coalition put up Doug Kidd, who was opposed by Hunt for Labour. Kidd won the vote 70 to 50, with Clark criticising the method of selection and Prebble expressing the hope that the position would be elevated beyond party appointments in the future. The attempt to elect a Deputy Speaker from the Opposition (Hunt was keenly interested in the position) was blocked. Instead Ian Revell (National) was elected Deputy, with Marie Hasler (National) and Geoff Braybrooke (Labour) as Assistant Speakers.

Prime Minister Jim Bolger, his cabinet and Cabinet Secretary after the coalition agreement with New Zealand First. The oval cabinet table made from selected indigenous wood was provided by the Timber Merchants' Federation in 1957. It was used until replaced in 2003 as part of the refurbishment of the Beehive.

Woolf, Parliamentary Service collection

The coalition agreement largely stymied National's hopes of further market liberalisation, and also tried to impose tight discipline on coalition members in the House. But serious conflicts arose and the government soon became incapacitated. Spending by the New Zealand First minister, Tukuroirangi Morgan, came under scrutiny, and the ill-fated development of Maori television plagued the coalition. Conflict between National's Minister of Health, Bill English, and the New Zealand First Associate Minister, Neil Kirton, eventually resulted in Kirton's resignation. The ill-feeling between the coalition partners was reflected in an alleged assault on Peters by Banks in 1997.[140]

The issue of superannuation contributed to the destabilisation.[141] Previous understandings between political parties that had produced an 'accord' on the issue broke down prior to the 1996 election. Labour and New Zealand First both promised to remove the surtax on superannuation. A central part of the coalition agreement was a referendum on compulsory superannuation – a strong commitment made by Peters – and this was held in 1997. New Zealanders registered overwhelming opposition, with more than 90 per cent of those voting rejecting the proposal.

MMP proponents who had expected politics to become more consensual were sorely disappointed by the continued conflict in the House. However, Labour and the Alliance repaired their differences after their disappointing showing in the election.[142] Following National's plunge in the polls, the more forceful Jenny Shipley replaced Bolger as Prime Minister in December 1997. She was prepared to use urgency much more readily, even invoking extraordinary urgency during the budget debate.[143]

Although the coalition staggered on, its days were numbered. Peters did not get on with Shipley in the way he had with Bolger. Bolger retired from the House not long after he was ousted as National's leader. As he delivered his valedictory there was confusion in the lobbies over the Local Government Amendment Bill (No. 5). He said (not in jest) that 'the whips have instructed me that I have to keep speaking until the Government has a majority'.[144] The division produced a tie, 60 apiece, after two Auckland National members, Christine Fletcher and John Banks, voted against the bill. Under the new rules, the second reading was lost – the only defeat of a government bill on its second reading in the twentieth century.

In August 1998 the coalition collapsed over the sale of the government's share of Wellington airport. The New Zealand First members walked out of cabinet. Peters was sacked, but National managed to hold onto power when six New Zealand First members left the party and with others continued to support the government. Shipley, in a move unprecedented under party government, chose to test confidence in the government by a motion in the House. She won 62 to 58.[145] On votes of confidence she regularly mustered a majority of 61 to 59, with the support of ACT, United and independents. Voting on other measures was haphazard. In one case, an Opposition bill on teacher registration was passed despite the government voting against it at every stage. The senior Opposition whip moved closure of the debate![146]

There was dismay and consternation at the chaotic results MMP seemed to be producing. On the initiative of the Association of Former Members, former Speakers Harrison, Gray and Tapsell prepared a report 'to help restore the perception of the importance and relevance of Parliament and of the democratic processes in the opinion of the public'. It was felt that the public's regard for Parliament was as low as it had ever been.[147]

The report sought to elevate the independence and authority of the Speaker. It suggested that the fundamental reason for the dismal view of Parliament was the failure among the public, media and politicians alike to understand the proper functions of Parliament. Other issues were the lack of leadership and discipline by party leaders, the conduct of members, and a poor relationship with the media that had led to perceptions that members' pay and allowances were excessive and not properly accounted for. Parliament, the former Speakers felt, should become more active in presenting itself to the public. The report was also critical of the standing orders, suggesting the reduction in sitting hours and opportunities for debate had gone too far. Question time had become too formal, with fewer off-the-cuff questions. Proxy voting was badly understood by the public, and the virtually empty chamber that resulted from the abolition of the quorum was a poor advertisement for Parliament.

Some amendments were made to the standing orders.[148] The House now sat on Tuesday evenings rather than Thursday mornings, to free up the latter for select committee work. Minor changes were made to speaking times and the procedure for the financial debates. The most important change concerned international treaties, which shaped New Zealand's domestic law much more than before. Up to a quarter of all legislation was being determined in this way, without Parliament having any role in the treaty-making. The government now had to present treaties to the House for scrutiny by the Foreign Affairs, Defence and Trade Select Committee prior to their ratification. Parliament's approval of treaties was not required, but it was understood that it should consider treaties before they were ratified.

The public was more concerned about the highly visible and frequent departure of members from their parties, the so-called 'party-hopping' or 'waka-jumping' that made a mockery of the principle of proportionality. The defection of Alamein Kopu from the Alliance in 1997 to become an independent was particularly damaging. Kopu had signed an agreement undertaking to resign her seat if she left the Alliance, but declined to do so.

The Alliance brought the matter before the Privileges Committee. The fundamental issue was whether 'the MMP system accorded primacy to proportional party representation in Parliament over the rights of the member as an individual'.[149] The committee determined that Kopu's letter to the Alliance did not constitute an effective resignation, and that it could not make a decision on whether members could bind themselves in this way. Labour's Cullen promoted a private member's bill requiring members to resign their seats if they resigned from their parties. Clerk McGee reflected that MMP might bind members to their parties in a way not envisaged even at the height of the two-party system. The Electoral Law Committee recommended that Cullen's bill not proceed, but both Labour and the Alliance remained committed to it. Meanwhile, in 1999 changes were made to the standing orders to tighten the definition of political parties and regulate the use of independent members' proxy votes.

A number of older and experienced members resigned in 1999 after the first Parliament under MMP. Some felt that the changes did not suit their style of politics. Paul East confessed that he was 'a little bit out of step with politics today'.[150] He believed that the high turnover of members and the trend towards a shorter stay of three to five terms was not in the best interests of the country, which needed the wisdom of age and reflection in the House. Birch, who was also retiring, felt that MMP was unsustainable. Shipley called for a new referendum on the electoral system and questioned whether government had been improved.[151] Clark, in response, criticised the lack of party loyalty shown by so many members. Backed vehemently by Cullen, she warned that Labour would deal with this matter.

Labour won the election of 1999 with 38.7 per cent of the party vote and 49 seats. It formed a minority government in coalition with the Alliance, which had ten seats. Alliance leader Jim Anderton became Deputy Prime Minister. Labour also secured an understanding that the Green Party (which had split from the Alliance and won seven seats) would support the government on supply and confidence votes. National's party vote had declined to 30.5 per cent and its seats to 39. Public opprobrium was clearly registered when the party-swapping members lost their seats.

Helen Clark won Mount Albert for Labour in 1981. She was Minister of Conservation, Housing and Health (1987–90), and Deputy Prime Minister under Palmer in 1989, the first woman to hold the position in New Zealand. Clark became Leader of the Labour Party in 1993, and in 1999 she was the first woman to be elected Prime Minister in New Zealand. Since that time more secure coalition arrangements have been forged by the Labour government, and politics has become more stable.

Jonathan Lucas Hunt was born in Lower Hutt on 2 December 1938. He was educated at Palmerston North Boys' High School and Auckland Grammar School. Hunt graduated from the University of Auckland with an MA (Hons) in 1961, and was a secondary schoolteacher until winning New Lynn for Labour in 1966. His experience in the House has been extensive. He was junior government whip (1972–4), and Chairman of Committees and Deputy Speaker (1974–5), acting as Speaker when Whitehead fell ill. Hunt was senior Opposition whip (1980–4), then Minister of Broadcasting, Postmaster-General, and later Minister of Housing and of Tourism, during the period 1984–90. He was also Leader of the House 1987–90, when he again assumed the position of senior Opposition whip. He has been Speaker since 1999.

Hunt, for some time Father of the House and considered something of an institution himself, finally became Speaker after 33 years in the House. He had an enduring interest in the standing orders and parliamentary procedure, a great love for the institution, and had been very actively involved in the PSC since its inception. He said that he was 'deeply moved' at his selection.[152] Labour's Geoff Braybrooke became Deputy Speaker and Jill Pettis Assistant Speaker, with National's Eric Roy as the other Assistant Speaker.

The Labour–Alliance coalition proved much more stable than the National–New Zealand First coalition. This helped restore some credibility to Parliament. Immediately on taking office in 1999, the new government introduced the controversial Electoral (Integrity) Amendment Bill, which required those who resigned their membership of a party to vacate their seats in Parliament. Despite a divided select committee, the bill was eventually passed under urgency in 2001, with the support of New Zealand First.[153] But the stresses on this coalition too were, in the end, too great. The ratification of the Singapore Free Trade Agreement in 2000 exposed internal disunity on the issue. It also raised the constitutional issue of collective responsibility in coalition governments. When Parliament voted 'symbolically' for ratification by noting the report of the Foreign Affairs, Defence and Trade Committee before the agreement was signed, Labour and National voted together against the smaller parties. Prime Minister Helen Clark and Foreign Affairs Minister Phil Goff were adamant that the executive retained control over the signing of treaties.[154]

In 2002, the Electoral (Integrity) Amendment Act came under close scrutiny when Deputy Prime Minister Anderton and other Alliance members avoided the intent of the legislation on a technicality after a serious split in the Alliance Party precipitated by New Zealand's involvement in the war in Afghanistan. The measure has proved not only defective in its application, but has had perverse consequences. Yet the epidemic of party-swapping has waned and the architect of the Act, Cullen, believes that parties are now sufficiently stable for it to be no longer required.[155] The Act contains provision for its removal from the statute book at the election of 2005, and it appeared in 2003 that the government would allow this to happen.

In 2002 Clark, encouraged by favourable opinion polls, called an election early, for July.[156] Parliament was not able to work effectively following the Alliance split and because of the Green Party's reluctance to concede urgency. In 2000, for example, the Greens had voted with National, ACT and New Zealand First to defeat Labour's closure motion, 60 to 59, during the passage of the Employment Relations Bill, which had been stuck in Committee for days of endless votes.[157]

Labour was re-elected as a minority government with 52 seats (41.3 per cent of the party vote). It was joined by Anderton and another Progressive Coalition member, and had the support of the eight

United Future members led by Dunne on confidence and supply. National fared poorly – it held only 27 seats (20.9 per cent of the party vote). Its ranks were severely depleted through the retirement of older, experienced hands such as Shipley, Kidd, Luxton, Wyatt Creech, and Max Bradford. New Zealand First won 13 seats, and ACT and the Greens 9 each.

With National's share of the House significantly diminished, the opposition parties could not agree on seating arrangements.[158] Prior to the election of the Speaker, members were allocated their places alphabetically. Hunt was re-elected as Speaker. Labour's Ann Hartley became Deputy Speaker and Ross Robertson an Assistant Speaker, with National's Clem Simich as the second Assistant Speaker. Normal seating arrangements could then be resumed.

MMP at work

In the early twenty-first century, public confidence in Parliament returned to some degree thanks to the greater stability in politics as MMP settled down.[159] But close attention continued to be paid to members' allowances. The apparent failure of the media and the public to appreciate their legitimacy has made it particularly difficult to counter the adverse publicity concerning allowances. This has distracted attention from the more important business of the House and reinforced negative perceptions of Parliament. From time to time, overuse or misuse of taxis, postage, air travel or accommodation in Wellington has been alleged.[160] A few politicians have fostered their careers by drawing attention to these allegations. Difficulties in assessing members' tax liability because of blurred lines between salaries and allowances and a controversy over the use of air points added fuel to the fire.

In 2002 a report commissioned by Parliament (following one by the Auditor-General) recommended a fundamental overhaul of the remuneration of members to improve transparency.[161] Legislation was introduced after the election to create an independent Remuneration Authority out of the Higher Salaries Commission. The Standing Orders Committee amended the bill to transfer responsibility for almost all allowances to the Speaker, arguing that 'a non-parliamentary body should not be responsible for determining what services should be funded'.[162] While this was constitutionally proper, it proved hard to persuade the public of the propriety of Parliament retaining control.

The role of select committees was greatly strengthened under MMP, making the New Zealand Parliament notable internationally. Changes in the standing orders freed up members for committee work and allowed committees to meet for up to three hours during sittings of the House. The increased scrutiny of government departments that resulted was assisted by funding for specialist assistance to committees.[163]

Under the energetic chairing of ACT member Derek Quigley in the late 1990s, the Foreign Affairs, Defence and Trade Committtee developed a wide-ranging policy function.[164] In 1999 it produced the radical and sweeping 'Defence Beyond 2000' report. This was followed in 2002 by a report on the economic and trading relationship between Australia and New Zealand. The committee's role was further enlarged by its scrutiny of international treaties from 2000.

At times, however, the integration of select committee deliberations into the business of the House left something to be desired. When the government tried in 2000 to rush a bill which reorganised the public health system through the House, the Health Select Committee failed to consult with the Greens and the Alliance. Its chair altered National's minority view in the report to the House.[165] After hasty negotiations Labour deferred the bill, allowing the Greens and National to make their contributions to an amended piece of legislation before its third reading. The Greens called this process 'MMP in action'; to the government it was more like an embarrassing mess.

The chairing of select committees took some time to adjust to MMP. In 1996 Labour wanted three chairs but got only the Regulations Review Committee. New Zealand First and ACT were also allocated one chair each in an understanding with National. As a result, appointments to chairs were seriously delayed, and the issue was resolved only after closure was applied to debate in the House.[166] In 1999 the Labour government argued that National had set a precedent and refused to give them additional chairs.[167] The Alliance was given one chair. Faced with the prospect of losing control of some committees, the government appointed special committees on which it had an assured majority, such as the committee on the Accident Insurance (Transitional Provisions) Bill.

In 2002 there was more substantial change to select committee arrangements. There was now a government majority only on the Government Administration Committee. Of the 14 select committees, 9 were chaired by Labour, 2 by National (Regulations Review and Primary Production) and 1 each by United Future, New Zealand First and the Greens.[168] The Deputy Chairs were allocated to create a rough proportionality overall. This approach met with more approval. The House began to grant non-voting membership of select committees to members from smaller parties to facilitate wider participation in committee work.

In the MMP environment private members' bills (now known as members' bills) experienced a resurgence. The Office of the Clerk provided a bill-drafting service.[169] Such measures were facilitated by the removal of the 'appropriation rule' that had traditionally disallowed any bills involving changes to government expenditure. This was replaced by a less draconian 'financial veto' that the government could apply to prevent a bill's third reading. In practice this veto was not used greatly. Governments preferred to use party support to defeat such initiatives in the House. The greater involvement of members did not extend to the budget, however. Only once has a select committee recommended an alteration to a vote.[170]

Individual members now took a more prominent role in the House, and the focus of attack shifted to select committees and question time, with its drama, theatrics and humour. But as Speaker Wall observed, the old rationale for question time as a means of obtaining public information has been supplanted by more immediate political motivations.[171] As well as Opposition grandstanding, question time provided the opportunity for governments to set up 'patsy' questions that praised their efforts. The number of written questions escalated to about 40,000 for the 1996–9 Parliament and 50,000 for the 1999–2002 Parliament. The high profile of question time, together with the increasingly independent and aggressive role of select committees, represented a definite shift in the balance of the functions of Parliament, towards more intense scrutiny of the government and government departments.

Although the public still believes that the chamber is the hub of Parliament, its role has diminished as a result of these changes. The burgeoning demands on members' time outside the chamber and the declining importance of votes have contributed to this trend.[172] Strict time limits on debate limited its function as a forum for a talkative, obstructive and stonewalling Opposition. The multiplication of opposition parties meant that their roles were no longer simply trenchant attacks on the government. Competing opposition positions had also to be taken into account.

The obverse of the attention given to question time was the tendency for the chamber (and the press gallery) to empty out once the show was over. The chamber became alarmingly thin when the government was dealing with its routine business. The traditional budget night disappeared, partly because of the Fiscal Responsibility Act. In 2002 the Serjeant-at-Arms had to ask parliamentary staff to fill the galleries for the budget announcement – a far cry, noted the *Dominion*, from 'the days of dramatic and dastardly budgets that had the whole country filling up the petrol tank and stocking up on ciggies and beer, before gluing itself to the television for the evening'.[173]

There was less cut and thrust to debate, perhaps due to the lack of experience of many members as well as the lifting of the prohibition on reading speeches.[174] Simon Upton, who had arrived in 1981 at the age of 23 as one of the youngest-ever members, expressed his disappointment at the decline of serious debate in his valedictory in 2000. He decried how the chamber had 'become a place of formulaic, partisan offerings' and denounced the five-minute general debate speeches as a 'travesty'.[175] Speaker Hunt, perhaps pointedly, congratulated Upton on 'one of the most distinguished valedictory speeches' that he had ever heard.

Redressing the balance: institutional reform and MMP, 1985–2003

The reduction to three sitting days a week with reduced hours, together with the difficulty of taking urgency in circumstances of coalition or minority government, has made it hard for governments to get their business through. The result has been a log-jam of government legislation and private members' bills (which have been chosen for introduction by ballot since 1992). The overloading also limited discussion of the reports of select committee. In 2003 the Clerk of the House suggested further changes to the standing orders to expedite business – a return to a four-day sitting week and, following the examples of Britain and Australia, the radical step of splitting the House to enable it to deal simultaneously with two pieces of legislation at different stages.[176] Parliament is likely to continue to adjust to the MMP environment for some time yet.

The changing House

The tumultuous events of the mid to late 1980s prepared the way for MMP. Many people saw executive power as excessive; public trust in the political system was eroded; the male domination of Parliament was broken down; and the two major parties were transformed. The massive intake of new members in 1990 prepared the ground for the changes to come.

The two major parties now drew upon similar social groupings. By 1990 National had substantially shed its farmer base, while Labour's takeover by middle-class professionals continued.[177] Farmers finally disappeared as a major component of the House in the 1990s, their numbers halving to 8 per cent of all members by 2002. Business, commerce, law, the public sector and accountancy now provided the bulk of members. Business made the largest contribution at almost 20 per cent of the total. Teachers had nearly doubled their representation to 18 per cent, while lawyers remained stable at around 10 per cent. Other professional occupations accounted for much of the remainder. More than three-quarters of members now had tertiary qualifications.

The number of women members rose steadily from 12 in 1984 to 21 in 1993 and 37 in 1999 (30.8 per cent of members). Women were increasingly appointed to senior positions. Of the ten female

Hunt abandoned the Speaker's wig altogether. Here a cartoonist speculates on the impact of dreadlocked Rastafarian member Nandor Tanczos on the House. Both Tanczos and Hunt had remarked on the drinking habits of members.

Labour members elected in 1984, Helen Clark, Margaret Shields, Fran Wilde, Annette King and Margaret Austin got cabinet posts in succeeding years, with Clark becoming Deputy Prime Minister in 1989–90. Ruth Richardson became Minister of Finance in 1990. By then there were eight female National members, including the Minister of Social Welfare, Jenny Shipley, who would be New Zealand's first female Prime Minister from 1997 to 1999. In late 1999 Shipley was replaced as Prime Minister by Helen Clark. Into the new century the proportion of female members remained at a steady 30 per cent. Women were appointed as Deputy and Assistant Speaker.

Under MMP there was a wider range of political parties, interests and people in the House. The 1990s brought a sprinkling of members of Pacific Island or Asian origin and those who represented alternative lifestyles, a greater variety of religions, including the first Muslim member and a Rastafarian, and members who were openly gay or trans-sexual.[178] The number of Maori members increased sharply. By 1996 their proportion of 13 per cent reflected that in the population at large. The first Pacific Island member, Taito Phillip Field, entered Parliament in 1993 and the first Asian member, Pansy Wong, in 1996.

The trend towards a younger age of entry to the House continued, with a little under 70 per cent of members in their thirties and forties. The average age remained around 45, with the average age at first entry just under 40. The 1990–3 Parliament was a particularly youthful one, with one-fifth of members in their thirties, half in their forties, and little more than one-fifth in their fifties. It was now rare for members to continue in the House beyond four or five terms – the average stay was just over seven years and only 14 members had more experience than this. Nearly two-thirds of members had been in Parliament for three terms at most.

The entry of younger age-groups and the increased 'professionalisation' of Parliament in the late 1980s and early 1990s meant, as East and others observed, that members generally had less experience of the outside world. But after the first MMP election in 1996, the trend was reversed. While there was a very large intake of 45 new members in that election (38 per cent of the larger House of 120), turnover in the House declined substantially thereafter. Following the election of 2002, the thirties and forties age-groups combined were down to 40 per cent of the total, while 44 per cent were in their fifties. Members in their sixties were, for the first time in a long while, a

Tom Scott, Evening Post, 9 August 2001

The Electoral Reform Committee rejects taking any action on the number of members after a referendum suggests that the public strongly favours a reduction.

significant group. With more stable parties and governments, Parliament had entered a more settled period.

Concern was expressed over the greater vulnerability of inexperienced members to the influence of single-issue groups.[179] The former farmer, business and trade union interest groups declined in importance, their places taken by new groups claiming to articulate either a broader public interest or more specific agendas. Accompanying this was a shift from smoke-filled back rooms to the more open arena of submissions and the public proceedings of select committees. These more diverse interests have been directly represented in the House through members who are, to a greater extent than in the past, identified and to some extent selected by parties or elected by the people on the basis of their commitments to specific causes or issues. McGee has raised the question of the implications for Parliament of magnified public expectations under MMP that representatives would act as 'ambassadors' for the 'aspirations of certain ethnic groups'.[180] Political scientist Keith Jackson has cautioned that political parties are no longer mass-democracy parties with hundreds of thousands of members, but cadre parties of smaller élite, professional groups.[181]

The old-style local electorate representative now has a much diminished role. The introduction of list members has promoted a broader arithmetical 'representativeness', but has also weakened the sense of local accountability and anchorage that all members had enjoyed in the interests of their electorates. MMP also finally broke the hold of the marginal provincial seats on national politics.

The trend towards greater stability in the last two Parliaments offers encouragement that the institution is once again settling down. MMP has made the legislative process more politically contestable and has given the House a greater role in shaping legislation and policy, particularly through the work of select committees, even if New Zealand politics remains characterised by 'realpolitik' rather than 'consensus'.[182] Minority government since 1999 has necessarily required much greater flexibility and more consultation in Parliament. MMP has also strengthened the link between party policy commitments and their actions once in office, although this has had to be tempered by the realities of coalition or minority government. Manifesto commitments have become sparser, more cautious and expressed as general principles, to leave room for manoeuvre.

The referendum held during the 1999 election on reducing the number of members to 99 gave very strong support (81.5 per cent) for a reduction. Nonetheless, the new Labour government said it would neither reduce numbers nor accept the further referendum on the electoral system proposed by National.[183] The referendum result and other surveys suggest that the public's regard for Parliament is still poor.[184] The antagonism towards the increased number of members under MMP reflects long and deeply held views on the size and expense of Parliament. Under MMP voting levels have continued to decline, and confusion over the significance of the two votes persists.[185] There remains some way to go in restoring faith and trust in Parliament and the system of representative democracy, even if the institution of Parliament has proved adaptable to the changing demands of the political system.

The reforming impulse of governments and the introduction of MMP in the late twentieth century have wrought far-reaching and fundamental changes and shifted the balance between Parliament and the executive significantly back towards the former. Representation has been broadened, decision-making has become more open and contestable, and it seems possible that governments might once again be made and unmade on the floor of the House.

Conclusion

The improvised beginnings of Parliament in makeshift quarters in Auckland on that wet day of 24 May 1854 gave little indication of what was to come. The formation of a stable executive and the assumption of responsible government was followed by a wresting of powers from the Governor. New Zealand's political leaders were chosen from the elected representatives in the House and its governments became accountable to that chamber. Through the medium of factional politics, the House was shaped into a workable institution providing New Zealand with effective government and a functional legal infrastructure. Meanwhile Parliament moved to Wellington, the institution grew and more democratic forms of suffrage were adopted. The extension of the franchise enlarged the basis of representation, brought new groups into the House, and created the conditions for the formation of political parties.

Into the new century, the House adapted to the emergence of a party system of government and a shifting balance between the powers of the executive and Parliament. The destruction of the Houses of Parliament by fire and their rebuilding, the experience of the two World Wars, the abolition of the Legislative Council, and the consolidation of the two-party system punctuated the first half-century, celebrated in 1954 by the centennial of the institution. The shifting social composition of the House reflected changing social groups and expectations of government and the state. In following decades the two-party system tightened its grip, amid growing concern over the means of representation and the balance between executive and Parliament.

Near the end of the twentieth century, a fundamental re-evaluation of the most appropriate form of political representation took place. This brought with it MMP, introduced more diversity among New Zealand's legislators, and broke down the rigid two-party system. This fundamental reappraisal of the place of the state and the nature of executive government required the House to adapt rapidly – and adapt it did.

This history of the House of Representatives fills a substantial gap in the story of the evolution of New Zealand's representative institutions. A.H. McLintock wrote on the constitutional beginnings of representative government prior to the calling of the first Parliament in 1854, and he and others examined the Legislative Council, abolished in 1950. The central theme throughout has been the way that political representation has evolved, the changing manner in which different forces have been expressed within the House, and the way that the House has responded to these changes, slowly at times but, in the long view of history, dramatically nonetheless. This history has also recorded the contributions made by a wide range of groups and individuals, together with the dramas that have unfolded on the floor of the House.

The history of the House tells us much about the changing relationship between the people of New Zealand and its political institutions. Shifting social definitions of political representation require new conditions for their fulfilment. The extent to which the House of Representatives at the beginning of the twenty-first century is no longer recognisable as that of the nineteenth century, or even of the mid to late twentieth century, is an indication of the magnitude of the changes. Understanding the House of Representatives – the representative forum for the people of New Zealand – and its complex evolution is integral to ensuring full and proper democratic representation itself.

Acknowledgements

Many people have helped me over the last three years. I can name here only some who have been of particular assistance. The Parliamentary Service and the Office of the Clerk jointly provided the funding for the project. I am very grateful for the comments of David McGee, Clerk of the House of Representatives, and Milton Hollard, Clerk-Assistant (Research), on drafts of the book. Staff in the Office of the Clerk, including Valerie Hellberg and Lisa Bognuda, have also assisted my research. Moira Fraser, Parliamentary Librarian, and the staff of the Parliamentary Library, especially Geoffrey Anderson and Barbara Stedman, have always been very helpful, interested in and supportive of the project. I have appreciated the library staff's rapid responses to my many requests for assistance. In the Parliamentary Service, Fred Albert provided files for research; Michelle Janse was extremely helpful in all sorts of ways, and I am very grateful for her support; John O'Sullivan warmly supported the project. Thanks also to Phillip O'Shea for his assistance.

Staff at the Alexander Turnbull Library, and especially Joan McCracken and Heather Mathie in the pictorial section and Linda Evans of the Oral History Archive, have been of great help. Numerous staff in the reference section at Archives New Zealand assisted with research. Emma Dewson's substantial contribution in researching aspects of the functioning of the House and in preparing a database of members should be acknowledged, as should Raewyn Dalziel's generous loan of her research files. Thanks to Hilary Stace for photographic research and to Fran McGowan, librarian, for her rapid response to my requests. (In a few instances copyright holders for illustrations could not be traced. If desired, a fee or other appropriate form of recognition could be negotiated with the holder.) I am grateful to my father, Lewis E. Martin, for guidance on architectural matters associated with the history. I would also like to acknowledge the valuable discussions I had with George Gair, Bob Tizard, Bert Bailey, Charles Littlejohn, Neale McMillan and Whetu Tirikatene-Sullivan. Jock Phillips, Claudia Orange, Bronwyn Dalley and Gavin McLean of the History Group set up and supervised the project, and commented on drafts. John Wilson, David Green and Gavin McLean did fine editing work. Finally, thanks to Sharmian Firth and Tracey Stagg of Dunmore Press for guiding the book through to publication on a tight schedule.

John E. Martin
February 2004

Notes

Abbreviations

AJHR	*Appendices to the Journal of the House of Representatives*
ArchNZ	Archives New Zealand, Wellington
ATL	Alexander Turnbull Library, Wellington
AUL	Auckland University Library
DNZB	*Dictionary of New Zealand Biography*
Dom	*Dominion*
DP	*Dominion Post*
EP	*Evening Post*
GBPP	*Great Britain, Parliamentary Papers*
JHR	*Journals of the House of Representatives*
JLC	*Journals of the Legislative Council*
NZH	*New Zealand Herald*
NZJH	*New Zealand Journal of History*
NZPD	*New Zealand Parliamentary Debates (Hansard)*
NZT	*New Zealand Times*
ODT	*Otago Daily Times*
PS	Parliamentary Service (files held in Parliament)
VP	*Votes and Proceedings*
Wheeler clippings	Political newspaper clippings, 1906–1950, Charles Edward Wheeler (4 vols), held in Parliamentary Library

Chapter 1 – Shaky beginnings, 1854–6

1. *New Zealander*, 20, 27, 31 May 1854. *Southern Cross*, 23, 26 May 1854. W. David McIntyre (ed.), *The Journal of Henry Sewell*, (2 vols), Christchurch, 1980, vol 2, pp. 11–28, entries 24–28 May 1854. *NZPD*, 1854, pp. 1–2.
2. *Southern Cross*, 26 May 1854.
3. 'A Letter From Sydney', p. 169, cited in Philip Temple, *A Sort of Conscience: The Wakefields*, Auckland, 2002, p. 128.
4. A.H. McLintock, *Crown Colony Government in NZ*, Wellington, 1958, p. 260.
5. See for the extent of the suffrage: J.E. FitzGerald, *The Representation of NZ*, Christchurch, 1864, p. 9; A.S. Thomson, *The Story of NZ*, London, 1859, vol 2, pp. 208–9; D.G. Herron, 'The structure and course of politics, 1853–1858', PhD, University of Otago, 1959; D.G. Herron, 'The franchise and NZ politics', *Political Science*, vol 12, no 1, 1960. The electoral system will be touched upon only as it affected Parliament and in relation to events in the House of Representatives. Otherwise, see *AJHR*, 1986, H-3, appendix A; Keith Jackson and Alan McRobie, *NZ Adopts Proportional Representation*, Christchurch, 1998, ch. 2; A. McRobie, *NZ Electoral Atlas*, Wellington, 1989; Leslie Lipson, *The Politics of Equality*, Chicago, 1948, chs 2, 8. Neill Atkinson, *Adventures in Democracy*, Dunedin, 2003.
6. McLintock, pp. 289–93. Alan Ward, *A Show of Justice*, Auckland, 1974, pp. 85–90.
7. Herron, 'Structure and course of politics', pp. 113–16. Herron, 'The franchise and NZ politics', p. 42. Lipson, *Politics of Equality*, pp. 38–43.
8. Election database, 1853–1876, and database of members, 1853–1938, Ministry for Culture and Heritage.
9. *Wellington Independent*, 31 Aug 1853.
10. McLintock, ch. 18. Raewyn Dalziel, 'The politics of settlement', pp. 92–4, in W.H. Oliver (ed.), *The Oxford History of NZ*, Wellington, 1981.
11. Wakefield letter, 24 Aug 1853, E.G. Wakefield papers, AUL.
12. McLintock, p. 377, citing *Otago Witness*, 31 Dec 1853.
13. McLintock, pp. 127–9.
14. *GBPP*, 1854, Cd. 1779, pp. 242–4.
15. W.P. Morrell, *The Provincial System in NZ, 1852–76* (revised edition), Christchurch, 1964, p. 81.
16. *NZPD*, 1860, p. 790; 1861, p. 321; 1863 pp. 900–3.
17. Colonial Secretary's Office/Department of Internal Affairs, IA1, 1855/705, ArchNZ. Herron, 'Structure and course of politics', pp. 389–405. Edmund Bohan, *'Blest Madman': FitzGerald of Canterbury*, Christchurch, 1998, chs 8, 9. Peter Stuart, *Edward Gibbon Wakefield in NZ*, Wellington, 1971. Rex Wright-St Clair, *Thoroughly a Man of the World: A Biography of Sir David Monro*, Christchurch, 1971, pp. 107–8.
18. Jeanine Graham, *Frederick Weld*, Auckland, 1983, p. 56.
19. McIntyre (ed.), vol 2, pp. 17–20, entries 22, 23 May 1854. Letters of Thomas King to Mary King, 26 May 1854, MS Papers 5641-02, ATL. William Fox ('Stranger in the gallery'), *Wellington Independent*, 29 Oct 1856.
20. McIntyre (ed.), vol 2, p. 20, entry 23 May 1854. Letters of Thomas King to Mary King, 28 May 1854. *Nelson Examiner*, 7 Oct 1854. Wright-St Clair, p. 108. Herron, 'Structure and course of politics', p. 403.
21. FitzGerald Letters, Fanny FitzGerald to Mr Vaux, 7 Jul, 20 Aug 1854, AUL. Bohan, *'Blest Madman'*, p. 108.
22. IA1, 1854/622, 784, 953, 1034, 1326, 2880, 2893. J.O. Wilson,

341

22. *NZ Parliamentary Record, 1840–1984*, Wellington, 1985, pp. 314–15. Article by Wilson, *Auckland Star*, 24 May 1954. John Stacpoole, *Colonial Architecture in NZ*, Wellington, 1976, pp. 62, 65.
23. McIntyre (ed.), vol 2, p. 26, entry 27 May 1854. *Wellington Independent*, 29 Oct 1856.
24. *Wellington Independent*, 29 Oct 1856.
25. R. Gaudin, 'Clifford of Stonyhurst – an account of the life of Charles Clifford in NZ', MA, Canterbury University College, 1950, p. 93.
26. *NZPD*, 1854, p. 113. McIntyre (ed.), vol 2, pp. 20–3, entry 24 May 1854.
27. *NZPD*, 1860, p. 805.
28. William Gisborne, *NZ Rulers and Statesmen, 1840 to 1897* (revised edition), London, 1897, p. 151.
29. *NZPD*, 1854, p. 21.
30. *NZPD*, 1854, p. 8.
31. For politics in these years, see McIntyre (ed.), vol 2, generally, and appendix 1, 'FitzGerald's account of the first General Assembly'; Gaudin, ch. 6; Guy H. Scholefield (ed.), *The Richmond–Atkinson Papers*, (2 vols), Wellington, 1960, chs 5–8; Bohan, *'Blest Madman'*; Edmund Bohan, *Edward Stafford: NZ's First Statesman*, Christchurch, 1994; Temple, ch. 29.
32. Editorial, *Southern Cross*, 29 Aug 1854.
33. McIntyre (ed.), vol 2, p. 22, entry 24 May 1854.
34. *NZPD*, 1854, p. 4. Letters of Thomas King to Mary King, 26 May 1854.
35. *NZPD*, 1854, p. 4. G.H. Scholefield (ed.), *A Dictionary of NZ Biography* (2 vols), Wellington, 1940, Clifford entry.
36. Graham, p. 56.
37. *VP*, session 1, 1854, (at end of which is the agreed form of prayer). This version, different from that of the House of Commons, continued to be used until the turn of the century when one based more on the Commons' prayer was adopted. *Dom*, 29 Jul 1950. This form of prayer was used until 1962 when it was revised. David McGee, *Parliamentary Practice in NZ*, (second edition), Wellington, 1994, pp. 84, 105. *JHR*, 1962, pp. 39–40. *AJHR*, 1962, I-17, pp. 6, 23.
38. C.E. Wheeler, 'Our Parliament', clipping, 10 Jun 1924, Wheeler clippings, vol 4, Parliamentary Library.
39. Legislative Department, LE1, 1854/7, ArchNZ. *VP*, session 1, 1854.
40. *Wellington Independent*, 31 Aug 1860.
41. *VP*, 1856, Standing Orders.
42. *AJHR*, 1892, I-6, p. 1.
43. *VP*, session 2, 1854, report of the select committee on estimates.
44. Herron, 'Structure and course of politics', pp. 180–6, 199.
45. Letters of Thomas King to Mary King, 6 Jul 1854.
46. *NZPD*, 1854, pp. 417–21; 1856, p. 265. W.A. Pierr, 'The history of the first NZ Parliament', MA, Canterbury University College, 1923, p. 221. Wilson, *Parliamentary Record*, pp. 302–5.
47. Editorial, *Southern Cross*, 30 May 1854. IA1, 1854/1886, 2216, 2880.
48. LE1, 1854/304, Speaker's letterbook, 1854–6, Campbell to Colonial Secretary, 4 Apr 1856, Campbell letter of 28 Sept 1854.
49. McIntyre (ed.), vol 2, p. 172, entry 10 Sept 1855.
50. See contemporary photographs, and plans of 1866 and 1876. Pers. comm., Sarah Macready, Historic Places Trust, Auckland, 2001.
51. *NZPD*, vol 54, 1886, p. 83. LE1, 1854/304; 1855/2848a, 3049.
52. *NZPD*, 1854, p. 181.
53. *NZPD*, 1854, p. 295.
54. LE1, 1863/2; 1864/2.
55. *Wellington Independent*, 29 Oct 1856.
56. IA1, 1858/395, 408, 423. LE1, 1864/2.
57. A.S. Atkinson to Emily E. Richmond, 18 Dec 1864, Scholefield (ed.), vol 2, p. 133.
58. IA1, 1854/1749, 2658. LE1, 1854/304, Clifford letter of 7 Jul 1854. *Southern Cross*, 8, 15 Sept 1854. *NZPD*, 1854, pp. 7, 96, 224.
59. *Wellington Independent*, 29 Oct 1856.
60. *NZ Gazette*, 21 Jul 1854.
61. IA1, 1884/12.
62. Sewell's journal, 14 Aug 1860, qMS 1783-8, ATL.
63. *Wellington Independent*, 29 Oct 1856.
64. LE1, 1854/304, Campbell to Colonial Secretary, 27 Feb 1856; 1866/103.
65. *NZPD*, 1854, p. 22. *GBPP*, 1854, Cd. 160.
66. Gaudin, pp. 100–4.
67. Graham, p. 58.
68. Alfred Saunders, *History of NZ, 1642–1861*, Christchurch, 1896, p. 304. W. Swainson, *NZ and its Colonisation*, London, 1859, chs 12, 13. Bohan, *'Blest Madman'*, pp. 125, 131–2.
69. *NZPD*, 1854, p. 269. Stuart, p. 150.
70. *NZPD*, 1854, p. 336. Pierr, pp. 167–72. Thomson, vol 2, pp. 219–20. McIntyre (ed.), vol 2, pp. 67–75, entry 22 Aug 1854. *Southern Cross*, 18, 22, 25 Aug 1854. *New Zealander*, 19, 26 Aug 1854. Saunders, p. 307. C.R. Carter, *Life and Recollections of a NZ Colonist*, London, 1866 and 1875, vol 2, pp. 110–11. Carol Rankin, 'Turmoil in the House', in David Wilson and Carol Rankin, *Tales of Two Contempts*, Wellington, 1998.
71. McIntyre (ed.), vol 1, introduction, p. 92.
72. Pierr, p. 171.
73. *NZPD*, 1854, p. 339. Saunders, p. 307.
74. Saunders, p. 307.
75. *NZPD*, 1854, p. 360.
76. *NZPD*, 1854, p. 444. Bohan, *'Blest Madman'*, p. 130. Herron, 'Structure and course of politics', pp. 382–3. *NZPD*, 1863, p. 927.
77. McIntyre (ed.), vol 2, pp. 83–7, entries 10, 17 Sept 1854.
78. The Otago members apparently returned home via Australia! Herron, 'Structure and course of politics', p. 391.
79. *NZPD*, 1854, p. 455.
80. Letters of Thomas King to Mary King, 12 Jul 1854.
81. McIntyre (ed.), vol 2, p. 89, entry 23 Sept 1854.
82. *GBPP*, 1855, Cd. 160, Earl Grey to Wynyard, 8 Dec 1854, p. 39. McIntyre (ed.), vol 1, introduction, pp. 96–100. Colonial Office correspondence, CO 209/124, pp. 121–4, Earl Grey's cancelled draft of 20 Nov 1854 (microfilm, ArchNZ).
83. B.J. Dalton, *War and Politics in NZ, 1855–1870*, Sydney, 1967, p. 23. Herron, 'Structure and course of politics', p. 396.
84. *NZPD*, 1855, p. 555. Herron, 'Structure and course of politics', p. 458ff.
85. *NZPD*, 1855, p. 557.
86. *NZPD*, 1856, pp. 16–17.
87. *Southern Cross*, 15 Apr 1856. Herron, 'Structure and course of politics', pp. 391, 393–4. *NZPD*, 1856, p. 246.
88. *Wellington Independent*, 29 Oct 1856.
89. J.K. Cunningham, 'Equality of electorates in NZ, 1854–1899', MA, Canterbury University College, 1953, vol 1, p. 19.
90. Database of NZ notables, Ministry for Culture and Heritage. I am grateful for access to this database compiled by Susan Butterworth.
91. Thomson, vol 2, p. 239.
92. *New Zealander*, 16 Apr 1856. *Wellington Independent*, 3 Sept 1856.

92. McIntyre (ed.), vol 2, pp. 228–40, entries 20 Apr–18 May 1856. G.A. Wood, 'The political structure of NZ, 1858–1861', PhD, University of Otago, 1965, p. 112.
93. McIntyre (ed.), vol 2, p. 237, entry 11 May 1856.
94. D.G. Herron, 'Provincialism and centralism, 1853–1858', in Robert Chapman and Keith Sinclair (eds) *Studies of a Small Democracy*, Auckland, 1963. Herron, 'The structure and course of politics'. Wood, 'Political structure', ch. 6.
95. *Wellington Independent*, 3 Sept 1856.
96. R.C.J. Stone, *Young Logan Campbell*, Auckland, 1982, pp. 218–19. *NZPD*, 1856, p. 69.
97. *NZPD*, 1856, p. 105.
98. 'Verax', *ODT*, 3 Sept 1881.
99. *NZPD*, 1856, pp. 85–6. *Wellington Independent*, 3 Sept 1856.
100. See for New South Wales, P. Loveday and A.W. Martin, *Parliament, Factions and Parties*, Melbourne, 1966.
101. Lipson, *Politics of Equality*, pp. 47–8, 81.
102. Leslie Lipson, 'The origins of caucus in NZ', *Historical Studies*, vol 2, no 5, 1942, p. 3. Wood, 'Political structure', p. 122n.
103. Ian R. Fletcher, 'Parties in the NZ House of Representatives, 1870–1890', MA, University of Canterbury, 1982, p. 14.
104. *NZPD*, vol 17, 1875, p. 33.
105. *NZPD*, vol 17, 1875, p. 12.
106. *Wellington Independent*, 3 Sept 1856.
107. *NZPD*, vol 22, 1876, pp. 91–4. Wheeler, 'The representative chamber', *LT*, 15 Jun 1922.
108. *NZPD*, 1856, pp. 131, 281; 1862, p. 626. *Southern Cross*, 10 Jun 1856. Carter, vol 2, p. 158. Sewell's journal, 26 Nov 1863; *Wellington Independent*, 21 Oct 1865.
109. *NZPD*, vol 98, 1897, pp. 636–54.
110. *NZPD*, vol 59, 1887, p. 1003.
111. McIntyre (ed.), vol 1, introduction, pp. 108–9; vol 2, p. 246, entry 1 Jun 1856. Dalton, pp. 34, 77.
112. Cabinet was defined only by membership of the Executive Council and often included ministers without portfolio (devices to reward politicians, provide the requisite balance in cabinet, or, from the 1870s, to include Maori representatives).
113. Morrell, p. 101. Wood, 'Political structure', p. 13. *VP*, 25 Jul 1856.
114. McIntyre (ed.), vol 2, p. 255, entry 13 Jul 1856.
115. *NZPD*, 1856, pp. 281, 307, 328–9.
116. *New Zealander*, 13 Aug 1856.
117. *NZPD*, 1856, pp. 14–15.
118. *New Zealander*, 20 Aug 1856. McIntyre (ed.), vol 2, pp. 259–62, entry 17 Aug 1855.

Chapter 2 – Establishing the foundations, 1858–75

1. W.K. Jackson, *The NZ Legislative Council*, Dunedin, 1972. A.H. McLintock and G.A. Wood, *The Upper House in Colonial NZ*, Wellington, 1987.
2. Jackson, *Legislative Council*, p. 103.
3. *NZPD*, 1856, p. 263. Wood, 'Political structure', pp. 58–9, *JHR*, 1860, pp. 247–8. LE1, 1860/25; 1861/14; 1862/14.
4. *JLC*, 1868, p. 22, tables. *NZPD*, vol 10, 1871, pp. 127–9; vol 11, 1871, pp. 891–5.
5. Wood, 'Political structure', p. 36. Bohan, *Stafford*, p. 120.
6. *NZPD*, 1858, pp. 373, 375. *Cyclopedia of NZ, Auckland*, Christchurch, 1902, p. 81. Thomson, vol 2, pp. 266–7. Herron, 'Structure and course of politics', p. 185.
7. IA1, 1856/1192, Clerk of House to Colonial Secretary, 12 Apr 1856; 1856/2109, report of committee. *NZPD*, 1856, p. 5. *LT*, 15 May 1858.
8. LE1, 1864/2.
9. A.H. Reed (ed.), *With Anthony Trollope in NZ*, Wellington, 1969, p. 35, referring to the Otago Provincial Council chamber.
10. *NZPD*, 1861, pp. 117, 153.
11. The Auckland Provincial Council used the premises outside of the parliamentary sessions.
12. The session of 1856 had been notable for its private members' bills, with select committees often piloting the legislation through the House. Wood, 'Political structure', pp. 95–6.
13. Morrell, p. 103ff.
14. Britain had disallowed the Waste Lands Act 1856 as contrary to the Constitution Act. M.M. Simpson, 'The history of the second NZ Parliament', MA, Canterbury University College, 1935, ch. 5. Wood, 'Political structure', p. 14ff.
15. McIntyre (ed.), vol 1, introduction, pp. 111–14. Dalton, ch. 2; Keith Sinclair, *The Origins of the Maori Wars* (second edition), Auckland, 1961, pp. 85–90.
16. Dalton, pp. 40–1, 48–9, ch. 3.
17. The Governor was to act on the advice of the Executive Council. Sinclair, *Origins of the Maori Wars*, p. 89.
18. *NZPD*, 1858, pp. 429, 467–8.
19. *NZPD*, 1858, pp. 64, 590.
20. Bohan, *Stafford*, p. 128.
21. Simpson, pp. 273–4. *NZPD*, 1861, pp. 241, 275; 1863, p. 900. Carter, vol 2, p. 151, 153, 167–8.
22. Morrell, pp. 16–20; Bohan, *Stafford*, pt 3, ch. 8.
23. *NZPD*, 1860, p. 600.
24. *NZPD*, 1860, p. 252. Saunders, vol 1, p. 406.
25. Sewell's journal, 14 Aug 1860. *NZPD*, 1860, pp. 379–81. Hadfield and McLean were followed by four Maori chiefs who delivered their (favourable) views on the Native Offenders Bill.
26. In 1872 a Wellington merchant was called to the bar over an alleged menacing of a member. *DNZB*, vol 2, John Martin. A.F. Campbell, 'The Speakership of the NZ House of Representatives, 1854–1912', MA, Canterbury University College, 1952, pp. 98–9. *NZPD*, vol 13, 1872, pp. 187–92, 201. *AJHR*, 1872, H-3.
27. *New Zealander*, 8 Aug 1860. Saunders, vol 1, p. 404.
28. *NZPD*, 1860, p. 582. *Wellington Independent*, 9 Oct 1860.
29. *NZPD*, 1860, p. 486. D.C. Doig, 'The history of the first session of the third NZ Parliament, 1861–1866', MA, Canterbury University College, 1935, p. 14. Carter, vol 2, pp. 151–3. Bohan, *Stafford*, p. 153.
30. Sewell's journal, 6, 9 June 1861.
31. Saunders, vol 1, p. 423.
32. Sewell's journal, 9 June 1861. Bohan, *Stafford*, p. 162. *NZPD*, 1861, p. 2.
33. *NZPD*, vol 6, 1869, p. 661, Vogel. Campbell, 'Speakership', pp. 108–19.
34. Wright-St Clair, pp. 171, 199.
35. *NZPD*, 1861, pp. 95–6. *JHR*, 1861, pp. 47–8. Wood, 'Political structure', pp. 151–3. Lipson, 'Origins of caucus', pp. 3–4.
36. *NZPD*, 1861, pp. 103, 168. Carter, vol 2, pp. 164–5. Scholefield (ed.), vol 1, p. 713.
37. Lipson, *Politics of Equality*, p. 54. Wood, 'Political structure', pp. 137–8.
38. Saunders, vol 1, pp. 449–51.
39. Sewell's journal, 15 Sept 1861.
40. Dalton, ch. 6.
41. Wright-St Clair, p. 181. Sewell's journal, 2, 9, 10, 13 July 1862. *Daily Southern Cross*, 14 July 1862. Ken Scadden, 'Problems of shipping the seat of government to Wellington, 1862–1865', NZ Society of Genealogists conference, 1995.

343

42. G.L. Meredith, *Adventuring in Maoriland in the Seventies* (ed. A.J. Harrop), Sydney, 1935, p. 35.
43. Sewell's journal, 15 July 1862.
44. Sewell's journal, 25 Dec 1861.
45. *NZPD*, 1862, pp. 436, 467, 476. *JHR*, 1862, pp. 36–7. Morrell, pp. 128–9. Bohan *Stafford*, pp. 173–6. Carter, vol 2, pp. 190–3. Campbell, 'Speakership', pp. 111–12. Wright-St Clair, p. 182.
46. *NZPD*, 1862, p. 482. Dalton, pp. 155–7.
47. *Press*, 23 Aug 1862. Sewell's journal, 13 Aug 1862.
48. *Press*, 13 Sept 1862. Wright-St Clair, pp. 183–6, 188, 253. *NZPD*, 1862, pp. 675–6, 696.
49. Later, the Speaker had his own desk clock. *NZPD*, vol 219, 1928, p. 34.
50. *AJHR*, 1863, E-7, Domett to Grey, 24 June 1863.
51. Sewell's journal, 31 May, 19 July, 2, 19, 23 Aug 1863.
52. *NZPD*, 1863, pp. 738, 740, 747–9, 900–3.
53. Bohan, *Stafford*, p. 183. T.B. Gillies to C.W. Richmond, 9 Nov 1863, Scholefield (ed.), vol 2, p. 73.
54. Wright-St Clair, pp. 188–9. Carter, vol 2, pp. 199–200. H.A. Atkinson to A.S. Atkinson, 8 Nov 1863, Scholefield (ed.), vol 2, pp. 69–70.
55. T.B. Gillies to C.W. Richmond, 9 Nov 1863, Scholefield (ed.), vol 2, p. 73.
56. Dalton, pp. 171–3. *AJHR*, 1863, E-7, no 4, Newcastle to Grey, 26 Feb 1863.
57. Saunders, vol 2, p. 112.
58. Sewell's journal, 18, 21 Nov 1863.
59. *NZPD*, 1863, p. 902.
60. *NZPD*, 1863, pp. 999–1005.
61. *NZPD*, vol 26, 1877, p. 189, Reynolds. The convention was that the House should not sit beyond midnight on Saturday.
62. Alfred Cox, *Recollections*, Christchurch, 1884, p. 129. Only in 1968 was it ruled that the term was not 'sufficiently abusive, offensive, or emotive' to be considered unparliamentary. *NZPD*, vol 355, 1968, p. 2473.
63. *NZPD*, 1863, p. 900.
64. *JHR*, 1863, pp. 86, 89, 103, 114, 150.
65. *NZPD*, 1854, p. 444; 1856, pp. 99–100, 251–62, 354–6, 365–6; 1863, pp. 927–8. *VP*, 1856, D-27. Bohan, *'Blest Madman'*, p. 130. Herron, 'Structure and course of politics', pp. 382–9. Edmund Bohan, 'Establishing the seat of government in Wellington', NZ Society of Genealogists conference, 1995. *Cyclopedia, Auckland*, pp. 79–82.
66. *NZPD*, 1860, p. 790. Wood, 'Political structure', p. 34n.
67. *NZPD*, 1861, p. 231. Gaudin, p. 154.
68. *NZPD*, 1862, pp. 594–600, 625–7.
69. Sewell's journal, 12 Jan 1864.
70. Carter, vol 2, pp. 202–8.
71. *NZPD*, 1863, pp. 912–15, 926–40.
72. *NZPD*, 1863, pp. 918, 921–2, 926–40. Sewell's journal, 21 Nov 1863. Bohan, 'Establishing the seat', pp. 5–6.
73. Fox's New Provinces Act amending bill was rejected by such means. *NZPD*, 1861, pp. 273–4.
74. Richmond cited five hour speeches by Fox's opposition, *NZPD*, 1861, p. 237.
75. Dalton, pp. 203–4.
76. J.C. Richmond to C.W. Richmond, 1 June 1865, Scholefield (ed.), vol 2, p. 162. *NZPD*, 1864, pp. 127–8.
77. Bohan, *Stafford*, p. 190.
78. *NZPD*, 1864, p. 146. *AJHR*, 1864, A-2. Graham, chs 5, 6 for 1864–5.
79. *AJHR*, 1864, D-2; 1865, B-9.
80. Sewell's journal, 11 Dec 1864.
81. *AJHR*, 1865, B-9.
82. IA1, 1864/2373.
83. Graham, pp. 98–9. IA1, 1860/307, including plan; 1865/746, 1258, 1475.
84. J.C. Richmond to Mary Richmond, 24 Aug 1862, Scholefield (ed.), vol 1, p. 784. Sewell's journal, 8 July, 13 Aug 1862.
85. Wright-St Clair, p. 196.
86. J.C. Richmond to Mary Richmond, 28 July 1865 (and other reports), Scholefield (ed.), vol 2, p. 171.
87. *NZPD*, 1865, pp. 222–3, 229, 285–6. Raewyn Dalziel, *Julius Vogel*, Auckland, 1986, pp. 63–7.
88. Morrell, p. 161.
89. The government won 28 to 5. Dalziel, *Vogel*, p. 65.
90. *NZPD*, 1865, p. 525. Morrell, p. 159.
91. Dalziel, *Vogel*, p. 66, citing diary of Alfred Buchanan, 13 Sept 1865.
92. *NZPD*, 1865, pp. 613, 616. *LT*, 2 Oct 1865.
93. *NZPD*, 1865, pp. 667–8, 672–5. Saunders, vol 2, p. 165. Wright-St Clair, p. 198.
94. Saunders, vol 2, p. 168. *NZPD*, vol 13, 1872, p. 567, Vogel.
95. For the debate over whether this move was constitutional, see *Otago Witness*, 28 Oct 1865; *NZPD*, 1865, pp. 697, 720; *JLC*, 1865, appendix 3; Sewell's journal, 15, 21, 29, 31 Oct 1865; Graham, p. 104; Bohan, *Stafford*, pp. 207–8, 217.
96. Roberta Nicholls, 'Elite society in Victorian and Edwardian Wellington', in David Hamer and Roberta Nicholls (eds), *The Making of Wellington, 1800–1914*, Wellington, 1990, p. 208. Timothy McIvor, *The Rainmaker: A Biography of John Ballance*, Auckland, 1989, p. 54. See O'Rorke papers, letters to wife in the period 1867–78 generally, AUL.
97. Dalziel, *Vogel*, p. 159.
98. IA1, 1866/1188, 1338, 1425, 1747, 1888. *AJHR*, 1866, D-2. *NZPD*, 1866, p. 787.
99. LE1, 1869/128. IA1, 1869/1281, 1345; 1871/628. *AJHR*, 1870, D-6, pp. 1, 4–5. *NZPD*, vol 7, 1870, p. 336. *JHR*, 1870, p. 179.
100. Peter Richardson, 'An architecture of empire: the government buildings of John Campbell in NZ', MA, University of Canterbury, 1988, pp. 224–7. Anne Crighton, 'William Henry Clayton: colonial architect', MA, University of Canterbury, 1985. Rod Cook, *Parliament: The Land and Buildings from 1840*, Wellington, 1988.
101. LE1, 1869/127. IA1, 1871/621. *JLC*, 1874, appendix 5.
102. *AJHR*, 1870, D-6.
103. *NZPD*, vol 7, 1870, pp. 319–20.
104. *NZPD*, vol 7, 1870, p. 408.
105. Wright-St Clair, pp. 207–8. *NZPD*, 1866, pp. 1024, 1035; vol 6, 1869, pp. 898–9, 909–11.
106. *NZPD*, vol 4, 1868, p. 334 (and pp. 333–8). A. Mulgan, *The City of the Strait*, Wellington, 1939, p. 213.
107. *NZPD*, vol 11, 1871, pp. 521–5, 819–26; vol 12, 1872, pp. 458–62. IA1, 1872/56. *Cyclopedia, Auckland*, p. 83.
108. Public Works Department, W1, 24/26, pt 0, 1874–82; PWD 15304, plans and elevations, ArchNZ. IA1, 1871/628. LE1, 1873/201. *AJHR*, 1872, G-11, G-42; 1873, E-3, appendix F, H-4. *NZPD*, vol 12, 1872, p. 16; vol 17, 1875, p. 568. *EP*, 11 Dec 1907.
109. *EP*, 17 May 1873.
110. *EP*, 4, 5 June, 19 Aug 1884. *NZT*, 18 May 1887.
111. *EP*, 18 July 1873.
112. *EP*, 14 July 1873.
113. *NZPD*, vol 15, 1873, pp. 1482–3. *AJHR*, 1875, E-3, appendix E. *JLC*, 1874, no 5. Wilson, *Parliamentary Record*, p. 318.
114. For the chamber, see LE1, 1867/11; 1893/3. *JHR*, 1864, p. 7; 1867, pp. 22, 27–8. *EP*, 17 May 1873. Cox, pp. 236–7. *The Observer*, 18 June 1881. *NZ Graphic*, 15 July 1893. *Cyclopedia, Wellington*, p. 93.
115. *Press*, 26 Aug 1898.

[116] *Auckland Star*, 11 Dec 1907. For the library, see LE1, 1861/8. IA1, 60/908; 63/281, 1323. *JHR*, 1860, pp. 235–6; 1861, p. 181; 1866, p. 301. *EP*, 23 August 1958, Wilson article.

[117] J.C. Richmond to Mary Richmond, 24 Aug 1862, Scholefield (ed.), vol 1, pp. 784–5.

[118] LE1, 1873/6; 1874/6. *JHR*, 1871, pp. 108–9; 1873, p. 210.

[119] Conrad Bollinger, *Grog's Own Country*, Auckland, 1967, p. 22.

[120] *NZ Graphic*, 16 Sept 1893.

[121] Meredith, pp. 74–5.

[122] Meredith, pp. 77–8. Silver Pen, *Parliamentary Skits and Sketches*, Wellington, 1872. *Dom*, 12 Dec 1907. *NZ Graphic*, 16 Sept 1893. Bollinger, pp. 23–4.

[123] LE1, 1875/7, 9. *Weekly Press*, 18 Dec 1875. *DNZB*, vol 1, Wakefield. Temple, pp. 521–2, 527–8, 530–3.

[124] *Nelson Examiner*, 30 June 1869. *NZPD*, vol 5, 1869, p. 122; vol 7, 1870, pp. 179–82; vol 28, 1878, p. 323.

[125] *NZPD*, vol 24, 1877, p. 5.

[126] *NZPD*, vol 26, 1877, pp. 98–103, 328–54. *AJHR*, 1877, I-8.

[127] *Press*, 5 Sept 1898.

[128] William Pember Reeves, *The Long White Cloud* (fourth edition), London, 1950, pp. 255–7. André Siegfried, *Democracy in NZ* (intro. by David Hamer), Wellington, 1982, p. 75.

[129] *NZPD*, vol 36, 1880, pp. 482–3.

[130] *ODT*, 20, 26 Sept 1881.

[131] Sheila Macdonald, *The Member for Mount Ida*, Wellington, 1938, pp. 46, 72.

[132] *Wellington Independent*, 3 Sept 1856.

[133] Cox, p. 256.

[134] *NZPD*, 1858, pp. 547–9.

[135] *NZPD*, 1866, pp. 917, 1000.

[136] *NZPD*, 1858, p. 383.

[137] *NZPD*, 1860, p. 465. Wright-St Clair, p. 234.

[138] LE1, 1868/2; 1869/9; 1870/14; 1871/14. *JHR*, 1869, pp. 218–19. *NZPD*, vol 10, 1871, p. 122. *AJHR*, 1869, F-8.

[139] W.A. Glue, *History of the Government Printing Office*, Wellington, 1966, chs 3, 4. *AJHR*, 1862, D-7. *JHR*, 1862, p. 129. LE1, 1862/15.

[140] Thomson, vol 2, p. 246.

[141] *NZPD*, 1854, pp. 179, 183ff. McIntyre (ed.), vol 2, p. 54, entry 9 July 1854. *Southern Cross*, 19 Sept 1854.

[142] *Wellington Independent*, 9 Oct 1860.

[143] *NZPD*, 1856, pp. 152–3, 158–63. *VP*, 1856, D-17.

[144] *Southern Cross*, 20 June 1856.

[145] LE1, 1858/301, Gisborne to Campbell, 18 June 1858.

[146] IA1, 1863/3299, note, 16 May 1864; 1865/461, Gisborne to Colonial Secretary, 25 Feb 1865. *NZPD*, 1861, pp. 221, 286; 1862, pp. 286–7, 452–3, 606, 964. *AJHR*, 1861, F-3.

[147] *JHR*, 1865, pp. 71–2. *NZPD*, 1865, pp. 256–8.

[148] *NZPD*, 1866, pp. 817, 852, 1011–12, 1016–17 and 'Postscript'; vol 11, 1871, p. 522; vol 57, 1887, p. 816. *LT*, 14 Sept 1865; 11 July, 4 Aug 1866. Bohan, *Stafford*, p. 213.

[149] IA1, 1867/1737, Barron to Colonial Secretary, 7 June 1867, 1867/2176, Barron and George Didsbury to Colonial Secretary, 9 July 1867. *NZPD*, vol 1, pt 1, 1867, p. 56.

[150] *NZPD*, vol 1, pt 1, 1867, pp. 17–22.

[151] *NZPD*, vol 1, pt 1, 1867, p. 57.

[152] L.S. Fanning, *Politics and the Public*, Wellington, 1919, p. 15.

[153] *JHR*, 1867, pp. 343–4.

[154] *NZPD*, vol 10, 1871, pp. 129–30; vol 17, 1875, p. 122. For *Hansard* 1854–66, see *NZPD*, vol 49, 1884, p. 353; vol 50, 1884, p. 496; Preface to *NZPD*, 1854-5.

[155] *NZPD*, vol 6, 1869, pp. 890–4; vol 8, 1870, pp. 310–15; vol 9, 1870, pp. 148–9; vol 11, 1871, p. 1079. *JHR*, 1869, pp. 218–19; 1870, pp. 66, 99. *AJHR*, 1869, F-8. LE1, 1870/14; 1871/14; 1872/14.

[156] William Law, *Our Hansard*, London, 1950, pp. 64–6.

[157] *NZPD*, vol 1, pt 2, 1867, pp. 788, 823–8.

[158] LE1, 1863/2. *NZPD*, 1863, p. 975. Wright-St Clair, pp. 190, 199.

[159] Standing Orders, 1865, Parliamentary Library.

[160] Reed (ed.), p. 121.

[161] *NZPD*, 1866, pp. 765, 767, 831, 975; vol 1, pt 1, 1867, p. 82; vol 2, 1868, p. 5; vol 6, 1869, pp. 473–4; vol 7, 1870, pp. 42–3, 78–9, 88, 94.

[162] Pierr, p. 215.

[163] The 1871 standing orders set the hour of 12 noon to no apparent effect.

[164] Campbell, 'Speakership', p. 86. *NZPD*, vol 3, 1868, p. 201.

[165] Wood, 'Political structure', p. 97. Campbell, 'Speakership', pp. 69–70. LE1, 1860/25; 1862/14; 1863/19. *AJHR*, 1870, A-30. McGee, *Parliamentary Practice*, pp. 252–3.

[166] *NZPD*, vol 7, 1870, pp. 169, 318.

[167] *NZPD*, vol 7, 1870, pp. 358–60; vol 8, 1870, p. 269; vol 11, 1871, pp. 671–3. *AJHR*, 1870, A-30. Monro diary, 26 July 1870, Micro MS 0412, ATL.

[168] E.P. Angus, 'Select committees of the House of Representatives, NZ', MA, Victoria University College, 1951.

[169] In 1888 the Public Petitions Committee was subdivided into two to cope with the huge numbers of petitions.

[170] Campbell, 'Speakership', p. 32. McGee, *Parliamentary Practice*, pp. 468–70. C.P. Littlejohn, 'Parliamentary privilege in NZ', Master of Laws, Victoria University, 1969.

[171] *NZPD*, 1854, pp. 95, 96, 121.

[172] *NZPD*, 1861, p. 4.

[173] Littlejohn, p. 29. The legislation was consolidated into the Legislature Act 1908 which provided the statutory basis for parliamentary privilege in the twentieth century.

[174] *JHR*, 1861, pp. 161–2. *NZPD*, 1861, pp. 239, 245; 1864, pp. 166–7, 175. *Daily Southern Cross*, 9 Dec 1864.

[175] *EP*, 16 Sept 1950. Tony Garnier, 'The parliamentary press gallery', in Stephen Levine (ed.), *Politics in NZ*, Auckland, 1978, p. 149.

[176] Patrick Day, *The Making of the NZ Press, 1840–1880*, Wellington, 1990, chs 9, 10.

[177] *Cyclopedia of NZ, Wellington*, Wellington, 1897, pp. 459–60. *DNZB*, vol 2, Gillon. *EP*, 20 Apr 1896. Monro diary, 29, 30 July 1869; 25, 26 May 1870. LE1, 1879/21. Jonathan L. Hunt, 'The election of 1875–76 and the abolition of the provinces', MA, Auckland University College, 1961, pp. 41, 241–2, 332.

[178] LE1, 1879/21.

[179] *The Press, 1861–1961*, Christchurch, 1963, pp. 202–3, 206.

[180] LE1, 1873/6, 17. *NZPD*, vol 14, 1873, pp. 10, 195, 210–14. *JHR*, 1873, p. 42. *EP*, 2 Aug 1873.

[181] For a later incident, see LE1, 1875/200.

[182] *NZPD*, vol 24, 1877, pp. 473–9; vol 25, 1877, pp. 54–81; vol 117, 1901, p. 649. *EP*, 29 Aug 1877; 29 June 1955; 7 Nov 1970. Saunders, vol 2, p. 391. Littlejohn, pp. 133–4. Scholefield (ed.), *DNZB*, Jones.

[183] Carleton challenged the propriety of a member belonging to the armed forces. *NZPD*, 1854, p. 95. The 1858 Disqualification Act merely excluded judges, magistrates and civil servants from becoming members.

[184] *NZPD*, 1865, pp. 196–7, 644.

[185] *NZPD*, vol 2, 1868, p. 558ff.

[186] *NZPD*, vol 5, 1869, pp. 498–9; vol 6, 1869, pp. 13–36, 715–31.

[187] For Fox's concerns, see *NZPD*, vol 10, 1871, p. 669.

[188] *NZPD*, vol 8, 1870, pp. 317–23, 407–18, 452–3, 485; vol 9, 1870, pp. 132–9, 660–1.

[189] McLintock and Wood, pp. 136–7.

[190] *LT*, 4 July 1866.

191 Dalziel, *Vogel*, p. 67. For the mace, see LE1, 1866/107; Scholefield, *Parliamentary Record*, p. 170; Allan Sutherland, 'Symbol of authority – the mace', NZ *Numismatic Journal*, vol 4, no 1, June–August 1947.
192 Bohan, *Stafford*, p. 224. Morrell, pp. 173–4. H.A.W. Gallagher, 'The history of the first and second sessions of the fourth NZ Parliament, 1866–7', MA, Canterbury University College, 1938.
193 *NZPD*, 1866, p. 863.
194 *NZPD*, 1866, p. 1035. IA1, 1866/3036, 3051.
195 A.S. Atkinson journal 8 Oct 1866, Scholefield (ed.), vol 2, p. 216.
196 Wright-St Clair, pp. 210, 211. Dalziel, *Vogel*, pp. 76–9.
197 Saunders, vol 2, p. 236. *NZPD*, vol 1, pt 2, pp. 979–85. *Wellington Independent*, 17 Feb 1871.
198 *NZPD*, vol 1, pt 1, 1867, pp. 157–74, 1167–9.
199 *NZPD*, vol 1, pt. 2, 1867, pp. 1167–9, 1182. Saunders, vol 2, pp. 226–7.
200 *NZPD*, vol 1, pt 2, 1867, pp. 974, 1214–15.
201 O'Rorke Papers, O'Rorke to his wife, 28 July 1867.
202 *NZPD*, vol 2, 1868, pp. 192, 270–2, 449.
203 W.K. Jackson and G.A. Wood, 'The NZ Parliament and Maori representation', *Historical Studies*, vol 11, no 43, 1964. Ward, pp. 98, 208–9. Keith Sinclair, *Kinds of Peace*, Auckland, 1991, ch. 7. Ranginui Walker, *Struggle Without End*, Auckland, 1990, pp. 112–13. Jackson, *Legislative Council*, pp. 80–6.
204 *NZPD*, 1862, p. 484. *AJHR*, 1860, E-7, p. 6; 1864, E-15. Jackson and Wood, pp. 384–6. M.P.K. Sorrenson, 'A history of Maori representation in Parliament', pp. 18–19, *AJHR*, 1986, H-3, appendix B.
205 Ward, pp. 209–10. Sinclair, *Kinds of Peace*, p. 88. *DNZB*, vol 1, Mete Kingi Paetahi.
206 Sinclair, *Kinds of Peace*, p. 92.
207 For their role, see *NZPD*, vol 2, 1868, pp. 499–500; vol 13, 1872, pp. 163, 168, 394; vol 14, 1873, p. 186; vol 19, 1875, p. 322; vol 33, 1879, p. 37; vol 36, 1880, p. 56. Ward, p. 270. Sinclair, *Kinds of Peace*, pp. 89–90. M.P.K. Sorrenson, 'The politics of land', p. 43, in J.G.A. Pocock (ed.), *The Maori and NZ Politics*, Auckland, 1965.
208 Bohan, *Stafford*, pp. 265, 272–3. *Press*, 25, 29 Aug, 22, 26 Sept, 1 Oct 1868.
209 *NZPD*, vol 3, 1868, pp. 224, 468–9. Monro diary, 18 Sept 1868. *Press*, 22, 26 Sept 1868.
210 *LT*, 1 Oct 1868. *NZPD*, vol 3, 1868, p. 378; vol 4, 1868, pp. 36, 39–40.
211 See later rulings referred to by Speaker Harrison, *NZPD*, vol 448, 1982, p. 4917.
212 *NZPD*, vol 4, 1868, pp. 59ff, 357–8. Saunders, vol 2, p. 260.
213 Monro diary, 1 June 1869.
214 *Nelson Examiner*, 30 June 1869. *NZPD*, vol 5, 1869, pp. 108, 304.
215 Dalziel, *Vogel*, ch. 7.
216 *NZPD*, vol 6, 1869, pp. 945–9. Monro diary, 20 Aug 1869.
217 *NZPD*, vol 6, 1869, p. 949.
218 *NZPD*, vol 5, 1869, pp. 423, 538.
219 *NZPD*, vol 6, 1869, pp. 572–6.
220 Monro diary, 3 Sept 1869.
221 Campbell, 'Speakership', ch. 1.
222 *NZPD*, 1861, p. 263; 1863, p. 958.
223 *NZPD*, vol 1, pt 2, 1867, p. 1196 (and pp. 1195–8, 1219–20). *AJHR*, 1867, D-12.
224 Campbell, 'Speakership', pp. 32–6.
225 IA1, 1867/3971; 1868/140. *AJHR*, 1868, A-13.
226 LE1, 1866/14; 1868/2; 1869/9. *NZPD*, vol 2, 1868, pp. 181–3, 318–20, 502–4.
227 *NZPD*, vol 3, 1868, pp. 371–2.
228 *AJHR*, 1867, D-13. IA1, 1867/1825, 2066, 3435, 3600; 1868/1059, 1158, 1611, 1892; 1869/837.
229 IA1, 1868/2006.
230 *NZPD*, vol 4, 1868, pp. 222–3.
231 LE1, 1870/4.
232 Clifford to Stafford, 4 June 1857, Stafford Papers, folder 31, MS Papers 28, ATL.
233 *NZPD*, vol 3, 1868, p. 524.
234 *AJHR*, 1862, D-19. LE1, 1862/142a.
235 *NZPD*, 1862, p. 660. *JHR*, 1862, pp. 115–16. IA1, 1862/971, 1234–5, 1382, 1670–3, 1844; 1884/12/1, incl 1863/2956, 1864/1947.
236 *AJHR*, 1868, D-2, p. 4.
237 *NZPD*, vol 13, 1872, pp. 302–4.
238 *AJHR*, 1886, I-10, pp. 19–20.
239 In 1854 an enquiry to Britain confirmed that the Council should not alter money bills. McLintock and Wood, pp. 55–60. *AJHR*, 1887, session I, A-8.
240 *NZPD*, 1862, pp. 712–17. *JLC*, 1862, pp. 97–8. *JHR*, 1864, pp. 17–18.
241 McLintock and Wood, pp. 60–1. Jackson, *Legislative Council*, pp. 57, 127. *NZPD*, vol 2, 1868, pp. 103–7; vol 39, 1881, p. 467.
242 *NZPD*, vol 11, 1871, pp. 219, 251–2, 743, 804, 891; vol 12, 1872, pp. 266–70. *JHR*, 1868, pp. 240–1, 262–3, 269. *JLC*, 1871, pp. 181–2, 218–23. McLintock and Wood, pp. 176–7.
243 *JLC*, 1871, appendix, pp. 222–3.
244 *NZPD*, vol 11, 1872, p. 267.
245 McLintock and Wood, pp. 66–8, 90–1. *NZPD*, vol 11, 1871, p. 920ff. *JLC*, 1872, no 2.
246 *NZPD*, vol 13, 1872, pp. 34–5.
247 *AJHR*, 1887, session I, A-8.
248 Monro diary, 28 June 1870.
249 *ODT*, 4 July 1870.
250 Morrell, p. 217.
251 *ODT*, 14 Sept 1870.
252 *AJHR*, 1871, B-2, p. 19.
253 *NZPD*, vol 9, 1870, p. 371.
254 A.M. Leslie, 'The general election of 1871 and its importance in the history of NZ', MA, Auckland University College, 1956.
255 *NZPD*, vol 10, 1871, p. 26.
256 *NZPD*, vol 10, 1871, pp. 3–4. Wright-St Clair, pp. 250, 254–5.
257 O'Rorke was replaced by A.P. Seymour for the 1873 session. *NZPD*, vol 13, 1872, p. 911; vol 14, 1873, p. 8.
258 Campbell, 'Speakership', pp. 119–23.
259 Saunders, vol 2, pp. 416–17.
260 *NZPD*, vol 10, 1871, pp. 12–13, 62–7. St Clair, pp. 256–62.
261 *NZPD*, vol 11, 1871, p. 40. St Clair, pp. 262–7. McLintock and Wood, p. 128n.
262 *NZPD*, vol 10, 1871, pp. 574, 606. Rolleston to Stafford, 20 July 1871, cited in W.D. Stewart, *William Rolleston*, Christchurch, 1940, pp. 89–90. Bohan, *Stafford*, p. 313n.
263 Dalziel, *Vogel*, p. 129.
264 *ODT*, 11 Nov 1871.
265 *NZPD*, vol 10, 1871, p. 606.
266 Morrell, p. 232.
267 Fletcher, p. 30, citing Vogel Papers, 1, p. 578.
268 *NZPD*, vol 13, 1872, p. 155.
269 Bohan, *Stafford*, pp. 329, 337. Dalziel, *Vogel*, p. 156.
270 *NZPD*, vol 13, 1872, pp. 533–9, 553–4, 579–80, 745. *AJHR*, 1872, H-7.
271 *LT*, 7 Oct 1872.
272 *NZPD*, vol 13, 1872, p. 678. Sinclair, *Kinds of Peace*, p. 89.
273 *NZPD*, vol 13, 1872, p. 751.

274	*NZPD*, vol 16, 1874, pp. 464–5, 571ff. Dalziel, *Vogel*, p. 173. *NZPD*, vol 26, 1877, p. 75. Bohan, *Stafford*, pp. 350–1. Saunders, vol 2, p. 382.		(ed.), vol 2, pp. 424–5. *NZPD*, vol 21, 1876, pp. 646–7; vol 22, 1876, pp. 10–19, 122–7, 256–7.
275	*NZPD*, vol 16, 1874, pp. 581–2, 638–9.	14	*NZPD*, vol 22, 1876, pp. 253–342. Meredith, pp. 75–6. *EP*, 4 Apr 1931.
276	Morrell, p. 253.	15	Meredith, p. 76.
277	Morrell, p. 256. *NZPD*, vol 17, 1875, p. 151. Edmund Bohan, *To Be a Hero: A Biography of Sir George Grey*, Auckland, 1998, pp. 249–51.	16	*NZPD*, vol 22, 1876, pp. 486–7.
		17	*NZPD*, vol 24, 1877, pp. 130–5.
		18	*NZPD*, vol 20, 1876, pp. 331–4, 353–5; vol 22, 1876, pp. 122–7, 241–7.
278	*Press*, 11 Sept 1875. *ODT*, 24 Sept 1875. Meredith, p. 76.	19	Saunders, vol 2, p. 370. *Press*, 27 Oct–1 Nov 1876.
279	Morrell, p. 260ff. *NZPD*, vol 18, 1875, p. 345. *EP*, 6–15 Sept 1875.	20	Stewart, *Rolleston*, p. 123. Bohan, *Stafford*, p. 363. *EP*, 1 Nov 1876.
280	Wood, 'Structure of politics', pp. 64–75. Lipson, *Politics of Equality*, ch. 6. Herron, 'Structure and course of politics', pp. 90–2. Leicester Webb, *Government in NZ*, Wellington, 1940, pp. 41–3. Susan Butterworth, 'The colonial savant in politics', NZ Society of Genealogists conference, 1995. Susan Butterworth, 'Scholars, gentlemen and floppy disks', in The Friends of the Turnbull Library (eds), *Edward Gibbon Wakefield and the Colonial Dream*, Wellington, 1997. Raewyn Dalziel, 'The "continuous ministry" revisited', *NZJH*, vol 21, no 1, 1987.	21	Robert Stout, 'Political parties in NZ', Melbourne, 1880, p. 65. See also Hall to Gisborne, 10 Aug 1882, Hall Papers, vol 27, MS Papers 1784, ATL.
		22	Bohan, *To Be a Hero*, pp. 255–6. Gardner, 'Abolition of the provinces', pp. 133, 137.
		23	*NZPD*, vol 24, 1877, p. 127. Bassett, *Atkinson*, ch. 5. McIvor, ch. 4. Gardner, 'Abolition of the provinces', pp. 144–8.
		24	McIvor, p. 67.
		25	Gardner, 'Abolition of the provinces', pp. 140–2, 152–61. *NZPD*, vol 24, 1877, pp. 344–61, 360. *Weekly Herald*, 18 May 1878.
281	Database of members, 1853–1938, and Butterworth database of NZ notables.		
282	Lipson, *Politics of Equality*, table 6, p. 121. Dalziel, 'Continuous ministry', table II, p. 53. J. Halligan, 'Continuity and change in the NZ Parliament', PhD, Victoria University, 1980, pp. 34–6, table 2.1.	26	*NZPD*, vol 26, 1877, p. 107 (also pp. 489, 542); vol 27, 1877, p. 798. Armstrong, p. 312. Macdonald, p. 48.
		27	*NZPD*, vol 26, 1877, pp. 269, 284. *EP*, *LT*, 10 Oct 1877. *Press*, 10 Oct 1877. Gardner, 'Abolition of the provinces', pp. 158–9.
283	Dalziel, 'Continuous ministry', pp. 55–6.		
284	Bohan, *Stafford*, p. 222.	28	*LT*, 14 Nov 1877.
285	Dalziel, *Vogel*, pp. 49–51, 74–5, 109–10.	29	*Weekly Herald*, 18 May 1878. David Hamer, 'The Agricultural Company and NZ politics, 1877–1886', *Historical Studies*, vol 10, no 38, 1962, pp. 142–3. McIvor, pp. 84–5, 120, 127–9. Fleur Snedden, *King of the Castle*, Auckland, 1997, p. 108. J. Rutherford, *Sir George Grey*, London, 1961, p. 602.
286	Election database, 1853–1876.		

Chapter 3 – Political realignment, retrenchment and depression, 1876–90

1	Bohan, *To Be a Hero*, chs 16–20. Dalziel, *Vogel*, chs 11, 13, 16–18. Judith Bassett, *Sir Harry Atkinson*, Auckland, 1975, chs 4–12. McIvor, chs 4–9. W.R. Armstrong, 'The politics of development: a study of the structure of politics from 1870 to 1890', MA, Victoria University College, 1960. T.G. Wilson, 'The rise of the Liberal Party in NZ, 1877–1890', MA, Auckland University College, 1951. John Young, 'The political conflict of 1875', *Political Science*, vol 13, no 2, 1961. Edmund Bohan, 'The general election of 1879 in Canterbury', MA, Canterbury University College, 1958.	30	*EP*, 10–20 Oct 1877.
		31	*NZPD*, vol 27, 1877, p. 22. *EP*, 27 Oct, 6–8 Nov 1877. *Press*, *LT*, 7 Nov 1877. Gardner, 'Abolition of the provinces', pp. 173–82. Stout, p. 66. C.W. Richmond to Sam Smith, 9 Nov 1877, Scholefield (ed.), vol 2, p. 439. Rutherford, p. 603.
		32	*NZPD*, vol 26, 1877, pp. 292–3; vol 27, 1877, pp. 109, 118–20. *LT*, 8, 12, 14 Nov 1877. Bohan, *To Be a Hero*, pp. 257–9. McIvor, p. 70. Rutherford, pp. 604–6.
		33	A Waste Lands Bill which included controversial pastoral license provisions.
2	Lipson, *Politics of Equality*, pp. 61, 131–5.	34	Saunders, vol 2, p. 385.
3	*NZPD*, vol 22, 1876, p. 246.	35	McIvor, pp. 70–1. Rutherford, pp. 606–7.
4	Hunt, p. 30. Fletcher, pp. 55–6. W.J. Gardner, 'The effect of the abolition of the provinces on political parties in the NZ House of Representatives, 1876–7', MA, Canterbury University College, 1936.	36	Rutherford, chs 39, 40.
		37	C.W. Richmond to Emily E. Richmond, 13, 22 Sept 1878, Scholefield (ed.), vol 2, pp. 454, 457. Saunders, vol 2, p. 399.
5	Stewart, *Rolleston*, p. 123.	38	*NZPD*, vol 28, 1878, p. 132; vol 41, 1882, p. 252.
6	Hunt, p. 313.	39	*NZPD*, vol 30, 1878, pp. 1264–5.
7	Dalziel, *Vogel*, p. 211. Stewart, *Rolleston*, pp. 120, 122–3. *NZPD*, vol 20, 1876, pp. 3–4. Saunders, vol 2, p. 355.	40	Rutherford, p. 616.
		41	Stewart, *Rolleston*, p. 132. Bohan, 'General election', pp. 16–19. Bassett, *Atkinson*, pp. 71–2.
8	*Wellington Independent*, 3 Sept 1856.	42	McIvor, pp. 83–7. Rutherford, p. 621.
9	Ignotus, *Peeps into Politics*, Wellington, 1881, p. 10.	43	*NZPD*, vol 31, 1879, pp. 3–4.
10	*NZPD*, vol 20, 1876, p. 53. Saunders, vol 2, pp. 355–6. Dalziel, *Vogel*, pp. 205–6, 211–12.	44	O'Rorke Papers, O'Rorke to his wife, 2 Feb, 5 Apr, 13, 14, 19, 29 June 1879.
11	Bohan, *To Be a Hero*, p. 253.	45	*NZPD*, vol 97, 1897, p. 4; vol 178, 1917, pp. 9–10, 35–7. Gisborne, pp. 227-8.
12	*NZPD*, vol 21, 1876, pp. 419, 421, 427. Gardner, 'Abolition of the provinces', pp. 58–9. W.H. Scotter, *A History of Canterbury, vol 3, 1876–1950*, Christchurch, 1965, pp. 8–9.	46	*ODT*, 20 Sept 1881.
		47	Dalziel, *Vogel*, p. 300. *DNZB*, vol 2, O'Rorke.
		48	*ODT*, 26 Aug 1881.
13	A.S. Atkinson to Emily Richmond, 18 Sept 1876, Scholefield	49	Gisborne, p. 227.
		50	*NZPD*, vol 31, 1879, pp. 17–18.

51. *NZPD*, vol 31, 1879, pp. 18–21. *JHR*, 1879, session I, p. 7.
52. R.C.J. Stone, 'The Maori lands question and the fall of the Grey government, 1879', *NZJH*, vol 1, no 1, 1967, p. 64. *NZPD*, vol 31, 1879, pp. 66–76, 190, 207–8, 254, 304; vol 32, 1879, p. 430. *JLC*, 1879, session II, no 6. Saunders, vol 2, pp. 385–6, 404.
53. *NZPD*, vol 31, 1879, p. 307.
54. A.L. Clark, 'Grant and refusal – a study of the requests for dissolution of the NZ Parliament in 1877 and 1879', MA essay, University of Otago, 1968, pp. 30–3. *NZT*, 1 Aug 1879. *ODT*, 4 Aug 1879.
55. *NZPD*, vol 32, 1879, p. 34.
56. *Press*, 29 July 1879. Bohan, 'General election', pp. 276–9.
57. Jean Garner, *By His Own Merits: Sir John Hall*, Hororata, 1995, p. 162.
58. *NZPD*, vol 32, 1879, pp. 8, 40, 162. Saunders, vol 2, p. 409. James Drummond, *The Life and Work of R.J. Seddon*, Christchurch, 1906, p. 42.
59. *DNZB*, vol 1, Whitaker. Hall to Oliver, 17 Mar 1882, Hall Papers, vol 27.
60. *ODT*, 10 Sept 1881.
61. *NZPD*, vol 32, 1879, p. 147. G.F. Thompson, 'The politics of retrenchment: the origin and some aspects of the politics of the Hall ministry, 1879–82', MA, Victoria University, 1967, pp. 46–8. Saunders, vol 2, p. 410.
62. *NZPD*, vol 32, 1879, pp. 178–81.
63. Saunders, vol 2, pp. 413–18. Stone, 'Maori lands question', pp. 70–1. Armstrong, p. 238.
64. *NZPD*, vol 32, 1879, p. 573 (see 517ff.). *Press*, 30 December 1879. Drummond, p. 63. Saunders, vol 2, p. 522.
65. Fletcher, pp. 96, 120, 124.
66. *NZPD*, vol 32, 1879, pp. 516–23.
67. *NZPD*, vol 32, 1879, p. 538. LE1, 1879/114.
68. Saunders, vol 2, p. 422.
69. *NZPD*, vol 189, 1920, p. 1009.
70. Keith Sinclair, 'The significance of "the Scarecrow Ministry", 1887–1891', p. 109, in Chapman and Sinclair (eds).
71. See G.N. Hawker, *The Parliament of New South Wales, 1856–1965*, Sydney, 1971, ch. 9, for Australia.
72. *NZPD*, vol 51, 1885, pp. 286, 293; vol 60, 1888, p. 551; vol 65, 1889, p. 327. Bassett, *Atkinson*, p. 132. Lipson, *Politics of Equality*, pp. 87–8.
73. C. Whitehead, 'The 1887 general election in Canterbury', MA, Canterbury University College, 1961, pp. 33–5. Fletcher, p. 151.
74. Fletcher, pp. 158–60.
75. Hazel Riseborough, *Days of Darkness*, Wellington, 1989.
76. *NZPD*, vol 36, 1880, pp. 309, 558–60.
77. *JHR*, 1880, p. 74. Saunders, vol 2, pp. 443–4.
78. G.J. Rosanowski, 'The West Coast railways and NZ politics, 1878–1888', *NZJH*, vol 4, no 1, 1970, pp. 35–7. Thompson, pp. 117–19. *NZPD*, vol 37, 1880, pp. 734–44.
79. *Press*, 20 Sept 1881. *NZPD*, vol 40, 1881, pp. 824–6.
80. *NZPD*, vol 37, 1880, p. 820.
81. *NZPD*, vol 38, 1881, pp. 119, 512.
82. *NZPD*, vol 38, 1881, pp. 251–64.
83. Thompson, pp. 143–5.
84. *Observer*, 30 July 1881. *NZPD*, vol 38, 1881, p. 535; vol 39, 1881, p. 176.
85. Cunningham, 'Equality of electorates'. The Representation Bill had been preceded by attempts to alter the duration of Parliament and have annual Parliaments adopted. *NZPD*, vol 39, 1881, pp. 453–6, 639–41.
86. *NZPD*, vol 39, 1881, p. 204.
87. *NZPD*, vol 40, 1881, pp. 137–9, 195–6. *LT*, 27 Aug 1881. *Observer*, 3 Sept 1881. *NZH*, 2, 3, 6 Sept 1881. 'Waratah' (W.H.S. Hindmarsh), *Tales of the Golden West*, Christchurch, 1906, pp. 119–20. Bohan, *To be a Hero*, pp. 286–7. R.M. Burdon, *King Dick*, Christchurch, 1955, pp. 49–52. Drummond, pp. 63–5.
88. Christopher Jones, *The Great Palace: The Story of Parliament*, London, 1983, p. 190.
89. *ODT*, 2 Sept 1881.
90. *ODT*, 26 Sept 1881.
91. Reeves Memoirs, folder 32, MS Papers 0129, ATL.
92. Bohan, *To Be a Hero*, p. 287.
93. *NZPD*, vol 40, 1881, p. 346.
94. *NZPD*, vol 40, 1881, pp. 232–45. *LT*, 27 Aug 1881. *ODT*, 5 Sept 1881.
95. *NZH*, 2, 3 Sept 1881.
96. *NZPD*, vol 40, 1881, p. 245.
97. *AJHR*, 1882, A-6. Hall to Fox, 21 Mar 1882, Hall Papers, vol 8. *NZPD*, vol 42, 1882, p. 251.
98. Bassett, *Atkinson*, pp. 103–6. Garner, pp. 188–91.
99. Fletcher, p. 120. Dalziel, 'Continuous ministry', p. 60. C. Campbell, 'Parties and special interests in NZ, 1890–1893', MA, Victoria University, 1978, p. 30. A.M. Evans, 'A study of Canterbury politics in the early 1880s', MA, Canterbury University College, 1959.
100. Saunders, vol 2, p. 477. H.A. Atkinson to E. Wakefield, 11 Apr 1882, Scholefield (ed.), vol 2, p. 507. Stewart, *Rolleston*, p. 139.
101. Hall to Fox, 15 Apr 1882, cited by Garner, p. 189.
102. *NZPD*, vol 41, 1882, pp. 135–8.
103. Hall to Fox, 7 Aug 1882, Hall to Gisborne, 10 Aug 1882, in Hall Papers, MS Papers 1784, vol 27. *NZPD*, vol 42, 1882, pp. 44–5.
104. *NZPD*, vol 40, 1881, p. 661; vol 42, 1882, pp. 296–306; vol 43, 1882, pp. 127–37. Ward, p. 290.
105. *Observer*, 12 Aug 1882.
106. Bassett, *Atkinson*, pp. 118–19.
107. Hall to Fox, 7 Aug 1882, Hall Papers, vol 27.
108. *NZPD*, vol 36, 1880, pp. 448–71, 481–6. Thompson, p. 100ff.
109. *JLC*, 1877, no 8, no 14, p. 2; 1878, pp. 27, 33. *JHR*, 1878, p. 32. *NZPD*, vol 28, 1878, pp. 185–8.
110. *NZPD*, vol 37, 1880, pp. 142–8.
111. *JLC*, 1885, no 12. *AJHR*, 1886, I-10. *JHR*, 1886, pp. 97–9, 263–4. *NZPD*, vol 54, 1886, pp. 632–8.
112. *NZPD*, vol 26, 1877, pp. 252, 453–5; vol 30, 1878, pp. 1094–9. *JLC*, 1877, no 8. *JHR*, 1877, p. 198.
113. *NZPD*, vol 18, 1875, pp. 624–31; vol 23, 1876, pp. 180–8; vol 28, 1878, pp. 188–91, 312–17.
114. *NZPD*, vol 35, 1880, p. 683. Erskine May confirmed that the British government was responsible for expenditure, *AJHR*, 1886, I-10, p. 19.
115. *AJHR*, 1886, I-10.
116. F.M.B. Fisher reminiscences, 1959, TX37, NZ Sound Archives.
117. *AJHR*, 1869, D-21; 1875, H-11; 1886, I-10.
118. IA1, 1896/1824. *Cyclopedia, Wellington*, p. 111.
119. *AJHR*, 1886, I-10, p. 18.
120. *NZPD*, vol 62, 1888, p. 144.
121. *NZPD*, vol 36, 1880, p. 461; vol 46, 1883, p. 571; vol 62, 1888, p. 143. IA1, 14/18/2, O'Rorke to Hall, 5 Aug 1880. *NZT*, 4 Aug 1880.
122. LE1, 1879/8.
123. *NZPD*, vol 33, 1879, pp. 223–4, 229–34; vol 35, 1880, pp. 689–90; vol 36, 1880, pp. 53–4, 481–5; vol 48, 1884, pp. 11–12; vol 50, 1884, p. 470; vol 51, 1885, pp. 37–8. LE1, 1902/14.
124. *NZPD*, vol 33, 1879, p. 230; vol 34, 1879, p. 637. LE1, 1880/12.
125. *NZPD*, vol 36, 1880, pp. 483, 484.
126. LE1, 1891/12; 1893/9; 1894/14. *NZPD*, vol 159, 1912, p. 746; vol 178, 1917, pp. 46–7.

[127] LE1, 1884/10; 1893/9. *AJHR*, 1886, I-10, pp. 9–10, 16. *NZPD*, vol 99, 1897, p. 421; vol 164, 1913, p. 219. Office of the Clerk, old Hansard files, incl. Marks to Seddon, 17 Aug 1899; interview with Spragg, 1916; J. McLean, 'Centenary of the NZ *Hansard*, 1867–1967'.
[128] *NZPD*, vol 23, 1876, pp. 441–2, 471–3. LE1, 1871/4; 1877/3.
[129] LE1, 1878/129; 1883/156. *NZPD*, vol 42, 1882, p. 472.
[130] *NZPD*, vol 30, 1878, pp. 1094, 1097; vol 40, 1881, p. 578; vol 42, 1882, p. 591.
[131] *EP*, 6 July 1883.
[132] *NZPD*, vol 30, 1878, p. 1097.
[133] *NZPD*, vol 43, 1882, pp. 867, 962–5, 974–6.
[134] *AJHR*, 1882, B-3A, p. 18.
[135] *JHR*, 1882, pp. 423, 466. *JLC*, 1877, no 8; 1882, no 15. *AJHR*, 1882, H-30. W1, 24/26, pt 0, 1874–82.
[136] LE1, 1883/156. W1, 24/26, pt 0, 1874–82. Chris Cochran, *Parliamentary Library, Parliament House*, NZHPT, 1989, pp. 39–43, 46.
[137] *NZPD*, vol 41, 1882, pp. 476, 605–6; vol 42, 1882, p. 472. *JHR*, 1882, pp. 79, 93. LE1, 1877/3; 1878/129; 1882/4. *AJHR*, 1883, H-27. *EP*, 4 July 1883.
[138] *NZPD*, vol 50, 1884, p. 376; vol 69, 1890, p. 449; vol 74, 1891, p. 734. *AJHR*, 1891, session II, I-15.
[139] LE1, 1875/7; 1877/3; 1883/5. *Cyclopedia, Wellington*, p. 92.
[140] *NZPD*, vol 24, 1877, p. 6.
[141] *NZPD*, vol 36, 1880, pp. 485–6. LE1, 1882/4; 1885/4.
[142] *NZPD*, vol 59, 1873, pp. 761–2. LE1, 1875/7; 1880/3; 1882/4; 1883/5; 1884/2; 1885/4; 1887/3.
[143] Snedden, p. 190.
[144] *Auckland Star*, 11 Dec 1907.
[145] *NZPD*, vol 87, 1895, p. 195. Fisher reminiscences.
[146] *JLC*, 1881, no 5. *LT*, 27 Aug 1881.
[147] *ODT*, 3 Sept 1881.
[148] Stewart, *Rolleston*, p. 207. *DNZB*, vol 2, Mackenzie. *NZPD*, vol 118, 1901, pp. 560–1.
[149] Macdonald, p. 46.
[150] *NZPD*, vol 2, 1868, pp. 258, 289. LE1, 1883/157. *DNZB*, vol 1, Mair; vol 2, Carroll.
[151] *NZPD*, vol 10, 1871, p. 473.
[152] *NZPD*, vol 36, 1880, p. 463; vol 62, 1888, p. 505; vol 82, 1893, p. 658.
[153] *NZPD*, vol 148, 1909, p. 624; vol 151, 1910, p. 635.
[154] Phil Parkinson, '"Strangers in the House"', *Victoria University Law Review*, vol 32, no 3, 2001.
[155] Parkinson, pp. 10–12. *JHR*, 1865, pp. 103–4.
[156] *JHR*, 1868, pp. 77–8, 83. Standing Orders in Maori, 1880.
[157] *NZPD*, vol 2, 1868, pp. 141–3; vol 9, 1870, pp. 514–17; vol 11, 1871, pp. 146, 157–8, 183; vol 13, 1872, p. 801; vol 14, 1873, pp. 637–8; vol 31, 1879, p. 540.
[158] *NZPD*, vol 33, 1879, p. 502.
[159] *NZPD*, vol 37, 1880, pp. 19–26; vol 60, 1887, pp. 331–2. *JHR*, 1895, p. 336.
[160] *NZPD*, vol 18, 1875, pp. 369–70; vol 23, 1876, pp. 664–5, 708. IA1, 1876/3322.
[161] *NZPD*, vol 25, 1877, pp. 264–5; vol 29, 1878, pp. 339–43.
[162] Lyn Waymouth, 'Parliamentary representation for Maori', in Jenifer Curnow et al. (eds), *Discovering History, Language and Politics in the Maori-Language Newspapers*, Auckland, 2002. Sinclair, *A Kind of Peace*, p. 92. Ward, p. 219.
[163] *NZPD*, vol 29, 1878, pp. 339–42; vol 36, 1880, pp. 55–7, 445; vol 38, 1881, pp. 289, 474. *JHR*, 1878, p. 159; 1879, session II, pp. 222–3; 1880, p. 105; 1881, pp. 55, 92. *JLC*, 1881, p. 19. LE1, 1878/11; 1879/21; 1880/12. IA1, 1881/2587.
[164] *NZPD*, vol 56, 1886, pp. 18–19; vol 59, 1887, pp. 527–8; vol 62, 1888, pp. 505, 507–9, 512; vol 69, 1890, pp. 178–9.

[165] The Government Printing Office was under great pressure to cut back its work. *AJHR*, 1906, I-8.
[166] Lipson, *Politics of Equality*, pp. 84–5.
[167] *NZPD*, vol 44, 1883, pp. 22, 358. *Observer*, 23 June 1883. LE1, 1882/4; 1883/16; 1883/156. Saunders, vol 2, p. 91.
[168] *NZPD*, vol 47, 1884, p. 75.
[169] *Observer*, 28 July, 4 Aug 1883.
[170] *NZPD*, vol 46, 1883, p. 55.
[171] *NZPD*, vol 46, 1883, pp. 645–6.
[172] Bassett, *Atkinson*, pp. 123–5.
[173] *NZPD*, vol 47, 1884, pp. 21–30. *EP*, 11 June 1884.
[174] *NZPD*, vol 47, 1884, pp. 35, 85–6, 126–7.
[175] *EP*, 14 June 1884.
[176] Campbell, 'Parties and special interests', p. 30. D.P. Millar, 'The general election of 1884 in Canterbury', MA, Canterbury University College, 1960, pp. 13, 61–2, 66, 184, 213.
[177] *EP*, 7, 8 Aug 1884.
[178] *NZPD*, vol 48, 1884, pp. 2–3.
[179] *NZPD*, vol 48, 1884, pp. 1–5, 38. Atkinson to A.S. Atkinson, 27 July, 14, 25 Aug 1884, Scholefield (ed.), vol 2, pp. 523–5. *EP*, 19 Aug 1884.
[180] *EP*, 2 Sept 1884.
[181] *NZH*, 2–4 Sept 1884. Bassett, *Atkinson*, p. 130. *NZPD*, vol 48, 1884, pp. 177–84.
[182] McIvor, p. 126.
[183] *NZPD*, vol 48, 1884, p. 360.
[184] *NZPD*, vol 49, 1884, pp. 384, 433; vol 50, 1884, pp. 88, 95–113. Rosanowski, pp. 42–3. Dalziel, *Vogel*, p. 258.
[185] *NZPD*, vol 50, 1884, p. 187. Dalziel, *Vogel*, pp. 258–9.
[186] *NZPD*, vol 51, 1885, pp. 256, 428; vol 52, 1885, p. 490; vol 53, 1885, pp. 277, 298, 310–11, 361–2, 573, 582, 733–4. *JHR*, 1885, pp. 337, 339–40.
[187] *NZPD*, vol 54, 1886, pp. 15, 290–1.
[188] *NZPD*, vol 54, 1886, pp. 229–34, 291; vol 56, 1886, pp. 567–83, 728. *JHR*, 1886, p. 45.
[189] *AJHR*, 1886, I-10. *JHR*, 1885, p. 313; 1886, pp. 97–9, 263–4. *NZPD*, vol 62, 1888, p. 144.
[190] *NZPD*, vol 56, 1886, pp. 739–41. *AJHR*, 1887, session I, B-6, p. v. *JHR*, 1887, session I, p. xxi.
[191] *NZPD*, vol 57, 1887, p. 9.
[192] *NZPD*, vol 57, 1887, p. 372 (and p. 230). Patricia Grimshaw, *Women's Suffrage in NZ*, Auckland, 1972, pp. 42–4. *Auckland Star*, 20 May 1887.
[193] *NZPD*, vol 57, 1887, pp. 80, 92–3, 298–9, 380. *NZT*, 18 May 1887. *NZH*, 3, 4 May 1887.
[194] *NZPD*, vol 57, 1887, pp. 535, 540.
[195] Whitehead, '1887 general election'. Dalziel, *Vogel*, p. 297.
[196] Sinclair, 'Scarecrow ministry', pp. 108–11. Keith Sinclair, *William Pember Reeves*, Oxford, 1965, p. 65ff.
[197] Sinclair, 'Scarecrow ministry', p. 116.
[198] *NZPD*, vol 61, 1888, p. 97.
[199] *NZPD*, vol 60, 1888, p. 511; vol 73, 1891, p. 491.
[200] *ODT*, 6 Aug 1888.
[201] *NZPD*, vol 58, 1887, pp. 233–4; vol 59, 1887, pp. 192, 854–7. *NZH*, 2 Dec 1887.
[202] *EP*, 3 May 1888. Fletcher, p. 170.
[203] *NZH*, 1, 25, 28, 29 Nov, 7, 8, 9 Dec 1887.
[204] *NZH*, 28 Nov 1887.
[205] Dalziel, *Vogel*, p. 300. *NZPD*, vol 58, 1887, p. 378ff; vol 59, 1887, pp. 427–8, 608–9.
[206] *Fair Play*, 27 Jan 1894.
[207] *NZPD*, vol 59, 1887, p. 75.
[208] *NZH*, 9 Dec 1887. *NZPD*, vol 59, 1887, pp. 411, 445.
[209] *NZH*, 9 Dec 1887.
[210] *NZPD*, vol 58, 1887, pp. 381–7, 478; vol 59, 1887, pp. 537–8.

211 Standing Orders, 1878. *NZPD*, vol 20, 1876, pp. 219–22, 246–51; vol 35, 1880, pp. 281–4; vol 36, 1880, pp. 138–44, 471–3; vol 44, 1883, pp. 54–5; vol 51, 1885, pp. 128–34, 165–6, 179–90; vol 58, 1887, pp. 556–61; vol 73, 1891, pp. 9–16. *JHR*, 1876, p. 17; 1879, session II, p. 185; 1880, pp. 40, 91–2, 203, 206; 1882, pp. 33, 55; 1887, session II, pp. 85, 137–8. *JLC*, session II, 1884, pp. 229–30; 1885, pp. 42–3.
212 Stewart, *Rolleston*, p. 174.
213 *NZPD*, vol 60, 1888, pp. 202–3; vol 72, 1891, p. 639.
214 *NZPD*, vol 62, 1888, pp. 139–87, 501–12. *NZH*, 7 Aug 1888.
215 *NZPD*, vol 54, 1886, p. 32.
216 IA1, 1884/12. *NZPD*, vol 67, 1890, pp. 3–4, 8–9.
217 *NZPD*, vol 60, 1888, pp. 437–42, 619; vol 61, 1888, p. 558; vol 66, 1889, p. 570.
218 *NZPD*, vol 62, 1888, pp. 407, 432–3. *NZH*, 3, 4, 8 Aug 1888.
219 Wilson, 'Rise of the Liberal Party', pp. 226–7.
220 *NZPD*, vol 64, 1889, pp. 128, 408.
221 *NZPD*, vol 64, 1889, pp. 643–4; vol 65, 1889, pp. 7, 19–20.
222 *Observer and Free Lance*, 3 Aug 1889. *NZH*, 27 July 1889. Cunningham, pp. 102–5. Sinclair, *Reeves*, p. 93.
223 *JHR*, 1889, pp. 91–8.
224 *NZPD*, vol 65, 1889, pp. 297–8.
225 Bassett, 'Atkinson', p. 215.
226 Bassett, 'Atkinson', p. 219. H.A. Atkinson to A.S. Atkinson, 23 May 1890, Scholefield (ed.), vol 2, p. 555.
227 Fletcher, p. 180.
228 *NZPD*, vol 67, 1890, pp. 191, 220.
229 *NZPD*, vol 67, 1890, pp. 351–63. John E. Martin, '1890: a turning point for labour', in Pat Walsh (ed.), *Pioneering NZ Labour History*, Palmerston North, 1994.
230 *NZPD*, vol 69, 1890, pp. 73–85.
231 *LT*, 1 Oct 1890, cited by Wilson, 'Rise of the Liberal Party', p. 255.
232 *NZPD*, vol 69, 1890, pp. 35–56.
233 Stewart, *Rolleston*, p. 146.
234 Halligan, p. 58, table 2.5.
235 McLintock and Wood, pp. 116–21, 233–5.
236 Halligan, pp. 34–6. See also A. von Tunzelmann, 'Membership of the NZ Parliament – a study of conditions, 1854–1979', Research paper, MPP, Victoria University, 1979. Webb, *Government in NZ*, pp. 43–4. Dalziel, 'Continuous ministry', pp. 55–61.
237 *AJHR*, 1890, H-48. Macandrew, with 29 years' service since 1854, had died in 1887.
238 Database of members, 1853–1938.
239 In the 1887–90 Parliament only 9 out of the 95 members were European NZ-born.
240 *ODT*, 26 Sept 1881.
241 In the period 1876–90 the balance between runholders and farmers was slowly shifting in favour of the latter, but the overall representation of farming remained relatively constant. Database of members, 1853–1938.
242 Sinclair, *Reeves*, pp. 56–7. *NZH*, 3 Nov 1884. O'Rorke, Notebook, 1887, speech notes of 1893, O'Rorke papers. *Observer and Free Lance*, 30 June 1894. *EP*, 3 July 1894. *NZT*, 23 Nov 1904. *Free Lance*, 9 Nov 1905; 20 July 1907. G.W. Russell, *NZ Parliamentary Guide Book*, 1895, p. 71.

Chapter 4 – From free-lance to disciplined private: the single party in the House, 1891–1912

1 Lipson, *Politics of Equality*, tables pp. 25, 172. *Censuses*, 1878–1891, figures for males 21 years and over and 'Representation' tables. *AJHR*, 1879, session II, H-17, H-18; 1882, H-1, H-1A; 1884, Session II, H-5; 1887, Session II, H-13; 1890, H-2. David Hamer, *The NZ Liberals*, Auckland, 1988, pp. 30–4. Campbell, 'Parties and special interests', p. 47. Wilson, 'Rise of the Liberal Party', pp. 259–65.
2 Sinclair, *Reeves*, ch. 7. Erik Olssen, 'The "working class" in NZ', *NZJH*, vol 8, no 1, 1974. W.H. Oliver, 'Reeves, Sinclair and the social pattern', in Peter Munz (ed.), *The Feel of Truth*, Wellington, 1969. Christopher Campbell, 'The "working class" and the Liberal party in 1890', *NZJH*, vol 9, no 1, 1975. Campbell, 'Parties and special interests', appendix 1, table, p. 98.
3 Campbell, 'Parties and special interests', ch. 2. H. Crook, 'The significance of the 1890 election', MA, Auckland University College, 1953, pp. 98–9. J.D. Salmond, *NZ Labour's Pioneering Days*, Auckland, 1950, ch. 9. Robert E. Weir, 'Whose left/who's left? The Knights of Labour and "radical progressivism"', pp. 30–2, in Pat Moloney and Kerry Taylor, (eds), *On the Left*, Dunedin, 2002.
4 Stewart, *Rolleston*, p. 177. Bassett, 'Atkinson', pp. 230, 233–5. *EP*, 23 Jan 1891. McIvor, p. 179. Draft memorandum, and C.W. Richmond to daughters, 20 Jan 1891, Scholefield (ed.), vol 2, pp. 573–5. Jackson, *Legislative Council*, pp. 141–4. By 1896 the traditional factional role in the House in forming governments had been eliminated. *NZPD*, vol 96, 1896, p. 918.
5 *NZPD*, vol 70, 1891, pp. 2–6. *EP*, 24 Jan 1891. Stewart, *Rolleston*, pp. 178–9.
6 Sinclair, *Reeves*, pp. 124–5.
7 Hamer, *Liberals*, chs 1, 2. B.J. Foster, 'Development of unity and organisation in the NZ political parties of the Liberal era, 1890–1912', MA, Victoria University College, 1956, p. 83ff. J.C. Clarke, 'The NZ Liberal Party and government, 1895–1906', MA, Auckland University College, 1962, p. 43. Campbell, 'Parties and special interests', pp. 92–6.
8 Hamer, *Liberals*, p. 123. Clarke, pp. 43–4. *NZPD*, vol 92, 1896, pp. 447, 453, 544.
9 *NZPD*, vol 92, 1896, p. 544; vol 94, 1896, pp. 466, 478–82.
10 Hamer, *Liberals*, pp. 82–5, 226–7. Foster, p. 117ff. Clarke, p. 99ff.
11 Lipson, *Politics of Equality*, p. 45. Wheeler clippings, vol 1, note on number of independents, 1890–1914.
12 *NZPD*, vol 188, 1920, p. 666, Jones.
13 *NZPD*, vol 74, 1891, p. 724.
14 *NZPD*, vol 74, 1891, pp. 92–100, 122–45. Stewart, *Rolleston*, p. 180. Campbell, 'Speakership', pp. 139–41. R. Walrond to F.J. Moss, 1 Sept 1891, Moss Papers, AUL. Later the censure of Bryce and five others was expunged. *NZPD*, vol 76, 1892, pp. 507–20.
15 Reeves, p. 256. See for example, *NZPD*, vol 77, 1892, pp. 17–27, 72–3, 212–20.
16 *NZPD*, vol 76, 1892, pp. 216–17.
17 Russell to Rolleston, 19 Apr 1893, in Stewart, *Rolleston*, p. 187.
18 *NZPD*, vol 74, 1891, p. 875. Jackson, *Legislative Council*, chs 6, 10, 12. McIvor, chs 10, 11.
19 Jackson, *Legislative Council*, p. 153.
20 *NZPD*, vol 75, 1892, pp. 42–6, 64–6. Saunders, vol 2, p. 532.
21 *NZ Mail*, 30 June 1892.
22 McIvor, pp. 220–3, Tom Brooking, *Lands for the People? The Highland Clearances and the Colonisation of NZ: A Biography of John McKenzie*, Dunedin, 1996, pp. 109–13. *NZPD*, vol 76, 1892, p. 526.
23 *NZPD*, vol 77, 1892, p. 430. Marcus Marks, *Memories (Mainly Merry) of Marcus Marks*, Sydney, 1934, p. 145.
24 *EP*, 11, 12 Oct 1892.
25 *NZPD*, vol 86, 1894, pp. 926–9, 938; vol 96, 1896, pp. 824–5. *Fair Play*, 1 Nov 1894. *EP*, 7 Apr 1897.

26. R.T. Shannon, 'The Liberal succession crisis in NZ, 1893', *Historical Studies,* vol 8, 1958.
27. Hamer, *Liberals,* pp. 195–8.
28. [Charles Lewis] One of the Elect, *Chosen of the People*, Napier, 1923, p. 21.
29. R.K. Newman, 'Liberal policy and the left wing, 1908–1911', MA, University of Auckland, 1965, p. 89.
30. O.T.J. Alpers, *Cheerful Yesterdays*, London, 1928, p. 60.
31. *NZPD*, vol 83, 1894, p. 330.
32. *NZPD*, vol 80, 1893, pp. 378–418. *NZ Graphic*, 12 Aug 1893. D. Hamer, 'The law and the prophet: a political biography of Sir Robert Stout, 1844–1930', MA, Auckland University College, 1960, ch. 18. B.H. Phipps, 'The NZ conservative party, 1891–1903', MA, Victoria University, 1990, pp. 137–41.
33. Constance A. Barnicoat, 'Life in NZ as it is', *The Empire Review*, vol 6, 1904, pp. 391–2.
34. Grimshaw, chs 7, 8. Judith Devaliant, *Kate Sheppard*, Auckland, 1992.
35. *Observer and Free Lance*, 5 Sept 1891. Devaliant, p. 62.
36. *NZ Graphic*, 5 Aug 1893.
37. *NZPD*, vol 82, 1893, p. 81. Grimshaw, p. 92.
38. R.T. Shannon, 'The fall of Reeves, 1893–1896', in Chapman and Sinclair (eds). *NZPD*, vol 84, 1894, p. 189.
39. Guy H. Scholefield, *The Right Honourable William Ferguson Massey*, Wellington, 1925, pp. 10–14.
40. *Fair Play*, 9 Dec 1893; 3 Feb 1894. *NZPD*, vol 83, 1894, p. 255; vol 153, 1910, p. 1299.
41. IA1, 1891/2028, Bellamy's accounts. *NZPD*, vol 72, 1891, pp. 188, 364–9.
42. A.W. Hogg Collection, folder 4, 'Through fire and water' MS Papers 1618, ATL. *NZPD*, vol 83, 1894, pp. 251–62, 275–6; vol 86, 1894, pp. 518–28; vol 87, 1895, pp. 22–3, 190–203. LE1, 1894/ 6. *JHR*, 1894, pp. 41, 45, 48, 347–8, 382; 1895, pp. 29–30. *EP*, 5 July 1894.
43. *ODT*, 7 July 1894.
44. Newman, pp. 219–20. *NZPD*, vol 88, 1895, p. 413; vol 90, 1895, p. 127; vol 91, 1895, p. 41; vol 98, 1897, pp. 226, 325–6, 553. Further attempts were made to close the bar. *NZPD*, vol 131, 1904, pp. 311, 423–4, 778–81; vol 132, 1905, p. 237. *JLC*, 1904, pp. 124–6.
45. *NZPD*, vol 91, 1895, p. 41. From 1961 the poll was abolished. Parliamentary privilege was now deemed to hold sway. *AJHR*, 1960, I-17, pp. 88–9. Nonetheless, a section still exempted Parliament from the Sale of Liquor Act 1962.
46. *NZPD*, vol 107, 1899, p. 632; vol 110, 1899, p. 434; vol 118, 1901, p. 649; vol 131, 1904, pp. 1023–4; vol 148, 1909, p. 1263. Phipps, p. 107.
47. *NZPD*, vol 148, 1909, pp. 1261, 1265; vol 153, 1910, pp. 1297–9.
48. *NZPD*, vol 184, 1919, pp. 12–15; vol 190, 1921, pp. 8–9, 11–12, 16–17, 19; vol 199, 1923, p. 40.
49. Michael Bassett, *Sir Joseph Ward*, Auckland, 1993, pp. 45, 55. *EP*, 15 May 1954. T.E.Y. Seddon, *The Seddons*, Auckland, 1968, p. 49.
50. *NZ Observer and Free Lance*, 5 Oct 1895. *NZPD*, vol 103, 1898, p. 220; vol 132, 1905, pp. 8–10. C.E. Major, 'Seventy years of life in NZ', pp. 99–100, qMS 1232, ATL. Bollinger, p. 77.
51. *Fair Play*, 1 Nov 1894. *NZPD*, vol 110, 1899, pp. 456–9. Tregear to Reeves, 8 Dec 1896, 5 Dec 1902, Letters written by men of mark, vol 1, qMS 1680, ATL.
52. D.A. Hamer (ed.), *The Webbs in NZ*, Wellington, 1974, pp. 41–2. O'Rorke Papers, O'Rorke to his wife, 10 Oct 1900. *Fair Play*, 27 Jan 1894.
53. *NZ Graphic*, 16 Sept 1893. *NZPD*, vol 184, 1919, p. 19.
54. Major, 'Seventy years', p. 65. Newman, pp. 73–4.
55. *NZPD*, vol 83, 1894, pp. 2–7. *NZT*, 22 June 1894.
56. Notebook, 1884, speech on election of Speaker, 21 June 1894, O'Rorke Papers.
57. Campbell, 'Speakership', pp. 60–6. *NZPD*, vol 83, 1894, p. 25. LE1, 1896/1824.
58. Campbell, 'Speakership', pp. 100–1, 135–7. *EP*, 7 Apr 1897.
59. *NZPD*, vol 82, 1893, p. 664, Rolleston. Hamer, 'Law and prophet', ch. 20. Phipps, p. 42. Shannon, p. 148.
60. *NZPD*, vol 80, 1893, pp. 282–3, 628–31.
61. *Fair Play*, 1 Aug 1894.
62. *NZ Graphic*, 26 Aug 1893.
63. *DNZB*, vol 2, McKenzie. Brooking, pp. 62, 139, 185–8. *NZPD*, vol 117, 1901, p. 285.
64. *NZPD*, vol 84, 1894, pp. 188–91, 229–30. *EP*, 28 July 1894. *ODT*, 3 Aug 1894.
65. Shannon, p. 140. Bassett, *Ward*, p. 53. *NZPD*, vol 91, 1895, p. 291.
66. Bassett, *Ward*, p. 59, chs 5, 6.
67. *NZPD*, vol 88, 1895, pp. 111, 600; vol 89, 1895, pp. 56, 89–90. Phipps, pp. 143–50. Bassett, *Ward*, pp. 60, 62. Hamer, *Liberals*, p. 122.
68. *NZPD*, vol 91, 1895, p. 822; vol 87, 1895, pp. 476–91. Clarke, pp. 29, 36–7. Shannon, pp. 148–9.
69. *NZH*, 30 Oct 1895.
70. David Wilson, 'A case of privilege' in Wilson and Rankin.
71. *NZPD*, vol 95, 1896, pp. 1–4.
72. *NZPD*, vol 90, 1895, p. 159; vol 91, 1895, p. 890; vol 92, 1896, p. 91; vol 95, 1896, p. 60.
73. *NZPD*, vol 93, 1896, pp. 517–18.
74. *NZPD*, vol 96, 1896, pp. 11–12, 24–7. Hamer, *Liberals*, p. 124.
75. *NZ Observer and Free Lance*, 31 Oct 1896.
76. Drummond, pp. 146–7. *NZPD*, vol 71, 1891, p. 45; vol 74, 1891, pp. 722–35.
77. *NZPD*, vol 80, 1893, p. 298.
78. *NZPD*, vol 78, 1892, p. 450; vol 80, 1893, pp. 293–302; vol 82, 1893, pp. 256–8, 984; vol 142, 1907, pp. 246–7. *Gazette*, 1894, p. 668. *JHR*, 1894, p. xxiii. *JLC*, 1893, nos 1, 7. *AJHR*, 1893, A-3, I-8, I-8A; 1894, I-1, p. 7. Audit Department register, A6, 3, 1891–4, ArchNZ. IA1, 1894/2726, 2727.
79. *NZPD*, vol 80, 1893, pp. 293, 296, 300; vol 82, 1893, pp. 659, 666. Old Hansard files, interview with Spragg, p. 14.
80. *NZPD*, vol 101, 1898, pp. 18–24; vol 105, 1898, pp 727–8, 756.
81. *AJHR*, 1893, I-8, p. 5. *NZPD*, vol 82, 1893, pp. 269–70, 309–11, 603–4.
82. *NZPD*, vol 89, 1895, p. 284; vol 91, 1895, pp. 163–4, 289–91, 578–9, 626–8; vol 93, 1896, p. 339; vol 96, 1896, pp. 36, 847–8. *AJHR*, 1895, I-8, I-8A. LE1, 1895/7; 1896/8, 124. Audit Department register, A6, 5, 1894–7. IA1, 1896/2748. Marks, pp. 274–5. Old Hansard files, interview with Spragg, p. 6.
83. Old Hansard files, Marks to Seddon, 17 Aug 1899, Spragg letter, 20 July 1909. A.B. Conway, 'The NZ Hansard staff', 1974. *EP*, 24 Mar 1973, McLean.
84. LE1, 1899/9; 1900/11. IA1, 1900/2659. *NZPD*, vol 112, 1900, pp. 12–53.
85. LE1, 1893/8; 1897/158. Audit Department registers, A6, 3, 1891–4; 6, 1897–1900. *NZPD*, vol 86, 1894, pp. 526–8; vol 99, 1897, pp. 404–13, 415–19, 475–9. IA1, 1893/2163. Letters in *EP*, 3, 4 May 1898.
86. *LT*, 26 Aug 1898. *NZPD*, vol 103, 1898, pp. 209–21.
87. Hamer, *Liberals*, pp. 109, 114. Audit Department register, A6, 3, 1891–4. IA1, 14/18/2. *Gazette*, 1894, p. 1924. *NZPD*, vol 83, 1894, pp. 22, 25–8, 70–84, 104–10, 314–58.
88. *NZPD*, vol 118, 1901, p. 578.
89. *NZPD*, vol 91, 1895, pp. 936–7; vol 87, 1895, p. 54, Stout.

90 *NZPD*, vol 73, 1891, pp. 13–14; vol 130, 1904, pp. 716–19. LE1, 1900/12.
91 *NZPD*, vol 98, 1897, pp. 506–25, 597, 656–7; vol 106, 1899, pp. 545–6.
92 *NZPD*, vol 118, 1901, p. 4; vol 188, 1920, p. 8. Later, accelerated passage of bills was occurring six weeks before the end of sessions. *NZPD*, vol 188, 1920, p. 8.
93 *NZPD*, vol 119, 1901, p. 602. 1903 Standing Orders.
94 The horse-racing fraternity, closely associated with Parliament, included John Ormond, William Herries, James Carroll, George McLean, Edwin Mitchelson and Heaton Rhodes.
95 *NZPD*, vol 78, 1892, pp. 282, 374–5; vol 92, 1896, p. 588; vol 95, 1896, p. 606. Campbell, 'Speakership', p. 45. Question time had been established in the Commons from 1869. Jones, *Great Palace*, p. 207.
96 *AJHR*, 1903, I-7A. *NZPD*, vol 128, 1904, pp. 370–1; vol 132, 1905, pp. 262–3; vol 307, 1955, pp. 3481–2.
97 *NZPD*, vol 164, 1913, pp. 148–50; vol 90, 1895, p. 302. Henry Otterson, *Notes in Connection with Procedure in Committee of the Whole*, 1897.
98 Fanning, p. 74.
99 *NZPD*, vol 70, 1891, pp. 106–7.
100 *NZPD*, vol 71, 1892, pp. 207–8; vol 75, 1892, p. 209.
101 *NZPD*, vol 82, 1893, pp. 1025–8; vol 82, 1893, pp. 856–8; vol 83, 1894, pp. 416–18; vol 160, 1912, p. 115. LE1, 1893/9; 1894/14. *AJHR*, 1893, I-10.
102 *NZPD*, vol 83, 1894, p. 9.
103 LE1, 1894/15. *JHR*, 1894, pp. 48–53, 57–8, 67–71, 75–82, 94. *NZPD*, vol 83, 1894, pp. 623–30. *AJHR*, 1892, I-6; 1894, H-11 (Standing Orders).
104 Burdon, *King Dick*, p. 164. *NZPD*, vol 91, 1895, pp. 163–4.
105 *NZPD*, vol 91, 1895, p. 488; vol 109, 1899, pp. 298–312; vol 118, 1901, p. 482.
106 Burdon, *King Dick*, pp. 159–69. Drummond, pp. 328–35. Phipps, pp. 80–3. Hamer, *Liberals*, pp. 146–9. Tregear to Reeves, 7 Oct 1896, Letters written by men of mark, vol 1.
107 *NZPD*, vol 100, 1897, pp. 167–208, 348 (largely unreported).
108 Burdon, *King Dick*, p. 166. *NZPD*, vol 104, 1898, p. 569.
109 *LT*, 26 Sept 1898.
110 *EP*, 6 Oct 1898. F. and N. Ross, *Mixed Grill*, Auckland, 1934, p. 229.
111 *NZPD*, vol 105, 1898, pp. 525–7, 570–87. *EP*, 28, 31 Oct 1898.
112 LE1, 1900/12; 1903/12. *AJHR*, 1900, I-9; 1903, I-7, I-7A. *NZPD*, vol 124, 1903, p. 194; vol 125, 1903, pp. 592–8; vol 126, 1903, pp. 137–64.
113 *NZPD*, vol 97, 1897, p. 3. *EP*, 7 Apr 1897. Phipps, pp. 61, 72ff. Hamer, *Liberals*, pp. 208–9.
114 Seddon, pp. 77–8.
115 Bassett, *Ward*, pp. 83–7. Littlejohn, pp. 151–3. Clarke, p. 66ff. *NZPD*, vol 98, 1897, pp. 69–70, 122–40; vol 100, 1897, pp. 446–7. *JHR*, 1897, session II, pp. 26–7. *NZT*, 23 June 1898. McKenzie to Reeves, 16 Feb 1898, Letters written by men of mark, vol 3.
116 Hamer, *Liberals*, pp. 122–4, 208–11, 224, 364. Campbell, 'Parties and special interests', pp. 64, 95. Clarke, pp. 25–70.
117 Clarke, p. 225ff. Hamer (ed.), *Webbs*, pp. 40–1, 'Bun Tuck' allegations.
118 *Press*, 9 Sept 1898. Ross, pp. 229–30.
119 McKenzie had attacked Hall through the map. *NZPD*, vol 71, 1891, p. 439; vol 103, 1898, pp. 123, 520–1. *Press*, 27, 29 Aug, 5, 9 Sept 1898. Marks, p. 96.
120 Day, *Making of the NZ Press*, pp. 107–10, 134–6, 175–81. Siegfried, ch. 25.
121 *Cyclopedia, Wellington*, p. 458.
122 *NZ Mail*, 21 May 1886. *Fair Play*, 1 Aug 1894. *NZPD*, vol 57, 1887, p. 196. *Observer and Free Lance*, 29 June 1889.
123 Clipping, c. 1912, Wheeler clippings, vol 2.
124 *AJHR*, 1894, H-5. *EP*, 4, 23, 24 Apr 1894. *DNZB*, vol 2, F.J. Fox. David Wilson, 'Privilege and the press gallery', in David Wilson, *Questions of Privilege*, Wellington, 1999, p. 31.
125 LE1, 1875/200, Luckie. *Observer*, 30 June 1884.
126 *NZPD*, vol 39, 1881, pp. 98–9; vol 45, 1883, pp. 448–9; vol 73, 1891, pp. 232–3.
127 *NZPD*, vol 73, 1891, pp. 232–3; vol 104, 1898, pp. 179–92; vol 113, 1900, pp. 411–14; vol 117, 1901, p. 648; vol 118, 1901, p. 277.
128 Wilson, 'Privilege and the press gallery', pp. 31–41. *Free Lance*, 7 July 1900.
129 *NZPD*, vol 125, 1903, p. 414; vol 126, 1903, pp. 83, 143–4, 722. *AJHR*, 1903, I-1, p. 11, I-8, p. 8; 1906, I-7.
130 LE1, 1903/12; 1904/14; 1906/12. *JHR*, 1903, pp. 392–3; 1906, p. 263. *NZPD*, vol 137, 1906, pp. 769–70, 790–8; vol 138, 1906, pp. 651–3. *AJHR*, 1906, I-7.
131 *NZPD*, vol 141, 1907, p. 204 (also pp. 203–15). *LT*, 22 Sept 1907. Fanning, p. 15.
132 T.L. Mills Papers, folder 16, reminiscences, MS Papers 7007, ATL. *NZ Magazine*, May–June 1945.
133 *DNZB*, vol 2, Suisted and Bullock. Charlotte Macdonald et al. (eds), *The Book of NZ Women*, Wellington, 1991, pp. 107–8, 639–40.
134 *NZ Graphic*, 16 Sept 1893.
135 LE1, 1898/9. *JHR*, 1898, petition no 285. *Press*, 26 Aug, 16, 23 Sept 1898. *LT*, 23 Sept 1898. *DNZB*, vol 2, Henderson. *Dom*, 12 Mar 1991. Macdonald et al. (eds), pp. 286–7. Wilson, 'Privilege and the press gallery', p. 30.
136 LE1, 1893/8; 1894/6. *NZPD*, vol 86, 1894, pp. 526–7. *JHR*, 1893, pp. 406–7. W1, 24/26, pt 0, 1874–82. *AJHR*, 1894, D-1, p. 40; 1898, D-1.
137 *AJHR*, 1891, session II, I-15; 1892, D-12, D-27; 1894, D-1, p. 40. W1, 24/26, pt 0, 1874–82. Wilson, *Parliamentary Record*, p. 319. *Dom*, 11 Dec 1907. *Fair Play*, 1 May 1894.
138 *Fair Play*, 2 July 1894.
139 *AJHR*, 1901, H-6F.
140 *NZPD*, vol 71, 1891, pp. 469–70; vol 73, 1891, p. 401; vol 78, 1892, pp. 110–16; vol 101, 1898, p. 42; vol 114, 1900, pp. 607–8, 692; vol 129, 1904, pp. 663, 678, 684; vol 131, 1904, p. 231; vol 134, 1905, pp. 599–600; vol 141, 1907, p. 505; vol 142, 1907, p. 1112. *AJHR*, 1892, D-12; 1893, D-1, p. 35; 1894, D-1, p. 40; 1897, D-1, p. 62; 1906, session II, H-33. LE1, 1892/144, 145. *Dom*, 11 Dec 1907.
141 *AJHR*, 1900, D-1, p. xiii. The House Committee lost control over Bellamy's. *NZPD*, vol 156, 1911, pp. 1011–14.
142 W1, 24/26, pt 0, 1874–82. *NZPD*, vol 70, 1891, pp. 52–6; vol 78, 1892, pp. 61, 450; vol 101, 1898, p. 44; vol 104, 1898, p. 507.
143 *JLC*, 1892, no 7. *AJHR*, 1893, H-30. *JLC*, 1894, no 11. *NZPD*, vol 83, 1894, pp. 448–52.
144 *NZPD*, vol 98, 1897, p. 473, vol 100, 1897, pp. 870–3; vol 101, 1898, pp. 40–1, 45, 52; vol 104, 1898, pp. 499, 506; vol 105, 1898, p. 655. PWD, W000, plan 18263, ArchNZ. *AJHR*, 1898, D-1. Newsletter, Wellington NZ Historic Places Trust, vol 1, no 4, 1977, articles. Howard Tanner, 'Parliament restored', *Historic Places*, July 1997, pp. 4–5.
145 *NZPD*, vol 101, 1898, pp. 24–49.
146 *NZPD*, vol 104, 1898, pp. 492–513. *AJHR*, 1899, D-1, p. xi.
147 *NZPD*, vol 105, 1898, p. 764.
148 *AJHR*, 1900–2, H-32, library reports.
149 *NZPD*, vol 109, 1899, pp. 506–12; vol 113, 1900, pp. 469–72. *AJHR*, 1958, H-32, p. 14. IA1, 1901/160.
150 Fanning, p. 40.
151 *NZPD*, vol 135, 1905, p. 145.

[152] *AJHR*, 1958, H-32, pp. 15–16.
[153] One of the Elect, pp. 29–31, 76.
[154] *NZPD*, vol 110, 1899, pp. 336, 779.
[155] Drummond, pp. 314–15. *NZPD*, vol 110, 1899, pp. 75–8. Seddon, p. 95. *EP*, 15 May 1954.
[156] Phipps, p. 100ff.
[157] Bassett, *Ward*, pp. 104–6.
[158] Hamer, *Liberals*, p. 214ff.
[159] *NZPD*, vol 112, 1900, pp. 480, 489–90; vol 113, 1900, pp. 465–72; vol 115, 1900, pp. 149–62.
[160] *NZPD*, vol 120, 1902, pp. 31, 36, 327–30. *NZT*, 3 Oct 1902.
[161] *NZPD*, vol 120, 1902, p. 9.
[162] Phipps, pp. 91–100. Clarke, p. 190ff.
[163] Clarke, p. 255. *NZPD*, vol 123, 1903, pp. 2–4. Mark Cohen to W.P. Reeves, 18 Apr 1903, Letters written to men of mark, vol 2.
[164] Campbell, 'Speakership', pp. 143–5, 154. Parliamentary Service, ABIK, 7663, 3/5/3, pt 2, Speaker to Wright-St Clair, 9 June 1954, ArchNZ.
[165] Phipps, p. 113ff. *NZPD*, vol 125, 1903, p. 495.
[166] *EP*, 4 Apr 1931. *NZPD*, vol 200, 1923, pp. 12, 19. *NZT*, 19 Dec 1911. Geoffrey W. Rice, *Heaton Rhodes of Otahuna*, Christchurch, 2001, pp. 125, 134–5.
[167] *NZPD*, vol 125, 1903, pp. 804, 817–18; vol 130, 1904, pp. 221–2; vol 153, 1910, p. 830.
[168] Foster, p. 248. *The Reformer*, no 1, Sept 1905, p. 7.
[169] *NZPD*, vol 133, 1905, pp. 182–6. Burdon, *King Dick*, pp. 309–11. Major, 'Seventy years', pp. 60–1. *JHR*, 1905, pp. 191–4.
[170] Drummond, pp. 359, 365–82. Seddon, p. 169.
[171] Foster, pp. 97–8. Seddon, p. 197. *NZPD*, vol 137, 1906, pp. 301–2, 445. Hamer, *Liberals*, pp. 254–65, ch. 8; Bassett, *Ward*, ch. 10.
[172] Seddon, pp. 178–9.
[173] *NZPD*, vol 140, 1907, pp. 696–700, 758–63. Seddon, pp. 197–8.
[174] *NZPD*, vol 141, 1907, pp. 34–5, 505–13; vol 148, 1909, p. 436; vol 165, 1913, p. 460. Seddon, p. 201.
[175] *Dom*, 11–13 Dec 1907. *EP*, *Auckland Star*, 11 Dec 1907. *AJHR*, 1958, H-32, pp. 17–18. David Wilson, 'The "hydra-headed fiend"', *NZ Legacy*, vol 11, no 1, 1999.
[176] *EP*, 11 Dec 1907.
[177] The *Journal* was recreated from Otterson's notes. ABIK, 7663, 2/3. A temporary wooden replacement mace was designed by John Campbell. *NZT*, 27 June 1908. Sutherland, 'Symbol of authority – the mace'.
[178] *NZPD*, vol 143, 1908, pp. 2, 39.
[179] Wilson, *Parliamentary Record*, pp. 320–1. J.O. Wilson, *Bellamy's, 1871–1969*, Wellington, 1969. Alan Henderson, 'Contested ground: the parliamentary precinct since 1840', *People's History*, no 30, May 1999. *NZPD*, vol 143, 1908, pp. 109–110, 456, 514–15; vol 144, 1908, pp. 74, 206, 681; vol 145, 1908, p. 7; vol 146, 1909, pp. 213–14; vol 147, 1909, pp. 544, 710; vol 148, 1909, pp. 629, 778, 786. *NZT*, 29 June 1908. The standing orders were altered to allow three rather than two minutes to return to the chamber for divisions.
[180] Ross, p. 231. *NZPD*, vol 156, 1911, p. 268; vol 157, 1912, p. 32; vol 158, 1912, pp. 622–4; vol 166, 1913, p. 86; vol 180, 1917, p. 232.
[181] *Otago Witness*, 8 July 1908. *NZT*, 27, 29, 30 June 1908. Hamer, *Liberals*, ch. 9.
[182] *NZT*, 19 Dec 1911. Bassett, *Ward*, ch. 12. *DNZB*, vol 3, McLaren. Barry Gustafston, *Labour's Path to Political Independence*, Auckland, 1980, pp. 18–19, 161; Newman, pp. 67, 75–6, 315–16.
[183] Newman, pp. 31–2. For Ngata and the 'Young Maori Party', see Ranginui Walker, *He Tipua: The Life and Times of Sir Apirana Ngata*, Auckland, 2001; Sorrenson, 'History of Maori representation', pp. 30–6.
[184] *EP*, 13 May 1909. A.W. Hogg Collection, folder 1, reminiscences notebook, p. 17.
[185] *NZPD*, vol 146, 1909, appendix, p. 1.
[186] *NZPD*, vol 146, 1909, pp. 146–9. Newman, p. 29.
[187] Newman, pp. 104–7. *NZPD*, vol 146, 1909, pp. 102–4.
[188] *NZPD*, vol 147, 1909, pp. 6–7.
[189] Newman, p. 173. Guy H. Scholefield, *NZ Parliamentary Record, 1840–1949*, Wellington, 1950, p. 170, mace.
[190] Newman, pp. 63–88, 184–95.
[191] *NZPD*, vol 148, 1909, pp. 434–9, 610–1, 981–90.
[192] *NZT*, 27, 30 Dec 1909. *NZPD*, vol 148, 1909, pp. 629–32, 1585–1624. Wheeler, 'Premier's personality', clipping, c. 10 May 1925, Wheeler clippings, vol 4. *EP*, 4 Apr 1931.
[193] *NZPD*, vol 150, 1910, pp. 807–16.
[194] *NZPD*, vol 161, 1912, pp. 961–2, 994–9.
[195] Bassett, *Ward*, pp. 185–6.
[196] *NZPD*, vol 149, 1910, p. 688; vol 152, 1910, pp. 3–5, 5–15, 724; vol 153, 1910, pp. 108–13, 1306–7. Tabulation of sessions and hours, 1875–1910, *NZPD*, vol 153, 1910, p. 1399.
[197] Bassett, *Ward*, ch. 13.
[198] Hamer, *Liberals*, ch. 10. Michael Bassett, *Three Party Politics in NZ, 1911–1931*, Auckland, 1982, pp. 3–14. The comparison with Atkinson's situation after the 1890 election is apposite.
[199] Seddon, pp. 204–10. L.C. Webb, 'The rise of the Reform Party', MA, Canterbury University College, 1928, pp. 42–5.
[200] *NZPD*, vol 157, 1912, pp. 40, 201–44, 356–9. *AJHR*, 1912, session I, I-7. Bruce Farland, *Coates' Tale*, Wellington, 1995, p. 12.
[201] Seddon, pp. 208–9. *NZPD*, vol 157, 1912, p. 339.
[202] Seddon, p. 209. A furious Massey suggested Labour member Payne had been bribed to switch his vote, quoting a letter. The House found that Massey had committed a breach of privilege; one of the few occasions before the mid 1970s on which a member was found to have breached privilege.
[203] *Dom*, 21–23 Mar 1912.
[204] *NZPD*, vol 158, 1912, pp. 104, 378–9.
[205] *NZT*, 8 July 1912. Webb, 'Reform Party', p. 51. Seddon, pp. 211–12. Ross, p. 231. Michael Bassett, *Coates of Kaipara*, Auckland, 1995, pp. 35–7.
[206] W.J. Gardner, 'The rise of W.F. Massey, 1891–1912', *Political Science*, vol 13, no 1, 1961, p. 23. Webb, 'Reform Party', p. 53.
[207] Lipson, *Politics of Equality*, pp. 340–3, table 16.
[208] Halligan, p. 58, table 2.5.
[209] Foster, p. 5, and Appendix I.
[210] Database of members, 1853–1938. Webb, *Government in NZ*, pp. 45–6. Lipson, *Politics of Equality*, tables 6 and 17, pp. 121, 355. Halligan, pp. 34–6. *AJHR*, 1913, H-27. Hamer, *Liberals*, appendix 1. Phipps, appendix B. Newman, pp. 19–40.
[211] W.J. Gardner, *The Farmer Politician in History*, Palmerston North, 1970, pp. 4–5.

Chapter 5 – Escaping the 'trammels of the past': organised party government, 1913–35

[1] *NZPD*, vol 158, 1912, p. 378.
[2] Gardner, 'The rise of Massey'. Webb, 'Reform Party'.
[3] Gardner, 'The rise of Massey', p. 11.
[4] *NZPD*, vol 206, 1925, p. 7.
[5] Wheeler, 'Premier's personality', clipping, c. 10 May 1925, Wheeler clippings, vol 4. *NZPD*, vol 206, 1925, p. 7. R.M. Burdon, *The New Dominion*, Wellington, 1965, p. 34.

6. William Downie Stewart, *Right Honourable Sir Francis H.D. Bell*, Wellington, 1937, p. 292.
7. Burdon, *New Dominion*, pp. 34–5.
8. *NZPD*, vol 186, 1920, p. 41 (and p. 268). Gardner, 'Massey in power', pp. 18–19. *EP*, 1 Nov 1956, George Sykes.
9. D.R. Hill, 'Organisation of the Reform Party in NZ', MA, Kansas State University of Agriculture and Applied Science, 1960, pp. 43, 70. Gardner, 'Massey in power', pp. 19–25; Foster, pp. 259–63.
10. *NZPD*, vol 158, 1912, pp. 445–6; vol 159, 1912, p. 2. Bassett, *Ward*, chs 14, 15. Bassett, *Three Party Politics*. Gardner, 'Massey in power'.
11. von Tunzelmann, 'Membership of Parliament', table 11. Stewart, *Bell*, p. 84. Burdon, *New Dominion*, pp. 35–6. *NZPD*, vol 224, 1930, pp. 81, 93.
12. *Spectator*, 13 July 1912. Gardner, 'Massey in power', p. 9. *NZPD*, vol 158, 1912, p. 405.
13. Bassett, *Ward*, pp. 215–16. *NZPD*, vol 158, 1912, p. 665.
14. *NZPD*, vol 161, 1912, p. 196; vol 178, 1917, p. 8.
15. *NZPD*, vol 161, 1912, pp. 1367–8.
16. *NZPD*, vol 162, 1913, pp. 2-4.
17. David Hamer, 'The second ballot', *NZJH*, vol 21, no 1, 1987. *NZPD*, vol 166, 1913, p. 637.
18. Seddon, pp. 213–14.
19. *NZPD*, vol 167, 1913, pp. 74–83, 134–5; vol 168, 1914, p. 524.
20. *NZPD*, vol 167, 1913, pp. 90, 92. *EP*, 4 Apr 1931. *NZT*, 24 Nov 1913. Seddon, pp. 213–15.
21. *NZPD*, vol 166, 1913, pp. 851–60. Seddon, pp. 216–17.
22. Ross, pp. 232–3. Webb, 'Reform Party', pp. 103–4.
23. Cited in P.J. Stewart, 'The Hon. J.A. Hanan', MA, University of Otago, 1955, p. 48.
24. *NZPD*, vol 174, 1915, pp. 651, 653.
25. *NZPD*, vol 168, 1914, pp. 329–38; vol 171, 1914, pp. 754–7, 892.
26. *NZPD*, vol 226, 1930, pp. 1206, 1242–3.
27. Webb, 'Reform Party', p. 121.
28. *NZPD*, vol 169, 1914, pp. 379–404.
29. Ian McGibbon (ed.), *Oxford Companion to NZ Military History*, Auckland, 2000, entry for First World War. Seddon, pp. 220–1. Webb, 'Reform Party', pp. 123–4.
30. Gardner, 'Massey in power', p. 10. Bassett, *Three Party Politics*, pp. 16–20.
31. Stewart, *Bell*, pp. 118–21.
32. *NZPD*, vol 172, 1915, pp. 67–8.
33. Gustafston, *Labour's Path*, p. 115.
34. Gardner, 'Massey in power', p. 13. *DNZB*, vol 3, Allen.
35. *NZPD*, vol 173, 1915, p. 188; vol 174, pp. 972–7; vol 175, 1916, p. 242. Bassett, *Coates*, pp. 46–7.
36. *NZPD*, vol 175, 1916, pp. 303, 786. Gustafston, *Labour's Path*, pp. 110–13.
37. *NZPD*, vol 177, 1916, pp. 940–4.
38. *NZPD*, vol 180, 1917, pp. 77, 217, 223.
39. *AJHR*, 1908, D-8, I-14. *NZPD*, vol 143, 1908, pp. 112, 330–65; vol 145, 1908, pp. 867–911; vol 147, 1909, p. 788; vol 156, 1911, p. 83. ABIK, 7662, special file no 15.
40. *NZPD*, vol 145, 1908, pp. 428–35, 869–70, 873.
41. *NZPD*, vol 152, 1910, pp. 300–1; vol 158, 1912, p. 163. *NZT*, 16 June 1910.
42. Cochran, pp. 49–51. *AJHR*, 1911, D-1, pp. xii–xiii. *NZ Building Progress*, supplement, Dec 1911. *NZPD*, vol 152, 1910, p. 304ff.
43. W1, 24/26, pt 1, 1913–14.
44. *NZPD*, vol 156, 1911, pp. 130–3. Richardson, 'Campbell', pp. 240–58.
45. Cochran, p. 33. *NZPD*, vol 160, 1912, pp. 192–201. *Dom*, 23 Mar 1912.
46. W1, 24/26, pts 1–6, 1913–23. LE1, 1921/237A; 1922/240. *NZPD*, vol 167, 1913, p. 1036; vol 172, 1915, p. 189; vol 173, 1915, p. 678; vol 174, 1915, pp. 526–8; vol 178, 1917, p. 471; vol 180, 1917, pp. 313–14; vol 196, 1922, p. 357. *AJHR*, 1923, D-1, p. 60. *EP*, 23 Nov 1914; 3 Oct 1970. *NZ Building Progress*, Oct 1914, p. 71; Oct 1915, pp. 445–6. *To House Parliament*, Wellington, 1996, p. 16. Cochran, pp. 35, 37.
47. Other wreaths were added in the early 1960s to commemorate the Second World War and other military engagements.
48. ABIK, 7662, special file no 15. W1, 24/26, pt 6, 1921–3.
49. *NZPD*, vol 193, 1921–2, pp. 369, 400.
50. Old Hansard files: 1924–35, Briggs letter, 21 July 1928; Hansard Roster Book, 1908–13. *NZ Women's Weekly*, 28 May 1984.
51. NZ had donated kauri for the Canadian Parliament Buildings. *NZPD*, vol 177, 1916, p. 801; vol 187, 1920, p. 814; vol 192, 1921, p. 657.
52. LE1, 1917/10; 1920/7. Works and Development Services Corporation, AAQB, 24/410, pt 2, 1923–62, ArchNZ.
53. *NZPD*, vol 177, 1916, p. 799; vol 183, 1918, pp. 554–8; vol 186, 1920, pp. 392–3. *NZT*, 2 Aug 1922. *AJHR*, 1922, I-3B.
54. *LT*, 15 June 1923. *NZPD*, vol 183, 1918, pp. 81, 553–8, 823; vol 187, 1920, pp. 558–9; vol 190, 1921, p. 365; vol 193, 1921–2, pp. 401, 474, 846. *AJHR*, 1919, I-11.
55. *NZPD*, vol 186, 1920, p. 75.
56. *NZPD*, vol 199, 1923, pp. 190, 339.
57. *NZPD*, vol 184, 1919, pp. 31, 110–11; vol 196, 1922, p. 1009; vol 204, 1924, p. 225. ABIK, 7663, 2/2/10, ArchNZ. Carol Rankin, *Women and Parliament, 1893–1993*, Wellington, 1993, p. 29.
58. *NZPD*, vol 206, 1925, pp. 245–6; vol 209, 1926, p. 805.
59. *NZPD*, vol 184, 1919, pp. 974–5.
60. *NZPD*, vol 192, 1921, p. 976.
61. *NZPD*, vol 192, 1921, p. 975.
62. ABIK, 7663, 2/1/15. *NZPD*, vol 240, 1934, pp. 143–51.
63. *NZPD*, vol 209, 1926, p. 786. ABIK, 7662, special file no 20A; 7663, 2/3/2.
64. Tschopp, landscape design, ATL pictorial collection, 6714. *NZPD*, vol 158, 1912, p. 141. Cochran, p. 35.
65. ABIK, 7663, 2/8/2, pt 1; 2/8/6. Farland, *Coates*, p 96.
66. LE7, special files, no 21, letter 18 Apr 1923, ArchNZ.
67. *AJHR*, 1912, H-34. *NZPD*, vol 176, 1916, p. 488; vol 194, 1921–2, p. 553.
68. ABIK, 7662, special files no 22. LE1, 1913/351. *NZPD*, vol 162, 1913, pp. 173–4, 494–5; vol 165, 1913, pp. 237, 283–4; vol 166, 1913, p. 86; vol 167, 1913, p. 1052.
69. *NZPD*, vol 174, 1915, pp. 920–1.
70. ABIK, 7662, no 6; 7663, 5/2/4. LE7, special files, no 26.
71. ABIK, 7662, special file no 6, Speaker to Clerk, 2 Dec 1920; 5/2/4. LE7, special files, no 26.
72. *NZPD*, vol 178, 1917, p. 45; vol 186, 1920, p. 363. IA1, 14/18/2.
73. LE7, special files, nos 3, 28. ABIK, 7662, special file no 20A. Memo, Nosworthy to Clerk, 7 Dec 1925, and 'Duties of Manager of Bellamy's and Officer-in-Charge of Parliament Buildings', 1920, Bailey collection. The Sergeant-at-Arms continued to keep the attendance roll of members, paid staff concerned with the buildings, and supervised the cleaning of the buildings during the session.
74. LE7, special files, no 34. ABIK, 7507, 5/26/31, ArchNZ. *DNZB*, vol 4, Andersen. Rachel Barrowman, *The Turnbull*, Auckland, 1995, p. 31. *NZPD*, vol 204, 1924, pp. 158–9; vol 205, 1924, pp. 1131–8; vol 209, 1926, pp. 778, 780–1, 803, 805; vol 213, 1927, pp. 694–700.
75. *AJHR*, 1926–35, H-32, library reports.
76. *AJHR*, 1958, H-32, pp. 16–17.

77. ABIK, 7507, 5/26/31, Scholefield to Coates, 28 Feb 1926. Grant Young, 'The construction of national storehouses of knowledge in post-war NZ', *Turnbull Library Record*, vol 35, 2002, pp. 67–8.
78. LE7, special files no 23; LE7, 1914; 1918/13. IA1, 14/20. ABIK, 7662, special file no 6; 7663, 5/1/1. Old Hansard files, Spragg interview, 1916.
79. ABIK, 7663, 5/8/3; 5/13/3. Old Hansard files, 1924–35, Briggs letter, 21 July 1928, Gray to Cameron, 7 Dec 1925, and reply, Cameron to Speaker, 11 Aug 1924.
80. *NZPD*, vol 230, 1931, pp. 977–8. ABIK, 7663, 5/2/4; 5/15/6.
81. *AJHR*, 1932, B-4, pp. 9, 14, 19–21; B-4A. *NZPD*, vol 233, 1932, p. 271. ABIK, 7663, 5/1/3; 5/2/4.
82. *NZPD*, vol 237, 1933, p. 519.
83. *NZPD*, vol 174, 1915, pp. 646–54; vol 177, 1916, p. 602. ABIK, 7663, 1/5/4; 3/3/16. LE7, special files no 3. LE1, 1916/239.
84. *NZT*, 19 Dec 1911.
85. Helen Wilson, *My First Eighty Years* (second edition), Hamilton, 1951, pp. 171–2.
86. *NZPD*, vol 186, 1920, p. 360; vol 215, 1927, p. 400; vol 234, 1932, p. 171; vol 343, 1965, p. 1397; vol 349, 1966, p. 3572. David Gee, *My Dear Girl*, Christchurch, 1993, p. 134. LE7, special files, no 3.
87. LE7, 1929/3. ABIK, 7663, 3/3/23, pt 1; 3/3/2; 3/3/3; 7/3/14, pt 2. *NZPD*, vol 215, 1927, pp. 380–2, 386, 409–10; vol 269, 1945, p. 816; vol 273, 1946, pp. 173–4. C.G. Scrimgeour et al., *The Scrim–Lee Papers*, Wellington, 1976, p. 96. Gwen Watts, *A Husband in the House*, Christchurch, 1969, p. 38.
88. *NZPD*, vol 343, 1965, p. 1397. *EP*, 27 Oct 1964, J.A. Lee.
89. *NZPD*, vol 185, 1919, pp. 1396–1402.
90. *NZPD*, vol 185, 1919, pp. 1399–1400.
91. Barry Gustafson, *From the Cradle to the Grave: A Biography of Michael Joseph Savage*, Auckland, 1988, pp. 112–13.
92. *NZPD*, vol 215, 1927, pp. 386, 421–4, 426, 429–33, 614–15, 682; vol 267, 1944, p. 654; vol 295, 1951, p. 176.
93. Clipping, 13 Nov 1929, Wheeler clippings, vol 4.
94. Gustafson, *Labour's Path*, pp. 91–4. Bruce Brown, The *Rise of NZ Labour*, Wellington, 1962, pp. 23–4, 32–4. B.M. Brown, 'The NZ Labour Party, 1916–35', MA, Victoria University College, 1955, pp. 29–33.
95. Gustafson, *Labour's Path*, pp. 133–4. *DNZB*, vol 3, Webb. *NZPD*, vol 178, 1917, p. 476.
96. Gustafson, *Labour's Path*, p. 137. Brown, *Rise of Labour*, p. 35. Brown, 'Labour Party', pp. 92–109.
97. Austin Mitchell, 'Caucus: the NZ parliamentary parties', *Journal of Commonwealth Political Studies*, vol 6, 1968, p. 7.
98. *NZPD*, vol 183, 1918, p. 92. Michael Bassett and Michael King, *Tomorrow Comes the Song: A Life of Peter Fraser*, Auckland, 2000, pp. 79–90.
99. Clyde Carr, *Politicalities*, Wellington, 1936, pp. 65, 80. Gee, p. 83.
100. Gustafson, *Labour's Path*, pp. 139, 151. Brown, *Rise of Labour*, pp. 55–60, 69–70, 76–7.
101. *NZPD*, vol 183, 1918, pp. 66, 355, 359, 368–70, 1041. Gustafson, *Labour's Path*, pp. 115, 134–6.
102. Webb, 'Reform Party', pp. 183–8. *NZPD*, vol 186, 1920, pp. 260–2. Gustafson, *Labour's Path*, p. 138. Bassett, *Coates*, chs 3, 4. B.M. O'Dowd, 'The post-war years of Massey's ministry, 1919–1925', MA, Auckland University College, 1949.
103. *NZPD*, vol 184, 1919, pp. 240–1, 278, 282, 896–7.
104. *LT*, 14 June 1923.
105. H.E. Holland, 'Mr Massey's Liberal Supporters', Wellington, 1924, and 'How the Liberals voted', Wellington, 1928. Wheeler, 'The representative chamber', *LT*, 15 June 1922. R.N. Kelson, 'Voting in the NZ House of Representatives, 1947–54', *Political Science*, vol 7, no 2, 1955, p. 102.
106. R.J. Harrison, 'Organisation and procedure in the NZ Parliament', PhD, Ohio State University, 1964, pp. 215–16.
107. Robin Hyde, *Journalese*, Auckland, 1934, pp. 37–8.
108. Burdon, *New Dominion*, p. 58.
109. *NZPD*, vol 184, 1919, pp. 963–80. Coney, *Standing in the Sunshine*, pp. 38–41. Burdon, *New Dominion*, pp. 50–1.
110. *NZPD*, vol 187, 1920, pp. 505, 543; vol 188, 1920, p. 8; vol 189, 1920, p. 1009; vol 190, 1921, pp. 5–6.
111. Clipping c. 4 Aug 1920, Wheeler clippings, vol 3.
112. *NZPD*, vol 186, 1920, pp. 257–63.
113. Fanning, p. 27. *LT*, 15 June 1922.
114. *NZPD*, vol 186, 1920, p. 269; vol 188, 1920, p. 668.
115. *NZPD*, vol 190, 1921, pp. 77, 183, 273–4, 437–8.
116. *NZPD*, vol 191, 1921, pp. 99, 286–7, 305, 340, 346; vol 194, 1922, p. 544.
117. Hyde, pp. 30–1.
118. *NZPD*, vol 193, 1921–2, pp. 500, 573, 711.
119. *NZPD*, vol 198, 1922, p. 830.
120. Bassett, *Three Party Politics*, pp. 26–33. Stewart, *Bell*, pp. 228–31.
121. *NZPD*, vol 199, 1923, pp. 190, 357.
122. *NZPD*, vol 199, 1923, pp. 2–12. Stewart, 'Hanan', p. 111.
123. Clippings, 16, 17 Feb 1923, Wheeler clippings, vol 3. *NZPD*, vol 199, pp. 110–13, 290–1.
124. Clipping, 15 Feb 1923, Wheeler clippings, vol 3. Wheeler, 'Premier's personality', clipping, c. 10 May 1925, Wheeler clippings, vol 4. Stewart, *Bell*, p. 231.
125. *NZPD*, vol 200, 1923, pp. 366–8, 398–400; vol 201, 1923, p. 348; vol 202, 1923, p. 689. Bassett, *Coates*, p. 82.
126. *NZPD*, vol 203, 1924, p. 670; vol 205, 1924, pp. 1211–12; vol 206, 1925, p. 9.
127. 'Premier's personality', c. 10 May 1925, Wheeler clippings, vol 4. *NZPD*, vol 218, 1928, pp. 444–5, 447.
128. *NZPD*, vol 205, 1924, pp. 723–9. Clippings, 22, 24 Oct 1924, Wheeler clippings, vol 4.
129. Farland, *Coates*, p. 46. Clippings, 30 Mar, 10 May 1925, Wheeler clippings, vol 4.
130. Bassett, *Coates*, pp. 94, 130–1.
131. Bassett, *Coates*, p. 86. Farland, *Coates*, pp. 41, 59, 67, 74–5. Wheeler, 'The new Prime Minister', 28 May 1925, Wheeler clippings, vol 4.
132. Bassett, *Ward*, p. 256. Holland, 'How the Liberals voted'. Hyde, pp. 36–7. *NZPD*, vol 206, 1925, pp. 473–4.
133. Clipping, 29 June 1925, Wheeler clippings, vol 4. *NZPD*, vol 206, 1925, pp. 22–3, 105, 386.
134. *NZPD*, vol 206, 1925, pp. 404, 414, 451, 459; vol 207, 1925, pp. 281–2.
135. *NZPD*, vol 208, 1925, pp. 926–32; vol 211, 1926, p. 604.
136. *NZPD*, vol 199, 1923, pp. 36–9; vol 209, 1926, pp. 803–4; vol 236, 1933, pp. 368, 377, 383; vol 237, 1933, p. 1356. *Press*, 8 Feb 1923. Bassett and King, *Tomorrow Comes*, pp. 100, 125. Sir Alister McIntosh, 'Working with Peter Fraser in wartime', p. 164, in Margaret Clark (ed.), *Peter Fraser*, Palmerston North, 1998.
137. One of the Elect, p. 64. *NZPD*, vol 198, 1922, p. 449; vol 206, 1925, p. 93; vol 224, 1930, pp. 181, 182.
138. *NZPD*, vol 208, 1925, p. 931.
139. Bassett, *Coates*, pp. 99–102. Bassett, *Three Party Politics*, pp. 34–7. Burdon, *New Dominion*, pp. 65–76.
140. LE7, 1926/34, letter of 19 May 1926.
141. *LT*, 27 Oct 1928.
142. Bassett, *Ward*, p. 259. *NZPD*, vol 209, 1926, p. 3.
143. Stewart, *Bell*, pp. 243, 296. Bassett, *Coates*, pp. 106–9, 118–27. *NZPD*, vol 211, 1926, pp. 415, 419, 453–6.

144. James Holt, *Compulsory Arbitration in NZ*, Auckland, 1986, pp. 175–80. B.H. Farland, 'The political career of J.G. Coates', MA, Victoria University, 1965, pp. 104–7. J.H. Gaudin, 'The Coates government, 1925–1928', MA, University of Auckland, 1971, pp. 107–9, 140–4. *NZPD*, vol 216, 1927, p. 186. Clipping, 30 Nov 1927, Wheeler clippings, vol 4.
145. *NZPD*, vol 216, 1927, pp. 866–7.
146. Bassett, *Ward*, pp. 262–3.
147. Bassett, *Ward*, pp. 265–70. Bassett, *Coates*, pp. 139–49.
148. *NZPD*, vol 220, 1928, pp. 2–4.
149. Clipping, 7 Dec 1928, Wheeler clippings, vol 4. *NZPD*, vol 220, 1928, pp. 15, 75.
150. LE1, 1913/20; 1920/21; 1923/19; 1925/19. *NZPD*, vol 186, 1920, p. 317; vol 192, 1921, p. 1105; vol 205, 1924, p. 1197; vol 215, 1927, p. 682; vol 216, 1927, p. 303; vol 218, 1928, pp. 425–57 passim.
151. *LT*, 6 Oct 1927.
152. *NZPD*, vol 220, 1929, pp. 163–4; vol 221, 1929, pp. 876–906. *AJHR*, 1929, I-18.
153. The new standing orders also gave the Speaker greater powers in calling members, a difficulty in the three-party system. *NZPD*, vol 221, 1929, p. 884.
154. *NZPD*, vol 222, 1929, p. 445. Clippings, 21–22 Aug, Wheeler clippings, vol 4.
155. Clippings, 24 Oct 1929, Wheeler clippings, vol 4.
156. *NZPD*, vol 223, 1929, pp. 1111–57.
157. Bassett, *Ward*, pp. 276–85. Clipping, 15 May 1930, Wheeler clippings, vol 4.
158. *DNZB*, vol 3, Forbes. Burdon, *New Dominion*, pp. 131–2. Bassett, *Coates*, p. 174.
159. *NZPD*, vol 223, 1929, p. 223; vol 225, 1930, pp. 458, 752; vol 226, 1930, p. 76.
160. *NZPD*, vol 226, 1930, pp. 1174–96. Clipping, 25 Oct 1930, Wheeler clippings, vol 4.
161. *NZPD*, vol 227, 1931, pp. 14, 29, 33, 105, 126.
162. *NZPD*, vol 227, 1931, pp. 433–720. H.E. Holland, 'Lest we forget! The salary and wage reductions and the record of the division lists', Wellington, 1931. Clippings, 31 Mar, 2 Apr 1931, Wheeler clippings, vol 4.
163. ABIK, 7663, 3/4/6, Clerk of the House to Clerk of Legislative Assembly, NSW, 1 Nov 1933.
164. *NZPD*, vol 227, 1931, pp. 668, 671, 682, 684, 695.
165. *NZPD*, vol 227, 1931, pp. 593, 597–8.
166. The Speaker had to rule on this matter later incorporated into the standing orders in 1932. ABIK, 7663, 3/4/6, Clerk of the House to Clerk of Legislative Assembly, NSW, 1 Nov 1933.
167. ABIK, 7663, 7/3/14, pt 2, letter and Standing Order 205A, 20 May 1931. Harrison, pp. 192–3.
168. *NZPD*, vol 229, 1931, pp. 468–77. Burdon, *New Dominion*, pp. 135–9.
169. *NZPD*, vol 230, 1931, pp. 297, 445.
170. Bassett, *Three Parties*, pp. 59–63.
171. *NZPD*, vol 231, 1932, p. 96ff. Bassett and King, *Tomorrow Comes*, p. 125.
172. *NZPD*, vol 231, 1932, p. 534ff. Erik Olssen, *John A. Lee*, Dunedin, 1977, pp. 55–6, 58. Scrimgeour et al., pp. 25–6.
173. Burdon, *New Dominion*, p. 146.
174. *NZPD*, vol 232, 1932, pp. 507, 776.
175. Bassett, *Coates*, pp. 189–98.
176. *NZPD*, vol 235, 1933, pp. 576–650. *EP*, 21 Feb 1933, 25 June 1935.
177. *NZPD*, vol 236, 1933, pp. 525–9. Bassett, *Coates*, p. 206. Wilson, *Parliamentary Record*, p. 304.
178. *NZPD*, vol 237, 1933, pp. 735–6. *EP*, 9 Feb 1972, Jack Young.
179. Bassett, *Coates*, pp. 204–5.
180. Burdon, *New Dominion*, p. 168.
181. *NZPD*, vol 243, 1935, p. 659.
182. Gustafson, *Cradle to the Grave*, pp. 166–7.
183. Halligan, table 2.5, p. 58.
184. Lipson, *Politics of Equality*, table 17, p. 355. Database of members, 1853–1938. Webb, *Government in NZ*, pp. 46–7. Gardner, *Farmer Politician*. *AJHR*, 1918, H-27A. E.M. McLeay, 'Parliamentary careers in a two-party system', PhD, University of Auckland, 1978, p. 96, table.

Chapter 6 – The consolidation of two-party government and Parliament, 1936–49

1. K.J. Scott, *The NZ Constitution*, Oxford, 1962, pp. 48–51.
2. A.D. Robinson, 'The rise of the NZ National Party, 1936–1949', MA, Victoria University College, 1957, ch. 2. Barry Gustafson, *The First 50 Years: A History of the NZ National Party*, Auckland, 1986, ch. 1.
3. Gustafson, *First 50 Years*, p. 12.
4. Robinson, pp. 204–5.
5. Louise Overacker, 'The NZ Labor Party', *American Political Science Review*, vol 49, no 3, 1955.
6. Keith Jackson, *The Dilemma of Parliament*, Wellington, 1987, ch. 1.
7. Gustafson, *Cradle to the Grave*, pp. 176–8. Carr, p. 47.
8. T.D.H. Hall, Manuscript on parliamentary procedure, Victoria University Library, ch. 3. *DNZB*, vol 4, Barnard.
9. Bassett and King, *Tomorrow Comes*, pp. 188–9.
10. Roy Jack, 'A Speaker looks at Parliament', pp. 83–4, in Sir John Marshall (ed.), *The Reform of Parliament*, Wellington, 1978. McLeay, 'Parliamentary careers', pp. 192–3.
11. ABIK, 7663, 3/5/3, pt 2, Speaker to Wright-St Clair, 9 June 1954. Bob Tizard interview with author, 21 Mar 2003.
12. Patrick Day, *The Radio Years*, Auckland, 1994, pp. 4, 213–15, 299–300. *NZPD*, vol 231, 1932, pp. 680, 690; vol 234, 1932, pp. 231, 244–5, 518.
13. *NZPD*, vol 247, 1936, pp. 32–3.
14. L. Cleveland, 'Is Parliament talking to itself?', in L. Cleveland and A.D. Robinson, (eds), *Readings in NZ Government*, Wellington, 1972, p. 125.
15. Charles Wheeler, 'NZ's first parliamentary broadcast', *NZ Railways Magazine*, 1 May 1936, pp. 15, 49–50. ABIK, 7663, 3/5/7, pt 1, pt 2, incl. H.N. Dollimore, 'Parliamentary broadcasting in NZ', 1966; 3/1/14, seating plan, 1945. Jim Sullivan, 'The House in your home', *NZ Listener*, 28 Mar 1981. *Waikato Times*, 8 Feb 1975. *NZPD*, vol 253, 1938, p. 505; vol 256, 1939, p. 842.
16. Ken G. Collins, *Broadcasting Grave and Gay*, Christchurch, 1967, p. 100, ch. 1. J.H. Hall, *The History of Broadcasting in NZ, 1920–1954*, Wellington, 1980, pp. 83–4. *EP*, 15 Jan 1986, Jack Hoare.
17. *NZ Radio Record*, 20, 27 Mar, 3 Apr 1936.
18. *NZPD*, vol 248, 1937–8, p. 455; vol 251, 1938, p. 288; vol 263, 1943, pp. 595, 606, 624. ABIK, 7663, 3/5/7, pt 1.
19. *NZPD*, vol 269, 1945, p. 810.
20. *NZPD*, vol 255, 1939, p. 446.
21. *NZPD*, vol 256, 1939, pp. 774–6, 840; vol 259, 1941, pp. 138, 146, 433.
22. *NZPD*, vol 257, 1940, pp. 6–18. Collins, ch. 11.
23. *Dom*, 23 July 1941.
24. D.E. McHenry, 'The broadcasting of parliamentary debates in NZ and Australia', *Political Science*, vol 7, 1955. Robert N. Kelson, *The Private Member of Parliament and the Formation of Public Policy*, Toronto, 1964, pp. 80–2.

25. *NZPD*, vol 306, 1955, p. 1693.
26. Day, *The Radio Years*, pp. 233–5. *NZPD*, vol 264, 1944, p. 505.
27. *Freedom*, 24 Aug 1949.
28. *NZPD*, vol 266, 1944, p. 505; vol 268, 1945, p. 52; vol 269, 1945, pp. 166–7.
29. ABIK, 7663, 3/5/7, pt 1. *EP*, 8 June 1950.
30. *NZPD*, vol 247, 1936, p. 1188.
31. *NZPD*, vol 271, 1945, p. 41.
32. *NZPD*, vol 244, 1936, pp. 170, 228–9, 867–76.
33. *NZPD*, vol 247, 1936, p. 1182; vol 252, 1938, p. 321; vol 260, 1941, p. 1244; vol 267, 1944, p. 830. Clipping, 29 Apr 1936, Wheeler Clippings, vol 4. *JHR*, 1937–9.
34. H.N. Dollimore, 'NZ "washing-up" bills', *The Table*, vol 37, 1968. Halligan, pp. 173–4, 187–8, table 6.7. Geoffrey Palmer, *Unbridled Power?*, Wellington, 1979, pp. 89–91. *NZPD*, vol 307, 1955, p. 3240; vol 380, 1972, p. 2547; vol 388, 1973, pp. 5231–4. See also Local Legislation Bill, first used in 1928. F.B. Stephens (ed.), *Local Government in NZ*, Wellington, 1949, pp. 37–8.
35. *NZPD*, vol 247, 1936, pp. 1093–1103.
36. *NZPD*, vol 250, 1938, pp. 395–6.
37. Elizabeth Hanson, *The Politics of Social Security*, Auckland, 1980.
38. *NZPD*, vol 252, 1938, p. 336; vol 253, 1938, pp. 160–70.
39. *NZPD*, vol 253, 1938, p. 173.
40. *NZPD*, vol 256, 1939, p. 20. ABIK, 7663, 7/1/14, 'Wartime activities of the Legislative Department'.
41. Gustafson, *Cradle to the Grave*, chs 12, 13.
42. Gustafson, *Cradle to the Grave*, pp. 271–2.
43. Austin Mitchell, *Government By Party*, Christchurch, 1966, p. 54.
44. *EP*, 12 July 1940.
45. Parliamentary (Secret Session) Emergency Regulations, 1940. ABIK, 7663, 7/1/14.
46. ABIK, 7663, 3/5/13.
47. Bassett, *Coates*, ch. 14.
48. Bassett and King, *Tomorrow Comes*, p. 194.
49. *NZPD*, vol 259, 1941, pp. 133–4; vol 347, 1966, pp. 1490–1.
50. Gustafson, *First 50 Years*, p. 40. Robinson, pp. 107–8, ch. 5.
51. *NZPD*, vol 260, 1941, pp. 1144, 1242. Bassett and King, *Tomorrow Comes*, p. 224.
52. *NZPD*, vol 259, 1942, pp. 286–7. Bassett and King, *Tomorrow Comes*, pp. 241–5.
53. ABIK, 7663, 7/1/14. Peter Cooke, *Defending NZ*, Wellington, 2000, vol 2, pp. 634–5, K-4.
54. *NZPD*, vol 266, 1944, p. 229. Bassett and King, *Tomorrow Comes*, pp. 187, 388. Wilson, *Parliamentary Record*, p. 328.
55. J.R. Marshall, 'The NZ cabinet', *Political Science*, vol 7, no 1, 1955, p. 3. H.N. Dollimore, *The Parliament of NZ and Parliament House* (revised edition), Wellington, 1973, p. 31.
56. *EP*, 25 Sept 1944. *NZPD*, vol 278, 1947, p. 473.
57. *NZPD*, vol 261, 1941–2, p. 718.
58. Bassett and King, *Tomorrow Comes*, pp. 243–5.
59. *NZPD*, vol 264, 1944, pp. 2–4. *EP*, 27 Oct 1943. Bassett and King, *Tomorrow Comes*, p. 259.
60. *EP*, 3, 31 Mar 1944.
61. Lipson, *Politics of Equality*, pp. 174–85.
62. *NZPD*, vol 270, 1945, pp. 765, 795–6; vol 271, 1945, pp. 39, 42, 76, 91, 144, 146–7, 157. Gustafson, *First 50 Years*, p. 52. Bassett and King, *Tomorrow Comes*, p. 302.
63. *NZPD*, vol 271, 1945, pp. 237–44.
64. Tizard interview.
65. *NZPD*, vol 260, 1941, pp. 1242–3; vol 276, 1947, pp. 2–5.
66. John Marshall, *Memoirs*, vol 1, Auckland, 1983, p. 101. Sorrenson, 'History of Maori representation', pp. 39–46. Claudia Orange, *The Treaty of Waitangi*, Wellington, 1987, pp. 232–4, 239–40. Pers. comm., Whetu Tirikatene-Sullivan, 20 Nov 2003.
67. *EP*, 23, 26 June 1947. *NZPD*, vol 276, 1947, pp. 185, 371; vol 284, 1948, p. 4349.
68. *Auckland Star*, 20 Sept 1969; 15 June 1977, Finlay. Hall, Manuscript on parliamentary procedure, ch. 2.
69. *NZPD*, vol 287, 1949, pp. 2369–70.
70. *NZPD*, vol 251, 1938, pp. 124–5; vol 254, 1939, pp. 140–1.
71. *NZPD*, vol 283, 1948, pp. 2447, 2465–6.
72. Walter Nash, 'The Leader of the Opposition', *Political Science*, vol 15, no 2, 1963.
73. *NZPD*, vol 285, 1949, p. 30ff; vol 287, 1949, p. 2081. Marshall, *Memoirs*, vol 1, pp. 131–2.
74. *NZPD*, vol 226, 1930, pp. 1239–43. ABIK, 7507, 5/13/4, Speaker to Fraser, 21 Mar 1945. Parliamentary Service, held in Parliament, PS, 5/10/3, Hall to Speaker, 19 July 1945. PS, 4/2, Clerk letter 9 Aug 1972.
75. *NZPD*, vol 249, 1937–8, p. 1098; vol 258, 1940, p. 592.
76. ABIK, 7663, 5/8/2, pt 1; 5/1/10, pt 1. *EP*, 20 Apr 1957.
77. ABIK, 7663, 5/13/3; 5/15/6.
78. Old Hansard files, selected papers, 1936–48, Briggs letter, 18 Feb 1936, Briggs to Weston, 8 Jan 1937, reply, 26 Jan 1937.
79. Old Hansard files, typists, messengers, 1937–77, Clerk to Chief Reporter Briggs, 22 June, 1 July 1937.
80. Old Hansard files: recruitment, 1960–72, Sutherland letter, 28 Nov 1960; selected papers, 1936–48, Briggs to Clerk, 16 Oct 1941; recruitment of reporters, 1945–61, Clerk to Briggs, 6 June 1939, Manderson letter, 19 May 1945. A.B. Conway, 'The NZ Hansard staff', 1974.
81. *EP*, 25 Nov 1974. *Dom*, 28 June 1979, Rosalie Hall.
82. *NZPD*, vol 314, 1957, p. 3327. Pers. comms, M. Hely, 20 August 2001, 28 October 2002.
83. *AJHR*, 1937–50, H-32, library reports.
84. *AJHR*, 1949, H-32, p. 4.
85. *NZPD*, vol 263, 1943, p. 1112; vol 267, 1944, p. 827. ABIK, 7507, 5/01/1. Hall, Manuscript on parliamentary procedure.
86. *NZPD*, vol 268, 1945, pp. 114–15; vol 272, 1944, p. 522. *EP*, 16 Dec 1944. *Dom*, 5 July 1945. ABIK, 7507, 5/13/4. Bert Bailey interview with author, 30 Apr 2003.
87. *NZPD*, vol 263, 1943, pp. 766–7, 1113; vol 264, 1944, p. 970; vol 266, 1944, pp. 213–14, 216, 227. ABIK, 7663, 2/1/1, pts 1, 2; 11/3. *Dom*, 5 Apr 1944.
88. Bailey interview.
89. ABIK, 7663, 11/1, telegram, 21 June 1944.
90. Bailey interview. *Dom*, 10 Jan 1951.
91. *NZPD*, vol 274, 1946, pp. 838–41. ABIK, 7663, 11/1; 11/3. Bailey interview.
92. Kelson, 'Voting in the House'. Lipson, *Politics of Equality*, p. 344. Hobby, p. 111.
93. Kelson, *Private Member*.
94. Mitchell, *Government By Party*, pp. 54–6. R.S. Milne, *Political Parties in NZ*, Oxford, 1966, pp. 133–6.
95. *NZPD*, vol 303, 1954, p. 765.
96. *Auckland Star*, 24 Sept 1977.
97. *Dom*, 29 June 1953; 8 Oct 1964.
98. *Auckland Star*, 15 June 1977, Finlay.
99. Watts, p. 111.
100. *Dom*, 20 July 1953.
101. *NZPD*, vol 307, 1955, pp. 1969–79, 3480–3; vol 313, 1957, pp. 2174–7. ABIK, 7663, 3/4/6, pt 2, Clerk of the House to Clerk of Legislative Assembly, Winnipeg, Canada, 19 June 1946. A.H. Nordmeyer, 'A critical examination of the functioning of Parliament', *Journal of Public Administration*, vol 8, 1946, pp. 3–5.
102. *NZH*, 16 June 1961, Halstead.
103. *NZPD*, vol 280, 1948, p. 590; vol 286, 1949, pp. 1229–31. Nordmeyer, p. 6.

104. P. Campbell, 'Politicians, public servants, and the people in NZ, I and II', *Political Studies*, vols 3, 4, 1955–6, p. 210. Angus, p. 51. ABIK, 7663, 3/3/43/2, Mason submission.
105. *Dom*, 17 Aug 1953. *NZPD*, vol 338, 1964, p. 255; vol 349, 1966, p. 3572. Watts, p. 78.
106. *JHR*, various years. Kelson, *Private Member*, p. 84.
107. Angus, p. 40, appendix 2, graph. Mitchell, *Government By Party*, p. 93.
108. Kelson, 'Voting in the House'. T. May, 'Parliamentary discipline', in Cleveland and Robinson, (eds). Hobby, pp. 120, 169–71, tables 3.3, 3.12, 3.13. Halligan, pp. 69–83, table 3.1.
109. ABIK, 7663, 3/4/6, pt 2, Clerk to Public Service Commission, 19 Feb 1947.
110. R.M. Algie, 'A system open to abuse', *NZ Law Journal*, 18 Apr 1933. *NZPD*, vol 265, 1944, pp. 392–7. R.M. Algie, 'A critical examination of the functioning of Parliament', *Journal of Public Administration*, vol 8, 1946, pp. 18–20. *EP*, 20 Nov 1940; 26 Aug 1943. A.C. Stephens, 'The abuse of delegated legislation', *NZ Law Journal*, 20 May 1947, p. 84. Nordmeyer, pp. 12–13.
111. Palmer, *Unbridled Power?*, p. 96, figure 2.
112. *NZPD*, vol 279, 1947, pp. 976, 1042–3. Kelson, *Private Member*, pp. 102–3. Marshall, *Memoirs*, vol 1, pp. 118–19.
113. Database of members, 1853–1938. Compilation of members, 1931–1996. Austin Mitchell, 'The NZ Parliaments of 1935–1960', *Political Science*, vol 13, no 1, 1961. Barry Gustafson, 'The Labour Party', table 1, p. 276, in Hyam Gold (ed.), *NZ Politics in Perspective* (third edition), Auckland, 1992. McLeay, 'Parliamentary careers', pp. 64, 67.
114. The majority of Labour members in the House prior to the 1935 election who remained were overseas born.
115. Rural seats were less well represented in Labour and National cabinets. McLeay, 'Parliamentary careers', pp. 168–72.
116. *NZPD*, vol 295, 1951, p. 176. For salary changes, *AJHR*, 1951, H-25, schedule B.
117. *NZPD*, vol 257, 1940, p. 495; vol 262, 1943, p. 817. *EP*, 13 July 1940.
118. ABIK, 7663, 3/3/43/1, letter to Blundell, 16 June 1951. Gustafson, *Cradle to Grave*, pp. 180–1. Bassett and King, *Tomorrow Comes*, p. 140.
119. *NZPD*, vol 267, 1944, pp. 654–7. *AJHR*, 1944, I-19.
120. *Dom*, 14 Dec 1944.
121. *EP*, 11 Nov 1932. *NZPD*, vol 272, 1945, p. 520; vol 279, 1947, pp. 726–8. *AJHR*, 1946, I-18.
122. Ross Galbreath, *Scholars and Gentlemen Both*, Wellington, 2002, pp. 290, 293.
123. *NZPD*, vol 279, 1947, pp. 895–7; vol 285, 1949, pp. 37–8, 46–7.
124. Janet McCallum, *Women in the House*, Picton, 1993, chs 2–6, 8.
125. *NZPD*, vol 260, 1941, pp. 25–8.
126. McCallum, p. 35.
127. *NZPD*, vol 262, 1943, p. 46.
128. Bassett and King, *Tomorrow Comes*, p. 316.
129. McCallum, p. 85. *NZPD*, vol 482, 1987, p. 10586.
130. McCallum, p. 55.
131. Halligan, p. 58, table 2.5.
132. Christopher Hollis, *Can Parliament Survive?*, London, 1949, p. 64.

Chapter 7 – Reform, efficiency and accountability, 1950–69

1. Watts, p. 30. Marshall, *Memoirs*, vol 1, pp. 140–1. Keith Eunson, *Mirrors on the Hill*, Palmerston North, 2001, 'Sidney Holland'. Bruce Brown, 'Nordmeyer, 1901–1989', pp. 43–4, in Margaret Clark (ed.), *Three Labour Leaders*, Palmerston North, 2001. Bruce Brown, 'Holyoake's precursors', in Margaret Clark (ed.), *Holyoake's Lieutenants*, Palmerston North, 2003. Neale McMillan, *Top of the Greasy Pole*, Dunedin, 1993, p. 43. *EP*, 22 Mar 1973, Nestor. Raymond Boord interview with Keith Sinclair about Nash, Oral History Centre, ATL.
2. *NZPD*, vol 289, 1950, pp. 4–5; vol 294, 1951, p. 24. ABIK, 7663, pt 2, Speaker to Wright-St Clair, 9 June 1954. *NZPD*, vol 314, 1957, pp. 3331–4. Marshall, *Memoirs*, vol 1, p. 110.
3. *NZPD*, vol 289, 1950, p. 10. Jackson, *Legislative Council*, chs 13–16.
4. Jackson, *Legislative Council*, pp. 187–9. Philip A. Joseph, *Constitutional and Administrative Law in NZ* (second edition), Wellington, 2001, pp. 445–7.
5. *NZPD*, vol 290, 1950, pp. 1573–5.
6. *NZPD*, vol 294, 1951, pp. 7–26. ABIK, 7663, 7/3/14, pt 1. *AJHR*, session II, 1951, I-17. Jackson, *Legislative Council*, pp. 198–9. From now on, we take the form of spelling of Serjeant-at-Arms (rather than Sergeant-at-Arms) as adopted by the House in the 1950s.
7. *AJHR*, 1982, I-6, pp. 7–8.
8. Bernard Crick, *The Reform of Parliament* (third edition), London, 1970, p. 12. Marshall, 'The NZ cabinet'. Hobby, p. 113, table 3.2. Mitchell, *Government By Party*, pp. 22–3.
9. Angus, pp. 74–5.
10. ABIK, 7663, 3/3/43/1, pt 3, A.E. Allen, Chief Government Whip, 22 Aug 1967. A.E. Allen, 'The role of the whips and the caucus in the NZ Parliament', *The Parliamentarian*, vol 52, no 1, 1971. Mitchell, *Government By Party*, pp. 66, 135–45. H.L.J. May, 'The whip', in Mitchell, *Government by Party*. *Auckland Star*, 15 Aug 1980, May. Tom Scott, *Ten Years Inside*, Christchurch, 1985, pp. 130–1.
11. *NZPD*, vol 377, 1971, pp. 5160–5. *EP*, 10 Dec 1971.
12. Milne, pp. 136–43.
13. *NZPD*, vol 303, 1954, pp. 762–6. *Dom*, 2 Aug 1954. Jack Young interview, Oral History Centre.
14. *NZPD*, vol 304, 1954, p. 1097.
15. Marshall, *Memoirs*, vol 1, pp. 161–2, 261. *DNZB*, vol 4, Mason. Watts, p. 80.
16. ABIK, 7663, 2/2/2, Holland to Speaker, 3 Oct 1950; 7/3/14, pt 1, Clerk to Speaker, 22 May 1951; 3/1/1, pt 2. Marcia Spencer, *The Incoming Tide*, Wellington, 1998, p. 144. Watts, pp. 33, 103. Bailey interview. *Dom*, 13 Apr 1953. *EP*, 7 Oct 1950.
17. *NZPD*, vol 314, 1957, p. 3325.
18. *EP*, 24, 26 June 1952.
19. Office of the Clerk, 5/2/1, 1972–5. *EP*, 25 June 1959.
20. F.L.W. Wood, *'Her Majesty Commands'*, Wellington, 1958. Jock Phillips, *Royal Summer*, Wellington, 1993, pp. 50–3. For the Auckland commemoration, see ABIK, 7663, 3/6/15, letter to Holland, 4 May 1954; 7665, box 45. IA1, 107/56; 107/56/1; 107/56/3. *NZH*, 25 May 1954; 29 February, 25 March, 23, 25 May 1956. *Auckland Star*, 25 May 1954; 23–25 May 1956. *Weekly News*, 30 May 1956.
21. *NZPD*, vol 291, 1950, pp. 2530–2.
22. Michael Bassett, *Confrontation '51*, Wellington, 1972. Nash amended the Act in 1960 to require a summoning of Parliament within seven days of an emergency being declared.
23. Marshall, *Memoirs*, vol 1, pp. 174–5. Sinclair, *Nash*, pp. 285–6.
24. *NZPD*, vol 294, 1951, pp. 88, 262.
25. *Dom*, 16 July 1951.
26. McLeay, 'Parliamentary careers', p. 137.
27. *NZPD*, vol 297, 1952, pp. 889–92; vol 298, 1952, pp. 1638–43. *EP*, 15 Aug 1952. *Dom*, 15 Aug, 29 Sept 1952.
28. Halligan, pp. 84–6, table 3.4.

29. *Dom*, 18 May 1953. Austin Mitchell, 'The people and the system', *NZ Journal of Public Administration*, vol 31, no 1, 1968, pp. 30–1. Raymond Miller, 'Social Credit/The Democrat Party', in Gold (ed.), *NZ Politics*.
30. *NZPD*, vol 303, 1954, pp. 821, 853–9. Bassett interview with Henry May, 1977, AUL.
31. *NZPD*, vol 307, 1955, p. 2570. *Dom*, 22, 26 Sept 1955.
32. ABIK, 7663, pt 2.
33. ABIK, 7663, pt 2, letter to Holland, 21 June 1957.
34. *NZPD*, vol 314, 1957, pp. 2743–4. May, 'Parliamentary discipline', pp. 111, 114. Ross Doughty, *The Holyoake Years*, Feilding, 1977, p. 127.
35. Sinclair, *Nash*, p. 303. Tizard interview.
36. Margaret Hayward, *Diary of the Kirk Years*, Wellington, 1981, p. 210. McLeay, 'Parliamentary careers', pp. 235–6. Tizard interview. *NZPD*, vol 455, 1983, p. 4725; vol 510, 1990, p. 4378. Bassett interview with May.
37. May, 'The whip', p. 140. Bassett interview with May. *Dom*, 1 Aug 1972, May.
38. *EP*, 30 Jan 1958. *NZPD*, vol 315, 1958, pp. 20–1, 194, 203–4, 212–15. Tizard interview.
39. *Dom*, 23–25 July 1958. May, 'Parliamentary discipline', p. 118. *Auckland Star*, 20 Sept 1969. *NZPD*, vol 315, 1958, pp. 193–4; vol 510, 1990, p. 4378, Tizard. Tizard interview.
40. Watts, p. 183. Doughty, p. 144.
41. *NZPD*, vol 317, 1958, pp. 922–3, 980, 1236–9, 1255–6. *Dom*, 18 Aug 1958. Doughty, p. 161. *DNZB*, vol 5, Shand.
42. *Dom*, 18 Aug 1958.
43. *EP*, 4 Oct, 2 Dec 1958. Sinclair, *Nash*, pp. 309–11, 319. Marshall, *Memoirs*, vol 1, pp. 277–9. Michael Bassett, *The Third Labour Government*, Palmerston North, 1976, p. 58. Sinclair's interviews concerning Nash, Oral History Centre.
44. Sinclair's interview with Boord.
45. Halligan, pp. 84–6, table 3.4.
46. *NZPD*, vol 321, 1959, pp. 2705–10. *EP*, 26 Oct 1959.
47. Tizard interview.
48. Tony Garnier et al., *The Hunter and the Hill*, Auckland, 1978, p. 82. Bassett interview with May.
49. *NZPD*, vol 321, 1959, pp. 2054–63, 2613. Doughty, p. 146.
50. *NZPD*, vol 321, 1959, p. 2190. *EP*, 2 Oct 1959. May, 'Parliamentary discipline', pp. 109–12. Mitchell, *Government By Party*, pp. 67–8.
51. ABIK, 7663, 3/5/3, pt 2. *EP*, 3, 7, 8 Sept 1960. *NZH*, 8, 9 Sept 1960.
52. *NZPD*, vol 324, 1960, pp. 2076–7, 2144–6.
53. Harrison, p. 360.
54. *Dom*, 8, 17 June 1961.
55. *NZPD*, vol 272, 1945, pp. 497–503.
56. *AJHR*, 1951, H-25. ABIK, 7663, 3/3/43/1, pt 1; 3/3/43/1, pt 3, Clerk of the House to Clerk of Parliament, Rhodesia, 27 June 1969.
57. Watts, p. 29. ABIK, 7663, 3/3/43/1, pt 1, submission of Shand.
58. ABIK, 7663, 3/3/43/2, submissions of Lake and Barnes. Barry Gustafson, *His Way: A Biography of Robert Muldoon*, Auckland, 2000, p. 64. *NZPD*, vol 482, 1987, p. 10599; vol 562, 1991, p. 3372. Mitchell, *Politics and People*, p. 251. PS, 6/3/7, pt 1, 1975–6, pt 3, 1981–4. Tizard interview. John Henderson, *Rowling*, Auckland, 1981, p. 72.
59. Watts, p. 38. Mitchell, 'M.Ps as seen by M.Ps', p. 251. Henderson, *Rowling*, pp. 70–1.
60. Mitchell, 'M.Ps as seen by M.Ps'. Bassett interview with Arnold Nordmeyer, 1977, AUL.
61. ABIK, 7663, 3/3/43/2. *NZPD*, vol 293, 1950, pp. 4760–1; vol 295, 1951, p. 172.
62. *AJHR*, 1951, H-25, p. 10.
63. *NZPD*, vol 295, 1951, pp. 171–8.
64. ABIK, 7663, 3/3/43/2. *NZPD*, vol 306, 1955, pp. 1879–84. *AJHR*, 1958–9, 1964, 1967–8, 1970, H-50. Neale McMillan, 'Parliamentary salaries in NZ', *The Parliamentarian*, vol 52, no 1, 1971.
65. *AJHR*, 1973, H-2.
66. Editorial, *Dom*, 5 Aug 1974.
67. For remuneration more recently: David McGee, *Parliamentary Practice*, Wellington, 1985, ch. 3, and second edition, 1994, ch. 3. G.A. Wood (ed.), *Ministers and Members in the NZ Parliament* (second edition), Dunedin, 1996, appendix 8.
68. *EP*, 22 Mar 1949; 17 Nov 1951. AAQB, 24/2537, pt 2, 1949–57, report on proposed government centre, 25 Aug 1950. ABIK, 7663, 2/1/15; 2/1/15/1.
69. *Weekly News*, 28 Dec 1949. *Southern Cross*, 13 Feb 1950. PS, 2/2/2.
70. Watts, p. 32. Marshall, *Memoirs*, vol 1, p. 116.
71. *NZPD*, vol 368, 1970, p. 2779; vol 442, 1981, p. 4352.
72. *Weekly News*, 8 Mar 1950.
73. *NZPD*, vol 295, 1950, p. 805. *EP*, 14 Nov 1951; 19 Nov 1952; 31 Jan 1963. AAQB, 24/1138. Wilson, *Parliamentary Record*, pp. 328–9. ABIK, 7663, 2/1/1, pt 2; 2/1/15. Cabinet Office, AAFD, 811, 170k, 42/8/1, ArchNZ. *Dom*, 22 June 1966. *Wanganui Herald*, 4 Sept 1969.
74. ABIK, 7663, 2/3/16, pt 2; 2/1/1, pt 2. AAQB, 24/1138, report to Speaker, 19 May 1952. *Dom*, 25 Sept 1957.
75. *NZPD*, vol 301, 1953, p. 2565; vol 310, 1956, pp. 2639–41, 2902, 2905, 2906; vol 343, 1965, p. 1731; vol 368, 1970, pp. 3187–9. *EP*, 22 Apr 1953; 15 Apr 1954. AAFD, 811, 170k, 42/8/1, cabinet approval, 28 Mar 1955.
76. AAQB, 24/410, pt 2, 1923–62. Hugh Templeton, *All Honourable Men*, Auckland, 1995, p. 64. AAFD, 811, 681, 42/8/1, pt 7, 1972–5, note on cabinet room table. Marshall, 'NZ cabinet', p. 65. The table was replaced when the Beehive was refurbished. *DP*, 14 Oct 2003.
77. AAQB, 24/410, pt 2, 1923–62; 24/817. *NZPD*, vol 330, 1962, pp. 982–3; vol 345, 1965, pp. 3377–8. R.D. Muldoon, *The Rise and Fall of a Young Turk*, Wellington, 1974, pp. 43–4.
78. ABIK, 7663, 2/1/15/1. *EP*, 16, 21 Oct 1953.
79. Sir Keith Holyoake Papers, folder 149:1, Ministry of Works proposal, Oct 1961, ATL. MS Papers 1814, ATL. AAQB, 24/817, Commissioner of Works to minister, 24 Sept 1962. AAFD, 811, 676, 42/8/1, pt 1, 1961–4. *Dom*, 16 Mar, 31 May 1962; 31 Jan 1963. *EP*, 27 Oct 1962.
80. ABIK, 7663, 2/1/15/1, Government Architect to ministerial committee, 13 Sept 1963. AAQB, 24/817, Commissioner of Works to minister, 24 Sept 1962. AAFD, 811, 676, 42/8/1, pt 1.
81. L.E. Martin, 'Memoirs', pp. 370–3, OHInt-0413-6, ATL.
82. ABIK, 7663, 2/1/15/1, ministerial committee, 24 Mar 1964. AAFD, 811, 676, 42/8/1, pt 1. *Designscape*, no 89, Mar 1977. *Hutt News*, 16 Mar 1971. *EP*, 26 Sept 1972. *NZH*, 21 Aug 1964; 16 Mar 1971.
83. AAFD, 811, 676, 42/8/1, pt 1, press statement, 1 Apr 1964. *NZPD*, vol 339, 1964, p. 1033. *Press*, 4 Apr 1964. *Dom*, 2–4, 15 Apr 1964. *EP*, 31 Aug 1964. Martin, 'Memoirs', p. 372.
84. AAFD, 811, 676, 42/8/1, pt 1, Sheppard reply, c. late 1964.
85. *Auckland Star*, 5 Aug 1964. *Press*, 4 Apr 1964. *Dom*, 2 Apr 1964. *NZPD*, vol 339, 1964, pp. 1033–4, 1055.
86. AAFD, 811, 676, 42/8/1, pt 1, Spence to Holyoake, 24 Apr 1964, papers Mar–June 1965; pt 3, McIntosh to Sheppard, 21 July 1965; pt 6, McIntosh note for file, 26 June 1965. *Additions to Parliament Buildings: Design Report*, Wellington, 1965.
87. *AJHR*, 1951, 1960, 1970, 1984, B-7, pt 1. ABIK 7663, 2/1/

88 15, list of staff, 1953. Charles Littlejohn interview with author, 21 May 2003.
88 LE7, special files no 23. ABIK, 7662, no 6; 7663, 3/4/6, pt 2; 5/8/1; 5/13/3; 5/15/6. *NZPD*, vol 276, 1947, p. 4. Old Hansard files, recruitment of reporters, 1945–61, Clerk to Higgie, 22 Apr 1947, Clerk to Speaker, 13 Apr 1953.
89 *EP*, 28 Apr 1953. Old Hansard files, recruitment of reporters, 1960–72, Sutherland letter, 28 Nov 1960, paper of 10 Nov 1960.
90 Old Hansard files: recruitment of reporters, 1960–72, senior reporter to Clerk, 11 Aug 1961; typists, messengers, 1937–77, letter, 22 July 1969. *EP*, 2, 5 May 1962; 1 Aug 1967; 24 Mar 1973, McLean; 25 Nov 1974. *Dom*, 28 June 1979. Pers. comm., M. Hely, 28 Oct 2002. ABIK, 7663, 3/5/3, pt 3, Clerk letter, 13 July 1964.
91 Bailey interview. *Wanganui Herald*, 26 Apr 1952. *Food and Catering*, vol 3, no 7, Mar 1968. *Catering in NZ*, vol 2, no 4, July 1968; vol 4, Jan–Feb 1967.
92 AAFD, 811, 170d, 42/14/1. *EP*, 31 Aug 1957. *Truth*, 13, 27 Aug 1957. ABIK, 7663, 4/6/1; 9/3/2; 11/1–4. PS, 4/5, pt 1. Bailey interview.
93 *NZPD*, vol 510, 1990, pp. 4376–7. Tizard interview. Eunson, p. 78.
94 McCallum, chs 7, 9.
95 McCallum, p. 85.
96 Hayward, p. 61. Rankin, p. 20.
97 *NZPD*, vol 267, 1944, pp. 408–10. ABIK, 7663, 2/2/10. *Dom*, 20 Nov 1945.
98 *Press*, 16 Aug 1972. Rankin, p. 30. *JHR*, 1948, p. 499. *NZPD*, vol 342, 1965, p. 491; vol 346, 1966, pp. 56, 217; vol 350, 1967, p. 67; vol 355, 1968, pp. 223, 253, 810–11; vol 356, pp. 909–10, 1338–40; vol 379, 1972, p. 1177. *AJHR*, 1967, I-14, p. 12. Hayward, p. 61. McCallum, p. 97. Pers. comm. Tirikatene-Sullivan.
99 ABIK, 7663, 11/4. Rankin, pp. 33–4. Bailey interview.
100 *NZPD*, vol 379, 1972, p. 1177. *EP*, 1 Nov 1972.
101 Gustafson, *His Way*, pp. 69–71. McLeay, 'Parliamentary careers', pp. 122–3. Tizard interview. *NZPD*, vol 510, 1990, pp. 4376–7; vol 521, 1991, p. 6457. George Gair interview with author, 20 Mar 2003.
102 Gustafson, *His Way*, pp. 100–2, 139–40.
103 Barrowman, pp. 103–9. Young, 'National storehouses'. *AJHR*, 1904, H-32, pp. 3–4. Penny Griffith et al., (eds) *Book and Print in NZ*, Wellington, 1997, pp. 193–5. P.A. Griffith, '1915 National Library prototype', *NZ Libraries*, vol 45, no 5, 1987.
104 AAQB, 24/2537, pt 1A, interdepartmental committee to Prime Minister, c. early 1937. LE7, 1928/1; special files, no 21. *NZPD*, vol 246, 1936, p. 514. ABIK, 7663, 2/2/17; 12/1/3; 12/1/3/1; 12/1/3/2. AAQB, 24/2537. *DNZB*, vol 5, McIntosh.
105 *AJHR*, 1958, I-17. ABIK, 7663, 2/1/1, pt 2.
106 *NZPD*, vol 345, 1965, pp. 4007–31.
107 *AJHR*, 1966, H-32. J.O. Wilson, 'Library of Parliament', *The Parliamentarian*, vol 52, no 1, 1971.
108 *AJHR*, 1969, H-32. *Auckland Star*, 24 Sept 1977, Freer.
109 Sinclair, *Nash*, pp. 349–50.
110 Bassett interview with May.
111 Tom McRae, *A Parliament in Crisis*, Wellington, 1994, pp. 62–3.
112 K.J. Holyoake, 'The Prime Minister', in Mitchell, *Government by Party*. Anthony Wood, 'Holyoake and the Holyoake years' and Barry Gustafson, 'Holyoake and the National Party', in Margaret Clark (ed.), *Sir Keith Holyoake*, Palmerston North, 1997. Barry Gustafson, 'The transition from Holland to Holyoake', in Clark (ed.), *Holyoake's Lieutenants*. Ian Templeton and Keith Eunson, *Election '69*, Wellington, 1969, ch. 3. Marshall, *Memoirs*, vol 2, pp. 150–6. McMillan, *Top of the Greasy Pole*, p. 46.
113 Comber, 'Personal reflections', p. 27, in Clark (ed.), *Holyoake*. Gair interview. Mitchell, *Government by Party*, pp. 56, 62–3, and K.J. Holyoake, 'The Prime Minister'. Allen, 'Whips and the caucus'.
114 Austin Mitchell, *Politics and People in NZ*, Christchurch, 1969, ch. 4. Muldoon, *Young Turk*, pp. 56–9. Marshall, *Memoirs*, vol 2, pp. 14–18.
115 *ODT*, 24 July 1978, obituary. *DNZB*, vol 4, Algie. Gustafson, *His Way*, p. 71. Gair interview.
116 ABIK, 7663, 7/3/14, pt 2. *NZPD*, vol 326, 1961, pp. 19–21; vol 333, 1962, p. 3458. *EP*, 15 July 1961. Harrison, p. 112. Ian Templeton and Keith Eunson, *In the Balance*, Dunedin, 1972, p. 68.
117 Muldoon, *Young Turk*, pp. 44–5. Gustafson, *His Way*, pp. 69–71. Eunson, pp. 96–7. *NZPD*, vol 580, 1999, p. 19773, Birch.
118 Templeton and Eunson, p. 52. PSC oral history project, Robin Gray interview, ATL. Gustafson, *His Way*, p. 75.
119 Muldoon, *Young Turk*, p. 47. Gustafson, *His Way*, p. 72.
120 *NZPD*, vol 328, 1961, pp. 2206, 2990; vol 361, 1969, p. 1708. Muldoon, *Young Turk*, pp. 48–51. Mitchell, *Government By Party*, p. 67. Marshall, *Memoirs*, vol 1, pp. 222–3.
121 Jackson, *Legislative Council*, ch. 17.
122 *AJHR*, 1952, I-18.
123 *AJHR*, 1961, I-2A; 1964, I-14. *NZPD*, vol 342, 1965, pp. 1149–51.
124 Wood, 'Holyoake', p. 46. Crick, pp. 276–89, for Britain.
125 *Dom*, 8, 17 June 1961.
126 ABIK, 7663, 7/3/14, pt 2, Clerk to Speaker, 31 July 1961, and Speaker to Standing Orders Committee, 1 Mar 1962. *AJHR*, 1961, B-1, pt 2, p. 7. *NZPD*, vol 316, 1958, pp. 173–6; vol 319, 1959, pp. 283–4.
127 ABIK, 7663, 7/3/14, pt 2, Standing Orders Committee, 16 May 1962; pt 3, Clerk to Roy Jack, 22 Feb 1967, Clerk, review of standing orders, 3 Mar 1967. *NZPD*, vol 330, 1962, pp. 24–50, 63–89, 322–38; vol 338, 1964, p. 255. *AJHR*, 1962, I-17, I-17A. Harrison, pp. 121–3, 130–4.
128 LT, 15 June 1922. *JHR*, 1921–2, 1926, 1936, 1951. Halligan, pp. 204, 207, tables 7.2, 7.3.
129 *NZPD*, vol 341, 1964, pp. 4102, 4104; vol 421, 1978, p. 4292.
130 *AJHR*, 1962, I-18.
131 *EP*, 26 Oct 1963.
132 Alex Frame and Robert McLuskie, 'Review of regulations under standing orders', *NZ Law Journal*, 7 Nov 1978. Palmer, *Unbridled Power?*, pp. 101–2. J.M. Smith, 'The parliamentary select committee for statutes revision', MA, University of Canterbury, 1974. Keith Jackson, 'NZ parliamentary committees', *The Parliamentarian*, vol 59, no 2, 1978, p. 101n.
133 Bryan Gilling, *The Ombudsman in NZ*, Palmerston North, 1998, ch. 1. Mitchell, *Government By Party*, pp. 93–6. S.N. Griffith, 'The effectiveness of parliamentary petitioning in NZ, 1969–1983', MA, University of Canterbury, 1985.
134 ABIK, 7663, 3/5/3, pt 3, Clerk to Austin Mitchell, 16 July 1963. *ODT*, 23 Oct 1972. McCallum, p. 76.
135 *NZPD*, vol 311, 1957, pp. 61, 75–8. Marshall, *Memoirs*, vol 2, p. 6. Eunson, p. 78.
136 Mitchell, *Government By Party*, pp. 66, 80–1.
137 *EP*, 26 Oct 1963. Muldoon, *Young Turk*, pp. 66–7.
138 *NZH*, 16 July 1969. *NZPD*, vol 335, 1963, pp. 676–7. *EP*, 20 July 1963. *Dom*, 8, 9 Oct 1964.
139 *AJHR*, 1962, H-41, p. 77. A.F. von Tunzelmann, 'The Public Expenditure Committee', MPP, Victoria University, 1977. R.D. Muldoon, 'The control of public expenditure in NZ', *The Parliamentarian*, vol 55, no 2, 1974.
140 *AJHR*, 1962, H-41, p. 64.
141 *AJHR*, 1958, B-1, pt 2, pp. 5–7. Geoff Skene, 'Parliament: reassessing its role', p. 129, in Gold (ed.), *NZ Politics*.

142. *NZPD*, vol 338, 1964, pp. 255–6. Mitchell, *Government By Party*, pp. 79–80.
143. von Tunzelmann, 'Public Expenditure Committee', ch. 3. Muldoon, *Young Turk*, pp. 65–6. Gustafson, *His Way*, p. 78.
144. ABIK, 7663, 3/5/3, pt 3, Clerk to Holyoake, 23 June 1967. Mitchell, *Government by Party*, p. 65.
145. *NZH*, 12 Apr 1961. *Dom*, 4 June 1962. *AJHR*, 1961, I-2A, pp. 60–6. ABIK, 7663, 7/3/14, pt 2, Standing Orders Committee, 1962. Mitchell, *Politics and People*, ch. 3.
146. Roy Jack, 'A Speaker looks at Parliament', p. 86, in Marshall (ed.). *NZ Listener*, 14 June 1986.
147. *NZPD*, vol 442, 1981, p. 4364, McLachlan.
148. *NZPD*, vol 350, 1967, p. 612; vol 352, 1967, pp. 2674–5. *NZ Statesman*, 30 May 1967. PS, 5/6/5, 1967–75.
149. *NZPD*, vol 350, 1967, pp. 63–71. ABIK, 7663, 7/3/14, pt 3, Clerk to Prime Minister, 20 Mar 1967, notes of committee, 29 Mar 1967. *AJHR*, 1967, I-14; 1968, I-14.
150. Hayward, p. 66n. Garnier et al., p. 81. Tizard interview. *NZ Listener*, 14 June 1986.
151. *NZPD*, vol 355, 1968, pp. 107–22.
152. Adopted since Statham's strict interpretation. Harrison, pp. 210–11.
153. *Press*, 27 Dec 1976.
154. *NZPD*, vol 338, 1964, pp. 79–90.
155. *EP*, 25 Nov 1967. Muldoon, *Young Turk*, p. 87. PSC oral history project, Jonathan Hunt interview. *NZPD*, vol 338, 1964, pp. 254–5, 612, Riddiford and Eyre.
156. Compilation of members, 1931–1996. von Tunzelmann, 'Membership of the NZ Parliament', tables 2, 4, 11. Mitchell: 'The Parliaments of 1935–60'; 'NZ Parliaments', p. 36; 'M.Ps as seen by M.Ps', pp. 238–40, 247, 251, 276–82. McLeay, 'Parliamentary careers', pp. 64–5, 76–8, 96, 156–9, 171–4. John Forster, 'A note on the background of parliamentarians', *Political Science*, vol 21, no 1, 1969, p. 47.
157. Mitchell, *Government By Party*, p. 69.
158. Douglas C. Webber, 'Trade unions and the Labour Party: the death of working-class politics in NZ', in Levine (ed.), *Politics in NZ*. Gustafson, 'The Labour Party', table 1. Hunt interview. Templeton and Eunson, p. 72. Garnier et al., pp. 57–8.
159. ABIK, 7663, 3/1/32. *EP*, 5 June 1968. *Dom*, 5 June 1968. Sinclair, *Nash*, p. 357.
160. Mitchell, *Government by Party*, pp. 72–6, 81–2 and table.
161. The Finance Bill lost its importance and became a minor 'washing up' bill.
162. Geoffrey Palmer, *Unbridled Power?* (second edition), Auckland, 1987, p. 112, table.
163. Mitchell, 'M.Ps as seen by M.Ps', pp. 267–9.
164. Mitchell, *Government by Party*, p. 18. *Auckland Star*, 3 Jan 1970. *Press*, 12 Dec 1970.
165. McLeay, 'Parliamentary careers', pp. 153, 166, 177–9.
166. *Dominion Sunday Times*, 12 June 1966. Mitchell, 'The people and the system', pp. 26–7, 35.
167. R.S. Milne, 'Voting in Wellington Central, 1957', *Political Science*, vol 10, 1958, p. 45. *EP*, 23 Oct 1959; 15 Aug 1964. *NZ Listener*, 16 Oct 1976; 4 June 1977. *Truth*, 23 Sept 1969.
168. ABIK, 7663, 3/5/7, pts 1, 2. *Dom*, 5 June 1962. *NZH*, 4 June 1962.
169. Office of the Clerk, 1/12/3, Speaker to Holyoake, 15 Oct 1970. *EP*, 11 Sept 1976.
170. Office of the Clerk, 5/2/1, 1972–5. *NZPD*, vol 350, 1967, p. 68. *EP*, 15 Aug 1964; 11 Apr 1970.
171. *NZPD*, vol 342, 1965, pp. 108, 282. *Dom*, 27 June 1968.
172. Templeton and Eunson, ch. 1.
173. *NZPD*, vol 352, 1967, p. 2067.
174. Crick, pp. 26–7, 80. Mitchell, *Government By Party*, pp. 68–9. Skene, 'Parliament'.

Chapter 8 – Executive and Parliament: the balance at issue, 1970–84

1. C.R. Marshall, 'The NZ Parliament and foreign policy', *The Parliamentarian*, vol 57, no 2, 1976. Graham Hill, 'The relationship between the NZ House of Representatives and NZ's international relations', *Legislative Studies*, vol 9, no 1, 1994.
2. Jack Young interview.
3. Keith Jackson, *NZ: Politics of Change*, Wellington, 1973, chs 11, 12.
4. Day, *Voice and Vision*, pp. 67–70, 100, 112, 139–44. G.A. Wood, 'The NZ news media', in Stephen Levine (ed.), *NZ Politics*, Melbourne, 1975.
5. Garnier, 'Parliamentary press gallery'. *Press*, 1 May 1993, Oliver Riddell.
6. Gustafson, *His Way*, ch. 9. Templeton and Eunson, pp. 45–7. Bassett interview with May. Hunt interview.
7. McLeay, 'Parliamentary careers', p. 137.
8. *NZPD*, vol 462, 1985, pp. 4331, 4333–4. Tizard interview.
9. *NZPD*, vol 372, 1971, pp. 2767, 2791–2, 3139–40; vol 381, 1972, pp. 3533, 3535. Tizard interview.
10. This became a custom for bills hard-fought in Committee which was then assumed into the standing orders, *AJHR*, 1986, I-18A, p. 7.
11. *NZH*, 8 June 1972. Muldoon had fallen asleep.
12. Templeton and Eunson, pp. 49–51. *NZPD*, vol 368, 1970, pp. 1166–9; vol 374, 1971, p. 3039; vol 375, 1971, p. 4084.
13. *NZPD*, vol 374, 1971, p. 3039. *ODT*, 4 Aug 1973.
14. *NZPD*, vol 377, 1971, pp. 5417–18. Hayward, p. 5. Templeton, p. 24. Templeton and Eunson, p. 57. This year there had been conflict over members' dress. *NZPD*, vol 371, 1971, pp. 51–6; vol 376, 1971, pp. 4540-1; vol 377, 1971, p. 5122ff. ABIK, 7663, 3/5/2. Tizard interview.
15. *NZPD*, vol 378, 1972, p. 125.
16. *NZPD*, vol 378, 1972, pp. 2–7. *ODT*, 23 Oct 1972. *NZH*, 8, 26 June 1976. *EP*, 8 June 1972.
17. Halligan, pp. 84–90, tables 3.4, 3.5.
18. J.O. Wilson, 'Party research units in the NZ Parliament', *The Parliamentarian*, vol 63, no 2, 1983. PS, 4/4/5.
19. Harrison, pp. 75–80. Martin Nestor, 'The role of research in NZ politics', *Political Science*, vol 15, 1963. *Dom*, 10 Aug 1970. *NZPD*, vol 442, 1981, pp. 4357–8.
20. *NZPD*, vol 482, 1987, p. 10593. *EP*, 27 July 1956.
21. PS, 4/4/5, D.W. Lloyd, 'Research support for MPs in NZ', 1983.
22. *AJHR*, 1972, I-19. *NZPD*, vol 378, 1972, pp. 43–60. E.A. Roussell, 'Revision of NZ standing orders', *The Parliamentarian*, vol 53, no 4, 1972. Keith Jackson, 'Parliamentary reform in NZ', *The Parliamentarian*, vol 60, no 4, 1979.
23. *NZPD*, vol 381, 1972, p. 3531; vol 388, 1973, p. 5419.
24. *AJHR*, 1979, I-14, p. 14.
25. Treatment of private members' bills involving appropriations had been a difficult issue. Campbell, 'Speakership', pp. 42–3. *NZPD*, vol 29, 1878, pp. 235–9. *AJHR*, 1910, I-7.
26. *NZPD*, vol 378, 1972, pp. 46–7, 51.
27. von Tunzelmann, 'Public Expenditure Committee', chs 3, 4. D.A. Shand, 'Parliamentary control of the public purse – how real?', Victoria University, Seminar – Can Parliament Survive Without Reform?, 1971.
28. Hunt interview.
29. Doug Kidd, 'What makes Parliament tick', 'Legislation Direct' seminar for lawyers, Aug 1999.
30. Hunt interview.
31. Hayward, [p. v]; and pp. 99–100, 104–5. Garnier et al., p. 26.
32. McMillan, *Top of the Greasy Pole*, p. 94.
33. 'Come in spinner', *Metro*, May 1999, p. 65.

34. *NZPD*, vol 382, 1973, pp. 2–3. Gustafson, *His Way*, p. 138. Bassett, *Third Labour Government*, p. 269. *NZH*, 26 June 1976.
35. R.D. Muldoon, 'An Opposition assessment', p. 24, in Ray Goldstein and Rod Alley, (eds), *Labour in Power*, Wellington, 1975. Templeton, p. 9.
36. Bassett, *Third Labour Government*, ch. 2.
37. *Press*, 23 June 1971, Kirk.
38. *NZPD*, vol 386, 1973, pp. 3676–7.
39. Garnier et al., pp. 95, 103.
40. Templeton, p. 30. Scott, *Ten Years Inside*, p. 15.
41. Gustafson, *His Way*, pp. 72–3, 138, 359. Templeton, pp. 30–1. Bassett, *Third Labour Government*, ch. 4, pp. 103–6.
42. Hunt interview.
43. *NZPD*, vol 384, 1973, pp. 2816–20.
44. Hayward, p. 154. Gustafson, *His Way*, p. 138. Bassett, *Third Labour Government*, p. 52. *ODT*, 4 Aug 1973.
45. Bassett, *Third Labour Government*, pp. 86–8. Hunt interview.
46. R.D. Alley, 'Committees of the House', Victoria University, Seminar – Can Parliament Survive Without Reform?, 1971.
47. *NZPD*, vol 343, 1965, p. 1670, Edwards.
48. Bassett, *Third Labour Government*, pp. 118–20, 123–5.
49. *NZPD*, vol 390, 1974, p. 1557; vol 391, 1974, pp. 2194–2200.
50. *NZPD*, vol 392, 1974, pp. 2729–31; vol 395, 1974, pp. 5579–80. Bassett, *Third Labour Government*, pp. 152–3. Hayward, p. 271.
51. *NZPD*, vol 393, 1974, pp. 3609–57. Hayward, pp. 288–9, 293. Hunt interview. Gair interview.
52. *NZPD*, vol 393, 1974, p. 4205.
53. Bassett, *Third Labour Government*, pp. 159–62. Hayward, pp. 307–11.
54. PS, 5/6/1, pt 2, 1972–84, Clerk to Standing Orders Committee, 1974. *ODT*, 10 Dec 1973. *EP*, 7 Nov 1974.
55. *AJHR*, 1974, I-14. *NZPD*, vol 395, 1974, pp. 5746–52.
56. *NZPD*, vol 395, 1974, p. 5752.
57. *NZPD*, vol 401, 1975, pp. 4192–3.
58. Bassett, *Third Labour Government*, pp. 179–84, 205, 211–13, 230–8.
59. Bassett, *Third Labour Government*, pp. 222–4.
60. *NZPD*, vol 396, 1975, pp. 740–1; vol 397, 1975, pp. 1188–9.
61. *NZPD*, vol 400, 1975, pp. 3295–3312. PS, 5/6/5, pt 0, 1967–75, Clerk letter, 28 July 1975.
62. *NZPD*, vol 400, 1975, pp. 3375–7. Bassett, *Third Labour Government*, p. 249.
63. *NZPD*, vol 407, 1976, p. 3167. PS, 5/6/5, pt 1, 1982–5. *AJHR*, 1979, I-14, p. 16. *NZH*, 31 Mar 1977. J.K. McLay, 'The Privileges Committee in NZ', *The Parliamentarian*, vol 65, no 3, 1984. Jackson, 'Parliamentary committees', p. 98. Bassett, *Third Labour Government*, p. 249.
64. *AJHR*, 1980, I-6, *NZPD*, vol 434, 1980, pp. 4665–84.
65. Bassett, *Third Labour Government*, p. 269. *NZPD*, vol 400, 1975, pp. 3875–6. Hunt interview.
66. *NZPD*, vol 402, 1975, p. 5470.
67. *NZPD*, vol 402, 1975, p. 5465.
68. Gustafson, *His Way*, pp. 190–1. Day, *Voice and Vision*, pp. 216–20, 320–3, 365–6.
69. Gustafson, *His Way*. Templeton, pp. 13–15. McMillan, *Top of the Greasy Pole*, pp. 48–9. Bob Jones, *Memories of Muldoon*, Christchurch, 1997, p. 121. Gair interview. *NZPD*, vol 528, 1992, pp. 10330, 10335.
70. Gustafson, *His Way*, pp. 178–82, chs 12, 13, 15.
71. Jim Bolger, *A View From the Top*, Auckland, 1998, p. 53.
72. McLeay, 'Parliamentary careers'. Marilyn Waring, 'Revitalisation of cabinet, Parliament, parties', in J. Stephen Hoadley (ed.), *Improving NZ's Democracy*, Auckland, 1979.
73. Keith Jackson, 'Cabinet and the Prime Minister', pp. 70–1, in Levine (ed.), *Politics in NZ*.
74. Templeton, p. 11. Paul Goldsmith, *John Banks*, Auckland, 1997, pp. 96–7.
75. Day, *Voice and Vision*, pp. 236–7. Jones, ch. 13.
76. Fran O'Sullivan, 'The parliamentary press gallery', *Cosmo*, Dec 1984.
77. Richard Harman comment, Revisiting Muldoon conference, Wellington, May 2002.
78. Scott, *Ten Years Inside*, p. 6.
79. *NZPD*, vol 395, 1974, p. 5755; vol 408, 1976, p. 4785; vol 428, 1979, p. 4813.
80. Palmer, *Unbridled Power?*, pp. 110–13. Gustafson, *His Way*, pp. 237–8.
81. McCallum, p. 127. Gustafson, *His Way*, p. 195. M. Minogue, 'Information and power', and M. Waring, 'Power and the NZ MP', in Levine (ed.), *Politics in NZ*.
82. Hunt interview.
83. *EP*, *Press*, 24 June 1976. *NZH*, 21 June 1976.
84. *Press*, 2 Dec 1976.
85. *Auckland Star*, 17 July 1976.
86. *NZPD*, vol 402, 1975, p. 5457; vol 403, 1976, pp. 2–6. *EP*, 17 Feb 1976.
87. *NZPD*, vol 405, 1976, p. 2007.
88. *NZPD*, vol 404, 1976, pp. 1552–6; vol 407, 1976, pp. 3157–69.
89. *NZPD*, vol 407, 1976, p. 3677. Gustafson, *His Way*, p. 199. Henderson, *Rowling*, pp. 162–5. Templeton, pp. 81–6. *Press*, 5, 6 Nov 1976. PSC oral history project, Hunt and Bill Birch interviews.
90. Bolger, pp. 79–80, regarded Muldoon's actions as 'perhaps the most vicious attack ever on another member in the House'.
91. Garnier et al., pp. 158–9. Henderson, *Rowling*, p. 167.
92. *NZPD*, vol 407, 1976, p. 3851; vol 408, 1976, p. 4787.
93. Vernon Wright, *David Lange*, Wellington, 1984, p. 114.
94. *NZPD*, vol 400, 1977, pp. 3710, 3751, 3761, 3780–1. PS, 5/1.
95. Birch interview.
96. *NZPD*, vol 416, 1977, pp. 5407–10. Scott, *Ten Years Inside*, p. 52.
97. *NZPD*, vol 417, 1978, pp. 1–4. *NZH*, 15 July 1978. *EP*, 27 Feb 1978. *ODT*, 24 July 1978.
98. *NZPD*, vol 455, 1983, p. 4271; vol 460, 1984, pp. 2780–1.
99. *NZPD*, vol 421, 1978, p. 4201.
100. *NZPD*, vol 421, 1978, pp. 3562–3636, 4418–23; vol 428, 1979, p. 4820. *NZH*, 21 Sept 1978.
101. In response to the Mount Egmont Vesting Bill. *EP*, 28 Sept 1978.
102. *NZPD*, vol 421, 1978, pp. 4294–4302.
103. *NZPD*, vol 421, 1978, p. 4285. *NZH*, 16, 23 Aug 1978.
104. Robert Muldoon, *Number 38*, Auckland, 1986, p. 27.
105. *EP*, 18 May 1979.
106. Gustafson, *His Way*, chs 16, 17.
107. Templeton, pp. 116, 121–2.
108. *NZPD*, vol 428, 1979, p. 4715. *JHR*, 1979, p. 469.
109. *EP*, 23 July 1981.
110. *ODT*, 24 Dec 1979.
111. *AJHR*, 1979, I-14. *NZPD*, vol 428, 1979, pp. 4810–24. Walter Iles, 'NZ experience of parliamentary scrutiny of legislation', *Statute Law Review*, vol 12, 1991.
112. *NZPD*, vol 428, 1979, p. 4816.
113. Halligan, table 6.1, p. 164.
114. Gustafson, *His Way*, p. 263. Richard Prebble, 'Muldoon and Parliament', Revisiting Muldoon conference, Wellington, May 2002.
115. *NZPD*, vol 457, 1984, p. 13.
116. The only exceptions were financial bills and those taken under urgency.

117. *Dom*, 7 Oct 1968. *NZH*, 30 May 1969.
118. Halligan, pp. 208–18, tables 7.4, 7.7. *JHR*, 1973–84.
119. *NZPD*, vol 408, 1976, p. 4447; vol 456, 1984, p. 6. *JHR*, 1976, p. 655. *Press*, 24 Nov 1976.
120. 'NZ: notes on the establishment of an advisory service for select committees', *The Parliamentarian*, vol 55, no 4, 1974. *AJHR*, 1970, I-15.
121. Jackson, 'Parliamentary committees'. Halligan, p. 171, table 6.2.
122. L.B. Hill, 'Parliamentary petitions, the Ombudsman and political change in NZ', *Political Studies*, vol 22, no 3, 1974.
123. Kidd, 'What makes Parliament tick', p. 1.
124. *NZH*, 31 Mar 1977.
125. *NZPD*, vol 428, 1979, pp. 4818, 4820; vol 425, 1979, p. 2664.
126. *NZPD*, vol 425, 1979, pp. 2790–2807; vol 436, 1980, pp. 5690–5701. Halligan, p. 272.
127. Keith Jackson and Alan McRobie, *NZ Adopts Proportional Representation*, Christchurch, 1998, pp. 40–6.
128. ABIK, 7663, 2/1/15/2. *NZPD*, vol 359, 1968, pp. 3877, 4055.
129. *EP*, 31 Oct, 28 Nov 1969. *Waikato Times*, 26 Nov 1969. *Putaruru Press*, 11 Nov 1969. *NZPD*, vol 363, 1969, p. 3214; vol 364, 1969, p. 3518. PS, 2/2/2. Bailey interview.
130. AAFD, 811, 678, 42/8/1 pt 3, report of Government Architect, c. mid 1967, Commissioner of Works to minister, 22 Sept 1967, Holyoake to minister, 1 Feb 1968, Commissioner of Works to minister, 14 Feb 1968.
131. AAFD, 811, 678, 42/8/1 pt 5. AAQB, W3950, 24/26/18, pt 1, Holyoake to Minister of Works, 1 Feb 1968.
132. *Designscape*, no 89, Mar 1977. PS, 2/5/3, parts 1–5, 1967 onwards. 'The Beehive', Ministry of Works and Development, Aug 1976. *NZPD*, vol 442, 1981, p. 4348.
133. *NZPD*, vol 388, 1973, p. 5427. 'Powerhouse' exhibition on Beehive, ArchNZ, Nov 2002.
134. Bailey interview. AAFD, 811, 680, 42/8/1, pt 6, House Committee to Holyoake, 26 Nov 1970. Hunt interview.
135. PS, 4/5, report of 22 May 1974. *NZH*, 26 Sept 1981. PS, 4/5, pts 1–3, 1969–88.
136. *EP*, 14 July 1973.
137. *Press*, 23 May 1977.
138. *NZH*, 19 Mar 1971; 7 Sept 1972; 12 Feb 1976. *EP*, 14 Apr, 6 Aug 1971; 26 Sept 1972; 14 Apr 1975. *Southland Times*, 19 Dec 1971. *Dom*, 16 Nov 1972.
139. *AJHR*, 1979, I-14A.
140. Gustafson, *His Way*, p. 186. Templeton, p. 68. *Auckland Star*, 7 Sept 1979. *ODT*, 3 Sept 1979. Muldoon, *Number 38*, p. 37.
141. Hayward. p. 105. *NZH*, 26 Sept 1981. *NZPD*, vol 425, 1979, p. 2773; vol 436, 1980, pp. 5944–5.
142. *NZPD*, vol 442, 1981, pp. 4348, 4351. PS, 2/4/6.
143. *NZPD*, vol 421, 1978, p. 4287. *AJHR*, 1988, A-2, p. 4. Roger McClay, 'Young New Zealanders take the floor', *The Parliamentarian*, vol 76, no 3, 1995.
144. PS, 2/4/3; 2/4/1. *NZPD*, vol 428, 1979, p. 4837. Garnier, 'The parliamentary press gallery'.
145. *AJHR*, 1982, I-6, p. 15; 1985, I-14, p. 11. *Auckland Star*, 29 July 1985.
146. *NZ Women's Weekly*, 1 Sept 1997.
147. AAFD, 811, 678, 42/8/1, pts 7, 8.
148. AAQB, W3950, 24/26/18, pt 1, Ministry of Works report, 31 Oct 1973, Minister of Works to Prime Minister, 1 July 1975, Treasury to Minister of Finance, 18 Dec 1975, and 18 Mar 1977.
149. *EP*, 4 Nov 1978.
150. PS, 2/7.
151. *NZPD*, vol 428, 1979, pp. 4814, 4836. *Auckland Star*, 7 Sept 1979.
152. *NZPD*, vol 430, 1980, pp. 1338–58; vol 436, 1980, pp. 5943–5.
153. Gustafson, *His Way*, pp. 359–60.
154. Muldoon, *Number 38*, pp. 6–8. O'Sullivan, pp. 41–2. *NZH*, 29 Sept 1983. PS, 2/4/3. Office of the Clerk, 1/12/2. *Dom*, 17 Apr 1984.
155. Office of the Clerk, 4/1/1.
156. *Auckland Star*, *NZH*, 22 Aug 1980.
157. Gustafson, *His Way*, ch. 17. Templeton, ch. 14.
158. Henderson, *Rowling*, ch. 1. Wright, pp. 118–20.
159. *NZPD*, vol 436, 1980, pp. 5631–7. *NZH*, 5 Dec 1980.
160. McCallum, pp. 131–2. Arthur Baysting et al. (eds), *Making Policy … Not Tea: Women in Parliament*, Auckland, 1993, p. 75.
161. Hunt interview.
162. *NZPD*, vol 439, 1981, pp. 1934–5. *NZH*, 24 July 1981. *Auckland Star*, 22 Oct 1981.
163. *NZPD*, vol 439, 1981, pp. 2066, 2085–7. *NZH*, 30 July 1981.
164. *NZPD*, vol 441, 1981, pp. 3301–15; vol 442, 1981, pp. 4315–25.
165. *NZPD*, vol 589, 2000, p. 7282.
166. Goldsmith, p. 92.
167. *EP*, 29 Jan, 15 Feb 1982.
168. *NZPD*, vol 443, 1982, pp. 70–1.
169. *NZPD*, vol 449, 1982, p. 5812.
170. *EP*, 16 Apr 1982.
171. *NZPD*, vol 448, 1982, pp. 4917–19. *NZH*, 7 Aug, 25 Nov 1982.
172. This became definitive of the casting vote. McGee, *Parliamentary Procedure* (second edition), pp. 180–2.
173. Gustafson, *His Way*, pp. 330–3.
174. Jibes about their 'billiard room retreat' accompanied Social Credit's abstention. *NZPD*, vol 455, 1983, pp. 4750–1.
175. Templeton, pp. 190–1.
176. *NZPD*, vol 455, 1983, p. 4647. Gustafson, *His Way*, pp. 338, 352. *EP*, 13 May 1983.
177. *NZH*, 19 Nov 1983.
178. *NZPD*, vol 455, 1983, p. 4775. Muldoon, *Number 38*, p. 147. This was the first time since 1928 that a government had been defeated on an important substantive division, Clerk of the House, pers. comm., Oct 2003.
179. Following a withdrawal by Lange, there was controversy over whether he could still vote. *NZPD*, vol 455, 1983, pp. 4269–77.
180. *EP*, 29 Sept 1983. *NZH*, 29 Sept, 3 Oct 1983. Gustafson, *His Way*, p. 365. Templeton, pp. 215–16, 222. Jones, p. 134.
181. Gustafson, *His Way*, pp. 360, 362–3.
182. *NZPD*, vol 455, 1983, p. 4719 (pp. 4718–32 for tributes).
183. Muldoon, *Number 38*, p. 148. Ruth Richardson, *Making a Difference*, Christchurch, 1995, p. 31.
184. *NZH*, 12 Oct 1983.
185. *EP*, 29 Nov 1983.
186. Gustafson, *His Way*, pp. 368–77.
187. Goldsmith, p. 108.
188. Muldoon continued to defend Allen strongly, *Number 38*, pp. 154-6.
189. *NZPD*, vol 456, 1984, pp. 89–90, 120–2, 175–81, 273–8.
190. *NZPD*, vol 456, 1984, p. 318. Muldoon, *Number 38*, p. 156. Templeton, pp. 188–9, 217–18.
191. *EP*, 26 Mar 1968; 3 Dec 1970. *NZPD*, vol 371, 1971, pp. 578–9. Littlejohn interview.
192. *NZPD*, vol 395, 1974, p. 5755.
193. PS, 4/4/3. Old Hansard files: production of Hansard, 1953–74; Conway, 'The NZ Hansard staff'.
194. *NZPD*, vol 436, 1980, p. 5948.
195. Old Hansard files, recruitment of reporters, 1972–80.
196. *NZPD*, vol 428, 1979, pp. 4837, 4839. *EP*, 10 Dec 1979.
197. Compilation of members, 1931–1996. Wilson, *Parliamentary Record*, pp. 296–7, table. von Tunzelmann, 'Membership of the

198 Palmer, *Unbridled Power?* (second edition), p. 112, table.
199 McLeay, 'Parliamentary careers', pp. 125–67.
200 Wilson, *Parliamentary Record*. Halligan, pp. 120, 127, tables 5.1, 5.3.
201 Jackson, *Dilemma of Parliament*, pp. 64–8. Palmer, *Unbridled Power?*, pp. 25–7. *Press*, 23 Mar 1982. *ODT*, 24 Dec 1979. Keith Jackson, 'Caucus: the anti-Parliament system?', in Hyam Gold (ed.), *NZ Politics in Perspective* (third edition), Auckland, 1992. Roderick M. Alley, 'Parliamentary parties in office', in Levine (ed.), *Politics in NZ*.
202 *NZPD*, vol 431, 1980, p. 1584.
203 Gustafson, 'The Labour Party', table 1, and pp. 276–7.
204 Ovenden, 'Parliament'. G.A. Wood, 'The National Party', p. 295, in Gold (ed.), *NZ Politics* (third edition).
205 *NZPD*, vol 482, 1987, p. 10585.
206 *NZPD*, vol 510, 1990, p. 4376.
207 *NZPD*, vol 460, 1984, p. 2654.
208 Richardson, *Making a Difference*, p. 28. *NZPD*, vol 541, 1994, p. 2892. Gair interview. Pers. comm., Tirikatene-Sullivan.
209 *EP*, 15 Oct 1982.
210 *EP*, 17 Mar, 16 Apr 1983. McCallum, p. 162. *NZH*, 9 Apr 1985. *EP*, 1 Nov 1985; 4 July 1990.
211 J. Theodore Anagnoson, 'Home style in NZ, *Legislative Studies Quarterly*, vol 8, no 2, 1983.
212 Some women members paid for their own secretaries. McCallum, pp. 127, 140.
213 *Press*, 9 May 1981. *Christchurch Star*, 16 May 1981. *ODT*, 3 Sept 1979.
214 *Auckland Star*, 30 Mar, 25 Aug, 24 Sept 1977. *EP*, 12 May 1978; 3 June 1981. PS, 6/3/7 pt 2, meeting of wives, 11 Aug 1977. Rankin, p. 32.
215 A room was allocated to wives in the Beehive. *EP*, 3 June 1981.
216 Gustafson, *His Way*, chs 19, 20.
217 Nigel S. Roberts, 'Proportional representation', in Hoadley (ed.), *Improving NZ's Democracy*. Bruce C. Beetham, 'The case for proportional representation', in Levine (ed.), *Politics in NZ*.
218 Arend Lijphart, *Democracies*, New Haven, 1984, pp. 16–19. Jackson, *Dilemma of Parliament*, p. ix, ch. 1. Elizabeth McLeay, *The Cabinet and Political Power in NZ*, Auckland, 1995, p. 7.
219 Lord Hailsham, *The Dilemma of Democracy*, London, 1978, ch. 20.

Chapter 9 – Redressing the balance: institutional reform and MMP, 1985–2003

1 Palmer, *Unbridled Power?*. Geoffrey Palmer, 'The fastest law-makers in the west', *NZ Listener*, 28 May 1977. Tom McRae, 'A study in attitudes of backbenchers to the parliamentary system', *Public Sector*, vol 6, nos 1, 2, 1983. Geoff Skene, 'Parliamentary reform', in Jonathan Boston and Martin Holland (eds), *The Fourth Labour Government*, Auckland, 1987. Brian Edwards, *Helen: Portrait of a Prime Minister*, Auckland, 2001, p. 177.
2 McRae, *Parliament in Crisis*, p. 134, 'Open government: the Labour plan for democracy in government', 1984.
3 Palmer, *Unbridled Power?* (second edition), appendix 1, NZ Labour Party, 1984 policy document.
4 Joseph, *Constitutional and Administrative Law*, p. 164. Palmer, *Unbridled Power?* (second edition), pp. 34–8. Bolger, p. 82.
5 Palmer, *Unbridled Power?* (second edition), p. 27.
6 *NZPD*, vol 464, 1985, p. 5599 (see pp. 5596–5612). *AJHR*, 1985, I-14.
7 Harrison, p. 373. *NZPD*, vol 442, 1981, p. 4352, Freer. *NZPD*, vol 316, 1958, pp. 360–1, 385; vol 335, 1963, pp. 660–2.
8 *NZPD*, vol 445, 1982, p. 2363. *EP*, 10 Dec 1979.
9 *AJHR*, 1985, I-14, p. 27.
10 *AJHR*, 1985, I-14, p. 35; 1986, I-18A, p. 10; 1989, I-14B. Palmer, *Unbridled Power?* (second edition), ch. 8.
11 David McGee, 'The House of Representatives', p. 96, in Gold (ed.), *NZ Politics* (third edition).
12 Iles, 'Parliamentary scrutiny'. McLeay, *Cabinet and Political Power*, pp. 116–20. Geoffrey Palmer, *NZ's Constitution in Crisis*, Dunedin, 1992, pp. 160–3. Richard Mulgan, 'The elective dictatorship in NZ', pp. 520–3, in Gold (ed.), *NZ Politics*.
13 *AJHR*, 1989, I-14B, p. 8. Iles, 'Parliamentary scrutiny', p. 174.
14 *AJHR*, 1986, A-2, p. 5; 1989, A-8, pp. 7–8, 18.
15 *NZPD*, vol 457, 1984, pp. 15–16. Palmer, *Unbridled Power?* (second edition), p. 133. Skene, 'Parliamentary reform', p. 78. Joseph, *Constitutional and Administrative Law*, pp. 247, 342. Doug Kidd, 'Executive v legislature – the struggle continues', NZ Centre for Public Law, lecture, May 2001.
16 The Labour government abandoned an inquiry by the committee into the foreign exchange crisis of 1984 when Muldoon attempted to interrogate key participants. John Roberts, 'Ministers, the cabinet, and public servants', pp. 92–5, in Boston and Holland (eds), *The Fourth Labour Government*. Muldoon, *Number 38*, pp. 180–2.
17 *NZPD*, vol 465, 1985, p. 6505; vol 510, 1990, p. 4397. *EP*, 10, 28 Aug 1984.
18 Hunt interview.
19 PS, 4/2/8, pt 1, 'Management audit', May 1982, N.S. Coad to SSC, 30 Apr 1984.
20 PS, 4/2/8, pt 1, SSC to Palmer, 18 July 1984, Clerk to Palmer, 20 July 1984.
21 In 2000, the Parliamentary Service Act was amended to strengthen the Speaker's powers as administrative head. *AJHR*, 1999, A-2, p. 7. Joseph, *Constitutional and Administrative Law*, pp. 382–3.
22 *EP*, 26 July 1985. Littlejohn interview.
23 *AJHR*, 1997, A-8.
24 For the PSC's work, see PSC oral history project, Oral History Centre.
25 The terms of employment of the General Manager and the Clerk of the House continued to provide for the separation of Parliament from the executive.
26 *AJHR*, 1988, A-2, pp. 8–9; 1990, A-2, pp. 4–5.
27 Palmer, *Constitution in Crisis*, pp. 117–18. McGee, *Parliamentary Practice* (second edition), p. 31. PS, 6/3/7, pt 3, 1981–4.
28 *AJHR*, 1986, A-2, p. 12.
29 PS, 4/4/8.
30 PS, 4/5/1. *AJHR*, 1988, A-2, pp. 6–7; 1990, A-2, pp. 13–15; 1991, A-2, p. 16. PSC oral history project, Keith Shirley, Peter Brooks, Margaret Austin interviews. *EP*, 8 Sept 1990; 3 Jan, 19 Oct 1991. *NZH*, 9 Nov 1991; 17 Oct 1992. *Sunday Times*, 3 Jan 1993. *Dom*, 21 Oct 1994.
31 *AJHR*, 1988, A-2, pp. 10, 12. 'Review of the Parliamentary Service, etc.', for Cabinet Expenditure Control Committee, Feb 1991, pp. 10, 24.
32 'Review', 1991. *AJHR*, 1990, A-2, p. 11; 1991, A-2, p. 11; 1992, A-8, pp. 10–11; 1994, A-2; 1997, A-2, p. 25; 2002, A-2, p. 28. Shirley interview. *EP*, 10 July, 5 Nov 1990. *NZH*, 2 Apr, 5 July 1990; 17 Oct 1991.
33 Birch interview.
34 *AJHR*, 1988, A-2, pp. 7–8; 1989, A-2, p. 16; 1990, A-2, p. 13.
35 PS, 11/2. *NZH*, 7, 8 Oct 1987. Office of the Clerk, 4/2/2, 1951–85.

36. *AJHR*, 1990, A-2, pp. 9–10; 1992, A-8, pp. 10–11; 1993, A-8, pp. 11–12. The number of staff was reduced.
37. PSC oral history project, Michael Cullen, Gray, Brooks, Shirley, Birch interviews.
38. *EP*, 18, 24, 27 Aug 1984. *NZPD*, vol 456, 1984, pp. 164, 171; vol 457, 1984, pp. 2–6.
39. *NZPD*, vol 462, 1985, pp. 4325–8. Cullen, Shirley interviews.
40. *EP*, 17 Aug 1985. *NZH*, 1 June 1985. Hunt, Austin, Cullen, Shirley interviews.
41. *NZPD*, vol 464, 1985, p. 5550; vol 465, 1985, p. 6737. Hunt interview. Bernard Steeds, 'Within the corridors of power', *NZ Geographic*, no 63, May–June 2003, p. 67.
42. *NZPD*, vol 468, 1985, pp. 9144–8.
43. *NZPD*, vol 466, 1985, pp. 7590–5; vol 467, 1985, p. 8254; vol 470, 1986, pp. 1530–1; vol 472, 1986, p. 2487; vol 473, 1986, p. 3177; vol 477, 1986–7, p. 6874; vol 478, 1986, pp. 7367, 7728; vol 480, 1986, pp. 9027–8; vol 482, 1987, p. 10588. *EP*, 2, 10 May 1986.
44. Gray interview.
45. *NZPD*, vol 471, 1986, pp. 1900–11. There had apparently been similar motions in 1966, 1970 and 1976 (Palmer, p. 1901). *AJHR*, 1986, I-15, pp. 8–13. PS, 5/6/5, pt 3, 1987. *NZH*, 5 June 1986.
46. *NZPD*, vol 474, 1986, pp. 4315–23. *NZH*, 17, 18 Sept 1986.
47. Goldsmith, pp. 103, 120, 125–6. *NZPD*, vol 465, 1985, pp. 6317–18; vol 469, 1986, pp. 72–4; vol 479, 1987, pp. 7785–6, 7824, 8096–7. *AJHR*, 1986, I-15. *EP*, 27 Mar 1987.
48. Bassett, *Third Labour Government*, pp. 138–41, 236–7. Laurie Guy, *Worlds in Collision*, Wellington, 2002.
49. *EP*, 30 Oct, 20 Nov 1968. *NZPD*, vol 357, 1968, pp. 2722–3; vol 358, 1968, pp. 2725–6, 3225–6.
50. *NZPD*, vol 467, 1985, p. 8068; vol 472, 1986, pp. 2602–3, 2823. *NZH*, 10 July 1986.
51. *NZPD*, vol 482, 1987, p. 10586.
52. *NZPD*, vol 468, 1985, p. 9147; vol 475, 1986, pp. 5470–9. Skene, 'Parliamentary reform', pp. 84–5. *AJHR*, 1986, I-18A, pp. 3–4.
53. Palmer, *Unbridled Power?* (second edition), p. 112, table. Joseph, *Constitutional and Administrative Law*, pp. 246–7. Geoffrey Palmer and Matthew Palmer, *Bridled Power*, Auckland, 1997, pp. 148–52.
54. Martin Holland, 'Engineering electoral success', in Martin Holland and Jonathan Boston, (eds), *The Fourth Labour Government* (second edition), Auckland, 1990.
55. Hunt, Austin, Cullen, Shirley interviews. *NZPD*, vol 485, 1987, p. 1907; vol 510, 1990, p. 4400.
56. Skene, 'Parliament', pp. 257–9. *AJHR*, 1990, A-8, pp. 2–3. *NZH*, 7 Sept 1990.
57. In 1978 Gerald O'Brien left and in 1980 Mat Rata departed. They were followed by Mel Courtney in 1981, John Kirk in 1983 and Brian MacDonell in 1984.
58. *NZPD*, vol 510, 1990, pp. 4085–6. *NZH*, *EP*, 1 Sept 1990.
59. *NZPD*, vol 504, 1989, p. 14798; vol 510, 1990, pp. 4397, 4401. *NZH*, 3 Jan 1990.
60. *AJHR*, 1989, I-14B, pp. 6–7, 13, 16. Austin interview.
61. *AJHR*, 1995, I-18A, p. 36. Skene, 'Parliament', p. 260. Iles, 'Parliamentary scrutiny', pp. 174–5.
62. *NZPD*, vol 510, 1990, p. 4401.
63. *NZPD*, vol 487, 1988, pp. 2783–4, 2787–9, 2795; vol 498, 1989, pp. 10774–5. J.F. Burrows and P.A. Joseph, 'Parliamentary law making', *NZ Law Journal*, Sept 1990. Joseph, *Constitutional and Administrative Law*, pp. 324–8. Hamish M. Finlay, 'Speed versus deliberation', Research Paper in Public Law, Victoria University, 1998.
64. *NZPD*, vol 503, 1989, p. 14082; vol 504, 1989 (12 Dec).
65. *Dom*, 3 May 1990. See Finance Bills (Nos 2 and 4) 1990, and 1991 budget. The use of 'omnibus' bills persisted beyond the new standing orders that sought to restrain the practice. *AJHR*, 1996, A-8, p. 15; 1998, A-8. Joseph, *Constitutional and Administrative Law*, pp. 327–8.
66. *NZPD*, vol 510, 1990, pp. 4395–8. *NZH*, 7 Sept 1990. Palmer, *Constitution in Crisis*, pp. 113–23. G.W.R. Palmer, 'The NZ legislative machine', *Victoria University Law Review*, vol 17, 1987.
67. Editorial, *EP*, 6 Sept 1990.
68. Jackson, 'Caucus', pp. 236–7.
69. *NZPD*, vol 511, 1990, pp. 9–13; vol 538, 1993, p. 18381.
70. Gray interview.
71. *NZPD*, vol 512, 1991, p. 1ff. *NZH*, 23 Jan 1991. Bolger, pp. 43, 45–6. Kidd, 'Executive v legislature', pp. 12–13.
72. *NZPD*, vol 540, 1994, pp. 972ff, 19461ff; vol 580, 1999, pp. 19461–99; vol 595, 2001, pp. 11996–12017.
73. McRae, *Parliament in Crisis*, p. 202.
74. *NZPD*, vol 514, 1991, pp. 1505–7, 1568–1647.
75. *NZPD*, vol 517, 1991, p. 3254ff.; vol 518, 1991, p. 3661ff. *AJHR*, 1992, A-8, p. 16. Richardson, *Making a Difference*, pp. 111–12.
76. Bolger, p. 30. Martin Hames, *Winston First*, Auckland, 1995, pp. 109–11.
77. *NZPD*, vol 521, 1991, pp. 6456–8. *NZH*, 20 Dec 1991.
78. *NZPD*, vol 528, 1992, pp. 10323, 10334.
79. For the election promises, see Colin James and Alan McRobie, *Turning Point*, Wellington, 1993, pp. 114–17.
80. *AJHR*, 1986, H-3. Jackson and McRobie, *Proportional Representation*. Jack Vowles, 'Introducing proportional representation', *Parliamentary Affairs*, vol 53, no 4, 2000.
81. *AJHR*, 1988, I-17B.
82. *AJHR*, 1989, A-2, p. 7. *EP*, 4, 7 Nov 1988. *NZH*, 21 Nov 1988.
83. Bolger, pp. 93–100.
84. *Press*, 26 June 1992.
85. Most supported the status quo. Jackson and McRobie, p. 155. However, only 55.2 per cent of voters turned out for the 1992 referendum. In 1993 the turnout was 83.3 per cent.
86. *NZPD*, vol 536, 1993, p. 16729.
87. Paul Harris and Elizabeth McLeay, 'The legislature', in G.R. Hawke, *Changing Politics? The Electoral Referendum 1993*, Wellington, 1993, p. 103.
88. Harris and McLeay, p. 125.
89. Bolger, p. 40.
90. *NZPD*, vol 529, 1992, pp. 11198–11201. Hames, pp. 170–6.
91. End of session summaries in *NZPD* to 1999. *AJHR*, 2000–3, A-8.
92. *Dom*, 21 Dec 2001.
93. *AJHR*, 1990, I-18B; 1991, I-18A; 1992, I-18B; 1993, A-8. *NZPD*, vol 522, 1992, pp. 6648–61. *NZH*, 2, 6 Mar 1992. Skene, 'Parliamentary reform', pp. 77–9.
94. *NZPD*, vol 512, 1991, pp. 315–75; vol 514, 1991, pp. 1505–7, 1568–1647.
95. Jack Vowles, 'Countdown to MMP', in Jack Vowles et al. (eds), *Voters' Victory?*, Auckland, 1998. Bolger, pp. 132–5.
96. Tapsell interview. *NZH*, 10 Dec 1993.
97. *NZPD*, vol 539, 1993–4, pp. 2–10.
98. *NZH*, 14 Mar 1994.
99. Richardson, *Making a Difference*, pp. 154, 178–81. Bolger, pp. 120–1, 196, 201.
100. Finlay, pp. 32–9. Mai Chen, 'The new Parliament under MMP', *Legislative Studies*, vol 11, no 2, 1997, p. 16.
101. *NZPD*, vol 540, 1994, p. 1702. Goldsmith, pp. 226–7.
102. *NZPD*, vol 551, 1995, p. 10176ff.
103. Bolger, p. 208, Peter Dunne, 'Improving perceptions of Parliament', *Legislative Studies*, vol 10, no 2, 1996.

104 James and McRobie, pp. 118, 124. *ODT*, 14 Apr 1989. *EP*, 11 Mar 1992. *Press*, 27 Feb 1992.
105 Al Morrison, 'Objectivity', Robert Muldoon, 'A politican's view of the parliamentary press gallery', in Judy McGregor and Margie Comrie (eds), *What's News?*, Palmerston North, 2002. *DP*, 19 Oct 2002, feature on Morrison.
106 Roberts, 'Ministers', p. 98. McLeay, *Cabinet and Political Power*, pp. 159–62. Eileen O'Leary, 'Political spin', p. 188, in McGregor and Comrie (eds), *What's News?* Deborah Coddington, 'Spinning, spinning, spinning', *North and South*, Nov 2001.
107 *AJHR*, 1986, I-18A. Palmer, *Unbridled Power?* (second edition), p. 128. PS, 3/4/2. *EP*, 31 May, 16, 21 June 1986.
108 *NZ Listener*, 14 June 1986. *NZH*, 18 June 1986.
109 *Dominion Sunday Times*, 16 Apr 1989. *NZH*, 3 Jan 1990. Hames, pp. 42–3.
110 *AJHR*, 1989, I-18A; 1992, I-22B. *EP*, 1 June 1990. Office of the Clerk, 1/12/3. *NZH*, 20 Feb, 31 Aug, 10 Sept 1992.
111 Ailsa Salt, 'Television broadcasting of Parliament', Presiding Officers and Clerks conference, 1993, Vanuatu. *AJHR*, 1989, I-18, p. 8. *NZPD*, vol 507, 1990, pp. 1828–9.
112 *DP*, 13 June 2003. Standing Orders Committee, 'Review of standing orders', Dec 2003.
113 *AJHR*, 1986–9, A-2.
114 PS, 2/5/3, pt 4, 1985–8; 4/5, pt 3, 1987–8, (Speaker) Chairman PSC note in cabinet paper, 23 Aug 1987; 2/7.
115 *To House Parliament*, pp. 16–18. *NZH*, 31 Dec 1990.
116 Austin interview.
117 Hunt, Brooks, Shirley interviews.
118 *AJHR*, 1989, A-2, pp. 5–6; 1990, A-2, pp. 20–1.
119 *NZH*, 22 Feb 1990. *NZPD*, vol 505, 1990, p. 30.
120 *NZH*, 31 Dec 1990; 3, 30 Jan 1991. Brooks interview.
121 *Press*, 27 July 1992. *EP*, 6 Jan 1993. *NZH*, 7 Jan 1993.
122 *AJHR*, 1992, A-2, pp. 31–2. Brooks interview.
123 *EP*, 29 Aug 1994.
124 *AJHR*, 1998, A-2, p. 6.
125 Geoffrey Palmer, 'What changes are likely to the legislative process and other functions of Parliament?', Institute for International Research, MMP, conference, Mar 1994. Mai Chen and Geoffrey Palmer, 'The impact of MMP on government', Ministries of Youth Affairs and Cultural Affairs, MMP seminar, Sept 1996.
126 David McGee, 'Parliamentary reform', memo to Speaker, 20 July 1992.
127 *AJHR*, 1995, I-18A. *NZPD*, vol 552, 1995, pp. 10786–10860. Mary Harris, 'How is Parliament performing under MMP?', *NZ Law Journal*, July 2002. Joseph, *Constitutional and Administrative Law*, pp. 312–16, 348–56. P.A. Joseph, 'Constitutional law', *NZ Law Review*, 1997. Doug Kidd, 'Parliament under MMP', *Canterbury Law Review*, vol 7, 2000. Chen, 'The new Parliament under MMP'.
128 For example, *NZPD*, vol 557, 1996, p. 14359.
129 Voting took nearly three hours on a part of the Maritime Transport Bill in 1994. Harris, 'How is Parliament performing?', p. 234. *JHR*, 1993–6, vol 1, p. 493.
130 A moment's lack of concentration could give the block vote the wrong way. Pam Corkery, *Pam's Political Confessions*, Auckland, 1999, p. 44.
131 A ruling of 1992 required a minister present during sittings. *NZPD*, vol 528, 1992, p. 10655.
132 Joseph, *Constitutional and Administrative Law*, pp. 343–4.
133 Palmer and Palmer, pp. 98–102, chs 6–9.
134 Hames, *Winston First*. G.W.R. Palmer, *Constitutional Conversations*, Wellington, 2002, p. 143.
135 *NZPD*, vol 559, 1997, pp. 885–6.
136 David McGee, 'Freedom of speech', *The Table*, vol 63, 1995.

137 Joseph, *Constitutional and Administrative Law*, pp. 356–60, 388. David Wilson, 'The development of natural justice procedures in the NZ House of Representatives', *Legislative Studies*, vol 13, no 1, 1998. David McGee, 'Parliament and the law', *Canterbury Law Review*, vol 6, no 2, 1996.
138 Bolger, pp. 234–43.
139 *NZPD*, vol 558, 1996–7, pp. 3–7, 18–42. *NZH*, 13 Dec 1996. Philip Joseph, 'The new Parliament', *NZ Law Journal*, July 1997.
140 *AJHR*, 1997, I-15A, p. 6. *NZPD*, vol 558, 1996–7, p. 672; vol 560, 1997, pp. 1896–1925. Bolger, pp. 246–7.
141 Bolger, pp. 238–9, 253, ch. 20.
142 Joseph, 'The new Parliament', p. 234.
143 *AJHR*, 1998, A-8. Palmer, *Constitutional Conversations*, pp. 272–3.
144 *NZPD*, vol 567, 1998, pp. 8193, 8195, 8160.
145 *NZPD*, vol 571, 1998, pp. 11806–41. Kidd, 'Parliament under MMP', pp. 511–12.
146 David McGee, 'Parliament and the executive in NZ', *Legislative Studies*, vol 11, no 2, 1997, p. 122.
147 'Restoring public confidence in Parliament', Committee of Former Speakers of the House, May 1998, p. i. Marcus Ganley, 'Public perceptions of the NZ Parliament', *Legislative Studies*, vol 14, no 2, 2000.
148 *AJHR*, 1996, A-8, I-18B (incl. annex D, Clerk paper); 1998, I-18A, 18B, 18C. *NZPD*, vol 568, 1998, pp. 9419–43; vol 574, 1998, pp. 14696–14700; vol 580, 1999, pp. 19431–2. Chen, 'The new Parliament under MMP', pp. 19–20. Michael Cullen, 'Courtiers of the executive?', *Legislative Studies*, vol 12, no 2, 1998. McGee, 'Parliament and the executive'. David Sanders, 'Changing role of Parliament', *The Parliamentarian*, vol 79, no 4, 1998. Kidd, 'Executive v legislature', p. 13. Derek Quigley, 'Making foreign policy', *The Parliamentarian*, vol 79, no 3, 1998. Mai Chen, 'A constitutional revolution?', *NZ Universities Law Review*, vol 19, no 4, 2001. David McGee, 'Parliamentarism and MMP', *Public Sector*, vol 25, no 4, 2002.
149 David McGee, 'The Member of Parliament – political existentialist or party delegate?', *The Table*, vol 66, 1998, p. 48. *AJHR*, 1997, I-15B.
150 *NZPD*, vol 580, 1999, p. 19778, Birch; vol 581, 1998, pp. 14535–6, East. Tapsell interview.
151 *NZPD*, vol 580, 1999, pp. 19757, 19762, 19798–9.
152 *NZPD*, vol 581, 1999–2000, p. 3. *Dom*, 13 Dec 1996; 24 Mar 2001. Austin, Cullen interviews.
153 *NZPD*, vol 597, 2001, p. 14074. *EP*, 14 Sept 2000. *Dom*, 15, 22 Sept 2000; 17 Apr 2001. In 2003 Donna Awatere-Huata continued to sit in the House while the ACT party first suspended and then expelled her over allegations of misuse of public funds. *DP*, 19 July 2003.
154 *NZPD*, vol 588, 2000, pp. 6329–57; vol 603, 2002, p. 839. *AJHR*, 2002, I-4A. Palmer, *Constitutional Conversations*, pp. 398–403.
155 *DP*, 19 July 2003.
156 *Dom*, 17 June 2002.
157 *NZPD*, vol 586, 2000, pp. 4233, 4236–51. *Dom*, 11 Aug 2000.
158 *DP*, 22 Aug 2002.
159 Harris, 'How is Parliament performing under MMP?'.
160 *Dom*, 23, 24 Feb 2001.
161 *DP*, 9, 27 Sept, 6 Dec 2002. *Sunday Star–Times*, 15 Dec 2002.
162 *NZPD*, vol 605, 2002, p. 2600. *Dom*, 17 May 2001, 25 July 2001; 19, 27 Mar 2002. In 2002 the Remuneration Authority (Members of Parliament) Amendment Bill was passed with ACT's Rodney Hide the sole member voting against it.
163 *AJHR*, 1997, A-8A.
164 *NZPD*, vol 558, 1996–7, pp. 552–3. *AJHR*, 1999, I-4D; 2002, I-4E.

[165] *NZPD*, vol 589, 2000, pp. 7236–50. *Dom*, 30 Nov 2000. *EP*, 2 Dec 2000.
[166] *NZPD*, vol 558, 1996–7, pp. 514–29. Alan Witcombe, 'The Berlin report', Aug 2002.
[167] *NZPD*, vol 581, 1999–2000, pp. 19–34, 106–13.
[168] *NZPD*, vol 602, 2002, pp. 36–7, 41. *AJHR*, 2003, A-8, p. 8.
[169] *AJHR*, 1995, I-18A, p. 61.
[170] *AJHR*, 1997, I-19A, p. 179.
[171] *NZPD*, vol 482, 1987, p. 10611. Palmer, *Constitutional Conversations*, pp. 376–8.
[172] Joseph, *Constitutional and Administrative Law*, pp. 349–50. Kidd, 'What makes Parliament tick', pp. 4–5.
[173] *Dom*, 23 May 2002.
[174] *Dom*, 19 Apr 2002, Assistant Speaker Eric Roy.
[175] *NZPD*, vol 589, 2000, pp. 7281–2, 7287.
[176] Clerk, 'Review of Standing Orders', May 2003. *AJHR*, 2003, A-8, p. 9. *DP*, 24 May 2003.
[177] Compilation of members, 1931–1996. *NZ Electoral Compendium* (third edition), Electoral Commission, 2002, pp. 176–7, 182–3, tables. Wood, 'The National Party', pp. 295–6, in Gold (ed.), *NZ Politics*, (third edition). Philip Temple, *Temple's Guide to the 44th NZ Parliament*, Dunedin, 1994, pp. 90–1. Wood (ed.), *Ministers and Members in the NZ Parliament*, appendix 4.
[178] Pansy Wong, 'Multicultural representation', *The Parliamentarian*, vol 79, no 3, 1998. Kidd, 'What makes Parliament tick', p. 4. McGee, 'Parliamentarism and MMP'.
[179] Chris Finlayson, 'A code of conduct for MPs?', *Victoria University Law Review*, vol 28, no 1, 1998, p. 177. Mulgan, 'Elective dictatorship', pp. 526–9.
[180] David McGee, 'Should Parliament be changed?', p. 352, in Colin James (ed.), *Building the Constitution*, Wellington, 2000.
[181] Keith Jackson, 'How should Parliament be changed?', p. 345, in James (ed.).
[182] McGee, 'Parliamentarism and MMP'.
[183] *AJHR*, 2001, I-23A. *Dom*, 16 Mar, 9 Aug 2001.
[184] Ganley, 'Public perceptions of Parliament'. James W. Lamare, 'Representational roles and proportional representation in NZ', *Journal of Legislative Studies*, vol 4, no 3, 1998.
[185] *NZ Electoral Compendium* (third edition), p. 174. Richard Mulgan, 'Should Parliament be changed?', p. 361, in James (ed.).

Select Bibliography

Books

Bassett, Judith, *Sir Harry Atkinson*, Auckland University Press, Auckland, 1975

Bassett, Michael and King, Michael, *Tomorrow Comes the Song: A Life of Peter Fraser*, Penguin, Auckland, 2000

Bassett, Michael, *Coates of Kaipara*, Auckland University Press, Auckland, 1995

Bassett, Michael, *Three Party Politics in New Zealand, 1911–1931*, Historical Publications, Auckland, 1982

Bassett, Michael, *Sir Joseph Ward: A Political Biography*, Auckland University Press, Auckland, 1993

Bohan, Edmund, *'Blest Madman': FitzGerald of Canterbury*, Canterbury University Press, Christchurch, 1998

Bohan, Edmund, *Edward Stafford: New Zealand's First Statesman*, Hazard Press, Christchurch, 1994

Bohan, Edmund, *To Be a Hero: A Biography of Sir George Grey, 1812–1898*, HarperCollins, Auckland, 1998

Bolger, Jim, *A View From the Top: My Seven Years as Prime Minister*, Viking, Auckland, 1998

Brown, Bruce, The *Rise of New Zealand Labour*, Price Milburn, Wellington, 1962

Burdon, R.M., *King Dick: A Biography of Richard John Seddon*, Whitcombe and Tombs, Christchurch, 1955

Chapman, Robert, and Sinclair, Keith, (eds), *Studies of a Small Democracy*, Blackwood and Janet Paul, Auckland, 1963

Cochran, Chris, *Parliamentary Library, Parliament House: Conservation Values*, New Zealand Historic Places Trust and Parliamentary Service Commission, Wellington, 1989

Cook, Rod, *Parliament: The Land and Buildings from 1840*, Parliamentary Service, Wellington, 1988

Crick, Bernard, *The Reform of Parliament* (third edition), Weidenfeld and Nicolson, London, 1970

Dalton, B.J., *War and Politics in New Zealand, 1855–1870*, Sydney University Press, Sydney, 1967

Dalziel, Raewyn, *Julius Vogel: Business Politician*, Auckland University Press, Auckland, 1986

Dollimore, H.N., *The Parliament of New Zealand and Parliament House* (revised edition), Government Printer, Wellington, 1973

Drummond, James, *The Life and Work of R.J. Seddon*, Whitcombe and Tombs, Christchurch, 1906

Fanning, L.S., *Politics and the Public*, Wellington Publishing Co., Wellington, 1919

Gardner, W.J., *The Farmer Politician in History*, Massey University, Palmerston North, 1970

Gisborne, William, *New Zealand Rulers and Statesmen, 1840 to 1897* (revised edition), Sampson Low, Marston, London, 1897

Graham, Jeanine, *Frederick Weld*, Auckland University Press, Auckland, 1983

Gustafson, Barry, *From the Cradle to the Grave: A Biography of Michael Joseph Savage*, Penguin, Auckland, 1988

Gustafson, Barry, *The First 50 Years: A History of the New Zealand National Party*, Reed Methuen, Auckland, 1986

Gustafston, Barry, *Labour's Path to Political Independence*, Auckland University Press, Auckland, 1980

Gustafson, Barry, *His Way: A Biography of Robert Muldoon*, Auckland University Press, Auckland, 2000

Hailsham, Lord, *The Dilemma of Democracy*, Collins, London, 1978

Hamer, David, *The New Zealand Liberals: The Years in Power*, Auckland University Press, Auckland, 1988

Hawker, G.N., *The Parliament of New South Wales, 1856–1965*, Government Printer, Sydney, 1971

Hollis, Christopher, *Can Parliament Survive?*, Hollis and Carter, London, 1949

Jackson, Keith, and McRobie, Alan, *New Zealand Adopts Proportional Representation*, Hazard Press, Christchurch, 1998

Jackson, Keith, *The Dilemma of Parliament*, Allen and Unwin, Wellington, 1987

Jackson, W.K., The *New Zealand Legislative Council*, Otago University Press, Dunedin, 1972

Jones, Christopher, *The Great Palace: The Story of Parliament*, BBC, London, 1983

Joseph, Philip A., *Constitutional and Administrative Law in New Zealand* (second edition), Brookers, Wellington, 2001

Kelson, Robert N., *The Private Member of Parliament and the Formation of Public Policy*, University of Toronto Press, Toronto, 1964

Lijphart, Arend, *Democracies*, Yale University Press, New Haven, 1984

Lipson, Leslie, *The Politics of Equality: New Zealand's Adventures in Democracy*, Chicago University Press, Chicago, 1948

Loveday, P., and Martin, A.W., *Parliament, Factions and Parties: The First Thirty Years of Responsible Government in New South Wales, 1856–1889*, Melbourne University Press, Melbourne, 1966

Marshall, Sir John (ed.), *The Reform of Parliament*, New Zealand Institute of Public Administration, Wellington, 1978

Marshall, John, *Memoirs* (2 vols), Collins, Auckland, 1983, 1989

McCallum, Janet, *Women in the House: Members of Parliament in New Zealand*, Cape Catley, Picton, 1993

McGee, David, *Parliamentary Practice in New Zealand*, Government Printer, Wellington, 1985

McGee, David, *Parliamentary Practice in New Zealand* (second edition), GP Publications, Wellington, 1994

McIntyre, W. David (ed.), *The Journal of Henry Sewell* (2 vols), Whitcoulls, Christchurch, 1980

McIvor, Timothy, *The Rainmaker: A Biography of John Ballance*, Heinemann Reed, Auckland, 1989

McLeay, Elizabeth, *The Cabinet and Political Power in New Zealand*, Oxford University Press, Auckland, 1995

McLintock, A.H., and Wood, G.A., *The Upper House in Colonial New Zealand*, Government Printer, Wellington, 1987

McLintock, A.H., *Crown Colony Government in New Zealand*, Government Printer, Wellington, 1958

Milne, R.S., *Political Parties in New Zealand*, Clarendon, Oxford, 1966

Mitchell, Austin, *Politics and People in New Zealand*, Whitcombe and Tombs, Christchurch, 1969

Mitchell, Austin, *Government By Party: Parliament and Politics in New Zealand*, Whitcombe and Tombs, Christchurch, 1966

Morrell, W.P., *The Provincial System in New Zealand, 1852–76* (revised edition), Whitcombe and Tombs, Christchurch, 1964

Muldoon, R.D., *The Rise and Fall of a Young Turk*, Reed, Wellington, 1974

Palmer, Geoffrey, *New Zealand's Constitution in Crisis: Reforming Our Political System*, McIndoe, Dunedin, 1992

Palmer, Geoffrey, *Unbridled Power? An Interpretation of New Zealand's Constitution and Government*, Oxford University Press, Wellington, 1979

Palmer, Geoffrey, *Unbridled Power? An Interpretation of New Zealand's Constitution and Government* (second edition), Oxford University Press, Auckland, 1987

Parliamentary Service Commission, *To House Parliament*, Parliamentary Service Commission, Wellington, 1996

Rankin, Carol, *Women and Parliament, 1893–1993: 100 Years of Institutional Change*, Office of the Clerk of the House of Representatives, Wellington, 1993

Rutherford, J., *Sir George Grey KCB, 1812–1898*, Cassell, London, 1961

Saunders, Alfred, *History of New Zealand, 1642–1861*, Whitcombe and Tombs, Christchurch, 1896

Scholefield, Guy H. (ed.), *The Richmond–Atkinson Papers* (2 vols), Government Printer, Wellington, 1960

Scholefield, Guy H., *New Zealand Parliamentary Record, 1840–1949*, Government Printer, Wellington, 1950

Scott, K.J., *The New Zealand Constitution*, Clarendon, Oxford, 1962
Seddon, T.E.Y., *The Seddons: An Autobiography*, Collins, Auckland, 1968
Stewart, William Downie, *Right Honourable Sir Francis H.D. Bell*, Butterworth, Wellington, 1937
Stewart, W.D., *William Rolleston*, Whitcombe and Tombs, Christchurch, 1940
Templeton, Hugh, *All Honourable Men: Inside the Muldoon Cabinet, 1975–1984*, Auckland University Press, Auckland, 1995
Ward, Alan, *A Show of Justice: Racial 'Amalgamation' in Nineteenth Century New Zealand*, Auckland University Press, Auckland, 1974
Watts, Gwen, *A Husband in the House*, Whitcombe and Tombs, Christchurch, 1969
Webb, Leicester, *Government in New Zealand*, Department of Internal Affairs, Wellington, 1940
Wilson, David, *Questions of Privilege: Case Studies from New Zealand's Parliament*, Office of the Clerk of the House of Representatives, Wellington, 1999
Wilson, David and Rankin, Carol, *Tales of Two Contempts: Two Episodes from New Zealand's Parliament in the Nineteenth Century*, Office of the Clerk of the House of Representatives, Wellington, 1998
Wilson, J.O., *New Zealand Parliamentary Record, 1840–1984*, Government Printer, Wellington, 1985
Wood, G.A. (ed.), *Ministers and Members in the New Zealand Parliament* (second edition), University of Otago Press, Dunedin, 1996
Wright-St Clair, Rex, *Thoroughly a Man of the World: A Biography of Sir David Monro, M.D.*, Whitcombe and Tombs, Christchurch, 1971

Articles and papers

Allen, A.E., 'The role of the whips and the caucus in the New Zealand Parliament', *The Parliamentarian*, vol 52, no 1, 1971
Dalziel, Raewyn, 'The "continuous ministry" revisited', *NZJH*, vol 21, no 1, 1987
Gardner, W.J., 'The rise of W.F. Massey, 1891–1912', *Political Science*, vol 13, no 1, 1961
Hamer, David, 'The Agricultural Company and New Zealand politics, 1877–1886', *Historical Studies: Australia and New Zealand*, vol 10, no 38, 1962
Herron, D.G., 'The franchise and New Zealand politics', *Political Science*, vol 12, no 1, 1960
Jackson, W.K., and Wood, G.A., 'The New Zealand Parliament and Maori representation', *Historical Studies: Australia and New Zealand*, vol 11, no 43, 1964
Kelson, R.N., 'Voting in the New Zealand House of Representatives, 1947–54', *Political Science*, vol 7, no 2, 1955
Lipson, Leslie, 'The origins of caucus in New Zealand', *Historical Studies: Australia and New Zealand*, vol 2, no 5, 1942
Mitchell, Austin, 'The New Zealand parliaments of 1935–1960', *Political Science*, vol 13, no 1, 1961
Mitchell, Austin, 'Caucus: the New Zealand parliamentary parties', *Journal of Commonwealth Political Studies*, vol 6, 1968
Sorrenson, M.P.K., 'A history of Maori representation', appendix B, *AJHR*, 1986, H-3
von Tunzelmann, A.F., 'The Public Expenditure Committee and parliamentary control of public expenditure', *Victoria University Law Review*, vol 10, 1979–80

Theses and unpublished papers

Angus, E.P., 'Select committees of the House of Representatives, New Zealand', MA thesis, Victoria University College, 1951
Armstrong, W.R., 'The politics of development: a study of the structure of politics from 1870 to 1890', MA thesis, Victoria University College, 1960

Campbell, A.F., 'The Speakership of the New Zealand House of Representatives, 1854–1912', MA thesis, Canterbury University College, 1952

Church, Stephen, 'Electoral systems, party systems and stability in New Zealand', PhD thesis, University of Canterbury, 1998

Cunningham, J.K., 'Equality of electorates in New Zealand, 1854–1899', MA thesis, Canterbury University College, 1953

Fletcher, Ian R., 'Parties in the New Zealand House of Representatives, 1870–1890', MA thesis, University of Canterbury, 1982

Gardner, W.J., 'The effect of the abolition of the provinces on political parties in the New Zealand House of Representatives, 1876–7', MA thesis, Canterbury University College, 1936

Halligan, J., 'Continuity and change in the New Zealand Parliament', PhD thesis, Victoria University of Wellington, 1980

Harrison, R.J., 'Organisation and procedure in the New Zealand Parliament', PhD thesis, Ohio State University, 1964

Herron, D.G., 'The structure and course of New Zealand politics, 1853–1858', PhD thesis, Otago University College, 1959

Hobby, M.G., 'The crack of the whip? Party cohesiveness and institutional consensus: the New Zealand House of Representatives, 1936–1985', MA thesis, University of Canterbury, 1987

Littlejohn, C.P., 'Parliamentary privilege in New Zealand', Master of Laws thesis, Victoria University of Wellington, 1969

McLeay, E.M., 'Parliamentary careers in a two-party system: cabinet selection in New Zealand', PhD thesis, University of Auckland, 1978

Phipps, B.H., 'The New Zealand conservative party, 1891–1903', MA thesis, Victoria University of Wellington, 1990

Robinson, A.D., 'The rise of the New Zealand National Party, 1936–1949', MA thesis, Victoria University College, 1957

von Tunzelmann, Adrienne, 'Membership of the New Zealand Parliament – a study of conditions, 1854–1979', Research paper in Public Policy, MPP, Victoria University of Wellington, 1979

Webb, L.C., 'The rise of the Reform Party', MA thesis, Canterbury University College, 1928

Wilson, T.G., 'The rise of the Liberal Party in New Zealand, 1877–1890', MA thesis, Auckland University College, 1951

Wood, G.A., 'The political structure of New Zealand, 1858–1861', PhD thesis, University of Otago, 1965

INDEX

Page numbers in bold indicate illustrations

Abolition of Provinces Act 1875, 68
abolition of the provinces, 62, 65, 68, 73, 74
abortion, 271, 279
accommodation, members, 14, 24, 43, 165, **245**
    Siberia, 247, 275, 288, 289, 300
ACT Party, 328, 331, 366 n.153
Ad Hoc (Whips) Committee, 309
Address-in-Reply, 26, 120, 122, 161, 192, 222, 223, 257, 260, 267, 298, 325, *see also* Speech from the Throne
Alexander Turnbull Library, 256
Algie, R.M., 222, 227, 243, **253**, 257, **258**, 259, 260, 261, 262, **266**
Allen, A.E., 242, 254, 273, 274, 296
Allen, James, 134, **143**, 145, 148, 149, 151, 152, 200
Alliance Party, 315, 319, 327, 329, 330, 331
Anderson, G.J., **185**
Anderton, Jim, 315, 329, 330
Angus, W.M., 288
Anzac Avenue, Auckland, 240
Anzac Day, 159
Appropriation bills, 120, 122, 198, 264
appropriation rule, 332
armed constabulary, 86
Arthur, Sir Basil, 250, 272, 311, 312
Association of Former Members, 328
Astor, Lady, 199
Atkinson ministries, 75–7, 95–6, 97–102, 117
Atkinson, A.S., 59
Atkinson, H.A., 25, 35, 69, 73–88 passim, 94–108 passim, **95**, 111, 121
Atmore, Harry, 142, 143, 186, 188, 189, 190, 213, 221, **222**
Auckland, 13, 23, 24, **28**, **29**, 34, 37, 39, 40, 41, 45, 81, 239, 240, 337
Auckland City Council, 50
Auckland members, 22, 25, 35, 38, 39, 40, 42, 58, 60, 81, 84, 96, 224, 328
    Auckland rats, 50, **80**, 81
Auckland Provincial Council, 32, 41, 44
Audit Committee, 56

Audit Office, 275
Auditor-General, 13, 331
Austin, Margaret, 312, 315, 322, 334
Austin, Rex, 298
Australia, 10, 17, 40, 41, 53, 58, 64, 65, 70, 79, 94, 118, 166, 185, 214, 238, 260, 268, 282, 333
Awatere-Huata, Donna, 366 n.153

Bailey, Ron, 277
Ballance ministry, 108–11
Ballance, John, 77, 79, 96, 97, 99, **101**, 102, 108, 109, **110**, 111, 121
    statue, 111, **130**
Bank of New Zealand, 41, 102, 117, 316
Banks, John, **291**, 294, 296, 313, 320, 328
Barnard, W.E., 204, 205, 207, 214, 239, 245
Barnes, J.G., 246
Barron, C.C.N., 53, **54**, 118, 122
Bartley, T.H., 15
Basin Reserve, 163, 196
Bassett, Michael, 188, 257, 279, **280**, 293
Batchelor, Mary, **299**, 314
Beehive, **170**, **175**, **184**, 248–51, **250**, **270**, 273, 281, **284**, 287–91, 297, 324, *see also* Parliament Buildings
    construction, 287–90, **289**, **290**
    Museum Street Annex, 288, 290, 324
    reception hall, 290
Beetham, Bruce, 274, 285, 286, 294, 295
Beetham, George, 96
Begg, Aubrey, **280**
Bell, Colonel Allen, 153
Bell, F.H.D., 112, 117, 141, 149, 185, 190
Bell, Francis Dillon, 13, 21, 24, 35, 38, 57, 58, 61, 63, 64, **66**, 67, 79, 112
Bell, W.H.D., 186
Bellamy's, **16**, 19, 32, 37, 41, 43, **45**, 47–9, 64, 67, 75, 83, 85, 87, 88–91, 113–15, 116, 128, 143, 154, 159, 160, 161, 188, 219, 221, 225, 237, 251–2, 254, **255**, 262, 266, 287, 288, **289**, 290, 294, 298, 308, 309–10, 311, 316, *see also* social activities, members

373

poll, 114
and women, 159, 199, 255
Benton, Eric, **253**
Berry, William, **94**, **119**
Bill of Rights 1688, 282
bills, *see also* government business; private members
    first reading, 18, 263, 279, 287, 325
    in Committee (of the Whole House), 18, 54, 55, 75, 122, 156, 192, 273, 279, 316, 325
    second reading, 18, 26, 122, 275, 283, 325
    third reading, 18, 286, 325
Birch, W.F., 275, 276, 281, 286, 294, 319, 327, 329
Blanchfield, Paddy, 261, **265**, 285
Bledisloe, Lord, 162
Bodkin, W.A., 194, 224
Bolger, Jim, 276, **310**, 312, **315**, 316, 317, 319, 320, 322, **327**, 328
Bollard, R.F., 190
Boord, Raymond, 244, 256
Bothamley, A.T., **162**, 218
Bothamley, C.M., 162, 235
Bothamley, G.F., 162, 218, **220**
Bowden, C.M., 271
Bowen House, **170**, **302**, 310, 311, 322, 324
    chamber, 316, 322
Bowen Street, 154, 159, 322
Bowen, Sir George, 60, 62, 67
Bradford, Max, 331
Braybrooke, Geoff, 327, 330
Britain, 9, 11, 23, 27, 29, 33, 38, 41, 53, 58, 63, 68, 110, 117, 124, 132, 138, 139, 152, 187, 197, 212, 213, 234, 301
Broadcasting House, 324
Broadcasting of Parliament Committee, 321
Broadfoot, W.J., 209, 215, 224
Brodie, W., 24
Brogden railway contractors, 67
Brooks, Peter, 309
Brown, J.C., 67
Brown, Major Charles, 58
Browne, Colonel Thomas Gore, 23, 29, 33, 34, 35, 36
Browne, Major H., 161
Browne, Harriet Gore, 32
Bryce, John, 77, 82, 83, 91, 109
Buchanan, Walter, 145, 187
Buck, Peter, 158
Buckland, W.F., 111
Buick, David, 167
Buller electorate, 246
Bunny, Henry, 90
Burdon, Philip, **291**
Burke, Kerry, 309, 314, 315, 316, 319, 321, 322
Business Committee, 325

cabinet, 25, 27, 32, 75, 108, 149, 195, 204, 230, 236, 281, 285, 317, 343 n.112, *see also* government business; Prime Minister
    collective responsibility, 25, 330
    committees, 236
    room, 130, 155, 156, 182, 214, 248, 290
    table, 182, 248, 290, **327**
Cabinet Expenditure Control Committee, 310
Cadman, A.J., 117
Cameron, D.H., **119**
Cameron, General Duncan, 41, 42
Campbell, F.E., **20**, **36**, 65, 87, 99
Campbell, John, 130, 152, 154, 155
Campbell, Logan, 24
Campion, Sir Gilbert, 220
Canada, 10, 17, 151, 152, 156, 321
Canterbury, 40, 58, 98
Canterbury members, 84, 96
capital punishment, 237, 245, 259
Cargill, William, **14**
Carleton, Hugh, 15, 19, **34**, 35, 44, 49, 59, 66
Carmen, 280
Carr, Clyde, 166
Carroll, James, 91, 114, 117, **124**, 134, 141, 142, 145, 158, 168, 200, 352 n.94
Carter, C.R., 35
Carthew, Alistair, 321
caucus, role of, 10, 109, 111, 124, 148, 162, 166, 167, 168, 185, 204, 212, 214, 221, 225, 226, 233, 236, 257, 258, 267, 281, 282, 285, 294, 296, 315, 317, *see also* party
    caucus committees, 212, 214, 222, 237, 247, 274, 298, 306
    caucuses (pre-party), 25, 43, 95, 97, 101
Caygill, David, 326
Cenotaph, 159, 196
centennial of Parliament, 1954, 239, 240, 337
centennial of Parliament in Wellington, 1965, **266**
Chairman of Committees, 35, 59, 64, 79, 86, 134, 155, 204, 210, 325
    election, 15, 26, 66, 79, 85, 96, 134, 135, 139, 140, 149, 257, 274, 294
    Deputy Chairman, 279, 325
chamber of the House, 19, 32, 39, 43, **45**, 45–6, **47**, **50**, 51, 88, 109, 128, **146**, **148**, 156–7, **179**, **208**, 248, **249**, **278**, 287, 354 n.47, *see also* Parliament Buildings; Parliament House
    bar of the House, 34, 58, 117, 187, 235, 343, n.25, n.26
    galleries, 21, 32, 39, 46, 47, 75, 85, 121, 132, 157, 159, 167, 213, 254, 284, 294
    ladies' gallery, 32, 46, 47, **48**, 49, 62, 83, 127, 128, 138, 198, 199, 229, 254
    Speaker's office, 155, 156, **182**, 324

temporary chamber, 137, **138**, 139, 151, 155, *see also* old wooden buildings
ventilation, 19, 32, 43, 45, 88, 128, 157
Chapman, Charles, 151
Chatham Islands, 36
Christchurch, 38, 40, 78
Christian Democrat Party, 320
Christie, Gordon, **273**
Citizens Initiated Referenda Act 1993, 308
Civil List Act, 247
civil service, 58, 82, 118, 134, 139, 160, *see also* public service
Clark, E.H., 299
Clark, Helen, **177**, 294, 298, 319, 322, 327, 329, 330, 334
Clark, Linda, 292
Clayton, William, 43
Clerk of Parliaments, 65, 99, 160, 162, 235
Clerk of Parliaments Act 1872, 65
Clerk of the House, 19, 46, 52, 63, 65, 99, 155, 160, 218, 220, 248, 297, 307, 308, 324
    Deputy Clerk, 308, 309
Clerk of the House of Representatives Act 1988, 308
Clifford, Charles, 12, 15, **17**, 20, 21, 32, 33, 34, 35, 52, 59, 63, 64, 66, 79, 136
Clifton, Jane, 292
Clinkard, C.H., 194
Clyde dam, 286, 295
Coalition for Open Government, 286
coalition government, 318, 320
    Labour–Alliance, 1999–2002, 329–30
    Labour–Progressive Coalition, 2002–, 330–1
    National, 1915–19, 151–2, 167
    National–NZ First, 1996–9, **327**, 327–9
    Second World War, 214
    United–Reform, 1931–5, 195–98, 201, 203, 204, 205
Coates, James, 19, 20
Coates, J.G. (Gordon), 142, 143, 152, 158, 161, **164**, 165, 167, **188**, **189**, 190–9 passim, **198**, 206, 212, 213, 214, 223, 227
Cobbe, J.G., 214
Cobham, Lord, **217**
Cohen, Albert, **94**, 127
Collett, B.F., **253**
Collier, James, 90, 91, 132
Collins, Ken, 207
Colman, Fraser, 274, 314
Colonial Bank of New Zealand, 117
Colvin, James, 140, 149
Committee of Supply, 55, 156, 261, 264
Committee of Ways and Means, 55, 264
Commons, House of, 17, 18, 20, 26, 37, 46–59 passim, 63, 64, 65, 79, 84, 94, 100, 102, 123, 127, 139, 159, 165, 187, 193, 199, 220, 222, 224, 236, 239, 260, 262, 280, 333, 342 n.37
Compact of 1856, 27–9, 42
compulsory military service, 152
compulsory military training, 218, 243, 268
computers, 311
conduct, members, *see also* standing orders
    absences, 38, 52, 59, 94, 224
    apology, 76, 119, 123, 241, 245, 263, 278, 283, 293
    censure, 40, 50, 109, 110, 119
    disorder, 22, 59, 75, 76, 81, **110**, 122, 123, 125, 243, 261, 274, 276, 277, 284, 292, 312, 313, 328
    naming, 50, 98, 99, 122, 123, 133, 151, 241, 244, 261, 312, 313
    reading newspapers, 51, 165, 321
    sin bin, 284, 306, 312
    suspension, 122, 151, 196, 273, 282, 313
    threats, violence, 22, 76, 77, 83, 86, 90, 91, 112, 119, 197, 258, 279, 313, 328
    unparliamentary language, 62, 75, 83, 109, 151, 189, 193, 195, 207, 241, 244, 262, 344 n.62
    walkouts, 22, 36, 42, 43, 95, 98, 99, 116, 121, 168, 185, 186, 194, 273, 283, 284
    withdrawals, 50, 215, 277, 279, 282, 283, 285, 294, 296, 311, 312, 313, 314, 363 n.179
    words taken down, 40, 119, 123, 151
confidence in ministry/government, *see* no-confidence
Connelly, Mick, 277
conscription, 152, 166
conservative/liberal, 73, 77
Constitution Act 1852, 11, 12, 27, 32, 58, 65, 235, 239
Constitution Act 1986, 305
Constitution Amendment Act 1857, 235
constitutional associations, **8**, 10, 11, 12, 74
constitutional issues, 9–12, 13, 16, 17, 19, 27, 38, 40, 41, 53, 58, 62–7 passim, 70, 77, 82, 99, 110, 118, 142, 234, 239, 259, 279, 282, 286, 301, 304, 307, 320, 343 n.14, *see also* executive versus Parliament; Speaker versus executive
    General Assembly, 11, 305
Constitutional Reform Committee, 1952, 258, 259
Constitutional Reform Committee, 1964, 259
Constitutional Society, 234, 259
contempt of Parliament, 50, 117, 313, *see also* privileges, breach of privilege
continuous ministry (1870s–80s), 25, 73, 107
Contraception, Sterilisation and Abortion Act 1977, 284
Controller and Auditor-General, 262

Conway, A.B., 219, **252**
Cooper, E.B., **252**, 297
Cooper, Warren, **291**, 294
Corbett, E.B., 158
corruption, 58, 73, 76, 116, 119, 124, 134, 135, 139, 353 n.202, *see also* patronage
Cosgrave, Michael, 87
Couch, Ben, 298
Country Party, 197
Cox, Michael, 285
Cracknell, Vernon, 262, 264
Creech, Wyatt, 331
Crick, Bernard, 269, 274
Crimes Act 1961, 259
Crombie, Charles M., **54**
Cross, Ihapera, 304
Crown Colony, 11
Crown Colony Government in New Zealand, 239
Crown Law Office, 118
Cullen, Michael, 294, **310**, 312, 313, 329, 330

Dasent, W.E., 162, 218
daylight saving, 224
Decimal Coinage bills, 237
Deck, 20
delegated legislation, 226, 227, 231, 260, 307, *see also* regulations
Democrat Party, 197
Department of External Affairs, 271
depression, late 1860s, 62
depression, 1880s, 73, 76, 78, 82, 103
depression, early 1930s, 162, 191, 193, 195–7
Dickie, H.G., 228
disqualification, 58, 75, 76, 166
Disqualification Act, 120
Disqualification Act 1858, 345 n.183
Disqualification Act 1870, 58
Disqualification Act 1876, 76
Disqualification bills, 1865, 1868, 43, 58
divisions, *see also* no-confidence; voting; whips
　　described, 21, 36, 40, 42, 68, 74, 83, 98, 134, 144, 192, 198, 236, 237, 241, 242, 243, 273, 286, 294, 296, 314, 315, 325, 328, 353 n.179
　　division bells, 19, 21, 46, 52, 206, 215, 290, 311
　　number of divisions in session, 116, 241, 244, 264, 274, 279, 314, 317
　　sand-glass, 52, 148
Doidge, F.W., 213
Dollimore, H.N., 162, **217**, 218, **220**, 226, 245, 251, 253, 261, 297
Domett ministry, 35, 37–8
Domett, Alfred, 12, 24, **37**, 38, 44, 53, 58, 119
Dominion, 292

Dominion Archives, 132, 161, 220, 256
Dominion status, 106, 128, 135
Douglas, Roger, **293**, 315
Downie, Edward, **54**
Downie, Gavin, 285
Drake, W., **54**
dreadnought, 138, 139, 141
Dreaver, Mary, 229
dress, **139**, 162, 192, 273, 309, 319, 320
　　hats, 22, 50, 51, 157, 159, 187, 188, 273
　　regalia, 15, 19, 20, 34, 87, *see also* mace; Parliament, opening
　　wigs, 59, 134, 148, 149, 150, 187, 309, 319, 333
Duke and Duchess of Cornwall and York, 133
Duke of Edinburgh, **232**
Duncan, T.Y., 132
Dunedin, 40, 44, 78
Dunne, Peter, 320, 327, 331
Durham Report, 1839, 10
Duthie, John, 130, 134

earthquakes, 39, 84, 221, 247, 248, 249, 287, 292, 322
East, A.W., 24
East, Paul, 317, 326, 329, 334
Economic Stabilisation Act, 295
Economic Stabilisation Act 1948, 227
Economic Stabilisation Emergency Regulations 1942, 227
economic summit, 1984, 312
Edwards, A.A., **252**
Edwards, Eileen, 297
Election Writs Act 1858, 63
elections, 15, 23, 60, 74, 80, 82, 85, 95, 107, 113, 152, 168, 186, 191, 195, 203, 204, 212, 214, 241, 243, 262, 275, 280, 285, 294, 296, 300, 316, 319, 320, 327, 329, 330
　　by-elections, 113, 129, 149, 190, 215, 272, 284, 285, 287, 293, 319
　　second ballot, 134, 149
　　vote-splitting, 190, 195, 203, 320
　　writs, 63, 305
elective executive, 102, 108, 109, 149, 168
electoral petitions, 67
electoral politics, 69, 70, 74, 80, 81, 85, 96, 105, 107, 203, 216, 268, 316, 317, 335
　　country quota, 12, 84, 101, 215, 245
electoral reform, 32, 73, 76–82 passim, 215, 300, 324, *see also* referenda; suffrage
Electoral Act, 268, 320
Electoral Act 1956, 259
Electoral Act 1986, 305
Electoral Act Committee, 279
Electoral Amendment Act 1945, 215
Electoral Amendment Bill, 1975, 279

Electoral Bill 1878, 78
Electoral Commission, 318, 327
Electoral (Integrity) Amendment Act 2001, 330
Electoral Law Committee, 307, 318, 329
Electoral Referendum Panel, 308
Electoral Reform Act 1993, 318
Electoral Reform Coalition, 317, 318
Electoral Reform Committee, 334
electorate work, 55, 83, 163, 165, 228, 246, 299, 300, 305, 309, 315, 335
    offices, 300, 309
    secretaries, 300, 309
electric lighting, 88, 128, **129**
Elliott, Charles, 27
Elworthy, Jonathan, **291**
Emergency Regulations Act 1939, 227
Emergency Regulations Select Committee, 227
emergency sessions, 193, 195, 212, 213
Employment Contracts Act 1991, 317
Employment Relations Act 2000, 330
English, Bill, 328
Ensor, Mr, **209**
Erskine May, Thomas, 55, 65
Erskine May (parliamentary procedure), 118, 210
estimates, 121, 218, 261, 263, 264, 274, 285, 286, 305, 311, 319, 326
European Economic Community, 268, 273
Evening Post, 57, 125, 126, 165, 313
Evening Star, 127
Executive Council, 10, 20, 23, 25, 33, 61, 124, 215, 231, 343 n.17
    room, 156
executive, versus Parliament, 34, 35, 36, 38, 43, 63–4, 86, 88, 97, 99, 116, 118, 147, 212, 231, 233, 236, 249, 251, 259, 260, 262, 267, 269, 281, 282, 286, 287, 290, 295, 300, 303, 311, 315, 316, 317, 318, 325, 333, 335, 337, 364 n.25, *see also* government business; Speaker, versus executive

factional system, 10, 23–7, 71, 73, 74, 81, 82, 93, 102, 105, 108, 112, 337
farmers, 103, 141, 145, 149, 186, 200–1, 227, 230, 265, 285, 298, 333, 350 n.241, *see also* pastoral élite
Farmers' Union, 134
Father of the House, 15, 34, 35, 108, 116, 237, 265, 284, 294, 330, 334
Featherston, 12, 24, 34, 39, 51, 75
Fergusson, Sir James, 43
Field, Mrs W.H., 164
Field, Taito Phillip, 334
Finance Act 1915, 152
Finance Act 1931, 193, 194
Finance Act 1932, 196
Finance and Expenditure Committee, 307, 326

Finance bills, 212, 267, 361 n.161, 362 n.116
financial statement/budget/debate, 27, 80, 120, 122, 192, 209, 222, 257, 260, 263, 264, 267, 321, 326, 329, 332
financial veto, 332
Finlay, Martyn, 251, 285, 287
fires, 129, 136, 214, 322
    1907, 59, 136, **137**, 337
    1992, **323**
First World War, 151, 167
Fiscal Responsibility Act 1994, 307, 319, 326, 332
Fish, Henry, 94, 112, 113, 121
Fisher, F.M.B., 115, 135
Fisher, George, **54**, 113, 114, 119
Fishers Catering, 310
FitzGerald ministry, 21–2
FitzGerald, J.E., 12, 13, 14, 18, 20, **21**, 22, 24, 37, 38, 40, 59, 60, 67
FitzGerald, Maurice, 54
Fitzgerald v. Muldoon, 282
Fitzherbert, William, 12, 24, 39, 40, 44, 53, 55, 67, 69, **74**, 79, 88, 97
Fletcher, Christine, 318, 328
Forbes, George, 188–99 passim, **192**, **195**, **198**, 206, 214, 223, 227
foreign affairs, 271
Foreign Affairs Committee, 271
Foreign Affairs, Defence and Trade Committee, 329, 330, 331
Forsaith ministry, 22
Fox ministries, 24, 35, 36–7, 49, 62–3, 65–7, 68
Fox, William, 12, 14, 19, 20, 24, 34–40 passim, **35**, 45, 49, 53, 55, 58–69 passim, 60, 74, 78, 80, 81, 87
Fox–Whitaker ministry, 35, 38, 40
FPP, 204, 300, 318
Fraser, A.L.D., 114
Fraser, Bill, 294
Fraser, Colonel W., 120
Fraser, Ian, 292
Fraser, Janet, 229
Fraser, Peter, 120, 159, 166, 168, 186, 188, 189, 191, 195, 207–15 passim, **213**, 218, 220, 221, 223, 227, 228, 233, 234, 235, 242, 247, 251, 271
Fraser, William, 148, 200
free trade, 98, 101, 117
Freer, Warren, 222, 243, 248, 256, 294
Friedlander, Tony, 313
Friend, George, 64, **87**, 99, 122
Furkert, F.W., 140
fusion (of Liberals, Reform), 151, 167, 186, 188, 189, 195, 203
Future New Zealand Party, 320

Gair, George, 279, 314
Galway, Lord, **211**
gambling, 141, 152, 187, 197, 237
Gang of Four, 295, 296
Garnier, Tony, 296
gas lighting, 43, 46, 88
Geddis, J.M., **119**
General Assembly Library Act 1903, 132
George, Joel, 309
Gerard, Jim, 316
Gerbic, Fred, 298
Gibson and O'Connor, 288
Gill, Frank, 257
Gillon, E.T., 57, **94**, 125, 126
Gisborne, William, 16, 50, 53, 54, 79, 85, 87
Glasgow, Earl of, 110
Glover, A.E., 224
Goff, Phil, 316, 330
Goosman, Stan, 222, 248
Gordon, Peter, **245**, 257
Gordon, Sir Arthur, 85
Gore, H.M., **119**
Götz, Leon, 261
Government Administration Committee, 307, 332
Government Buildings, 49, 88
government business, 18, 55, 60, 99, 101, 120, 121, 122, 135, 144, 192, **198**, 200, 224, 231, 242, 267, 297, 315, 316, 333, 352 n.92, *see also* executive versus Parliament; sessions; sittings
    defeat in division, 197, 215, 272, 295, 328
    urgency, 120, 142, 147, 152, 193, 195, 196, 197, 210, 215, 216, 231, 241, 242, 280, 282, 285, 305, 314, 315, 316, 319, 320, 328, 330, 333, 362 n.116
    extraordinary urgency, 305, 317, 328
Government Centre, 247, 249, 254
government departments, 41, 43, 45, 49, 88
Government House, 40, 41, 294
Government House, Auckland, 9, **15**, 32
Government Printing Office, 41, 52, 53, 64, 311
governments, *see* individual governments (from 1891); coalition government; minority government, *see also* ministries (to 1890)
Governor, 10, 11, 18, 19, 23, 25, 26, 27, 33, 36, 39, 40, 41, 46, 56, 60, 63, 64, 77, 88, 337
    messages, 21, 50, 51
    royal assent, 11, 21, 27, 63, 77, 305
Governor-General, 227, 238, 260, 282, 284, 305, 311
    messages, 264
Grace, John, 158
Graham, Doug, 319
Gray, J., **119**
Gray, Robin, 312, 316, 319, 328
Great White Fleet, 140

Green Party, 329, 330, 331
Green, M.W., 95
Greenwood, J., 24
Grey ministry, 73, 77–80, 81
Grey, George, 11, 12, 13, 14, 28, 33, 36–43 passim, 60, 67, 68, 73–86 passim, **76**, 91–101 passim, 105, 134, 150
Grey, J. Grattan, **119**
Griffin, Richard, 282
Grigg, Mary, 229
Guinness, Arthur, 59, 118, 119, 121, 123, **134**, 138, 142, 143, 145, 149, 150
Gulf War, 316
Guthrie, D.H., **185**

Hackett, Fred, 241
Hadfield, Archbishop, 34
Hailsham, Lord, 300
Hall ministry, 81–5
Hall, John, 25, 49, 73, 80–7 passim, **81**, 102, 112, **113**, 114, 118, 125
Hall, Rosalie, 251, **252**
Hall, T.D.H., 59, **161**, 193, **218**, 219, 220, 297
Halstead, Eric, 224
Hamilton, Adam, 203, 212, 213, 214, 216
Hamlin, Ebenezer, 81, 85, 96
Hammond, E.E., 204
Hanan, Ralph, 237, 245, 257, 259, 272
Hansard, 47, 52–55, 57, 59, 68, 80, 87, 88, 92, 93, 116, 119, 121, 122, 125, 135, 137, 160, 161, 205, 208, 213, 219, 220, 244, 251, 297, 308, 310, 311, 315, 326, *see also* parliamentary reporting; press gallery
    Editor of Debates, 220, 251, 252, 297
    gallery, 53
    Reader, 54
    reporting in Committee, 264, 297, 311, 326
    reporters, 46, **54**, 57, 76, 84, 86, 97, 98, 114, 117, 118, **119**, 121, 156, 159, 161, 219, 249, **251**, **252**, 285, 297
    Supervisor, 118, 125, 218, 251
    typists, 161, **219**, 220
    women, 161, 251, 252, 254, **278**, 297
Hansford, Mills and Hardie, 155
Hardie Boys, Sir Michael, 176, **177**
Hardy, C.A.C., 134
Harkness, J.G. **144**
Harman, Richard, 282
Harrier, 36
Harrison, J.R., **245**, 257, 274, 284, **285**, 286, 293, 294, 296, 306, 328
Hart, George R., 57
Hartley, Ann, 331
Hasler, Marie, 327
Hauk-Willis, Angela, **326**

Index

Havelock, 41
Hayward, Margaret, 253
Health Select Committee, 331
Heaphy, Charles, 62
Heke, Hone, 114
Hely, Madeleine, 219
Henare, Raymond Tau, 319
Henare, Taurekareka, 151
Henderson, Stella, **128**
Hercus, Ann, 298
Herdman, Alexander, 148
Herekino, Northland, 153
Herries, W.H., 134, 140, 148, **185**, 352 n.94
Hide, Rodney, 366 n.162
Higher Salaries Commission, 247, 331
Hill Street, 46, 87, 154
Hill, Morris, 217
Hindmarsh, A.H., 139, 166, 167
Hine, J.B., 152, 167
Hinemoa, 76, 95
Hislop, T.W., 77
Historic Places Trust, 292, 322
Hobson, William, 28
Hogg, Alexander, 112, 139
Holland, H.E., 166, 167, 168, 185–97 passim, 223
Holland, Sidney, 204, 209, 213–18 passim, 227, **233**, 234, 235, 238, **240**, 241–9 passim, 257, 259, 261, 267, 271
Hollard, Milton, **326**
Hollis, Christopher, 231
Holloway, Philip, 256
Holmes Consulting Group, 322
Holyoake, Keith, **217**, 233, 237, 242, 243, 244, 250, 251, 253, 254, **257**, 259, 262, 263, 264, 272, 273, 275, 277, 279, 284, 287, 290, 291, 296, 307, 313
homosexual law reform, 245, 268, 271, 279, 313–14
Homosexual Law Reform Act 1986, 313, 314
Horne, Commander, 161
Hororata estate, Canterbury, 125
horse racing, 121, 152, 163, 187, 197, 242, 352 n.94, *see also* social activities
    New Zealand Cup, 121
    New Zealand Racing Conference, 197
House, business of, 102, 103, 198, 216, 284, 286, 305, 314, *see also* private members; standing orders
    adjournment, 81, 96, 111, 117, 141, 143, 149, 152, 167, 185, 186, 192, 194, 195, 198, 210, 212, 213, 214, 243, 260, 264, 267, 279, 303, 305, 312, 315
    notices of motion, 186, 260, 261, 263, 277, 279, 285, 286, 298, 305
    order paper, 27, 52, 121, 216, 244, 316
    quorum, 22, 27, 28, 32, 52, 75, 85, 95, 111, 121, 123, 277, 293, 296, 306, 325, 329

House and Legislative Council, *see* Legislative Council, versus House
House Committee, 19, 64, 89, 221, 230, 254, 288, 307
House Committee (PSC), 309
Howard, E.J., 168, 210, 230
Howard, Mabel, **230**, 248, 253, 254, 265
Hunt, Jonathan, **6**, 230, 265, 272, **273**, 275, 277–87 passim, 293, 294, **295**, 300, **310**, 313, 317, 327, **330**, 331, 332, **333**
Hunter, George, 299
Hunter, J., 251, **252**
Hurst, W.J., 85
Hursthouse, Richmond, 83
Hutcheson, John, 123
Hutchison, George, 102, 124
Hyde, Robin, 128

Immigration and Public Works Act 1870, 66
Imperial Conferences, 138, 141, 185, 190, 193
Imprest Supply bills, debate, 120, 121, 263, 264, 286
independent members, 26, 82, 108, 109, 116, 117, 120, 124, 132, 142, 143, 168, 185, 186, 187, 189, 191, 204, 212, 213, 221, 222, 226, 285, 328, 329
influenza epidemic, 167
Ingles, H.A., 67
Isbey, Eddie, 314, 315
Isitt, L.M., 165, 186
Islington, Baron, 142

Jack, Roy, 205, 257, 262, **263**, 264, 268, 273, 274, 282, 284, 285, 291, 306
Jackson, Sylvia, 219
James, Colin, 282
James, H.L., 91, 129, 132
Japan, 213
Jelicich, Dorothy, 298, **299**
Jennings, W.T., 163
Jervois, Sir William, 95, 98
Johnstone, H., 209
Jones, Bob, 295
Jones, Dail, 296
Jones, Fred, 208, 241
Jones, George, 58
Jones, Norman, 312
journalists, 12, 69, 103, 112, 125, 126, 127, 145, 201, 228, 230, 282, 291, 292, 298, 321, *see also Hansard*; newspapers; press gallery
Joyce, John, 77, 105
Judd, Hugo, **326**

Kane, E.W., 160, 161, 218
Katene, Wiremu, 61
Kay, A.M., **119**
Keane, M.C., **126**

379

Kearins, Paddy, 222, 237
Keefe, John, 87
Keeling, Reg, 241, 243, 244, 256
Kent, Jim, 241
Kidd, Doug, 285, 307, 322, 327, 331
King Country, 237
King George VI, 240
    coronation, 212
King Movement, 33, 35, 36, 37, 124
King, Annette, 334
King, Thomas, 18, 22
Kingi, Wiremu, 33, 34
Kirk, John, 295, 365 n.57
Kirk, Norman, 243, 244, 251, 262, 263, 265, 268, 269, 272–9 passim, **276**, 295, 314
Kirton, Neil, 328
Knapp, Gary, 293, 295, 317
Knights of Labour, 108, 113
Kohukohu, Northland, 153
Kopu, Alamein, 329

Labour Disputes Investigation Act 1913, 151
Labour Governments
    1935–49, 203–32
    1957–60, 243–45
    1972–5, 275–80, 305
    1984–90, 311–16
Labour members, 138, 139, 142, 143, 150, 152, 166, 358 n.114
labour movement, 107, 110, 138, 141, 190, 193
Labour Party, 145, 159, 166–7, 188, 197, 201, 203, 204, 205, 213, 215, 218, 226, 227, 228, 241, 263, 265, 266, 268, 282, 287, 293, 295, 298, 314, 320, 330, 333
labour policy, 107, 109
Lake, Harry, 264
Lambton Quay, 88, 159, 196
Land Act 1892, 111
Land for Settlements Act 1894, 116
land march, **283**
land policy, 11, 27, 33, 34, 73, 98, 103, 107, 139
land tax, 94, 109
Lang, F.W., 140, **148**, 149, **150**, 151, 157, 186, 216
Lange, David, 284, **293**, 295, 298, 303, 312, 314, 315, 316, 317, 319
Langstone, Frank, 215, 224
Lapwood, Harry, 257, 263, 277, 279, 284, 285
Larnach, William, 89, **123**
Law Drafting Office, 159, 160, 218, 287, 288
Law Reform (Miscellaneous Provisions) bills, 316
Laws, Michael, 320
lawyers, 12, 145, 285, 298, 333
Leader of the House, 68, 85, 120, 195, 216, 242, 286, 308, 325, 327
leasehold/freehold, 111, 134, 135, 139, 140

Lee, E.P., **185**, 190
Lee, Graeme, 320
Lee, John A., 163, 190, 195, 204, 209, 212, 213, 221, 224
Lee, Walter, 17, 51
left-wing Liberals, 116, 123, 124, 132, 133, 134
Legislative Council, 11, 14–20 passim, 32, 37, 38, 43, 47, 56, 61, 68, 79, 81, 86, 91, 92, 103, 108, 110, 112, 113, 114, 118, 121, 123, 132, 134, 137, 149, 160, 162, 190, 218, 337
    abolition of, 233–5, **235**
    Black Rod, 16, 20, 86, **162**, 218, 304
    chamber, 15, 22, **45**, 46, 49, 88, 128, **177**, **217**, 268, 324
    Clerk, 99, 160, 162
    reform, 65, 67, 110
    Speaker, 74, 97, 108, 118
    versus House, 34, 43, 63, 64, 65, 68, 69, 78, 86, 96, 109, 110, 116, 123, 346 n.239
Legislative Council Abolition Act 1950, 235
Legislative Department, 63, 86, 159, 160, 162, 218, 225, 251, 275, 296, 297, 304, 307, *see also* parliamentary staff
    estimates, 64, 99, 274
    expenditure, 86, 97, 98, 99, 116, 118, 159, 161, 307
Legislative Officers Salaries Act 1867, 63
Legislature Act 1908, 114, 304, 345 n. 173
Legislature Amendment Act 1913, 150
Legislature Amendment Act 1977, 284
Leslie, W., **119**
Letham, W., 87
Lewis, Charles, 132
Liberal and Labour Federation, 109
Liberal Associations, 80, 109
Liberal government, 108–43
Liberal Party, 77, 101, 108, 111, 132, 135, 138, 144, 145, 147, 148, 152, 158, 190, 234
Libraries Association, 161
Library Committee, 56, 130, 132, 256, 307
Library Committee (PSC), 309
Licensing Act 1881, 49, 114
Licensing Amendment Act 1854, 19, 64
Licensing Amendment Bill 1927, 190
Lipson, Leslie, 109
liquor licensing, 114, 141, 168, 237, 252, 259, 269, 351 n.45
Littlejohn, C.P., 218, 285, **297**, 308, **311**
Liverpool, Lord, 151, **163**
Lloyd, Rev. F.J., 17
lobbies, 47, 50, 52, 89, 97, 116, 137, 140, 154, 190, 300, 325, *see also* divisions; voting
Local Bills Committee, 56, 86, 226, 260, 264, 286, 307

Index

local body politics, 144, 265
Lockwood buildings, 287, 288, 289
Long, Richard, 282
Lowe, A.F., 160
Luke, Sir John, 186
Lusk, H.H., 50
Luxton, John, 294, 299, 314, 331
Lynsar, W.D., 224
Lyttelton Times, 128

Macandrew, James, 17, 54, 70, 77, 81, 82, 83, 103
Macdonald, Ritchie, 244
Macdonald, W.D.S., 168
MacDonell, Brian, 295, 296, 365 n.57
mace, 15, 16, **59**, 116, **136**, **139**, **182**, **309**, **311**, 353 n.177
Macfarlane, R.M., 205, 218, **243**, 244
MacIntyre, Duncan, 158, 257, 280, 293
Mackay, James, 77
Mackay, James (member, 1853–5), 22
Mackenzie, Scobie, 51, 91, 97, 113
Mackenzie, Thomas, 105, 135, 138, 143, 145, 149
Maher, J.J., 252
Mahuta (Maori King), 124
Mainzeal Group, 322
Mair, Gilbert, 91
Malcolm, A.S., 149, 150, 186
male culture, 162, 252, 253, 292, 297, 298, *see also* women
Mana Motuhake Party, 277
Manderson, Fred, 161, 220, 251
Mantell, Walter, 58, 92
manual workers, 100, 103, 145, 201, 227–8, 265, 298
Maori/Native affairs, 11, 12, 29, 33, 36, 37, 38, 40, 41, 73
Maori/Native Affairs Committee, 56, 91, 127, 158
Maori/Native Affairs Committee room, 155, 157, **158**, **180**, 290
Maori Affairs Committee Room (Maui Tikitiki a Taranga), **180**, **181**, 324
Maori Councils, 124
Maori language, 61, 91, 216
    Hansard, 93
    interpreters, 86, 91, 118, 124, 136, 216
Maori Language Act 1987, 216
Maori members, 48, 56, 60, 61, 80, 82, 91–93, 215, 243, 246, 247, 253, 334
Maori Parliaments, 124
Maori representation, 11, 56, 60, 317, 318, 343 n.112
    seats, 215, 279, 317, 318, 327
Mapourika, 141
marginal lands loan affair, 280
maritime strike, 1890, 101
Marshall, Jack, 235, 247, 251, 254, 257, 259, 273, 274, 277, 278, 279, 280, 286, 296

Martin, William, 15
Mason, H.G.R. (Rex), 190, 212, 228, **237**, 265, 313
Massey, J.N., 252
Massey, William, 82, 113, **131**, 134, 137–54 passim, **143**, **147**, **148**, 157, 159, **163**, 165, 167, 168, **185**, 186, 187, 188, 200, 234
Matakohe, Northland, 164
Mathison, Jock, 243
Maxwell, Ralph, 287
May, Henry, 241, **242**, 244
Mayne, Edward, **36**
McColl, C.R., **252**
McColl, Ewen, 90, **91**
McCombs, Elizabeth, **199**, 229
McCombs, James, 186, 187, 191, 199, **225**
McCombs, Terence, 199, 241
McCully, Murray, 314, 316, 318
McDavitt, J.P., 254
McDougall, David, 224
McGee, D.G., 218, 306, **308**, **311**, 324, 325, **326**, 329, 335
McGregor, Angus, 91
McIntosh, Alister, 230
McKay, Wing Commander R.M., **311**
McKeen, Robert, 205, 215, 218, 227, 229, 233
McKenzie, John (Jock), 109, 111, 112, **116**, 117, 118, 124, **125**, 132
McKenzie, Roderick, 115, 123, 133, 135, 139, 143
McKinnon, Don, **295**, **310**
McLachlan, Colin, 277, 282
McLachlan, John, **114**, 115
McLaren, David, 138, **139**
McLay, Jim, 298, 304, 312
McLean, Donald, 25, 34, 60, 62, 66, 69, 73
McLean, Ian, 285
McLean, J., 219, **252**
McLean, William, 142
McLintock, A.H., 10, 239, 337
McMillan, Ethel, 261
McMillan, Neale, **253**
McNab, Robert, 236
McSkimming, Peter, 224
Melville, Ellen, 168, 190, 199
Members Services Committee, 309
Members' Superannuation Committee 1945, 228
Mentiplay, Cedric, **253**
Merriman, F.W., 15
Meurant, Ross, 320
military, 9, 11, 29, 33, 38, 41, 43, 64, 73
    58th Regiment, 16
Millar, J.A., 134, 143
Mills, C.H., 116
ministries, *see* individual ministries (to 1890) and governments (from 1891)

381

Ministry of Works, 248, 249, 287, 288, 292
Minogue, Mike, 282, 284, 286, 295, 296
minority government, 318, 320, 329, 330, 335
Mitchell, Austin, 267
Mitchell, William, **54**
mixed ministry, 21, 22
MMP, 308, 317, 318, 319, 320, 324, 329, 331, 333, 337
Molesworth Street, 87, 112, 128, 129, 132, 154, 169, 294, 324
Monk, Richard, 125
Monro, David, 13, **34**, 35, **36**, 37, 41, 51, 55, 57–67 passim, 79
Montgomery, William, 76, 82, 86, 95, 97
Moohan, Mick, 215, 241, 252, 261
Moore, Mike, 275, **293**, 315, 316, 319
Moorhouse, William, 59
Morgan, Tukuroirangi, 328
Morrison, Tom **94**
Morton, Harry, 224
Moss, F.J., 50
Motueka, 155
Moyle affair, 283
Moyle, Colin, 283, 284
Muldoon, Rob, **245**, 254, 256, 257, 259, 262, 264, 274–86 passim, **277**, 281, 289–304 passim, 307, 311, 312, 313, 317, 321, 362 n.90, 364 n.16
Munro, James, 224
Munro, Leslie, 254, 262, 272
Murdoch, A.J., 252
Museum Street, 154, 287

Nash, Walter, 212, **217**, 219, 233, 237, **240**, 241, 243, 244, 257, 263, 265
Nathan, Colonel W.C., 304
national anthem, 152, 304
National Council of Women, 128
National Development Act 1979, 286
National Expenditure Adjustment Act 1932, 196
National Expenditure Commission, 162
National government
    1949–57, 233–42
    1960–72, 256–64, 272–4
    1975–84, 281–7, 292–6
    1990–6, 316–20
'National' government, wartime, 213
National Historic Places Trust Bill, 1952, 237
National Library, 91, 132, 254, 256, 309
National Party, 203, 204, 209, 212, 213, 214, 215, 226, 227, 229, 258, 259, 266, 274, 284, 293, 298, 312, 319, 320, 330, 333
National Party (1920s), 188, 190
Native Land Court, 60, 61, 124
Native Lands Act 1862, 37, 65

Native Offenders Bill 1860, 34, 343 n.25
Neilson, Peter, 224
Nelson, 13, 22, 23, 39, 40, 41, 95
Nelson cotton mill, 257
Nelson members, 24, 39, 40, 84
Nestor, Martin, 233, 274
New Plymouth, 140
New Provinces Act 1858, 33, 34
New Zealand Bill of Rights Act 1990, 326
New Zealand Broadcasting Corporation, 268
New Zealand Broadcasting Service, 209
New Zealand Company, 10, 27
New Zealand First Party, 319, 320, 327, 328, 330, 331
New Zealand Graphic, 127
New Zealand Legion, 197
New Zealand Local Time Bill, 224
New Zealand Party, 295
New Zealand Times, 127, 287
New Zealand wars, 33–8, 58, 60
NewLabour Party, 315
Newman, A.K., 95, 102
newspapers, 19, 24, 43, 52, 53, 57, 69, 95, 125, 205, 271, 274, 279, *see also* journalism; press gallery; individual newspapers
    photography, **217**
Ngata, Apirana, 114, 138, 150, 156, **158**, 191, 227
Ngatata, W.T., 92
no-confidence (matters of confidence in ministry/government)
    government defeat, 22, 24, 35, 37, 62, 67, 77, 80, 81, 95, 97, 143, 191
    motions of, 26, 34, 42, 59, 61, 62, 77, 81, 82, 85, 96, 97, 101, 109, 117, 120, 122, 124, 132, 134, 142, 168, 185, 186, 187, 188, 189, 192, 193, 195, 214, 216, 218, 241, 244, 296, 325, 328
Nordmeyer, Arnold, 233, 244, 251, 263, 264, 265
Normanby, Marquis of, 75, 77, 78
North Auckland Development Board, 153
Northern Club, 164
Northland, 153
Nosworthy, William, **185**

O'Brien, Gerald, 285, 365 n.57
O'Brien, James, 166
obstruction, 18, 37, 38, 85, 99, 103, 141, 187, 195, 210, 332, *see also* speeches; standing orders
    adjourning the House, 81, 84, 116, 117, 121, 122, 143, 150, 193
    previous question, 37, 81, 83, 236
    reporting progress, 75, 84, 85, 117, 150, 190, 193
    stonewalls, 38, 55, 62, 68, 75, 76, 84, 85, 90, 94,

Index

97, 98, 99, 101, 112, 121–5, 139, 140, 150,
   186, 187, 188, 192, 193, 194, 279, 285, 317
      tedious repetition, 75, 122, 150, 192, 196, 257
Office of the Clerk, 307, 308, 310, 321, 332
O'Flynn, Frank, 314
old wooden buildings (Government House), 137,
   138, 149, **154**, 159, 220, 238, 247–51 passim, 288,
   289, *see also* Government House; Parliament
   Buildings
      ballroom, **138**
      Social Hall, 159, 248, 249
old-age pensions, 122
Omana, Tiaki, 209, 215
Ombudsman, 257, 259, 260, 261, 286
omnibus bills, 210, 316, *see also* Finance bills
      Local Legislation bills, 357 n.34
      Statutes Amendment Bill 1936, 212
      Statutes Amendment bills, 210, 226, 267, 316
Onehunga, 14, 23, 29, 140
Onslow, Earl of, 110
Opposition, role of, 46, 144, 190, 274, 307, *see also*
   party
      Leader of, 159, 190, 216, 246, 247, 275, 308,
         319, 324, 325
Oram, Matthew, 216, 233, **234**, 236–42 passim, 262,
   306
Orders in Council, 197, 226, 247, 286, *see also*
   regulations
O'Regan, P.J., 109
Ormond, J.D., 83, 101, 103, 352 n.94
O'Rorke, Maurice, 27, 35, 59, 60, 63, 66, 68, 76, **79**,
   83, 85, 86, 87, 88, 96, 97, 98, 99, 102, 103, 108,
   113, 115, 116, 118, 119, 122, 123, 133, 134, 149,
   187, 189
Osborne, A.G., 241
O'Sullivan, John, 309
Otago, 33, 37, 40, 58, 70, 98
Otago members, 13, 14, 15, 24, 37, 40, 42, 58, 60,
   70, 84, 96
Otago Witness, 127
Otterson, Henry, 87, 99, **122**, 160

Paikea, P.K., 215
Paikea, T.P. (Dobbie), 215, **216**, 244
pairing, 27, 43, 83, 113, 215, 216, 221, 236, 237, 243,
   244, 272, 294, 325, *see also* whips
Palmer, Geoffrey, 286, 287, 296, 303, **305**, 307, 313–
   17 passim, 321, 322
Palmer, Jackson, **49**
Parata, Taare, 149
Parata, Tame, 149
Parata, Wiremu, **61**
Parihaka, 82
Parliament, calling of, **13**, 34, 282, 316, 358 n.22

Parliament, dissolution of, 43, 62, 67, 77, 80, 93, 95,
   97, 98, 101, 102, 117, 135, 150, 186, 191, 240, 282,
   283, 305, **326**
Parliament, life of, 152, 168, 196, 212, 214, 348 n.85,
   see also electoral politics; electoral reform
      term, 11, 76, 78, 82, 262, 269, 295, 304
Parliament, opening **1**, 36, 41, **46**, 55, 57, 59, 62, **136**,
   138, **211**, **217**, 236, 238, 268, 273, 282, 285, 303, 311
      ceremony, 16, **176**, **177**, 206, 211, **238**, **304**
      royal, 232, 240, 248, 272
      swearing in, members, 11, 15, 51, 55, 199, 206
Parliament, proroguing, 11, 21, 55, 139, 198, 212,
   303, 315, 316
Parliament, public's view of, 229, 267, 284, 316, 318,
   320, 321, 324, 328, 331, 333, 335
Parliament Buildings, **2**, **3**, 39–42 passim, **39**, **42**, 43–
   9, **44**, **45**, 64, **72**, 86, **89**, 88–91, 94, 124, 126, 128–
   30, **129**, **130**, **133**, 136–8, **137**, 152–9, **160**, **169**, 239,
   247–51, **249**, 290, 308, 312, 322–4, *see also* Beehive;
   chamber of the House; old wooden buildings;
   Parliament House; Parliamentary Library
      committee rooms, 41, 43, 45, 88, 89, 128, 129,
         130, 154, 156, 324
      ladies' tearoom, 129, 159
      Lobby, 89, 90, **92**, **93**, 114, 126, 162, 324
      smoking room, 19, 35, 46, 67, 90, 155
      whips' room, 88, 163
Parliament Buildings, Auckland, 9, 14, **15**, **16**, 19, 32,
   41, 240
Parliament Buildings, refurbishment, 310, 322–4
Parliament grounds, 111, 117, 128, **129**, **154**, 159,
   196, **200**, **270**, 271, **272**, 282, **283**, **284**, 288, 290,
   308, 324
      protest, **196**, **200**, 268, 269, **270**, 271, **272**, 282,
         283, **284**, 285, 294, 300, 301
            Springbok tour, 293, 294
      public events, **133**, **202**, 272
      tennis court, 89, 118
      Twopenny tube, 137, **154**, 155
Parliament House, 170, **171**, **175**, **178**, **182**, **183**, 220,
   254, 292, 317, 324, *see also* chamber of the House;
   Parliament Buildings
      construction, 152–9, **156**, **157**
      Grand Hall, **178**, 324
      lounge lobby/billiard room, 149, 155, 166, **167**,
         178, 262, 298, 299, 324
      penthouse, 156, 214, 248, 271, 322
      proposed Parliament House, **155**
      south wall, 156, **157**, 250, 287, **289**
Parliament Street, Auckland, 240
Parliament Weeks, 290
Parliamentary debating societies, 104
Parliamentary Honorarium and Privileges Act 1884,
   100

Parliamentary (General Assembly) Library, 37, 41, **44**, 47, 49, 88, 89, **90**, 91, 99, 128–30, **131**, 136, 137, 154, 160, 161, 220, 225, 230, 254, 256, 274, 308, 309, 311
    building, **44**, **106**, 129–30, **130**, 136, 149, 151, **154**, 156, 159, **169**, **171**, **172**, **173**, **174**, 247, 275, 282, 292, 322, 324, *see also* Parliament Buildings

Parliamentary Practice in New Zealand, 308

Parliamentary Privileges Act 1865, 57, 65

parliamentary record, *see also* Hansard
    Appendix to the Journals of the House of Representatives, 52
    Journal, 47, 50, 52
    Votes and Proceedings, 52

parliamentary reform, 233, 256, 257, 258, 259, 267, 274, 277, 281, 285, 287, 300, 303, 314, 317, 324, *see also* electoral reform; Legislative Council; referenda

Parliamentary Representation Bill 1878, 78

Parliamentary Service, 307, 308, 310, 311

Parliamentary Service Act 1985, 307, 308, 364 n.21

Parliamentary Service building, 312, 322

Parliamentary Service Commission, 307, 308, 309, **310**, 311, 322, 330

parliamentary staff, 19, 41, 86, 133, 162, 251, 254, *see also* Clerk of the House; *Hansard*; Legislative Council; Legislative Department; Sergeant/Serjeant-at-Arms
    appointments, 63, 64, 86, 116, 118, 119, 218
    charwomen, 86, 119, 128, 155, 161, 219
    Chief Hansard Reporter, 54, 119, 161
    Chief Librarian, 161
    Chief Messenger, 87
    Clerk-Assistant, 155
    clerks, 20, 118, 160, 218
    custodian, 87, 128, 161
    Examiner of Standing Orders on Private Bills, 55, 86, 99
    housekeeper, 19, 49
    messengers, 20, 119, 155, 159, 160, 161, 219, 252, 255, 310
    nightwatchmen, 128, 136
    officer in charge of the buildings, 128
    Reader of Bills, 86, 162
    salaries, 59, 63, 64, 86, 87, 98, 99, 133
    Second Clerk-Assistant, 118, 162

parliamentary tours, **104**, *see also* travel
    voyage to Pacific Islands, 1903, **141**
    'winterless north' tour, 1917, **153**

Parliamentary Wives' Association, 300

Parr, C.J., 190

Parry, W.E., 165, 168, 194, 227, 241

party, 10, 25, 52, 71, 73, 74, 80, 81, 94, 105, 107, 112, 116, 120, 144, 147, 185, 233, 300, 337, *see also* caucus; independent members; Opposition, role of; whips; and individual parties
    discipline, 109, 124, 134, 135, 144, 186, 190, 204, 216, 222, 226, 237, 244, 297, 317, 325
    organisation, 81, 94, 98, 186, 197, 203, 335

party-hopping, 329, 330

party research units, 214, 262, 274, 275

pastoral élite, 12, 24, 31, 69, 70, 73, 103, 145, 350 n.241, *see also* farmers

patronage, 118, 119, 120, 126, 129, 132, 139, 160, 234, *see also* corruption

Patterson, John, 60, 62

Paul, J.T., 213

Payment of Members Act 1892, 100

Payment to Provinces Act 1871, 65

Payne, John, 139, 150, 151, 166

Peace Treaty, Versailles, **131**, 167

Pere, Wiremu, 124

Peters, Winston, 298, 313, 319, 321, 326, 327, 328

petitions, 56, 91, 97, 109, 113, 128, 215, 226, 259, 260, 261, 267, 287, 313, 314, 324

Pettis, Jill, 330

Piako swamp, sale, 75

Picton, 40, 41, 95

Pirani, Fred, 133

Political Reform League, 148

politicians, self-made, 70, 104, 111

politics as career, 58, 69, 103, 104, 116, 228, 231, 266

Pollen ministry, 68

Pollen, Daniel, 68

Polson, W.J., 197, 230, 235

Pomare, Maui, 149, 156, 158, 299

populism, 77, 105, 109, 189

Porritt, Sir Arthur, 268

Port Underwood, 41

post office, 159, 287

Powles, Guy, 286

prayer, 17, 18, 208, 216, 259, 263, 342 n.37

Prebble, Richard, 292, 326, 327

Premier House, 112, 132

Press, 127

Press Association, 57

press gallery, 39, 46, 47, 57, 58, 68, **94**, 125, **126**, 127, 128, 159, 213, 230, 249, 252, **253**, 254, 261, 268, 271, 282, 283, 291, 292, 293, 321, *see also Hansard*; journalists; newspapers
    reporters, 19, 57, 126, 127, 161, 188
    women, 127, 128, 253, 254, 291, 292

Primary Products Marketing Act 1936, 210

Prime Minister, *see also* cabinet
    annual statement of, 325
    Department of, 214, 271, 281

Index

office, 130, 155, 156, 276
    role of, 286
Printing Committee, 56
private bills, 55, 56, 279
Private Bills Committee, 56, 307
Private Bills Office, 55
private members, 109, 120, 220, 226, 231, 242, 257, 260, 261, 319, *see also* independent members
    bills, 86, 108, 144, 152, 168, 190, 197, 224, 237, 264, 275, 279, 286, 287, 294, 305, 320, 332, 333, 343, n.12
    business, 18, 103, 222, 224, 225, 314
privileges, 56–8, 64, 65, 86, 118, 291, 297, 326, 345 n.173, 351 n.45, *see also* Legislative Council, versus House
    breach of privilege, 127, 263, 274, 279, 280, 282, 286, 294, 313, 353 n.202
    fines, 50, 83, 85, 94, 117, 127
Privileges Act 1856, 50, 57
Privileges Committee, 56, 127, 263, 279, 280, 287, 294, 307, 313, 329
Progressive Coalition Party, 330
prohibition, 112, 113, 115, 116, 141, 168, 190, 234, *see also* temperance
Prolongation of Parliament Act 1941, 213
property tax, 83, 96, 107
proportional representation, 300, 317, 318, *see also* MMP
protectionism, 73, 98, 101
Protestant Political Association, 168
provincial system, 11, 32, 33, 36, 43, 59, 66, 73
provincialism, 12, 16, 24, 25, 27, 32, 35, 43, 58, 59, 60, 63, 68, 71, 73, 74, 102, 144
Public Accounts Committee, 56, 226, 259, 261
Public Debts and Loan Consolidation Act 1867, 65
Public Expenditure Committee, 258, 261, 262, 267, 274, 275, 282, 286, 307, 319, 364 n.16
Public Finance Act 1989, 308, 315, 319
Public Petitions Committee, 56, 226, 307
Public Safety Conservation Act 1932, 196, 240
public service, 186, 196, *see also* civil service
Public Service Commission, 251
public works, 25, 36, 58, 63, 73, 74, 77, 81, 82, 84, 95, 96, 97, 102, 107
Public Works Department, 130, 140, 213
Pyke, Vincent, 50, 81, 82, **83**, 102

Qualifications of Electors Act 1879, 82
Queen, 41
Queen Elizabeth II, **232**, 239, **240**, 272, 289, 324
Queen Victoria, 9, 124, 128, 133
Quigley, Derek, 295, 296, 331
Quinton's Corner, Lambton Quay, **154**, 159
Quirke, M., **252**

radio, 205, 209, 321
    broadcasting debates, 205–10, **205**, **206**, 216, 231, 268, 305, 321
    The Day in Parliament, 321
    The Week in Parliament, 321
Rae, D.M., 237
railways, 63, 65, 67, 73, 78, 82, 83, 96, 140
    medallion passes, **164**
    Parliament Special (train), **140**
Ralston, Bill, 321
Rankin, Carol, 308, **309**, 313
Rata, Matiu, 263, 276, **277**, 285, 365 n.57
Ratana movement, 215, 216, 253
Ratana, H.T., 215
Ratana, Iriaka, **253**
Ratana, Matiu, 253
Rees, W.L., 75, 76, 80
Reeves, R.H., 84, 89, 90, 113
Reeves, W.P., 50, 103, 105, 108, 109, 117
referenda, 141, 218, 235, 259, 269, 295, 304, 308, 317, 318, 319, 328, 329, 334, 335, 365 n.85, *see also* electoral reform; parliamentary reform
Reform Act 1832, 10
Reform government, 143, 147–91
Reform of Parliament Bill, 1979, 287
Reform Party, 109, 135, 139, 144, 145, 148, 201, 203, 215
Regulation of Elections Act 1870, 64
regulations, 227, 257, 260
Regulations Act 1936, 227
Regulations Review Committee, 307, 331
Reilly, T.F., **252**
Remuneration Authority, 331, 366 n.162
Reporting Debates Committee, 58
Reporting Debates and Printing Committee, 53, 56, 121
Representation Act, 101
Representation Act 1860, 33
Representation Act 1881, 84
Representation Act 1887, 97
Representation Act Amendment Act 1889, 101
Representation Acts Amendment Act 1887, 98
Reserve Bank of New Zealand Act 1936, 210
Reserve Bank of New Zealand Amendment Act 1939, 207
responsible government, 11, 17, 20–3, 24, 26, 33, 36, 63, 337, *see also* constitutional issues
retrenchment, 73, 81, 82, 86, 97, 98, 100, 101, 103, 105, 160, 162, 196, *see also* depression
Revell, Ian, 327
Rhodes, Heaton, 134, 148, 353 n.94
Rhodes, W.B., 40
Richards, A.S., 215
Richardson, Ruth, 294, 295, 296, 298, **300**, 317, 319, 334

385

Richmond, C.W., 24, 47, 69
Richmond, J.C., 35, 41
Ridley, Jack, **280**
Right of Centre Party, 320
Robertson, J., 139
Robertson, Ross, 331
Robinson, Sir Hercules, 80, 81, 82
Rolleston, William, 76, 86, 91, 103, 108, 109, **110**, 111, 113, 117, 118
Ross, Forrest, 127
Ross, Hilda, 230, **231**, 253, 254
Ross, Malcolm, **126**
Roussell, E.A., 218, 243, **278**, 279, 283, 291, 297
Rowling, Bill, 272, 277–85 passim, 293, 295, 297
Roy, Eric, 330
Royal Commission on the Electoral System, 1986, 304, 317
Royal Commission on Parliamentary Salaries and Allowances, 245, 246, 247, 274
RSA, 159
Russell, Captain William, 97, 101, 110, 117, 120, 132
Russell, Frederick Nene, 60
Russell, G.W., 109, 123, 168
Russell, Thomas, 75
Russell, W.H., **119**

salaries/honorarium, members, 18, 80, 97, 98, 100, 105, 163, 165, 166, 228, 245, **246**, 247, 328, 331
 allowances, 18, 228, 247, 328, 331
 superannuation, 165, 228, **229**
Sale of Liquor Restriction Act 1917, 152
Salt, Ailsa, **326**
Sandle, Major S.G., **161**
Saunders, Alfred, 22, 34, 81, 102, 113
Savage, M.J. (Micky), 165, 168, 194, 197, **198**, 204–12 passim, **205**, 219, 229
Scholefield, G.H., **126**, 161, 220, 254, 256
Schramm, F.W., 205, 214, 215, 221
Schwabe, Emil, 127
Scott, Tom, 255, 282, 292, 321
Scrimgeour, Colin, 207
seat of government, 9, 13, 17, 25, 28, 38–41, 44, 68
Seath, David, 272
seats, number of, 33, 37, 40, 58, 60, 69, 74, 84, 134, 259, 262, 267, 269, 278, 279, 289, 317, 334, 335, *see also* electoral reform; Maori representation
 reduction in seats, 97, 98, 101, 109, **195**
Second Ballot Act 1908, 138
second chamber, 258, 259, 318, *see also* Legislative Council
Second World War, 208, 210, 212–14
secret sessions, 208, 213, 214
secretarial assistance, members, **131**, 246, 247, 274, 304
Security Intelligence Service Act 1977, 270, 284

Seddon ministry, 111–35
Seddon, Captain Richard, 135
Seddon, R.J., 50, 77, 81, 83, **84**, 85, 94, 99, 104, 108–35 passim, **141**, 143, 144, 147, 148, 150, 152, 159, 186, 203, 251, 269
 statue, 159
Seddon, T.E.Y., 135, 167
select committees, 56, 120, 129, 225, 226, 247, 257, 259, 260, 267, 275, 278, 282, 284, 286, 287, 292, 298, 304, 306, 308, 315, 316, 319, 325, 329, 331, 332, *see also* House, business of
 chairing, 331, 332
 proceedings, 94, 127, 286
 subject committees, 306
 witnesses, 327
self-government, 9–12, 17, *see also* responsible government
self-reliance, 33, 40, 42
Sellars, Roy, 197
Semple, Robert, 159, 166, 206, 215, 221, 222, **223**
separation movement, 35, 37, 40, 41, 42, 58, 70, 75
Sergeant/Serjeant-at-Arms, 17, 20, 21, 29, 34, 49, 51, 58, 59, 83, 87, 120, **139**, 151, 155, 160, 161, 166, 239, 278, 293, 304, 308, **309**, **311**, 313, 354 n.73
sessions, *see also* Parliament, life of
 length, 103, 141, 144, 149, 185, 190, 197, 198, 273, 278, 279, 284, 298, 305, 312, 319
 pattern, 13, 120, 135, 193, 197, 213, 264, 267, 275, 277, 282, 298, 303, 325
Sewell ministry, 24
Sewell, Henry, 13, 14, 17, 21–9 passim, **22**, 34–40 passim, 51, 52, 53, 58, 69
Seymour, Arthur, 79, 85
Shand, Tom, 244, 254, 257, 258, 272
Shearer, Ian, 286
Sheat, W.A., 262
Sheehan, John, 77, **78**, 80, 84, 87
Shepherd, Major T.V., **59**, **139**, 161
Sheppard, Fergus, 248, 249, 250
Shields, Margaret, 298, 316, 334
Shipley, Jenny, **177**, 314, 328, 329, 331, 334
Sidey, T.K., 165, **224**
Sim, Geoffrey, 209
Simich, Clem, 331
Singapore Free Trade Agreement, 330
sittings
 days, 18, 99, 120, 242, 263, 275, 305, 333
  Mondays, 63, 76, 85, 120, 123, 135, 141, 150, 187, 192, 195, 197, 317
  Saturdays, 22, 38, 76, 85, 123, 150, 193, 197, 279, 315, 317
 hours, 18, 55, 99, 103, 163, 191, 225, 231, 260, 267, 279, 286, 305, 314, 315, 319, 325, 328, 329, 344 n.61, 345 n.163

length, 37, 60, 76, 101, 123, 140, 194, 257, 273, 282, 317
Skinner, C.F. (Jerry), 256
Smith, E.M., **112**
Smith, S.G., 192
Smith, W.C., 95
Snowdon, B.A., **252**
social activities, members, 90, 91, 95, **163**, 298, 299, *see also* horse racing
    balls, 24, 43, 101, 238, 240
    cricket, **163**, **277**, 305
    jogging, **291**
    liquor, 19, 43, 48, 49, 77, 78, 79, 89, 94, 98, 114, 115, 116, 123, 127, 243, 252, 254, 255, 296, 299, 333
    smoking, 51
    snuff, 51
social composition, House, 12, 24, 69, 103, 144–5, 200–1, 227–8, 230, 264–6, 297–8, 318, 333–5, *see also* Maori members; women members; individual occupations
    characters, 114, 115, 230, 265
    turnover by election, 23, 35, 66, 69, 74, 103, 113, 124, 145, 191, 200, 227, 264, 297, 316, 329, 333
Social Credit Political League, 241, 262, 264, 268, 274, 284, 285, 293, 294, 295, 296, 300, 314, 317
Social Democratic Party, 166
Social Security Act 1938, 212
social security scheme, 205, 212
South Africa, 193, 194, 268
South African War, 128, 132
Southern Maori, 204, 246, 247, 276
Southland, 33
Speaker, 11, 18, 46, 63, 64, 88, 109, 120, 127, 192, 208, 213, 263, 276, 279, 280, 298, 305, 306, *see also* House, business of; standing orders
    censure motion, 286, 313
    chair, 14, 46, **187**, **208**, **239**
    election, 15, 26, 35, 55, 66, 74, 79, 96, 108, 116, 134, 138, 149, 186, 190, 191, 204, 214, 215, 233, 243, 257, 274, 276, 282, 284, 311, 312, 316, 319, 327, 330, 331
    in Committee, 63, 67, 79, 134, 187, 204, 205, 215, 233, 243, 262, 276
    role of, 10, 50, 62, 63, 79, 109, 161, 205, 234, 262, 294, 304, 311, 313, 314, 316, 319, 320, 324, 325, 328, 364 n.21
    rulings, 79, 96, 120, 121, 122, 216, 356 n.166
    salary, 59, 63, 86
    versus executive, 63–4, 86, 118, 126, 307
Speaker, Assistant/Deputy 316, 325, 327, 330, 331
Speech from the Throne, 26, 199, *see also* Address-in-Reply

speeches, 17, **50**, **51**, 52, 53, 54, 122, 207, 208, 209, 213, 221, 222, **223**, 224, 251, *see also* obstruction; standing orders
    call of the Speaker, 192, 213, 224, 325
    closure, 40, 55, 76, 195, 196, 197, **210**, 215, 227, 231, 241, 244, 261, 264, 273, 279, 293, 313, 315, 328, 330
        introduction of, 84, 99, 102, 121–3, 141, 147, 150, 190, 191, 193–4, **194**
    guillotine, 123, 279, 325
    general debates, 305, 314, 325
    interjections, 54, 141, 189, 192, 206, 220, 241, 261, 263, 277, 311
    maiden speeches, 26, 78, 84, 95, 135, 166, 230, 259, 264, 284, 298
    question time, questions, 121, 224, 236, 260, 261, 263, 267, 279, **306**, 321, 325, 328, 332
    special debates, 260, 261, 263, 264, 267, 271
    reading speeches, 17, 50, 189, 224, 234, 259, 306, 325, 332
    time of, 75, 76, 99, 118, 122, 147, 191, 260, 305, 325
Spence, Sir Basil, 249, 250
Spragg, Silas, **119**, 161
St Mary's, Hill Street, **169**
Staff Committee, 309
Stafford ministries, 24–5, 27–9, 32–5, 39, 43, 58–62, 67
Stafford, Edward, 12, 15, 24, 25, 26, 27, 28, **32**, 34, 35, 36, 37, 39, 40, 42, 43, 49, 52, 53, 55, 58, 59, 60, 61, 62, 63, 64, 65, 66, 67, 68, 69
standing orders, 11, 27, 28, 37, 38, 40, 43, 50, 52, 55, 84, 85, 91, 99, 121, 127, 191, 193, 215, 220, 242, 259, 279, 280, 286, 308, 316, 324, 325, 328, 329, 333, 353 n.179, 356 n.166, 361 n.10
    (by year) 1854, 18; 1856, 18; 1865, 35, 51, 55, 57, 91, 127; 1871, 92; 1894, 99, 118, 120, 121; 1903, 120, 121; 1929, 51, 127, 161, **192**, 356 n.153; 1951, 236; 1962, 258; 1967, 263, 264; 1985, 216, 305, 306; 1992, 216, 316, 319; 1996, 325, 326
    amendment of, 18, 122
    suspension of, 19, 21, 22, 55, 60, 74, 75, 79, 120, 122, 150, 296
Standing Orders Committee, 56, 85, 165, 191, 260, 263, 274, 275, 284, 285, 286, 292, 307, 319, 321, 326, 331
state funerals, 111, 135, 188, 192, 212, 214, 265, 279
state of emergency, 240
State Sector Act 1988, 309, 315
State Services Act 1962, 307
State Services Commission, 307
Statham, Charles, 151, 157, 159, **161**, 168, 185, 186, **187**, 189, 190, 191, 193, 194, 195, 197, 204, 205, 218, 220

Statute of Westminster, 234
Statutes Revision Committee, 56, 205, 212, 226, 256, 258, 260
Stella, 76
Stevens, E.C.J., 62
Stevenson, Rona, 254
Steward, Major W.J., 95, 96, 102, **108**, 109, **110**, 116, 118, 120, 121, 122, 134, 135, 139, 141, 234
Stewart, Catherine, 229
Stewart, William Downie, 151, 152, 167, 195, 197
Storey, Rob, **310**
Stormbird, 36
Stout, Robert, **51**, 54, 76, 77, 79, 82, **96**, 97, 111, 112, 113, 117, 120, 126
Stout–Vogel ministry, 73, 96–7
Stowe, Leonard, 160
Studholme, John, 103
suffrage, 10, 76, 78, 82, 107, 337, *see also* electoral reform
    female, 97, 112, 113, 127
    franchise, 11, 33, 60, 69, 81, 103, 105
    plural voting, 11, 78, 82, 101
    property qualification, 11
    secret ballot, 66
Suisted, Laura, 127
Sullivan, D.G., 168, 191, 221, 230
Sullivan, William, 233
Summer Time Act 1927, 224
superannuation, 278, 279, 282, 317, 328
Superannuation Act 1947, 229
supply, 22, 23, 26, 43, 62, 68, 77, 95, 122, 320, 329, 331
Supreme Court, 58
Sutherland, Allan, 161, 251
Swanson, William, 48, **50**, 67, 89
Sydney, 24
Sydney Street, 43, 45, 128, 137, 154, 169
Symmans, Gerry, 321

Taiaroa, H.K., 61, 92
Takaka marble, 155, **157**, 249, 288, 324
Takamoana, Karaitiana, 61
Talbot, Rob, **245**, 257, 272, 279
Talboys, Brian, **245**, 257, 293, 294
Talboys, Pat, 300
Tanczos, Nandor, 333
Tapsell, Peter, 216, 319, **320**, 328
Taranaki, 82
Taranaki war, 33, 34, 37, 39, 41
tariffs, 98, 117, 133
Taylor, R.M., **115**
Taylor, T.E., **115**, 119, 124
Te Kooti, 62
Te Moananui, Tareha, 60
Te Rangi Paetahi, Mete Kingi, 60, **61**

Te Waka Maori, 92
Te Wananga, 92
Te Wheoro, Wiremu, 81
Te Whiti, 79
telegraph, 57, 95
television, 209, 268, 271, 272, 280, 286, 291, 292
    televising the House, 268, 317, 321
temperance, 49, 78, 89, 113, 116, *see also* prohibition
Templeton, Hugh, 277
Templeton, Ian **253**
Terrace, The 154
Terris, John, **310**, 312, 313, 316
Thacker, Dr H.T.J., 157, 224
'Think Big' energy projects, 286, 295
Thomson, David, 257, 284, 286
Thomson, G.M., 228
Thomson, J.W., 77
three-party politics, 145, 147, 166–95
Timber Merchants' Federation, 248, 327
Tinakori Road, 112
Tirikatene, E.T., 215, 216, 251, 276
Tirikatene-Sullivan, Whetu, 254, 255, **276**, 299
Titokowaru, 62
Tizard, Bob, 244, 252, 256, 272, **273**, 282, 283, 298
Tombleson, Esmé, 248, 253
Tomoana, Henare, 81, 85, 86, 124
Tourist Hotel Corporation, 288, 310
trade unions, 108, 145, 167, 201, 227, 240, 265, 298
travel, **104**, 140, 163, 164, 263
    air, **225**
    motor car, **142**, **153,** 163, 246
    passes, **164**
    rail, 163
    ship, 13, 23
Travers, W.T.L., 44
treaties, 271, 329, 330, 331
Treaty of Waitangi, 9, 215, 300, 303
Treaty of Waitangi Act 1975, 277
Triennial Parliaments Act 1879, 82
Triennial Parliaments Bill 1878, 78
Trimble, Colonel Robert, 91
Trollope, Anthony, 32, 55
Turnbull, Thomas, 88, 129, 130
Turnbull, William, 89
Tutanekai, 124
TV3, 321
TVNZ, 321, 326
two-party system, 200, 203, 204, 214, 216, 221, 226, 227, 231, 236, 268, 280, 281, 300, 303, 314, 318, 319, 324, 329, 337
typewriters, 87, 118, 159

Unbridled Power?, 303
unemployment, 190, 193, 195, 196, **200**

Index

Union Steam Ship Company, 140, 164
United Future Party, 331
United government, 191–5
United New Zealand Party, 328
United Party, 190, 191, 192, 320, 327
United States, 268, 274, 301
United–Labour alliance, 1928–30, 191, 192, 193
Upton, Simon, 294, 332
Uruti Point, Wairarapa, 36

Values Party, 274
VE Day, **202**
Veitch, W.A., 139, 152, 166, 190
Vernon, Colonel, 154
Victoria, 9, 13, 14, 20
Vietnam War, 268, 271, 272
Vogel ministries, 68, 74–5
Vogel, Julius, 31, 40, 42, 43, 50, 51, 56–70 passim, **63**, 74, 75, 82, 95, 96, 97, 98, **99**, 132
    development plan, 62, 65, 73
von Tunzelmann, Adrienne, 308, 309
voting, 52, 82, 218, **236**, 325, 366 n.130, *see also* divisions; no-confidence
    across the floor, 204, 231, 237, 244, 259, 285, 286, 295, 296, 328
    casting votes, 34, 37, 43, 62, 75, 77, 86, 95, 96, 97, 117, 143, 242, 272, 273, 294, 315, 320, 325, 363 n.172
    conscience/free votes, 109, 112, 141, 226, 237, 259, 279, 295, 325
    proxy, 325, 329
voucher incident, 1905, 135

Waihi strike, 1912, 149
Waikato, 33, 36
Waikato war, 37
Waitangi Tribunal, 277
Waitara, 33
Wakefield, E.G., 10, 13–23 passim, 52
Wakefield, E.J., 21, **49**, 52, 67
Walker, H.J., 285
Walker, Simon, 286, 292
Wall, Gerard, 291, **310**, **311**, **312**, **313**, 314, 321, 322, 332
Wanganui, 41
War Administration, 214
war cabinet, 213, 214
Ward, J.G., **106**, 111, 114, 117, 119, 124, 127, 132, 135, **136**, **138**, 139–54 passim, **140**, **163**, 166, 167, 168, 186, 190, 191, 192, 200, 234, 236
Waring, Marilyn, 282, 286, **291**, 293, 295, 296, 298
Warren and Mahoney, 322
Washers and Manglers Bill 1892, 111
waterfront dispute, 1951, 240

waterfront strike, 1913, 150, 151
Waterhouse ministry, 68
Waterhouse, G.M., 68
Watson, William, 117
Watt, Hugh, 244, 277, **278**
Watts, Jack, 224, 244, 245
Webb, P.C. (Paddy), 150, 151, 152, **166**, 197
Webb, Sidney, 115
Webb, T.C., 233
Weld ministry, 35, 41–3
Weld, F.A., 12, 13, 17, 18, 21, 35, 40, **41**, 42, 43, 58, 69
Wellbrock, W., **252**
Wellington, 12, 13, 34, 36, 38, 39, 40, 41, 43, 44, 68, 96, 132, 337
Wellington City Council, 139, 154
Wellington Club, 164
Wellington members, 25, 28, 32, 33, 34, 35, 39, 40, 60, 154
Wellington Province, 15, 27
Wellington, Merv, 312
West Coast members, 60, 84
Western Maori, 204
Westminster system, 10, 300
Wetere, Koro, 216
Wheeler, C.E., **126**, 206
whips, 27, 34, 48, 49, 62, 67, 77, 80, 101, 113, 116, 120, 132, 144, 204, 209, 215, 221, 222, 237, 241, 242, 274, 282, 295, 298, 312, 315, 325, *see also* divisions; no-confidence; pairing; voting
Whitaker, Frederick, 19, 24, 25, 38, 58, 59, 69, 73, 78, 79, 81, 85, 95, 102
Whitaker–Atkinson ministry, 85–6
Whitaker–Fox ministry, see Fox–Whitaker ministry
White Swan, 33, 36
Whitehead, Stan, 276, 277, 278, 280
Wild, Chief Justice, 282
Wilde, Fran, 298, 313, 314, 334
Wilford, T.M., 139, 140, 147, 152, 168, 188
Wilkinson, C.A., 221
Williamson, Maurice, 314
Wilson, Charles, 132, 161, 254
Wilson, C.K., 163
Wilson, J.O., 256
wine box affair, 326
Witty, George, 186
wives/spouses of members, 238, 246, 278, 300, 364 n.215
women, *see also* Bellamy's; chamber of the House; *Hansard*; male culture; press gallery; women members
    and Bellamy's, 221, 254
    in Parliament, 159, 161, 276, 297, 299, 300, 308, 309
    on floor of House, 254

women members, 113, 199, 229, 230, 231, 252, 253, 254, 298, 299, 317, 333
Women's Parliamentary Rights Act 1919, 168
Wong, Pansy, 334
Wonga Wonga, 38
Wood, Reader, 69, 81
Wynyard, R.H., 9, 13, 16, 17, 20, 21, 22, 23, 28

Young Maori Party, 158

Young Turks, 254, 257
Young, J.A., 187
Young, Jane, 292
Young, Venn, **245**, 314
Young, W.L., **288**
Youth Parliaments, 291

Zingari, 23, 24, 29